JLA
JUSTICE FOR ALL

JENETTE KAHN
President & Editor-in-Chief

PAUL LEVITZ
Executive Vice President & Publisher

MIKE CARLIN
Executive Editor

DAN RASPLER
Editor-original series

DALE CRAIN
Editor-collected edition

TONY BEDARD
Associate Editor-original series

MICHAEL WRIGHT
Assistant Editor-collected edition

GEORG BREWER
Design Director

ROBBIN BROSTERMAN
Art Director

RICHARD BRUNING
VP-Creative Director

PATRICK CALDON
VP-Finance & Operations

DOROTHY CROUCH
VP-Licensed Publishing

TERRI CUNNINGHAM
VP-Managing Editor

JOEL EHRLICH
Senior VP-Advertising & Promotions

ALISON GILL
Exec. Director-Manufacturing

LILLIAN LASERSON
VP & General Counsel

JIM LEE
Editorial Director-WildStorm

JOHN NEE
VP & General Manager-WildStorm

BOB WAYNE
VP-Direct Sales

JLA: JUSTICE FOR ALL

DC Comics, 1700 Broadway, New York, NY 10019
A division of Warner Bros. - A Time Warner Entertainment Company
Printed in Canada. First Printing.
ISBN: 1-56389-511-0
Cover illustration by Howard Porter and John Dell.
Cover color by Lee Loughridge.
Publication design by Steve Vance/Modern Art & Design

JLA
JUSTICE FOR ALL

GRANT MORRISON
MARK WAID
MARK MILLAR
DEVIN GRAYSON
WRITERS

HOWARD PORTER
MARK PAJARILLO
PENCILLERS

JOHN DELL
WALDEN WONG
MARLO ALQUIZA
INKERS

PAT GARRAHY
JOHN KALISZ
COLORISTS

KEN LOPEZ
LETTERER

SUPERMAN

Last son of the planet Krypton, Superman is the world's greatest super-hero. The guiding force behind the formation of this new incarnation of the Justice League, Superman has become the example all metahumans on Earth strive to equal and has changed his adopted planet forever by his very existence. Powered by the sun itself, Superman is capable of great feats of strength, matchless invulnerability, the gift of flight and other fantastic powers.

BATMAN

Just as Superman is the perfection all superhumans aspire to, Batman embodies everything Man can ever hope to be. Driven by a desire to use the persona of the Dark Knight to ensure that others will never experience the tragedy that has shaped his life, Batman uses his keen intellect, a body honed to physical perfection and a vast arsenal of technological and financial resources to wage a personal war on crime on its own shadowy terrain.

WONDER WOMAN

Born Diana, warrior Princess of Themyscira, home of the fabled Amazons, Wonder Woman was chosen above all her sisters to journey into the Patriarch's World as an ambassador of peace. Gifted by the gods with great speed and strength and the power of flight, and possessing indestructible bracelets and the magical Lasso of Truth, spun from the girdle of the Earth Goddess Gaea, she struggles to defend the ideals she was sent to represent.

THE FLASH

His name is Wally West—and he is the Fastest Man Alive. The third in a long tradition of super-speedsters, the Flash is the only former sidekick to fulfill the job's unspoken duty when he took over the Flash identity. By tapping into an extradimensional "speed force," the Flash is able to reach velocities that approach the speed of light itself and perform other feats of whirlwind wizardry.

GREEN LANTERN

One of the youngest members of the team, Green Lantern makes up for what he lacks in experience with an unmatched enthusiasm—despite his insecurity about being chosen to be Green Lantern through a simple twist of fate. His power ring, the most powerful weapon in the universe, is able to create solid light images which can be shaped to take any form he can imagine—and imagination is an ability that artist Kyle Rayner has in abundance.

AQUAMAN

Born of an Atlantean queen and an ancient wizard, King of the Seas and sworn protector of almost three-quarters of the Earth, Aquaman is known—and often feared—both above and below the waves. Quiet, regal, serious as the tides, Aquaman is incredibly strong and amazingly fast both in water and on land. Unlike other Atlanteans, he alone possesses the power to telepathically communicate with sea creatures.

J'ONN J'ONZZ
THE MANHUNTER FROM MARS

Pulled through space from his native Mars by Earth science, J'onn J'onzz was left stranded on a strange new world. An intensely silent figure, as is common among telepaths, he has been a founding member of every incarnation of the JLA. Among his many inhuman abilities are the powers of flight, super-strength, super-speed, telepathy Martian vision and the natural Martian ability to alter his physical shape and density.

ZAURIEL

A Guardian Angel in Heaven's Eagle Host for over a million years, Zauriel renounced his immortality to serve as Heaven's official champion on Earth. One of the JLA's newest members, he accepted their offer to join after twice aiding the League in defeating renegade king-angel Asmodel. Naturally comfortable in the role of a super-hero, Zauriel's enhanced strength, angel wings, potent sonic cry and supernatural expertise are valuable assets to his teammates.

PLASTIC MAN

While it is easy to believe that Plastic Man was brought into the Justice League to be the team's comic relief, he was instead chosen for his amazing shapechanging powers and ability to think fast on his feet—but being able to make even some of the more stern Leaguers crack a smile didn't hurt. One of its most versatile and creative members, he serves in the League with a dedication and fortitude that often contradicts his playful demeanor.

STEEL

A man of strong morals and unshakable ethics, John Henry Irons was once saved from certain death by Superman. The Man of Steel then told a grateful Irons, "Then make sure it counts for something." Inspired by those words, Irons now uses his greatest creations—a suit of flight-capable armor and a formidable hi-tech hammer—as the hero Steel, the Justice League's resident scientist and techno-artisan.

THE HUNTRESS

The "Anastasia of Gotham," Helena Bertinelli is the sole survivor of a brutal attack that killed her parents and closest relations, the Bertinelli crime family. Echoing Batman's own history, Helena became the Huntress and preys on the criminals of the inner city, using her own brand of harsh justice. She has been brought into the League by Batman in an effort to curb her violent methods and combative attitude.

ORION

Orion of the New Gods lives for one thing, and one thing alone: combat. Son of the evil lord Darkseid, Orion has been sent to Earth to stand alongside the JLA in preparation for a coming threat of cosmic proportions. His fearsome rage held in check only by his sentient Mother Box computer, Orion grudgingly assists the League, waiting to unleash his mighty strength and the awesome power of the Astro-Force upon his enemies on the field of battle.

BIG BARDA

Drilled in the savage art of war in the orphanages of Granny Goodness, Barda was the leader of Darkseid's elite Female Furies battalion until she fell in love with Scott Free—a.k.a. the super-escape artist Mister Miracle—and left to join him on Earth. One of the few to escape from dark Apokolips and live, Barda was also sent by Highfather, leader of New Genesis, to aid the Justice League and to keep an eye on the ever unpredictable Orion.

ORACLE

No stranger to super-heroics, Barbara Gordon once patrolled the streets of Gotham as the masked heroine Batgirl—until a vicious attack by the Joker ended her career and left her wheelchair-bound. Never one to give up, Barbara created the identity of Oracle, a mysterious freelance information broker who specializes in metahuman activities. Oracle now divides her time between serving as Data Central and computer link for the JLA and troubleshooting global crises with League founder Black Canary.

EXECUTIVE ACTION!

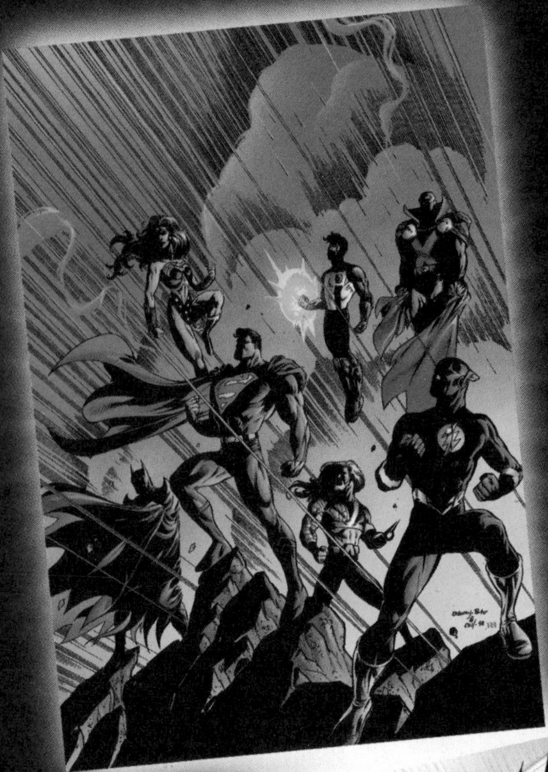

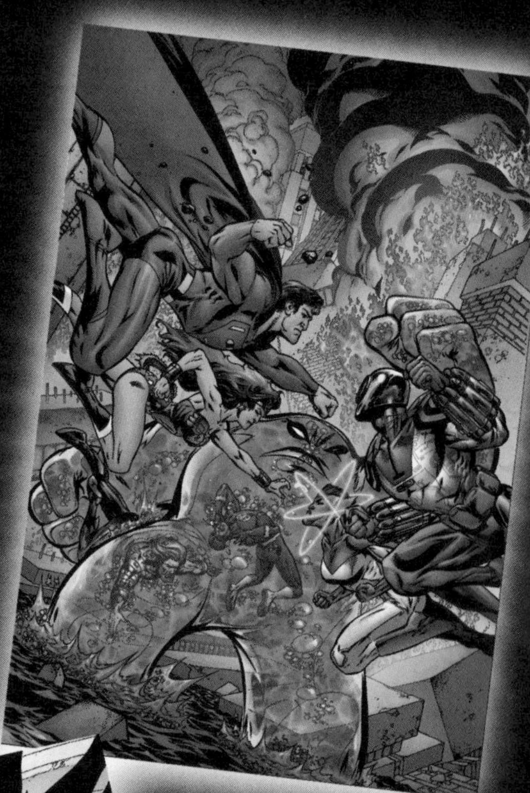

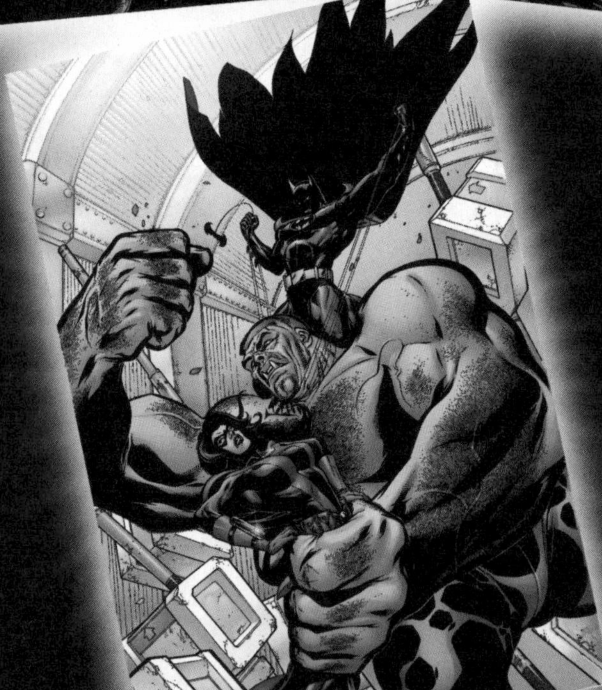

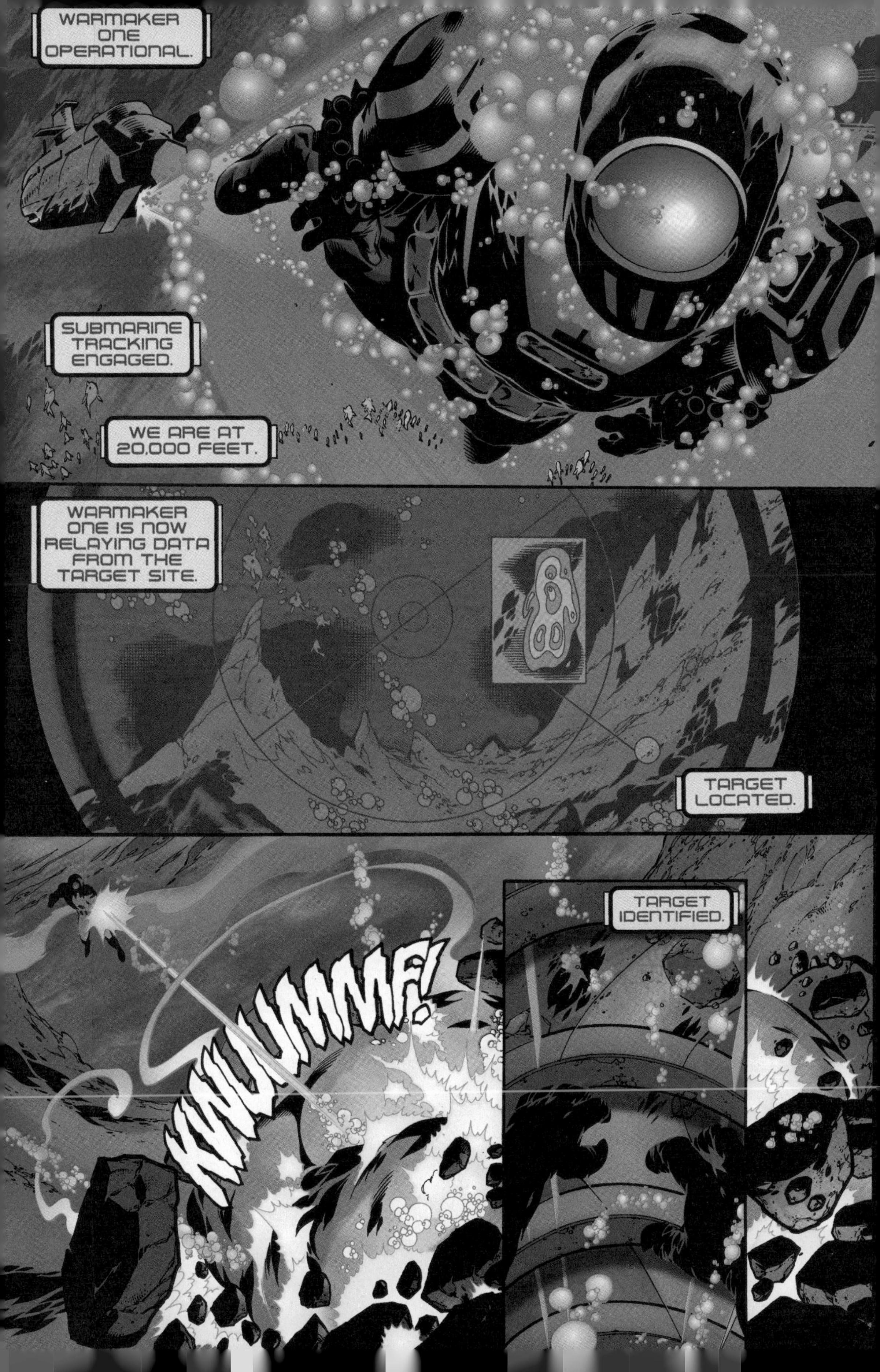

WARMAKER ONE OPERATIONAL.
SUBMARINE TRACKING ENGAGED.
WE ARE AT 20,000 FEET.
WARMAKER ONE IS NOW RELAYING DATA FROM THE TARGET SITE.
TARGET LOCATED.
KWUUMMF!
TARGET IDENTIFIED.

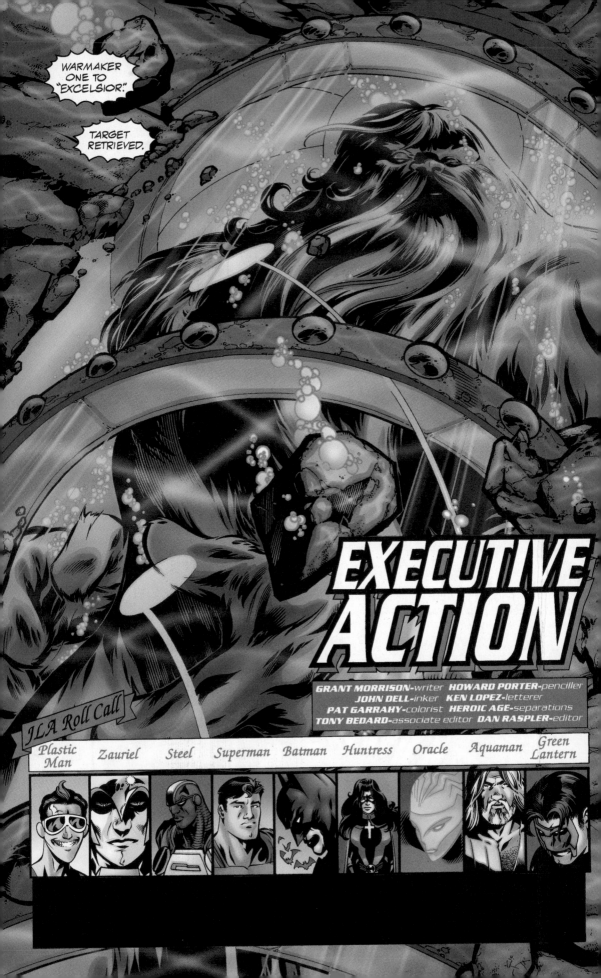

WARMAKER ONE TO "EXCELSIOR."

TARGET RETRIEVED.

EXECUTIVE ACTION

GRANT MORRISON-writer **HOWARD PORTER**-penciller
JOHN DELL-inker **KEN LOPEZ**-letterer
PAT GARRAHY-colorist **HEROIC AGE**-separations
TONY BEDARD-associate editor **DAN RASPLER**-editor

JLA Roll Call

Plastic Man | Zauriel | Steel | Superman | Batman | Huntress | Oracle | Aquaman | Green Lantern

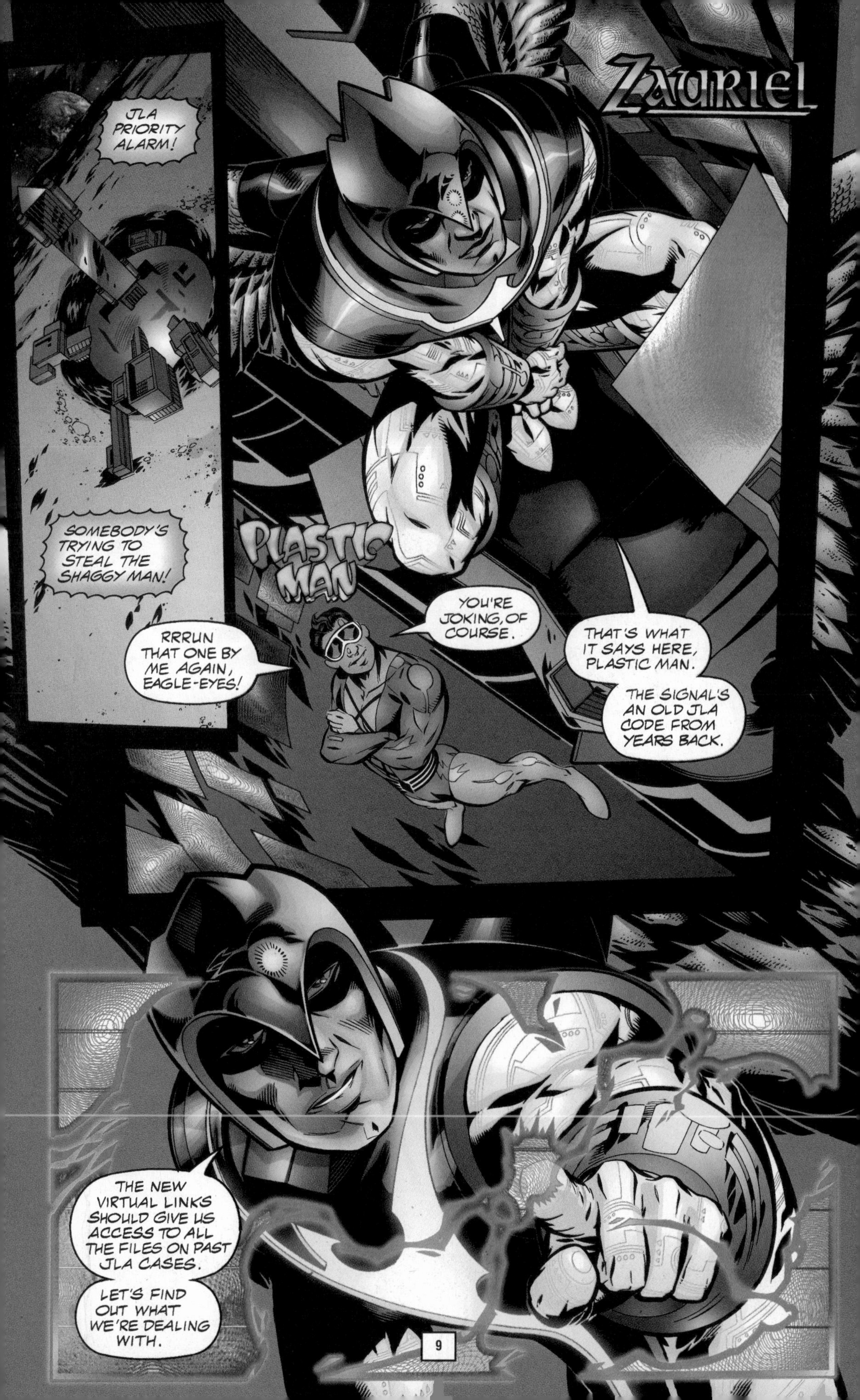
ZAURIEL
JLA PRIORITY ALARM!
SOMEBODY'S TRYING TO STEAL THE SHAGGY MAN!
PLASTIC MAN
RRRUN THAT ONE BY ME AGAIN, EAGLE-EYES!
YOU'RE JOKING, OF COURSE.
THAT'S WHAT IT SAYS HERE, PLASTIC MAN.
THE SIGNAL'S AN OLD JLA CODE FROM YEARS BACK.
THE NEW VIRTUAL LINKS SHOULD GIVE US ACCESS TO ALL THE FILES ON PAST JLA CASES.
LET'S FIND OUT WHAT WE'RE DEALING WITH.

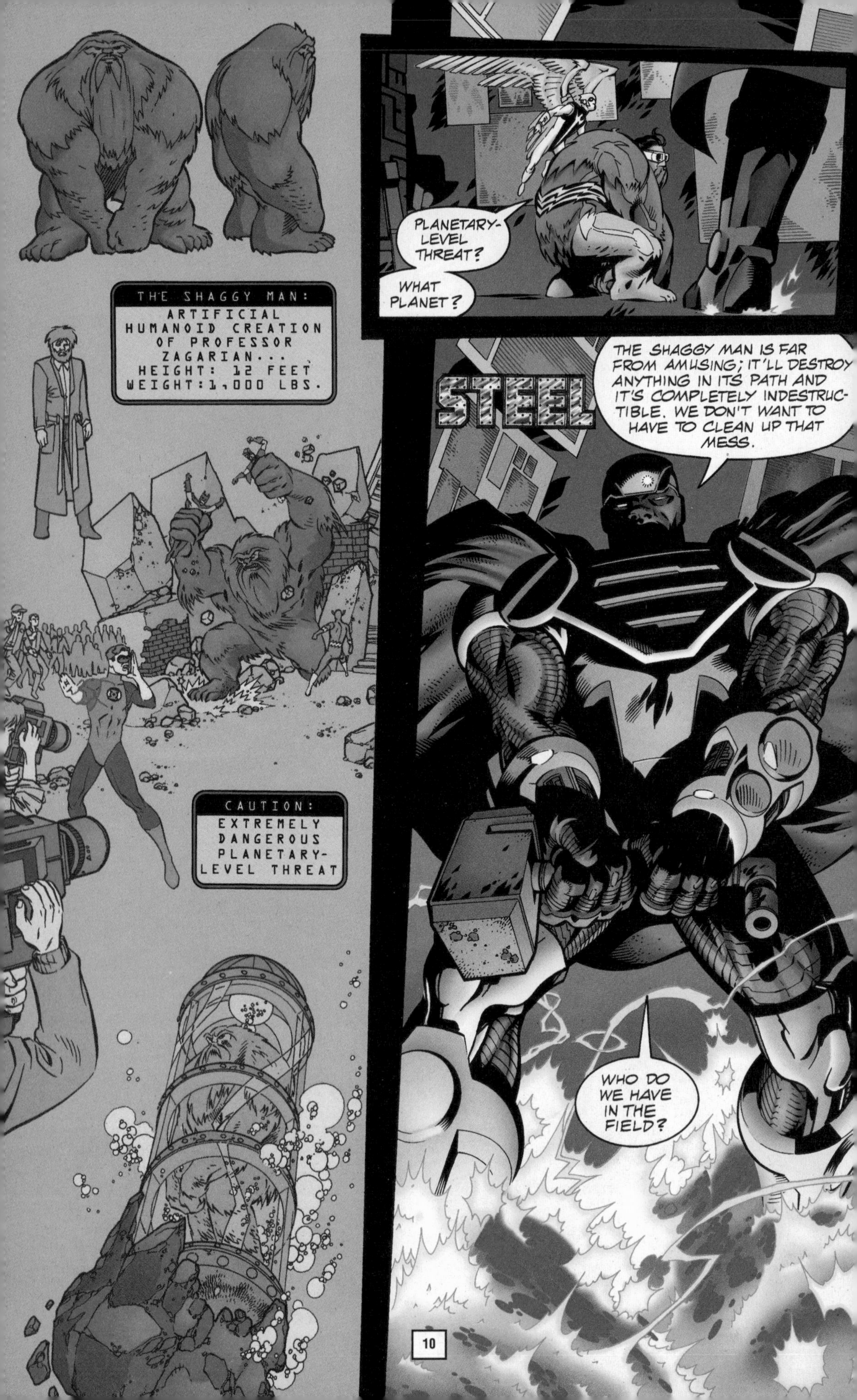
THE SHAGGY MAN:
ARTIFICIAL HUMANOID CREATION OF PROFESSOR ZAGARIAN... HEIGHT: 12 FEET WEIGHT:1,000 LBS.
CAUTION:
EXTREMELY DANGEROUS PLANETARY-LEVEL THREAT
PLANETARY-LEVEL THREAT?
WHAT PLANET?
STEEL
THE SHAGGY MAN IS FAR FROM AMUSING; IT'LL DESTROY ANYTHING IN ITS PATH AND IT'S COMPLETELY INDESTRUCTIBLE. WE DON'T WANT TO HAVE TO CLEAN UP THAT MESS.
WHO DO WE HAVE IN THE FIELD?

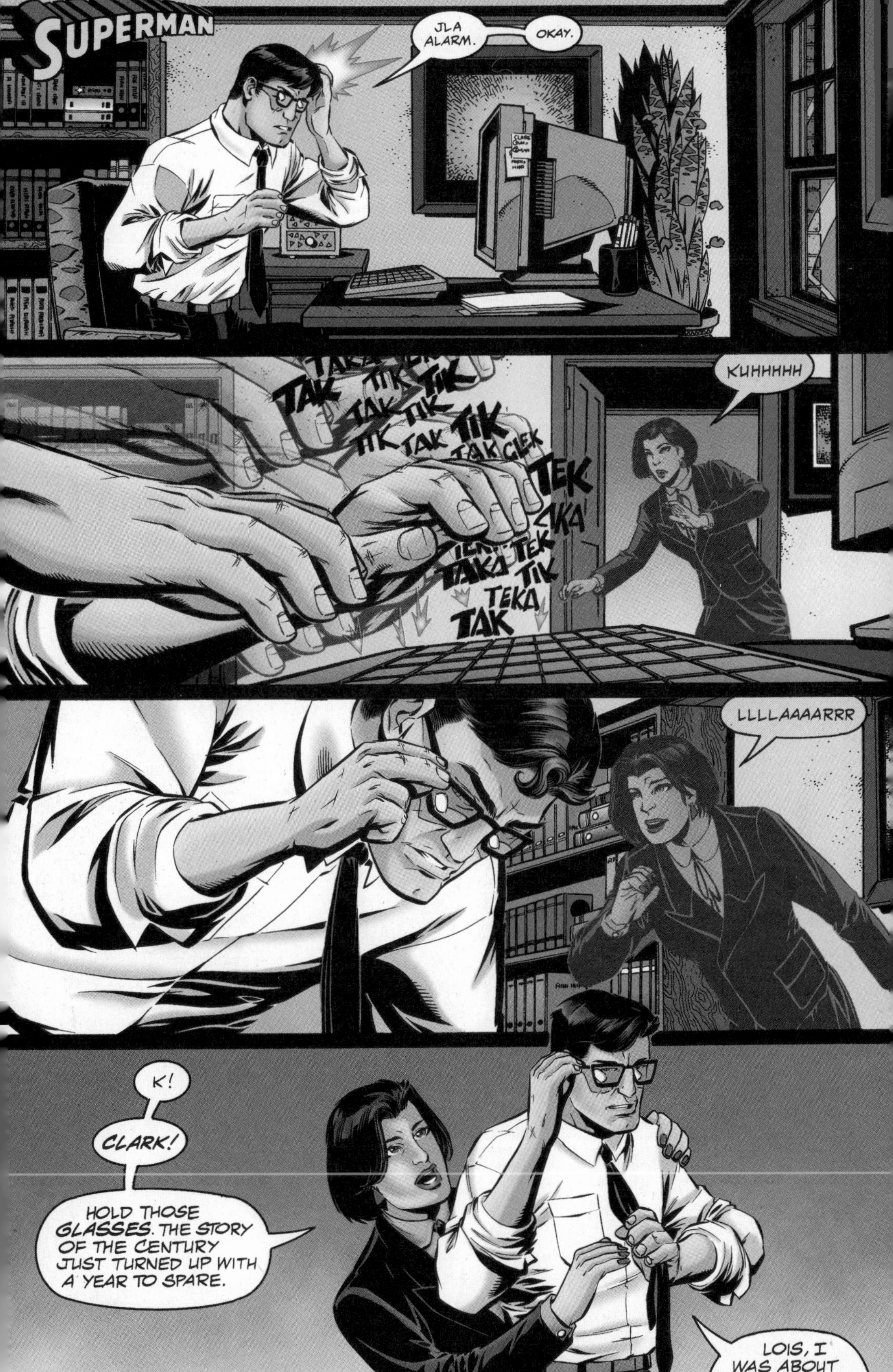
SUPERMAN
JLA ALARM.
OKAY.
TAK TIK TAK TIK TIK TIK TAK TIK TAK CLEK TEK CKA TEKA TEK TIK TEKA TAK
KUHHHHH
LLLLAAAARRR
K!
CLARK!
HOLD THOSE GLASSES. THE STORY OF THE CENTURY JUST TURNED UP WITH A YEAR TO SPARE.
LOIS, I WAS ABOUT TO RESPOND TO A JLA EMERGENCY...

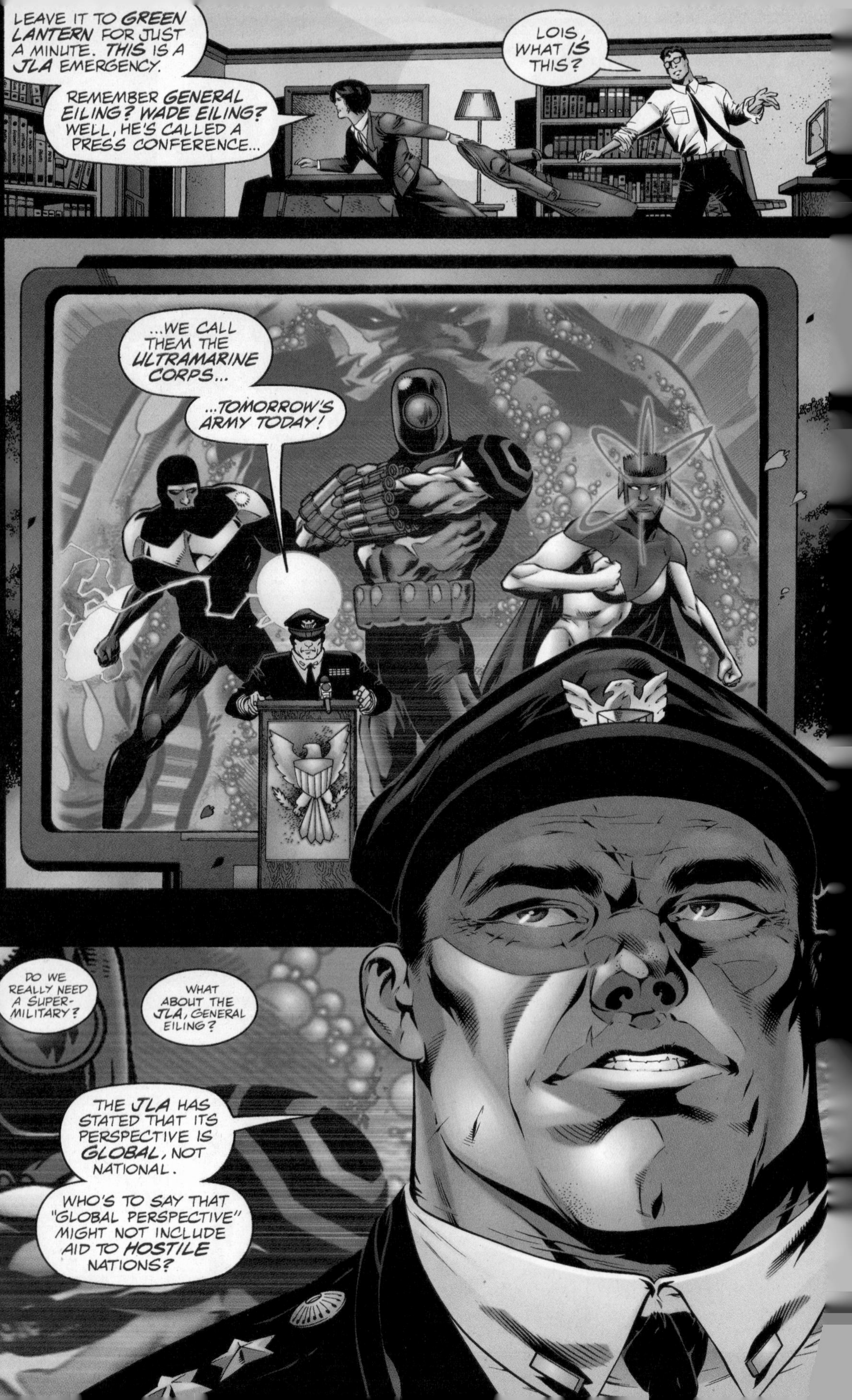
LEAVE IT TO GREEN LANTERN FOR JUST A MINUTE. THIS IS A JLA EMERGENCY.
REMEMBER GENERAL EILING? WADE EILING? WELL, HE'S CALLED A PRESS CONFERENCE...
LOIS, WHAT IS THIS?
...WE CALL THEM THE ULTRAMARINE CORPS...
...TOMORROW'S ARMY TODAY!
DO WE REALLY NEED A SUPER-MILITARY?
WHAT ABOUT THE JLA, GENERAL EILING?
THE JLA HAS STATED THAT ITS PERSPECTIVE IS GLOBAL, NOT NATIONAL.
WHO'S TO SAY THAT "GLOBAL PERSPECTIVE" MIGHT NOT INCLUDE AID TO HOSTILE NATIONS?

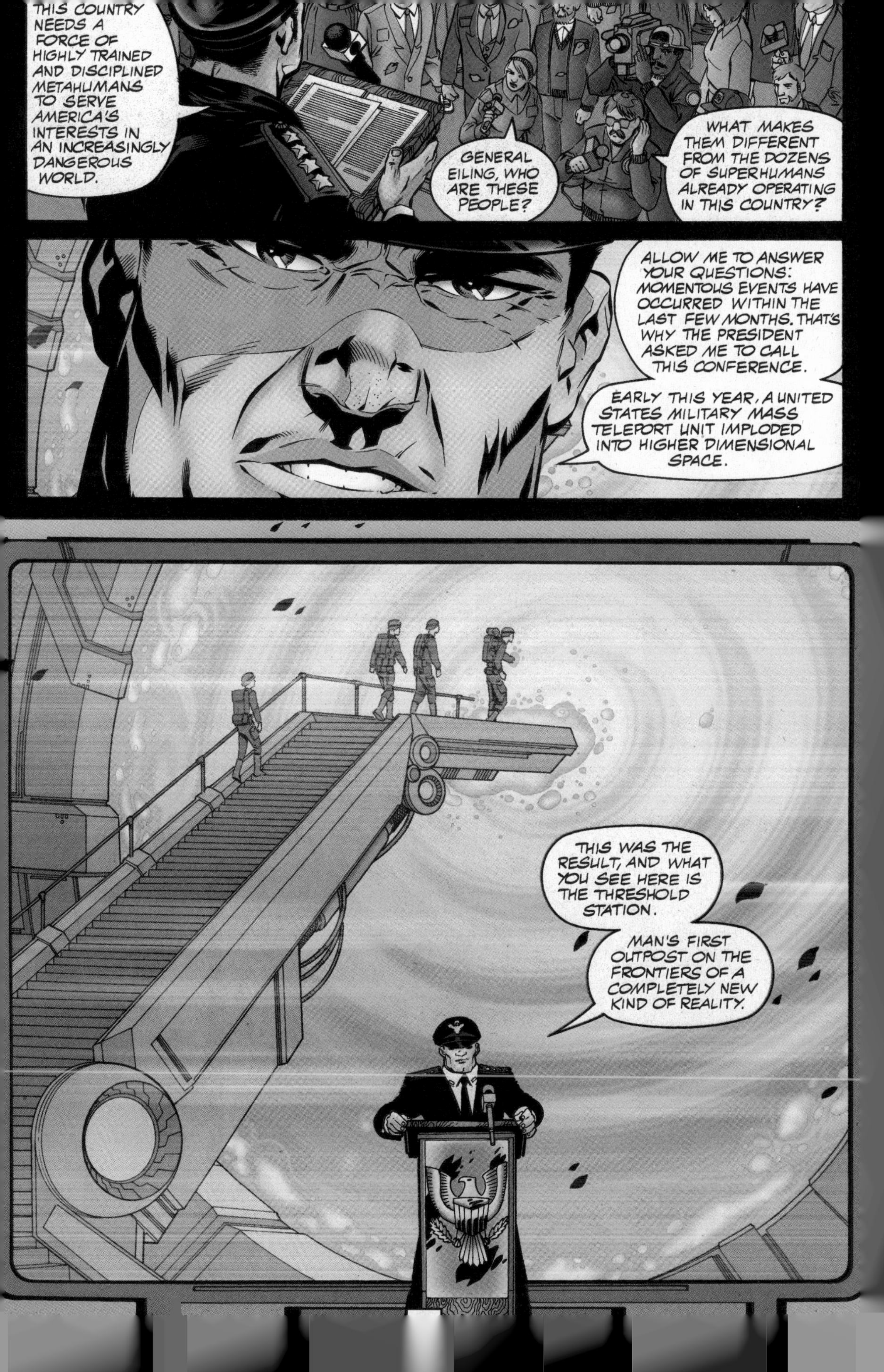
THIS COUNTRY NEEDS A FORCE OF HIGHLY TRAINED AND DISCIPLINED METAHUMANS TO SERVE AMERICA'S INTERESTS IN AN INCREASINGLY DANGEROUS WORLD.
GENERAL EILING, WHO ARE THESE PEOPLE?
WHAT MAKES THEM DIFFERENT FROM THE DOZENS OF SUPERHUMANS ALREADY OPERATING IN THIS COUNTRY?
ALLOW ME TO ANSWER YOUR QUESTIONS: MOMENTOUS EVENTS HAVE OCCURRED WITHIN THE LAST FEW MONTHS. THAT'S WHY THE PRESIDENT ASKED ME TO CALL THIS CONFERENCE.
EARLY THIS YEAR, A UNITED STATES MILITARY MASS TELEPORT UNIT IMPLODED INTO HIGHER DIMENSIONAL SPACE.
THIS WAS THE RESULT, AND WHAT YOU SEE HERE IS THE THRESHOLD STATION.
MAN'S FIRST OUTPOST ON THE FRONTIERS OF A COMPLETELY NEW KIND OF REALITY.

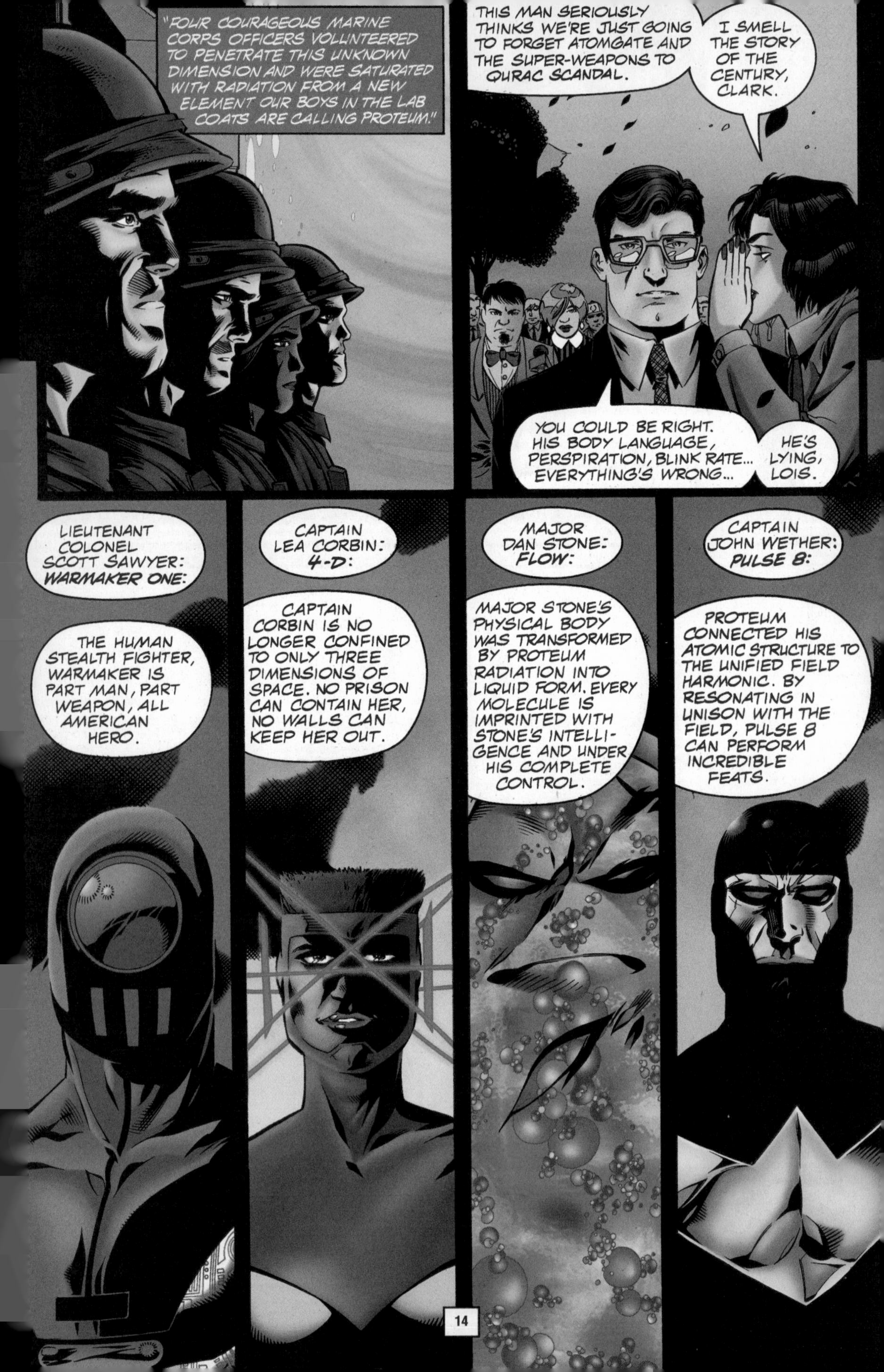
"FOUR COURAGEOUS MARINE CORPS OFFICERS VOLUNTEERED TO PENETRATE THIS UNKNOWN DIMENSION AND WERE SATURATED WITH RADIATION FROM A NEW ELEMENT OUR BOYS IN THE LAB COATS ARE CALLING PROTEUM."
THIS MAN SERIOUSLY THINKS WE'RE JUST GOING TO FORGET ATOMGATE AND THE SUPER-WEAPONS TO QURAC SCANDAL.
I SMELL THE STORY OF THE CENTURY, CLARK.
YOU COULD BE RIGHT. HIS BODY LANGUAGE, PERSPIRATION, BLINK RATE... EVERYTHING'S WRONG...
HE'S LYING, LOIS.
LIEUTENANT COLONEL SCOTT SAWYER: WARMAKER ONE:
THE HUMAN STEALTH FIGHTER, WARMAKER IS PART MAN, PART WEAPON, ALL AMERICAN HERO.
CAPTAIN LEA CORBIN: 4-D:
CAPTAIN CORBIN IS NO LONGER CONFINED TO ONLY THREE DIMENSIONS OF SPACE. NO PRISON CAN CONTAIN HER, NO WALLS CAN KEEP HER OUT.
MAJOR DAN STONE: FLOW:
MAJOR STONE'S PHYSICAL BODY WAS TRANSFORMED BY PROTEUM RADIATION INTO LIQUID FORM. EVERY MOLECULE IS IMPRINTED WITH STONE'S INTELLIGENCE AND UNDER HIS COMPLETE CONTROL.
CAPTAIN JOHN WETHER: PULSE 8:
PROTEUM CONNECTED HIS ATOMIC STRUCTURE TO THE UNIFIED FIELD HARMONIC. BY RESONATING IN UNISON WITH THE FIELD, PULSE 8 CAN PERFORM INCREDIBLE FEATS.

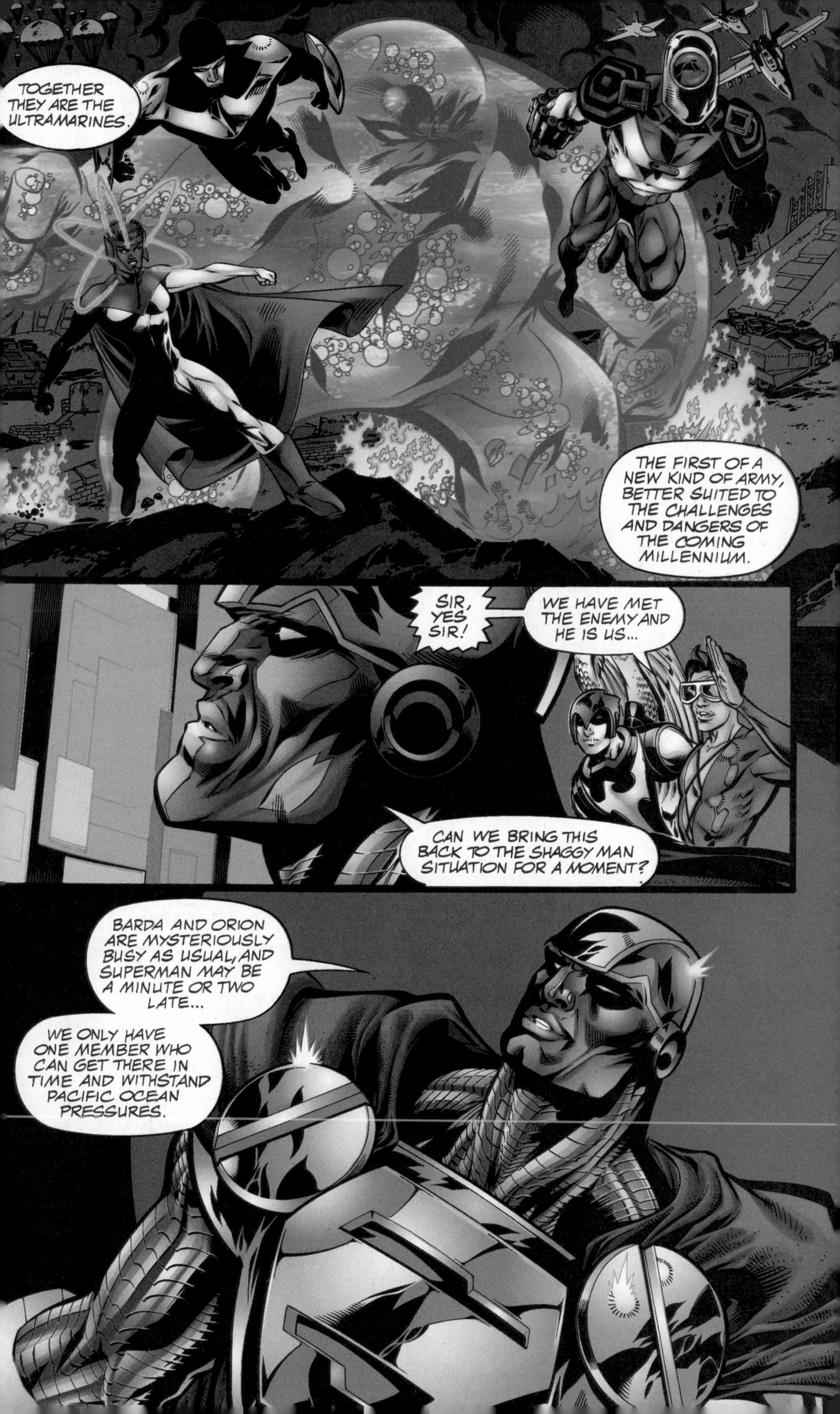
TOGETHER THEY ARE THE ULTRAMARINES.
THE FIRST OF A NEW KIND OF ARMY, BETTER SUITED TO THE CHALLENGES AND DANGERS OF THE COMING MILLENNIUM.
SIR, YES SIR!
WE HAVE MET THE ENEMY AND HE IS US...
CAN WE BRING THIS BACK TO THE SHAGGY MAN SITUATION FOR A MOMENT?
BARDA AND ORION ARE MYSTERIOUSLY BUSY AS USUAL, AND SUPERMAN MAY BE A MINUTE OR TWO LATE...
WE ONLY HAVE ONE MEMBER WHO CAN GET THERE IN TIME AND WITHSTAND PACIFIC OCEAN PRESSURES.

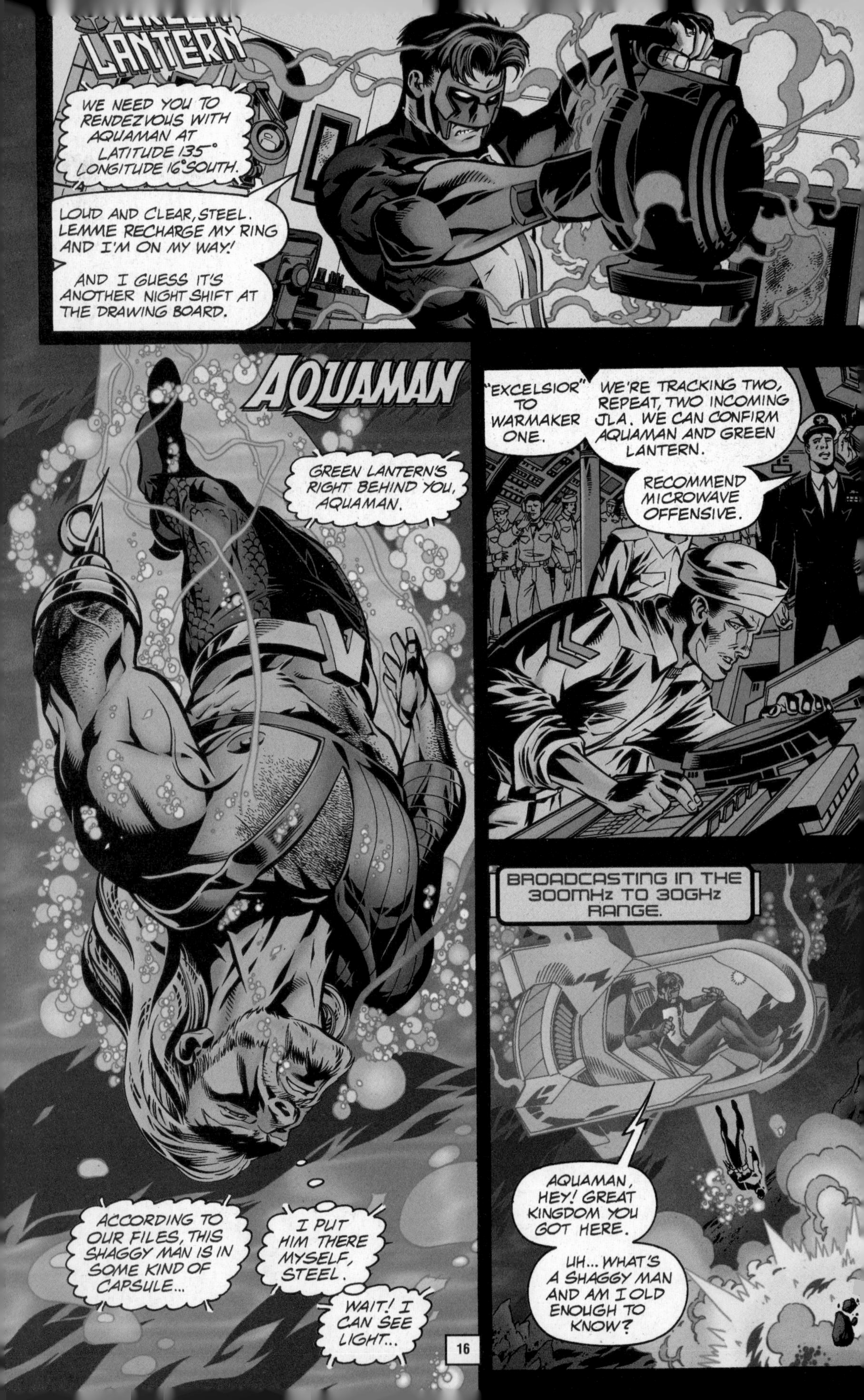
GREEN LANTERN
WE NEED YOU TO RENDEZVOUS WITH AQUAMAN AT LATITUDE 135° LONGITUDE 16° SOUTH.
LOUD AND CLEAR, STEEL. LEMME RECHARGE MY RING AND I'M ON MY WAY!
AND I GUESS IT'S ANOTHER NIGHT SHIFT AT THE DRAWING BOARD.
AQUAMAN
GREEN LANTERN'S RIGHT BEHIND YOU, AQUAMAN.
ACCORDING TO OUR FILES, THIS SHAGGY MAN IS IN SOME KIND OF CAPSULE...
I PUT HIM THERE MYSELF, STEEL.
WAIT! I CAN SEE LIGHT...
"EXCELSIOR" TO WARMAKER ONE.
WE'RE TRACKING TWO, REPEAT, TWO INCOMING JLA. WE CAN CONFIRM AQUAMAN AND GREEN LANTERN.
RECOMMEND MICROWAVE OFFENSIVE.
BROADCASTING IN THE 300MHz TO 30GHz RANGE.
AQUAMAN, HEY! GREAT KINGDOM YOU GOT HERE.
UH... WHAT'S A SHAGGY MAN AND AM I OLD ENOUGH TO KNOW?

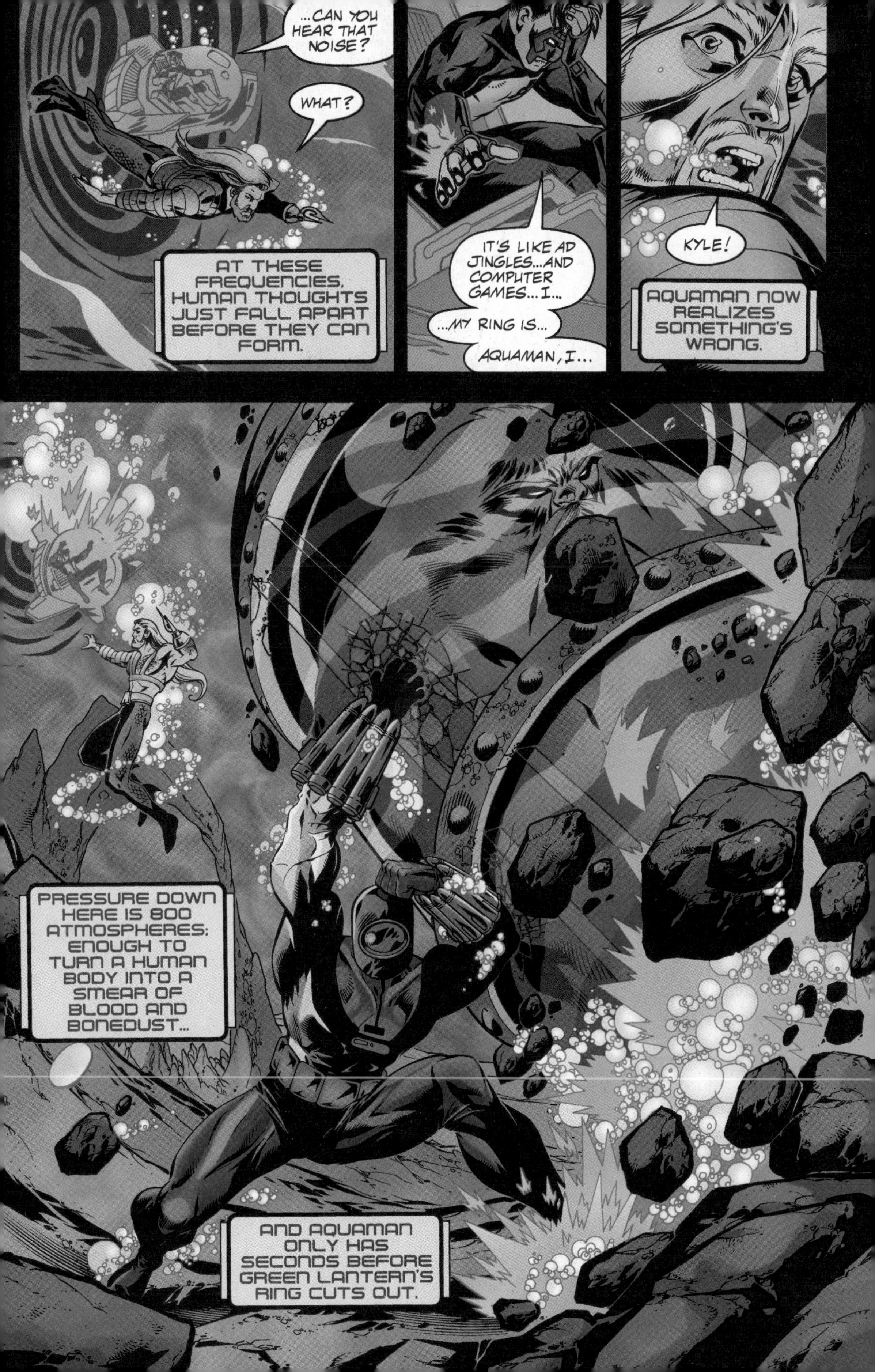

...CAN YOU HEAR THAT NOISE?
WHAT?
AT THESE FREQUENCIES, HUMAN THOUGHTS JUST FALL APART BEFORE THEY CAN FORM.
IT'S LIKE AD JINGLES...AND COMPUTER GAMES... I...
...MY RING IS...
AQUAMAN, I...
KYLE!
AQUAMAN NOW REALIZES SOMETHING'S WRONG.
PRESSURE DOWN HERE IS 800 ATMOSPHERES: ENOUGH TO TURN A HUMAN BODY INTO A SMEAR OF BLOOD AND BONEDUST...
AND AQUAMAN ONLY HAS SECONDS BEFORE GREEN LANTERN'S RING CUTS OUT.

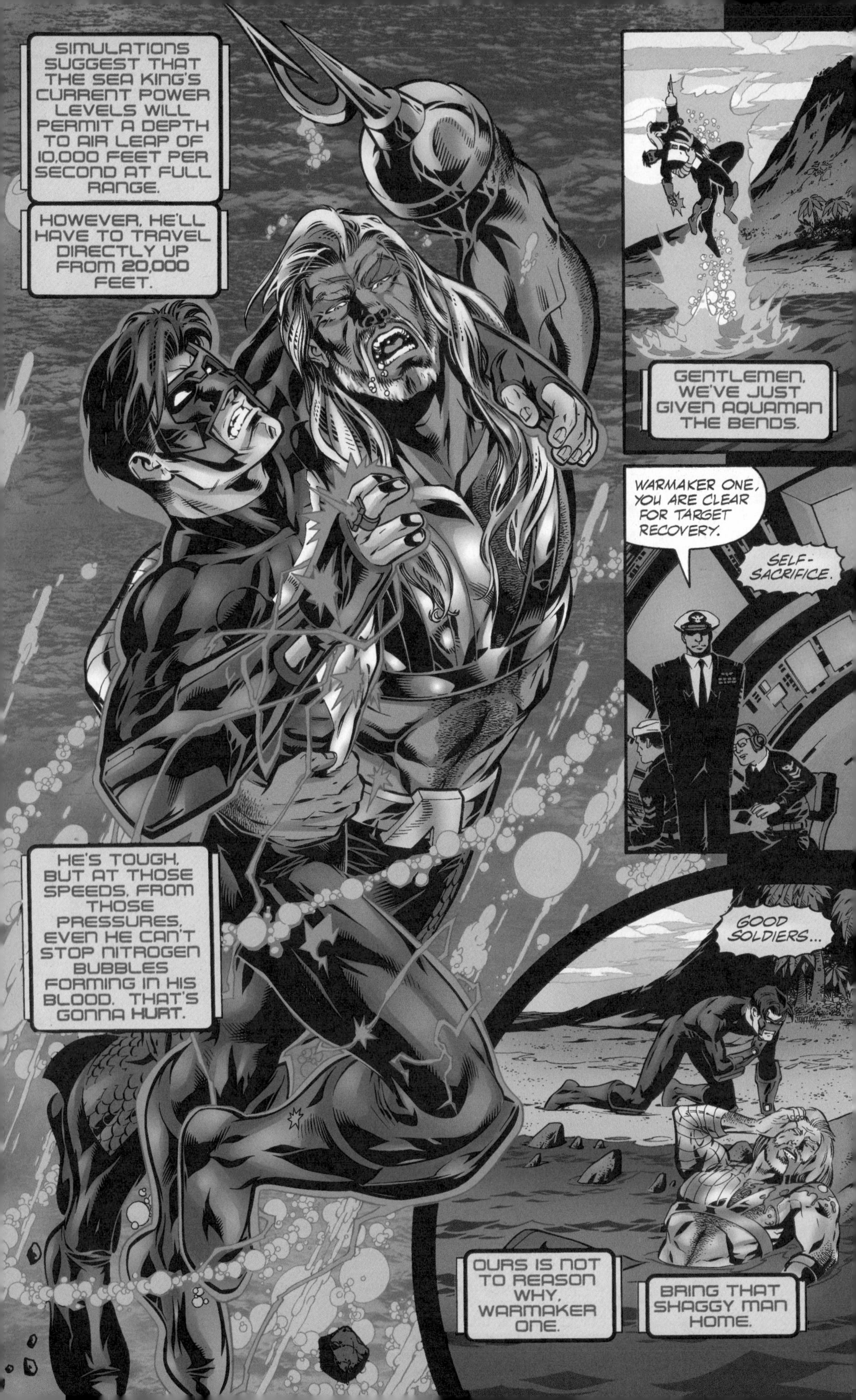
SIMULATIONS SUGGEST THAT THE SEA KING'S CURRENT POWER LEVELS WILL PERMIT A DEPTH TO AIR LEAP OF 10,000 FEET PER SECOND AT FULL RANGE.
HOWEVER, HE'LL HAVE TO TRAVEL DIRECTLY UP FROM 20,000 FEET.
GENTLEMEN. WE'VE JUST GIVEN AQUAMAN THE BENDS.
WARMAKER ONE, YOU ARE CLEAR FOR TARGET RECOVERY.
SELF-SACRIFICE.
HE'S TOUGH, BUT AT THOSE SPEEDS, FROM THOSE PRESSURES, EVEN HE CAN'T STOP NITROGEN BUBBLES FORMING IN HIS BLOOD. THAT'S GONNA HURT.
GOOD SOLDIERS...
OURS IS NOT TO REASON WHY, WARMAKER ONE.
BRING THAT SHAGGY MAN HOME.

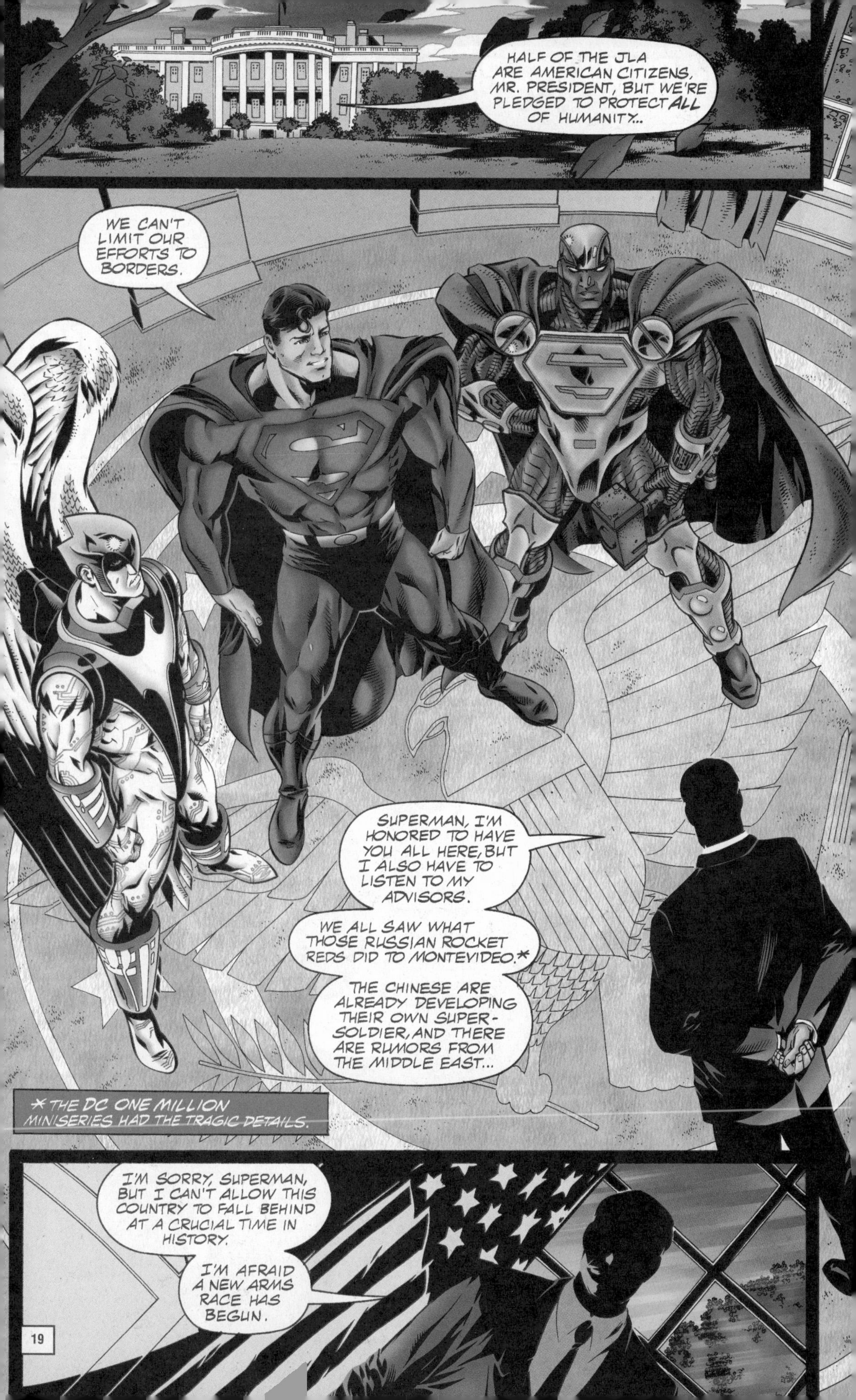
HALF OF THE JLA ARE AMERICAN CITIZENS, MR. PRESIDENT, BUT WE'RE PLEDGED TO PROTECT ALL OF HUMANITY...
WE CAN'T LIMIT OUR EFFORTS TO BORDERS.
SUPERMAN, I'M HONORED TO HAVE YOU ALL HERE, BUT I ALSO HAVE TO LISTEN TO MY ADVISORS.
WE ALL SAW WHAT THOSE RUSSIAN ROCKET REDS DID TO MONTEVIDEO.*
THE CHINESE ARE ALREADY DEVELOPING THEIR OWN SUPER-SOLDIER, AND THERE ARE RUMORS FROM THE MIDDLE EAST...
*THE DC ONE MILLION MINISERIES HAD THE TRAGIC DETAILS.
I'M SORRY, SUPERMAN, BUT I CAN'T ALLOW THIS COUNTRY TO FALL BEHIND AT A CRUCIAL TIME IN HISTORY.
I'M AFRAID A NEW ARMS RACE HAS BEGUN.

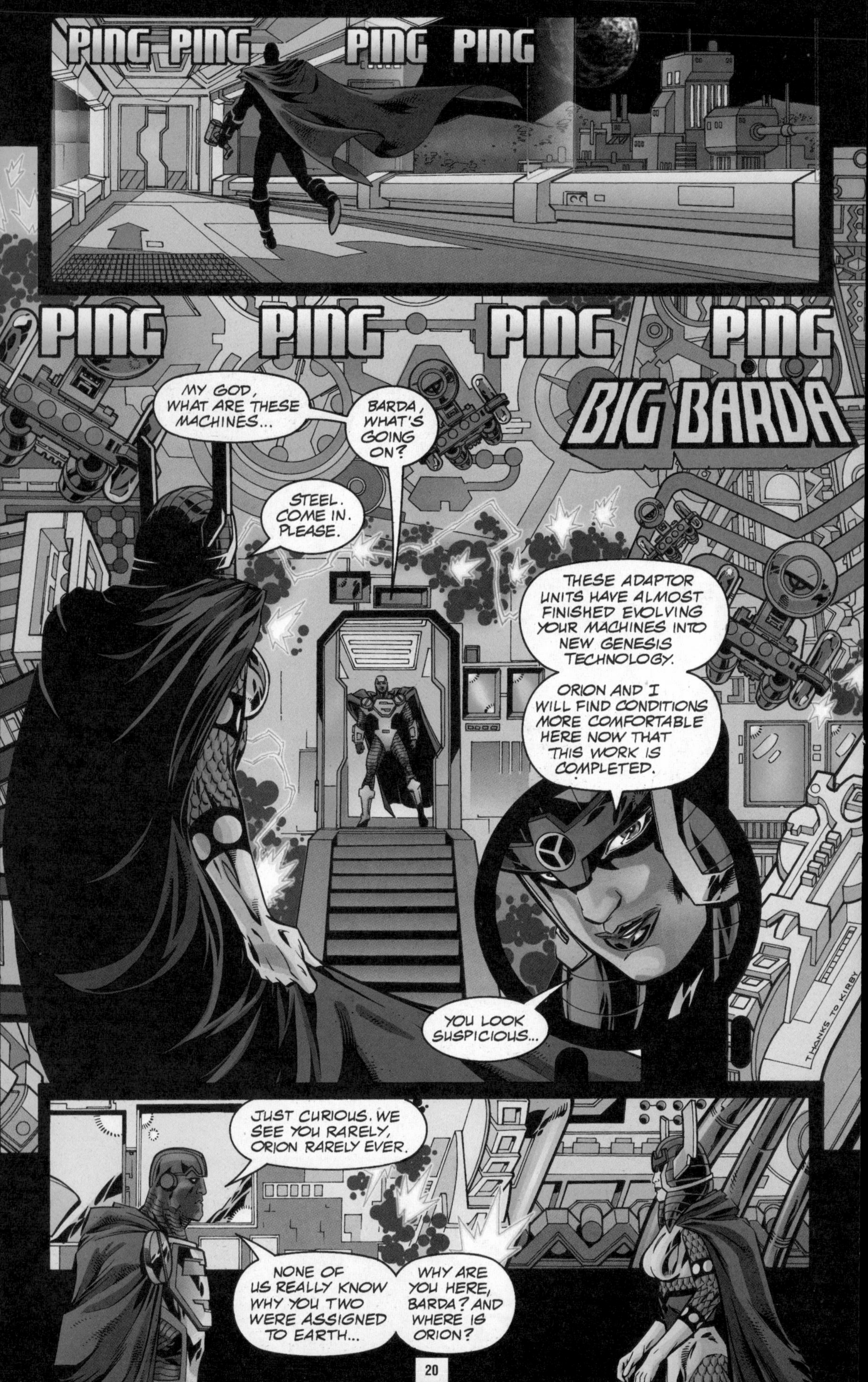
PING PING PING PING
PING PING PING PING
BIG BARDA
MY GOD, WHAT ARE THESE MACHINES...
BARDA, WHAT'S GOING ON?
STEEL. COME IN. PLEASE.
THESE ADAPTOR UNITS HAVE ALMOST FINISHED EVOLVING YOUR MACHINES INTO NEW GENESIS TECHNOLOGY.
ORION AND I WILL FIND CONDITIONS MORE COMFORTABLE HERE NOW THAT THIS WORK IS COMPLETED.
YOU LOOK SUSPICIOUS...
THANKS TO KIRBY
JUST CURIOUS. WE SEE YOU RARELY, ORION RARELY EVER.
NONE OF US REALLY KNOW WHY YOU TWO WERE ASSIGNED TO EARTH...
WHY ARE YOU HERE, BARDA? AND WHERE IS ORION?

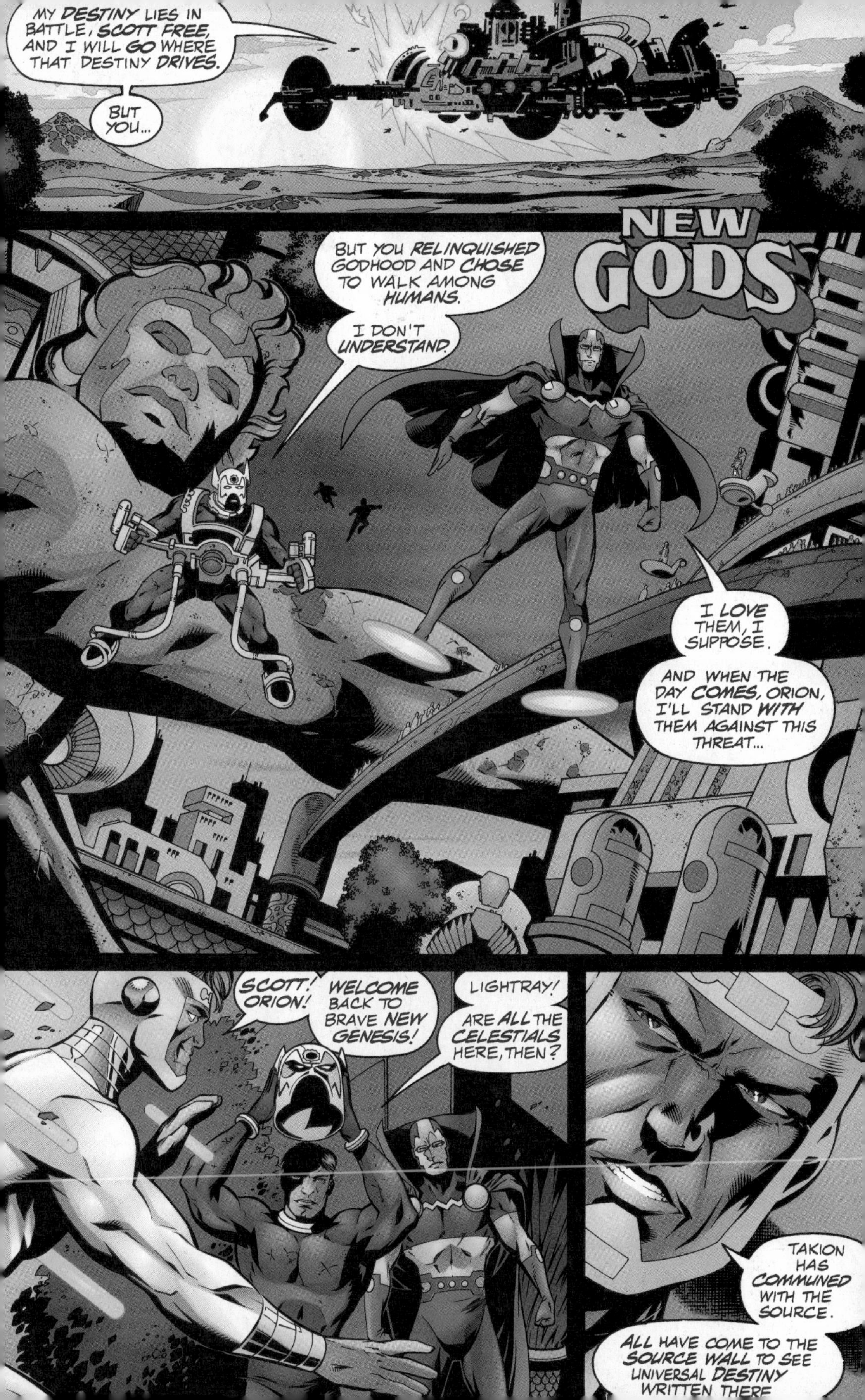

MY DESTINY LIES IN BATTLE, SCOTT FREE, AND I WILL GO WHERE THAT DESTINY DRIVES.
BUT YOU...
NEW GODS
BUT YOU RELINQUISHED GODHOOD AND CHOSE TO WALK AMONG HUMANS.
I DON'T UNDERSTAND.
I LOVE THEM, I SUPPOSE.
AND WHEN THE DAY COMES, ORION, I'LL STAND WITH THEM AGAINST THIS THREAT...
SCOTT! ORION!
WELCOME BACK TO BRAVE NEW GENESIS!
LIGHTRAY!
ARE ALL THE CELESTIALS HERE, THEN?
TAKION HAS COMMUNED WITH THE SOURCE.
ALL HAVE COME TO THE SOURCE WALL TO SEE UNIVERSAL DESTINY WRITTEN THERE

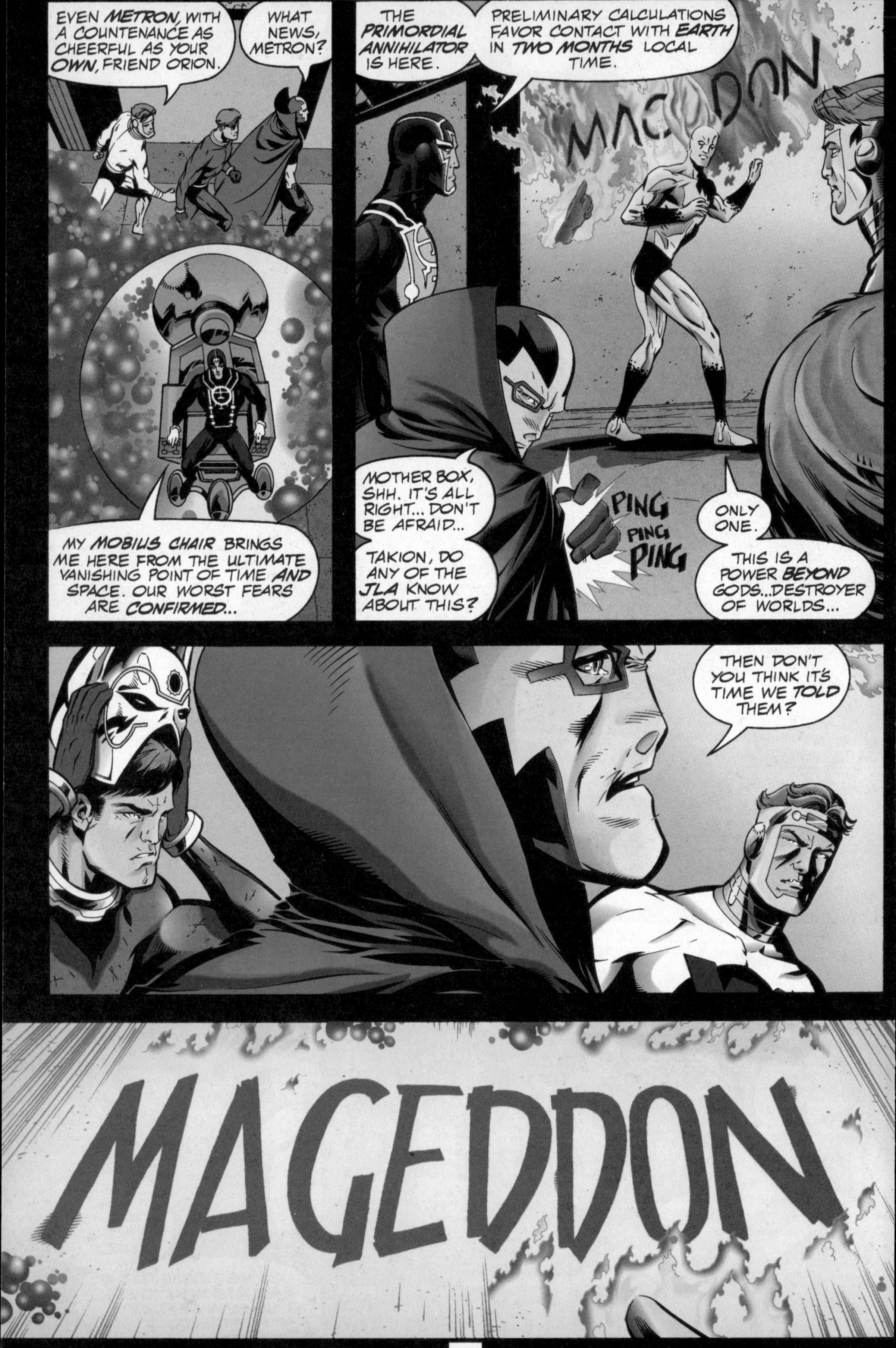
EVEN METRON, WITH A COUNTENANCE AS CHEERFUL AS YOUR OWN, FRIEND ORION.
WHAT NEWS, METRON?
MY MOBIUS CHAIR BRINGS ME HERE FROM THE ULTIMATE VANISHING POINT OF TIME AND SPACE. OUR WORST FEARS ARE CONFIRMED...
THE PRIMORDIAL ANNIHILATOR IS HERE.
PRELIMINARY CALCULATIONS FAVOR CONTACT WITH EARTH IN TWO MONTHS LOCAL TIME.
MAGEDDON
MOTHER BOX, SHH. IT'S ALL RIGHT... DON'T BE AFRAID...
PING PING PING
TAKION, DO ANY OF THE JLA KNOW ABOUT THIS?
ONLY ONE.
THIS IS A POWER BEYOND GODS...DESTROYER OF WORLDS...
THEN DON'T YOU THINK IT'S TIME WE TOLD THEM?
MAGEDDON

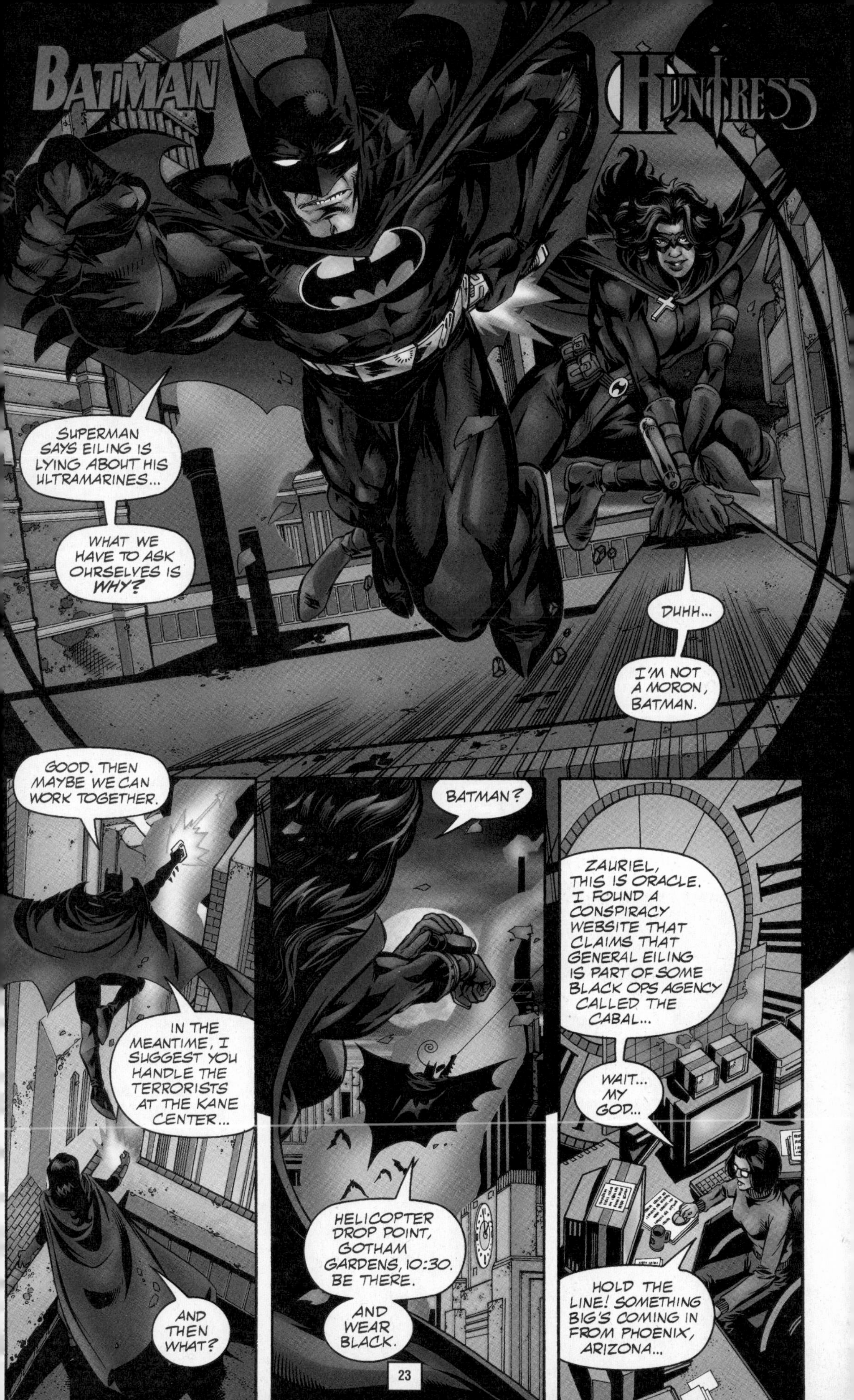
BATMAN
HUNTRESS
SUPERMAN SAYS EILING IS LYING ABOUT HIS ULTRAMARINES...
WHAT WE HAVE TO ASK OURSELVES IS *WHY?*
DUHH...
I'M NOT A MORON, BATMAN.
GOOD. THEN MAYBE WE CAN WORK TOGETHER.
IN THE MEANTIME, I SUGGEST YOU HANDLE THE TERRORISTS AT THE KANE CENTER...
AND THEN WHAT?
BATMAN?
HELICOPTER DROP POINT, GOTHAM GARDENS, 10:30. BE THERE.
AND WEAR BLACK.
ZAURIEL, THIS IS ORACLE. I FOUND A CONSPIRACY WEBSITE THAT CLAIMS THAT GENERAL EILING IS PART OF SOME BLACK OPS AGENCY CALLED THE CABAL...
WAIT... MY GOD...
HOLD THE LINE! SOMETHING BIG'S COMING IN FROM PHOENIX, ARIZONA...

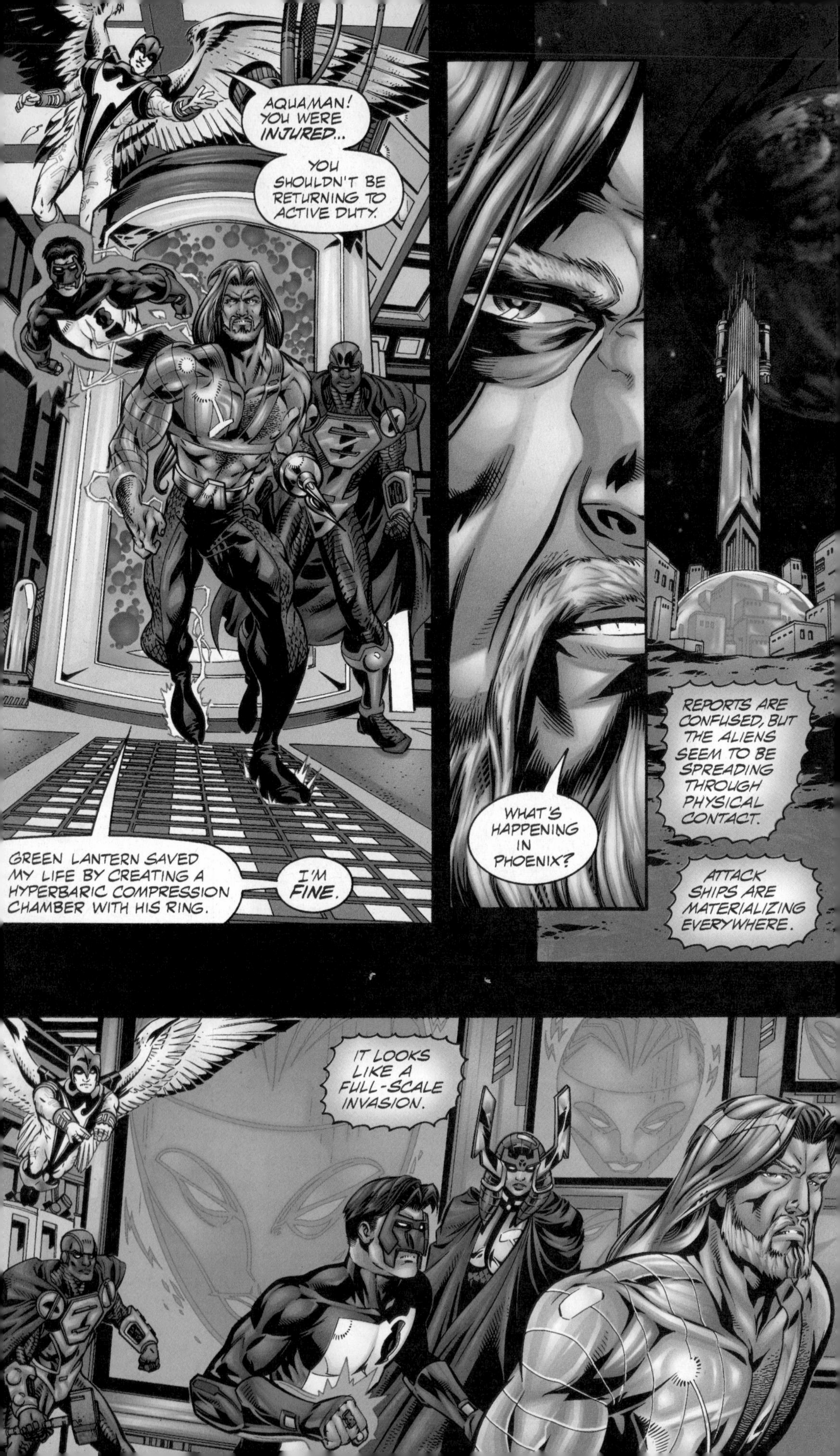
AQUAMAN! YOU WERE INJURED...
YOU SHOULDN'T BE RETURNING TO ACTIVE DUTY.
GREEN LANTERN SAVED MY LIFE BY CREATING A HYPERBARIC COMPRESSION CHAMBER WITH HIS RING.
I'M FINE.
WHAT'S HAPPENING IN PHOENIX?
REPORTS ARE CONFUSED, BUT THE ALIENS SEEM TO BE SPREADING THROUGH PHYSICAL CONTACT.
ATTACK SHIPS ARE MATERIALIZING EVERYWHERE.
IT LOOKS LIKE A FULL-SCALE INVASION.

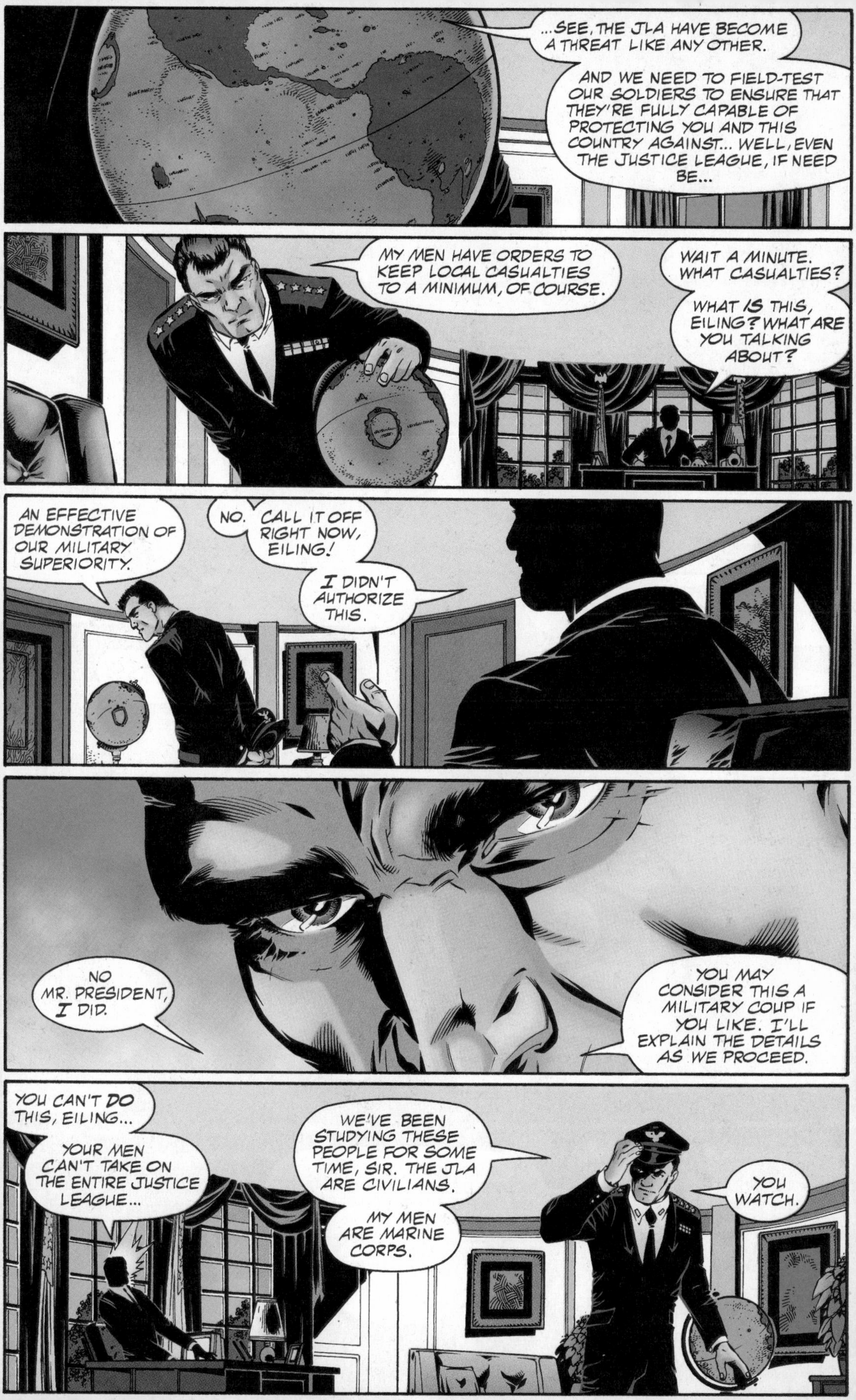
...SEE, THE JLA HAVE BECOME A THREAT LIKE ANY OTHER.
AND WE NEED TO FIELD-TEST OUR SOLDIERS TO ENSURE THAT THEY'RE FULLY CAPABLE OF PROTECTING YOU AND THIS COUNTRY AGAINST... WELL, EVEN THE JUSTICE LEAGUE, IF NEED BE...
MY MEN HAVE ORDERS TO KEEP LOCAL CASUALTIES TO A MINIMUM, OF COURSE.
WAIT A MINUTE. WHAT CASUALTIES?
WHAT IS THIS, EILING? WHAT ARE YOU TALKING ABOUT?
AN EFFECTIVE DEMONSTRATION OF OUR MILITARY SUPERIORITY.
NO.
CALL IT OFF RIGHT NOW, EILING!
I DIDN'T AUTHORIZE THIS.
NO MR. PRESIDENT, I DID.
YOU MAY CONSIDER THIS A MILITARY COUP IF YOU LIKE. I'LL EXPLAIN THE DETAILS AS WE PROCEED.
YOU CAN'T DO THIS, EILING...
YOUR MEN CAN'T TAKE ON THE ENTIRE JUSTICE LEAGUE...
WE'VE BEEN STUDYING THESE PEOPLE FOR SOME TIME, SIR. THE JLA ARE CIVILIANS.
MY MEN ARE MARINE CORPS.
YOU WATCH.

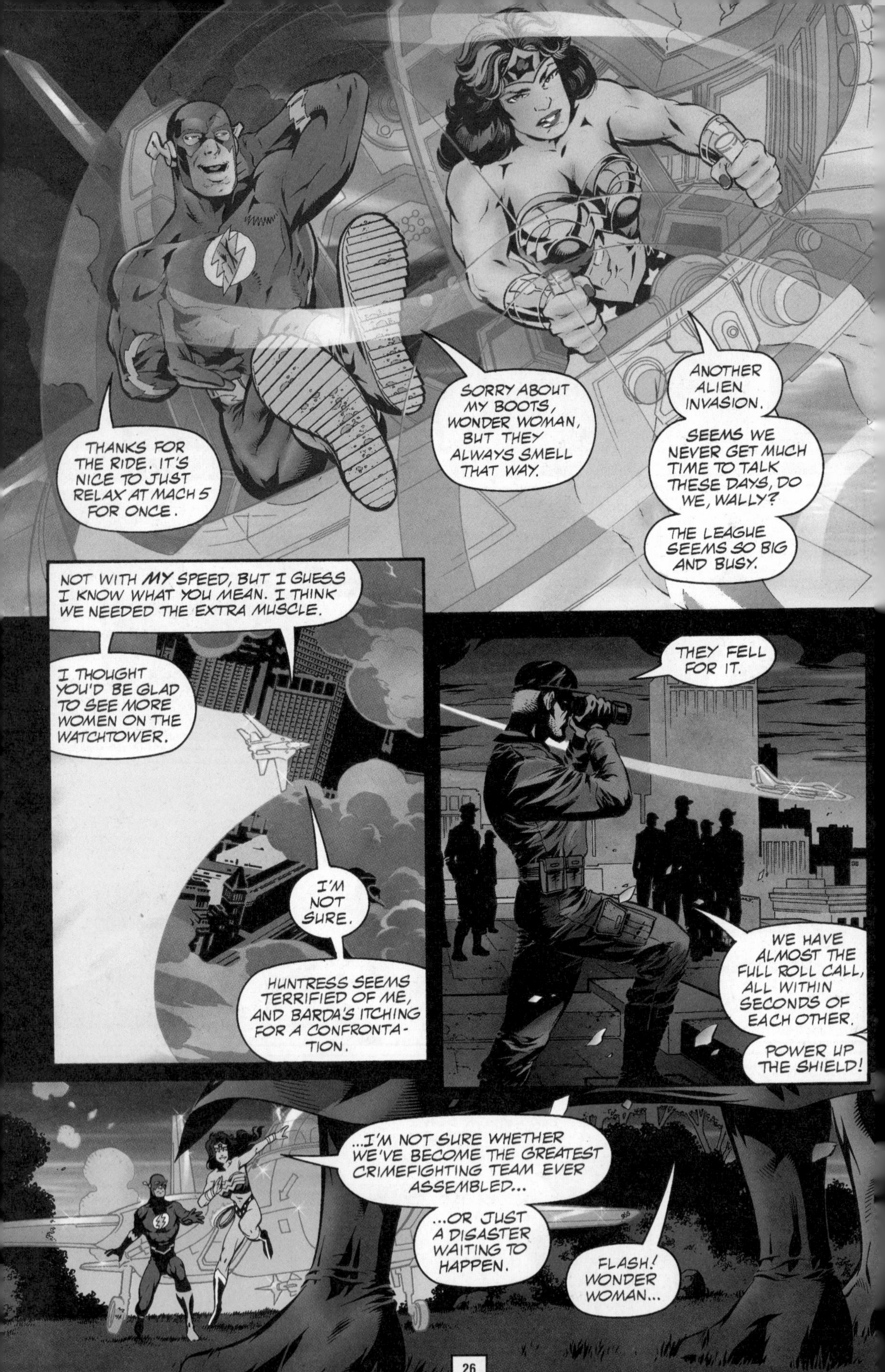
THANKS FOR THE RIDE. IT'S NICE TO JUST RELAX AT MACH 5 FOR ONCE.
SORRY ABOUT MY BOOTS, WONDER WOMAN, BUT THEY ALWAYS SMELL THAT WAY.
ANOTHER ALIEN INVASION.
SEEMS WE NEVER GET MUCH TIME TO TALK THESE DAYS, DO WE, WALLY?
THE LEAGUE SEEMS SO BIG AND BUSY.
NOT WITH MY SPEED, BUT I GUESS I KNOW WHAT YOU MEAN. I THINK WE NEEDED THE EXTRA MUSCLE.
I THOUGHT YOU'D BE GLAD TO SEE MORE WOMEN ON THE WATCHTOWER.
I'M NOT SURE.
HUNTRESS SEEMS TERRIFIED OF ME, AND BARDA'S ITCHING FOR A CONFRONTA-TION.
THEY FELL FOR IT.
WE HAVE ALMOST THE FULL ROLL CALL, ALL WITHIN SECONDS OF EACH OTHER.
POWER UP THE SHIELD!
...I'M NOT SURE WHETHER WE'VE BECOME THE GREATEST CRIMEFIGHTING TEAM EVER ASSEMBLED...
...OR JUST A DISASTER WAITING TO HAPPEN.
FLASH! WONDER WOMAN...

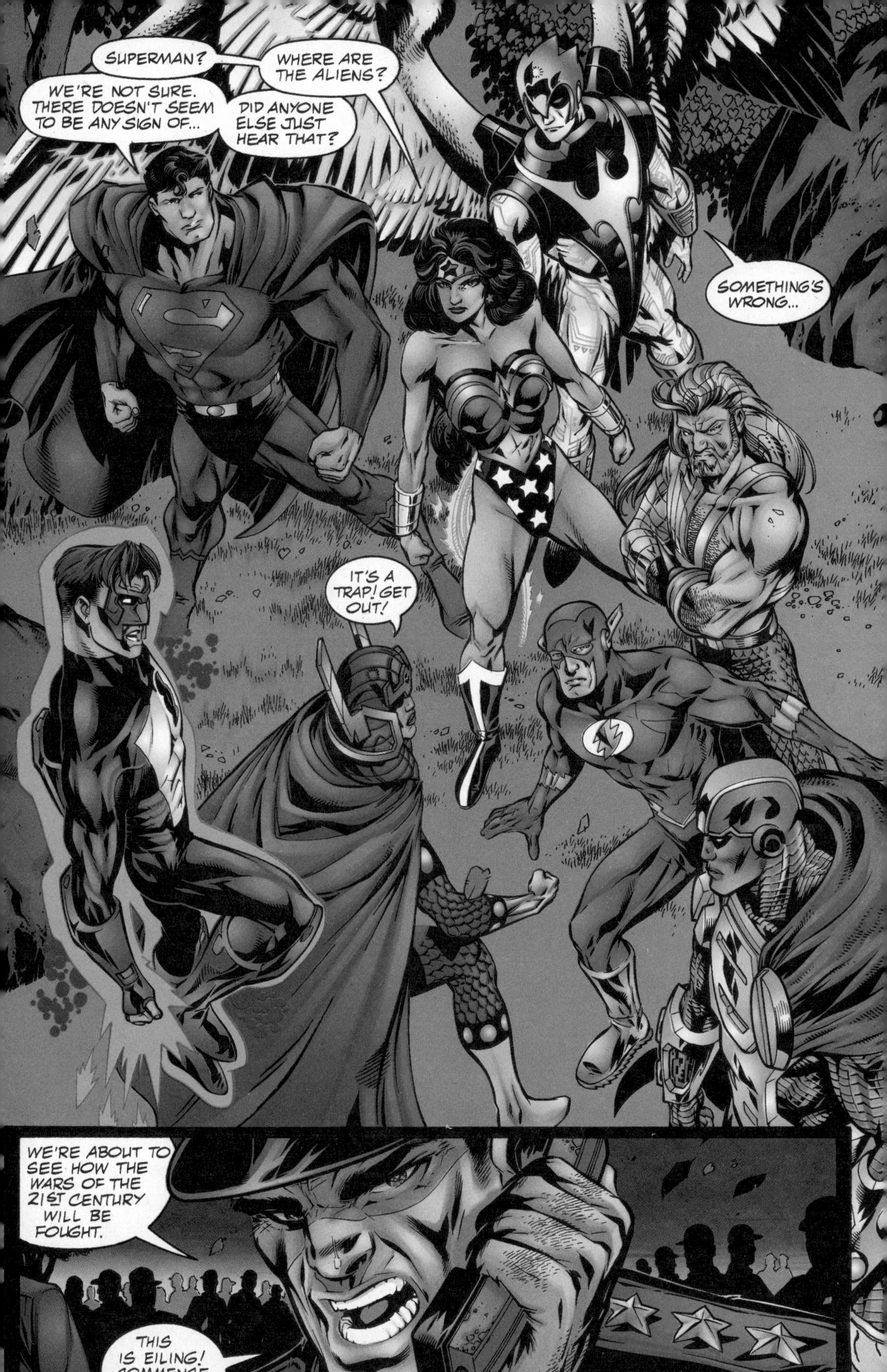
SUPERMAN?
WHERE ARE THE ALIENS?
WE'RE NOT SURE. THERE DOESN'T SEEM TO BE ANY SIGN OF...
DID ANYONE ELSE JUST HEAR THAT?
SOMETHING'S WRONG...
IT'S A TRAP! GET OUT!
WE'RE ABOUT TO SEE HOW THE WARS OF THE 21ST CENTURY WILL BE FOUGHT.
THIS IS EILING! COMMENCE OPERATION!

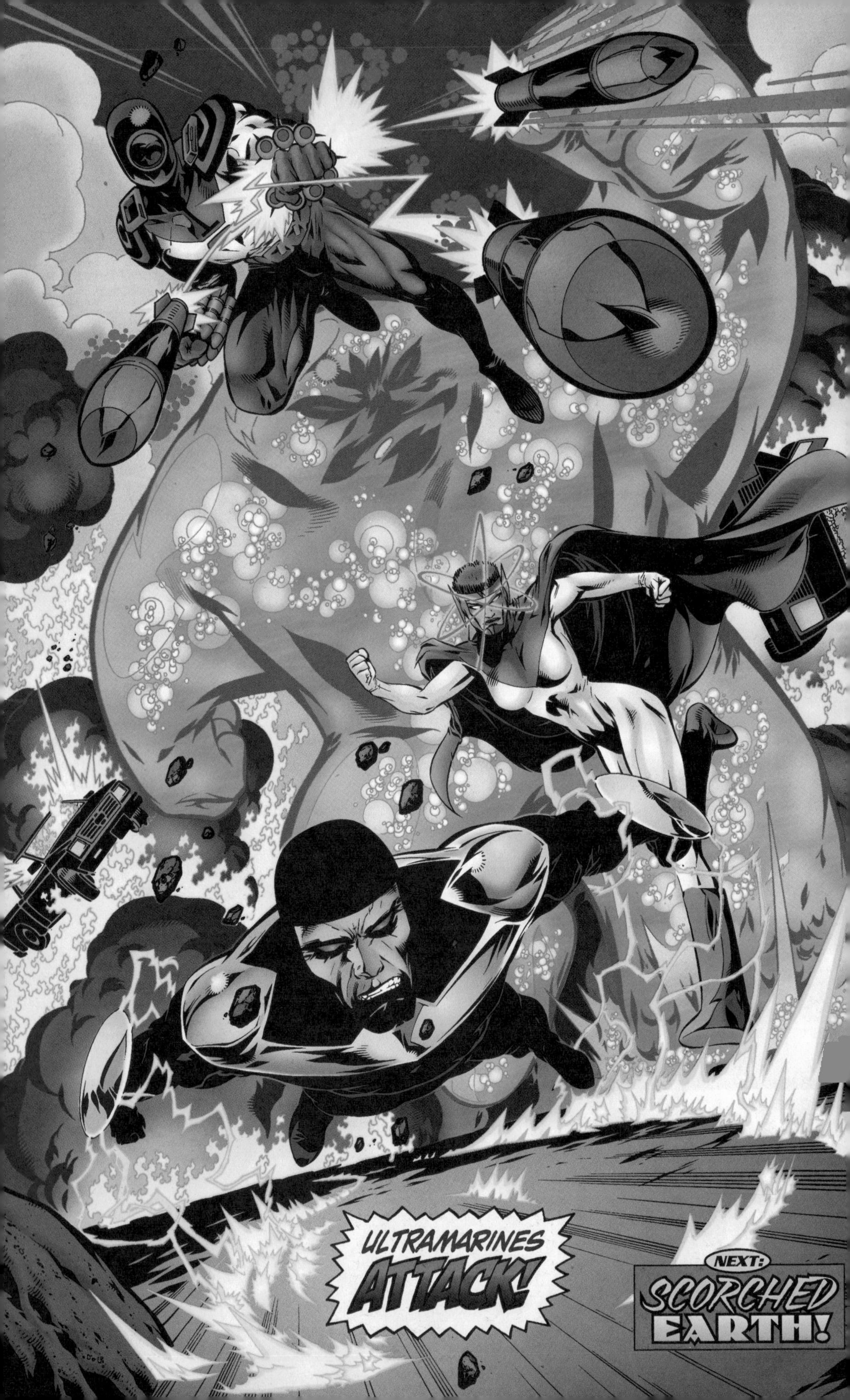
ULTRAMARINES
ATTACK!
NEXT:
SCORCHED
EARTH!

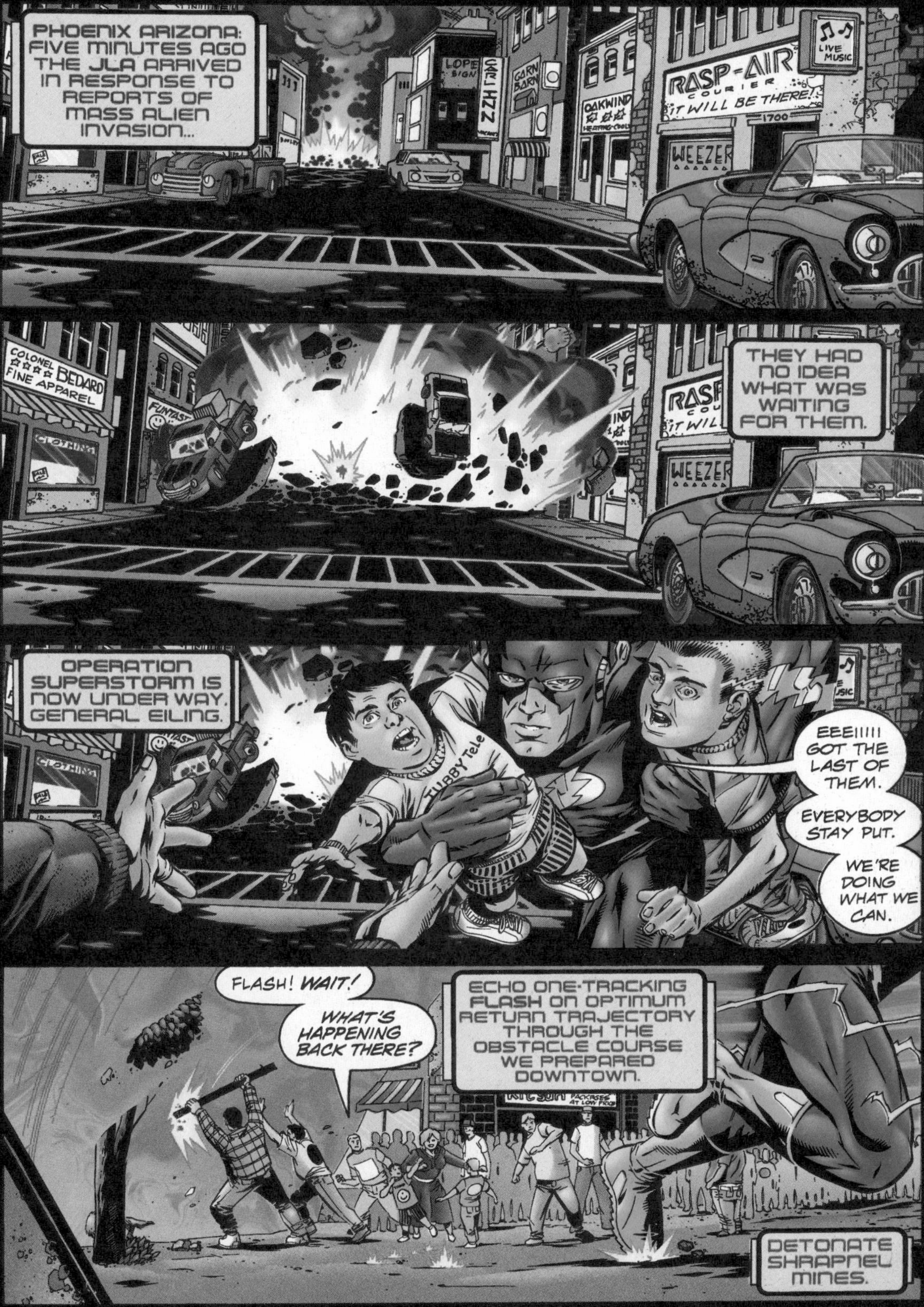
PHOENIX ARIZONA: FIVE MINUTES AGO THE JLA ARRIVED IN RESPONSE TO REPORTS OF MASS ALIEN INVASION...
RASP-AIR COURIER IT WILL BE THERE!
LIVE MUSIC
WEEZER
OAKWIND
THEY HAD NO IDEA WHAT WAS WAITING FOR THEM.
COLONEL BEDARD FINE APPAREL
CLOTHING
OPERATION SUPERSTORM IS NOW UNDER WAY, GENERAL EILING.
TUBBY TeLe
EEE!!!!! GOT THE LAST OF THEM.
EVERYBODY STAY PUT.
WE'RE DOING WHAT WE CAN.
FLASH! WAIT!
WHAT'S HAPPENING BACK THERE?
ECHO ONE-TRACKING FLASH ON OPTIMUM RETURN TRAJECTORY THROUGH THE OBSTACLE COURSE WE PREPARED DOWNTOWN.
DETONATE SHRAPNEL MINES.

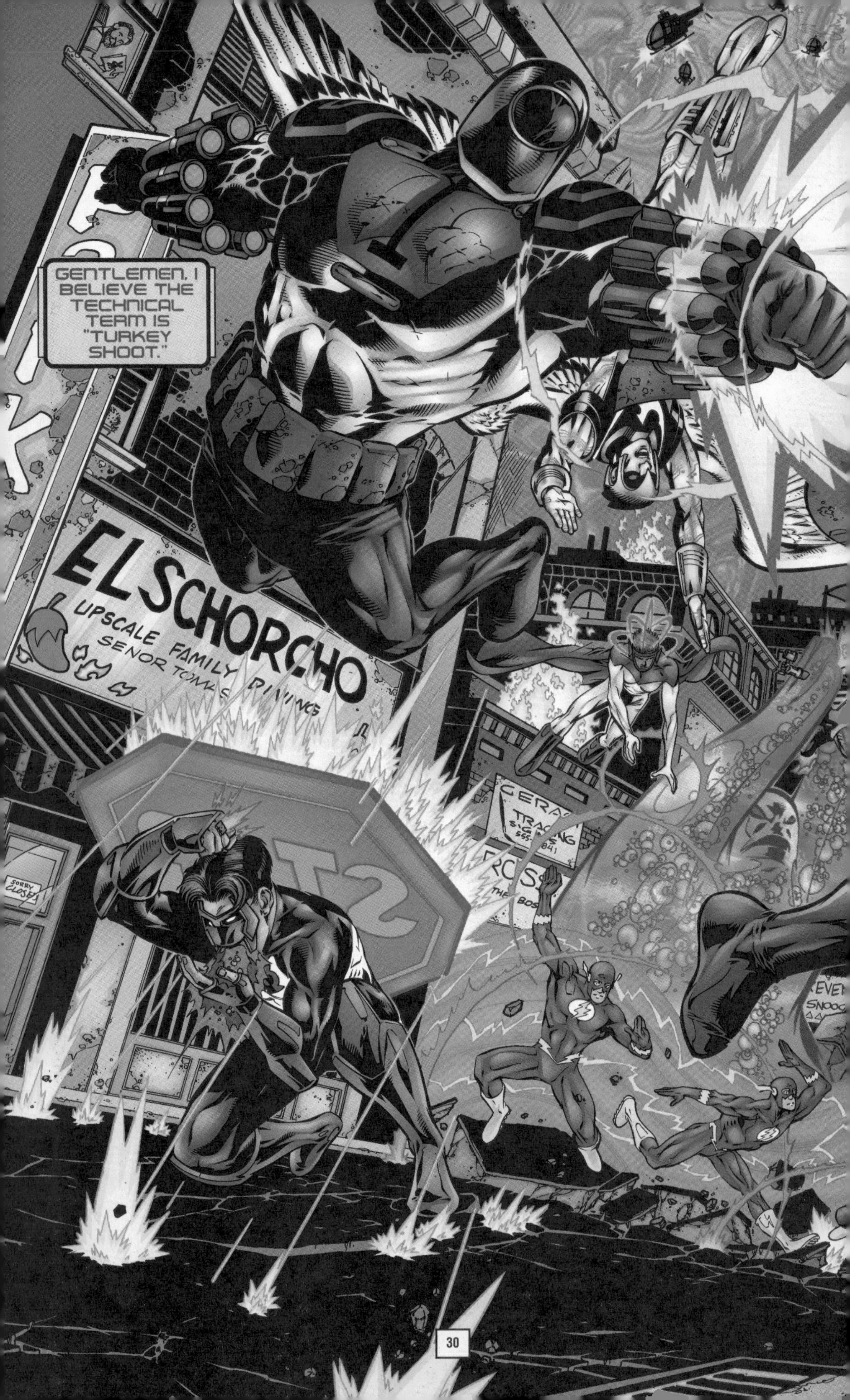
GENTLEMEN, I BELIEVE THE TECHNICAL TERM IS "TURKEY SHOOT."
EL SCHORCHO
UPSCALE FAMILY DINING
SENOR TOMKS
SORRY CLOSED

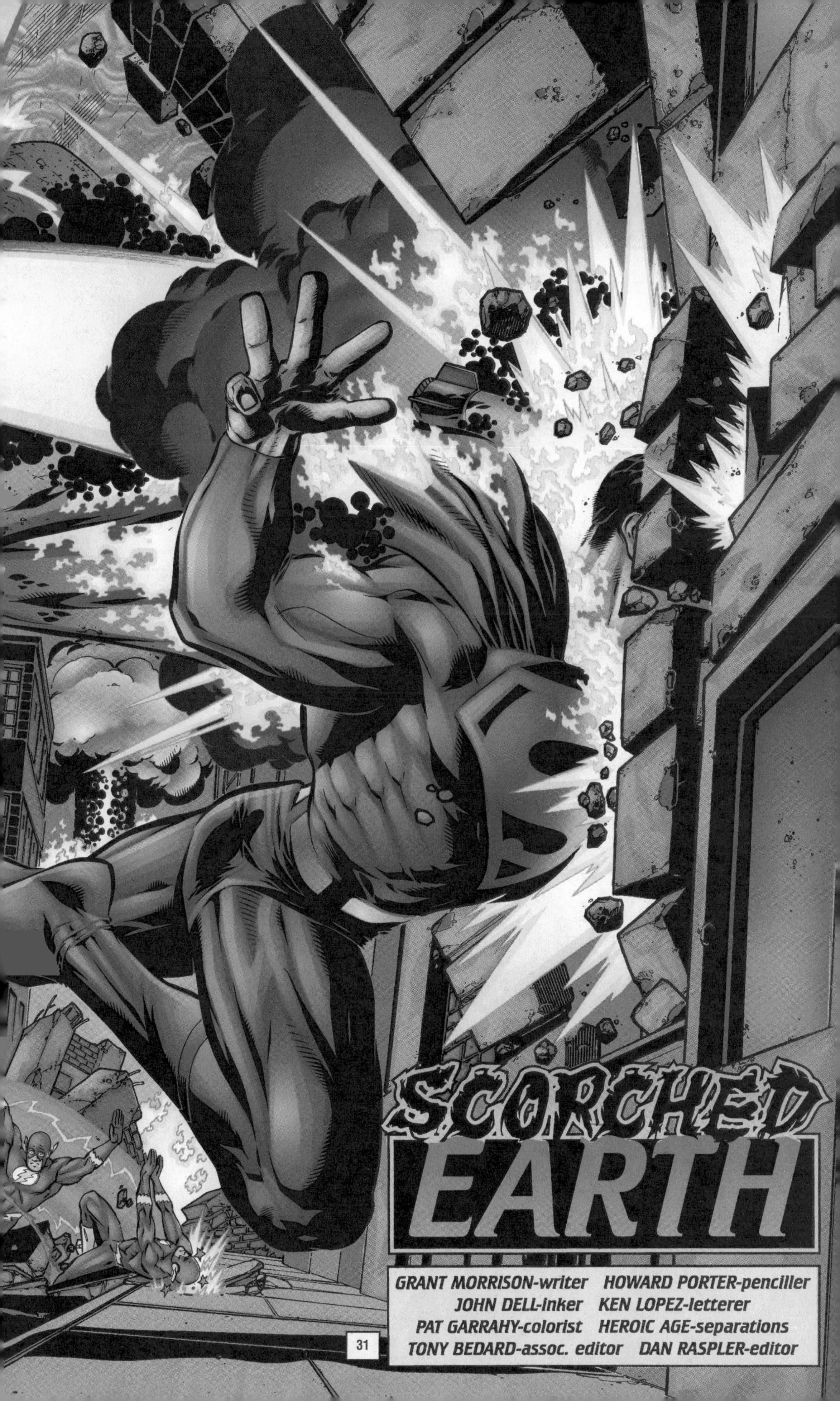
SCORCHED
EARTH
GRANT MORRISON-writer HOWARD PORTER-penciller
JOHN DELL-inker KEN LOPEZ-letterer
PAT GARRAHY-colorist HEROIC AGE-separations
TONY BEDARD-assoc. editor DAN RASPLER-editor

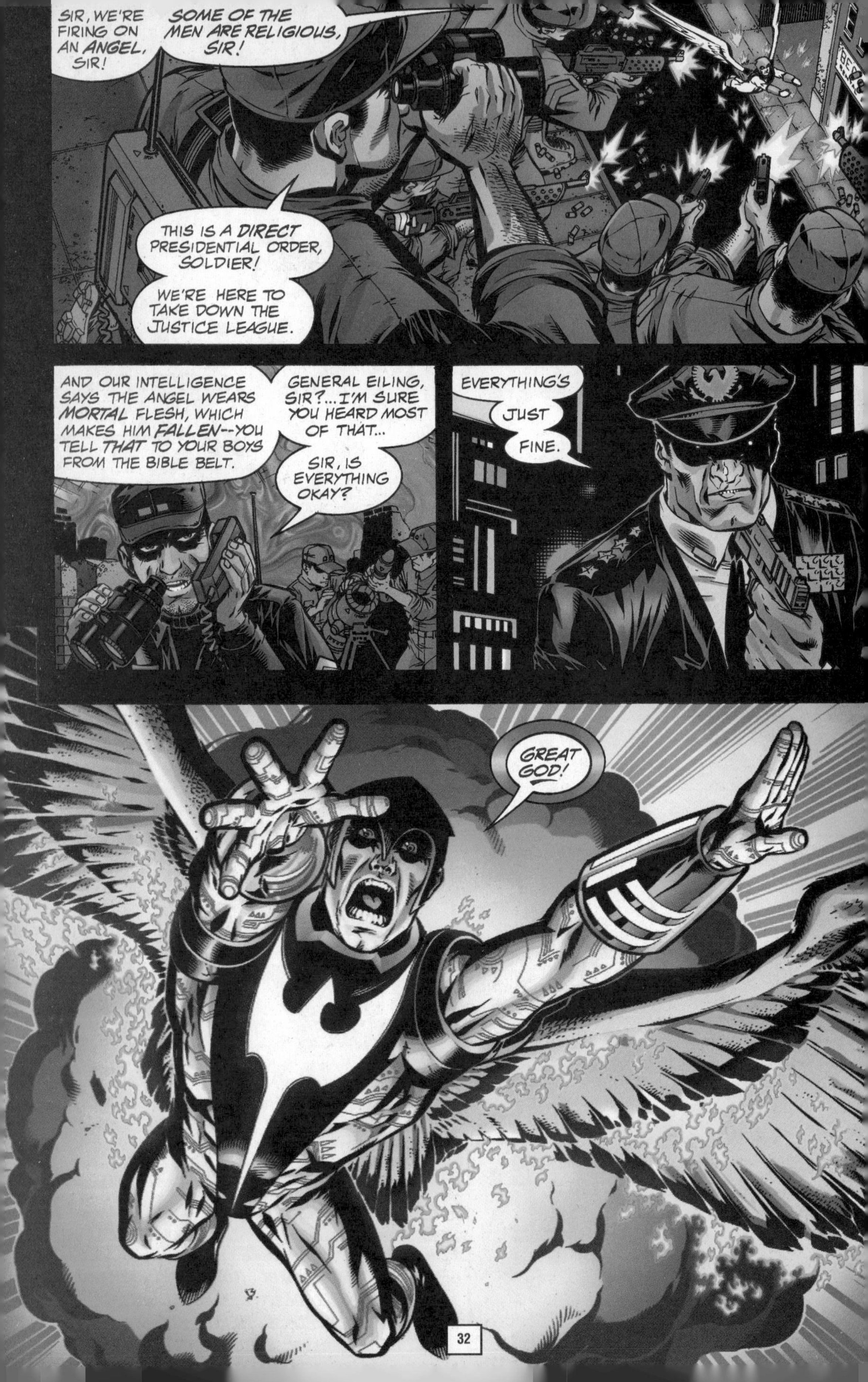
SIR, WE'RE FIRING ON AN ANGEL, SIR!
SOME OF THE MEN ARE RELIGIOUS, SIR!
THIS IS A DIRECT PRESIDENTIAL ORDER, SOLDIER!
WE'RE HERE TO TAKE DOWN THE JUSTICE LEAGUE.
AND OUR INTELLIGENCE SAYS THE ANGEL WEARS MORTAL FLESH, WHICH MAKES HIM FALLEN--YOU TELL THAT TO YOUR BOYS FROM THE BIBLE BELT.
GENERAL EILING, SIR?...I'M SURE YOU HEARD MOST OF THAT...
SIR, IS EVERYTHING OKAY?
EVERYTHING'S
JUST
FINE.
GREAT GOD!

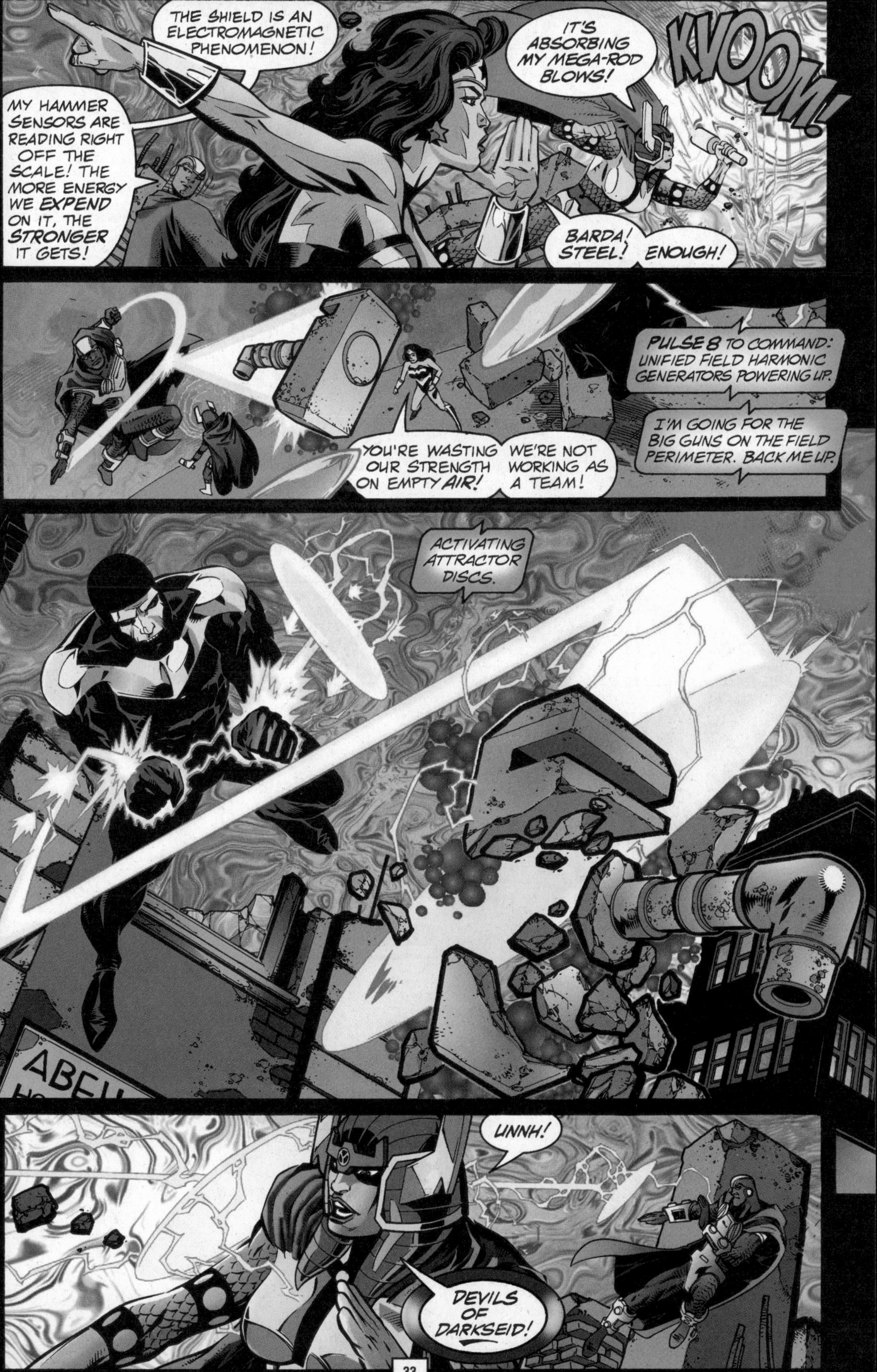
THE SHIELD IS AN ELECTROMAGNETIC PHENOMENON!
IT'S ABSORBING MY MEGA-ROD BLOWS!
KVOOM!
MY HAMMER SENSORS ARE READING RIGHT OFF THE SCALE! THE MORE ENERGY WE EXPEND ON IT, THE STRONGER IT GETS!
BARDA! STEEL! ENOUGH!
PULSE 8 TO COMMAND: UNIFIED FIELD HARMONIC GENERATORS POWERING UP.
I'M GOING FOR THE BIG GUNS ON THE FIELD PERIMETER. BACK ME UP.
YOU'RE WASTING OUR STRENGTH ON EMPTY AIR!
WE'RE NOT WORKING AS A TEAM!
ACTIVATING ATTRACTOR DISCS.
UNNH!
DEVILS OF DARKSEID!

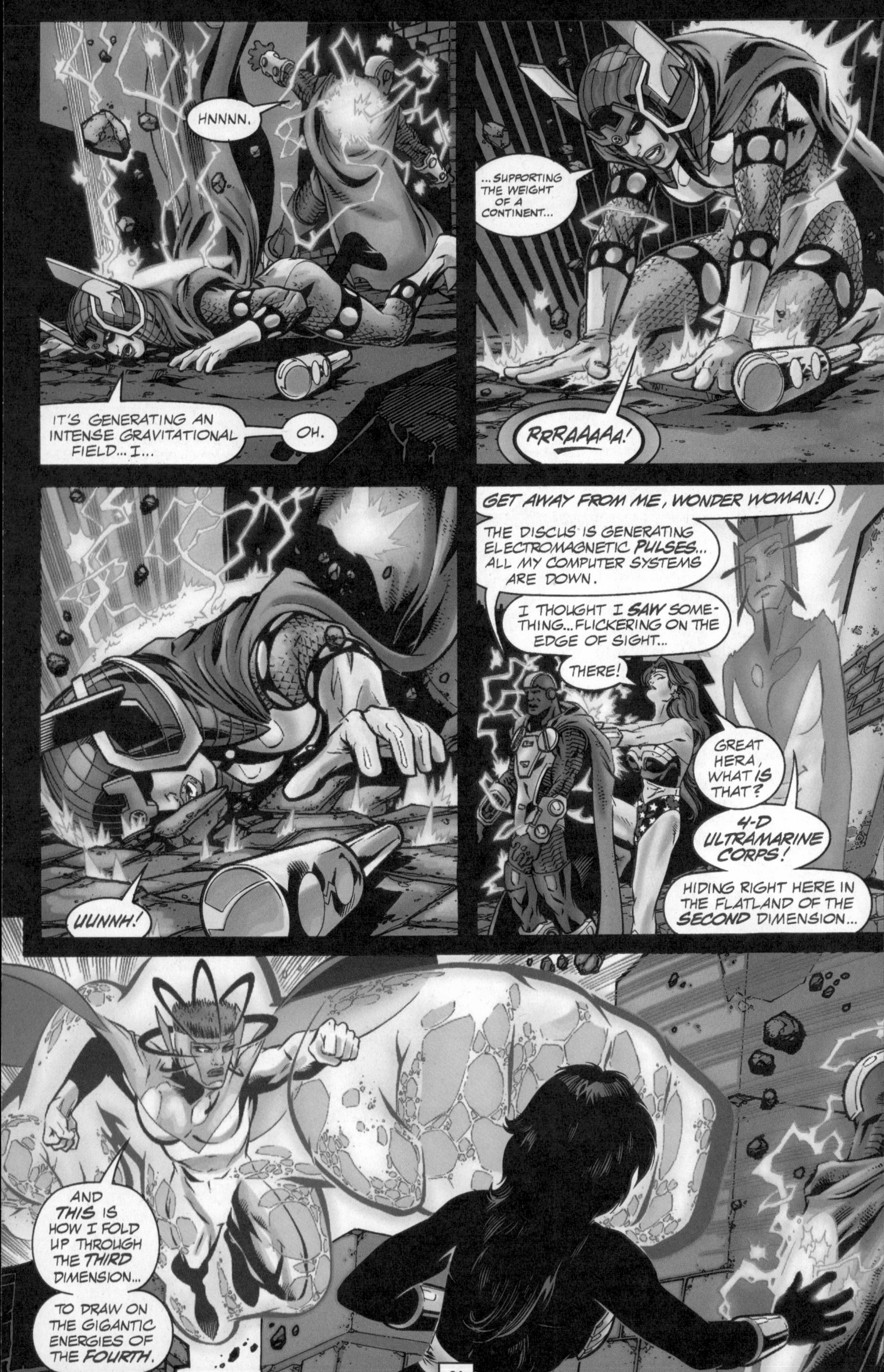
HNNNN.
IT'S GENERATING AN INTENSE GRAVITATIONAL FIELD... I...
OH.
...SUPPORTING THE WEIGHT OF A CONTINENT...
RRRAAAAA!
UUNNH!
GET AWAY FROM ME, WONDER WOMAN!
THE DISCUS IS GENERATING ELECTROMAGNETIC PULSES... ALL MY COMPUTER SYSTEMS ARE DOWN.
I THOUGHT I SAW SOME-THING... FLICKERING ON THE EDGE OF SIGHT...
THERE!
GREAT HERA, WHAT IS THAT?
4-D ULTRAMARINE CORPS!
HIDING RIGHT HERE IN THE FLATLAND OF THE SECOND DIMENSION...
AND THIS IS HOW I FOLD UP THROUGH THE THIRD DIMENSION...
TO DRAW ON THE GIGANTIC ENERGIES OF THE FOURTH.

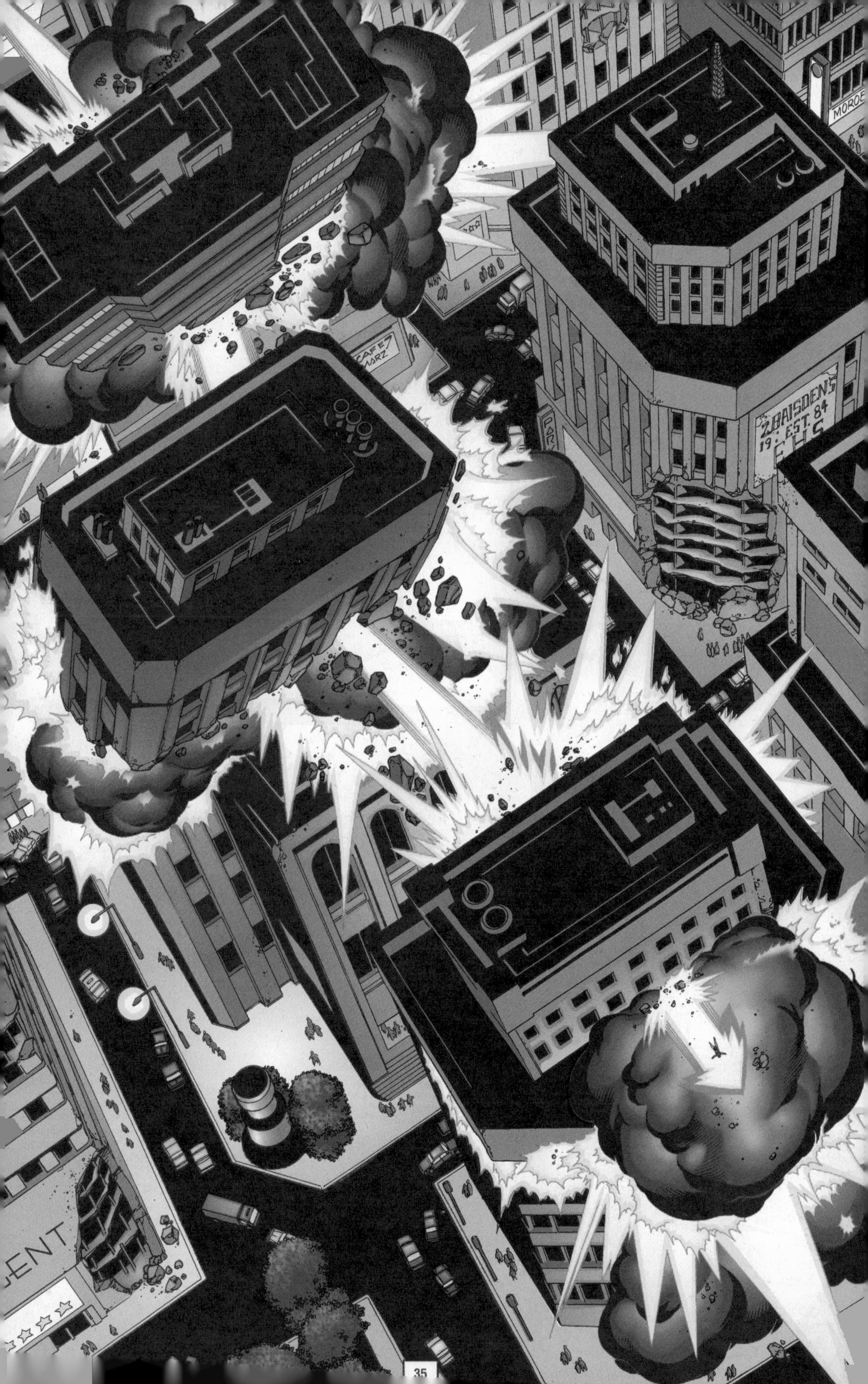

ZBAISDEN'S
19 EST. 84

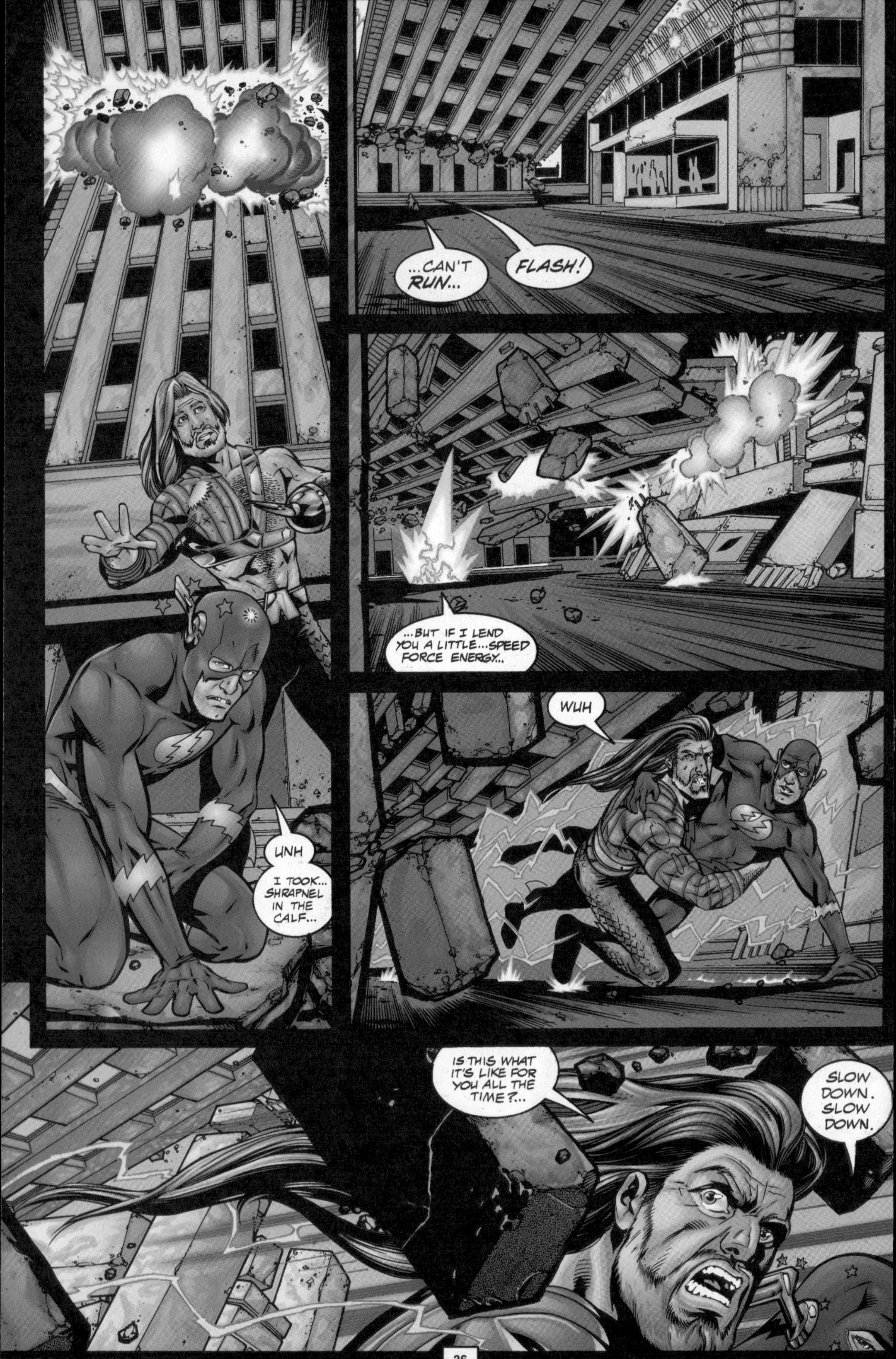
...CAN'T RUN...
FLASH!
...BUT IF I LEND YOU A LITTLE...SPEED FORCE ENERGY...
UNH
I TOOK... SHRAPNEL IN THE CALF...
WUH
IS THIS WHAT IT'S LIKE FOR YOU ALL THE TIME?...
SLOW DOWN. SLOW DOWN.

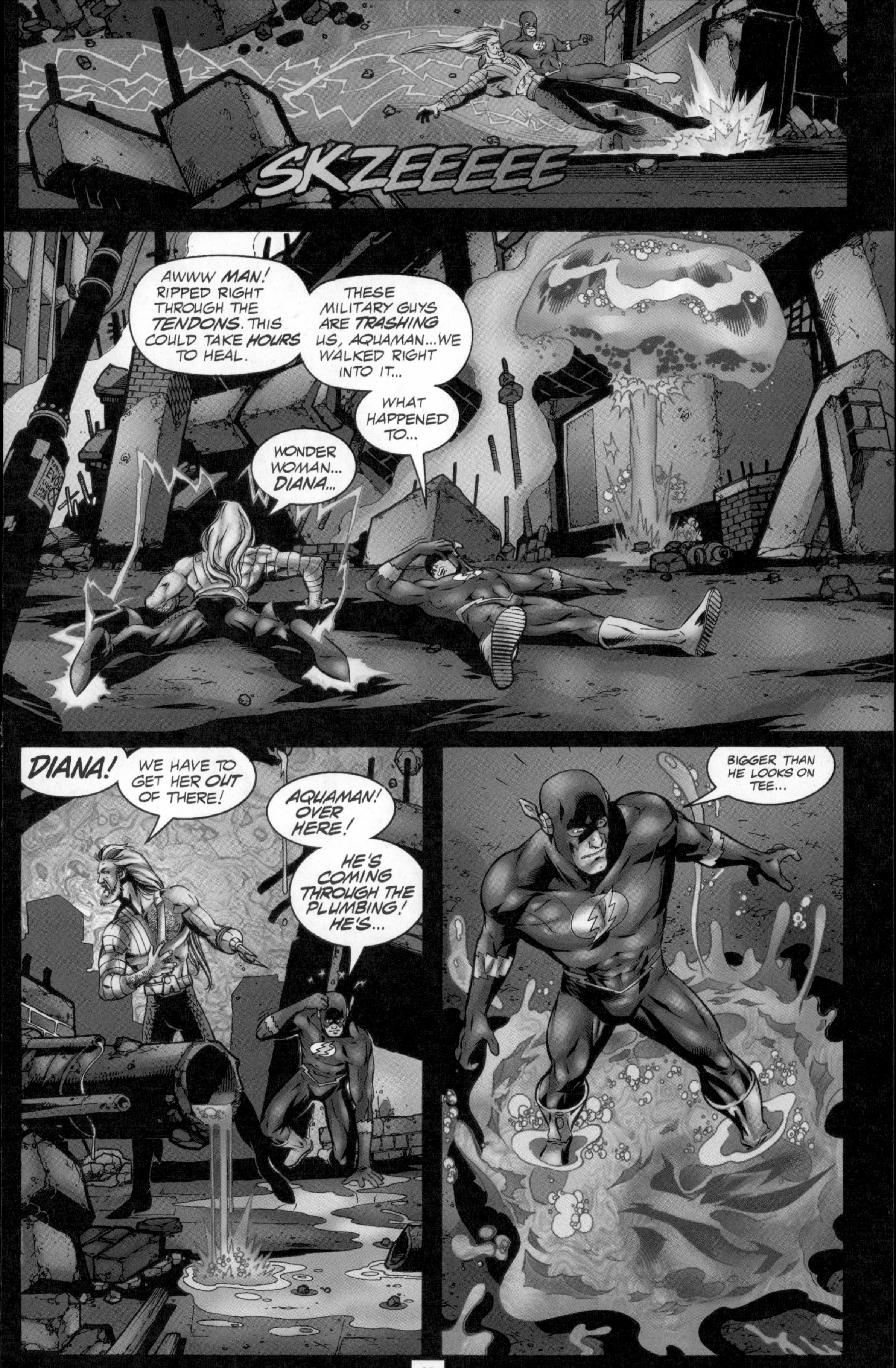
SKZEEEEE
AWWW MAN! RIPPED RIGHT THROUGH THE TENDONS. THIS COULD TAKE HOURS TO HEAL.
THESE MILITARY GUYS ARE TRASHING US, AQUAMAN... WE WALKED RIGHT INTO IT...
WHAT HAPPENED TO...
WONDER WOMAN... DIANA...
DIANA!
WE HAVE TO GET HER OUT OF THERE!
AQUAMAN! OVER HERE!
HE'S COMING THROUGH THE PLUMBING! HE'S...
BIGGER THAN HE LOOKS ON TEE...

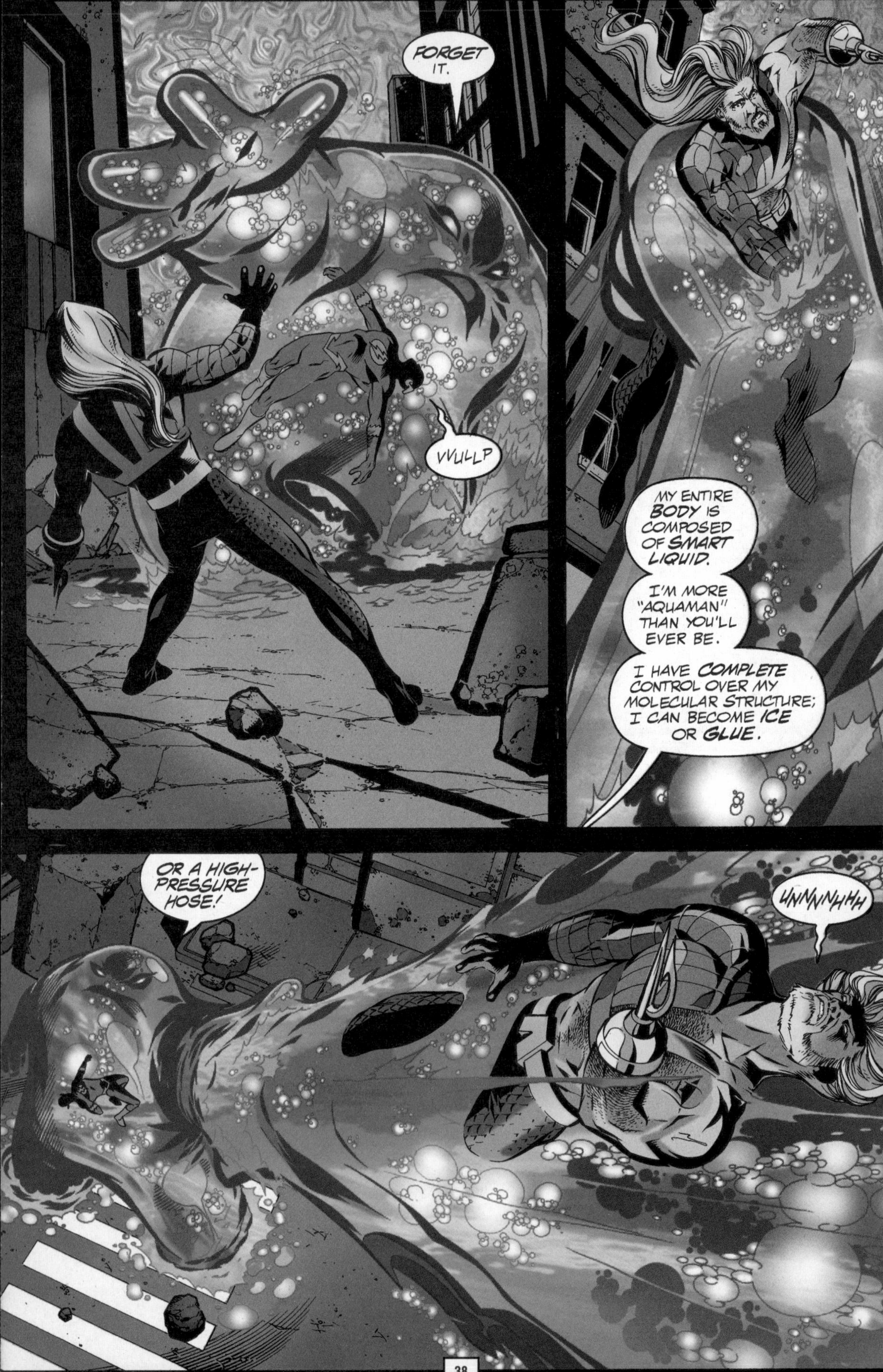
FORGET IT.
VVULLP
MY ENTIRE BODY IS COMPOSED OF SMART LIQUID.
I'M MORE "AQUAMAN" THAN YOU'LL EVER BE.
I HAVE COMPLETE CONTROL OVER MY MOLECULAR STRUCTURE; I CAN BECOME ICE OR GLUE.
OR A HIGH-PRESSURE HOSE!
UNNNNHHH

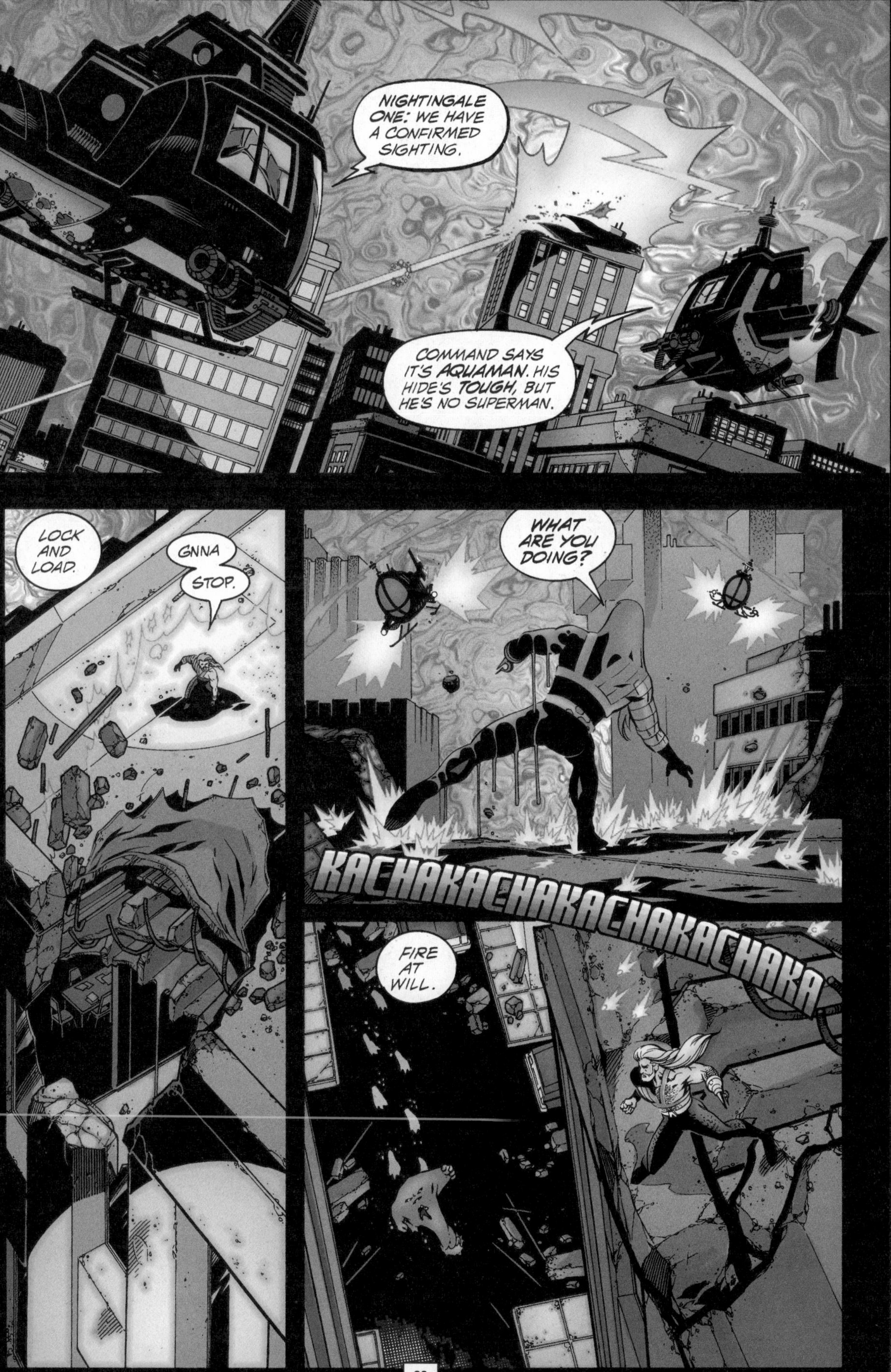
NIGHTINGALE ONE: WE HAVE A CONFIRMED SIGHTING.
COMMAND SAYS IT'S AQUAMAN. HIS HIDE'S TOUGH, BUT HE'S NO SUPERMAN.
LOCK AND LOAD.
GNNA
STOP.
WHAT ARE YOU DOING?
KACHAKACHAKACHAKACHAKA
FIRE AT WILL.

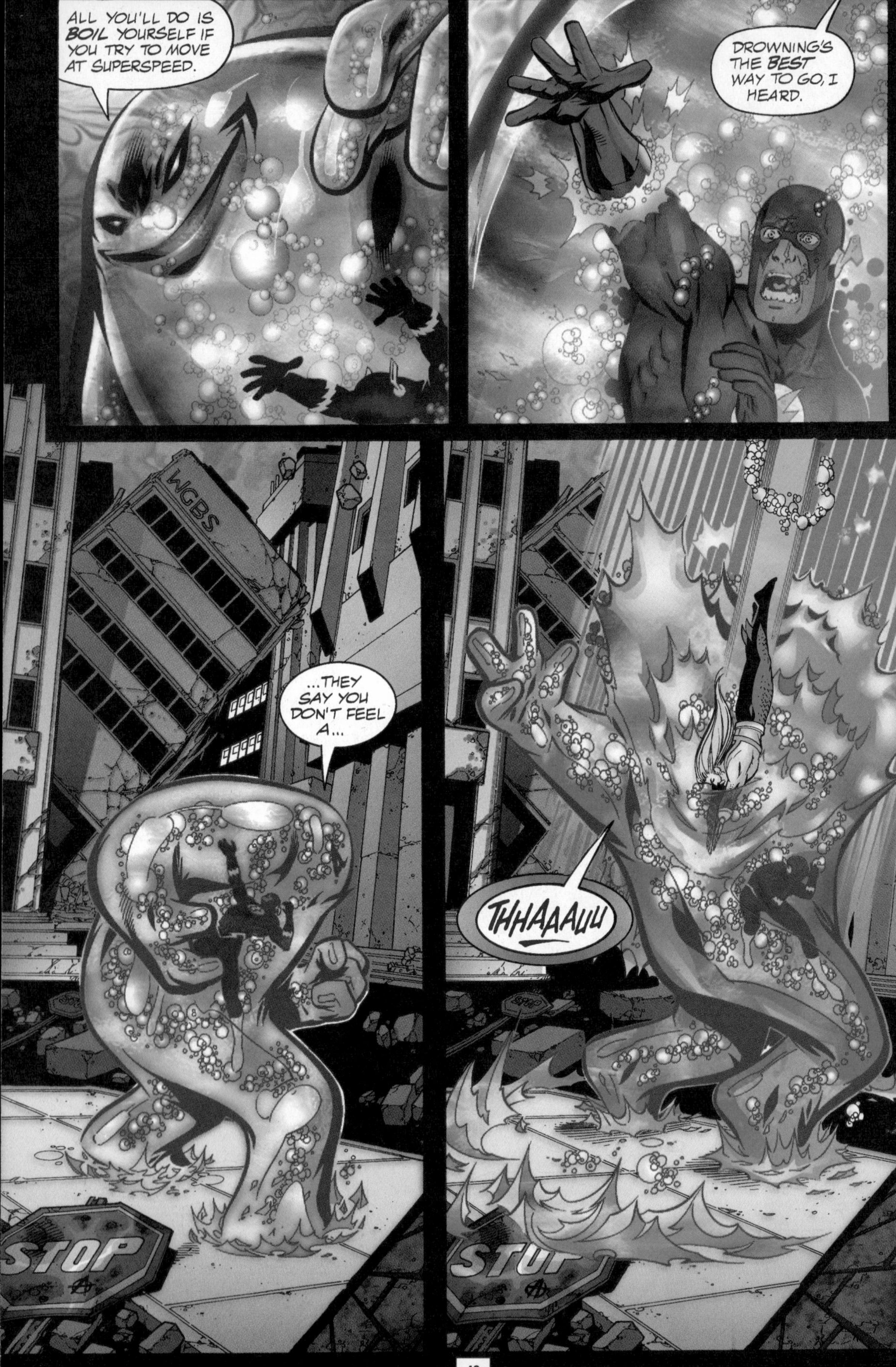
ALL YOU'LL DO IS BOIL YOURSELF IF YOU TRY TO MOVE AT SUPERSPEED.
DROWNING'S THE BEST WAY TO GO, I HEARD.
WGBS
...THEY SAY YOU DON'T FEEL A...
THHAAAUU
STOP
STOP

HUNHH

ALKGGHH

LET'S GO, FLASH!

WUUHHH!

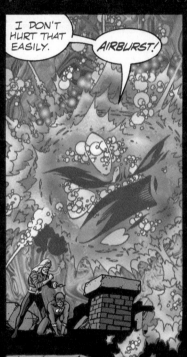

I DON'T HURT THAT EASILY.

AIRBURST!

SEE? I CAN EVEN ATTACK YOU IN THE FORM OF RAIN

HE'S CONDENSING AROUND US, FLASH!

AND I'M SUPER-ACCELERATING HIS MOLECULES.

NNUUHH

HE'S STEAM!

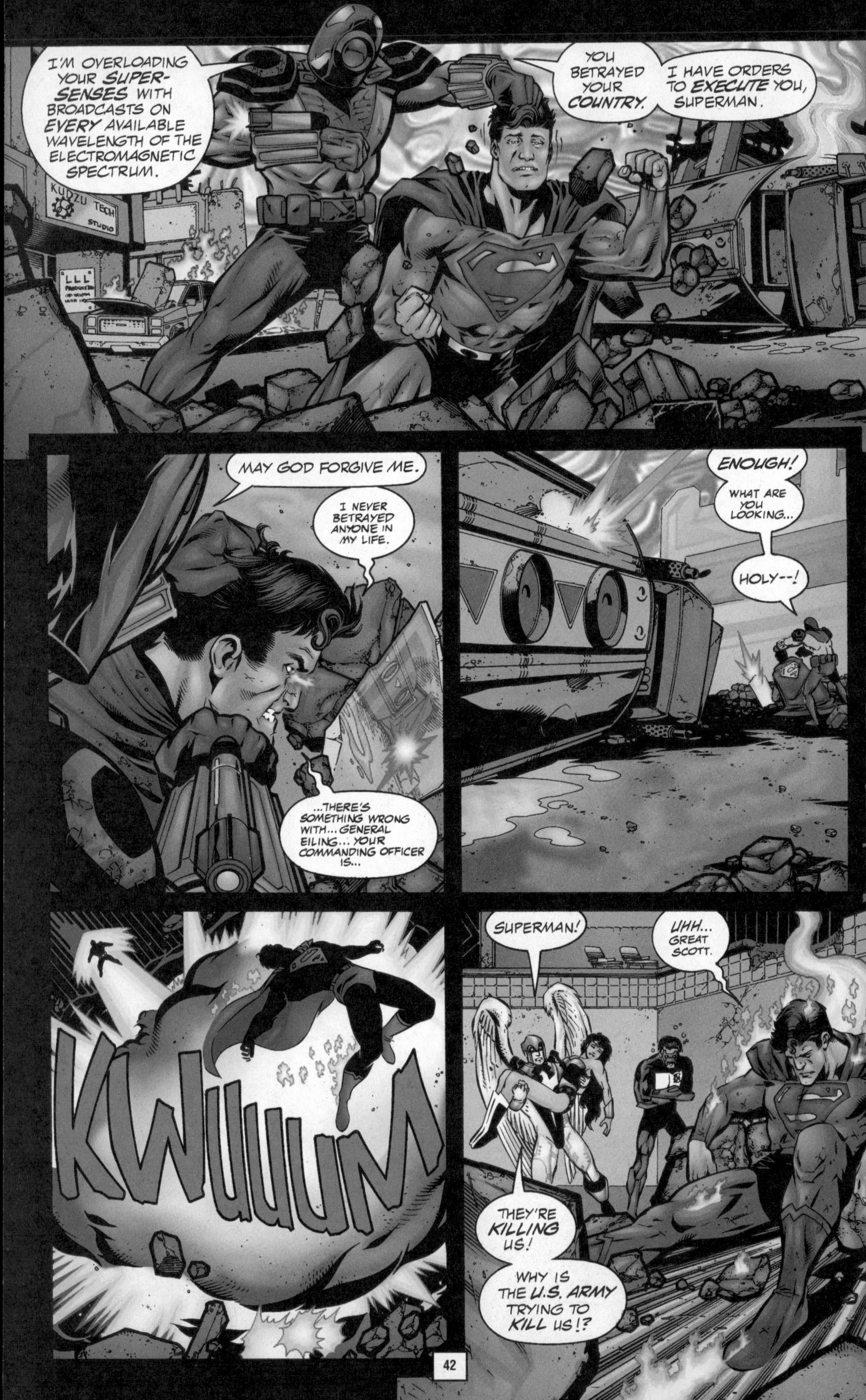
I'M OVERLOADING YOUR SUPER-SENSES WITH BROADCASTS ON EVERY AVAILABLE WAVELENGTH OF THE ELECTROMAGNETIC SPECTRUM.
YOU BETRAYED YOUR COUNTRY.
I HAVE ORDERS TO EXECUTE YOU, SUPERMAN.
KUDZU TECH STUDIO
MAY GOD FORGIVE ME.
I NEVER BETRAYED ANYONE IN MY LIFE.
...THERE'S SOMETHING WRONG WITH... GENERAL EILING... YOUR COMMANDING OFFICER IS...
ENOUGH!
WHAT ARE YOU LOOKING...
HOLY--!
KWUUUM
SUPERMAN!
UHH... GREAT SCOTT.
THEY'RE KILLING US!
WHY IS THE U.S. ARMY TRYING TO KILL US!?

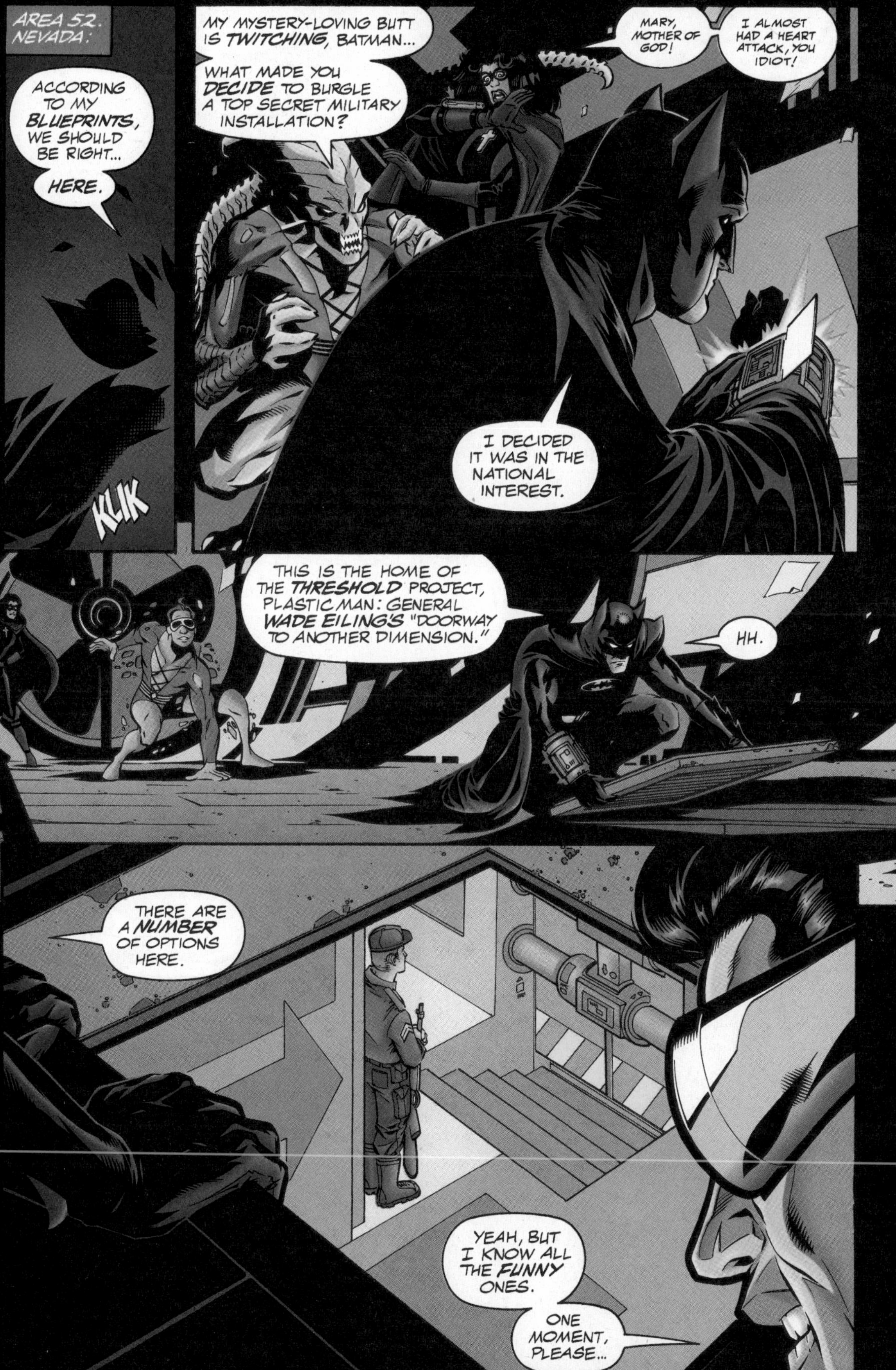
AREA 52. NEVADA:
ACCORDING TO MY BLUEPRINTS, WE SHOULD BE RIGHT... HERE.
KLIK
MY MYSTERY-LOVING BUTT IS TWITCHING, BATMAN...
WHAT MADE YOU DECIDE TO BURGLE A TOP SECRET MILITARY INSTALLATION?
MARY, MOTHER OF GOD!
I ALMOST HAD A HEART ATTACK, YOU IDIOT!
I DECIDED IT WAS IN THE NATIONAL INTEREST.
THIS IS THE HOME OF THE THRESHOLD PROJECT, PLASTIC MAN: GENERAL WADE EILING'S "DOORWAY TO ANOTHER DIMENSION."
HH.
THERE ARE A NUMBER OF OPTIONS HERE.
YEAH, BUT I KNOW ALL THE FUNNY ONES.
ONE MOMENT, PLEASE...

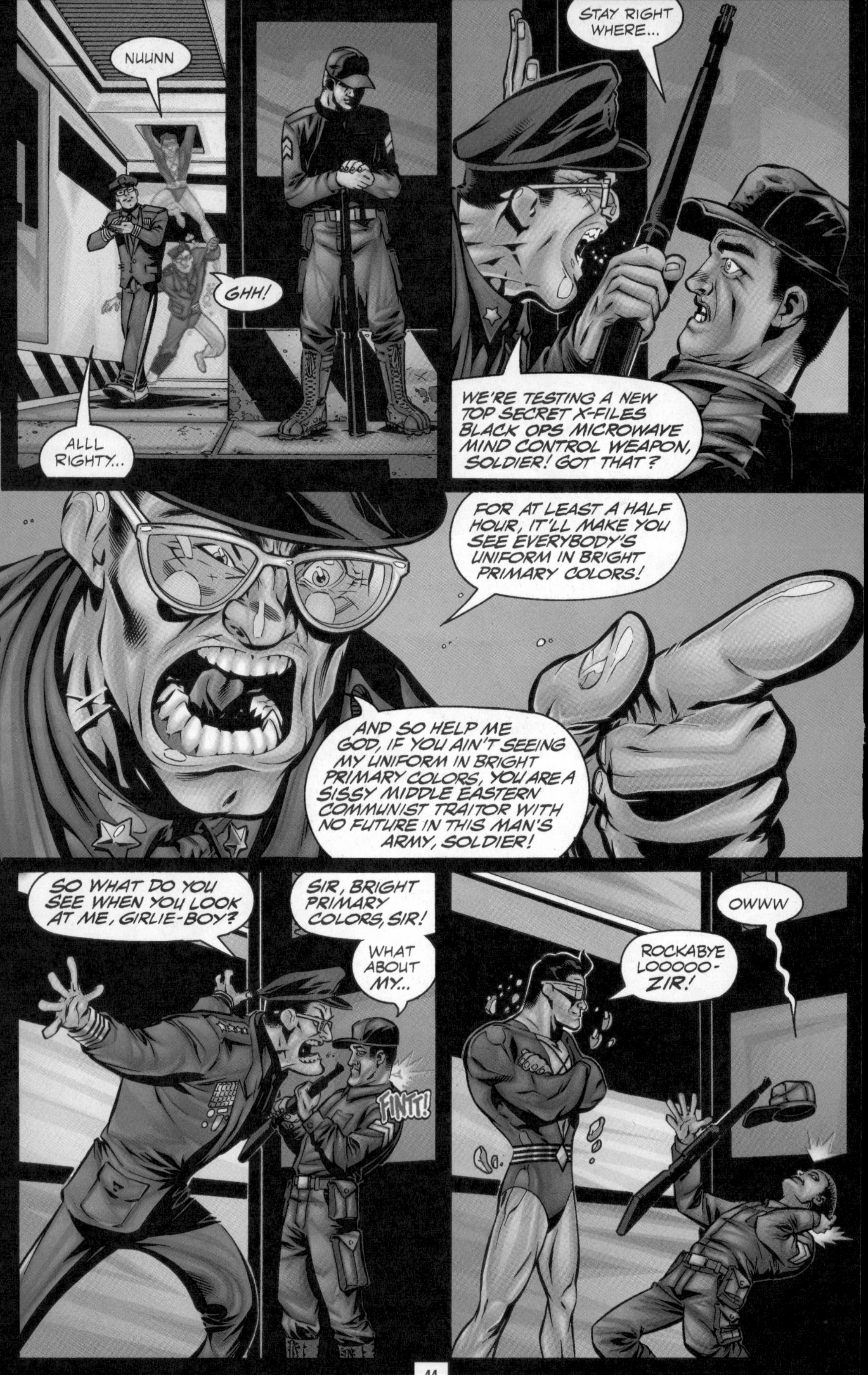
NUUNN
GHH!
ALLL RIGHTY...
STAY RIGHT WHERE...
WE'RE TESTING A NEW TOP SECRET X-FILES BLACK OPS MICROWAVE MIND CONTROL WEAPON, SOLDIER! GOT THAT?
FOR AT LEAST A HALF HOUR, IT'LL MAKE YOU SEE EVERYBODY'S UNIFORM IN BRIGHT PRIMARY COLORS!
AND SO HELP ME GOD, IF YOU AIN'T SEEING MY UNIFORM IN BRIGHT PRIMARY COLORS, YOU ARE A SISSY MIDDLE EASTERN COMMUNIST TRAITOR WITH NO FUTURE IN THIS MAN'S ARMY, SOLDIER!
SO WHAT DO YOU SEE WHEN YOU LOOK AT ME, GIRLIE-BOY?
SIR, BRIGHT PRIMARY COLORS, SIR!
WHAT ABOUT MY...
FNTT!
ROCKABYE LOOOOO-ZIR!
OWWW

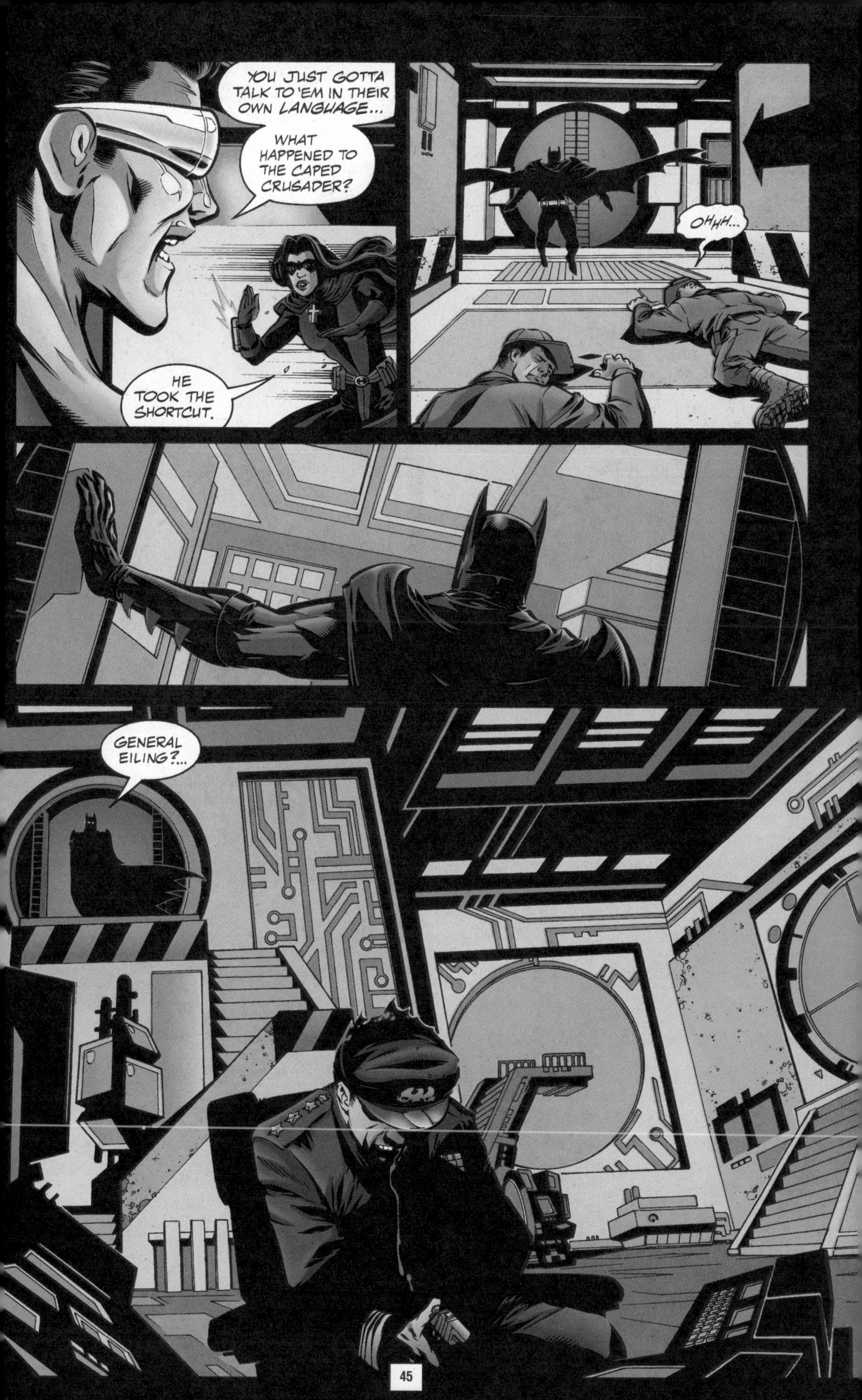
YOU JUST GOTTA TALK TO 'EM IN THEIR OWN LANGUAGE...
WHAT HAPPENED TO THE CAPED CRUSADER?
HE TOOK THE SHORTCUT.
OHHH...
GENERAL EILING?...

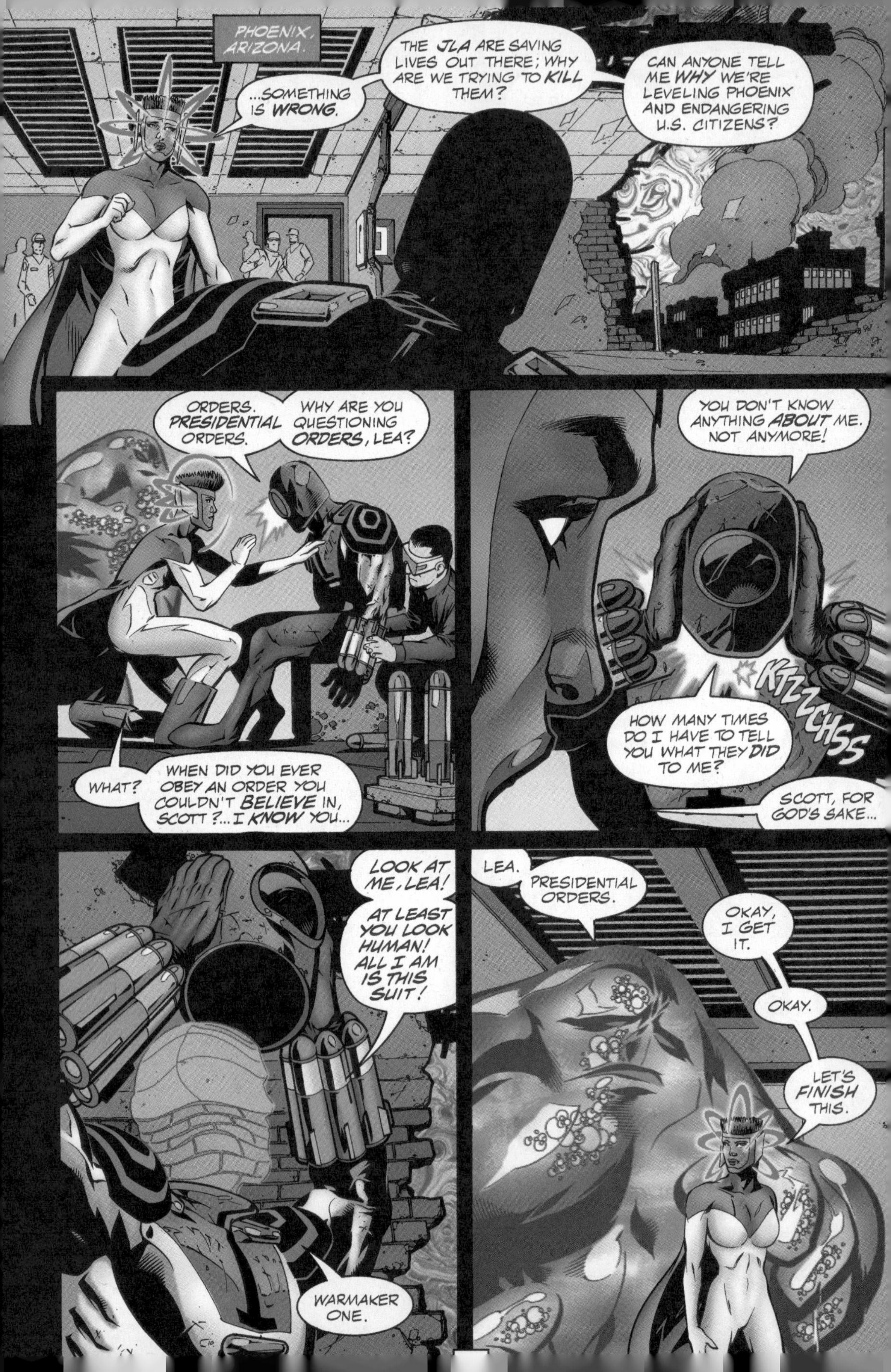
PHOENIX, ARIZONA.
...SOMETHING IS WRONG.
THE JLA ARE SAVING LIVES OUT THERE; WHY ARE WE TRYING TO KILL THEM?
CAN ANYONE TELL ME WHY WE'RE LEVELING PHOENIX AND ENDANGERING U.S. CITIZENS?
ORDERS. PRESIDENTIAL ORDERS.
WHY ARE YOU QUESTIONING ORDERS, LEA?
WHAT?
WHEN DID YOU EVER OBEY AN ORDER YOU COULDN'T BELIEVE IN, SCOTT?... I KNOW YOU...
YOU DON'T KNOW ANYTHING ABOUT ME. NOT ANYMORE!
KTZZCHSS
HOW MANY TIMES DO I HAVE TO TELL YOU WHAT THEY DID TO ME?
SCOTT, FOR GOD'S SAKE...
LOOK AT ME, LEA!
AT LEAST YOU LOOK HUMAN! ALL I AM IS THIS SUIT!
WARMAKER ONE.
LEA.
PRESIDENTIAL ORDERS.
OKAY, I GET IT.
OKAY.
LET'S FINISH THIS.

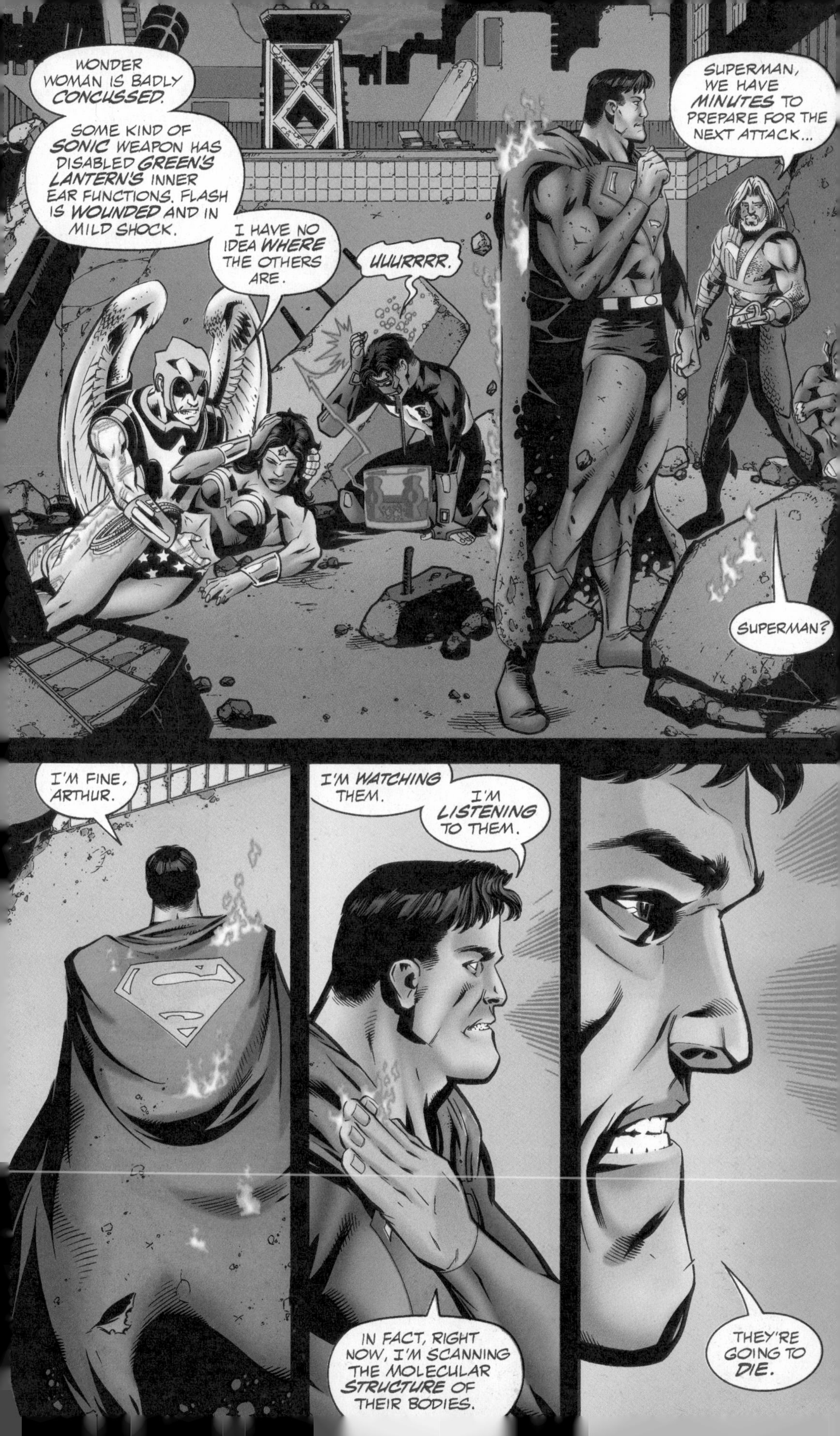
WONDER WOMAN IS BADLY CONCUSSED.
SOME KIND OF SONIC WEAPON HAS DISABLED GREEN'S LANTERN'S INNER EAR FUNCTIONS. FLASH IS WOUNDED AND IN MILD SHOCK.
I HAVE NO IDEA WHERE THE OTHERS ARE.
UUURRRR.
SUPERMAN, WE HAVE MINUTES TO PREPARE FOR THE NEXT ATTACK...
SUPERMAN?
I'M FINE, ARTHUR.
I'M WATCHING THEM.
I'M LISTENING TO THEM.
IN FACT, RIGHT NOW, I'M SCANNING THE MOLECULAR STRUCTURE OF THEIR BODIES.
THEY'RE GOING TO DIE.

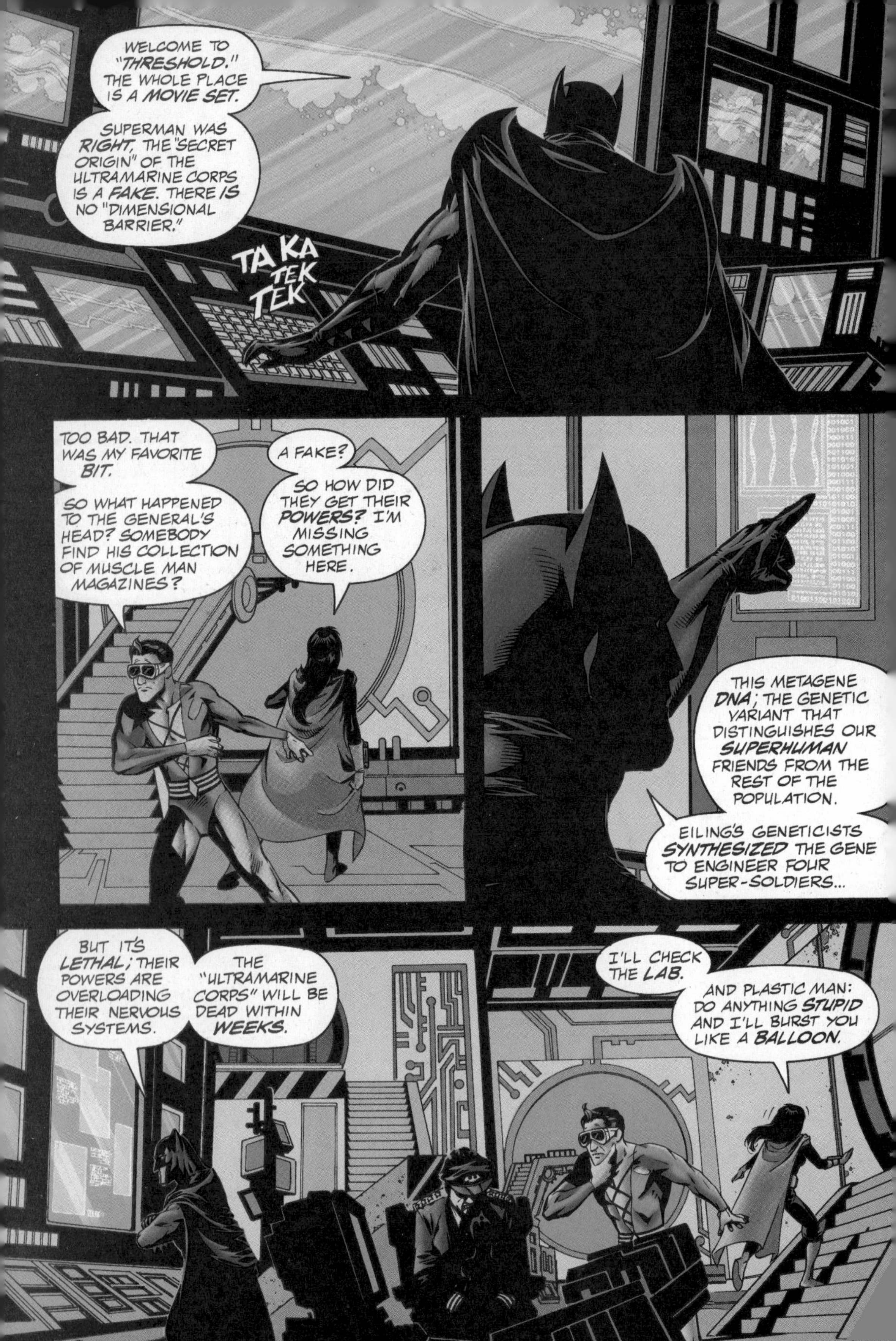
WELCOME TO "THRESHOLD." THE WHOLE PLACE IS A MOVIE SET.
SUPERMAN WAS RIGHT, THE "SECRET ORIGIN" OF THE ULTRAMARINE CORPS IS A FAKE. THERE IS NO "DIMENSIONAL BARRIER."
TA KA TEK TEK
TOO BAD. THAT WAS MY FAVORITE BIT.
SO WHAT HAPPENED TO THE GENERAL'S HEAD? SOMEBODY FIND HIS COLLECTION OF MUSCLE MAN MAGAZINES?
A FAKE?
SO HOW DID THEY GET THEIR POWERS? I'M MISSING SOMETHING HERE.
THIS METAGENE DNA; THE GENETIC VARIANT THAT DISTINGUISHES OUR SUPERHUMAN FRIENDS FROM THE REST OF THE POPULATION.
EILING'S GENETICISTS SYNTHESIZED THE GENE TO ENGINEER FOUR SUPER-SOLDIERS...
BUT IT'S LETHAL; THEIR POWERS ARE OVERLOADING THEIR NERVOUS SYSTEMS.
THE "ULTRAMARINE CORPS" WILL BE DEAD WITHIN WEEKS.
I'LL CHECK THE LAB.
AND PLASTIC MAN: DO ANYTHING STUPID AND I'LL BURST YOU LIKE A BALLOON.

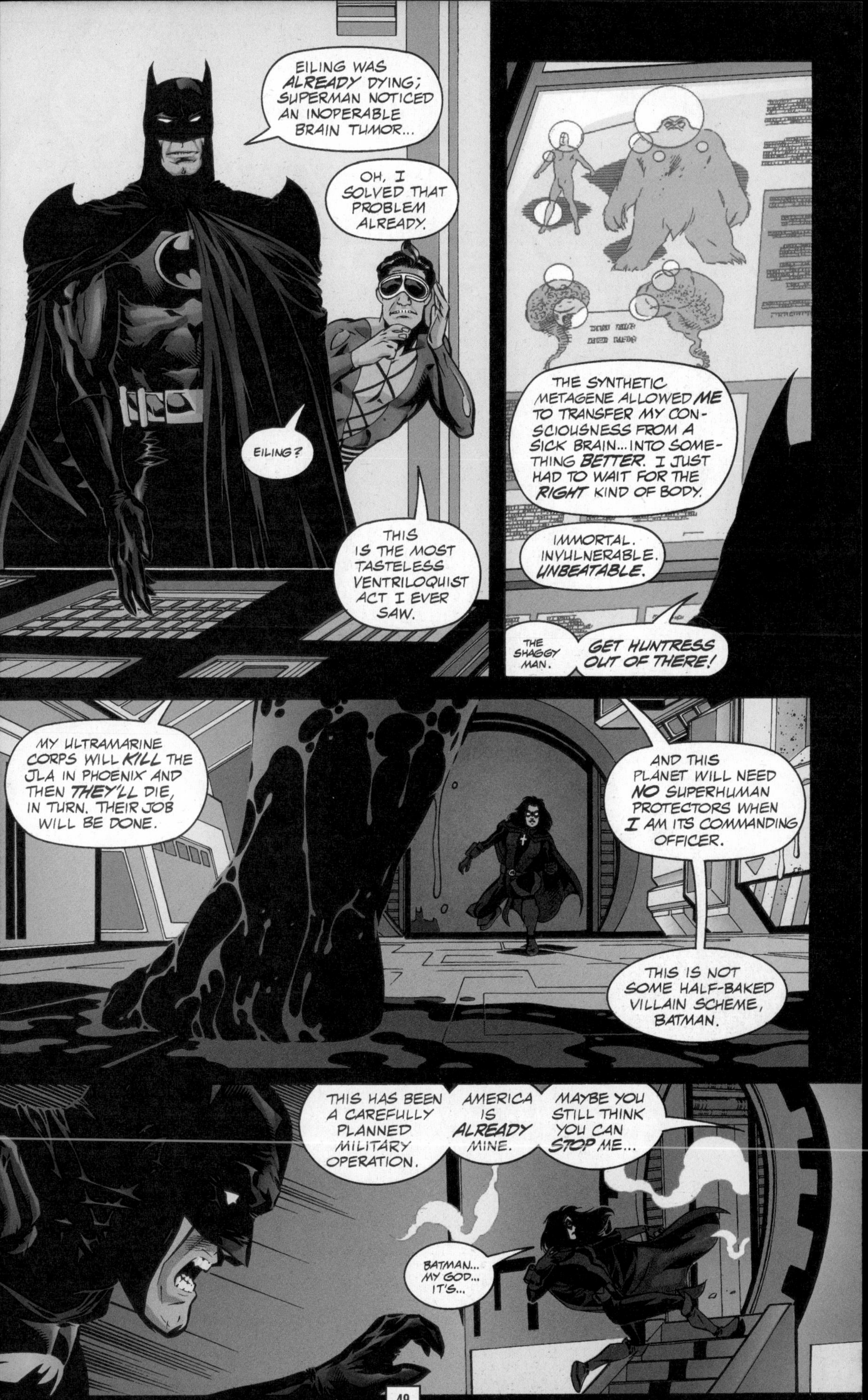

EILING WAS ALREADY DYING; SUPERMAN NOTICED AN INOPERABLE BRAIN TUMOR...
OH, I SOLVED THAT PROBLEM ALREADY.
EILING?
THIS IS THE MOST TASTELESS VENTRILOQUIST ACT I EVER SAW.
THE SYNTHETIC METAGENE ALLOWED ME TO TRANSFER MY CONSCIOUSNESS FROM A SICK BRAIN...INTO SOMETHING BETTER. I JUST HAD TO WAIT FOR THE RIGHT KIND OF BODY.
IMMORTAL. INVULNERABLE. UNBEATABLE.
THE SHAGGY MAN.
GET HUNTRESS OUT OF THERE!
MY ULTRAMARINE CORPS WILL KILL THE JLA IN PHOENIX AND THEN THEY'LL DIE, IN TURN. THEIR JOB WILL BE DONE.
AND THIS PLANET WILL NEED NO SUPERHUMAN PROTECTORS WHEN I AM ITS COMMANDING OFFICER.
THIS IS NOT SOME HALF-BAKED VILLAIN SCHEME, BATMAN.
THIS HAS BEEN A CAREFULLY PLANNED MILITARY OPERATION.
AMERICA IS ALREADY MINE.
MAYBE YOU STILL THINK YOU CAN STOP ME...
BATMAN... MY GOD... IT'S...

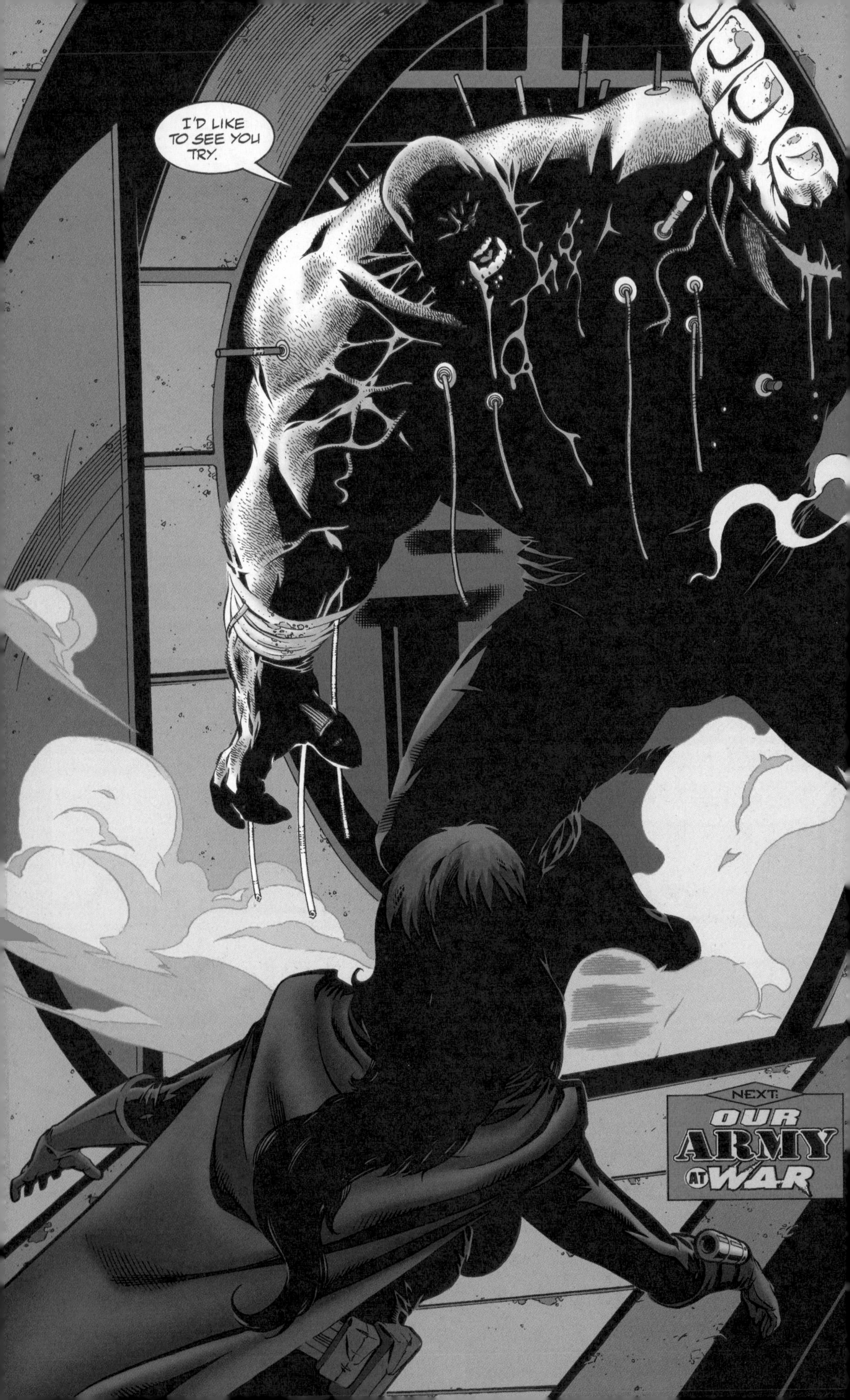
I'D LIKE TO SEE YOU TRY.
NEXT:
OUR ARMY AT WAR

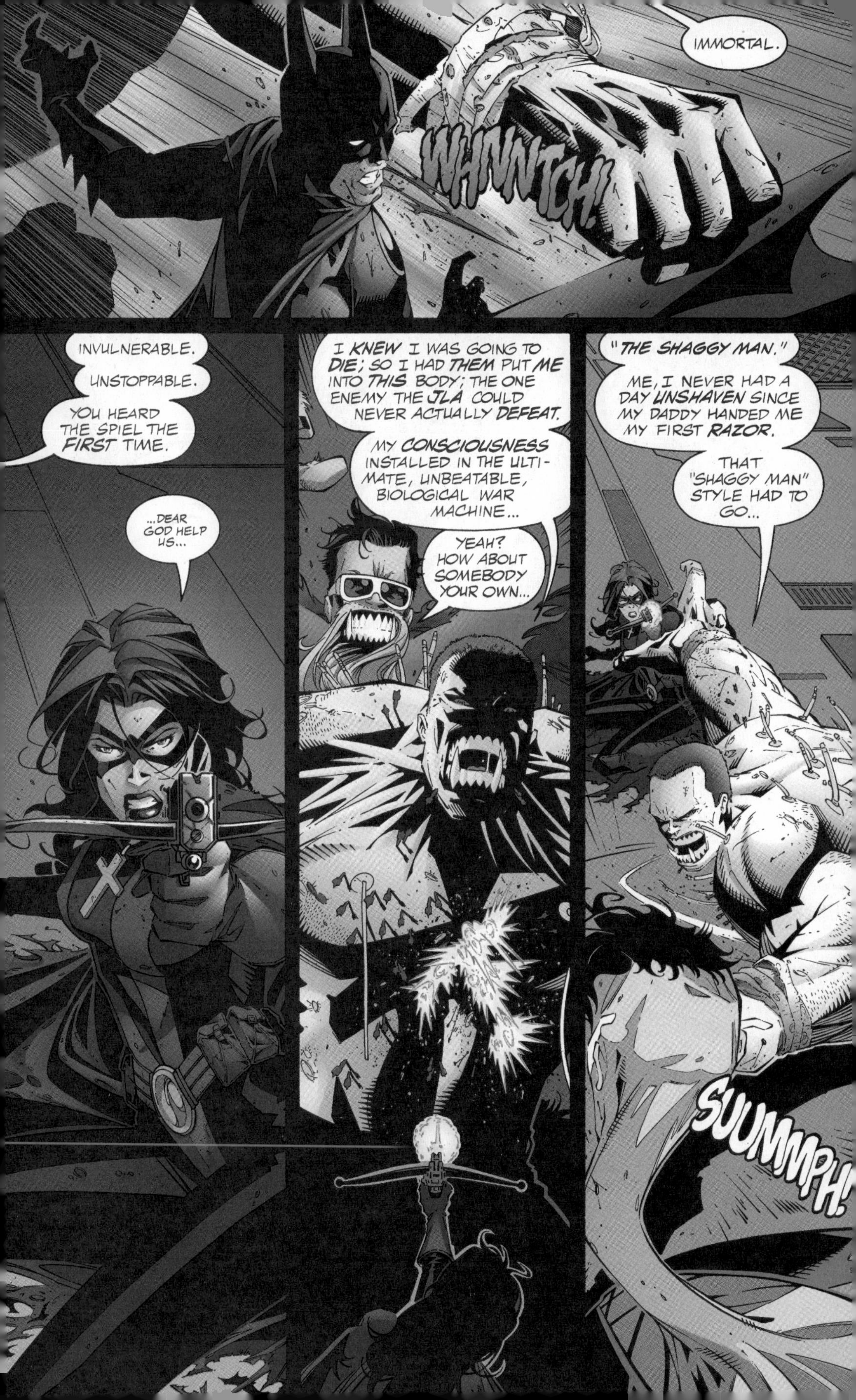
IMMORTAL.
WHUNNTCH!
INVULNERABLE.
UNSTOPPABLE.
YOU HEARD THE SPIEL THE FIRST TIME.
...DEAR GOD HELP US...
I KNEW I WAS GOING TO DIE; SO I HAD THEM PUT ME INTO THIS BODY; THE ONE ENEMY THE JLA COULD NEVER ACTUALLY DEFEAT.
MY CONSCIOUSNESS INSTALLED IN THE ULTIMATE, UNBEATABLE, BIOLOGICAL WAR MACHINE...
YEAH? HOW ABOUT SOMEBODY YOUR OWN...
"THE SHAGGY MAN."
ME, I NEVER HAD A DAY UNSHAVEN SINCE MY DADDY HANDED ME MY FIRST RAZOR.
THAT "SHAGGY MAN" STYLE HAD TO GO...
SUUMMPH!

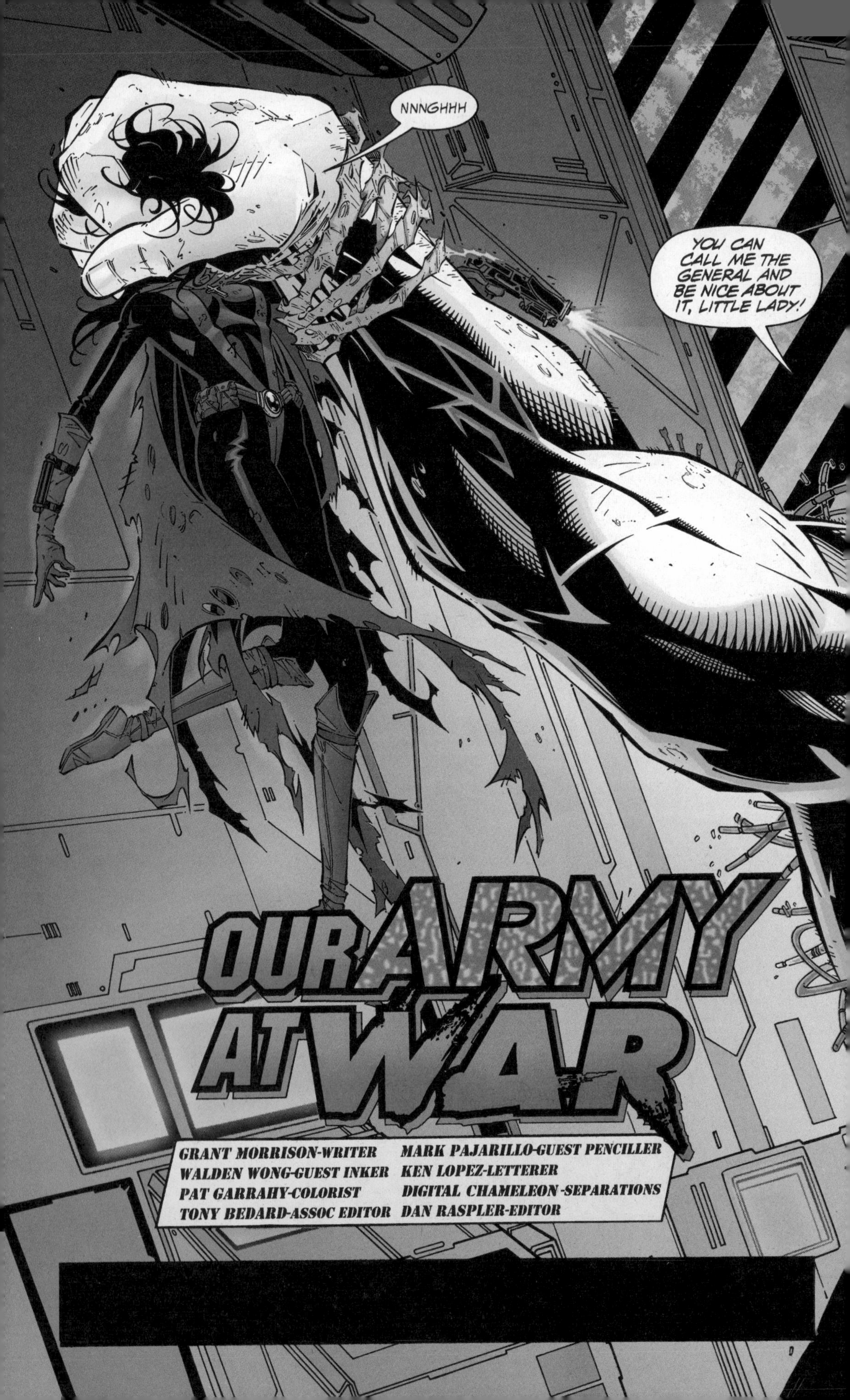
NNNGHHH
YOU CAN CALL ME THE GENERAL AND BE NICE ABOUT IT, LITTLE LADY!
OUR ARMY AT WAR
GRANT MORRISON-WRITER
MARK PAJARILLO-GUEST PENCILLER
WALDEN WONG-GUEST INKER
KEN LOPEZ-LETTERER
PAT GARRAHY-COLORIST
DIGITAL CHAMELEON -SEPARATIONS
TONY BEDARD-ASSOC EDITOR
DAN RASPLER-EDITOR
[redacted]

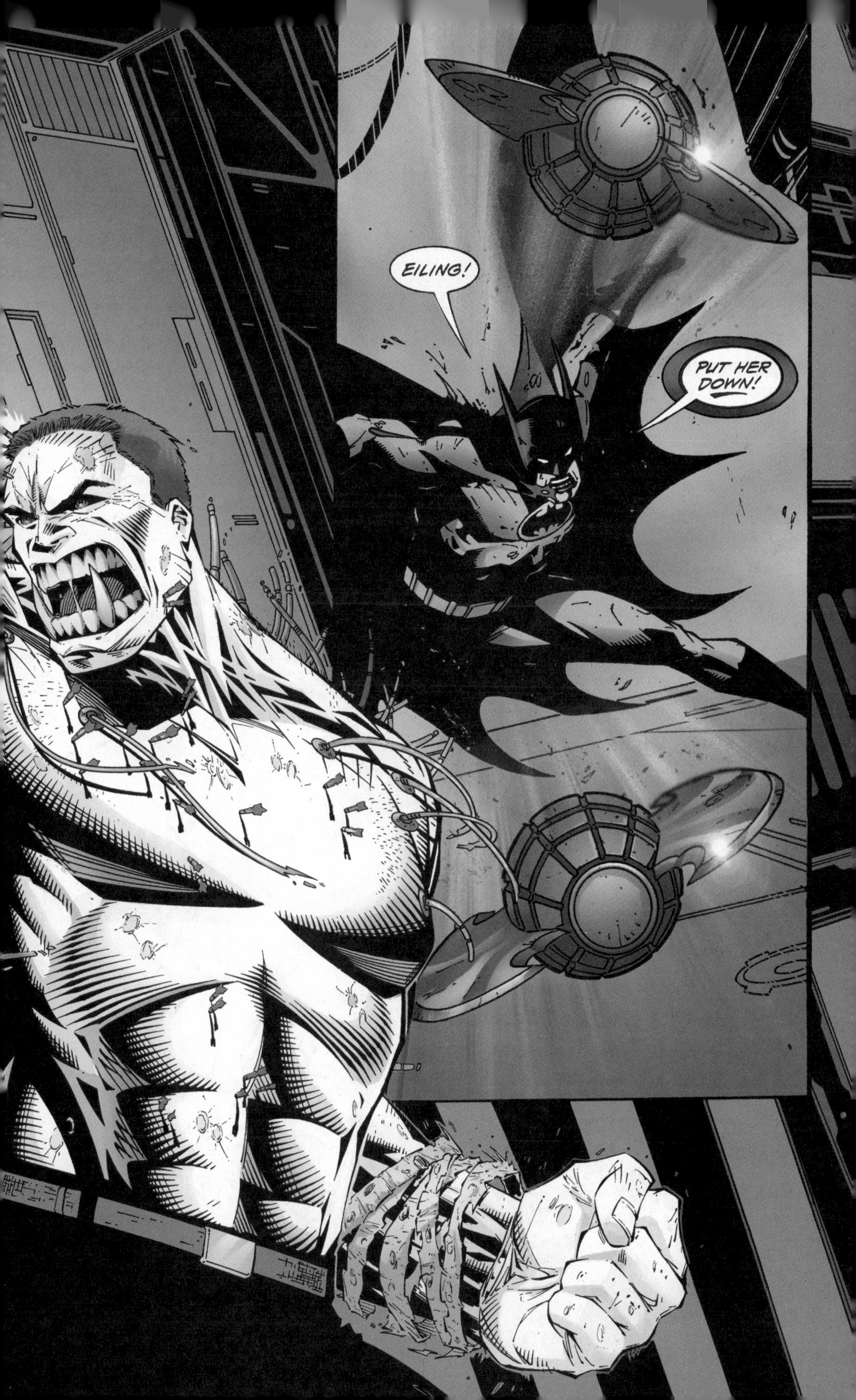
EILING!
PUT HER DOWN!

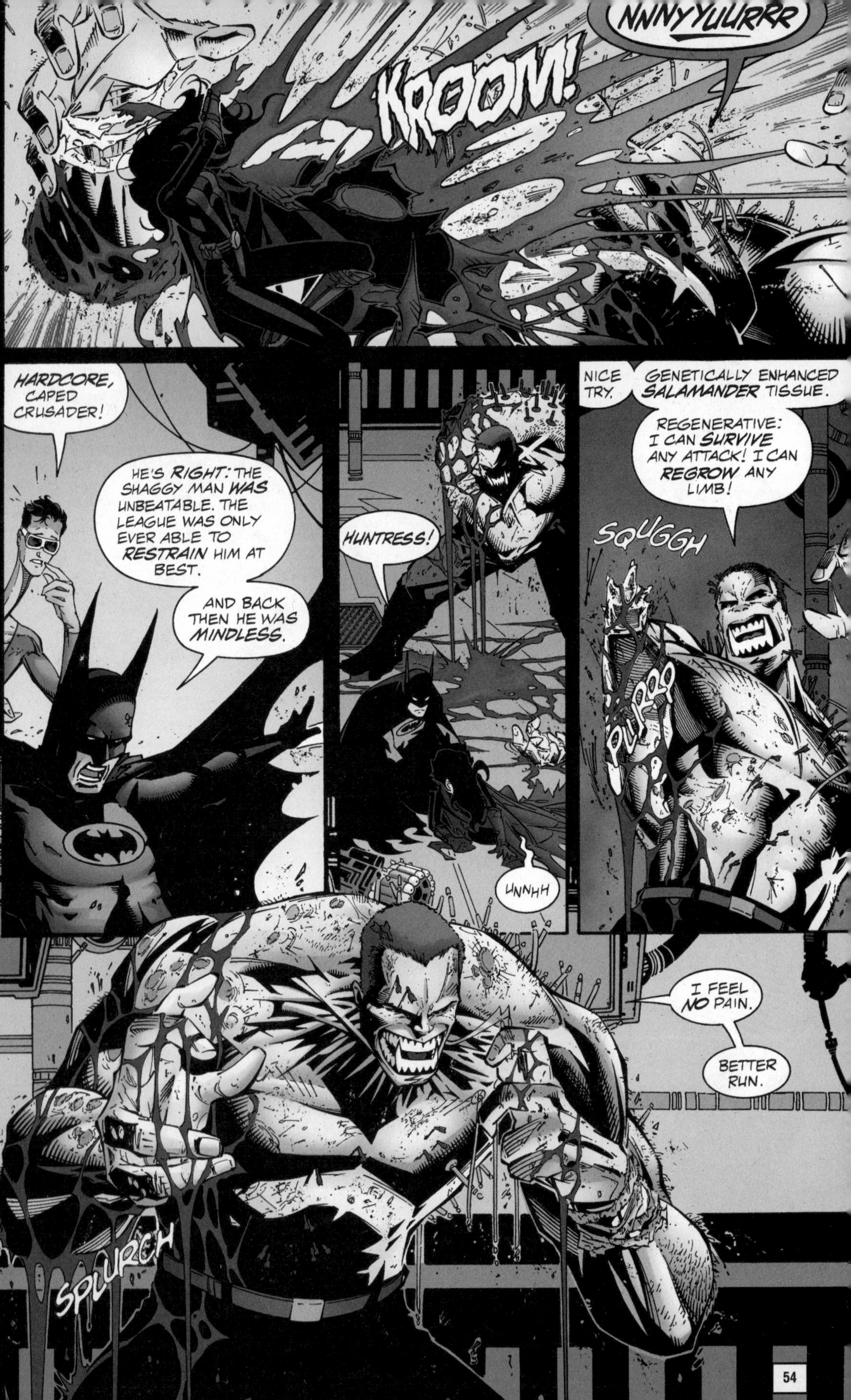
NNNYYUURRR
KROOM!
HARDCORE, CAPED CRUSADER!
HE'S RIGHT: THE SHAGGY MAN WAS UNBEATABLE. THE LEAGUE WAS ONLY EVER ABLE TO RESTRAIN HIM AT BEST.
AND BACK THEN HE WAS MINDLESS.
HUNTRESS!
UNNHH
NICE TRY.
GENETICALLY ENHANCED SALAMANDER TISSUE.
REGENERATIVE: I CAN SURVIVE ANY ATTACK! I CAN REGROW ANY LIMB!
SQUGGH
PURRR
I FEEL NO PAIN.
BETTER RUN.
SPLURCH

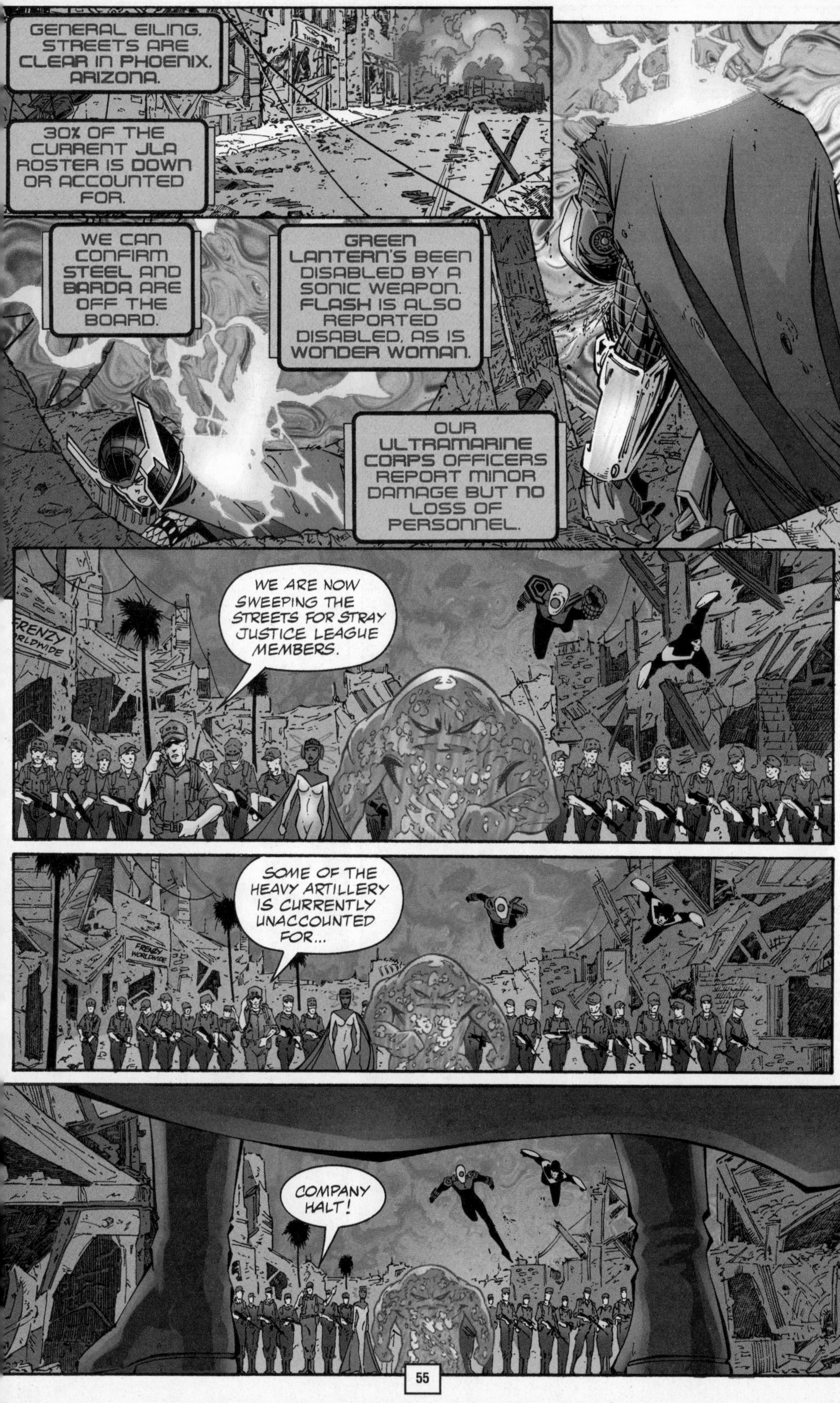
GENERAL EILING. STREETS ARE CLEAR IN PHOENIX, ARIZONA.
30% OF THE CURRENT JLA ROSTER IS DOWN OR ACCOUNTED FOR.
WE CAN CONFIRM STEEL AND BARDA ARE OFF THE BOARD.
GREEN LANTERN'S BEEN DISABLED BY A SONIC WEAPON. FLASH IS ALSO REPORTED DISABLED, AS IS WONDER WOMAN.
OUR ULTRAMARINE CORPS OFFICERS REPORT MINOR DAMAGE BUT NO LOSS OF PERSONNEL.
FRENZY WORLDWIDE
WE ARE NOW SWEEPING THE STREETS FOR STRAY JUSTICE LEAGUE MEMBERS.
SOME OF THE HEAVY ARTILLERY IS CURRENTLY UNACCOUNTED FOR...
FRENZY WORLDWIDE
COMPANY HALT!

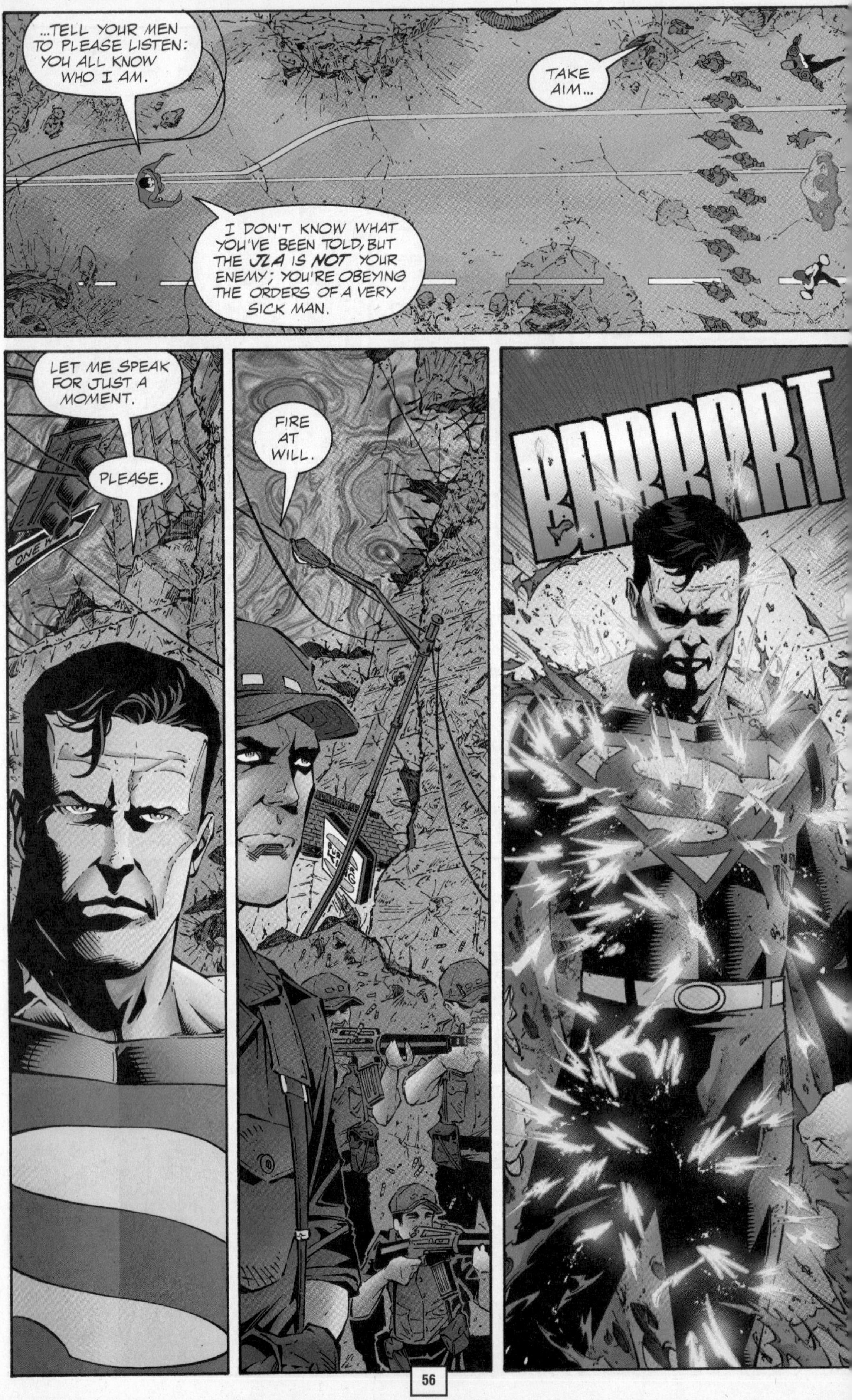
...TELL YOUR MEN TO PLEASE LISTEN: YOU ALL KNOW WHO I AM.
TAKE AIM...
I DON'T KNOW WHAT YOU'VE BEEN TOLD, BUT THE JLA IS NOT YOUR ENEMY; YOU'RE OBEYING THE ORDERS OF A VERY SICK MAN.
LET ME SPEAK FOR JUST A MOMENT.
PLEASE.
ONE WAY
FIRE AT WILL.
BRRRRRT

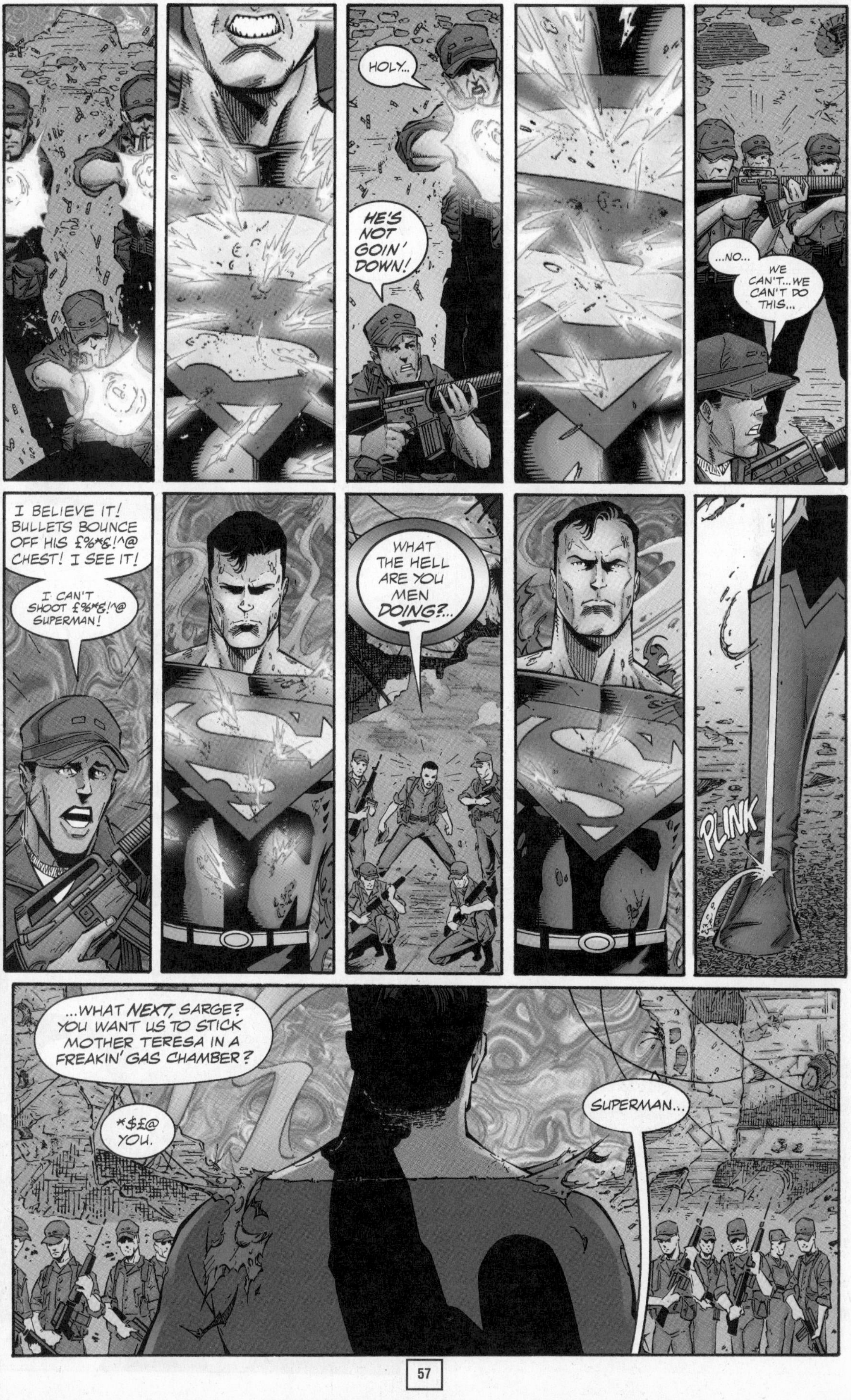
HOLY...
HE'S NOT GOIN' DOWN!
...NO...
WE CAN'T...WE CAN'T DO THIS...
I BELIEVE IT! BULLETS BOUNCE OFF HIS £%*&!^@ CHEST! I SEE IT!
I CAN'T SHOOT £%*&!^@ SUPERMAN!
WHAT THE HELL ARE YOU MEN DOING?...
PLINK
...WHAT NEXT, SARGE? YOU WANT US TO STICK MOTHER TERESA IN A FREAKIN' GAS CHAMBER?
*$£@ YOU.
SUPERMAN...

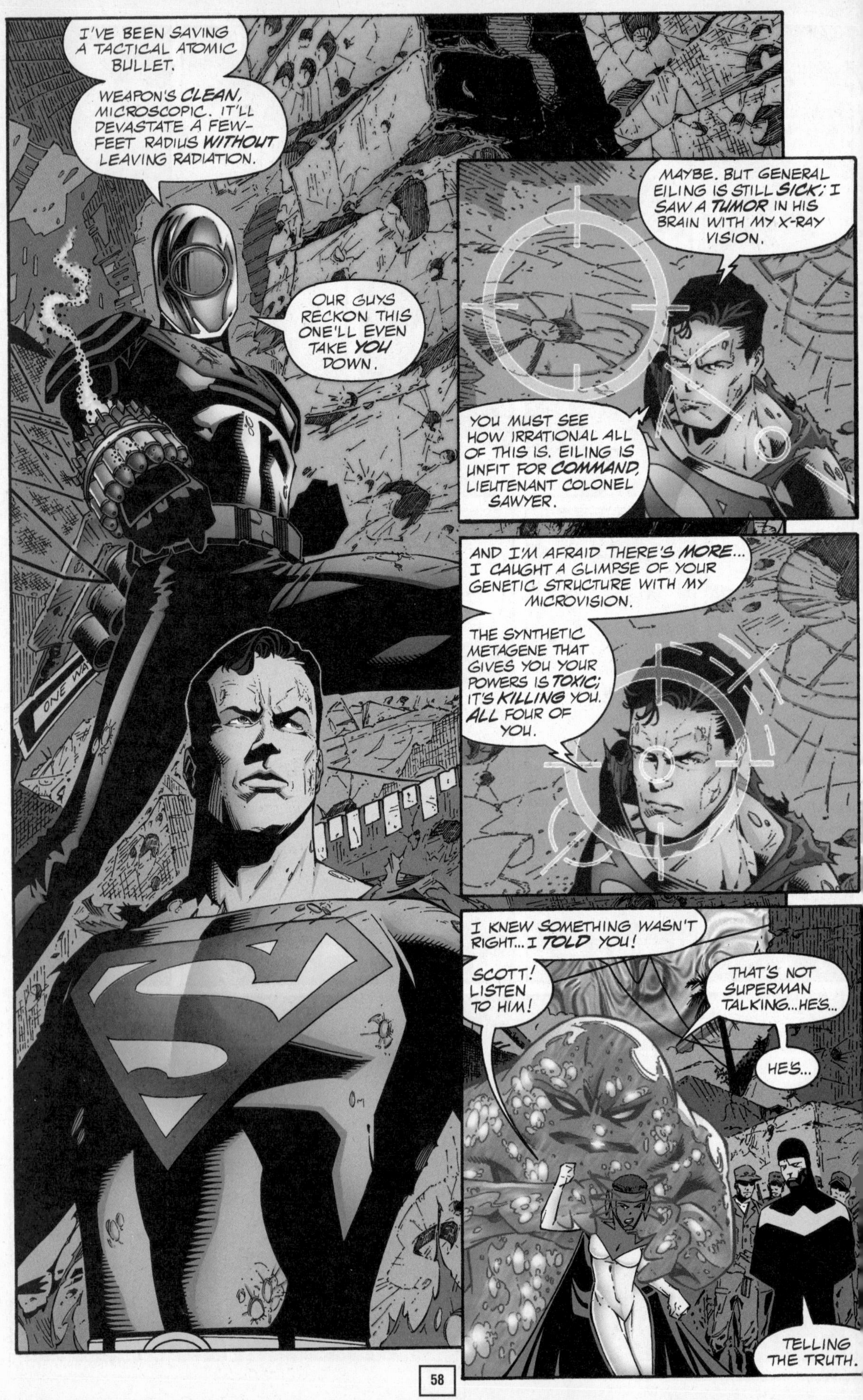
I'VE BEEN SAVING A TACTICAL ATOMIC BULLET.
WEAPON'S CLEAN, MICROSCOPIC. IT'LL DEVASTATE A FEW-FEET RADIUS WITHOUT LEAVING RADIATION.
OUR GUYS RECKON THIS ONE'LL EVEN TAKE YOU DOWN.
ONE WA
MAYBE. BUT GENERAL EILING IS STILL SICK; I SAW A TUMOR IN HIS BRAIN WITH MY X-RAY VISION.
YOU MUST SEE HOW IRRATIONAL ALL OF THIS IS. EILING IS UNFIT FOR COMMAND, LIEUTENANT COLONEL SAWYER.
AND I'M AFRAID THERE'S MORE... I CAUGHT A GLIMPSE OF YOUR GENETIC STRUCTURE WITH MY MICROVISION.
THE SYNTHETIC METAGENE THAT GIVES YOU YOUR POWERS IS TOXIC; IT'S KILLING YOU. ALL FOUR OF YOU.
I KNEW SOMETHING WASN'T RIGHT... I TOLD YOU!
SCOTT! LISTEN TO HIM!
THAT'S NOT SUPERMAN TALKING... HE'S...
HE'S...
TELLING THE TRUTH.

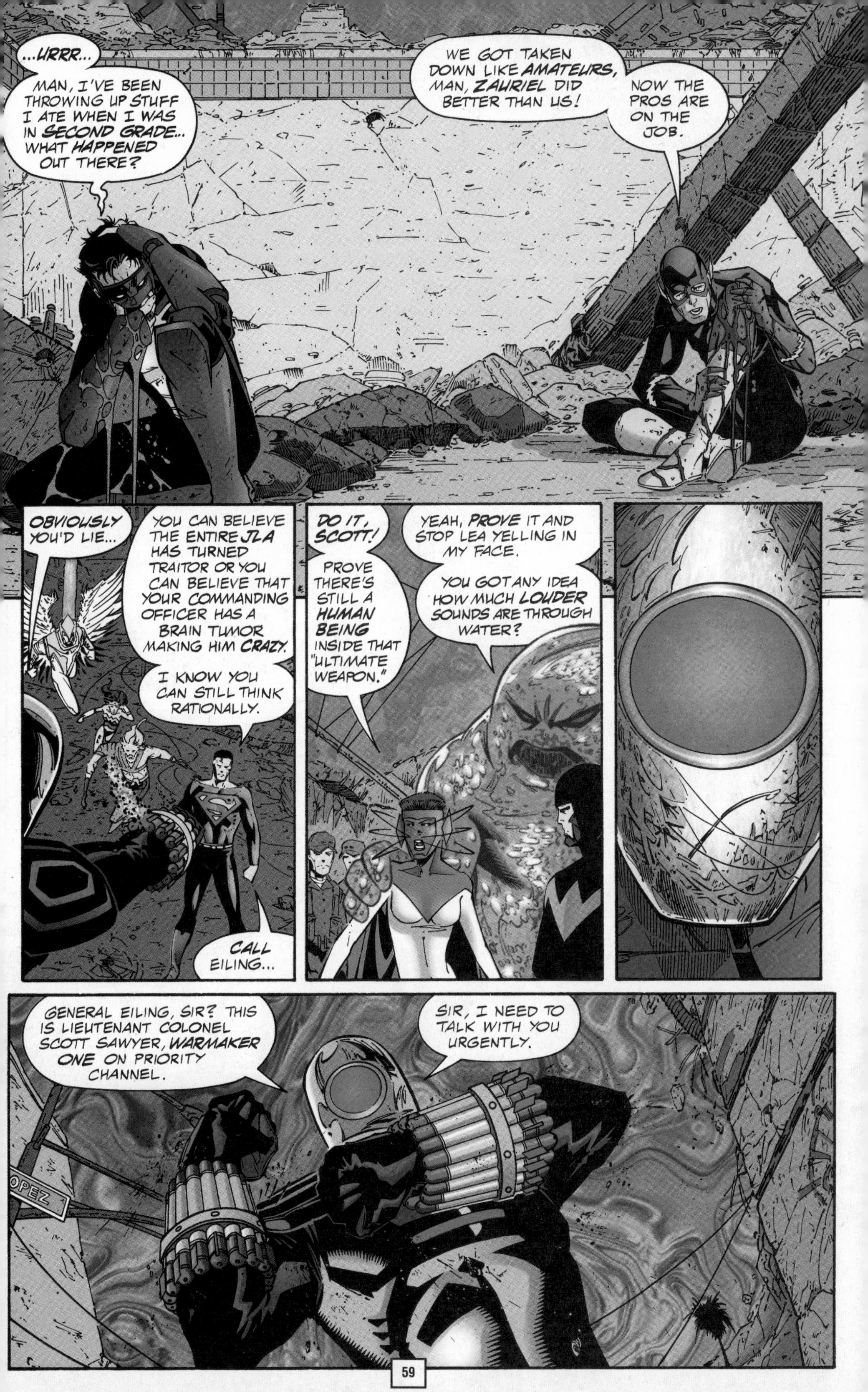

...URRR...
MAN, I'VE BEEN THROWING UP STUFF I ATE WHEN I WAS IN SECOND GRADE... WHAT HAPPENED OUT THERE?
WE GOT TAKEN DOWN LIKE AMATEURS, MAN, ZAURIEL DID BETTER THAN US!
NOW THE PROS ARE ON THE JOB.
OBVIOUSLY YOU'D LIE...
YOU CAN BELIEVE THE ENTIRE JLA HAS TURNED TRAITOR OR YOU CAN BELIEVE THAT YOUR COMMANDING OFFICER HAS A BRAIN TUMOR MAKING HIM CRAZY.
I KNOW YOU CAN STILL THINK RATIONALLY.
CALL EILING...
DO IT, SCOTT!
PROVE THERE'S STILL A HUMAN BEING INSIDE THAT "ULTIMATE WEAPON."
YEAH, PROVE IT AND STOP LEA YELLING IN MY FACE.
YOU GOT ANY IDEA HOW MUCH LOUDER SOUNDS ARE THROUGH WATER?
GENERAL EILING, SIR? THIS IS LIEUTENANT COLONEL SCOTT SAWYER, WARMAKER ONE ON PRIORITY CHANNEL.
SIR, I NEED TO TALK WITH YOU URGENTLY.
LOPEZ

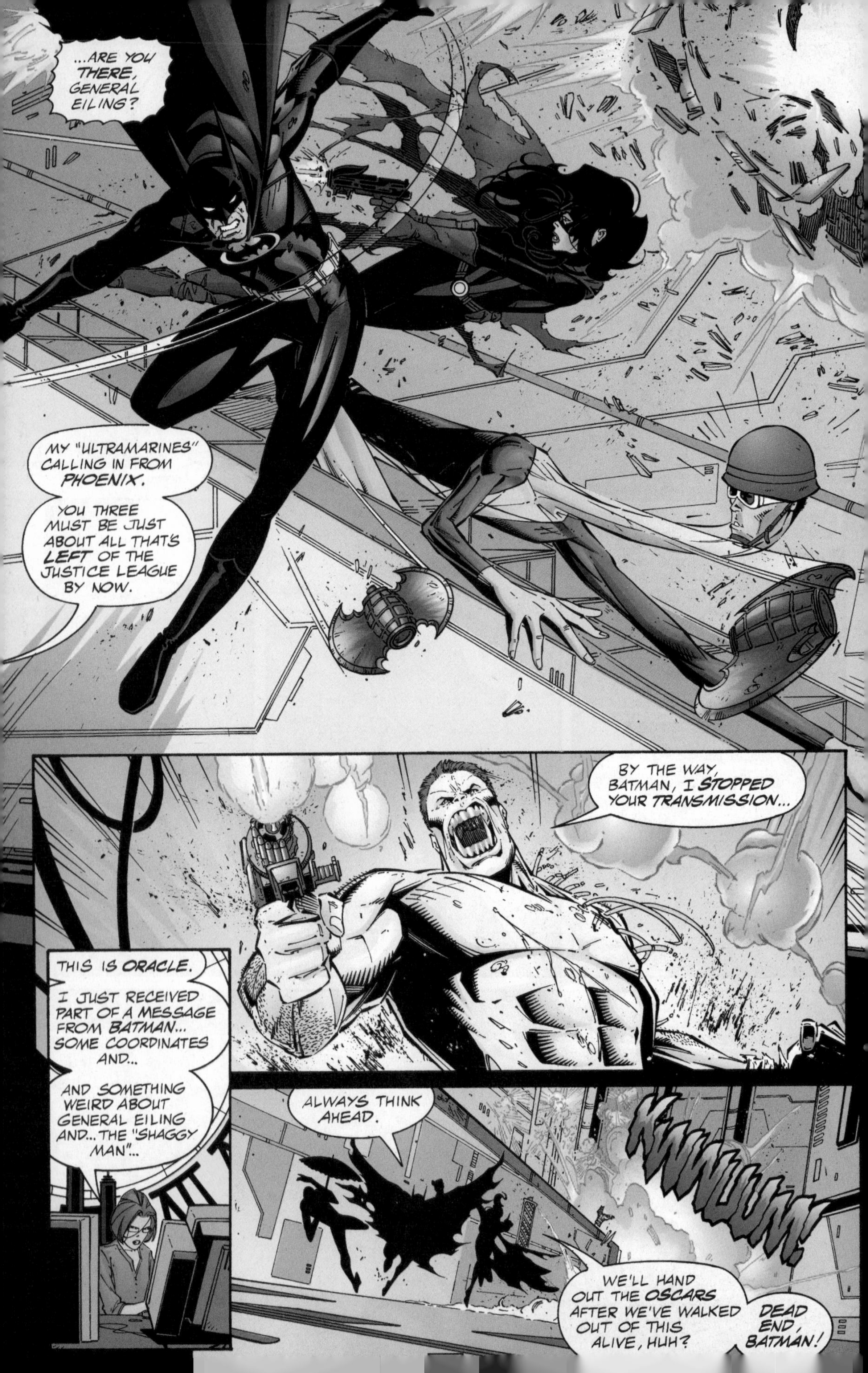
...ARE YOU THERE, GENERAL EILING?
MY "ULTRAMARINES" CALLING IN FROM PHOENIX.
YOU THREE MUST BE JUST ABOUT ALL THAT'S LEFT OF THE JUSTICE LEAGUE BY NOW.
BY THE WAY, BATMAN, I STOPPED YOUR TRANSMISSION...
THIS IS ORACLE.
I JUST RECEIVED PART OF A MESSAGE FROM BATMAN... SOME COORDINATES AND...
AND SOMETHING WEIRD ABOUT GENERAL EILING AND... THE "SHAGGY MAN"...
ALWAYS THINK AHEAD.
KWUUUM!
WE'LL HAND OUT THE OSCARS AFTER WE'VE WALKED OUT OF THIS ALIVE, HUH?
DEAD END, BATMAN!

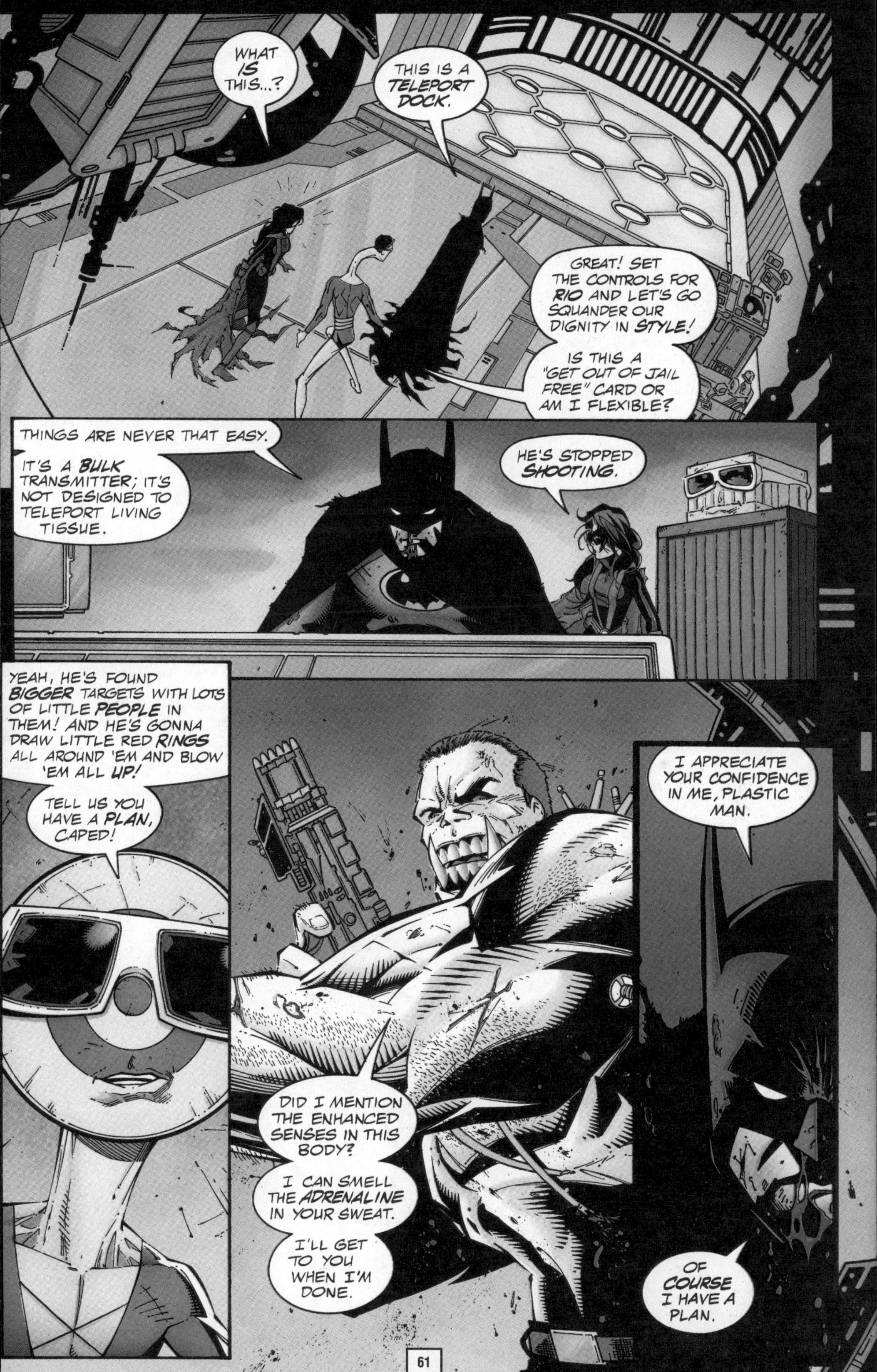
WHAT IS THIS...?
THIS IS A TELEPORT DOCK.
GREAT! SET THE CONTROLS FOR RIO AND LET'S GO SQUANDER OUR DIGNITY IN STYLE!
IS THIS A "GET OUT OF JAIL FREE" CARD OR AM I FLEXIBLE?
THINGS ARE NEVER THAT EASY.
IT'S A BULK TRANSMITTER; IT'S NOT DESIGNED TO TELEPORT LIVING TISSUE.
HE'S STOPPED SHOOTING.
YEAH, HE'S FOUND BIGGER TARGETS WITH LOTS OF LITTLE PEOPLE IN THEM! AND HE'S GONNA DRAW LITTLE RED RINGS ALL AROUND 'EM AND BLOW 'EM ALL UP!
TELL US YOU HAVE A PLAN, CAPED!
DID I MENTION THE ENHANCED SENSES IN THIS BODY?
I CAN SMELL THE ADRENALINE IN YOUR SWEAT.
I'LL GET TO YOU WHEN I'M DONE.
I APPRECIATE YOUR CONFIDENCE IN ME, PLASTIC MAN.
OF COURSE I HAVE A PLAN.

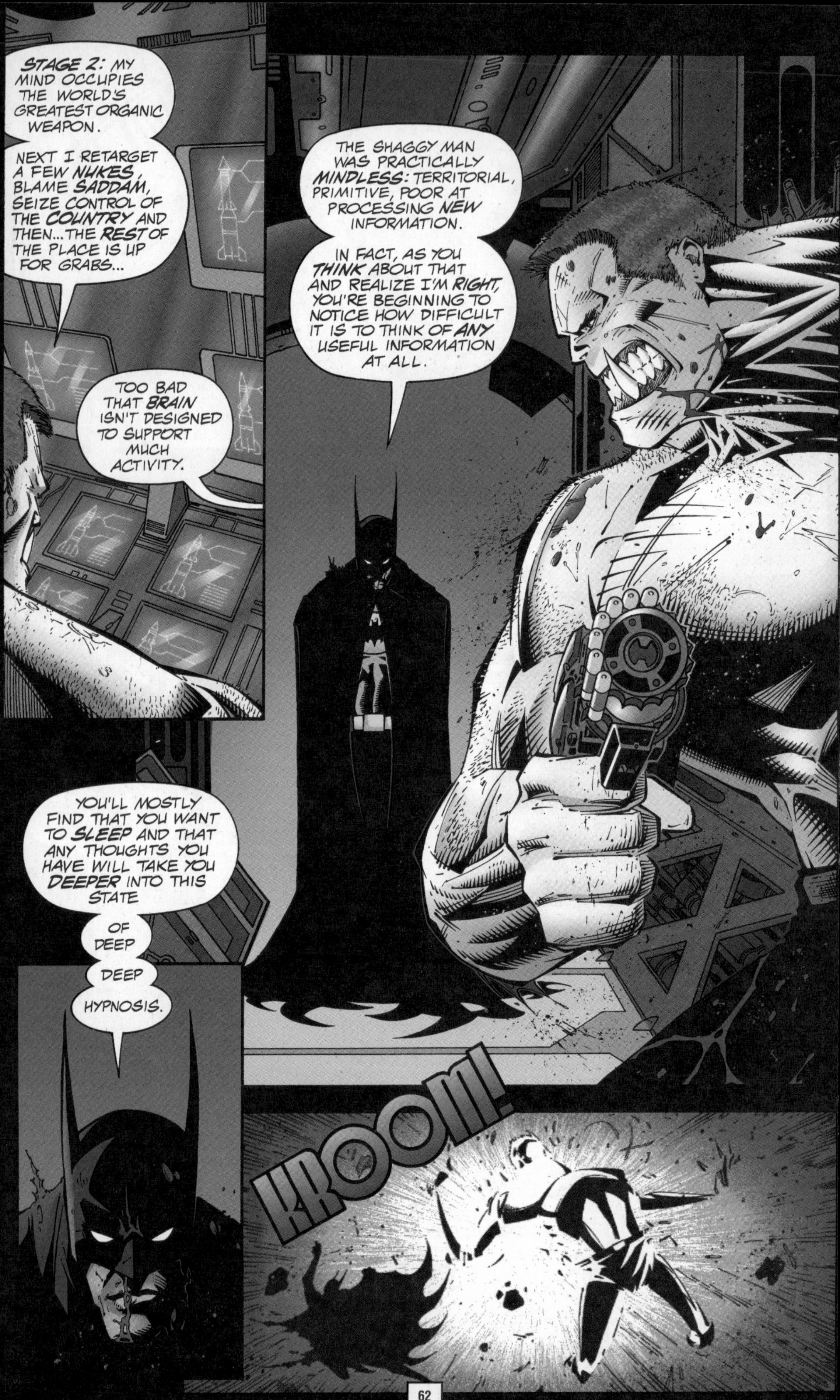
STAGE 2: MY MIND OCCUPIES THE WORLD'S GREATEST ORGANIC WEAPON.
NEXT I RETARGET A FEW NUKES, BLAME SADDAM, SEIZE CONTROL OF THE COUNTRY AND THEN...THE REST OF THE PLACE IS UP FOR GRABS...
TOO BAD THAT BRAIN ISN'T DESIGNED TO SUPPORT MUCH ACTIVITY.
THE SHAGGY MAN WAS PRACTICALLY MINDLESS: TERRITORIAL, PRIMITIVE, POOR AT PROCESSING NEW INFORMATION.
IN FACT, AS YOU THINK ABOUT THAT AND REALIZE I'M RIGHT, YOU'RE BEGINNING TO NOTICE HOW DIFFICULT IT IS TO THINK OF ANY USEFUL INFORMATION AT ALL.
YOU'LL MOSTLY FIND THAT YOU WANT TO SLEEP AND THAT ANY THOUGHTS YOU HAVE WILL TAKE YOU DEEPER INTO THIS STATE
OF DEEP
DEEP
HYPNOSIS.
KROOOM!

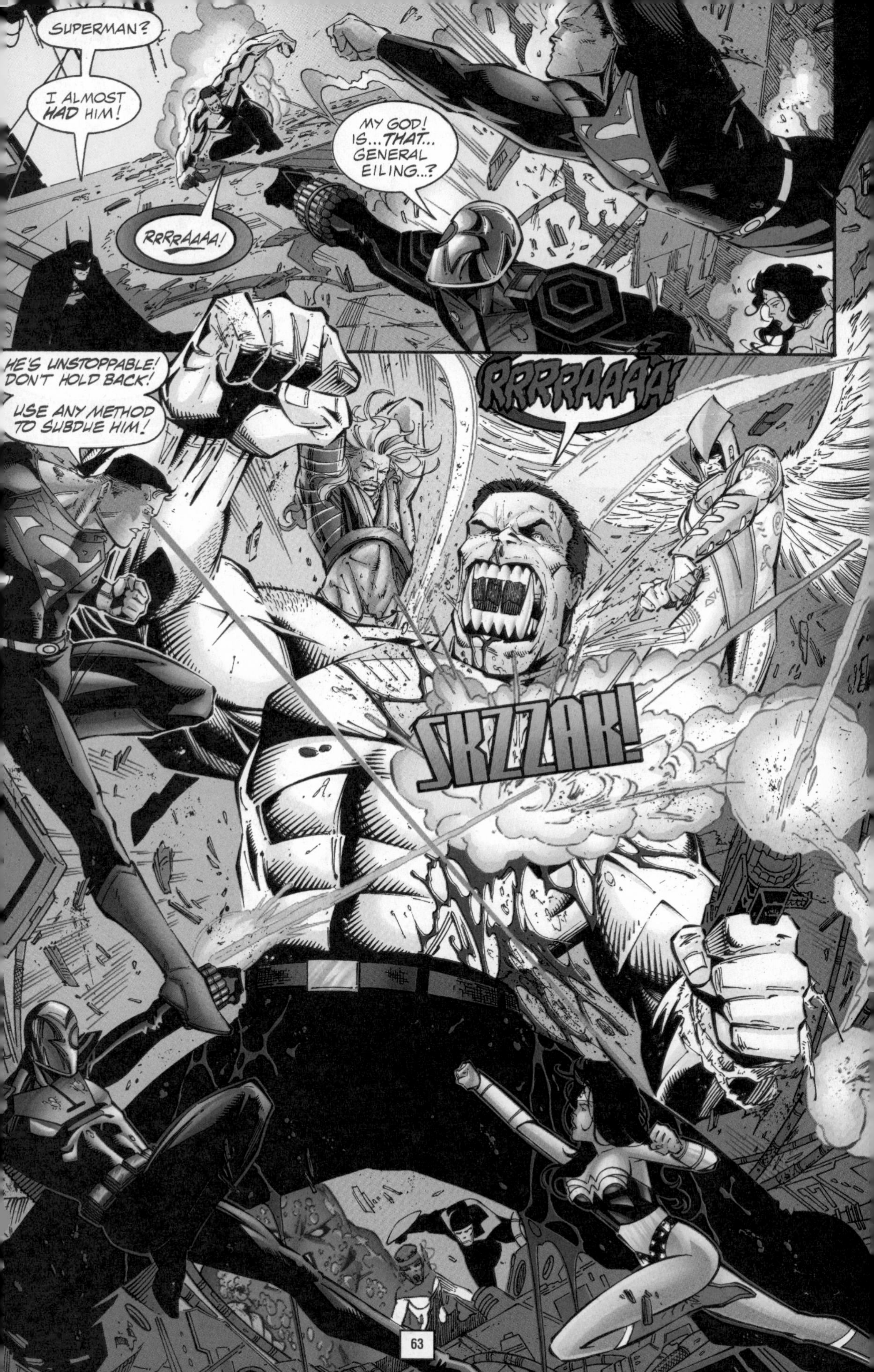
SUPERMAN?
I ALMOST HAD HIM!
MY GOD! IS...THAT... GENERAL EILING...?
RRRRAAAA!
HE'S UNSTOPPABLE! DON'T HOLD BACK!
USE ANY METHOD TO SUBDUE HIM!
RRRRAAAAA!
SKZZAK!

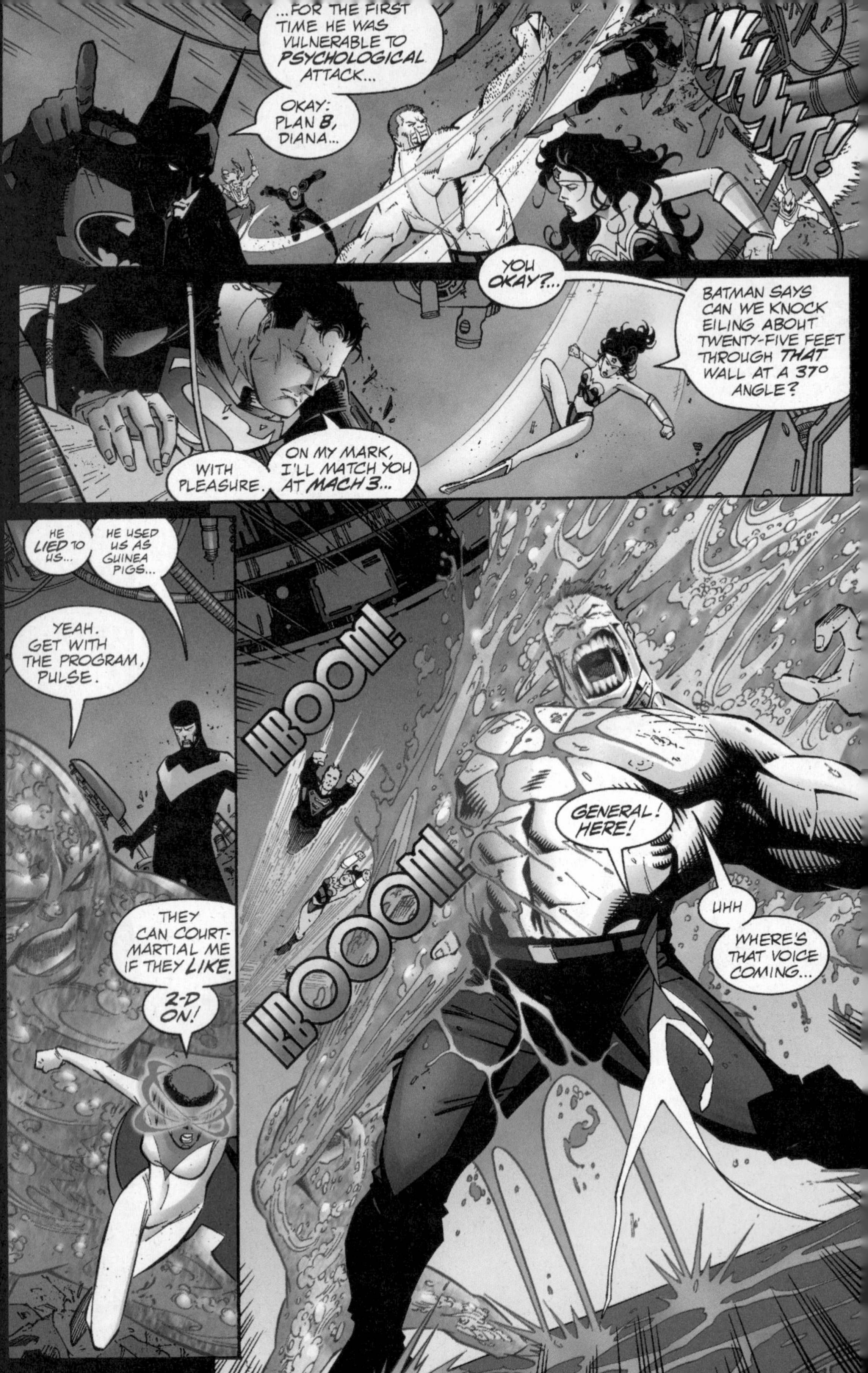
...FOR THE FIRST TIME HE WAS VULNERABLE TO PSYCHOLOGICAL ATTACK...
OKAY: PLAN B, DIANA...
WHUNT!
YOU OKAY?...
BATMAN SAYS CAN WE KNOCK EILING ABOUT TWENTY-FIVE FEET THROUGH THAT WALL AT A 37° ANGLE?
WITH PLEASURE.
ON MY MARK, I'LL MATCH YOU AT MACH 3...
HE LIED TO US...
HE USED US AS GUINEA PIGS...
YEAH. GET WITH THE PROGRAM, PULSE.
THEY CAN COURT-MARTIAL ME IF THEY LIKE.
2-D ON!
KBOOM!
KBOOOM!
GENERAL! HERE!
UHH
WHERE'S THAT VOICE COMING...

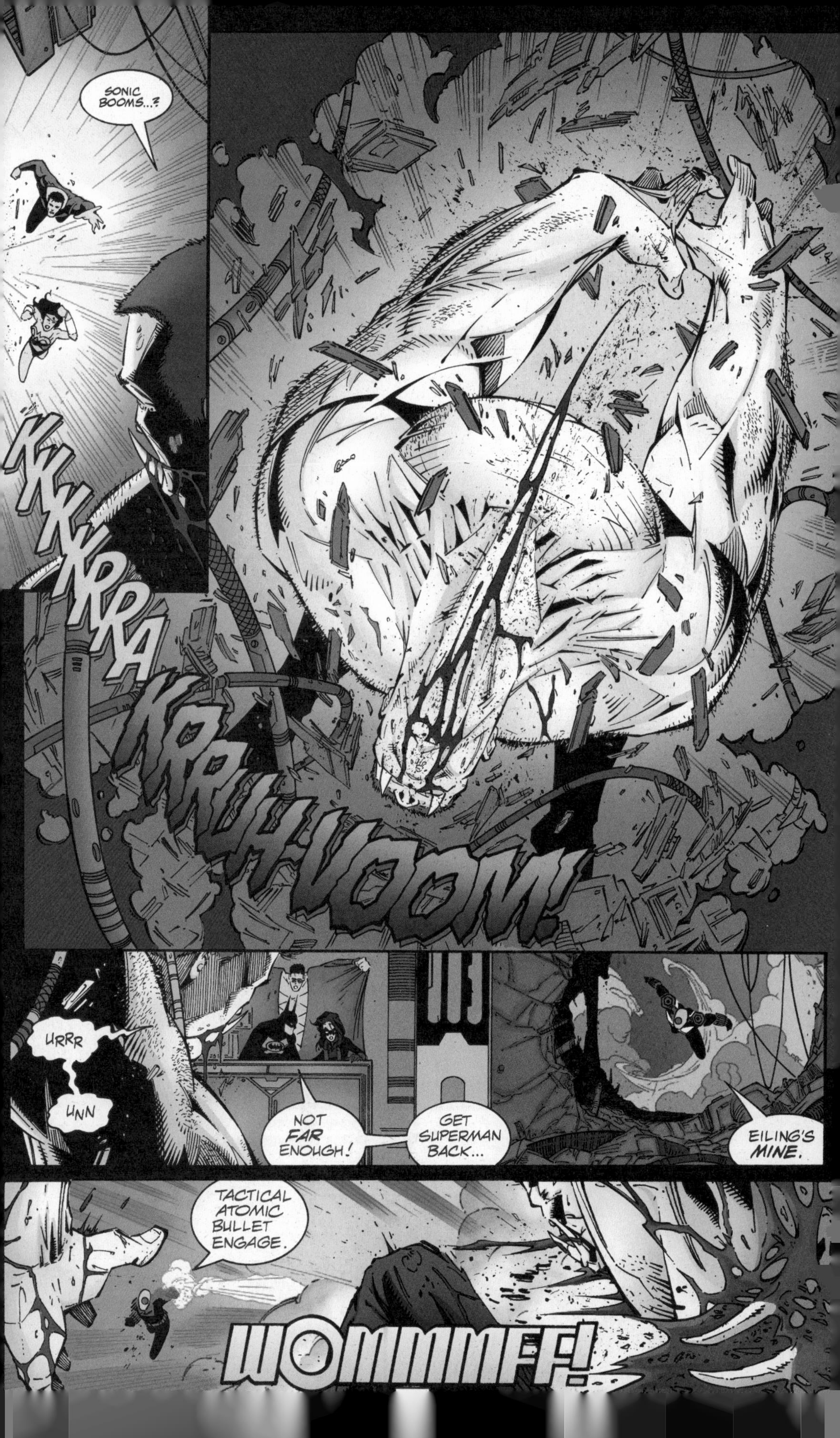

SONIC BOOMS...?
KKKKRRA
KRUH-VOOM!
URRR
UNN
NOT FAR ENOUGH!
GET SUPERMAN BACK...
EILING'S MINE.
TACTICAL ATOMIC BULLET ENGAGE.
WOMMMMFF!

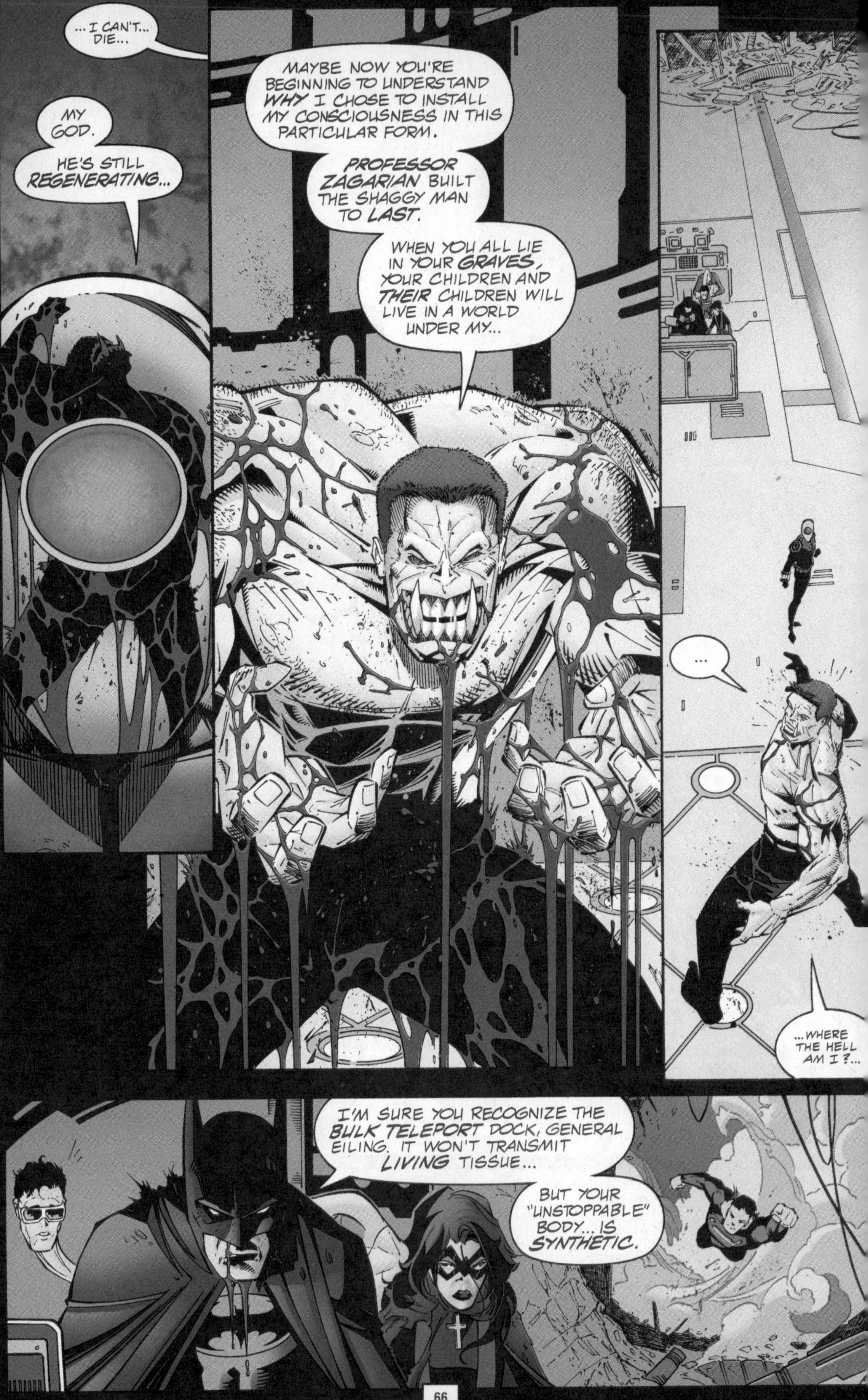
...I CAN'T... DIE...
MY GOD.
HE'S STILL REGENERATING...
MAYBE NOW YOU'RE BEGINNING TO UNDERSTAND WHY I CHOSE TO INSTALL MY CONSCIOUSNESS IN THIS PARTICULAR FORM.
PROFESSOR ZAGARIAN BUILT THE SHAGGY MAN TO LAST.
WHEN YOU ALL LIE IN YOUR GRAVES, YOUR CHILDREN AND THEIR CHILDREN WILL LIVE IN A WORLD UNDER MY...
...
...WHERE THE HELL AM I?...
I'M SURE YOU RECOGNIZE THE BULK TELEPORT DOCK, GENERAL EILING. IT WON'T TRANSMIT LIVING TISSUE...
BUT YOUR "UNSTOPPABLE" BODY... IS SYNTHETIC.

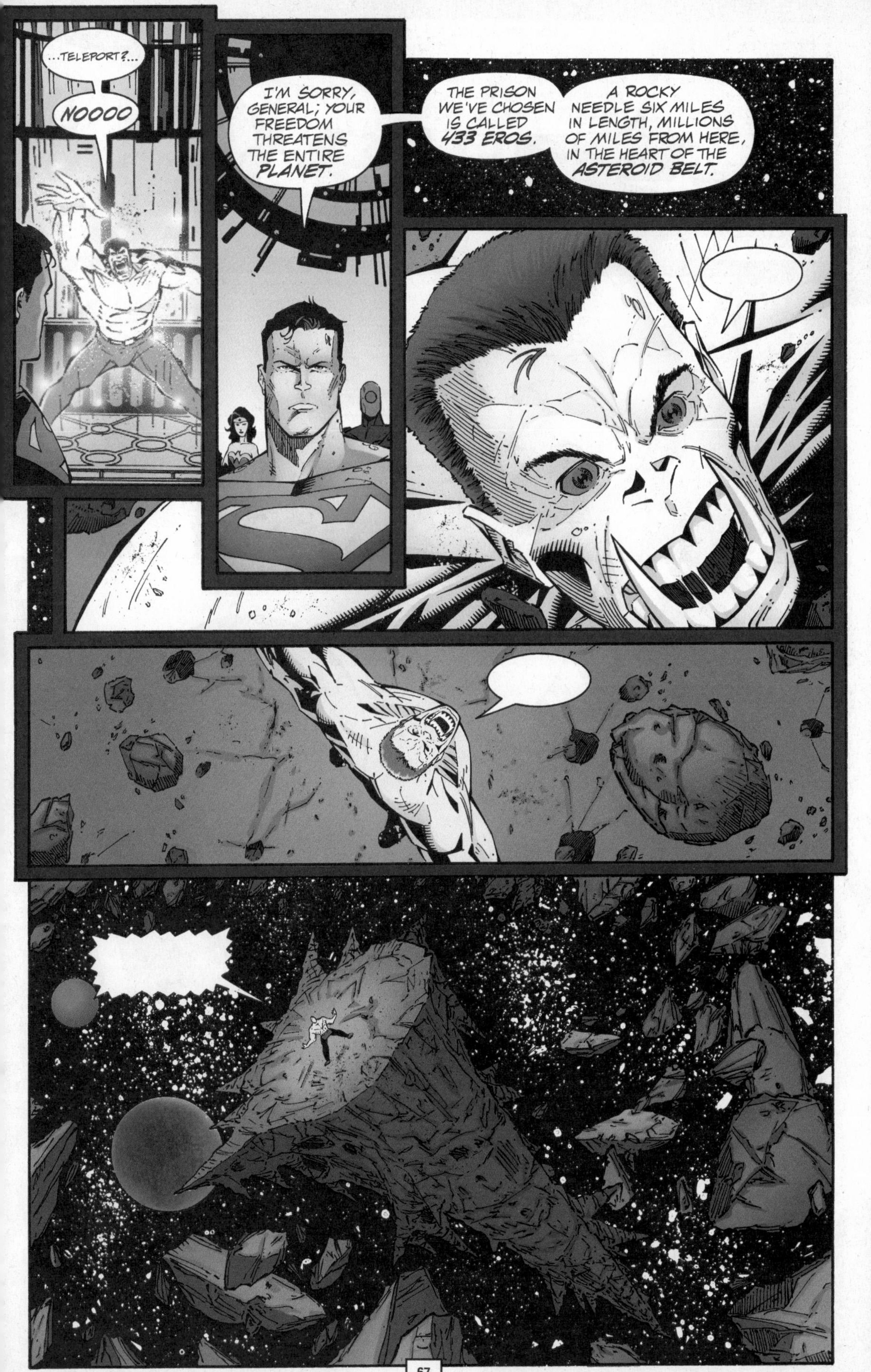
...TELEPORT?...
NOOOO
I'M SORRY, GENERAL; YOUR FREEDOM THREATENS THE ENTIRE PLANET.
THE PRISON WE'VE CHOSEN IS CALLED 433 EROS.
A ROCKY NEEDLE SIX MILES IN LENGTH, MILLIONS OF MILES FROM HERE, IN THE HEART OF THE ASTEROID BELT.

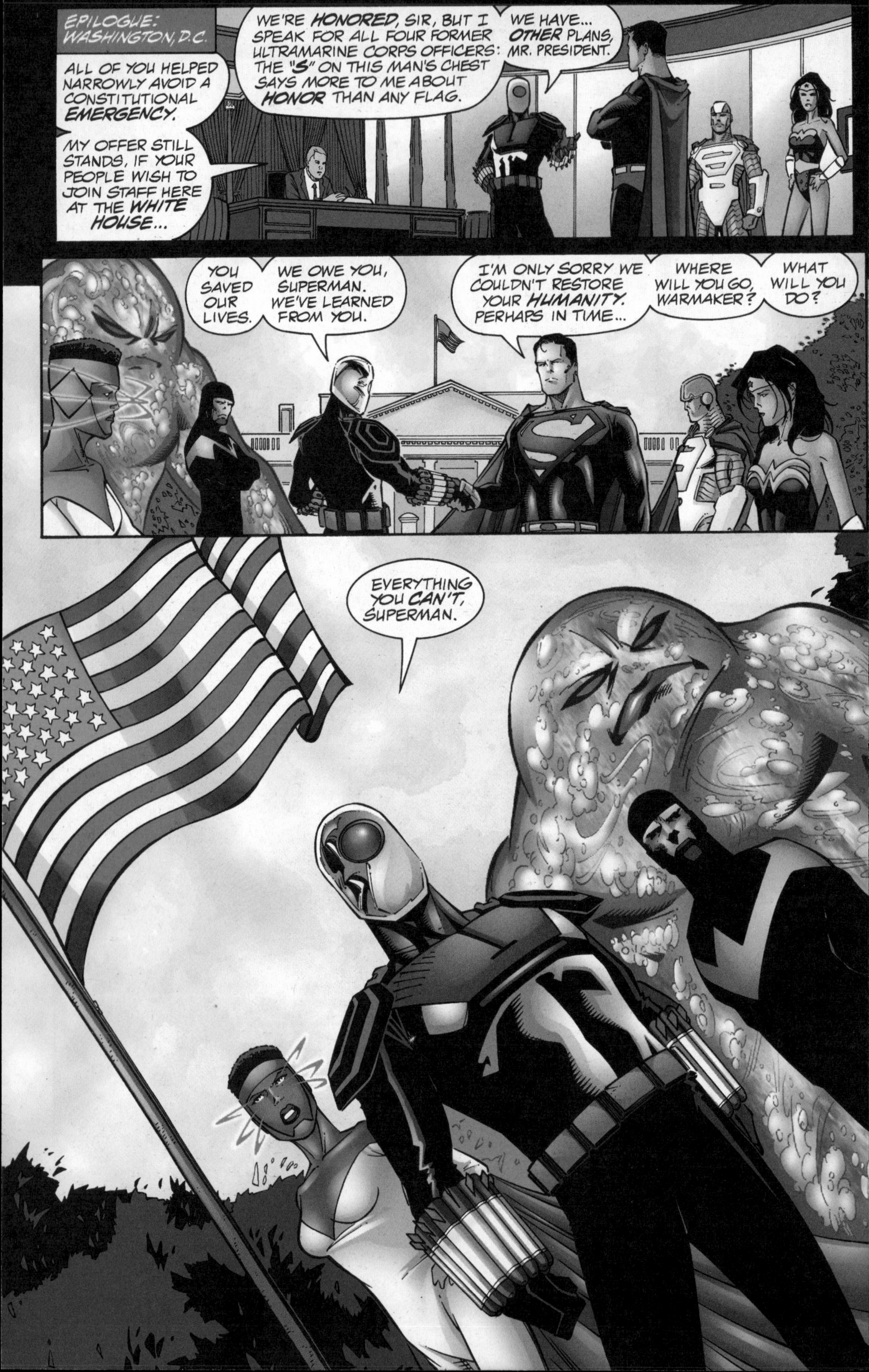
EPILOGUE: WASHINGTON, D.C.
ALL OF YOU HELPED NARROWLY AVOID A CONSTITUTIONAL EMERGENCY.
MY OFFER STILL STANDS, IF YOUR PEOPLE WISH TO JOIN STAFF HERE AT THE WHITE HOUSE...
WE'RE HONORED, SIR, BUT I SPEAK FOR ALL FOUR FORMER ULTRAMARINE CORPS OFFICERS: THE "S" ON THIS MAN'S CHEST SAYS MORE TO ME ABOUT HONOR THAN ANY FLAG.
WE HAVE... OTHER PLANS, MR. PRESIDENT.
YOU SAVED OUR LIVES.
WE OWE YOU, SUPERMAN. WE'VE LEARNED FROM YOU.
I'M ONLY SORRY WE COULDN'T RESTORE YOUR HUMANITY. PERHAPS IN TIME...
WHERE WILL YOU GO, WARMAKER?
WHAT WILL YOU DO?
EVERYTHING YOU CAN'T, SUPERMAN.

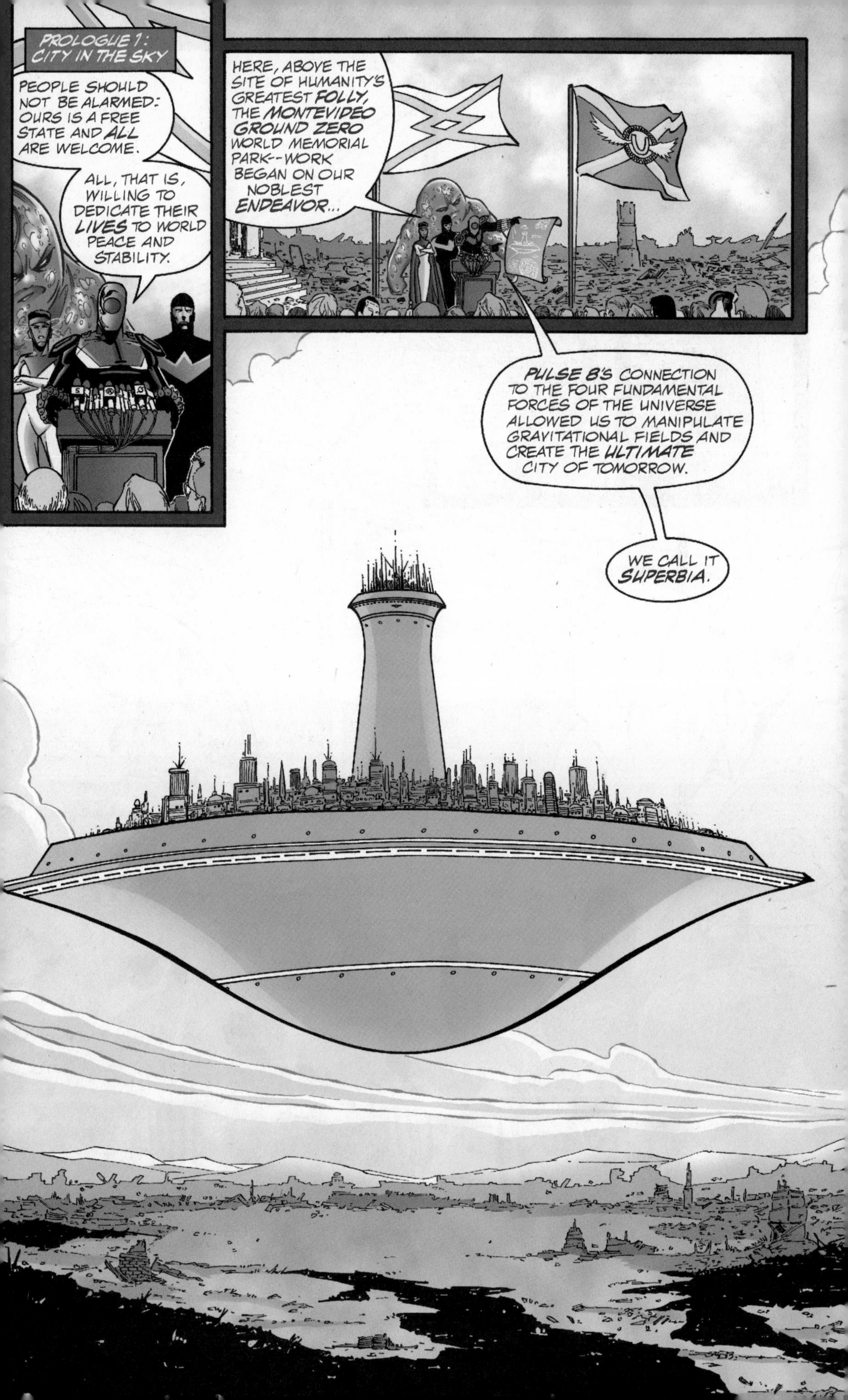
PROLOGUE 1: CITY IN THE SKY
PEOPLE SHOULD NOT BE ALARMED: OURS IS A FREE STATE AND ALL ARE WELCOME.
ALL, THAT IS, WILLING TO DEDICATE THEIR LIVES TO WORLD PEACE AND STABILITY.
HERE, ABOVE THE SITE OF HUMANITY'S GREATEST FOLLY, THE MONTEVIDEO GROUND ZERO WORLD MEMORIAL PARK--WORK BEGAN ON OUR NOBLEST ENDEAVOR...
PULSE 8'S CONNECTION TO THE FOUR FUNDAMENTAL FORCES OF THE UNIVERSE ALLOWED US TO MANIPULATE GRAVITATIONAL FIELDS AND CREATE THE ULTIMATE CITY OF TOMORROW.
WE CALL IT SUPERBIA.

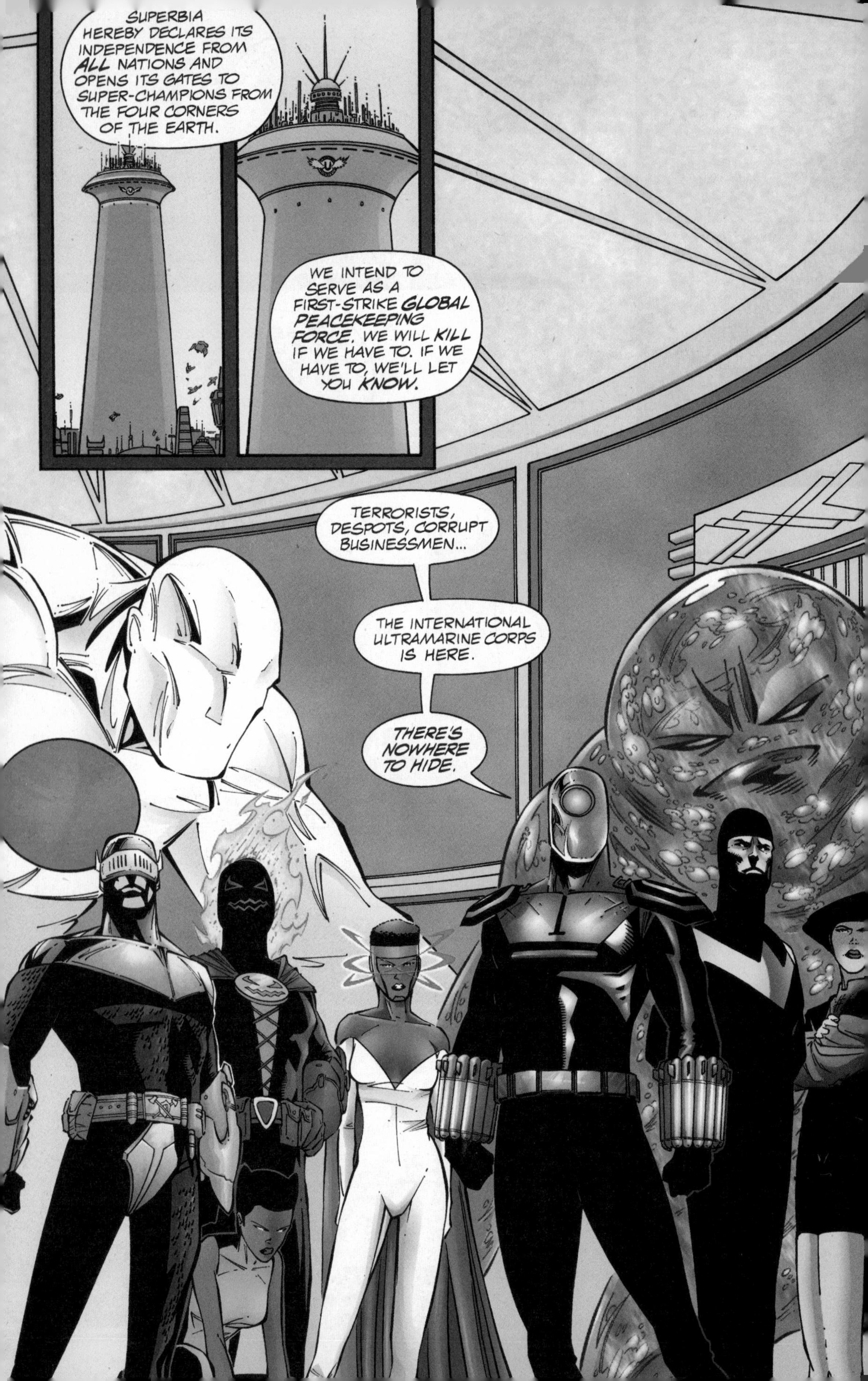
SUPERBIA HEREBY DECLARES ITS INDEPENDENCE FROM ALL NATIONS AND OPENS ITS GATES TO SUPER-CHAMPIONS FROM THE FOUR CORNERS OF THE EARTH.
WE INTEND TO SERVE AS A FIRST-STRIKE GLOBAL PEACEKEEPING FORCE. WE WILL KILL IF WE HAVE TO. IF WE HAVE TO, WE'LL LET YOU KNOW.
TERRORISTS, DESPOTS, CORRUPT BUSINESSMEN...
THE INTERNATIONAL ULTRAMARINE CORPS IS HERE.
THERE'S NOWHERE TO HIDE.

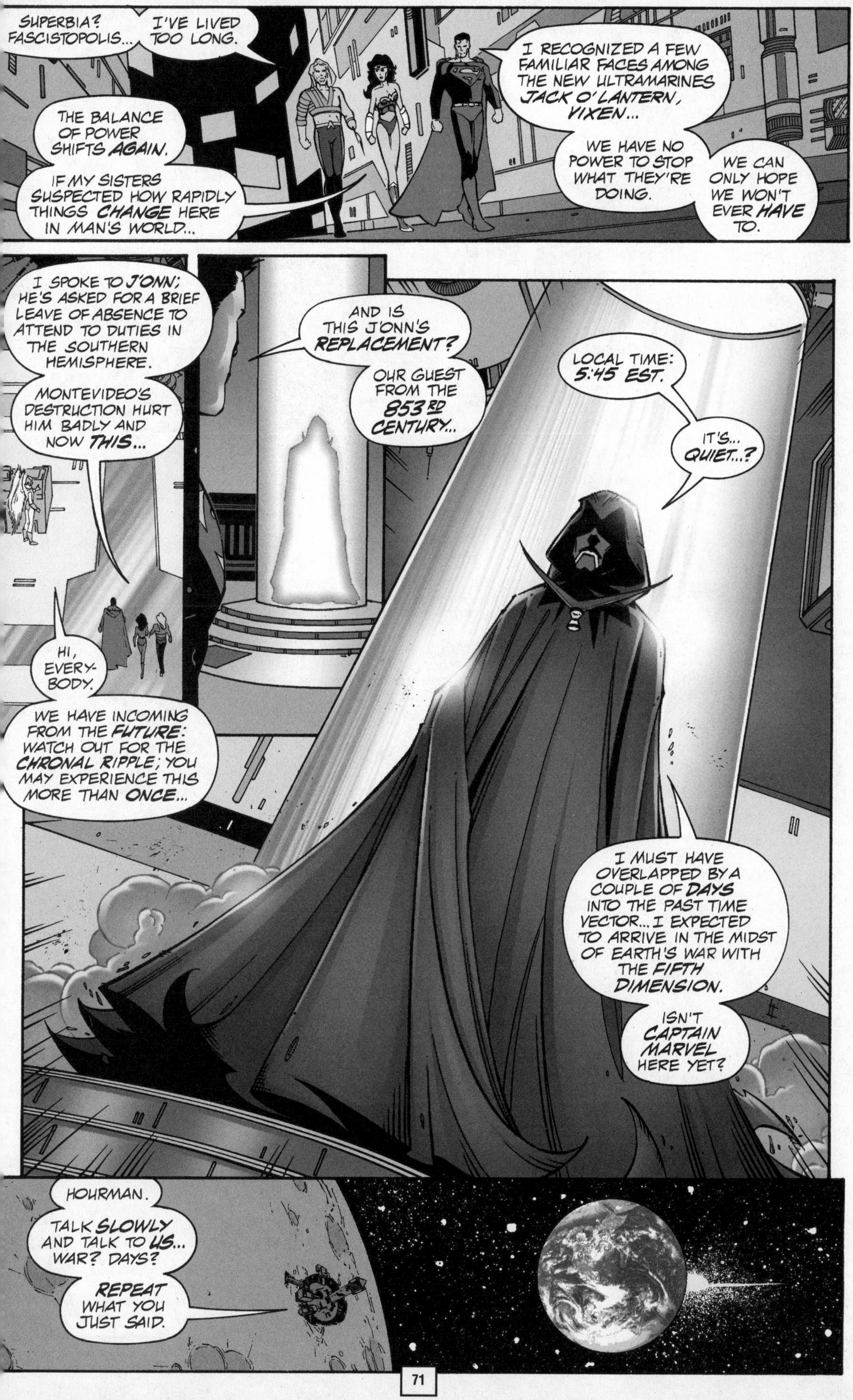
SUPERBIA? FASCISTOPOLIS...
I'VE LIVED TOO LONG.
THE BALANCE OF POWER SHIFTS AGAIN.
IF MY SISTERS SUSPECTED HOW RAPIDLY THINGS CHANGE HERE IN MAN'S WORLD...
I RECOGNIZED A FEW FAMILIAR FACES AMONG THE NEW ULTRAMARINES JACK O'LANTERN, VIXEN...
WE HAVE NO POWER TO STOP WHAT THEY'RE DOING.
WE CAN ONLY HOPE WE WON'T EVER HAVE TO.
I SPOKE TO J'ONN; HE'S ASKED FOR A BRIEF LEAVE OF ABSENCE TO ATTEND TO DUTIES IN THE SOUTHERN HEMISPHERE.
MONTEVIDEO'S DESTRUCTION HURT HIM BADLY AND NOW THIS...
AND IS THIS J'ONN'S REPLACEMENT?
OUR GUEST FROM THE 853RD CENTURY...
LOCAL TIME: 5:45 EST.
IT'S... QUIET...?
HI, EVERY-BODY.
WE HAVE INCOMING FROM THE FUTURE: WATCH OUT FOR THE CHRONAL RIPPLE; YOU MAY EXPERIENCE THIS MORE THAN ONCE...
I MUST HAVE OVERLAPPED BY A COUPLE OF DAYS INTO THE PAST TIME VECTOR... I EXPECTED TO ARRIVE IN THE MIDST OF EARTH'S WAR WITH THE FIFTH DIMENSION.
ISN'T CAPTAIN MARVEL HERE YET?
HOURMAN.
TALK SLOWLY AND TALK TO US... WAR? DAYS?
REPEAT WHAT YOU JUST SAID.

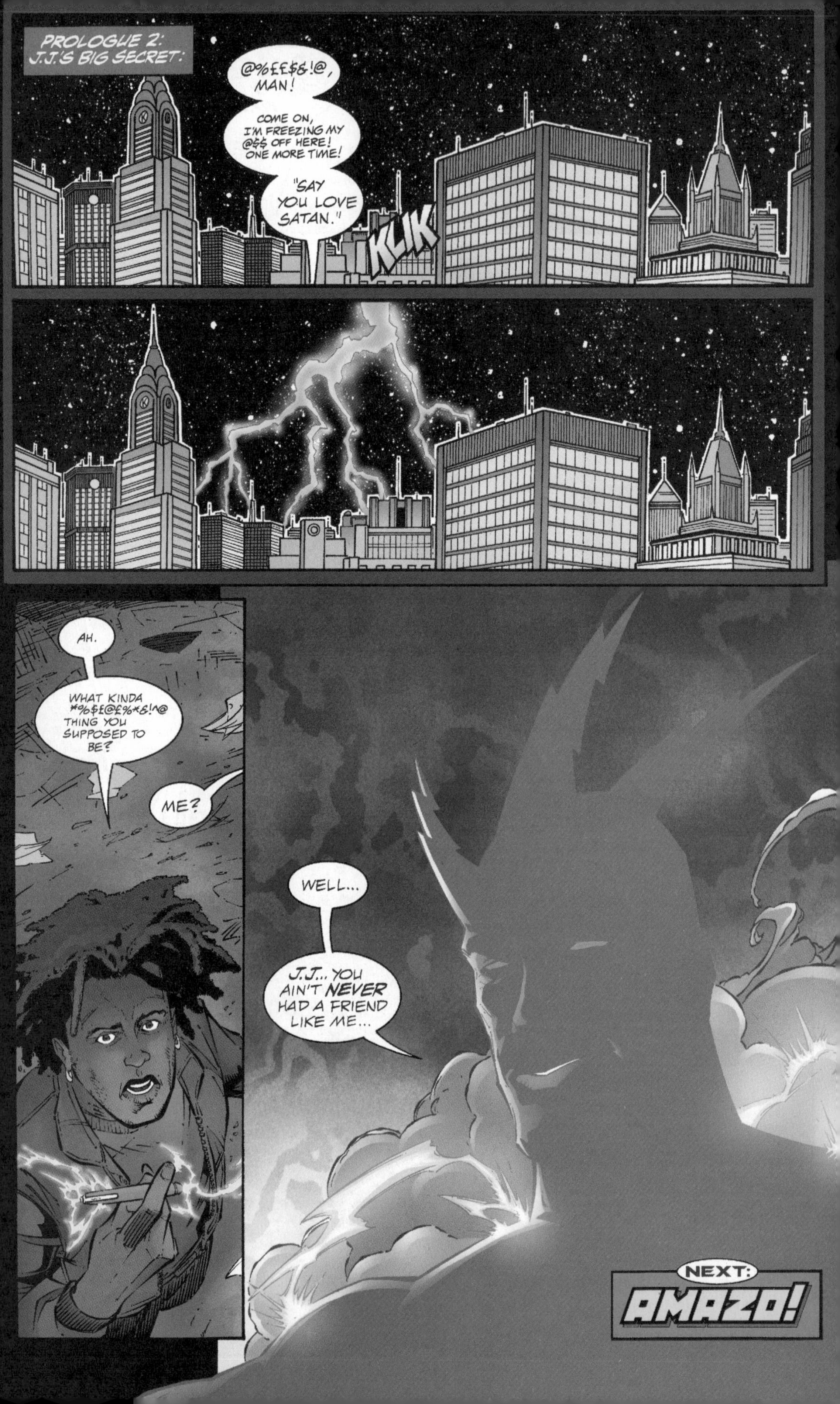
PROLOGUE 2: J.J.'S BIG SECRET:
@%££$&!@, MAN!
COME ON, I'M FREEZING MY @$$ OFF HERE! ONE MORE TIME!
"SAY YOU LOVE SATAN."
KLIK
AH.
WHAT KINDA *%$£@£%*&!@ THING YOU SUPPOSED TO BE?
ME?
WELL...
J.J... YOU AIN'T NEVER HAD A FRIEND LIKE ME...
NEXT: AMAZO!

THE BIGGER THEY COME...

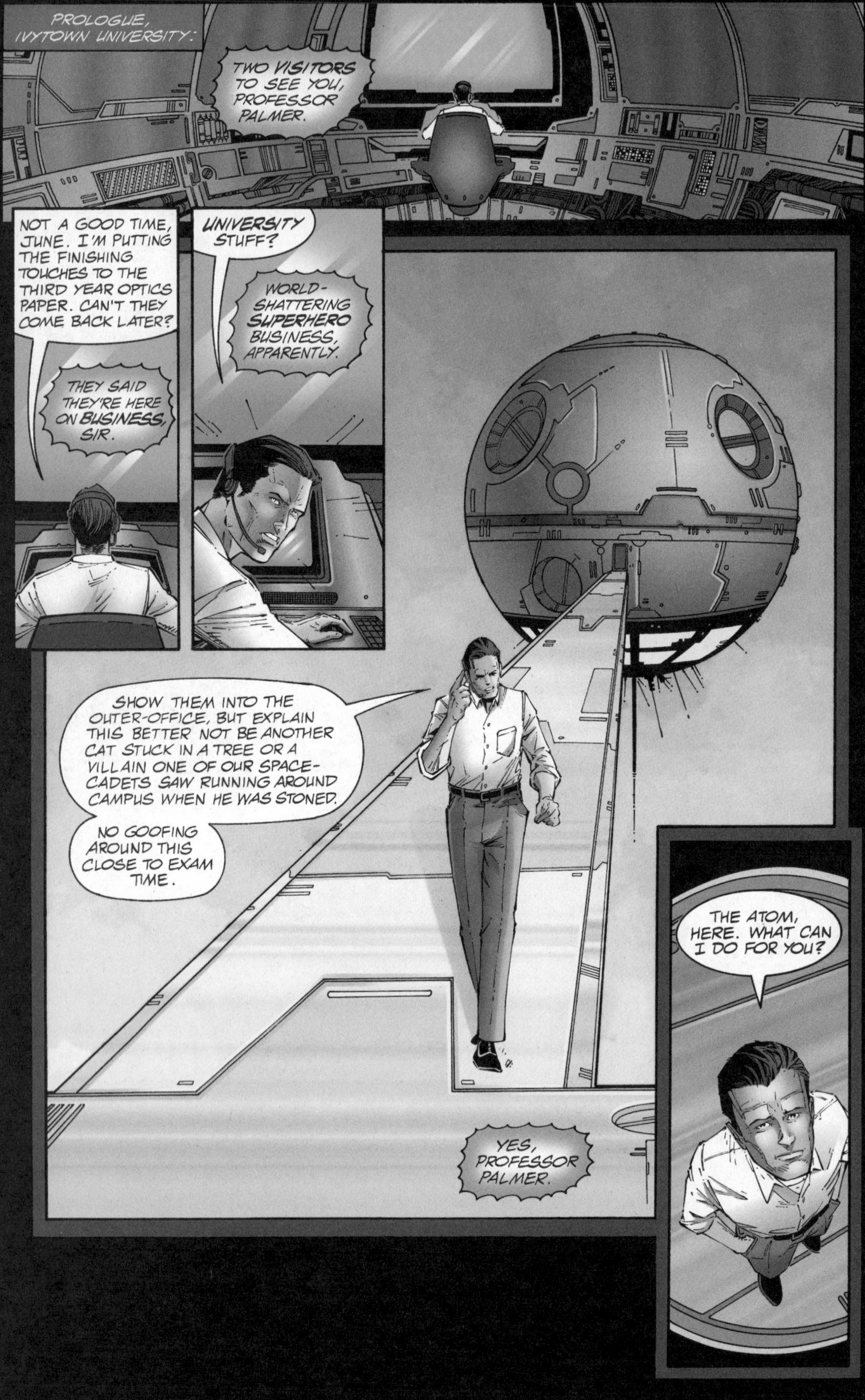
PROLOGUE, IVYTOWN UNIVERSITY:
TWO VISITORS TO SEE YOU, PROFESSOR PALMER.
NOT A GOOD TIME, JUNE. I'M PUTTING THE FINISHING TOUCHES TO THE THIRD YEAR OPTICS PAPER. CAN'T THEY COME BACK LATER?
THEY SAID THEY'RE HERE ON BUSINESS, SIR.
UNIVERSITY STUFF?
WORLD-SHATTERING SUPERHERO BUSINESS, APPARENTLY.
SHOW THEM INTO THE OUTER-OFFICE, BUT EXPLAIN THIS BETTER NOT BE ANOTHER CAT STUCK IN A TREE OR A VILLAIN ONE OF OUR SPACE-CADETS SAW RUNNING AROUND CAMPUS WHEN HE WAS STONED.
NO GOOFING AROUND THIS CLOSE TO EXAM TIME.
YES, PROFESSOR PALMER.
THE ATOM, HERE. WHAT CAN I DO FOR YOU?

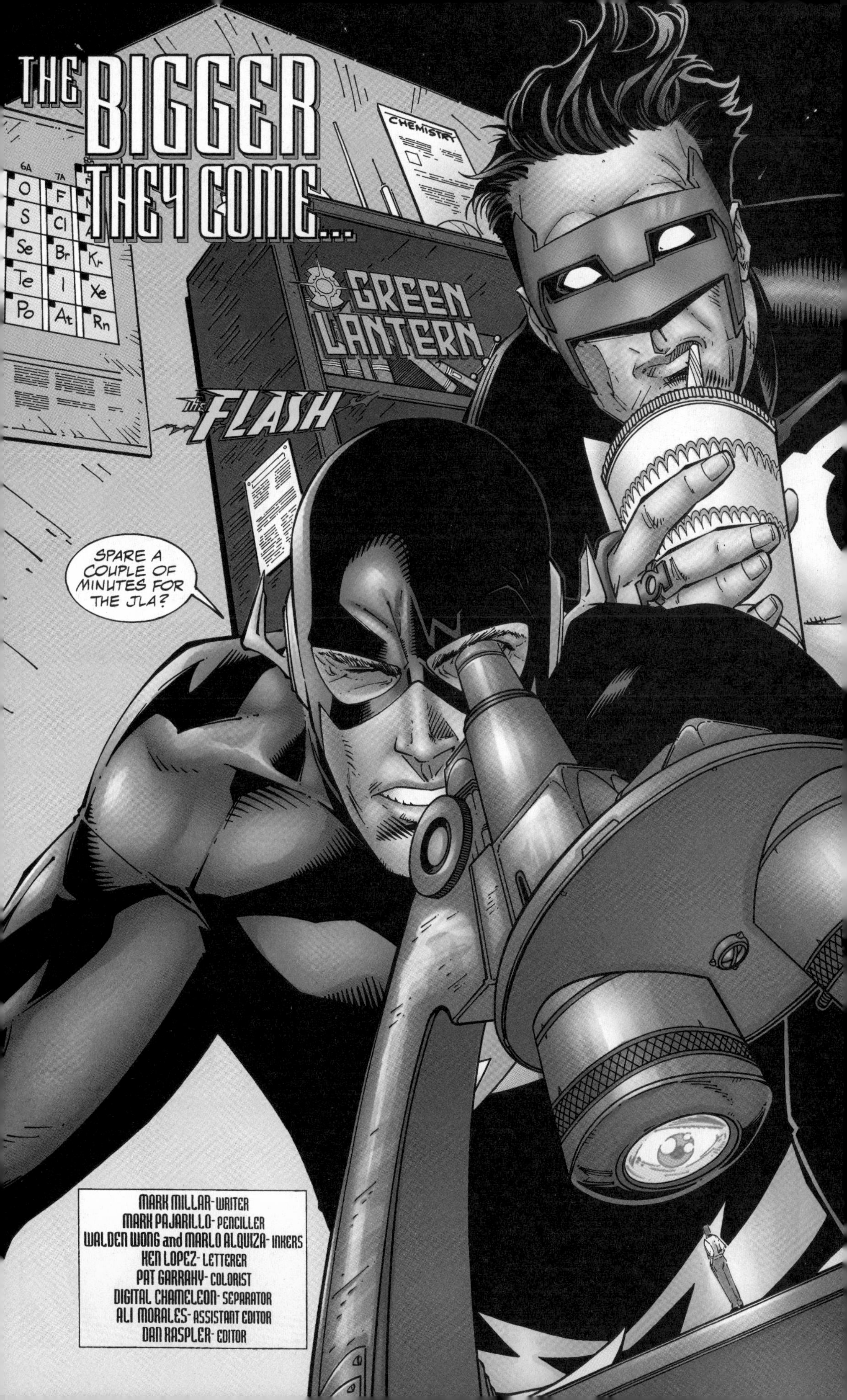
THE BIGGER THEY COME...
CHEMISTRY
6A 7A
O F
S Cl
Se Br Kr
Te I Xe
Po At Rn
GREEN LANTERN
THE FLASH
SPARE A COUPLE OF MINUTES FOR THE JLA?
MARK MILLAR- WRITER
MARK PAJARILLO- PENCILLER
WALDEN WONG and MARLO ALQUIZA- INKERS
KEN LOPEZ- LETTERER
PAT GARRAHY- COLORIST
DIGITAL CHAMELEON- SEPARATOR
ALI MORALES- ASSISTANT EDITOR
DAN RASPLER- EDITOR

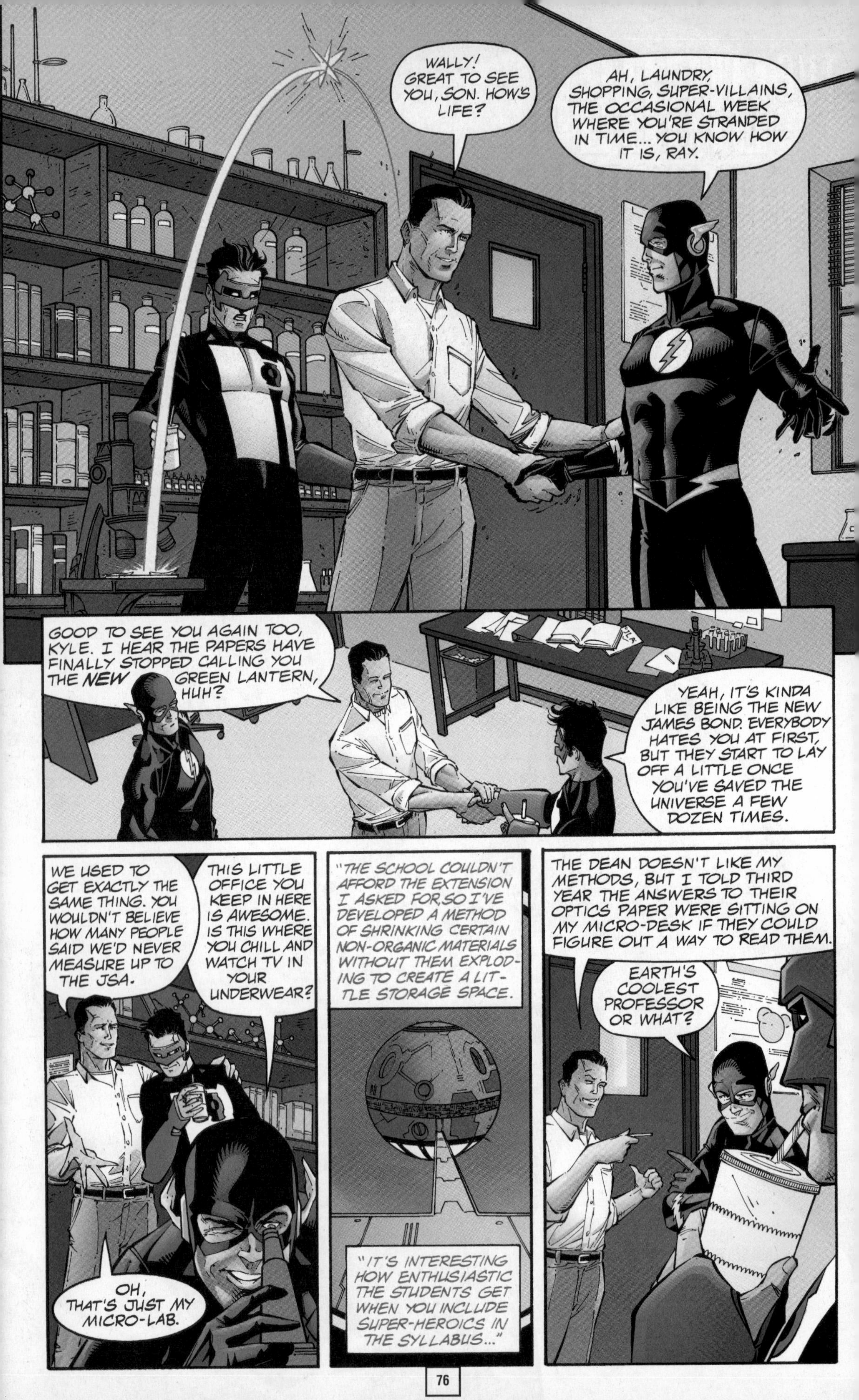
WALLY! GREAT TO SEE YOU, SON. HOW'S LIFE?
AH, LAUNDRY, SHOPPING, SUPER-VILLAINS, THE OCCASIONAL WEEK WHERE YOU'RE STRANDED IN TIME... YOU KNOW HOW IT IS, RAY.
GOOD TO SEE YOU AGAIN TOO, KYLE. I HEAR THE PAPERS HAVE FINALLY STOPPED CALLING YOU THE NEW GREEN LANTERN, HUH?
YEAH, IT'S KINDA LIKE BEING THE NEW JAMES BOND. EVERYBODY HATES YOU AT FIRST, BUT THEY START TO LAY OFF A LITTLE ONCE YOU'VE SAVED THE UNIVERSE A FEW DOZEN TIMES.
WE USED TO GET EXACTLY THE SAME THING. YOU WOULDN'T BELIEVE HOW MANY PEOPLE SAID WE'D NEVER MEASURE UP TO THE JSA.
THIS LITTLE OFFICE YOU KEEP IN HERE IS AWESOME. IS THIS WHERE YOU CHILL AND WATCH TV IN YOUR UNDERWEAR?
OH, THAT'S JUST MY MICRO-LAB.
"THE SCHOOL COULDN'T AFFORD THE EXTENSION I ASKED FOR, SO I'VE DEVELOPED A METHOD OF SHRINKING CERTAIN NON-ORGANIC MATERIALS WITHOUT THEM EXPLODING TO CREATE A LITTLE STORAGE SPACE.
"IT'S INTERESTING HOW ENTHUSIASTIC THE STUDENTS GET WHEN YOU INCLUDE SUPER-HEROICS IN THE SYLLABUS..."
THE DEAN DOESN'T LIKE MY METHODS, BUT I TOLD THIRD YEAR THE ANSWERS TO THEIR OPTICS PAPER WERE SITTING ON MY MICRO-DESK IF THEY COULD FIGURE OUT A WAY TO READ THEM.
EARTH'S COOLEST PROFESSOR OR WHAT?

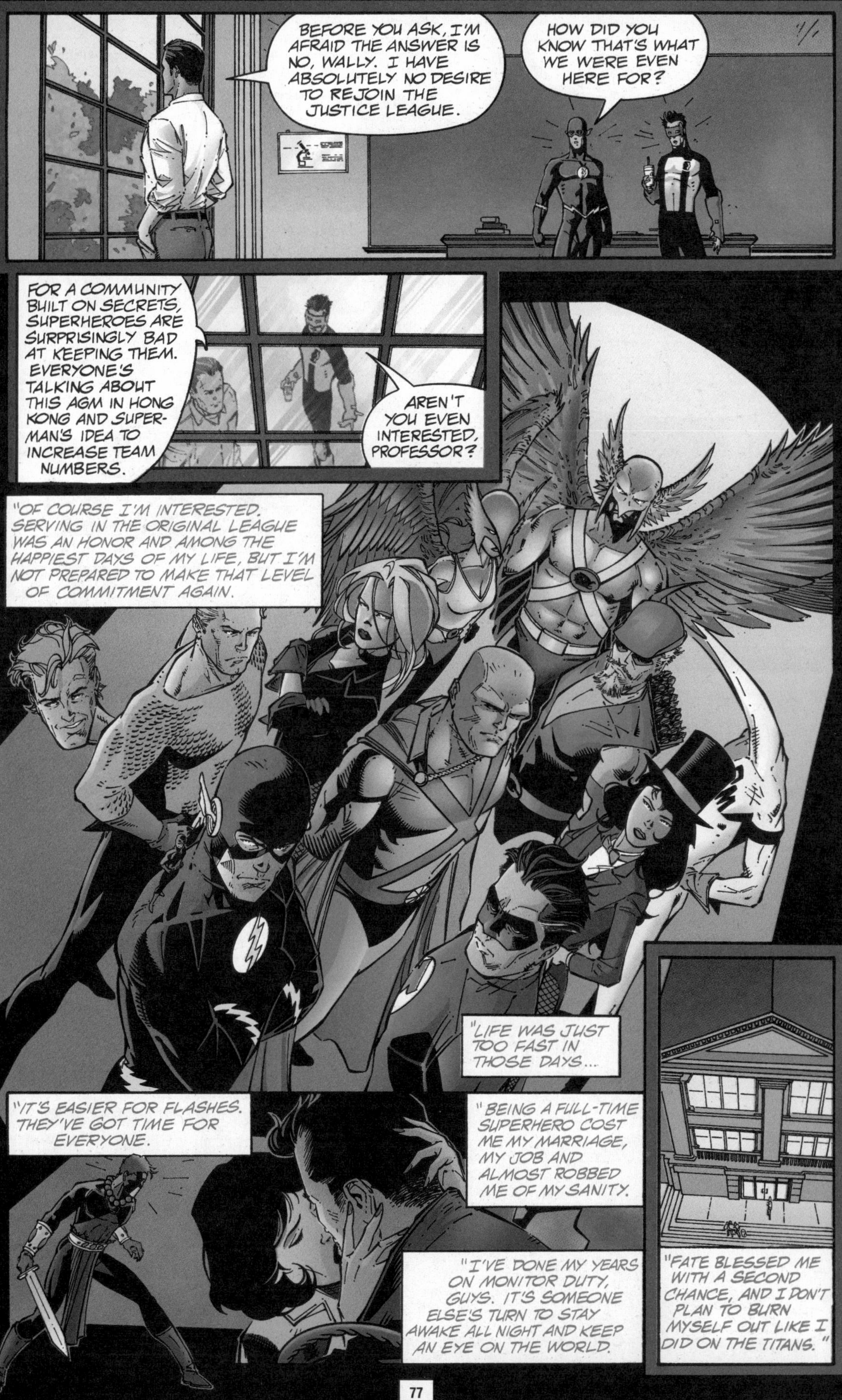
BEFORE YOU ASK, I'M AFRAID THE ANSWER IS NO, WALLY. I HAVE ABSOLUTELY NO DESIRE TO REJOIN THE JUSTICE LEAGUE.
HOW DID YOU KNOW THAT'S WHAT WE WERE EVEN HERE FOR?
FOR A COMMUNITY BUILT ON SECRETS, SUPERHEROES ARE SURPRISINGLY BAD AT KEEPING THEM. EVERYONE'S TALKING ABOUT THIS AGM IN HONG KONG AND SUPER-MAN'S IDEA TO INCREASE TEAM NUMBERS.
AREN'T YOU EVEN INTERESTED, PROFESSOR?
"OF COURSE I'M INTERESTED. SERVING IN THE ORIGINAL LEAGUE WAS AN HONOR AND AMONG THE HAPPIEST DAYS OF MY LIFE, BUT I'M NOT PREPARED TO MAKE THAT LEVEL OF COMMITMENT AGAIN.
"LIFE WAS JUST TOO FAST IN THOSE DAYS...
"IT'S EASIER FOR FLASHES. THEY'VE GOT TIME FOR EVERYONE.
"BEING A FULL-TIME SUPERHERO COST ME MY MARRIAGE, MY JOB AND ALMOST ROBBED ME OF MY SANITY.
"I'VE DONE MY YEARS ON MONITOR DUTY, GUYS. IT'S SOMEONE ELSE'S TURN TO STAY AWAKE ALL NIGHT AND KEEP AN EYE ON THE WORLD.
"FATE BLESSED ME WITH A SECOND CHANCE, AND I DON'T PLAN TO BURN MYSELF OUT LIKE I DID ON THE TITANS."

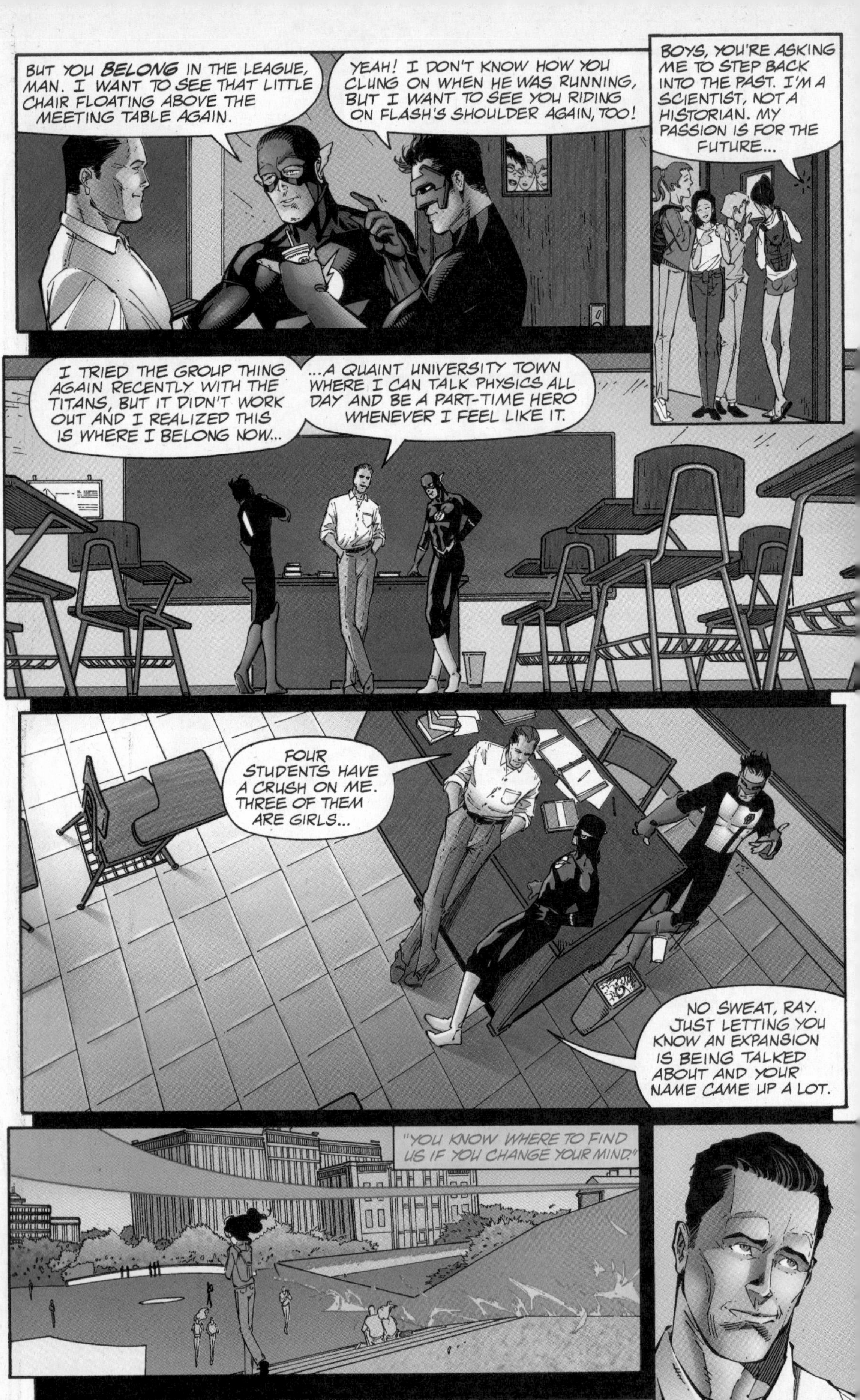
BUT YOU BELONG IN THE LEAGUE, MAN. I WANT TO SEE THAT LITTLE CHAIR FLOATING ABOVE THE MEETING TABLE AGAIN.
YEAH! I DON'T KNOW HOW YOU CLUNG ON WHEN HE WAS RUNNING, BUT I WANT TO SEE YOU RIDING ON FLASH'S SHOULDER AGAIN, TOO!
BOYS, YOU'RE ASKING ME TO STEP BACK INTO THE PAST. I'M A SCIENTIST, NOT A HISTORIAN. MY PASSION IS FOR THE FUTURE...
I TRIED THE GROUP THING AGAIN RECENTLY WITH THE TITANS, BUT IT DIDN'T WORK OUT AND I REALIZED THIS IS WHERE I BELONG NOW...
...A QUAINT UNIVERSITY TOWN WHERE I CAN TALK PHYSICS ALL DAY AND BE A PART-TIME HERO WHENEVER I FEEL LIKE IT.
FOUR STUDENTS HAVE A CRUSH ON ME. THREE OF THEM ARE GIRLS...
NO SWEAT, RAY. JUST LETTING YOU KNOW AN EXPANSION IS BEING TALKED ABOUT AND YOUR NAME CAME UP A LOT.
"YOU KNOW WHERE TO FIND US IF YOU CHANGE YOUR MIND."

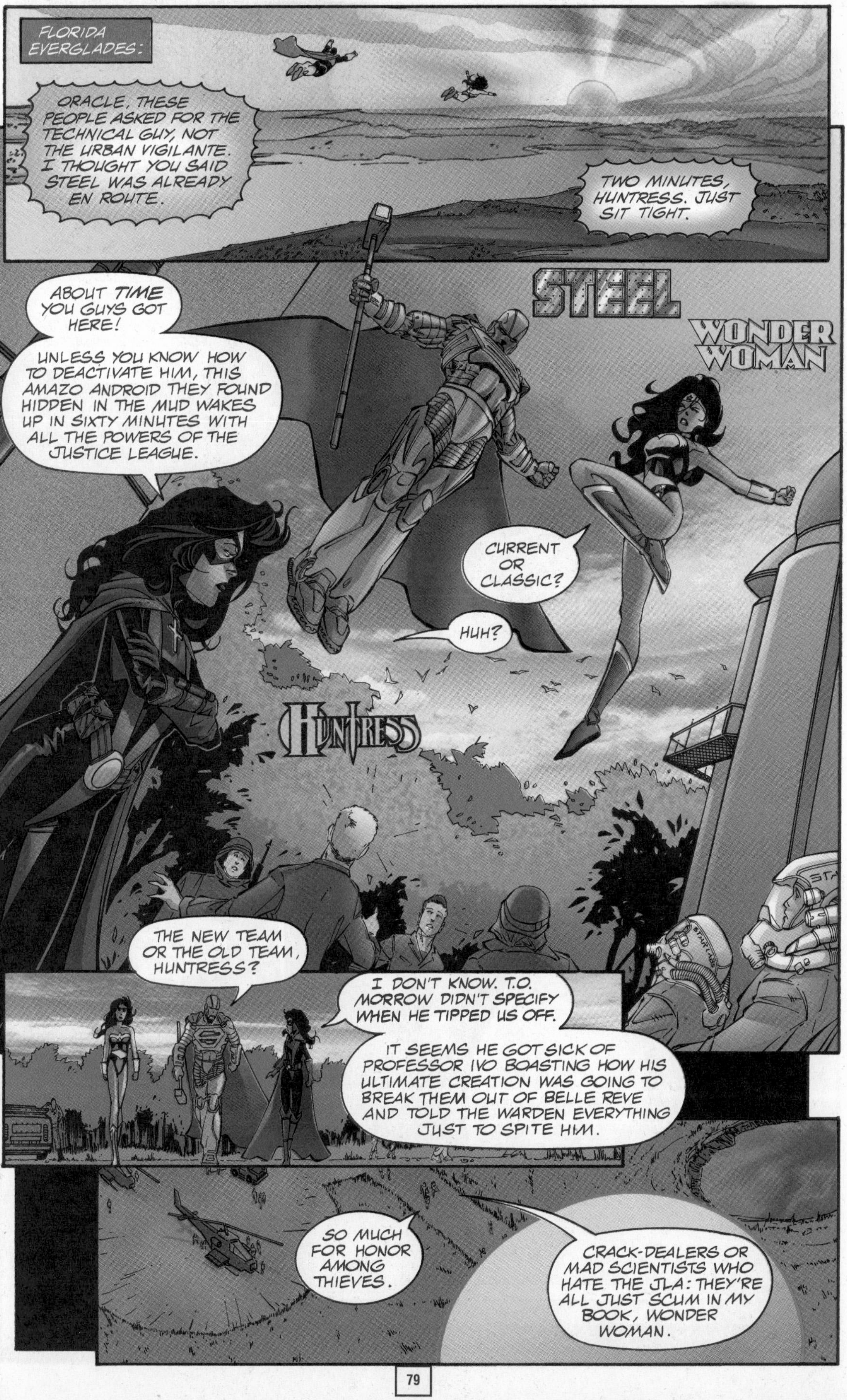
FLORIDA EVERGLADES:
ORACLE, THESE PEOPLE ASKED FOR THE TECHNICAL GUY, NOT THE URBAN VIGILANTE. I THOUGHT YOU SAID STEEL WAS ALREADY EN ROUTE.
TWO MINUTES, HUNTRESS. JUST SIT TIGHT.
STEEL
WONDER WOMAN
ABOUT TIME YOU GUYS GOT HERE!
UNLESS YOU KNOW HOW TO DEACTIVATE HIM, THIS AMAZO ANDROID THEY FOUND HIDDEN IN THE MUD WAKES UP IN SIXTY MINUTES WITH ALL THE POWERS OF THE JUSTICE LEAGUE.
CURRENT OR CLASSIC?
HUH?
HUNTRESS
THE NEW TEAM OR THE OLD TEAM, HUNTRESS?
I DON'T KNOW. T.O. MORROW DIDN'T SPECIFY WHEN HE TIPPED US OFF.
IT SEEMS HE GOT SICK OF PROFESSOR IVO BOASTING HOW HIS ULTIMATE CREATION WAS GOING TO BREAK THEM OUT OF BELLE REVE AND TOLD THE WARDEN EVERYTHING JUST TO SPITE HIM.
SO MUCH FOR HONOR AMONG THIEVES.
CRACK-DEALERS OR MAD SCIENTISTS WHO HATE THE JLA: THEY'RE ALL JUST SCUM IN MY BOOK, WONDER WOMAN.

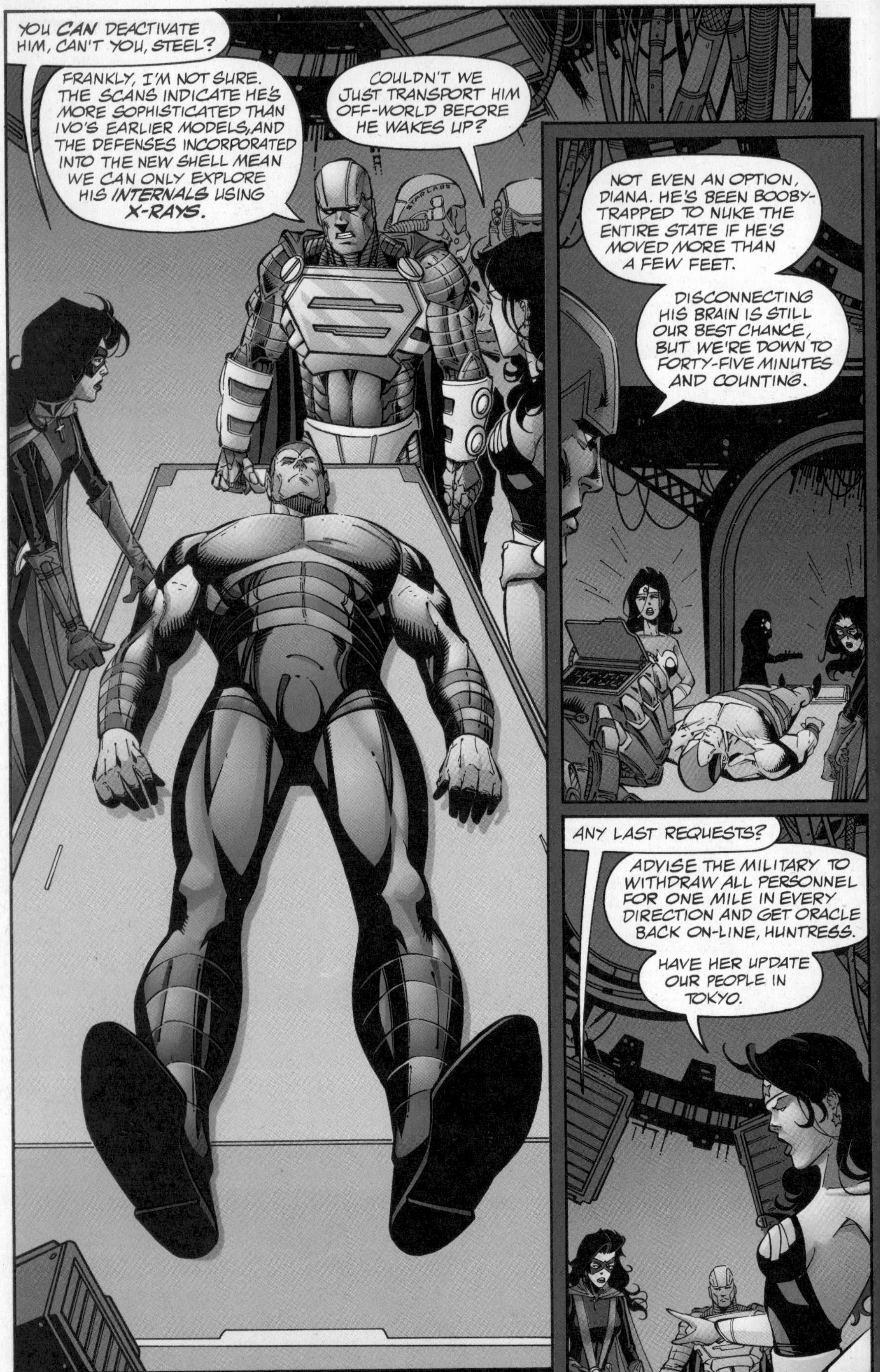
YOU *CAN* DEACTIVATE HIM, CAN'T YOU, STEEL?
FRANKLY, I'M NOT SURE. THE SCANS INDICATE HE'S MORE SOPHISTICATED THAN IVO'S EARLIER MODELS, AND THE DEFENSES INCORPORATED INTO THE NEW SHELL MEAN WE CAN ONLY EXPLORE HIS *INTERNALS* USING **X-RAYS**.
COULDN'T WE JUST TRANSPORT HIM OFF-WORLD BEFORE HE WAKES UP?
NOT EVEN AN OPTION, DIANA. HE'S BEEN BOOBY-TRAPPED TO NUKE THE ENTIRE STATE IF HE'S MOVED MORE THAN A FEW FEET.
DISCONNECTING HIS BRAIN IS STILL OUR BEST CHANCE, BUT WE'RE DOWN TO FORTY-FIVE MINUTES AND COUNTING.
ANY LAST REQUESTS?
ADVISE THE MILITARY TO WITHDRAW ALL PERSONNEL FOR ONE MILE IN EVERY DIRECTION AND GET ORACLE BACK ON-LINE, HUNTRESS.
HAVE HER UPDATE OUR PEOPLE IN TOKYO.

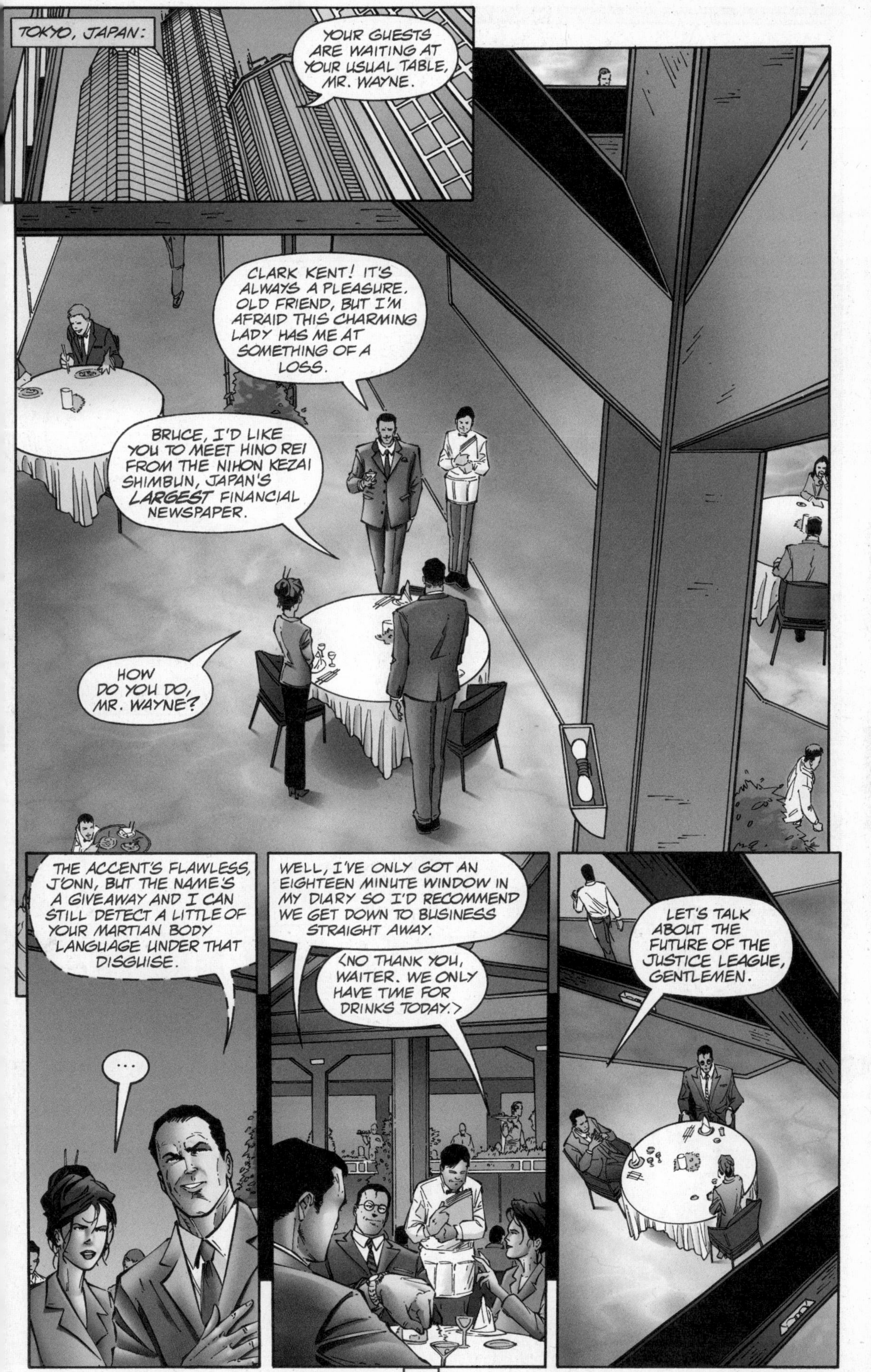
TOKYO, JAPAN:
YOUR GUESTS ARE WAITING AT YOUR USUAL TABLE, MR. WAYNE.
CLARK KENT! IT'S ALWAYS A PLEASURE, OLD FRIEND, BUT I'M AFRAID THIS CHARMING LADY HAS ME AT SOMETHING OF A LOSS.
BRUCE, I'D LIKE YOU TO MEET HINO REI FROM THE NIHON KEZAI SHIMBUN, JAPAN'S LARGEST FINANCIAL NEWSPAPER.
HOW DO YOU DO, MR. WAYNE?
THE ACCENT'S FLAWLESS, J'ONN, BUT THE NAME'S A GIVEAWAY AND I CAN STILL DETECT A LITTLE OF YOUR MARTIAN BODY LANGUAGE UNDER THAT DISGUISE.
...
WELL, I'VE ONLY GOT AN EIGHTEEN MINUTE WINDOW IN MY DIARY SO I'D RECOMMEND WE GET DOWN TO BUSINESS STRAIGHT AWAY.
<NO THANK YOU, WAITER. WE ONLY HAVE TIME FOR DRINKS TODAY.>
LET'S TALK ABOUT THE FUTURE OF THE JUSTICE LEAGUE, GENTLEMEN.

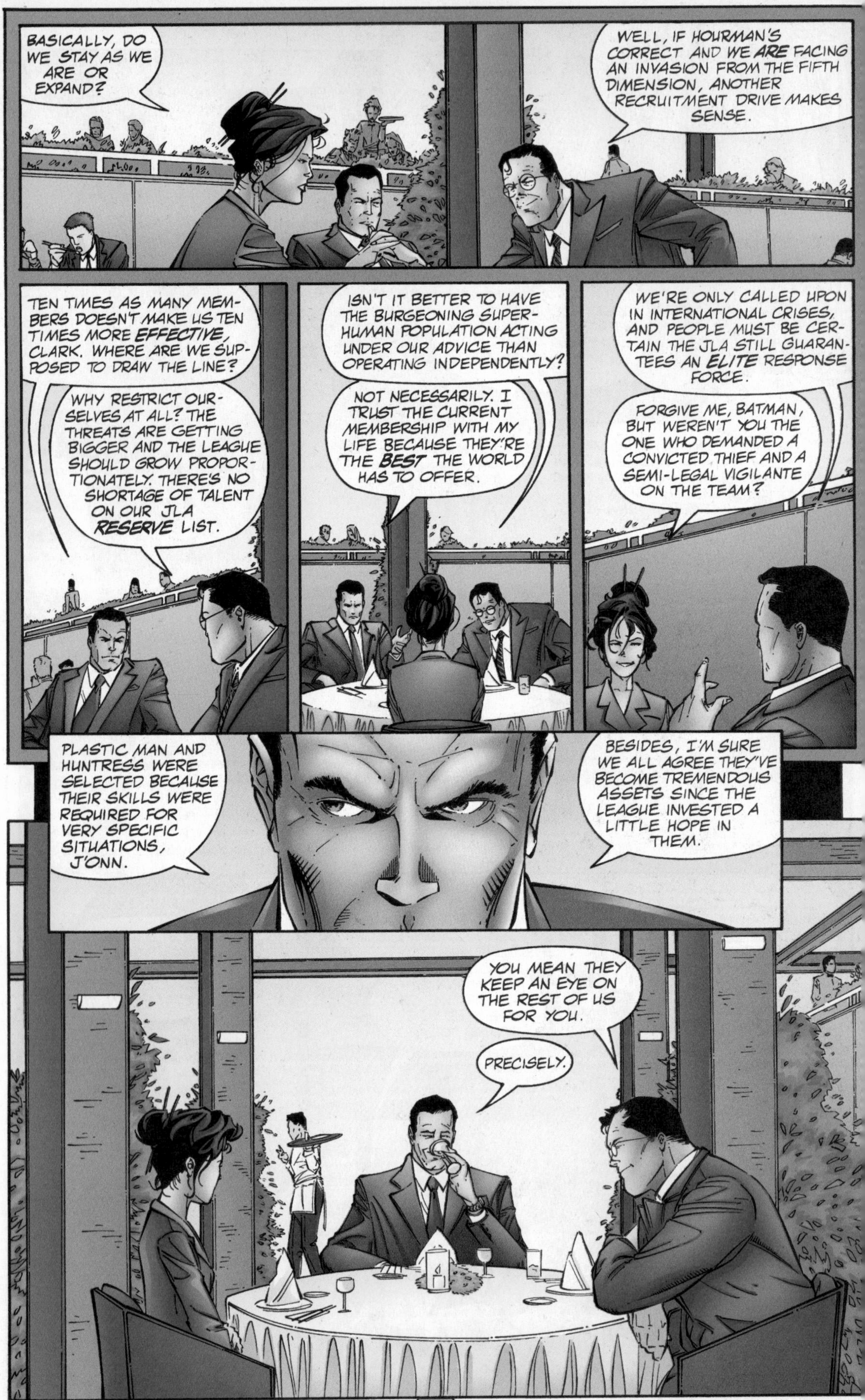

BASICALLY, DO WE STAY AS WE ARE OR EXPAND?
WELL, IF HOURMAN'S CORRECT AND WE ARE FACING AN INVASION FROM THE FIFTH DIMENSION, ANOTHER RECRUITMENT DRIVE MAKES SENSE.
TEN TIMES AS MANY MEMBERS DOESN'T MAKE US TEN TIMES MORE EFFECTIVE, CLARK. WHERE ARE WE SUPPOSED TO DRAW THE LINE?
WHY RESTRICT OURSELVES AT ALL? THE THREATS ARE GETTING BIGGER AND THE LEAGUE SHOULD GROW PROPORTIONATELY. THERE'S NO SHORTAGE OF TALENT ON OUR JLA RESERVE LIST.
ISN'T IT BETTER TO HAVE THE BURGEONING SUPER-HUMAN POPULATION ACTING UNDER OUR ADVICE THAN OPERATING INDEPENDENTLY?
NOT NECESSARILY. I TRUST THE CURRENT MEMBERSHIP WITH MY LIFE BECAUSE THEY'RE THE BEST THE WORLD HAS TO OFFER.
WE'RE ONLY CALLED UPON IN INTERNATIONAL CRISES, AND PEOPLE MUST BE CERTAIN THE JLA STILL GUARANTEES AN ELITE RESPONSE FORCE.
FORGIVE ME, BATMAN, BUT WEREN'T YOU THE ONE WHO DEMANDED A CONVICTED THIEF AND A SEMI-LEGAL VIGILANTE ON THE TEAM?
PLASTIC MAN AND HUNTRESS WERE SELECTED BECAUSE THEIR SKILLS WERE REQUIRED FOR VERY SPECIFIC SITUATIONS, J'ONN.
BESIDES, I'M SURE WE ALL AGREE THEY'VE BECOME TREMENDOUS ASSETS SINCE THE LEAGUE INVESTED A LITTLE HOPE IN THEM.
YOU MEAN THEY KEEP AN EYE ON THE REST OF US FOR YOU.
PRECISELY.

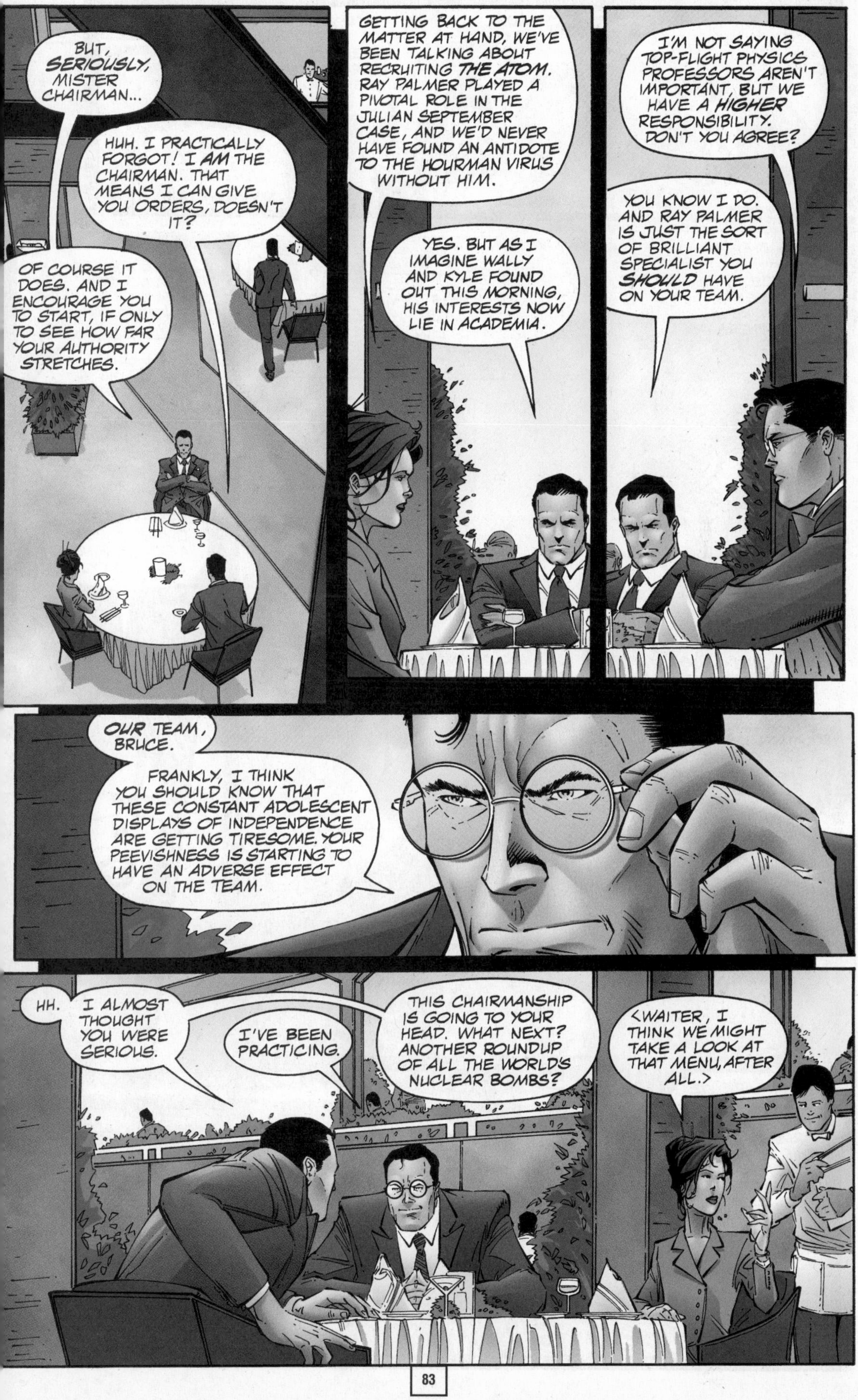
BUT, SERIOUSLY, MISTER CHAIRMAN...
HUH. I PRACTICALLY FORGOT! I AM THE CHAIRMAN. THAT MEANS I CAN GIVE YOU ORDERS, DOESN'T IT?
OF COURSE IT DOES. AND I ENCOURAGE YOU TO START, IF ONLY TO SEE HOW FAR YOUR AUTHORITY STRETCHES.
GETTING BACK TO THE MATTER AT HAND, WE'VE BEEN TALKING ABOUT RECRUITING THE ATOM. RAY PALMER PLAYED A PIVOTAL ROLE IN THE JULIAN SEPTEMBER CASE, AND WE'D NEVER HAVE FOUND AN ANTIDOTE TO THE HOURMAN VIRUS WITHOUT HIM.
YES. BUT AS I IMAGINE WALLY AND KYLE FOUND OUT THIS MORNING, HIS INTERESTS NOW LIE IN ACADEMIA.
I'M NOT SAYING TOP-FLIGHT PHYSICS PROFESSORS AREN'T IMPORTANT, BUT WE HAVE A HIGHER RESPONSIBILITY. DON'T YOU AGREE?
YOU KNOW I DO. AND RAY PALMER IS JUST THE SORT OF BRILLIANT SPECIALIST YOU SHOULD HAVE ON YOUR TEAM.
OUR TEAM, BRUCE.
FRANKLY, I THINK YOU SHOULD KNOW THAT THESE CONSTANT ADOLESCENT DISPLAYS OF INDEPENDENCE ARE GETTING TIRESOME. YOUR PEEVISHNESS IS STARTING TO HAVE AN ADVERSE EFFECT ON THE TEAM.
HH.
I ALMOST THOUGHT YOU WERE SERIOUS.
I'VE BEEN PRACTICING.
THIS CHAIRMANSHIP IS GOING TO YOUR HEAD. WHAT NEXT? ANOTHER ROUNDUP OF ALL THE WORLD'S NUCLEAR BOMBS?
<WAITER, I THINK WE MIGHT TAKE A LOOK AT THAT MENU, AFTER ALL.>

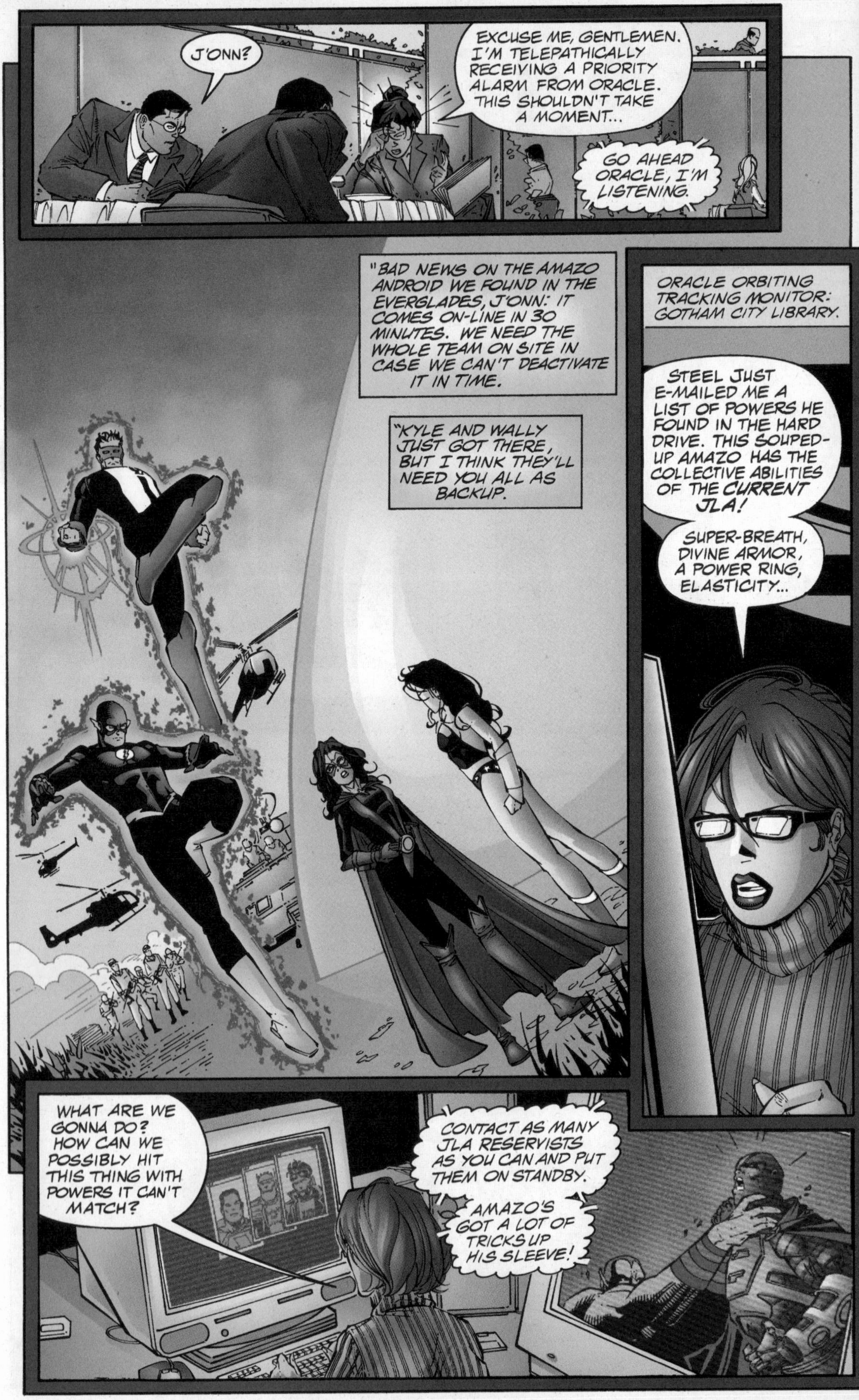
J'ONN?
EXCUSE ME, GENTLEMEN. I'M TELEPATHICALLY RECEIVING A PRIORITY ALARM FROM ORACLE. THIS SHOULDN'T TAKE A MOMENT...
GO AHEAD ORACLE, I'M LISTENING.
"BAD NEWS ON THE AMAZO ANDROID WE FOUND IN THE EVERGLADES, J'ONN: IT COMES ON-LINE IN 30 MINUTES. WE NEED THE WHOLE TEAM ON SITE IN CASE WE CAN'T DEACTIVATE IT IN TIME.
"KYLE AND WALLY JUST GOT THERE, BUT I THINK THEY'LL NEED YOU ALL AS BACKUP.
ORACLE ORBITING TRACKING MONITOR: GOTHAM CITY LIBRARY.
STEEL JUST E-MAILED ME A LIST OF POWERS HE FOUND IN THE HARD DRIVE. THIS SOUPED-UP AMAZO HAS THE COLLECTIVE ABILITIES OF THE CURRENT JLA!
SUPER-BREATH, DIVINE ARMOR, A POWER RING, ELASTICITY...
WHAT ARE WE GONNA DO? HOW CAN WE POSSIBLY HIT THIS THING WITH POWERS IT CAN'T MATCH?
CONTACT AS MANY JLA RESERVISTS AS YOU CAN AND PUT THEM ON STANDBY.
AMAZO'S GOT A LOT OF TRICKS UP HIS SLEEVE!

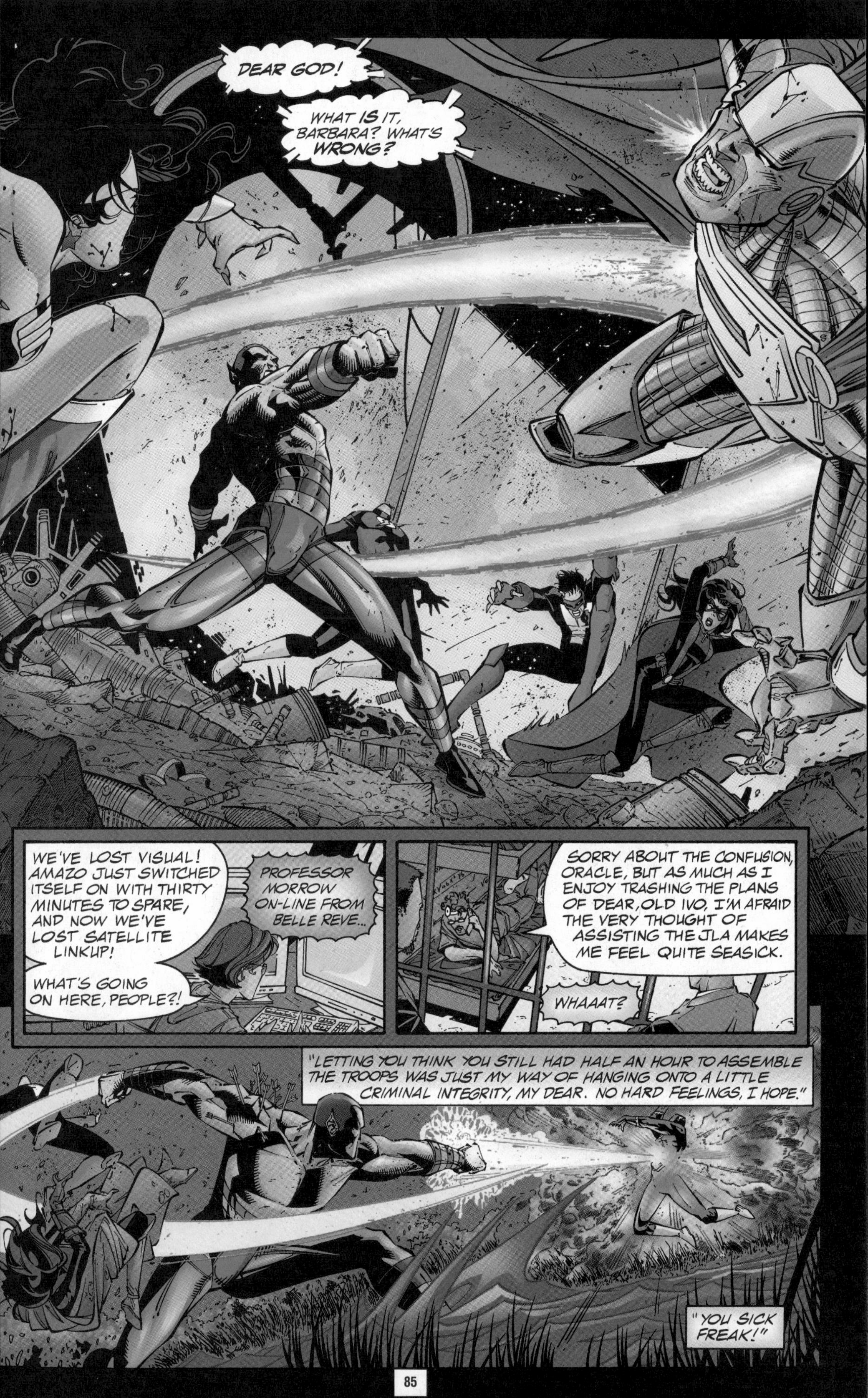
DEAR GOD!
WHAT IS IT, BARBARA? WHAT'S WRONG?
WE'VE LOST VISUAL! AMAZO JUST SWITCHED ITSELF ON WITH THIRTY MINUTES TO SPARE, AND NOW WE'VE LOST SATELLITE LINKUP!
WHAT'S GOING ON HERE, PEOPLE?!
PROFESSOR MORROW ON-LINE FROM BELLE REVE...
SORRY ABOUT THE CONFUSION, ORACLE, BUT AS MUCH AS I ENJOY TRASHING THE PLANS OF DEAR, OLD IVO, I'M AFRAID THE VERY THOUGHT OF ASSISTING THE JLA MAKES ME FEEL QUITE SEASICK.
WHAAAT?
"LETTING YOU THINK YOU STILL HAD HALF AN HOUR TO ASSEMBLE THE TROOPS WAS JUST MY WAY OF HANGING ONTO A LITTLE CRIMINAL INTEGRITY, MY DEAR. NO HARD FEELINGS, I HOPE."
"YOU SICK FREAK!"

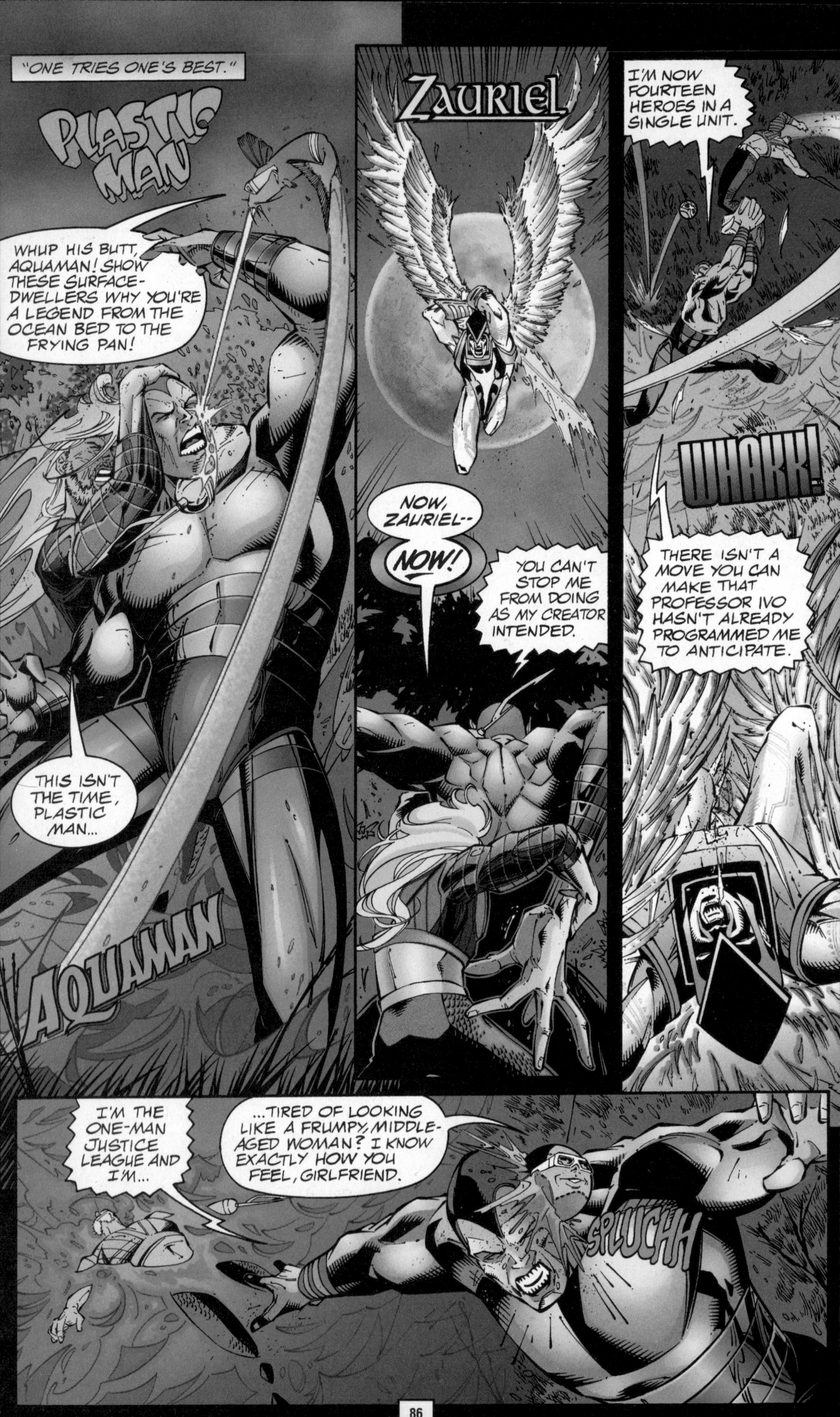
"ONE TRIES ONE'S BEST."
PLASTIC MAN
WHUP HIS BUTT, AQUAMAN! SHOW THESE SURFACE-DWELLERS WHY YOU'RE A LEGEND FROM THE OCEAN BED TO THE FRYING PAN!
THIS ISN'T THE TIME, PLASTIC MAN...
AQUAMAN
ZAURIEL
NOW, ZAURIEL--
NOW!
YOU CAN'T STOP ME FROM DOING AS MY CREATOR INTENDED.
I'M NOW FOURTEEN HEROES IN A SINGLE UNIT.
WHAKK!
THERE ISN'T A MOVE YOU CAN MAKE THAT PROFESSOR IVO HASN'T ALREADY PROGRAMMED ME TO ANTICIPATE.
I'M THE ONE-MAN JUSTICE LEAGUE AND I'M...
...TIRED OF LOOKING LIKE A FRUMPY, MIDDLE-AGED WOMAN? I KNOW EXACTLY HOW YOU FEEL, GIRLFRIEND.
SPLUCHH

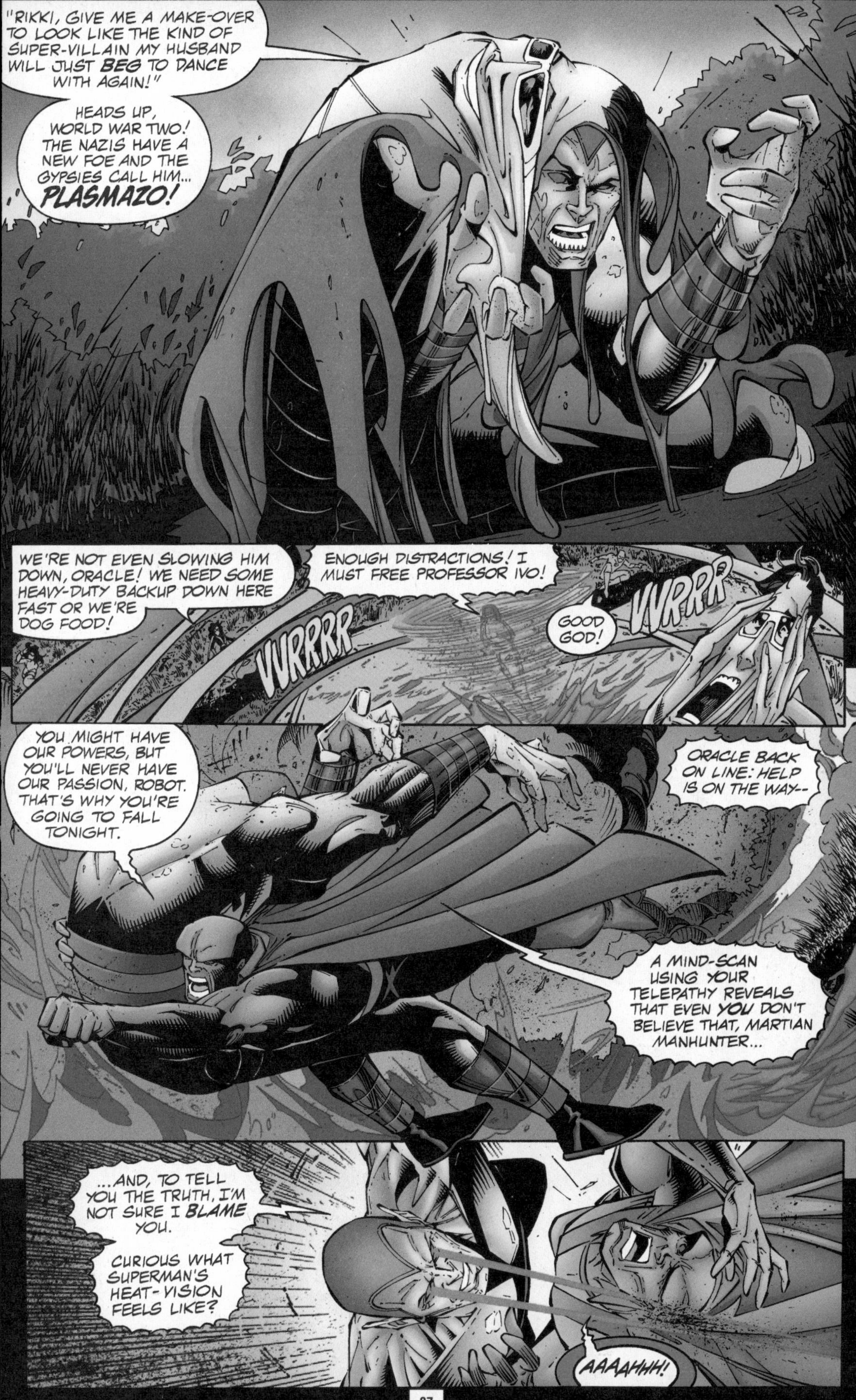
"RIKKI, GIVE ME A MAKE-OVER TO LOOK LIKE THE KIND OF SUPER-VILLAIN MY HUSBAND WILL JUST BEG TO DANCE WITH AGAIN!"
HEADS UP, WORLD WAR TWO! THE NAZIS HAVE A NEW FOE AND THE GYPSIES CALL HIM... PLASMAZO!
WE'RE NOT EVEN SLOWING HIM DOWN, ORACLE! WE NEED SOME HEAVY-DUTY BACKUP DOWN HERE FAST OR WE'RE DOG FOOD!
ENOUGH DISTRACTIONS! I MUST FREE PROFESSOR IVO!
VVRRRR
GOOD GOD!
VVRRRR
YOU MIGHT HAVE OUR POWERS, BUT YOU'LL NEVER HAVE OUR PASSION, ROBOT. THAT'S WHY YOU'RE GOING TO FALL TONIGHT.
ORACLE BACK ON LINE: HELP IS ON THE WAY--
A MIND-SCAN USING YOUR TELEPATHY REVEALS THAT EVEN YOU DON'T BELIEVE THAT, MARTIAN MANHUNTER...
...AND, TO TELL YOU THE TRUTH, I'M NOT SURE I BLAME YOU.
CURIOUS WHAT SUPERMAN'S HEAT-VISION FEELS LIKE?
AAAAHHH!

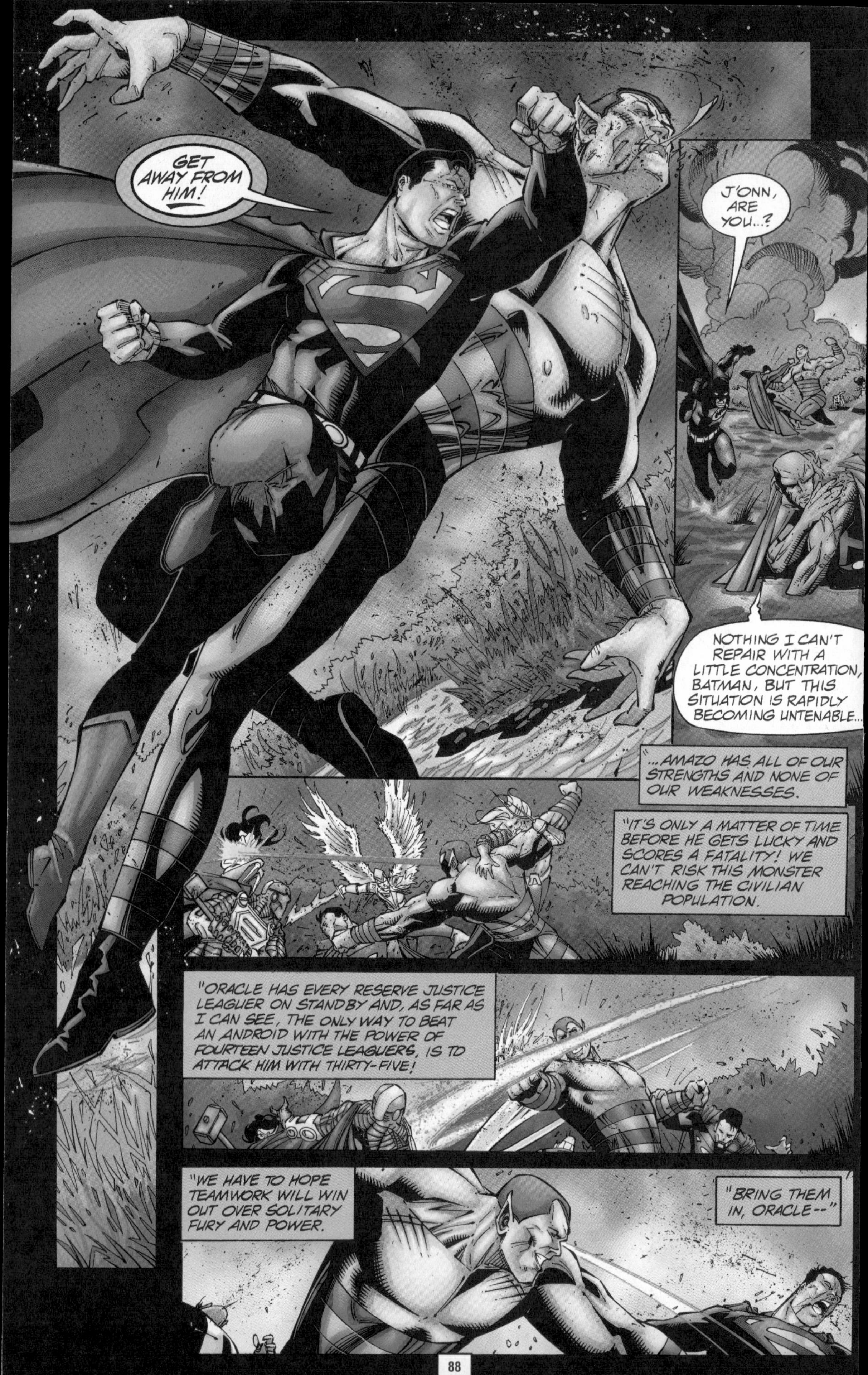
GET AWAY FROM HIM!
J'ONN, ARE YOU...?
NOTHING I CAN'T REPAIR WITH A LITTLE CONCENTRATION, BATMAN, BUT THIS SITUATION IS RAPIDLY BECOMING UNTENABLE...
"...AMAZO HAS ALL OF OUR STRENGTHS AND NONE OF OUR WEAKNESSES.
"IT'S ONLY A MATTER OF TIME BEFORE HE GETS LUCKY AND SCORES A FATALITY! WE CAN'T RISK THIS MONSTER REACHING THE CIVILIAN POPULATION.
"ORACLE HAS EVERY RESERVE JUSTICE LEAGUER ON STANDBY AND, AS FAR AS I CAN SEE, THE ONLY WAY TO BEAT AN ANDROID WITH THE POWER OF FOURTEEN JUSTICE LEAGUERS, IS TO ATTACK HIM WITH THIRTY-FIVE!
"WE HAVE TO HOPE TEAMWORK WILL WIN OUT OVER SOLITARY FURY AND POWER.
"BRING THEM IN, ORACLE--"

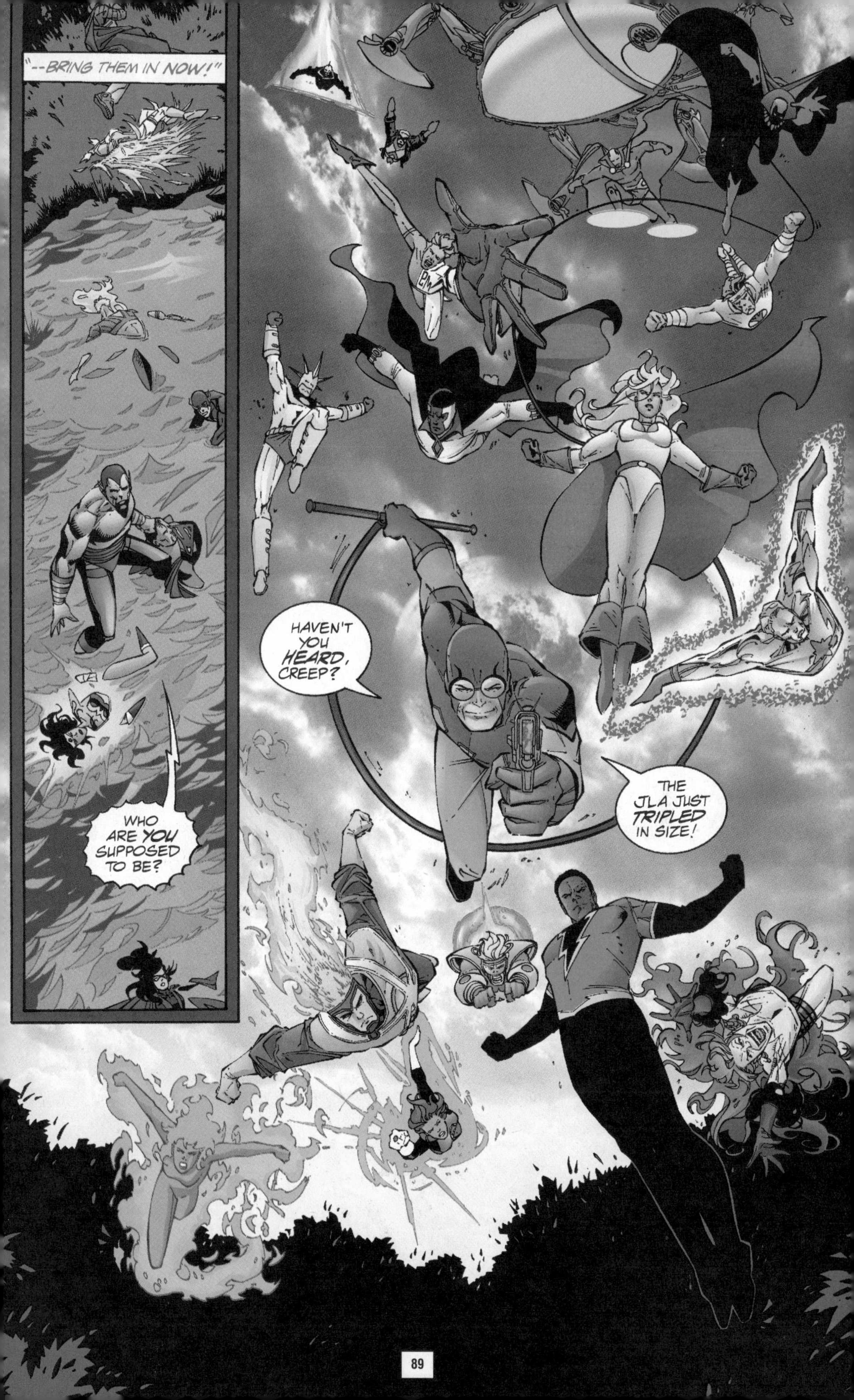
"--BRING THEM IN NOW!"
WHO ARE YOU SUPPOSED TO BE?
HAVEN'T YOU HEARD, CREEP?
THE JLA JUST TRIPLED IN SIZE!

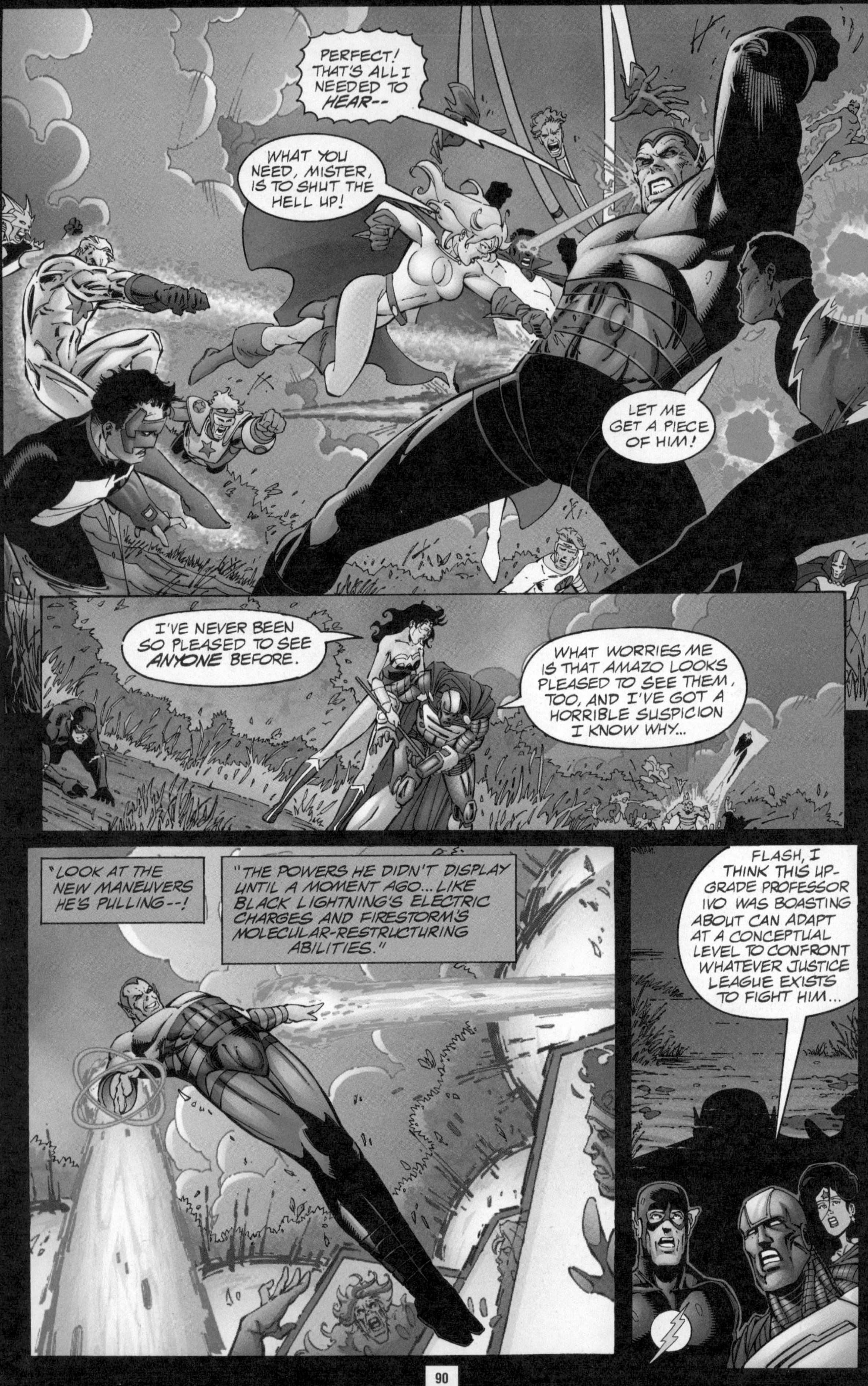
PERFECT! THAT'S ALL I NEEDED TO HEAR--
WHAT YOU NEED, MISTER, IS TO SHUT THE HELL UP!
LET ME GET A PIECE OF HIM!
I'VE NEVER BEEN SO PLEASED TO SEE ANYONE BEFORE.
WHAT WORRIES ME IS THAT AMAZO LOOKS PLEASED TO SEE THEM, TOO, AND I'VE GOT A HORRIBLE SUSPICION I KNOW WHY...
"LOOK AT THE NEW MANEUVERS HE'S PULLING--!
"THE POWERS HE DIDN'T DISPLAY UNTIL A MOMENT AGO... LIKE BLACK LIGHTNING'S ELECTRIC CHARGES AND FIRESTORM'S MOLECULAR-RESTRUCTURING ABILITIES."
FLASH, I THINK THIS UPGRADE PROFESSOR IVO WAS BOASTING ABOUT CAN ADAPT AT A CONCEPTUAL LEVEL TO CONFRONT WHATEVER JUSTICE LEAGUE EXISTS TO FIGHT HIM...

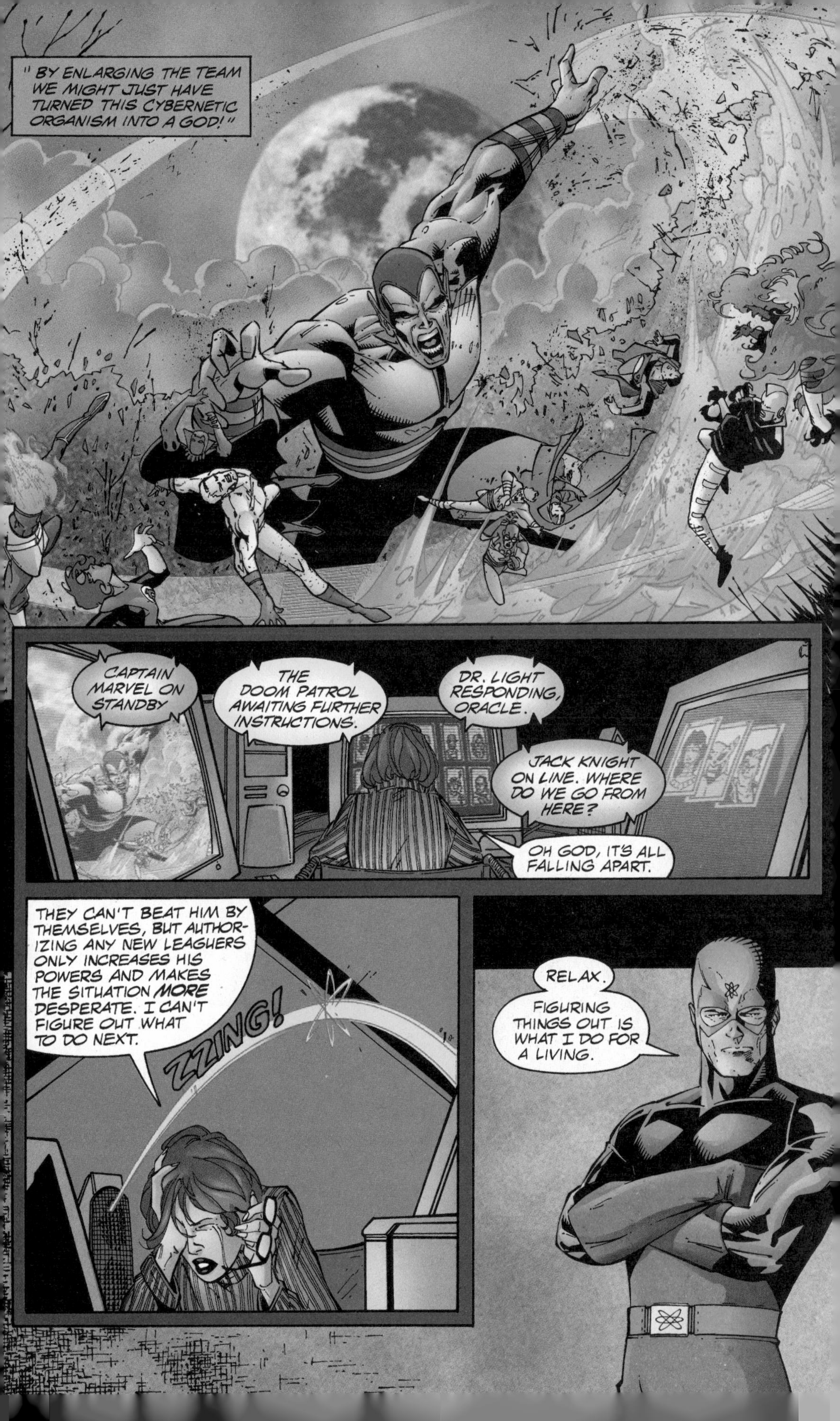
"BY ENLARGING THE TEAM WE MIGHT JUST HAVE TURNED THIS CYBERNETIC ORGANISM INTO A GOD!"
CAPTAIN MARVEL ON STANDBY
THE DOOM PATROL AWAITING FURTHER INSTRUCTIONS.
DR. LIGHT RESPONDING, ORACLE.
JACK KNIGHT ON LINE. WHERE DO WE GO FROM HERE?
OH GOD, IT'S ALL FALLING APART.
THEY CAN'T BEAT HIM BY THEMSELVES, BUT AUTHORIZING ANY NEW LEAGUERS ONLY INCREASES HIS POWERS AND MAKES THE SITUATION MORE DESPERATE. I CAN'T FIGURE OUT WHAT TO DO NEXT.
ZZING!
RELAX.
FIGURING THINGS OUT IS WHAT I DO FOR A LIVING.

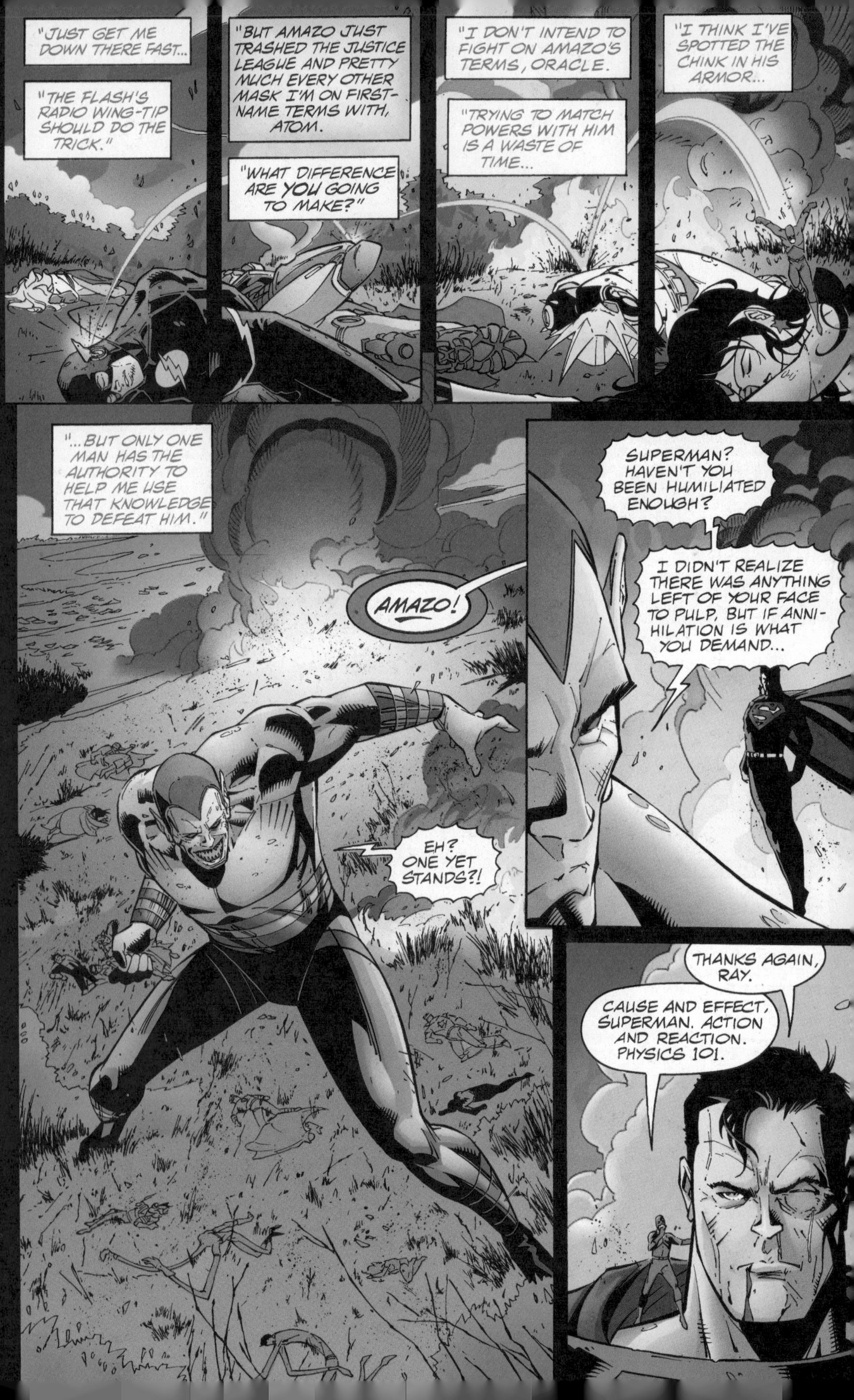
"JUST GET ME DOWN THERE FAST...
"THE FLASH'S RADIO WING-TIP SHOULD DO THE TRICK."
"BUT AMAZO JUST TRASHED THE JUSTICE LEAGUE AND PRETTY MUCH EVERY OTHER MASK I'M ON FIRST-NAME TERMS WITH, ATOM.
"WHAT DIFFERENCE ARE YOU GOING TO MAKE?"
"I DON'T INTEND TO FIGHT ON AMAZO'S TERMS, ORACLE.
"TRYING TO MATCH POWERS WITH HIM IS A WASTE OF TIME...
"I THINK I'VE SPOTTED THE CHINK IN HIS ARMOR...
"...BUT ONLY ONE MAN HAS THE AUTHORITY TO HELP ME USE THAT KNOWLEDGE TO DEFEAT HIM."
AMAZO!
EH? ONE YET STANDS?!
SUPERMAN? HAVEN'T YOU BEEN HUMILIATED ENOUGH?
I DIDN'T REALIZE THERE WAS ANYTHING LEFT OF YOUR FACE TO PULP, BUT IF ANNIHILATION IS WHAT YOU DEMAND...
THANKS AGAIN, RAY.
CAUSE AND EFFECT, SUPERMAN. ACTION AND REACTION. PHYSICS 101.

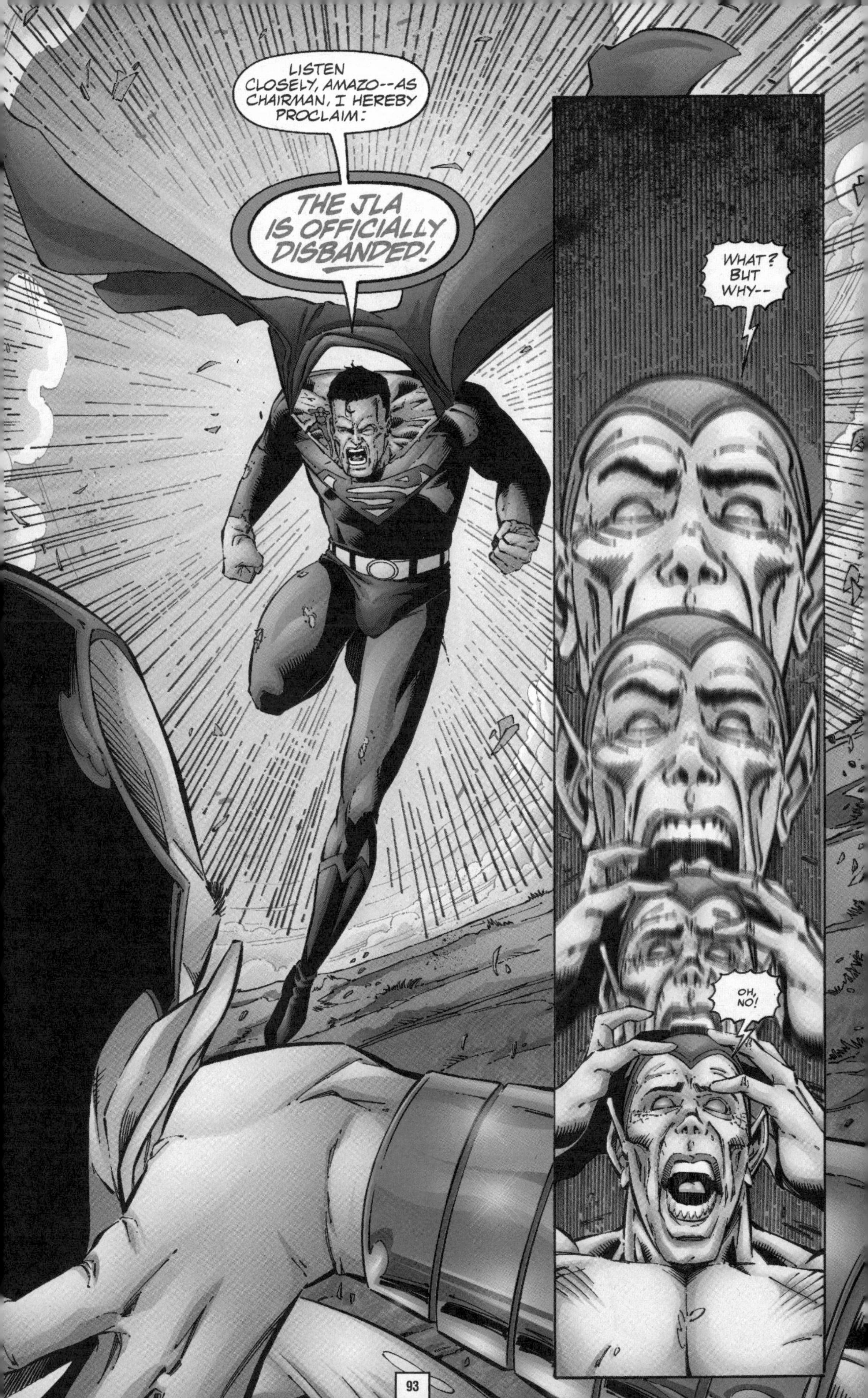

LISTEN CLOSELY, AMAZO--AS CHAIRMAN, I HEREBY PROCLAIM:
THE JLA IS OFFICIALLY DISBANDED!
WHAT? BUT WHY--
OH, NO!

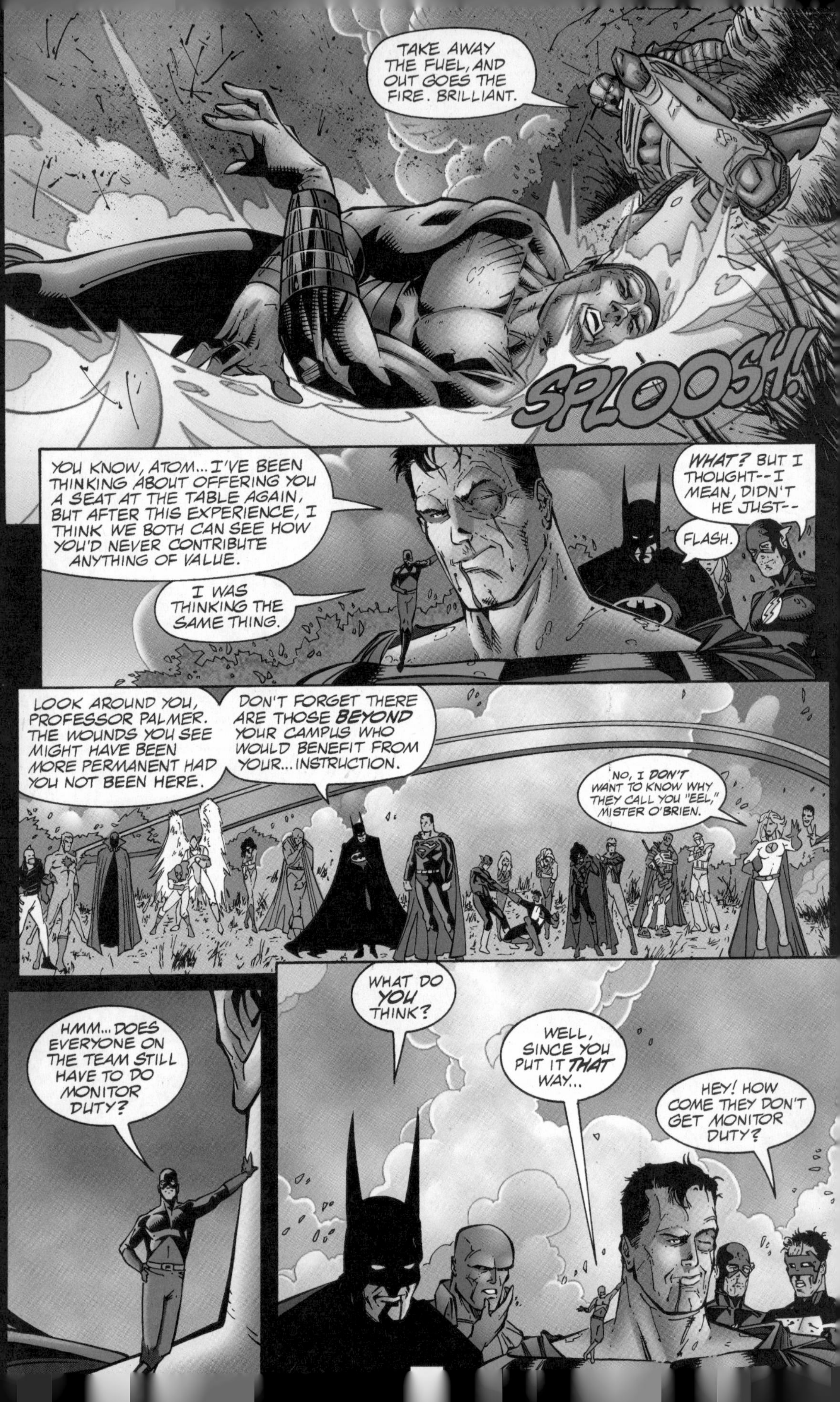
TAKE AWAY THE FUEL, AND OUT GOES THE FIRE. BRILLIANT.
SPLOOSH!
YOU KNOW, ATOM... I'VE BEEN THINKING ABOUT OFFERING YOU A SEAT AT THE TABLE AGAIN, BUT AFTER THIS EXPERIENCE, I THINK WE BOTH CAN SEE HOW YOU'D NEVER CONTRIBUTE ANYTHING OF VALUE.
I WAS THINKING THE SAME THING.
WHAT? BUT I THOUGHT-- I MEAN, DIDN'T HE JUST--
FLASH.
LOOK AROUND YOU, PROFESSOR PALMER. THE WOUNDS YOU SEE MIGHT HAVE BEEN MORE PERMANENT HAD YOU NOT BEEN HERE.
DON'T FORGET THERE ARE THOSE BEYOND YOUR CAMPUS WHO WOULD BENEFIT FROM YOUR... INSTRUCTION.
NO, I DON'T WANT TO KNOW WHY THEY CALL YOU "EEL," MISTER O'BRIEN.
HMM... DOES EVERYONE ON THE TEAM STILL HAVE TO DO MONITOR DUTY?
WHAT DO YOU THINK?
WELL, SINCE YOU PUT IT THAT WAY...
HEY! HOW COME THEY DON'T GET MONITOR DUTY?

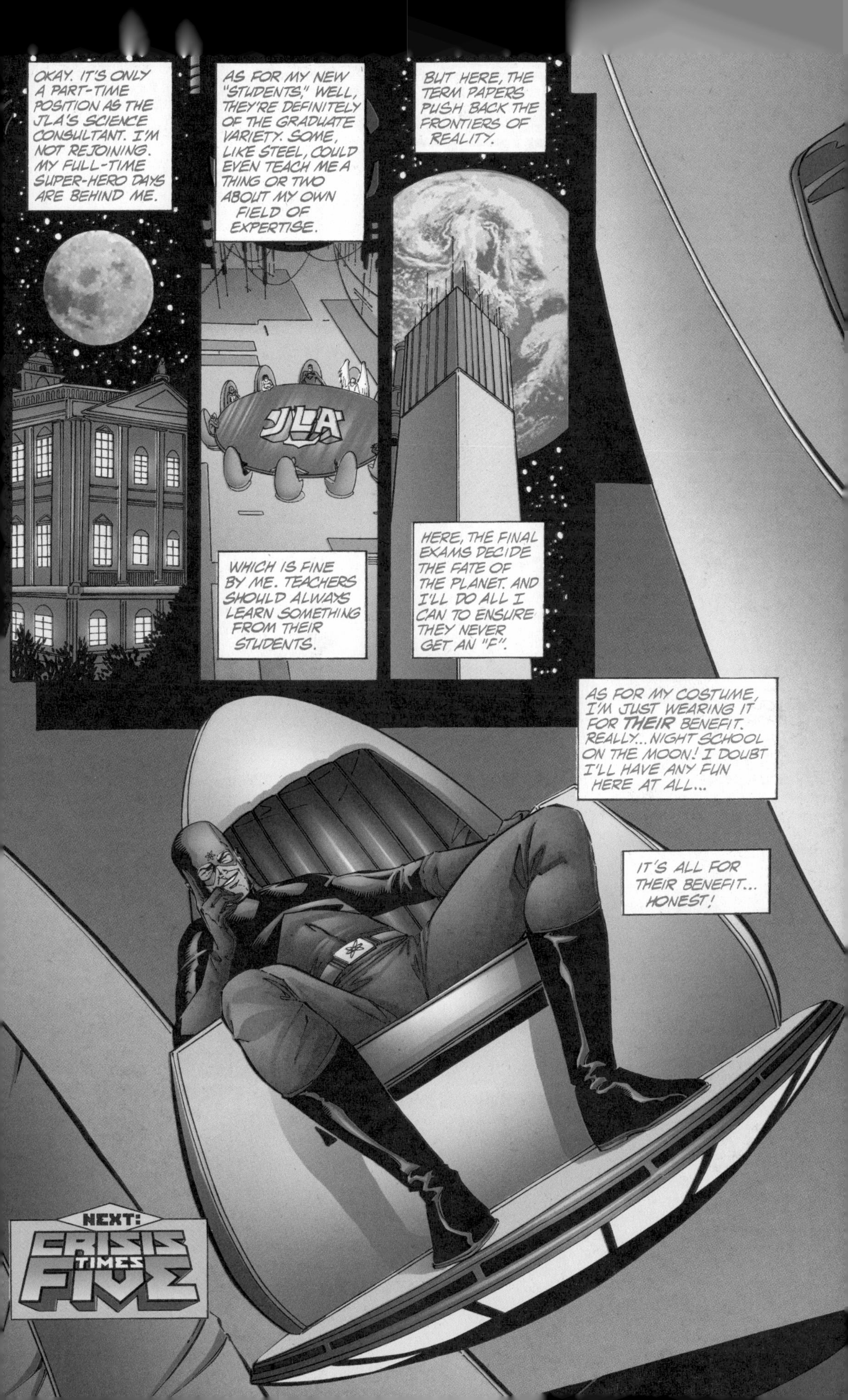
OKAY. IT'S ONLY A PART-TIME POSITION AS THE JLA'S SCIENCE CONSULTANT. I'M NOT REJOINING. MY FULL-TIME SUPER-HERO DAYS ARE BEHIND ME.
AS FOR MY NEW "STUDENTS," WELL, THEY'RE DEFINITELY OF THE GRADUATE VARIETY. SOME, LIKE STEEL, COULD EVEN TEACH ME A THING OR TWO ABOUT MY OWN FIELD OF EXPERTISE.
JLA
WHICH IS FINE BY ME. TEACHERS SHOULD ALWAYS LEARN SOMETHING FROM THEIR STUDENTS.
BUT HERE, THE TERM PAPERS PUSH BACK THE FRONTIERS OF REALITY.
HERE, THE FINAL EXAMS DECIDE THE FATE OF THE PLANET. AND I'LL DO ALL I CAN TO ENSURE THEY NEVER GET AN "F".
AS FOR MY COSTUME, I'M JUST WEARING IT FOR THEIR BENEFIT. REALLY... NIGHT SCHOOL ON THE MOON! I DOUBT I'LL HAVE ANY FUN HERE AT ALL...
IT'S ALL FOR THEIR BENEFIT... HONEST!
NEXT: CRISIS TIMES FIVE

CRISIS TIMES FIVE!

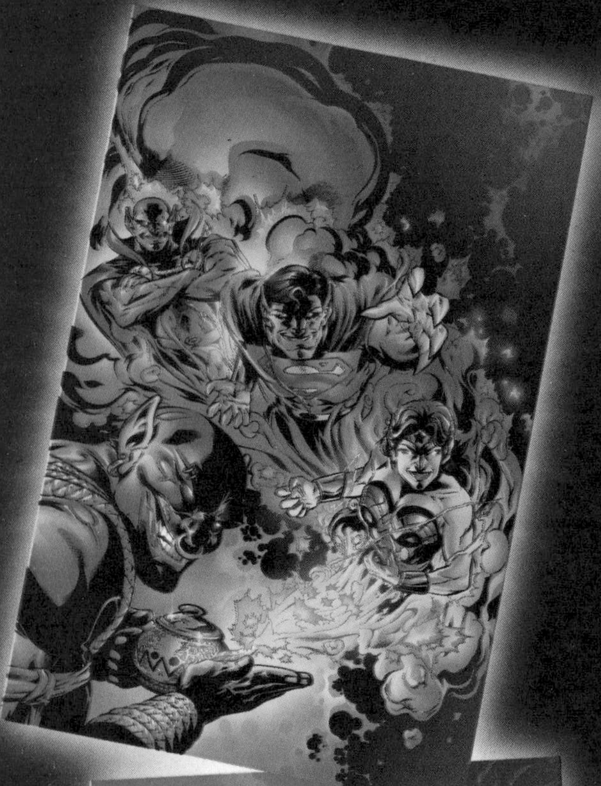

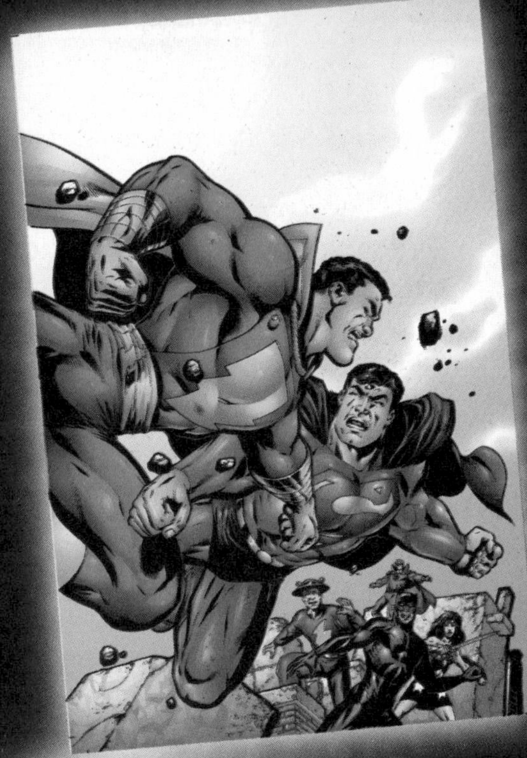

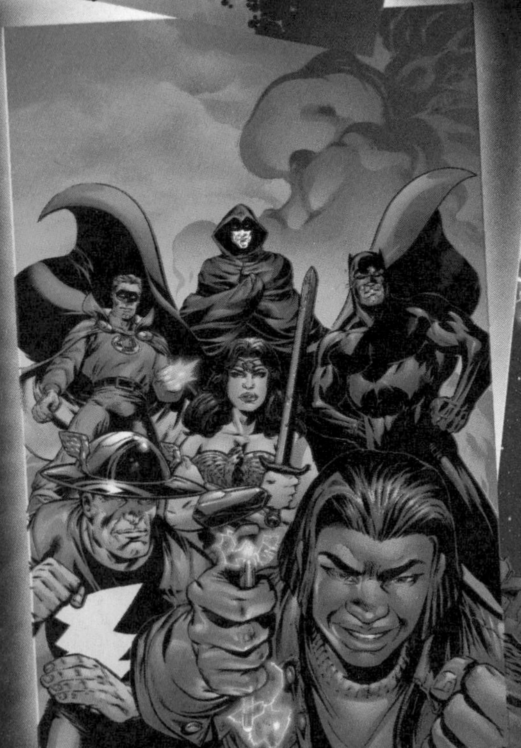

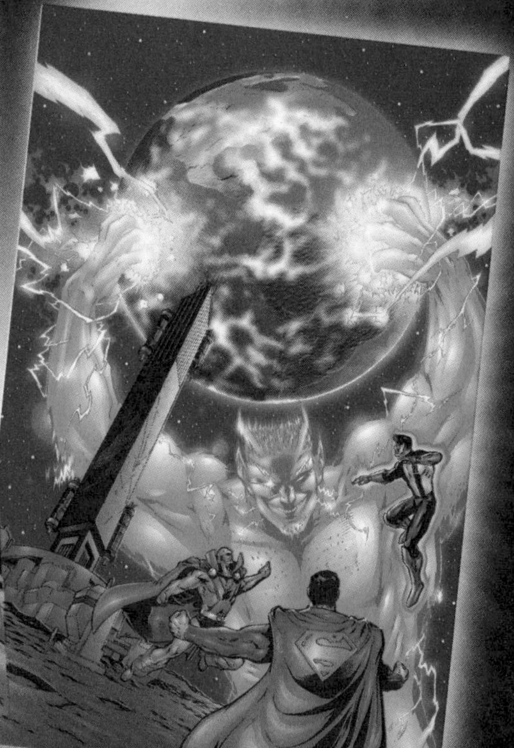

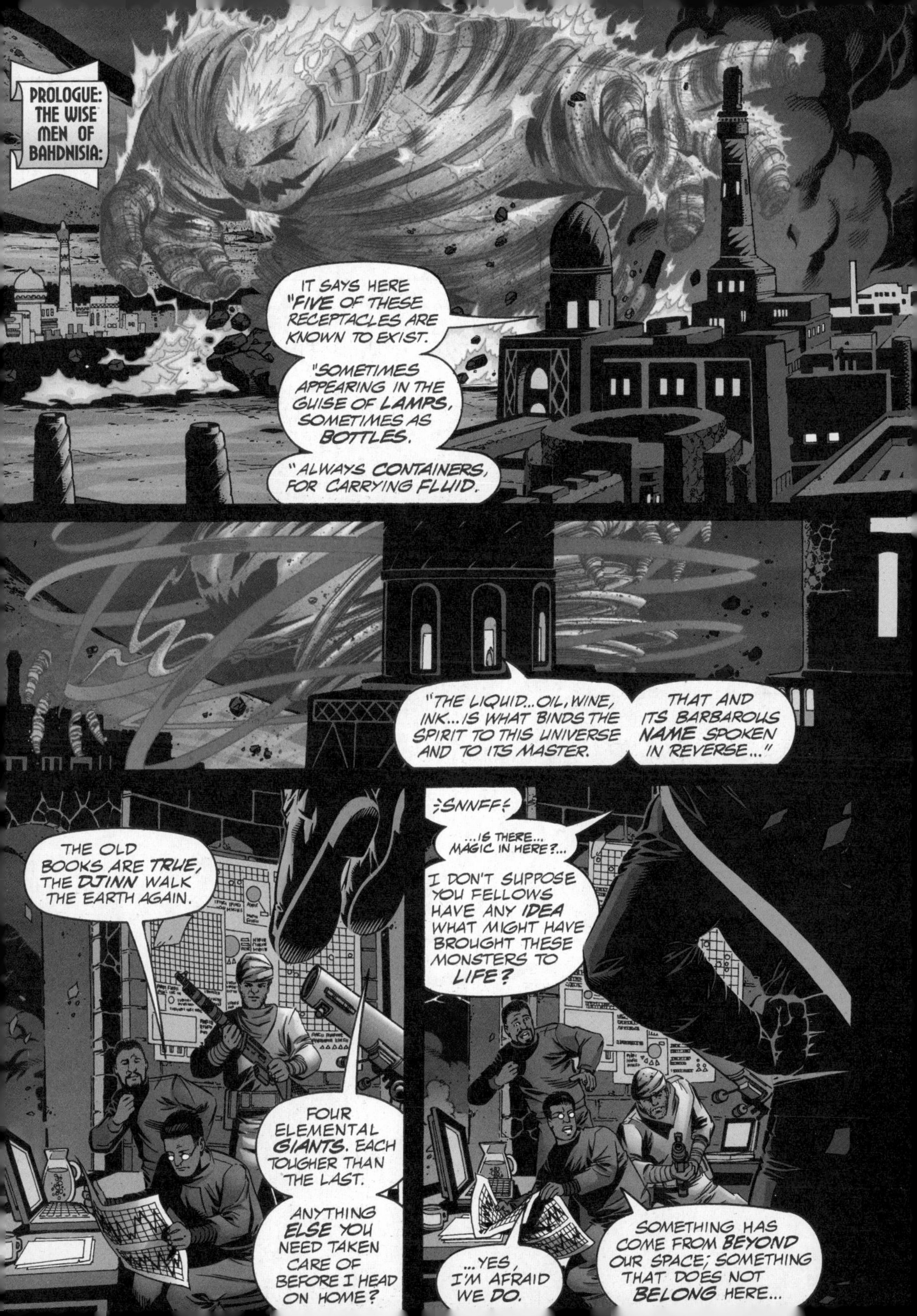
PROLOGUE: THE WISE MEN OF BAHDNISIA:
IT SAYS HERE "FIVE OF THESE RECEPTACLES ARE KNOWN TO EXIST.
"SOMETIMES APPEARING IN THE GUISE OF LAMPS, SOMETIMES AS BOTTLES.
"ALWAYS CONTAINERS, FOR CARRYING FLUID.
"THE LIQUID...OIL, WINE, INK...IS WHAT BINDS THE SPIRIT TO THIS UNIVERSE AND TO ITS MASTER.
THAT AND ITS BARBAROUS NAME SPOKEN IN REVERSE..."
THE OLD BOOKS ARE TRUE, THE DJINN WALK THE EARTH AGAIN.
FOUR ELEMENTAL GIANTS. EACH TOUGHER THAN THE LAST.
ANYTHING ELSE YOU NEED TAKEN CARE OF BEFORE I HEAD ON HOME?
SNNFF
...IS THERE... MAGIC IN HERE?...
I DON'T SUPPOSE YOU FELLOWS HAVE ANY IDEA WHAT MIGHT HAVE BROUGHT THESE MONSTERS TO LIFE?
...YES, I'M AFRAID WE DO.
SOMETHING HAS COME FROM BEYOND OUR SPACE; SOMETHING THAT DOES NOT BELONG HERE...

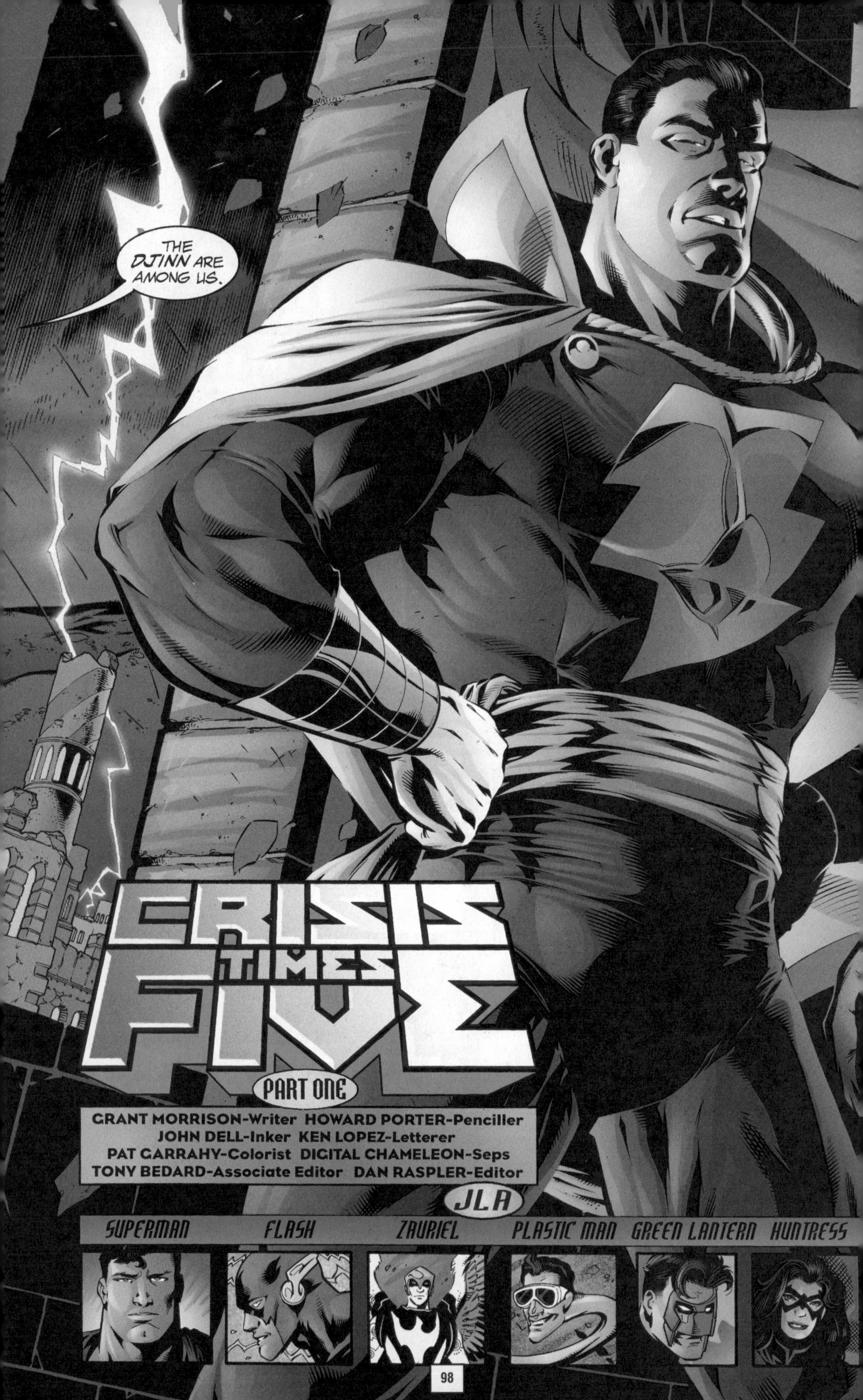
THE DJINN ARE AMONG US.
CRISIS TIMES FIVE
PART ONE
GRANT MORRISON-Writer HOWARD PORTER-Penciller
JOHN DELL-Inker KEN LOPEZ-Letterer
PAT GARRAHY-Colorist DIGITAL CHAMELEON-Seps
TONY BEDARD-Associate Editor DAN RASPLER-Editor
JLA
SUPERMAN
FLASH
ZAURIEL
PLASTIC MAN
GREEN LANTERN
HUNTRESS

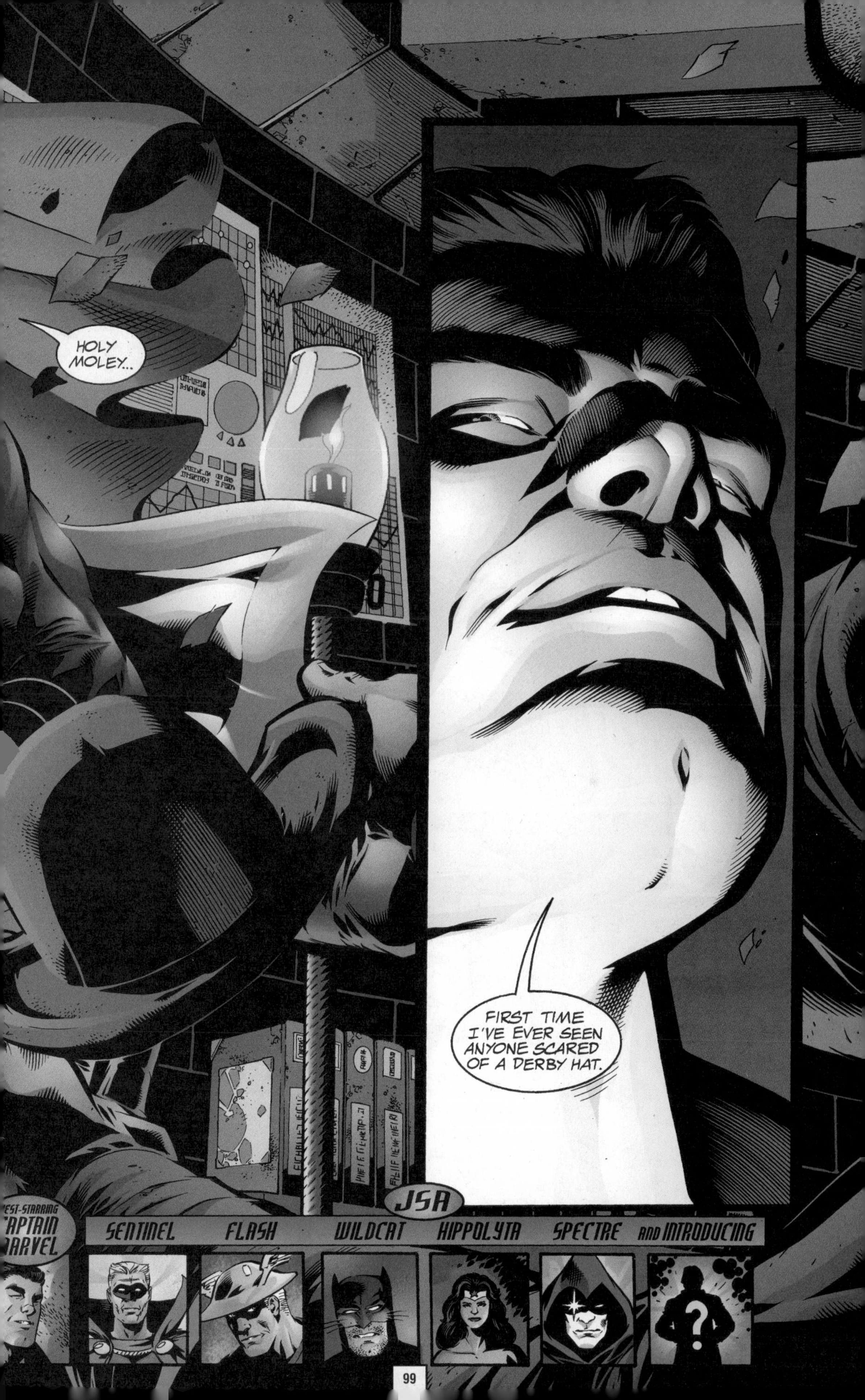
HOLY MOLEY...
FIRST TIME I'VE EVER SEEN ANYONE SCARED OF A DERBY HAT.
JSA
SENTINEL
FLASH
WILDCAT
HIPPOLYTA
SPECTRE
AND INTRODUCING

CHAPTER 1: MILE HIGH GRAFFITI

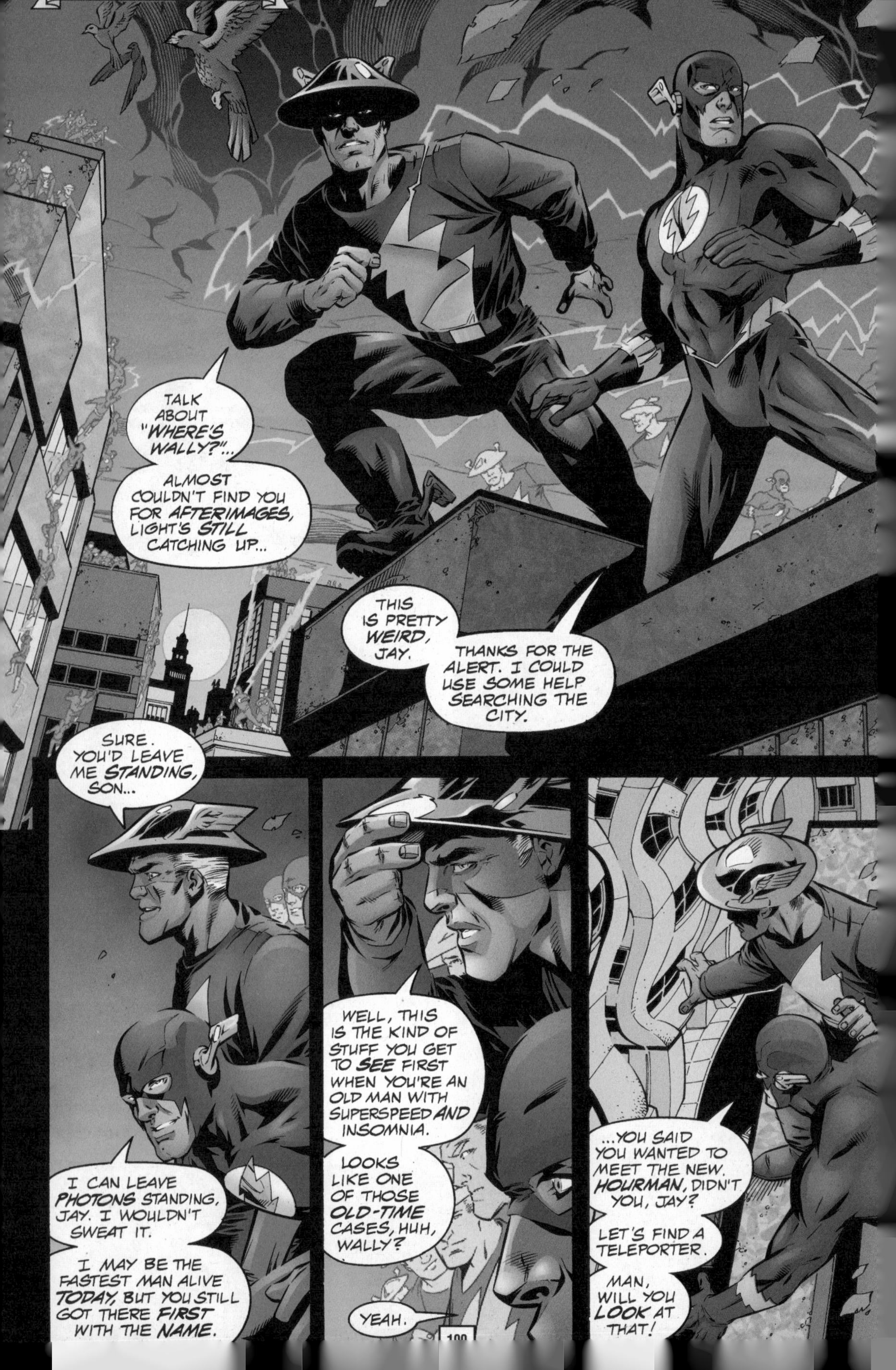
TALK ABOUT "WHERE'S WALLY?"...
ALMOST COULDN'T FIND YOU FOR AFTERIMAGES, LIGHT'S STILL CATCHING UP...
THIS IS PRETTY WEIRD, JAY.
THANKS FOR THE ALERT. I COULD USE SOME HELP SEARCHING THE CITY.
SURE. YOU'D LEAVE ME STANDING, SON...
I CAN LEAVE PHOTONS STANDING, JAY. I WOULDN'T SWEAT IT.
I MAY BE THE FASTEST MAN ALIVE TODAY, BUT YOU STILL GOT THERE FIRST WITH THE NAME.
WELL, THIS IS THE KIND OF STUFF YOU GET TO SEE FIRST WHEN YOU'RE AN OLD MAN WITH SUPERSPEED AND INSOMNIA.
LOOKS LIKE ONE OF THOSE OLD-TIME CASES, HUH, WALLY?
YEAH.
...YOU SAID YOU WANTED TO MEET THE NEW HOURMAN, DIDN'T YOU, JAY?
LET'S FIND A TELEPORTER.
MAN, WILL YOU LOOK AT THAT!

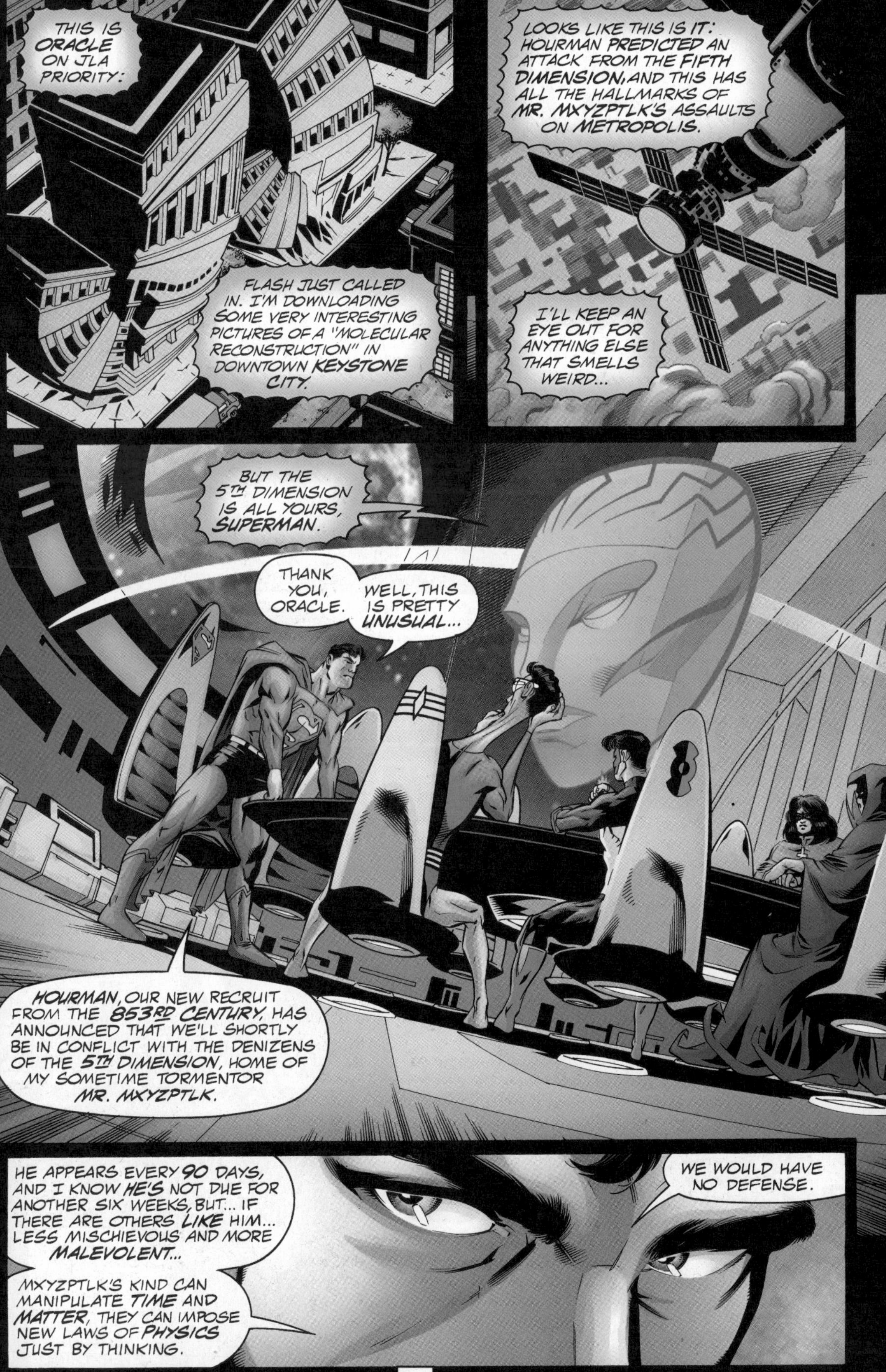
THIS IS ORACLE ON JLA PRIORITY:
FLASH JUST CALLED IN. I'M DOWNLOADING SOME VERY INTERESTING PICTURES OF A "MOLECULAR RECONSTRUCTION" IN DOWNTOWN KEYSTONE CITY.
LOOKS LIKE THIS IS IT: HOURMAN PREDICTED AN ATTACK FROM THE FIFTH DIMENSION, AND THIS HAS ALL THE HALLMARKS OF MR. MXYZPTLK'S ASSAULTS ON METROPOLIS.
I'LL KEEP AN EYE OUT FOR ANYTHING ELSE THAT SMELLS WEIRD...
BUT THE 5TH DIMENSION IS ALL YOURS, SUPERMAN.
THANK YOU, ORACLE.
WELL, THIS IS PRETTY UNUSUAL...
HOURMAN, OUR NEW RECRUIT FROM THE 853RD CENTURY, HAS ANNOUNCED THAT WE'LL SHORTLY BE IN CONFLICT WITH THE DENIZENS OF THE 5TH DIMENSION, HOME OF MY SOMETIME TORMENTOR MR. MXYZPTLK.
HE APPEARS EVERY 90 DAYS, AND I KNOW HE'S NOT DUE FOR ANOTHER SIX WEEKS, BUT... IF THERE ARE OTHERS LIKE HIM... LESS MISCHIEVOUS AND MORE MALEVOLENT...
MXYZPTLK'S KIND CAN MANIPULATE TIME AND MATTER, THEY CAN IMPOSE NEW LAWS OF PHYSICS JUST BY THINKING.
WE WOULD HAVE NO DEFENSE.

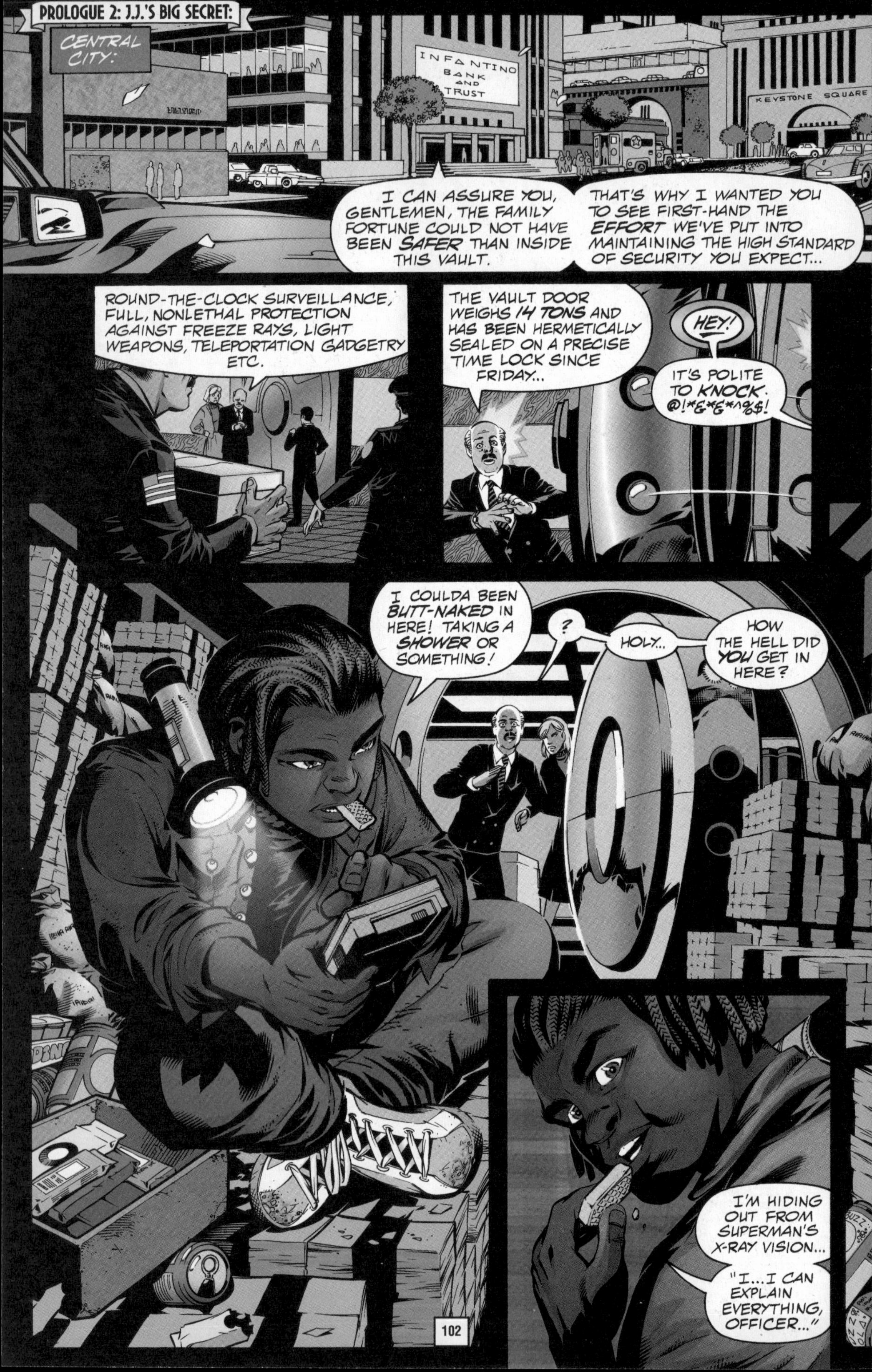
PROLOGUE 2: J.J.'S BIG SECRET:
CENTRAL CITY:
INFANTINO BANK AND TRUST
KEYSTONE SQUARE
I CAN ASSURE YOU, GENTLEMEN, THE FAMILY FORTUNE COULD NOT HAVE BEEN SAFER THAN INSIDE THIS VAULT.
THAT'S WHY I WANTED YOU TO SEE FIRST-HAND THE EFFORT WE'VE PUT INTO MAINTAINING THE HIGH STANDARD OF SECURITY YOU EXPECT...
ROUND-THE-CLOCK SURVEILLANCE, FULL, NONLETHAL PROTECTION AGAINST FREEZE RAYS, LIGHT WEAPONS, TELEPORTATION GADGETRY ETC.
THE VAULT DOOR WEIGHS 14 TONS AND HAS BEEN HERMETICALLY SEALED ON A PRECISE TIME LOCK SINCE FRIDAY...
HEY!
IT'S POLITE TO KNOCK. @!*&*&*^%$!
I COULDA BEEN BUTT-NAKED IN HERE! TAKING A SHOWER OR SOMETHING!
?
HOLY...
HOW THE HELL DID YOU GET IN HERE?
I'M HIDING OUT FROM SUPERMAN'S X-RAY VISION...
"I...I CAN EXPLAIN EVERYTHING, OFFICER..."

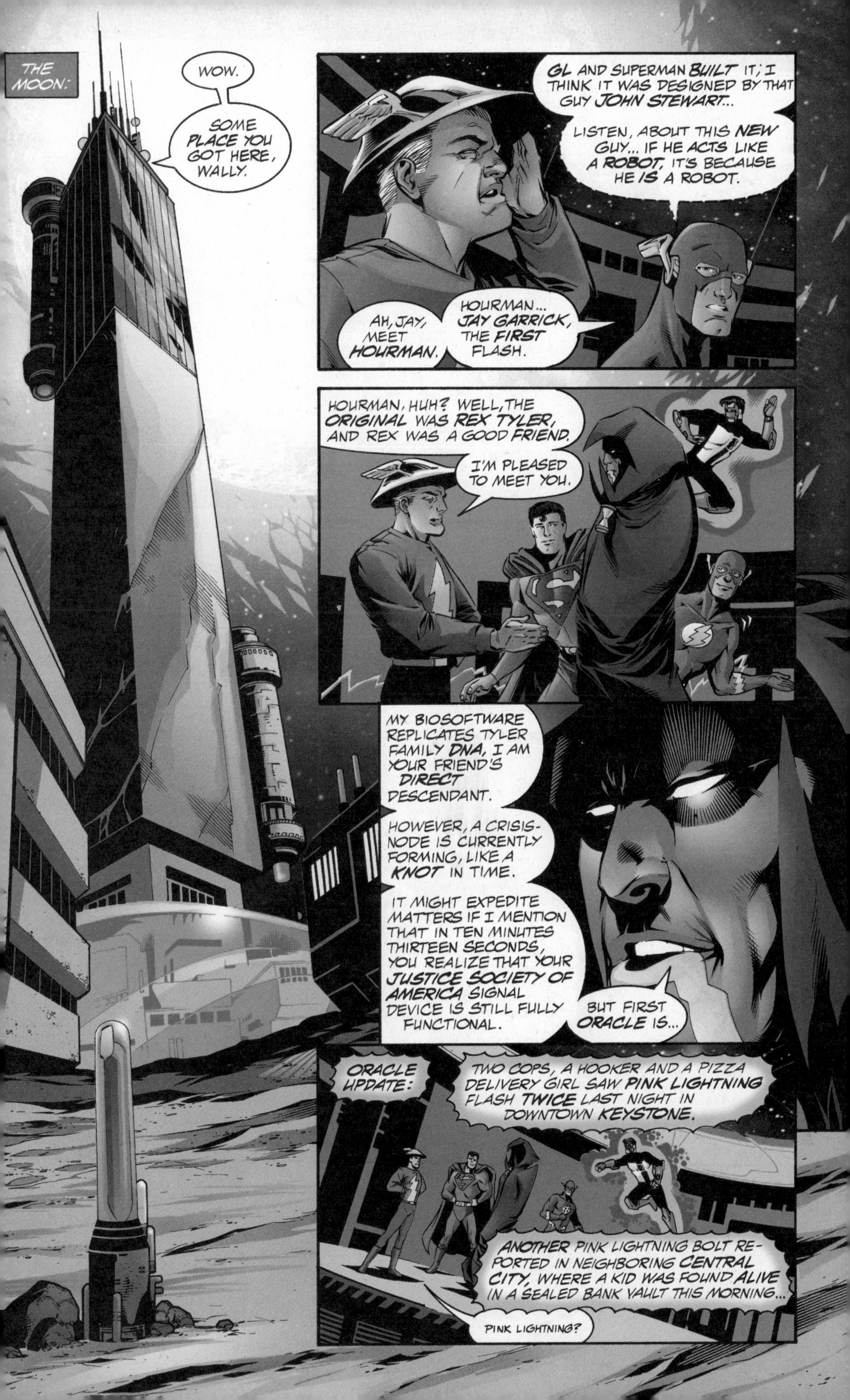
THE MOON:
WOW.
SOME PLACE YOU GOT HERE, WALLY.
GL AND SUPERMAN BUILT IT; I THINK IT WAS DESIGNED BY THAT GUY JOHN STEWART...
LISTEN, ABOUT THIS NEW GUY... IF HE ACTS LIKE A ROBOT, IT'S BECAUSE HE IS A ROBOT.
AH, JAY, MEET HOURMAN.
HOURMAN... JAY GARRICK, THE FIRST FLASH.
HOURMAN, HUH? WELL, THE ORIGINAL WAS REX TYLER, AND REX WAS A GOOD FRIEND.
I'M PLEASED TO MEET YOU.
MY BIOSOFTWARE REPLICATES TYLER FAMILY DNA, I AM YOUR FRIEND'S DIRECT DESCENDANT.
HOWEVER, A CRISIS-NODE IS CURRENTLY FORMING, LIKE A KNOT IN TIME.
IT MIGHT EXPEDITE MATTERS IF I MENTION THAT IN TEN MINUTES THIRTEEN SECONDS, YOU REALIZE THAT YOUR JUSTICE SOCIETY OF AMERICA SIGNAL DEVICE IS STILL FULLY FUNCTIONAL.
BUT FIRST ORACLE IS...
ORACLE UPDATE:
TWO COPS, A HOOKER AND A PIZZA DELIVERY GIRL SAW PINK LIGHTNING FLASH TWICE LAST NIGHT IN DOWNTOWN KEYSTONE.
ANOTHER PINK LIGHTNING BOLT RE-PORTED IN NEIGHBORING CENTRAL CITY, WHERE A KID WAS FOUND ALIVE IN A SEALED BANK VAULT THIS MORNING...
PINK LIGHTNING?

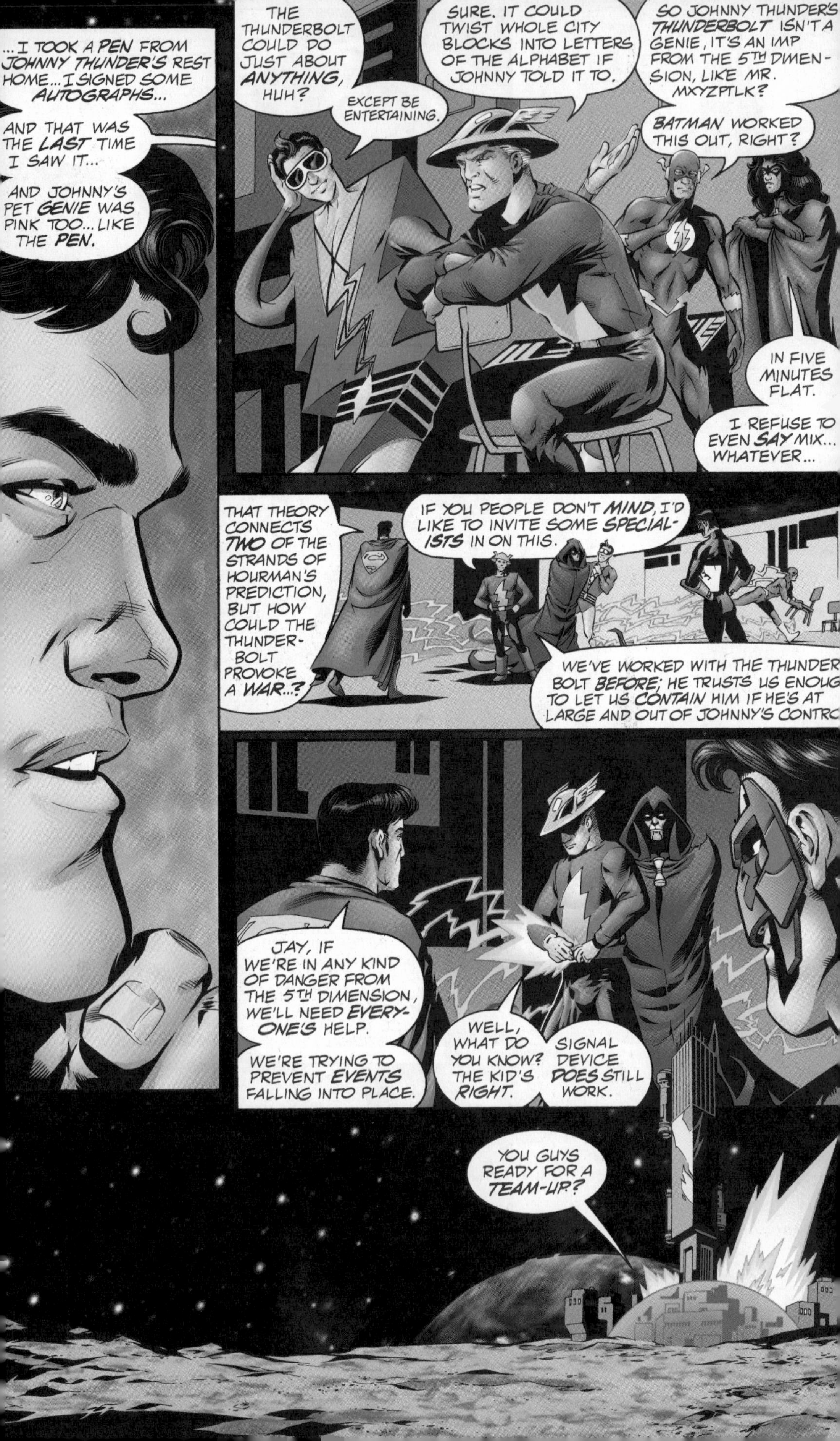

...I TOOK A PEN FROM JOHNNY THUNDER'S REST HOME... I SIGNED SOME AUTOGRAPHS...
AND THAT WAS THE LAST TIME I SAW IT...
AND JOHNNY'S PET GENIE WAS PINK TOO... LIKE THE PEN.
THE THUNDERBOLT COULD DO JUST ABOUT ANYTHING, HUH?
EXCEPT BE ENTERTAINING.
SURE. IT COULD TWIST WHOLE CITY BLOCKS INTO LETTERS OF THE ALPHABET IF JOHNNY TOLD IT TO.
SO JOHNNY THUNDER'S THUNDERBOLT ISN'T A GENIE, IT'S AN IMP FROM THE 5TH DIMENSION, LIKE MR. MXYZPTLK?
BATMAN WORKED THIS OUT, RIGHT?
IN FIVE MINUTES FLAT.
I REFUSE TO EVEN SAY MIX... WHATEVER...
THAT THEORY CONNECTS TWO OF THE STRANDS OF HOURMAN'S PREDICTION, BUT HOW COULD THE THUNDERBOLT PROVOKE A WAR...?
IF YOU PEOPLE DON'T MIND, I'D LIKE TO INVITE SOME SPECIALISTS IN ON THIS.
WE'VE WORKED WITH THE THUNDERBOLT BEFORE; HE TRUSTS US ENOUG TO LET US CONTAIN HIM IF HE'S AT LARGE AND OUT OF JOHNNY'S CONTRO
JAY, IF WE'RE IN ANY KIND OF DANGER FROM THE 5TH DIMENSION, WE'LL NEED EVERYONE'S HELP.
WE'RE TRYING TO PREVENT EVENTS FALLING INTO PLACE.
WELL, WHAT DO YOU KNOW? THE KID'S RIGHT.
SIGNAL DEVICE DOES STILL WORK.
YOU GUYS READY FOR A TEAM-UP?

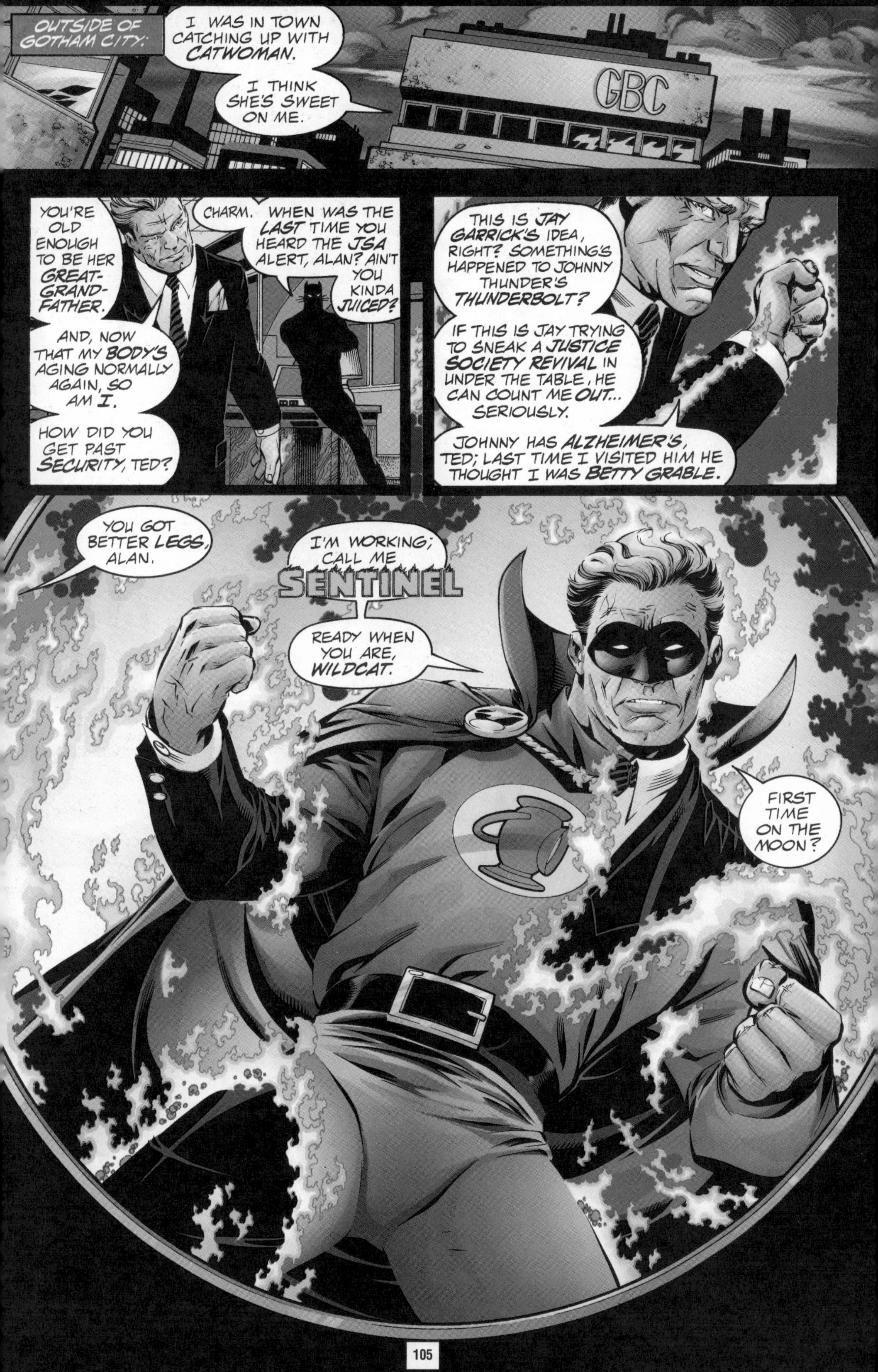
OUTSIDE OF GOTHAM CITY:
I WAS IN TOWN CATCHING UP WITH CATWOMAN.
I THINK SHE'S SWEET ON ME.
GBC
YOU'RE OLD ENOUGH TO BE HER GREAT-GRAND-FATHER.
AND, NOW THAT MY BODY'S AGING NORMALLY AGAIN, SO AM I.
HOW DID YOU GET PAST SECURITY, TED?
CHARM. WHEN WAS THE LAST TIME YOU HEARD THE JSA ALERT, ALAN? AIN'T YOU KINDA JUICED?
THIS IS JAY GARRICK'S IDEA, RIGHT? SOMETHING'S HAPPENED TO JOHNNY THUNDER'S THUNDERBOLT?
IF THIS IS JAY TRYING TO SNEAK A JUSTICE SOCIETY REVIVAL IN UNDER THE TABLE, HE CAN COUNT ME OUT... SERIOUSLY.
JOHNNY HAS ALZHEIMER'S, TED; LAST TIME I VISITED HIM HE THOUGHT I WAS BETTY GRABLE.
YOU GOT BETTER LEGS, ALAN.
I'M WORKING; CALL ME SENTINEL
READY WHEN YOU ARE, WILDCAT.
FIRST TIME ON THE MOON?

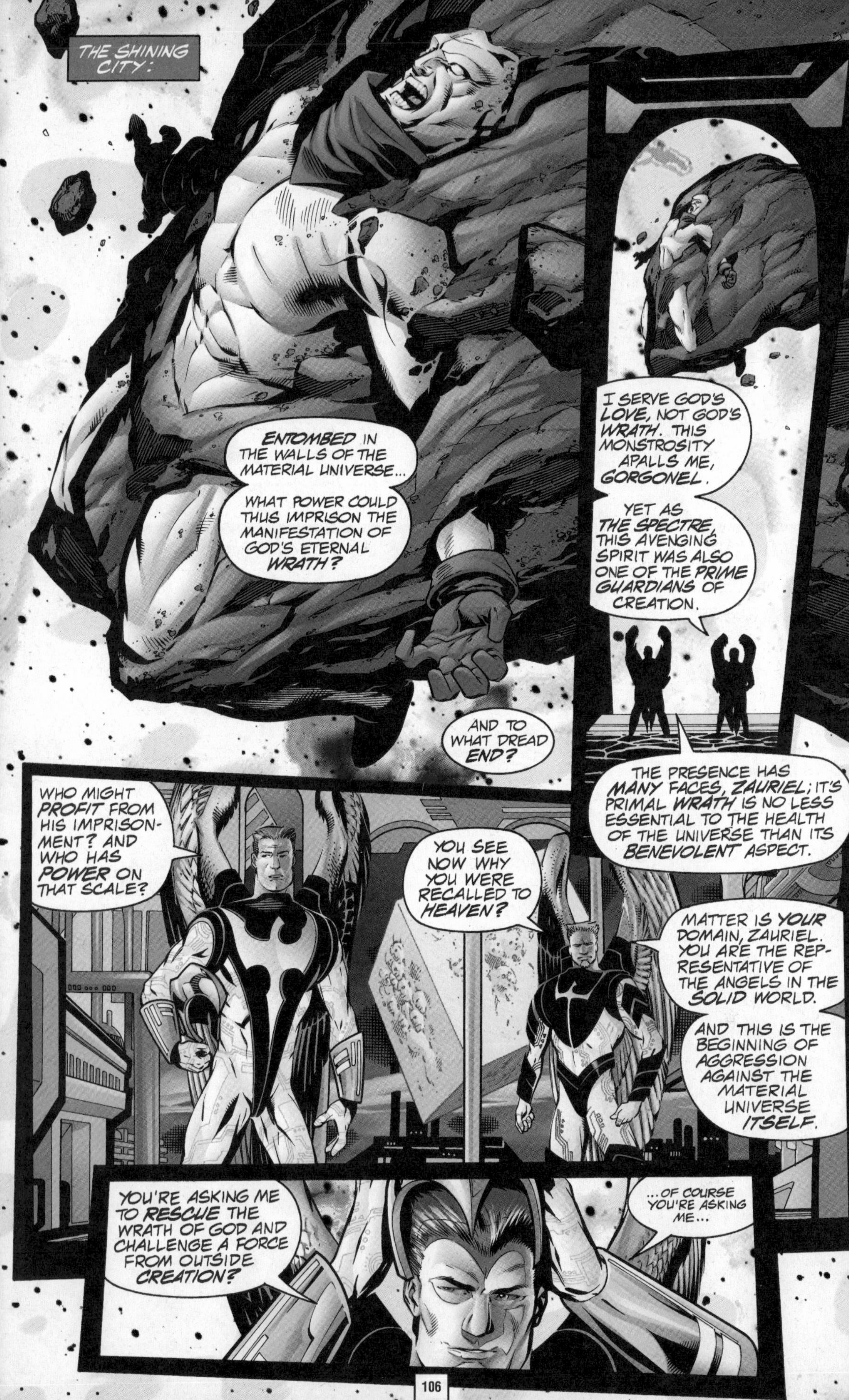
THE SHINING CITY:
ENTOMBED IN THE WALLS OF THE MATERIAL UNIVERSE...
WHAT POWER COULD THUS IMPRISON THE MANIFESTATION OF GOD'S ETERNAL WRATH?
AND TO WHAT DREAD END?
I SERVE GOD'S LOVE, NOT GOD'S WRATH. THIS MONSTROSITY APALLS ME, GORGONEL.
YET AS THE SPECTRE, THIS AVENGING SPIRIT WAS ALSO ONE OF THE PRIME GUARDIANS OF CREATION.
THE PRESENCE HAS MANY FACES, ZAURIEL; IT'S PRIMAL WRATH IS NO LESS ESSENTIAL TO THE HEALTH OF THE UNIVERSE THAN ITS BENEVOLENT ASPECT.
WHO MIGHT PROFIT FROM HIS IMPRISONMENT? AND WHO HAS POWER ON THAT SCALE?
YOU SEE NOW WHY YOU WERE RECALLED TO HEAVEN?
MATTER IS YOUR DOMAIN, ZAURIEL. YOU ARE THE REPRESENTATIVE OF THE ANGELS IN THE SOLID WORLD.
AND THIS IS THE BEGINNING OF AGGRESSION AGAINST THE MATERIAL UNIVERSE ITSELF.
YOU'RE ASKING ME TO RESCUE THE WRATH OF GOD AND CHALLENGE A FORCE FROM OUTSIDE CREATION?
...OF COURSE YOU'RE ASKING ME...

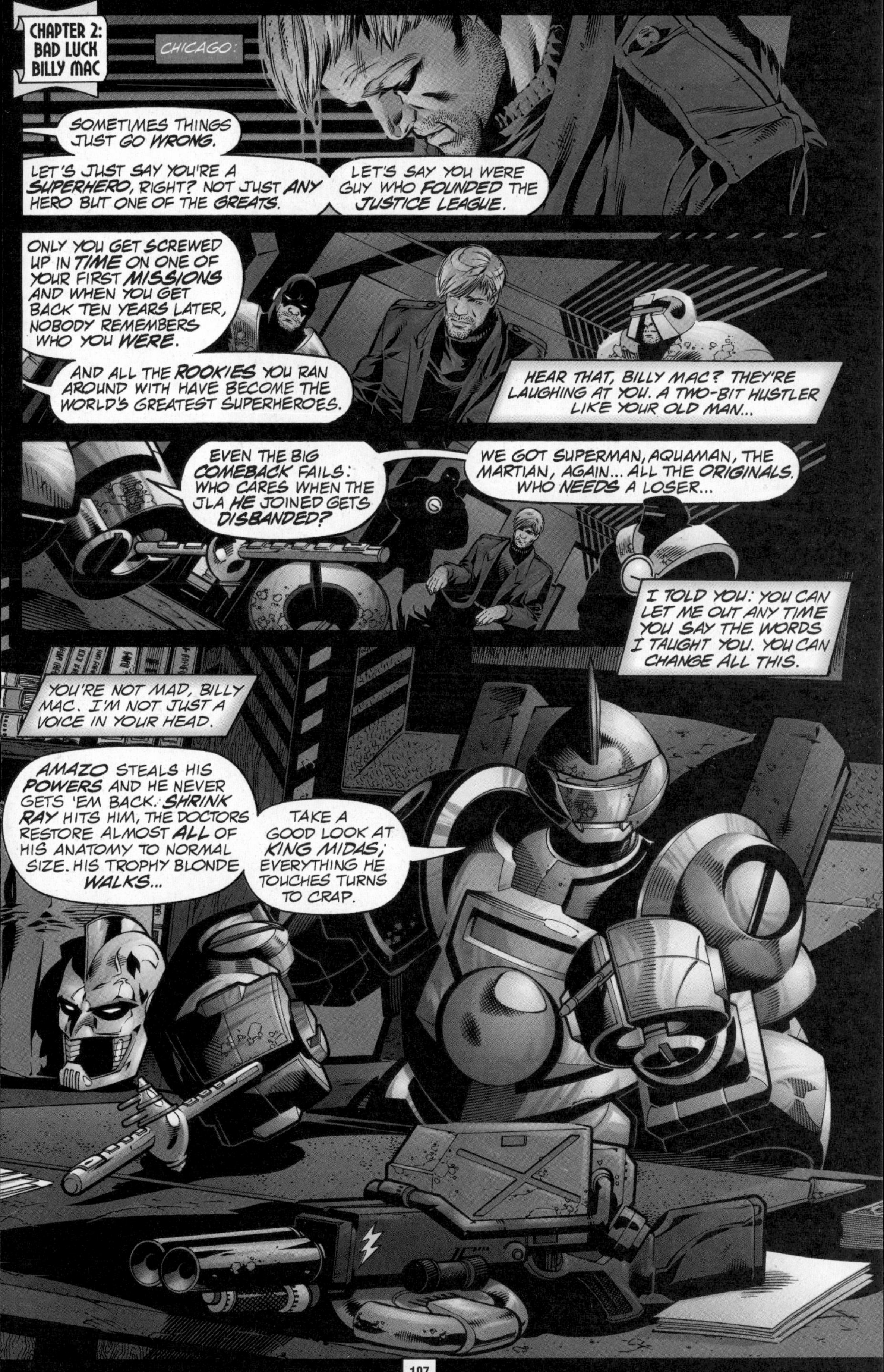

CHAPTER 2: BAD LUCK BILLY MAC
CHICAGO:
SOMETIMES THINGS JUST GO WRONG.
LET'S JUST SAY YOU'RE A SUPERHERO, RIGHT? NOT JUST ANY HERO BUT ONE OF THE GREATS.
LET'S SAY YOU WERE GUY WHO FOUNDED THE JUSTICE LEAGUE.
ONLY YOU GET SCREWED UP IN TIME ON ONE OF YOUR FIRST MISSIONS AND WHEN YOU GET BACK TEN YEARS LATER, NOBODY REMEMBERS WHO YOU WERE.
AND ALL THE ROOKIES YOU RAN AROUND WITH HAVE BECOME THE WORLD'S GREATEST SUPERHEROES.
HEAR THAT, BILLY MAC? THEY'RE LAUGHING AT YOU. A TWO-BIT HUSTLER LIKE YOUR OLD MAN...
EVEN THE BIG COMEBACK FAILS: WHO CARES WHEN THE JLA HE JOINED GETS DISBANDED?
WE GOT SUPERMAN, AQUAMAN, THE MARTIAN, AGAIN... ALL THE ORIGINALS. WHO NEEDS A LOSER...
I TOLD YOU: YOU CAN LET ME OUT ANY TIME YOU SAY THE WORDS I TAUGHT YOU. YOU CAN CHANGE ALL THIS.
YOU'RE NOT MAD, BILLY MAC. I'M NOT JUST A VOICE IN YOUR HEAD.
AMAZO STEALS HIS POWERS AND HE NEVER GETS 'EM BACK. SHRINK RAY HITS HIM, THE DOCTORS RESTORE ALMOST ALL OF HIS ANATOMY TO NORMAL SIZE. HIS TROPHY BLONDE WALKS...
TAKE A GOOD LOOK AT KING MIDAS; EVERYTHING HE TOUCHES TURNS TO CRAP.

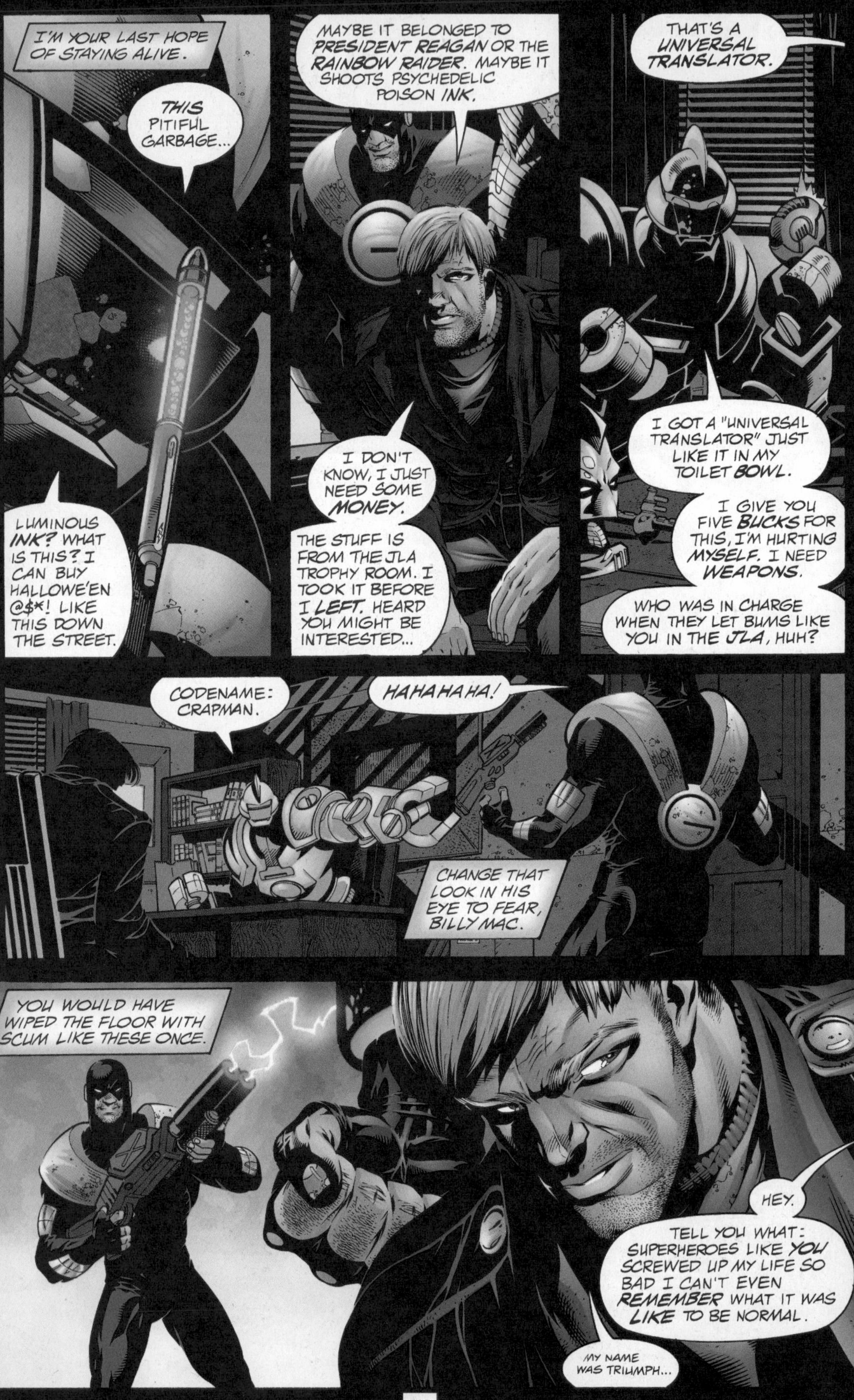
I'M YOUR LAST HOPE OF STAYING ALIVE.
THIS PITIFUL GARBAGE...
LUMINOUS INK? WHAT IS THIS? I CAN BUY HALLOWE'EN @$*! LIKE THIS DOWN THE STREET.
MAYBE IT BELONGED TO PRESIDENT REAGAN OR THE RAINBOW RAIDER. MAYBE IT SHOOTS PSYCHEDELIC POISON INK.
I DON'T KNOW, I JUST NEED SOME MONEY.
THE STUFF IS FROM THE JLA TROPHY ROOM. I TOOK IT BEFORE I LEFT. HEARD YOU MIGHT BE INTERESTED...
THAT'S A UNIVERSAL TRANSLATOR.
I GOT A "UNIVERSAL TRANSLATOR" JUST LIKE IT IN MY TOILET BOWL.
I GIVE YOU FIVE BUCKS FOR THIS, I'M HURTING MYSELF. I NEED WEAPONS.
WHO WAS IN CHARGE WHEN THEY LET BUMS LIKE YOU IN THE JLA, HUH?
CODENAME: CRAPMAN.
HAHAHAHA!
CHANGE THAT LOOK IN HIS EYE TO FEAR, BILLY MAC.
YOU WOULD HAVE WIPED THE FLOOR WITH SCUM LIKE THESE ONCE.
HEY.
TELL YOU WHAT: SUPERHEROES LIKE YOU SCREWED UP MY LIFE SO BAD I CAN'T EVEN REMEMBER WHAT IT WAS LIKE TO BE NORMAL.
MY NAME WAS TRIUMPH...

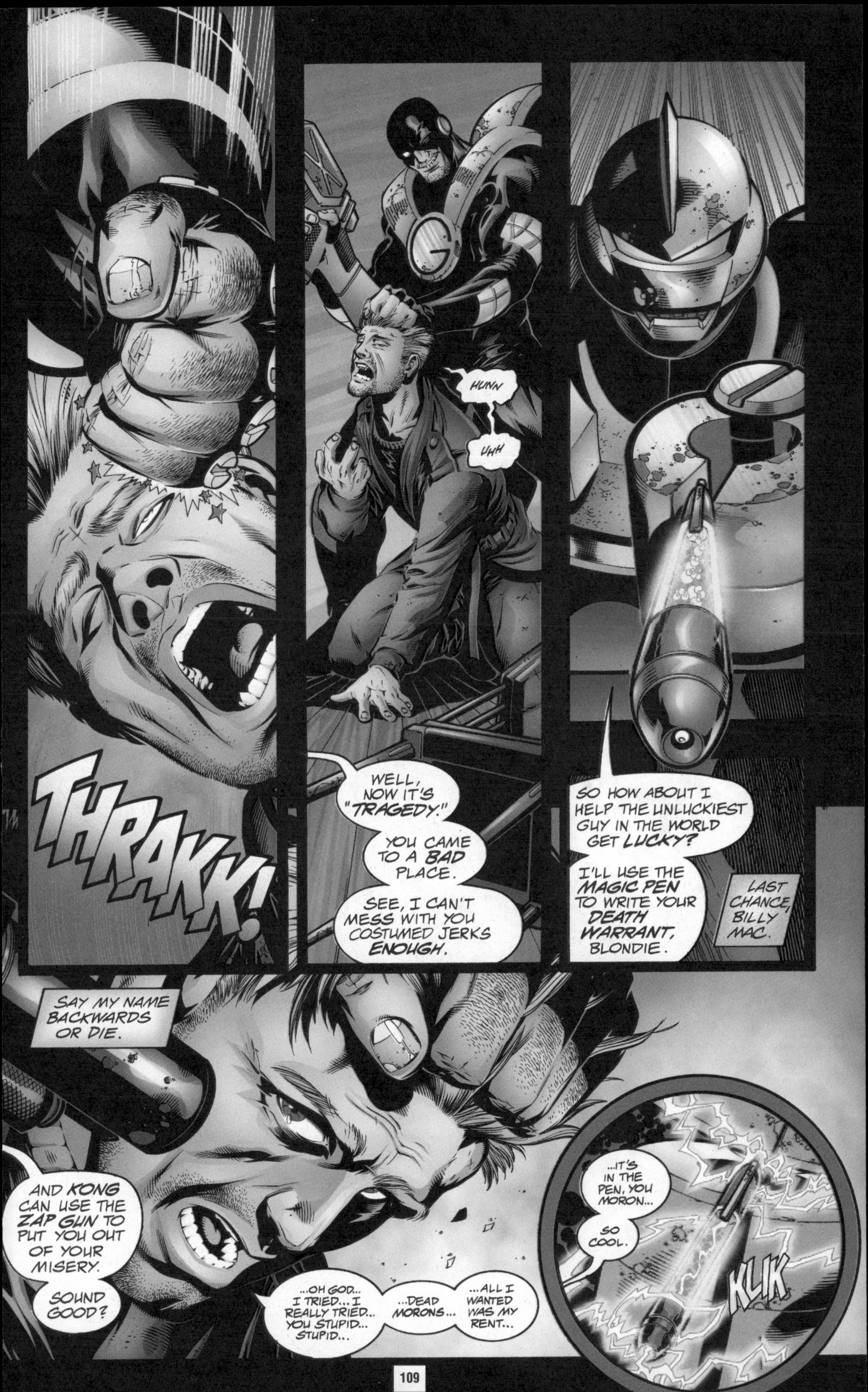
THRAKK!
HUNN
UHH
WELL, NOW IT'S "TRAGEDY."
YOU CAME TO A BAD PLACE.
SEE, I CAN'T MESS WITH YOU COSTUMED JERKS ENOUGH.
SO HOW ABOUT I HELP THE UNLUCKIEST GUY IN THE WORLD GET LUCKY?
I'LL USE THE MAGIC PEN TO WRITE YOUR DEATH WARRANT, BLONDIE.
LAST CHANCE, BILLY MAC.
SAY MY NAME BACKWARDS OR DIE.
AND KONG CAN USE THE ZAP GUN TO PUT YOU OUT OF YOUR MISERY.
SOUND GOOD?
...OH GOD... I TRIED... I REALLY TRIED... YOU STUPID... STUPID...
...DEAD MORONS...
...ALL I WANTED WAS MY RENT...
...IT'S IN THE PEN, YOU MORON...
SO COOL.
KLIK

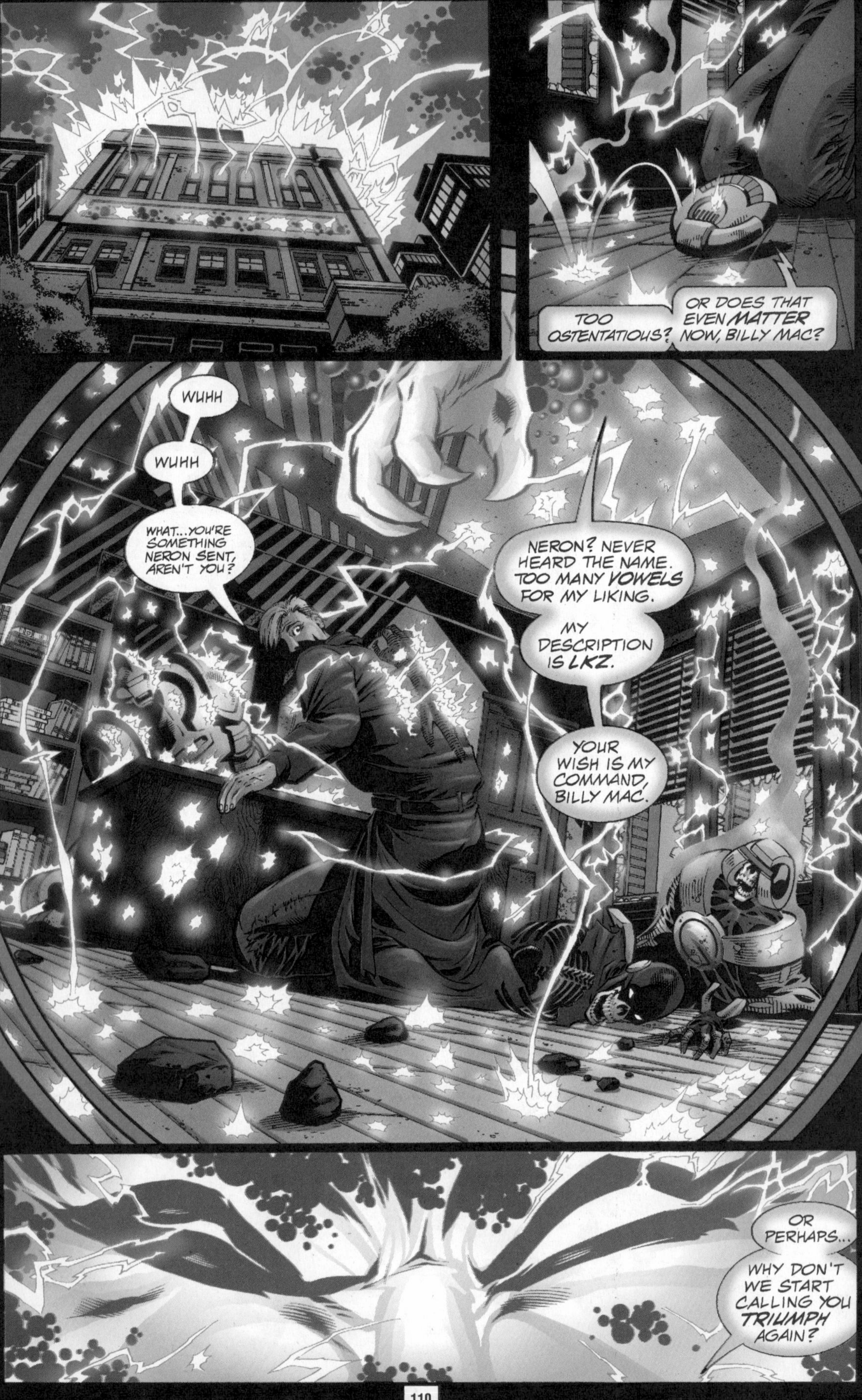

TOO OSTENTATIOUS?
OR DOES THAT EVEN MATTER NOW, BILLY MAC?
WUHH
WUHH
WHAT...YOU'RE SOMETHING NERON SENT, AREN'T YOU?
NERON? NEVER HEARD THE NAME. TOO MANY VOWELS FOR MY LIKING.
MY DESCRIPTION IS LKZ.
YOUR WISH IS MY COMMAND, BILLY MAC.
OR PERHAPS...
WHY DON'T WE START CALLING YOU TRIUMPH AGAIN?

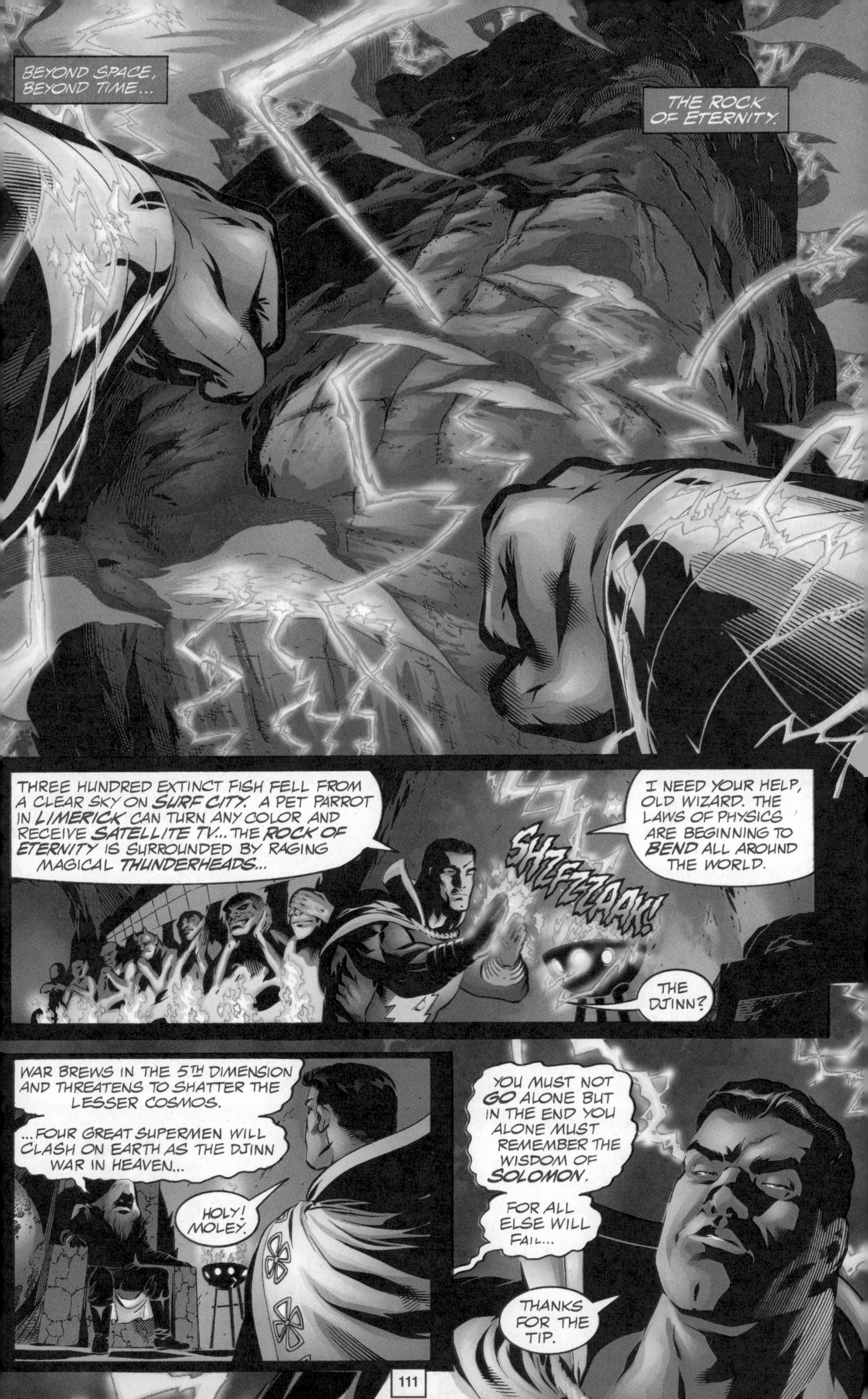

BEYOND SPACE, BEYOND TIME...
THE ROCK OF ETERNITY.
THREE HUNDRED EXTINCT FISH FELL FROM A CLEAR SKY ON SURF CITY. A PET PARROT IN LIMERICK CAN TURN ANY COLOR AND RECEIVE SATELLITE TV... THE ROCK OF ETERNITY IS SURROUNDED BY RAGING MAGICAL THUNDERHEADS...
I NEED YOUR HELP, OLD WIZARD. THE LAWS OF PHYSICS ARE BEGINNING TO BEND ALL AROUND THE WORLD.
SHZZZAAK!
THE DJINN?
WAR BREWS IN THE 5TH DIMENSION AND THREATENS TO SHATTER THE LESSER COSMOS.
...FOUR GREAT SUPERMEN WILL CLASH ON EARTH AS THE DJINN WAR IN HEAVEN...
HOLY! MOLEY.
YOU MUST NOT GO ALONE BUT IN THE END YOU ALONE MUST REMEMBER THE WISDOM OF SOLOMON.
FOR ALL ELSE WILL FAIL...
THANKS FOR THE TIP.

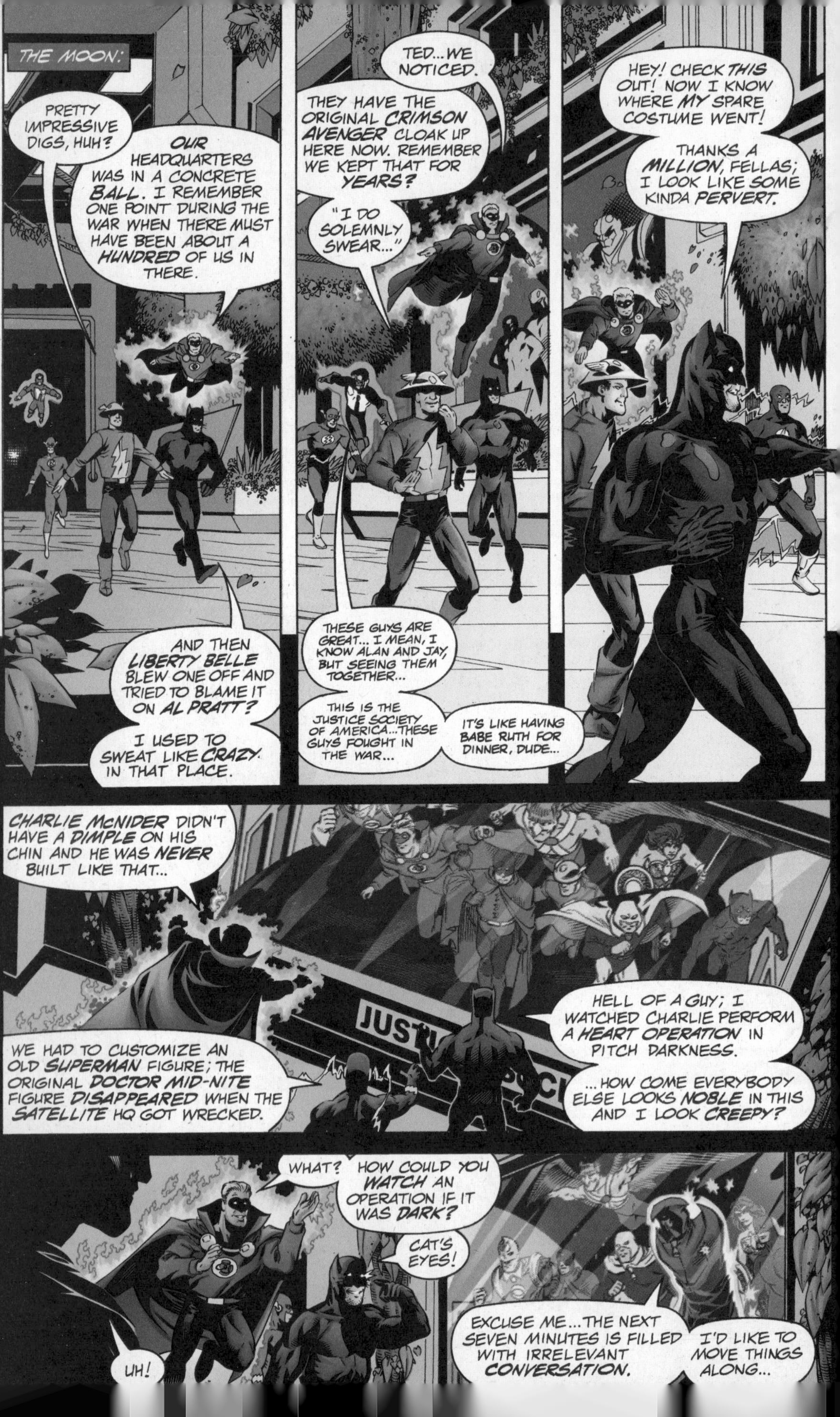
THE MOON:
PRETTY IMPRESSIVE DIGS, HUH?
OUR HEADQUARTERS WAS IN A CONCRETE BALL. I REMEMBER ONE POINT DURING THE WAR WHEN THERE MUST HAVE BEEN ABOUT A HUNDRED OF US IN THERE.
AND THEN LIBERTY BELLE BLEW ONE OFF AND TRIED TO BLAME IT ON AL PRATT?
I USED TO SWEAT LIKE CRAZY IN THAT PLACE.
TED... WE NOTICED.
THEY HAVE THE ORIGINAL CRIMSON AVENGER CLOAK UP HERE NOW. REMEMBER WE KEPT THAT FOR YEARS?
"I DO SOLEMNLY SWEAR..."
THESE GUYS ARE GREAT... I MEAN, I KNOW ALAN AND JAY, BUT SEEING THEM TOGETHER...
THIS IS THE JUSTICE SOCIETY OF AMERICA... THESE GUYS FOUGHT IN THE WAR...
IT'S LIKE HAVING BABE RUTH FOR DINNER, DUDE...
HEY! CHECK THIS OUT! NOW I KNOW WHERE MY SPARE COSTUME WENT!
THANKS A MILLION, FELLAS; I LOOK LIKE SOME KINDA PERVERT.
CHARLIE McNIDER DIDN'T HAVE A DIMPLE ON HIS CHIN AND HE WAS NEVER BUILT LIKE THAT...
WE HAD TO CUSTOMIZE AN OLD SUPERMAN FIGURE; THE ORIGINAL DOCTOR MID-NITE FIGURE DISAPPEARED WHEN THE SATELLITE HQ GOT WRECKED.
HELL OF A GUY; I WATCHED CHARLIE PERFORM A HEART OPERATION IN PITCH DARKNESS.
...HOW COME EVERYBODY ELSE LOOKS NOBLE IN THIS AND I LOOK CREEPY?
WHAT?
HOW COULD YOU WATCH AN OPERATION IF IT WAS DARK?
CAT'S EYES!
UH!
EXCUSE ME... THE NEXT SEVEN MINUTES IS FILLED WITH IRRELEVANT CONVERSATION.
I'D LIKE TO MOVE THINGS ALONG...

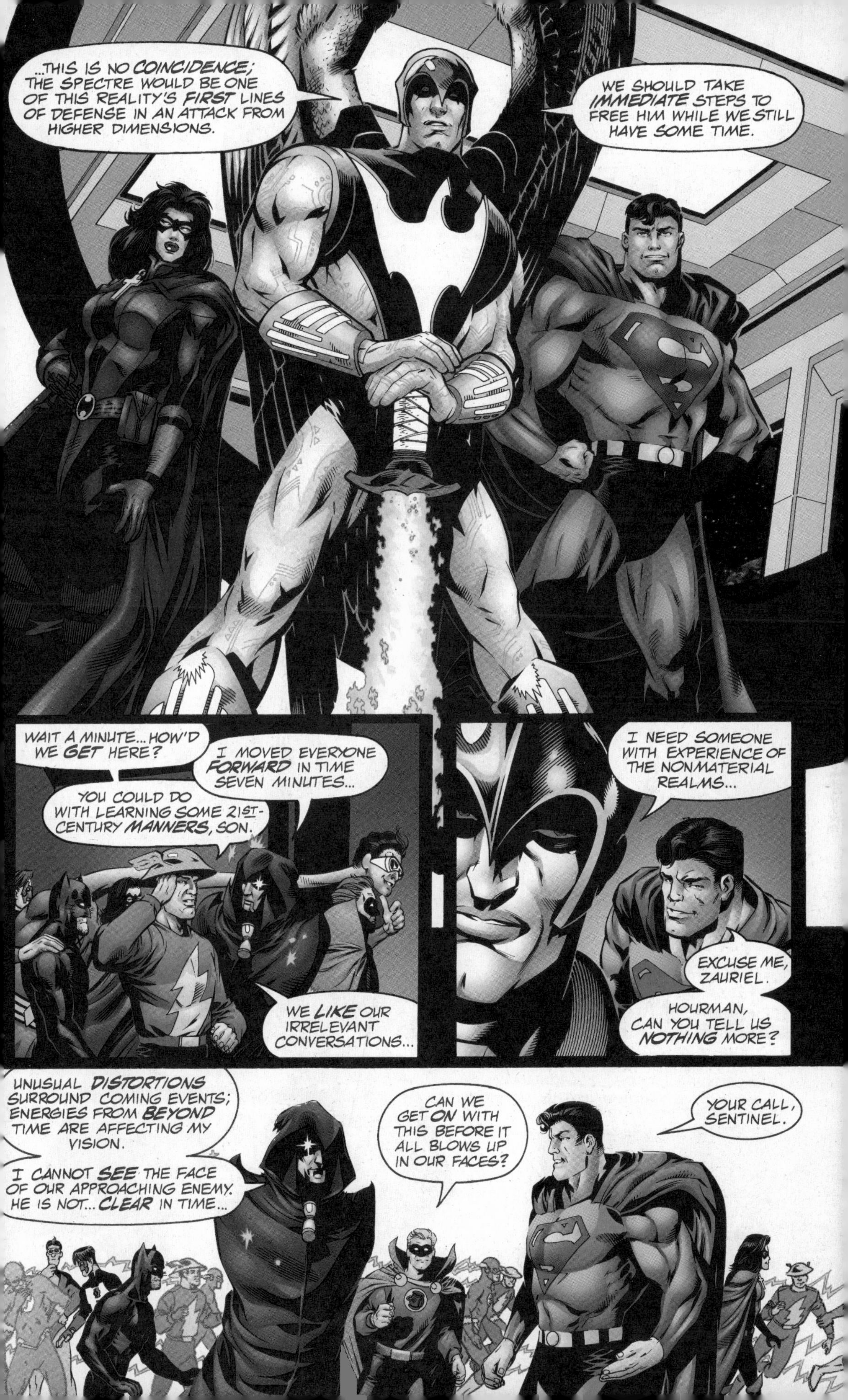
...THIS IS NO COINCIDENCE; THE SPECTRE WOULD BE ONE OF THIS REALITY'S FIRST LINES OF DEFENSE IN AN ATTACK FROM HIGHER DIMENSIONS.
WE SHOULD TAKE IMMEDIATE STEPS TO FREE HIM WHILE WE STILL HAVE SOME TIME.
WAIT A MINUTE... HOW'D WE GET HERE?
I MOVED EVERYONE FORWARD IN TIME SEVEN MINUTES...
YOU COULD DO WITH LEARNING SOME 21ST-CENTURY MANNERS, SON.
WE LIKE OUR IRRELEVANT CONVERSATIONS...
I NEED SOMEONE WITH EXPERIENCE OF THE NONMATERIAL REALMS...
EXCUSE ME, ZAURIEL.
HOURMAN, CAN YOU TELL US NOTHING MORE?
UNUSUAL DISTORTIONS SURROUND COMING EVENTS; ENERGIES FROM BEYOND TIME ARE AFFECTING MY VISION.
I CANNOT SEE THE FACE OF OUR APPROACHING ENEMY. HE IS NOT... CLEAR IN TIME...
CAN WE GET ON WITH THIS BEFORE IT ALL BLOWS UP IN OUR FACES?
YOUR CALL, SENTINEL.

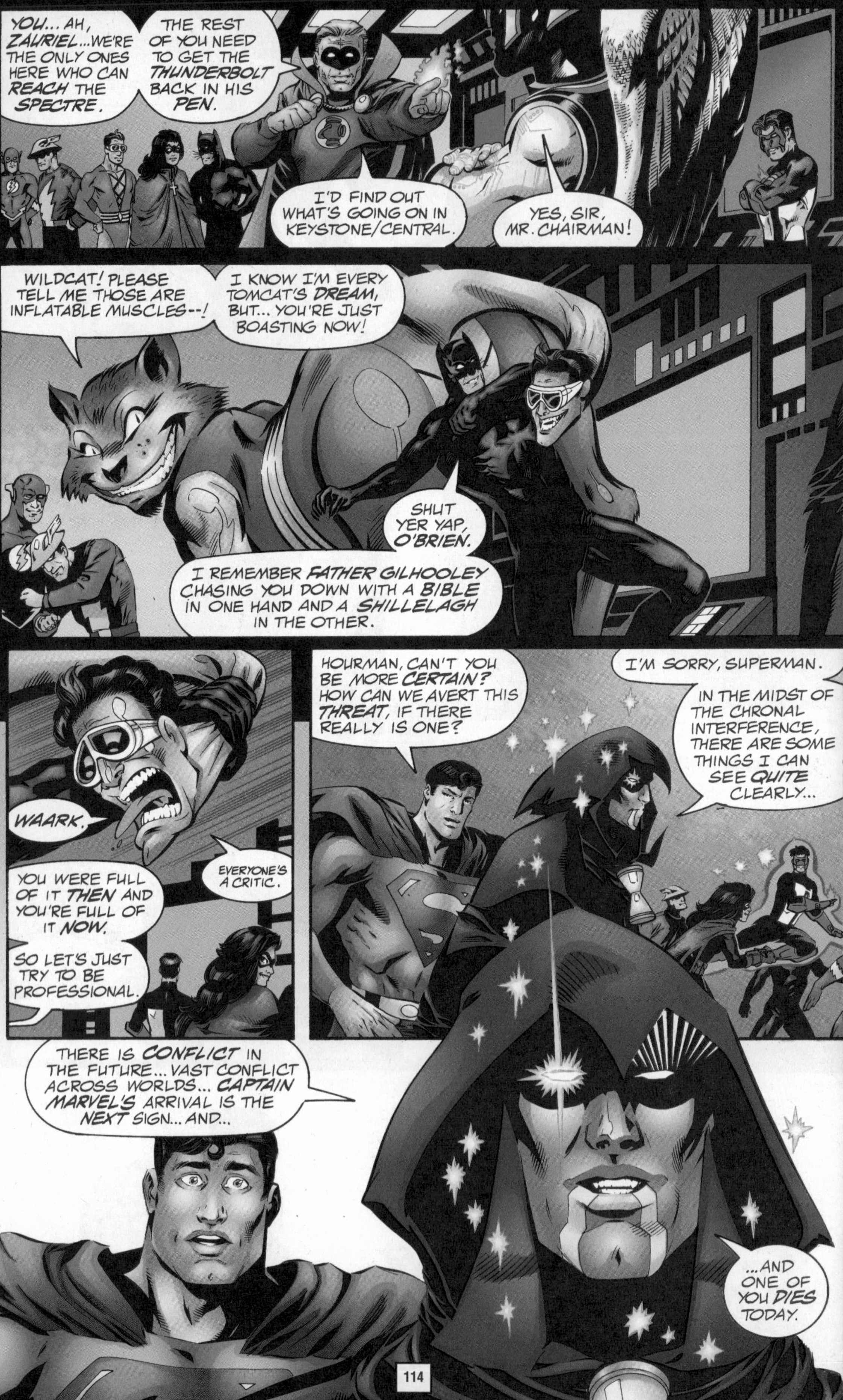
YOU... AH, ZAURIEL...WE'RE THE ONLY ONES HERE WHO CAN REACH THE SPECTRE.
THE REST OF YOU NEED TO GET THE THUNDERBOLT BACK IN HIS PEN.
I'D FIND OUT WHAT'S GOING ON IN KEYSTONE/CENTRAL.
YES, SIR, MR. CHAIRMAN!
WILDCAT! PLEASE TELL ME THOSE ARE INFLATABLE MUSCLES--!
I KNOW I'M EVERY TOMCAT'S DREAM, BUT... YOU'RE JUST BOASTING NOW!
SHUT YER YAP, O'BRIEN.
I REMEMBER FATHER GILHOOLEY CHASING YOU DOWN WITH A BIBLE IN ONE HAND AND A SHILLELAGH IN THE OTHER.
WAARK.
EVERYONE'S A CRITIC.
YOU WERE FULL OF IT THEN AND YOU'RE FULL OF IT NOW.
SO LET'S JUST TRY TO BE PROFESSIONAL.
HOURMAN, CAN'T YOU BE MORE CERTAIN? HOW CAN WE AVERT THIS THREAT, IF THERE REALLY IS ONE?
I'M SORRY, SUPERMAN.
IN THE MIDST OF THE CHRONAL INTERFERENCE, THERE ARE SOME THINGS I CAN SEE QUITE CLEARLY...
THERE IS CONFLICT IN THE FUTURE... VAST CONFLICT ACROSS WORLDS... CAPTAIN MARVEL'S ARRIVAL IS THE NEXT SIGN... AND...
...AND ONE OF YOU DIES TODAY.

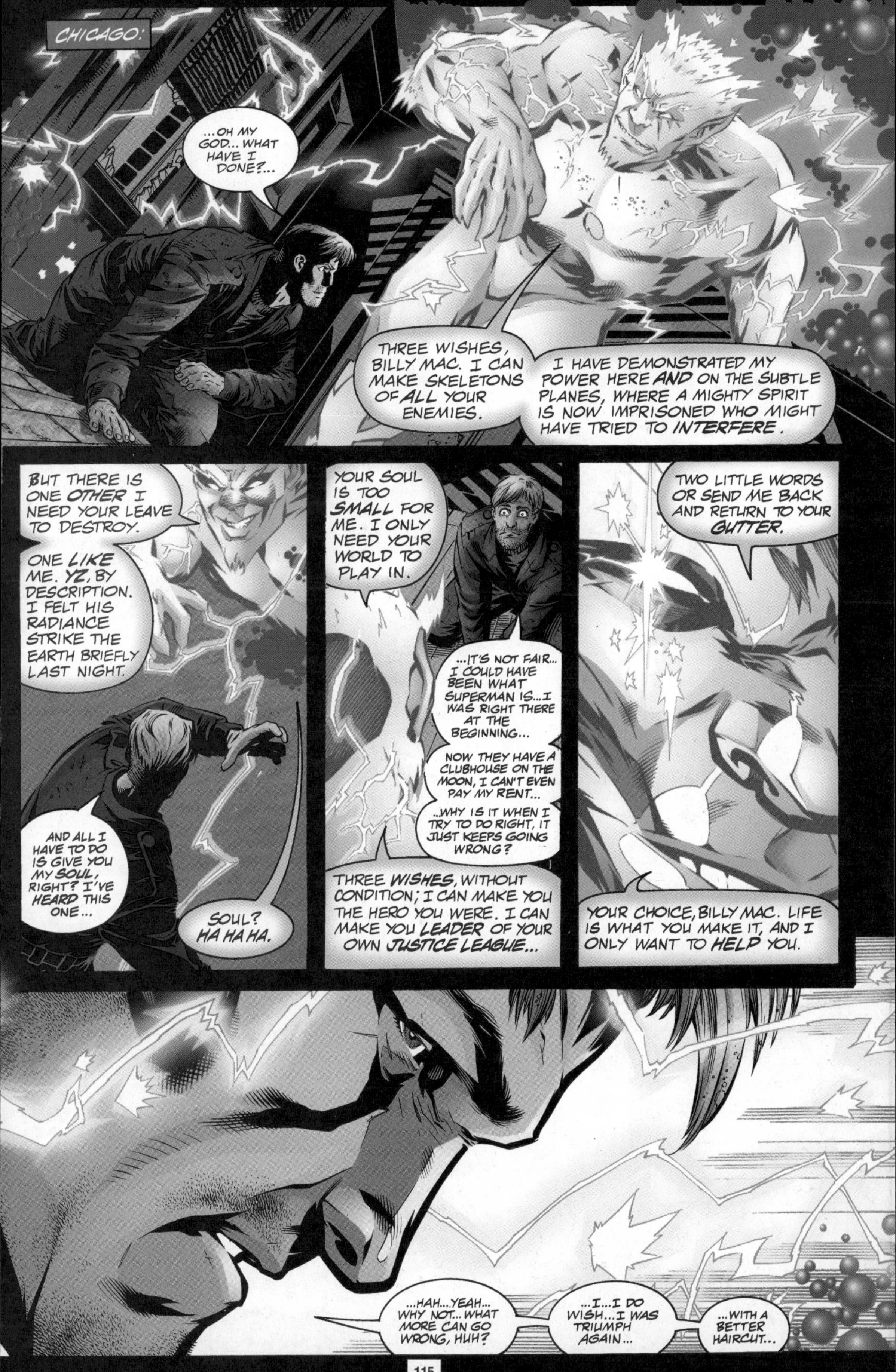
CHICAGO:
...OH MY GOD... WHAT HAVE I DONE?...
THREE WISHES, BILLY MAC. I CAN MAKE SKELETONS OF ALL YOUR ENEMIES.
I HAVE DEMONSTRATED MY POWER HERE AND ON THE SUBTLE PLANES, WHERE A MIGHTY SPIRIT IS NOW IMPRISONED WHO MIGHT HAVE TRIED TO INTERFERE.
BUT THERE IS ONE OTHER I NEED YOUR LEAVE TO DESTROY.
ONE LIKE ME. YZ, BY DESCRIPTION. I FELT HIS RADIANCE STRIKE THE EARTH BRIEFLY LAST NIGHT.
AND ALL I HAVE TO DO IS GIVE YOU MY SOUL, RIGHT? I'VE HEARD THIS ONE...
SOUL? HA HA HA.
YOUR SOUL IS TOO SMALL FOR ME. I ONLY NEED YOUR WORLD TO PLAY IN.
...IT'S NOT FAIR... I COULD HAVE BEEN WHAT SUPERMAN IS... I WAS RIGHT THERE AT THE BEGINNING...
NOW THEY HAVE A CLUBHOUSE ON THE MOON, I CAN'T EVEN PAY MY RENT...
...WHY IS IT WHEN I TRY TO DO RIGHT, IT JUST KEEPS GOING WRONG?
THREE WISHES, WITHOUT CONDITION; I CAN MAKE YOU THE HERO YOU WERE. I CAN MAKE YOU LEADER OF YOUR OWN JUSTICE LEAGUE...
TWO LITTLE WORDS OR SEND ME BACK AND RETURN TO YOUR GUTTER.
YOUR CHOICE, BILLY MAC. LIFE IS WHAT YOU MAKE IT, AND I ONLY WANT TO HELP YOU.
...HAH...YEAH... WHY NOT... WHAT MORE CAN GO WRONG, HUH?
...I...I DO WISH...I WAS TRIUMPH AGAIN...
...WITH A BETTER HAIRCUT...

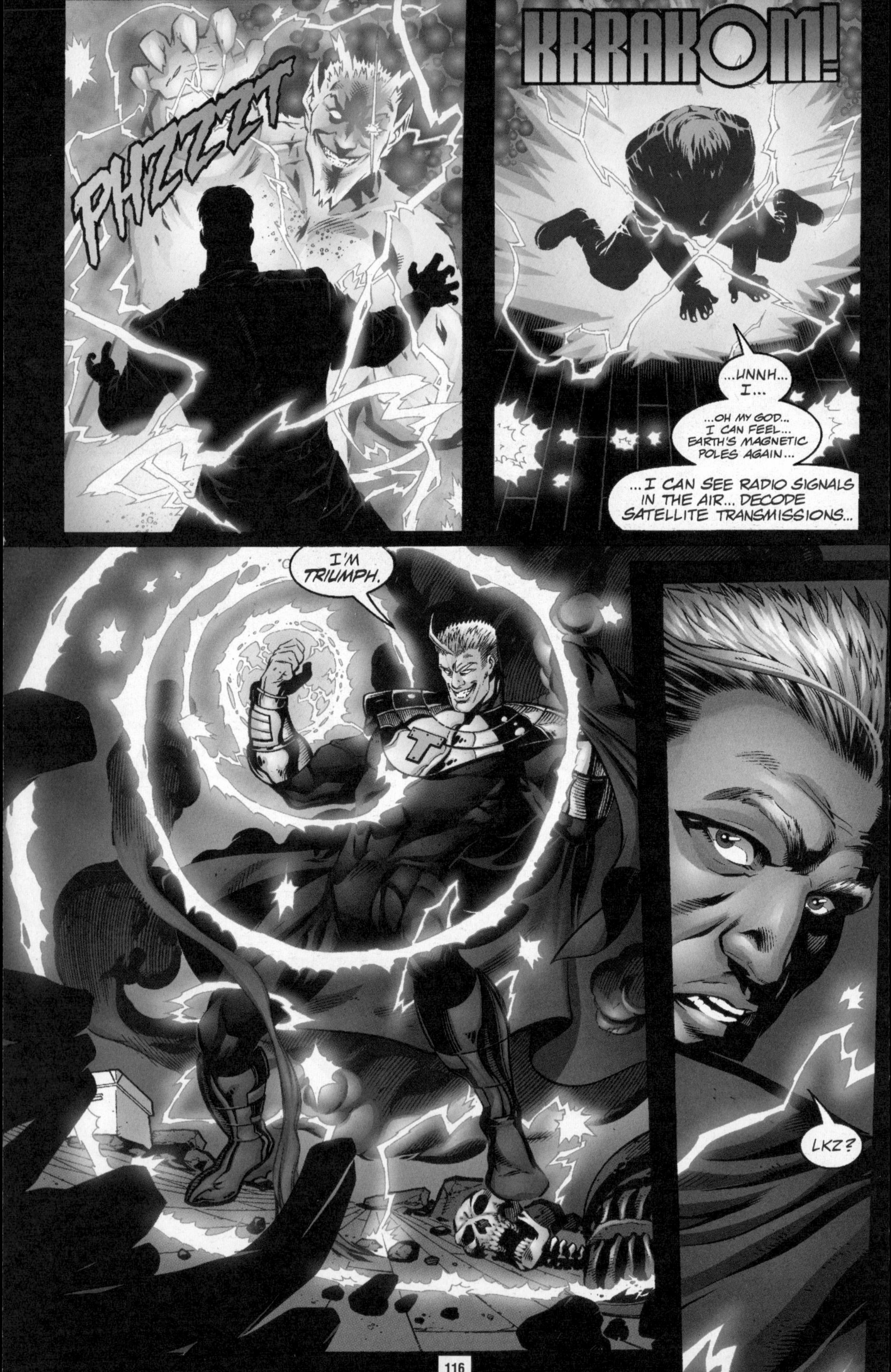
PHZZZT
KRRAKOM!
...UNNH... I...
...OH MY GOD... I CAN FEEL... EARTH'S MAGNETIC POLES AGAIN...
...I CAN SEE RADIO SIGNALS IN THE AIR... DECODE SATELLITE TRANSMISSIONS...
I'M TRIUMPH.
LKZ?

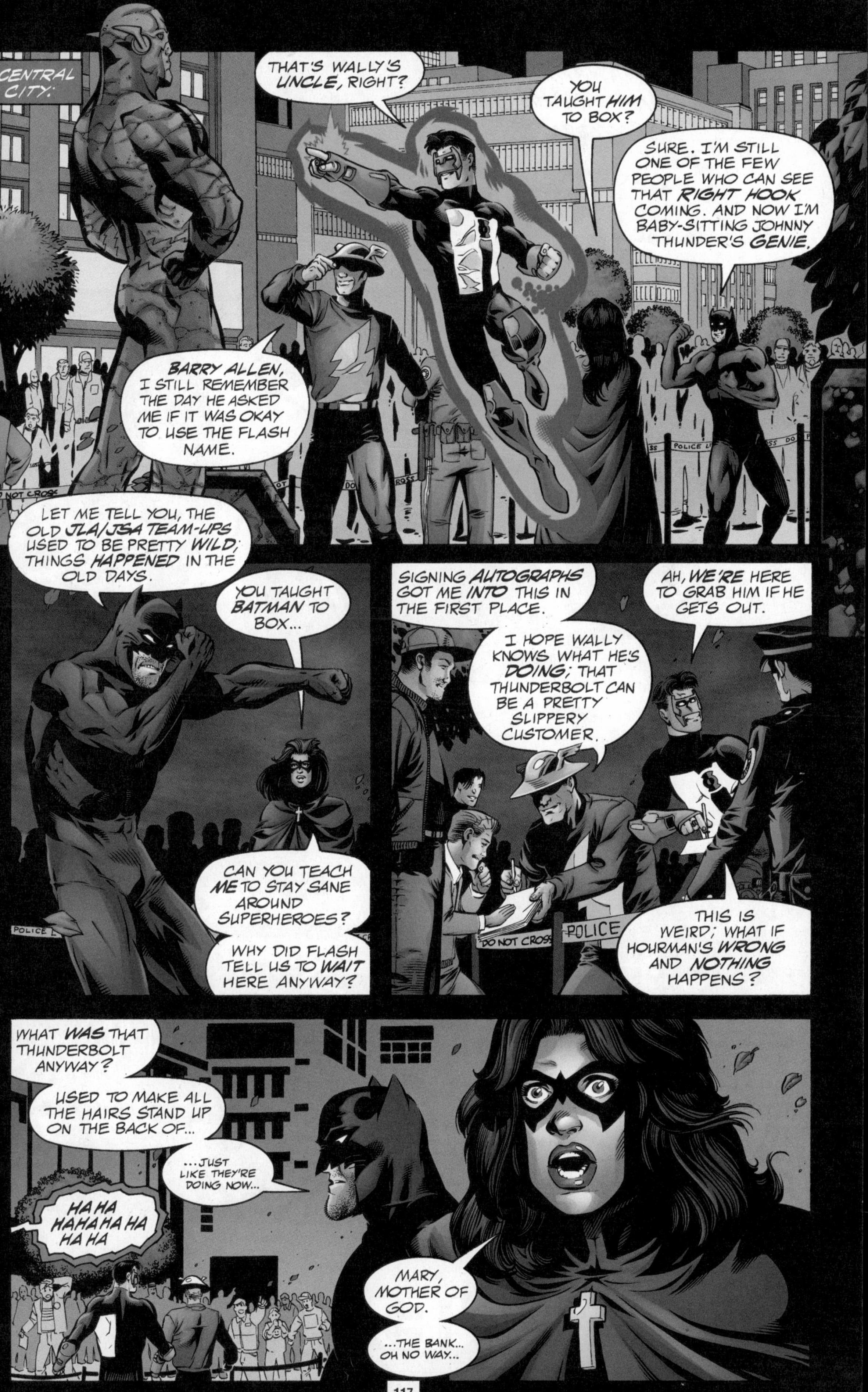
CENTRAL CITY:
THAT'S WALLY'S UNCLE, RIGHT?
YOU TAUGHT HIM TO BOX?
SURE. I'M STILL ONE OF THE FEW PEOPLE WHO CAN SEE THAT RIGHT HOOK COMING. AND NOW I'M BABY-SITTING JOHNNY THUNDER'S GENIE.
BARRY ALLEN, I STILL REMEMBER THE DAY HE ASKED ME IF IT WAS OKAY TO USE THE FLASH NAME.
LET ME TELL YOU, THE OLD JLA/JSA TEAM-UPS USED TO BE PRETTY WILD; THINGS HAPPENED IN THE OLD DAYS.
YOU TAUGHT BATMAN TO BOX...
CAN YOU TEACH ME TO STAY SANE AROUND SUPERHEROES?
WHY DID FLASH TELL US TO WAIT HERE ANYWAY?
SIGNING AUTOGRAPHS GOT ME INTO THIS IN THE FIRST PLACE.
AH, WE'RE HERE TO GRAB HIM IF HE GETS OUT.
I HOPE WALLY KNOWS WHAT HE'S DOING; THAT THUNDERBOLT CAN BE A PRETTY SLIPPERY CUSTOMER.
DO NOT CROSS POLICE
THIS IS WEIRD; WHAT IF HOURMAN'S WRONG AND NOTHING HAPPENS?
WHAT WAS THAT THUNDERBOLT ANYWAY?
USED TO MAKE ALL THE HAIRS STAND UP ON THE BACK OF...
...JUST LIKE THEY'RE DOING NOW...
HA HA HAHAHAHA HA HA
MARY, MOTHER OF GOD.
...THE BANK... OH NO WAY...

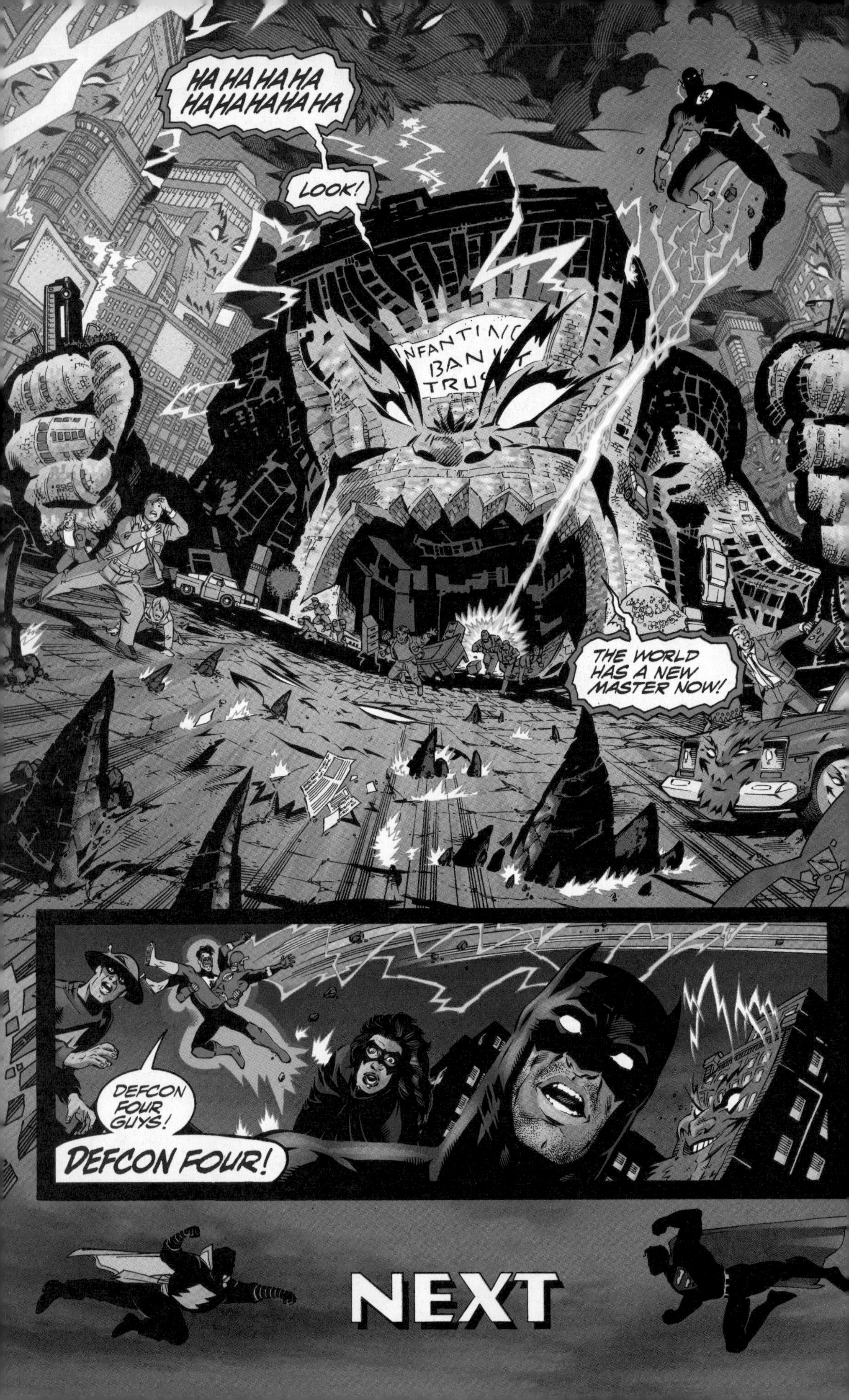
HA HA HA HA
HAHAHAHAHA HA
LOOK!
THE WORLD HAS A NEW MASTER NOW!
DEFCON FOUR GUYS!
DEFCON FOUR!
NEXT

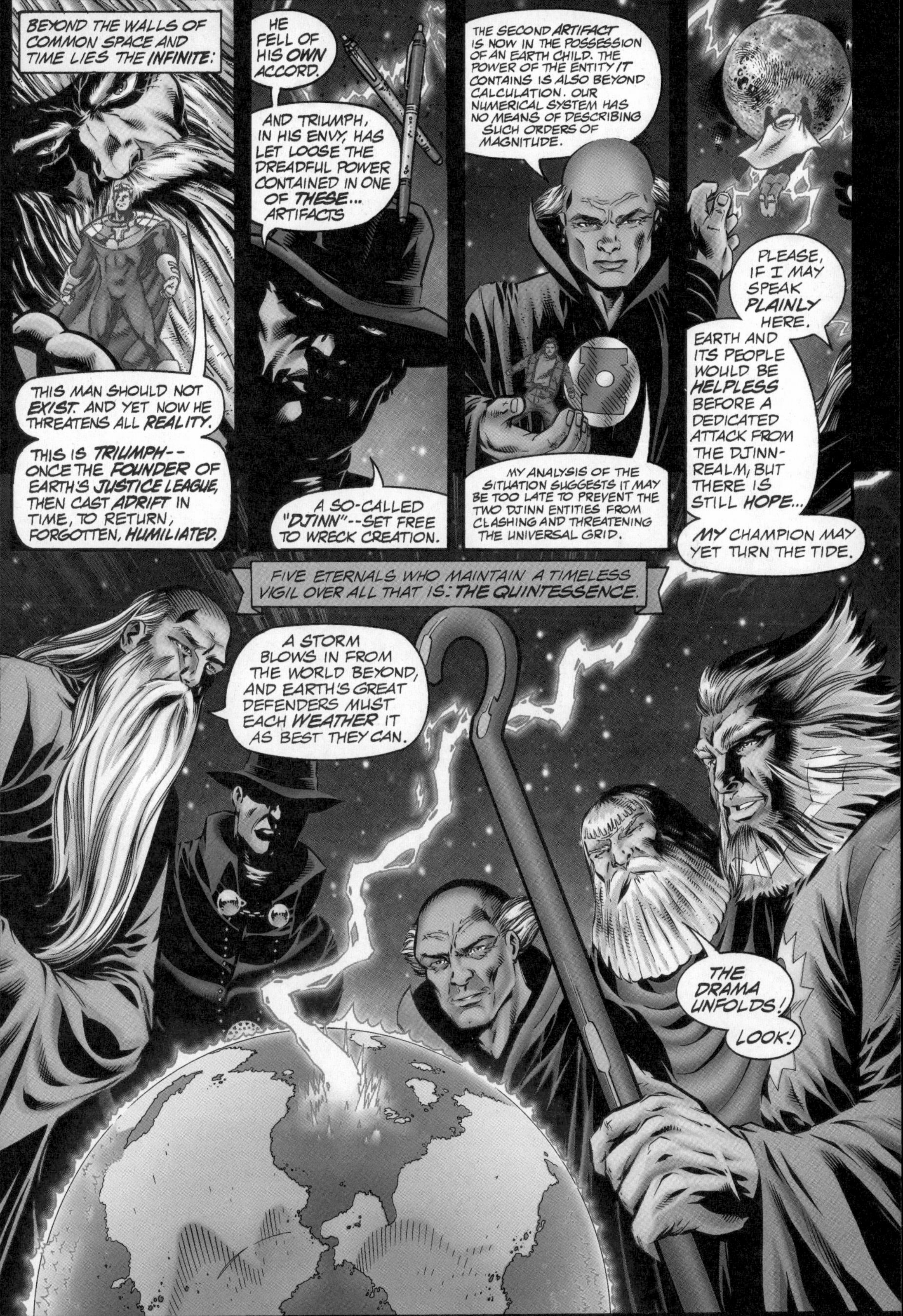
BEYOND THE WALLS OF COMMON SPACE AND TIME LIES THE INFINITE:
THIS MAN SHOULD NOT EXIST. AND YET NOW HE THREATENS ALL REALITY.
THIS IS TRIUMPH-- ONCE THE FOUNDER OF EARTH'S JUSTICE LEAGUE, THEN CAST ADRIFT IN TIME, TO RETURN, FORGOTTEN, HUMILIATED.
HE FELL OF HIS OWN ACCORD.
AND TRIUMPH, IN HIS ENVY, HAS LET LOOSE THE DREADFUL POWER CONTAINED IN ONE OF THESE... ARTIFACTS
A SO-CALLED "DJINN"--SET FREE TO WRECK CREATION.
THE SECOND ARTIFACT IS NOW IN THE POSSESSION OF AN EARTH CHILD. THE POWER OF THE ENTITY IT CONTAINS IS ALSO BEYOND CALCULATION. OUR NUMERICAL SYSTEM HAS NO MEANS OF DESCRIBING SUCH ORDERS OF MAGNITUDE.
MY ANALYSIS OF THE SITUATION SUGGESTS IT MAY BE TOO LATE TO PREVENT THE TWO DJINN ENTITIES FROM CLASHING AND THREATENING THE UNIVERSAL GRID.
PLEASE, IF I MAY SPEAK PLAINLY HERE.
EARTH AND ITS PEOPLE WOULD BE HELPLESS BEFORE A DEDICATED ATTACK FROM THE DJINN-REALM, BUT THERE IS STILL HOPE...
MY CHAMPION MAY YET TURN THE TIDE.
FIVE ETERNALS WHO MAINTAIN A TIMELESS VIGIL OVER ALL THAT IS: THE QUINTESSENCE.
A STORM BLOWS IN FROM THE WORLD BEYOND, AND EARTH'S GREAT DEFENDERS MUST EACH WEATHER IT AS BEST THEY CAN.
THE DRAMA UNFOLDS!
LOOK!

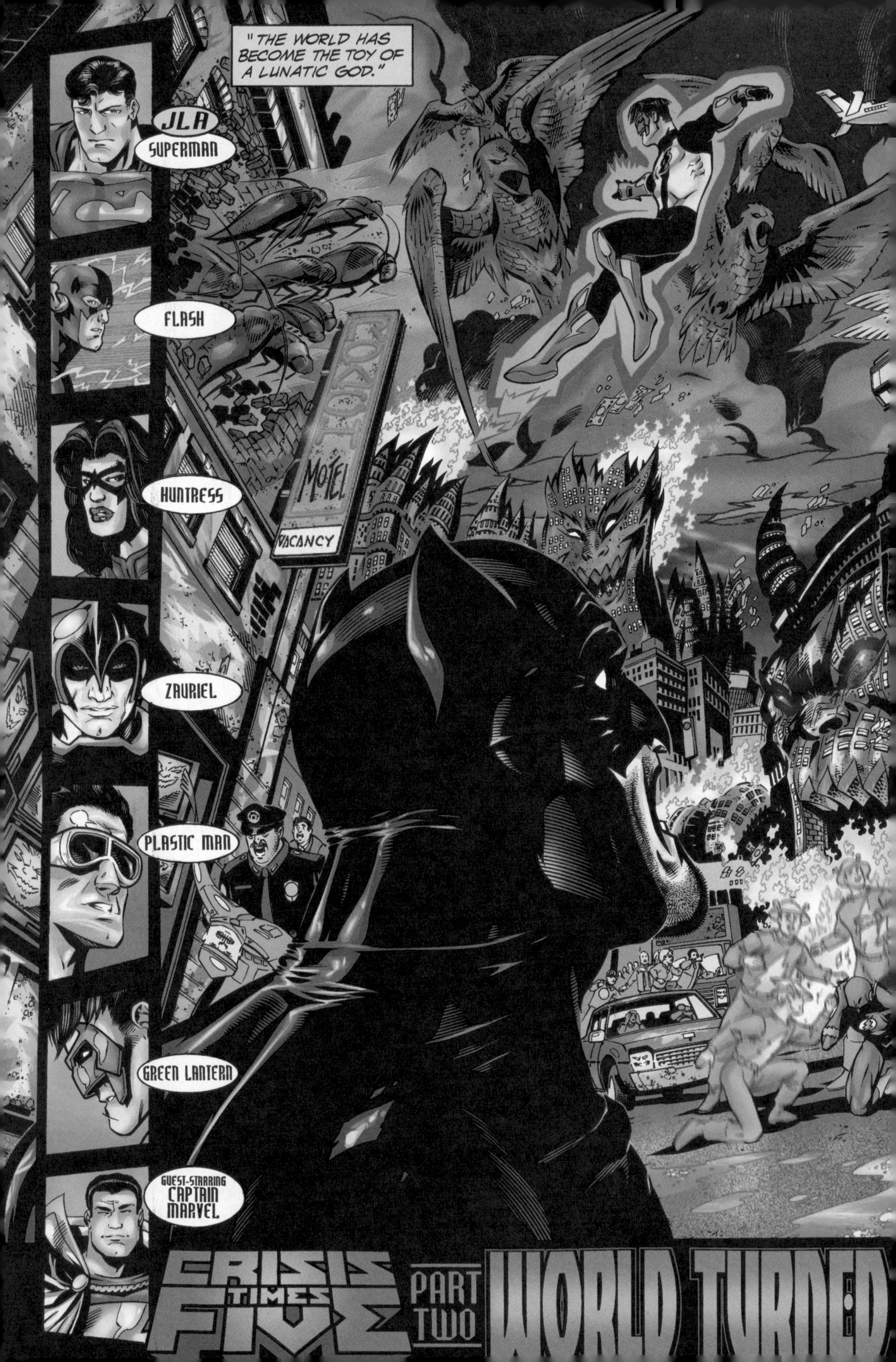
"THE WORLD HAS BECOME THE TOY OF A LUNATIC GOD."
JLA
SUPERMAN
FLASH
HUNTRESS
ZAURIEL
PLASTIC MAN
GREEN LANTERN
GUEST-STARRING CAPTAIN MARVEL
MOTEL
VACANCY
CRISIS TIMES FIVE
PART TWO
WORLD TURNED

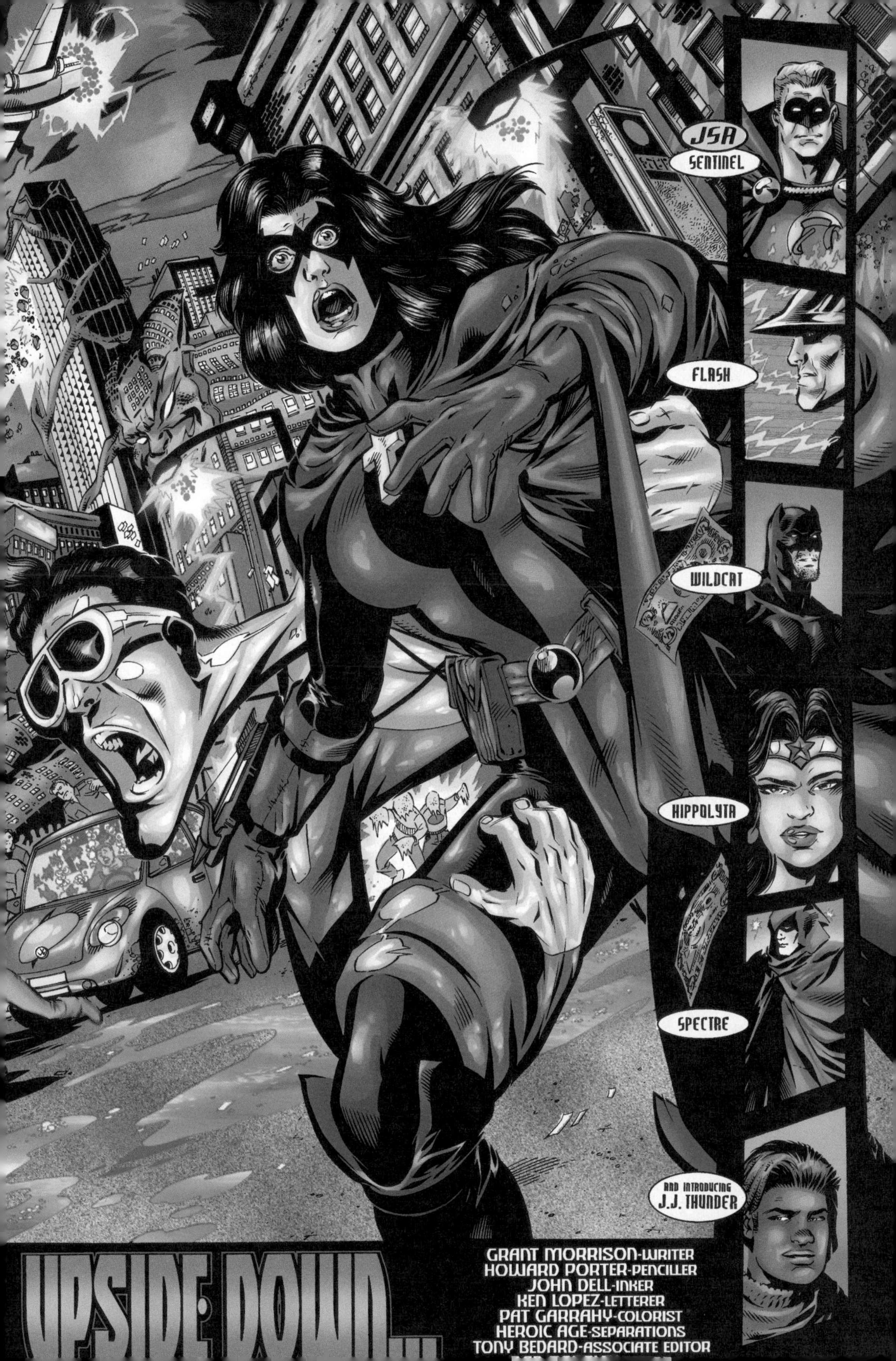
JSA
SENTINEL
FLASH
WILDCAT
HIPPOLYTA
SPECTRE
AND INTRODUCING
J.J. THUNDER
UPSIDE DOWN...
GRANT MORRISON-WRITER
HOWARD PORTER-PENCILLER
JOHN DELL-INKER
KEN LOPEZ-LETTERER
PAT GARRAHY-COLORIST
HEROIC AGE-SEPARATIONS
TONY BEDARD-ASSOCIATE EDITOR

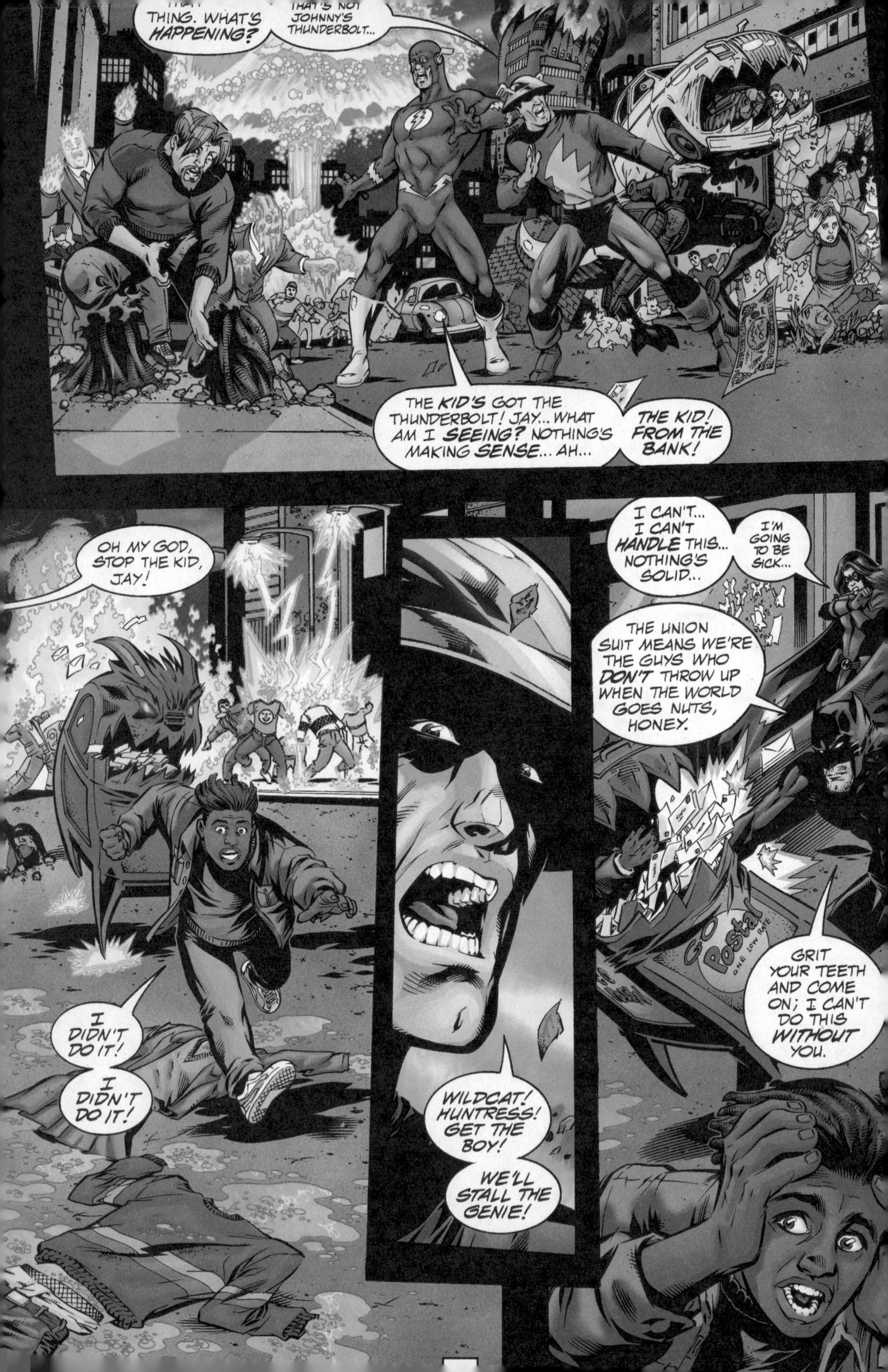
THING. WHAT'S HAPPENING?
THAT'S NOT JOHNNY'S THUNDERBOLT...
THE KID'S GOT THE THUNDERBOLT! JAY... WHAT AM I SEEING? NOTHING'S MAKING SENSE... AH...
THE KID! FROM THE BANK!
OH MY GOD, STOP THE KID, JAY!
I DIDN'T DO IT!
I DIDN'T DO IT!
WILDCAT! HUNTRESS! GET THE BOY!
WE'LL STALL THE GENIE!
I CAN'T... I CAN'T HANDLE THIS... NOTHING'S SOLID...
I'M GOING TO BE SICK...
THE UNION SUIT MEANS WE'RE THE GUYS WHO DON'T THROW UP WHEN THE WORLD GOES NUTS, HONEY.
GRIT YOUR TEETH AND COME ON; I CAN'T DO THIS WITHOUT YOU.
GO Postal ONE LOW RATE

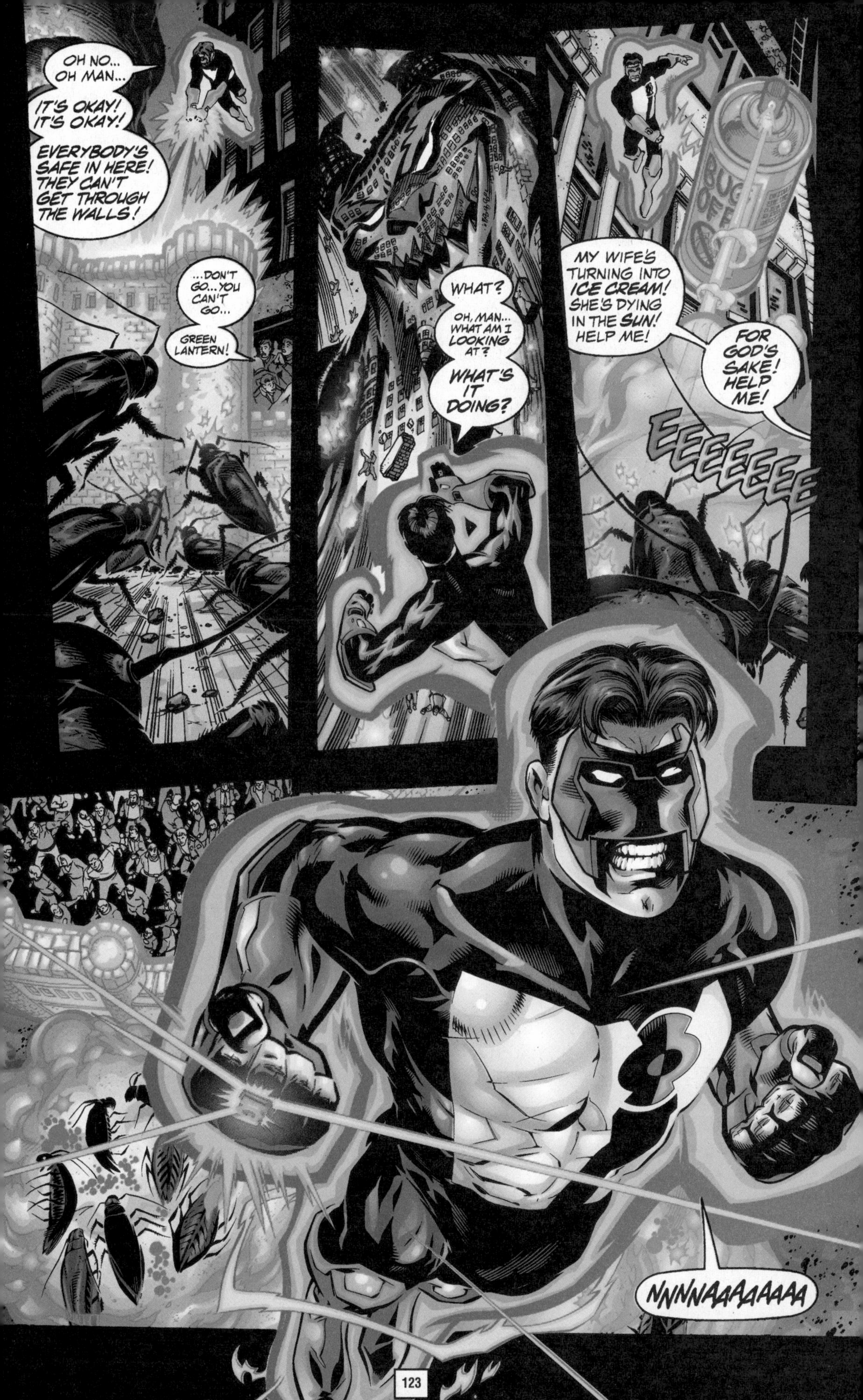
OH NO... OH MAN...
IT'S OKAY! IT'S OKAY!
EVERYBODY'S SAFE IN HERE! THEY CAN'T GET THROUGH THE WALLS!
...DON'T GO... YOU CAN'T GO...
GREEN LANTERN!
WHAT?
OH, MAN... WHAT AM I LOOKING AT?
WHAT'S IT DOING?
BUG OFF
MY WIFE'S TURNING INTO ICE CREAM! SHE'S DYING IN THE SUN! HELP ME!
FOR GOD'S SAKE! HELP ME!
EEEEEEEE
NNNNAAAAAAAA

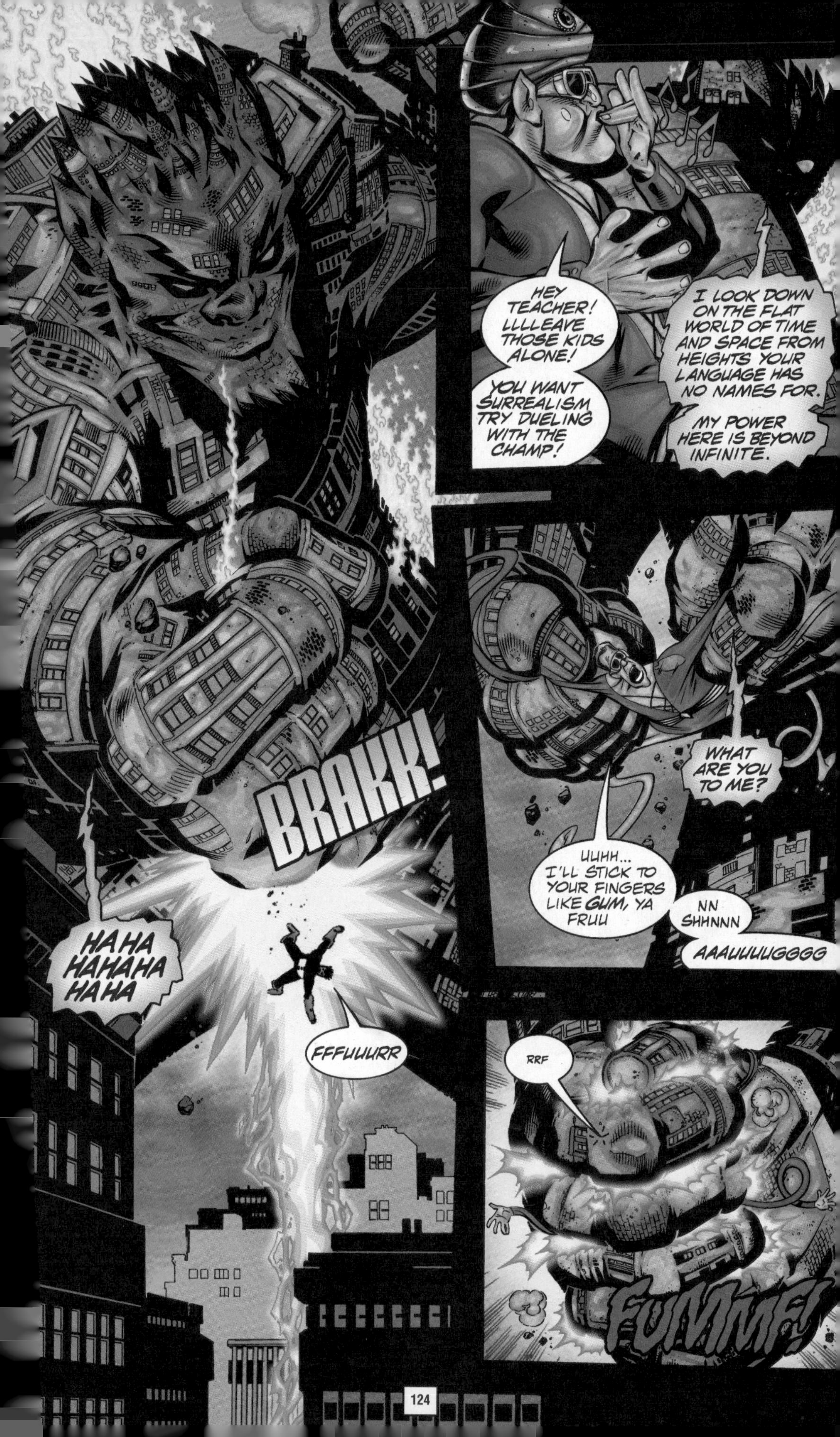
HEY TEACHER! LLLLEAVE THOSE KIDS ALONE!
YOU WANT SURREALISM TRY DUELING WITH THE CHAMP!
I LOOK DOWN ON THE FLAT WORLD OF TIME AND SPACE FROM HEIGHTS YOUR LANGUAGE HAS NO NAMES FOR.
MY POWER HERE IS BEYOND INFINITE.
BRAKK!
HA HA HAHAHA HA HA
FFFUUURR
WHAT ARE YOU TO ME?
UUHH... I'LL STICK TO YOUR FINGERS LIKE GUM, YA FRUU
NN SHHNNN
AAAUUUUGGGG
RRF
FUMMF!

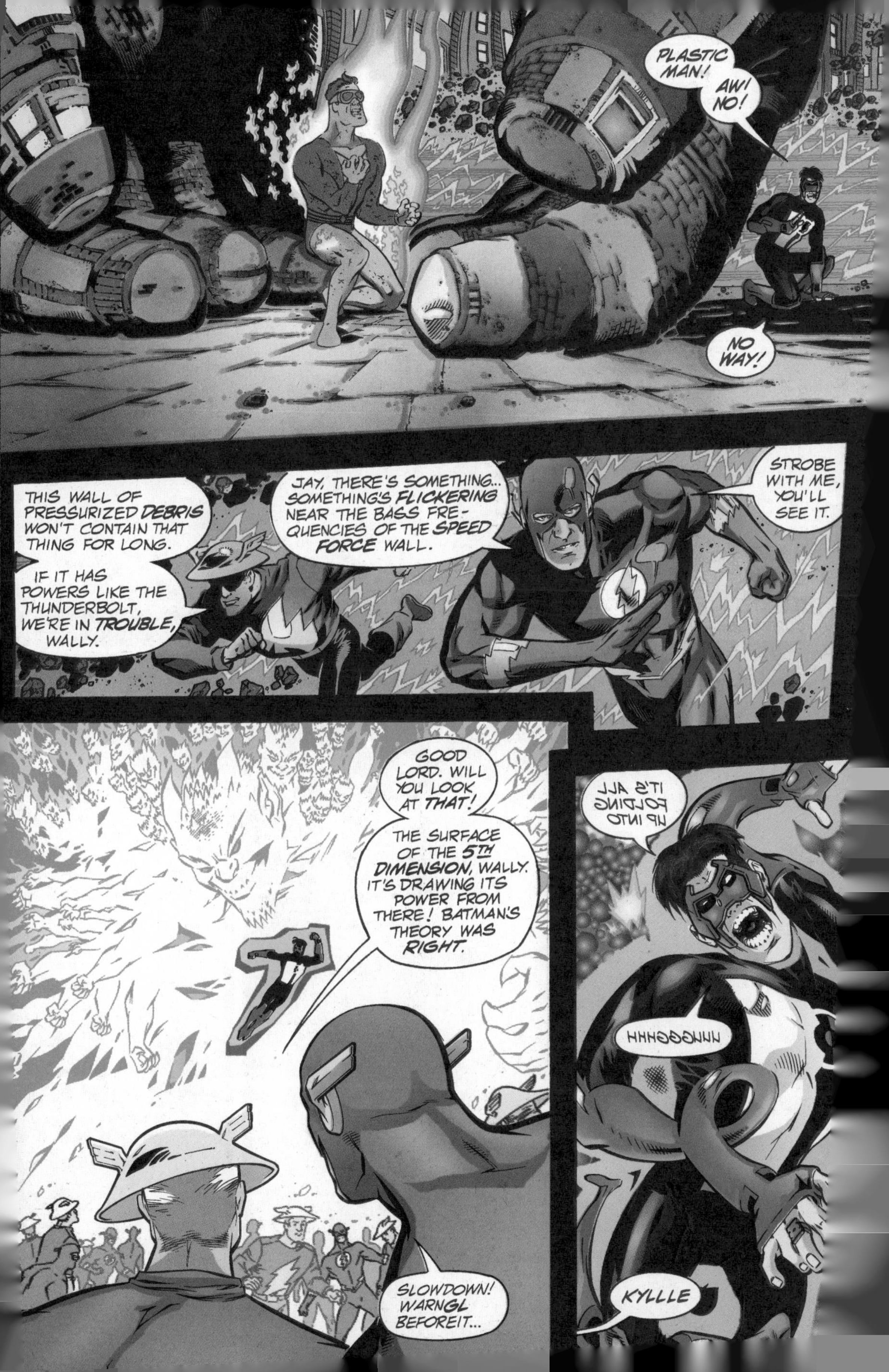
PLASTIC MAN!
AW! NO!
NO WAY!
THIS WALL OF PRESSURIZED DEBRIS WON'T CONTAIN THAT THING FOR LONG.
IF IT HAS POWERS LIKE THE THUNDERBOLT, WE'RE IN TROUBLE, WALLY.
JAY, THERE'S SOMETHING... SOMETHING'S FLICKERING NEAR THE BASS FRE-QUENCIES OF THE SPEED FORCE WALL.
STROBE WITH ME, YOU'LL SEE IT.
GOOD LORD. WILL YOU LOOK AT THAT!
THE SURFACE OF THE 5TH DIMENSION, WALLY. IT'S DRAWING ITS POWER FROM THERE! BATMAN'S THEORY WAS RIGHT.
SLOWDOWN! WARNGL BEFOREIT...
IT'S ALL FOLDING UP INTO
UNNGGHHH
KYLLLE

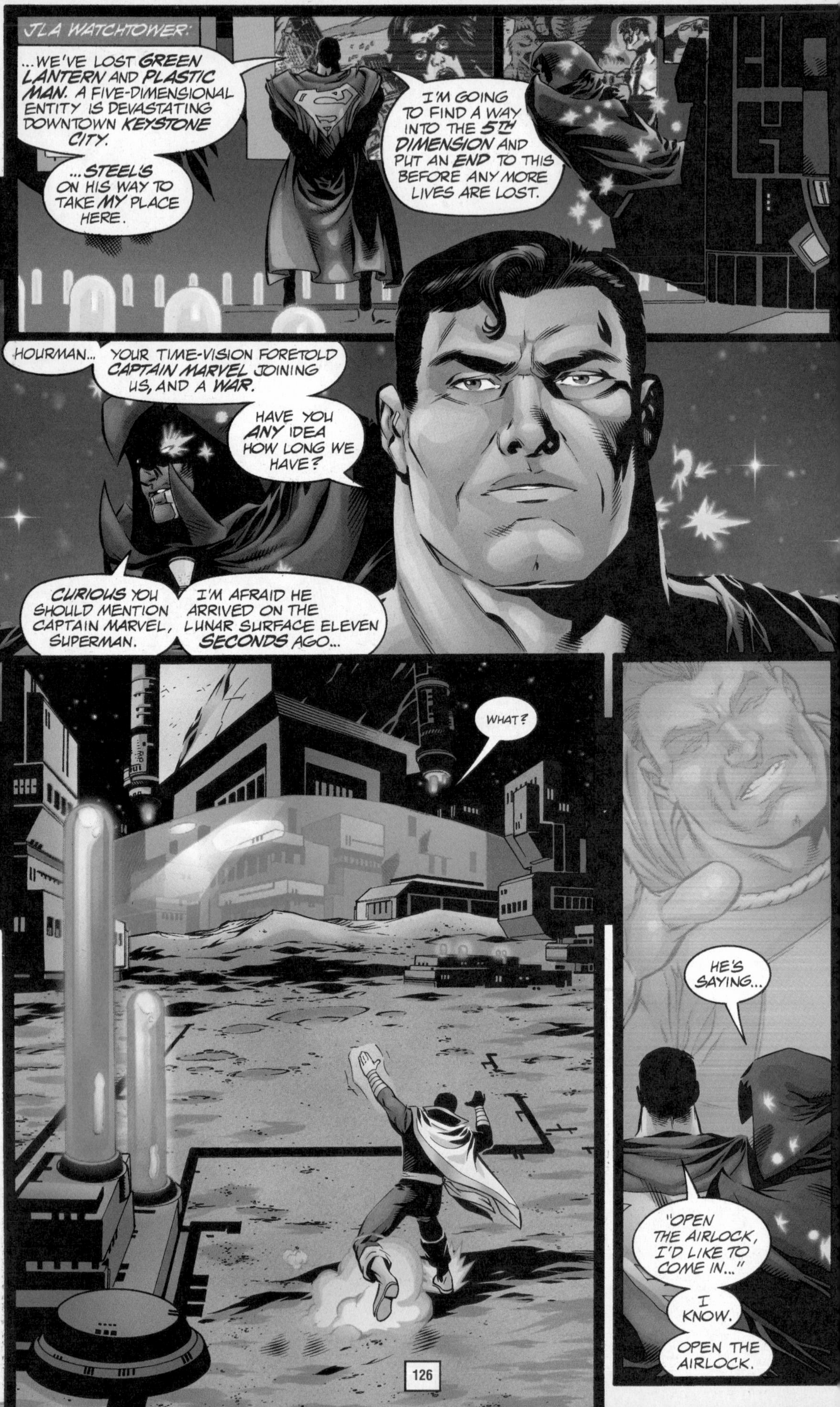
JLA WATCHTOWER:
...WE'VE LOST GREEN LANTERN AND PLASTIC MAN. A FIVE-DIMENSIONAL ENTITY IS DEVASTATING DOWNTOWN KEYSTONE CITY.
...STEEL'S ON HIS WAY TO TAKE MY PLACE HERE.
I'M GOING TO FIND A WAY INTO THE 5TH DIMENSION AND PUT AN END TO THIS BEFORE ANY MORE LIVES ARE LOST.
HOURMAN...
YOUR TIME-VISION FORETOLD CAPTAIN MARVEL JOINING US, AND A WAR.
HAVE YOU ANY IDEA HOW LONG WE HAVE?
CURIOUS YOU SHOULD MENTION CAPTAIN MARVEL, SUPERMAN.
I'M AFRAID HE ARRIVED ON THE LUNAR SURFACE ELEVEN SECONDS AGO...
WHAT?
HE'S SAYING...
"OPEN THE AIRLOCK, I'D LIKE TO COME IN..."
I KNOW.
OPEN THE AIRLOCK.

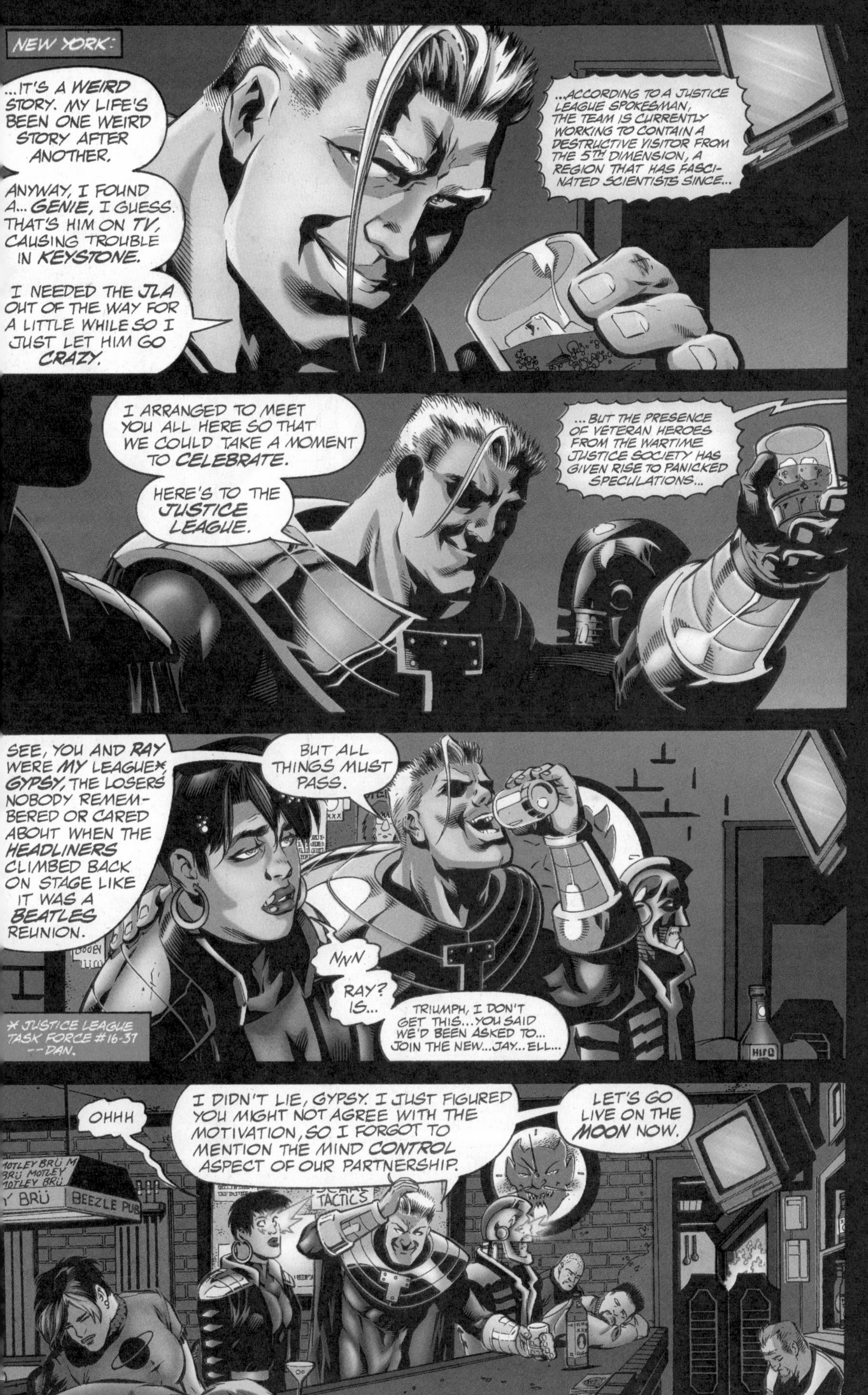
NEW YORK:
...IT'S A WEIRD STORY. MY LIFE'S BEEN ONE WEIRD STORY AFTER ANOTHER.
ANYWAY, I FOUND A... GENIE, I GUESS. THAT'S HIM ON TV, CAUSING TROUBLE IN KEYSTONE.
I NEEDED THE JLA OUT OF THE WAY FOR A LITTLE WHILE SO I JUST LET HIM GO CRAZY.
...ACCORDING TO A JUSTICE LEAGUE SPOKESMAN, THE TEAM IS CURRENTLY WORKING TO CONTAIN A DESTRUCTIVE VISITOR FROM THE 5TH DIMENSION, A REGION THAT HAS FASCI-NATED SCIENTISTS SINCE...
I ARRANGED TO MEET YOU ALL HERE SO THAT WE COULD TAKE A MOMENT TO CELEBRATE.
HERE'S TO THE JUSTICE LEAGUE.
...BUT THE PRESENCE OF VETERAN HEROES FROM THE WARTIME JUSTICE SOCIETY HAS GIVEN RISE TO PANICKED SPECULATIONS...
SEE, YOU AND RAY WERE MY LEAGUE*, GYPSY, THE LOSERS NOBODY REMEM-BERED OR CARED ABOUT WHEN THE HEADLINERS CLIMBED BACK ON STAGE LIKE IT WAS A BEATLES REUNION.
BUT ALL THINGS MUST PASS.
NNN
RAY? IS...
TRIUMPH, I DON'T GET THIS... YOU SAID WE'D BEEN ASKED TO... JOIN THE NEW... JAY... ELL...
* JUSTICE LEAGUE TASK FORCE #16-37 --DAN.
OHHH
I DIDN'T LIE, GYPSY. I JUST FIGURED YOU MIGHT NOT AGREE WITH THE MOTIVATION, SO I FORGOT TO MENTION THE MIND CONTROL ASPECT OF OUR PARTNERSHIP.
LET'S GO LIVE ON THE MOON NOW.
MOTLEY BRÜ MOTLEY BRÜ MOTLEY BRÜ
BEEZLE PUB
SCARE TACTICS

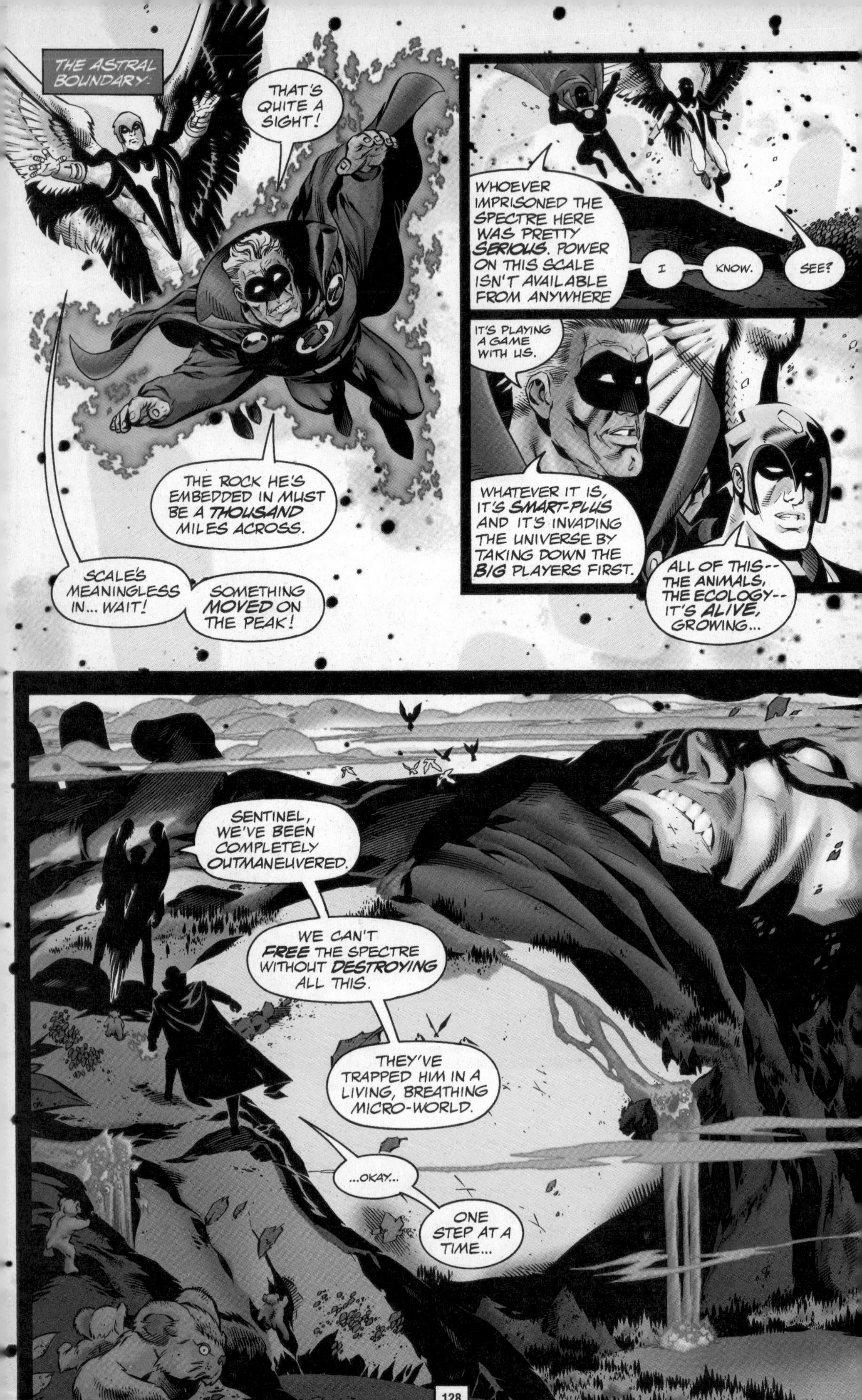
THE ASTRAL BOUNDARY:
THAT'S QUITE A SIGHT!
THE ROCK HE'S EMBEDDED IN MUST BE A THOUSAND MILES ACROSS.
SCALE'S MEANINGLESS IN... WAIT!
SOMETHING MOVED ON THE PEAK!
WHOEVER IMPRISONED THE SPECTRE HERE WAS PRETTY SERIOUS. POWER ON THIS SCALE ISN'T AVAILABLE FROM ANYWHERE
I
KNOW.
SEE?
IT'S PLAYING A GAME WITH US.
WHATEVER IT IS, IT'S SMART-PLUS AND IT'S INVADING THE UNIVERSE BY TAKING DOWN THE BIG PLAYERS FIRST.
ALL OF THIS-- THE ANIMALS, THE ECOLOGY-- IT'S ALIVE, GROWING...
SENTINEL, WE'VE BEEN COMPLETELY OUTMANEUVERED.
WE CAN'T FREE THE SPECTRE WITHOUT DESTROYING ALL THIS.
THEY'VE TRAPPED HIM IN A LIVING, BREATHING MICRO-WORLD.
...OKAY...
ONE STEP AT A TIME...

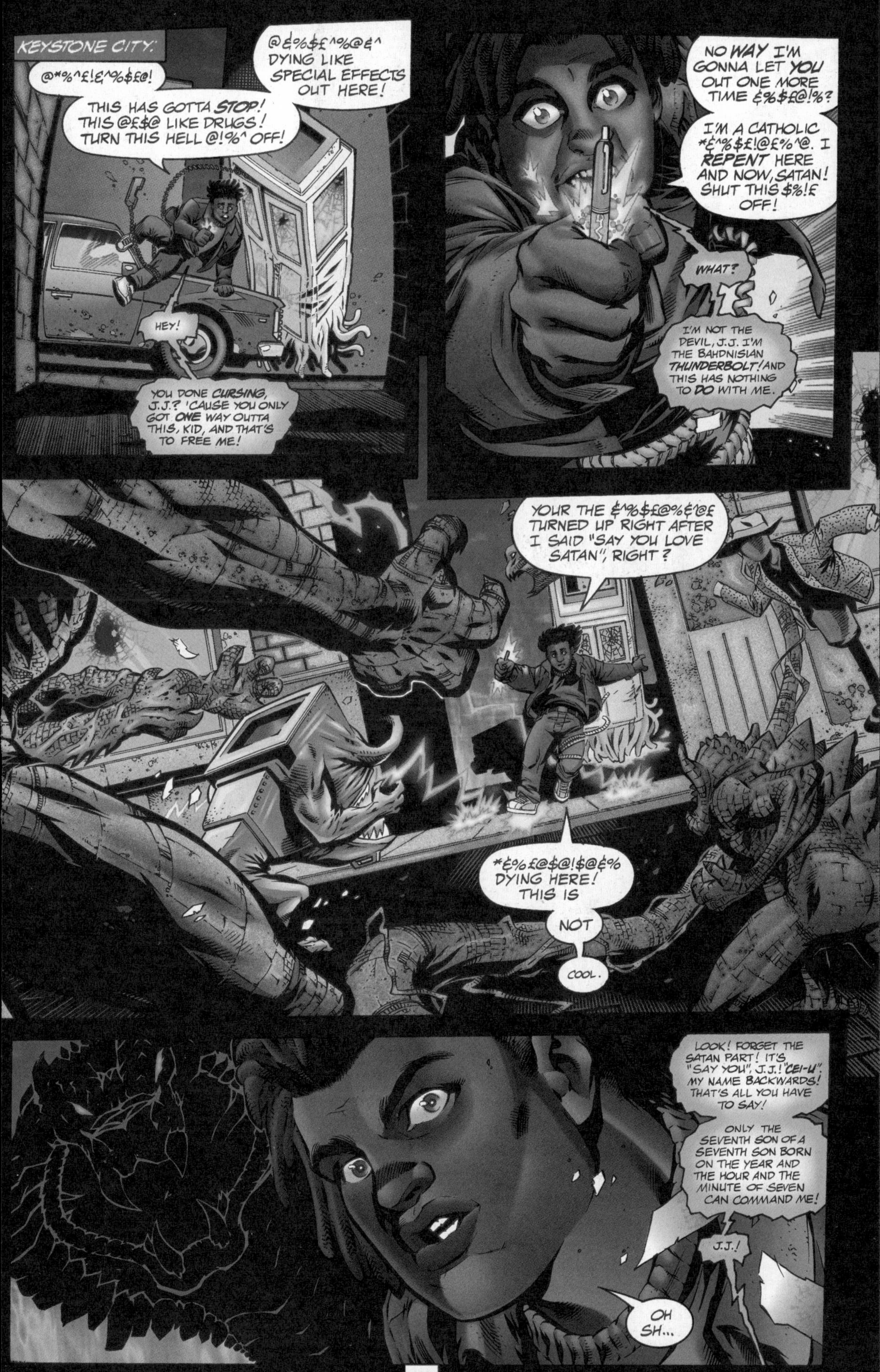
KEYSTONE CITY:
@*%^£!£^%$£@!
THIS HAS GOTTA STOP! THIS @£$@ LIKE DRUGS! TURN THIS HELL @!%^ OFF!
@£%$£^%@£^ DYING LIKE SPECIAL EFFECTS OUT HERE!
HEY!
YOU DONE CURSING, J.J.? 'CAUSE YOU ONLY GOT ONE WAY OUTTA THIS, KID, AND THAT'S TO FREE ME!
NO WAY I'M GONNA LET YOU OUT ONE MORE TIME £%$£@!%?
I'M A CATHOLIC *£^%$£!@£%^@. I REPENT HERE AND NOW, SATAN! SHUT THIS $%!£ OFF!
WHAT?
I'M NOT THE DEVIL, J.J. I'M THE BAHDNISIAN THUNDERBOLT! AND THIS HAS NOTHING TO DO WITH ME.
YOUR THE £^%$£@%£^@£ TURNED UP RIGHT AFTER I SAID "SAY YOU LOVE SATAN", RIGHT?
*£%£@$@!$@£% DYING HERE! THIS IS
NOT
COOL.
LOOK! FORGET THE SATAN PART! IT'S "SAY YOU", J.J.! "CEI-U". MY NAME BACKWARDS! THAT'S ALL YOU HAVE TO SAY!
ONLY THE SEVENTH SON OF A SEVENTH SON BORN ON THE YEAR AND THE HOUR AND THE MINUTE OF SEVEN CAN COMMAND ME!
J.J.!
OH SH...

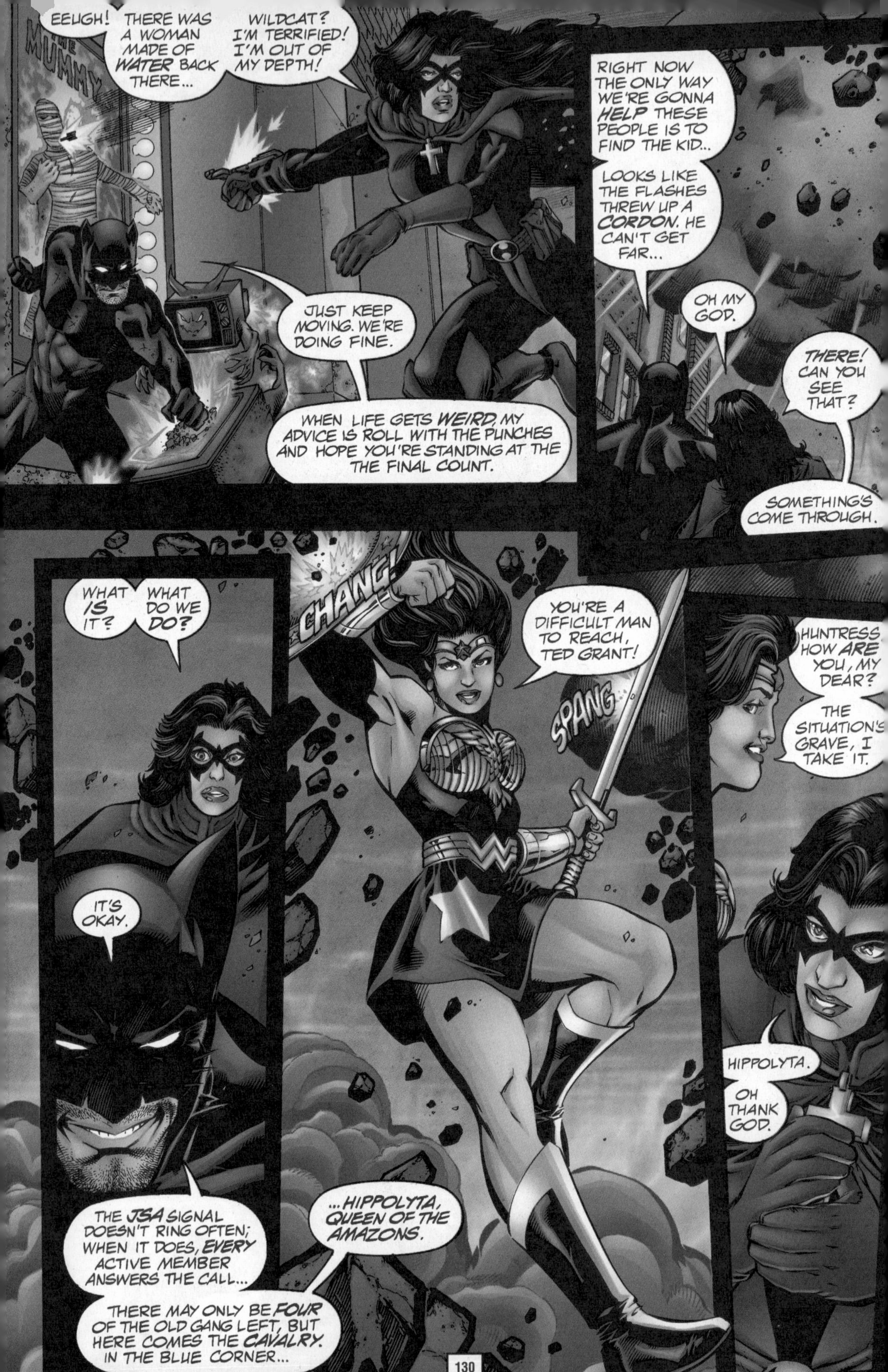

EEUGH!
THERE WAS A WOMAN MADE OF WATER BACK THERE...
WILDCAT? I'M TERRIFIED! I'M OUT OF MY DEPTH!
JUST KEEP MOVING. WE'RE DOING FINE.
WHEN LIFE GETS WEIRD, MY ADVICE IS ROLL WITH THE PUNCHES AND HOPE YOU'RE STANDING AT THE THE FINAL COUNT.
RIGHT NOW THE ONLY WAY WE'RE GONNA HELP THESE PEOPLE IS TO FIND THE KID...
LOOKS LIKE THE FLASHES THREW UP A CORDON. HE CAN'T GET FAR...
OH MY GOD.
THERE! CAN YOU SEE THAT?
SOMETHING'S COME THROUGH.
WHAT IS IT?
WHAT DO WE DO?
IT'S OKAY.
THE JSA SIGNAL DOESN'T RING OFTEN; WHEN IT DOES, EVERY ACTIVE MEMBER ANSWERS THE CALL...
THERE MAY ONLY BE FOUR OF THE OLD GANG LEFT, BUT HERE COMES THE CAVALRY. IN THE BLUE CORNER...
...HIPPOLYTA, QUEEN OF THE AMAZONS.
CHANG!
YOU'RE A DIFFICULT MAN TO REACH, TED GRANT!
SPANG
HUNTRESS HOW ARE YOU, MY DEAR?
THE SITUATION'S GRAVE, I TAKE IT.
HIPPOLYTA.
OH THANK GOD.

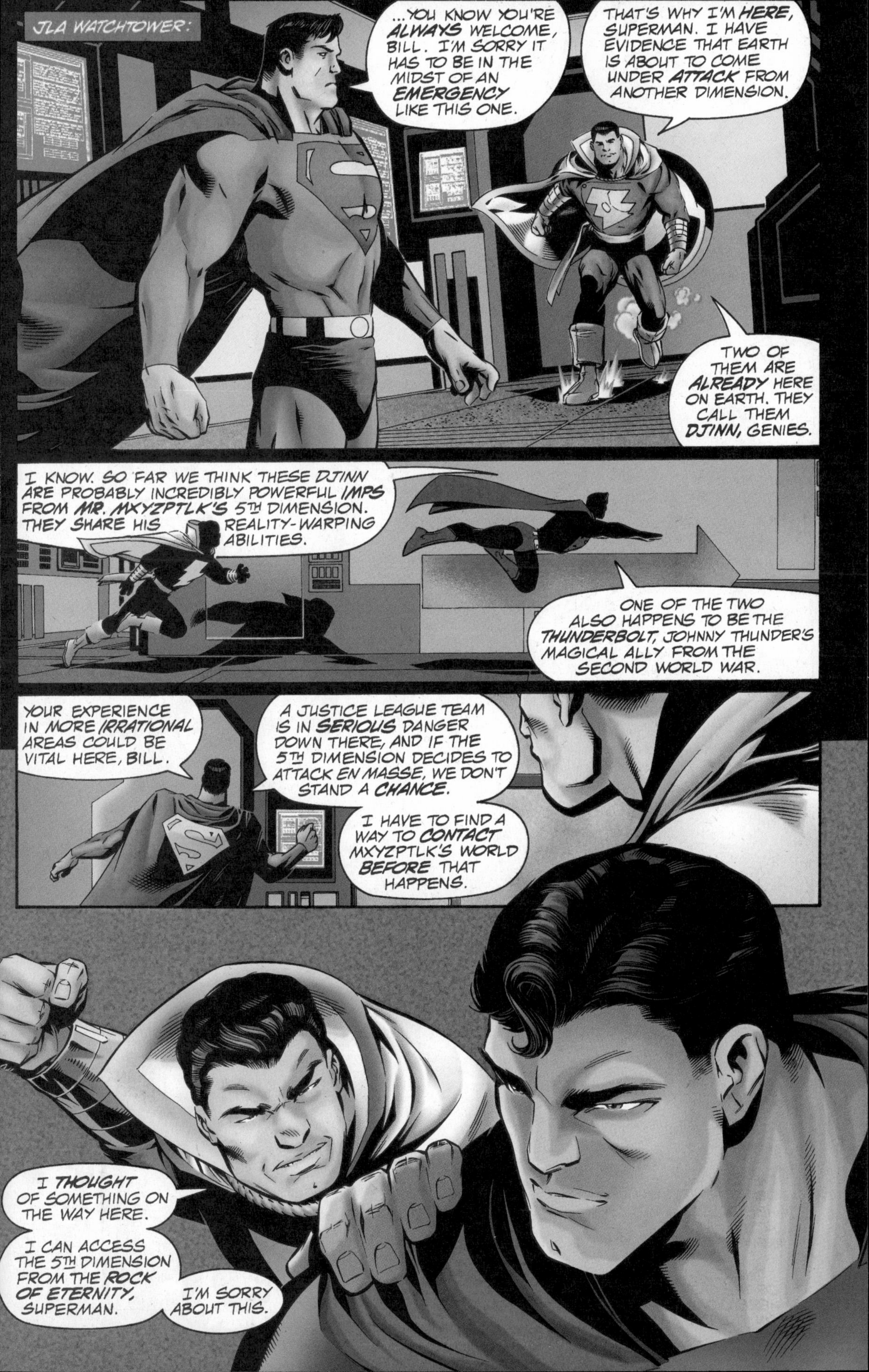
JLA WATCHTOWER:
...YOU KNOW YOU'RE ALWAYS WELCOME, BILL. I'M SORRY IT HAS TO BE IN THE MIDST OF AN EMERGENCY LIKE THIS ONE.
THAT'S WHY I'M HERE, SUPERMAN. I HAVE EVIDENCE THAT EARTH IS ABOUT TO COME UNDER ATTACK FROM ANOTHER DIMENSION.
TWO OF THEM ARE ALREADY HERE ON EARTH. THEY CALL THEM DJINN, GENIES.
I KNOW. SO FAR WE THINK THESE DJINN ARE PROBABLY INCREDIBLY POWERFUL IMPS FROM MR. MXYZPTLK'S 5TH DIMENSION. THEY SHARE HIS REALITY-WARPING ABILITIES.
ONE OF THE TWO ALSO HAPPENS TO BE THE THUNDERBOLT, JOHNNY THUNDER'S MAGICAL ALLY FROM THE SECOND WORLD WAR.
YOUR EXPERIENCE IN MORE IRRATIONAL AREAS COULD BE VITAL HERE, BILL.
A JUSTICE LEAGUE TEAM IS IN SERIOUS DANGER DOWN THERE, AND IF THE 5TH DIMENSION DECIDES TO ATTACK EN MASSE, WE DON'T STAND A CHANCE.
I HAVE TO FIND A WAY TO CONTACT MXYZPTLK'S WORLD BEFORE THAT HAPPENS.
I THOUGHT OF SOMETHING ON THE WAY HERE.
I CAN ACCESS THE 5TH DIMENSION FROM THE ROCK OF ETERNITY, SUPERMAN.
I'M SORRY ABOUT THIS.

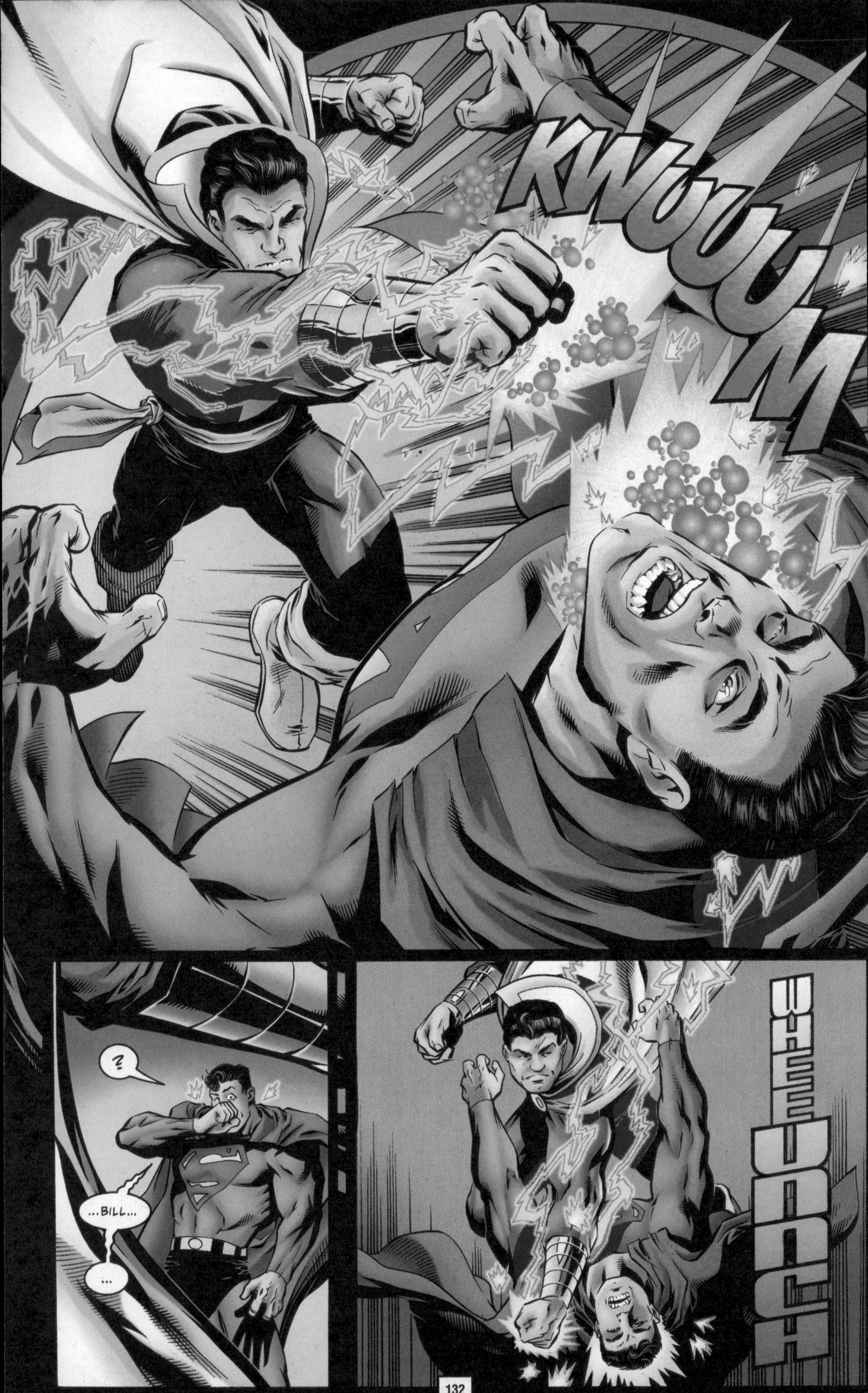
KWOOOM
?
...BILL...
...
WHEEUNCH

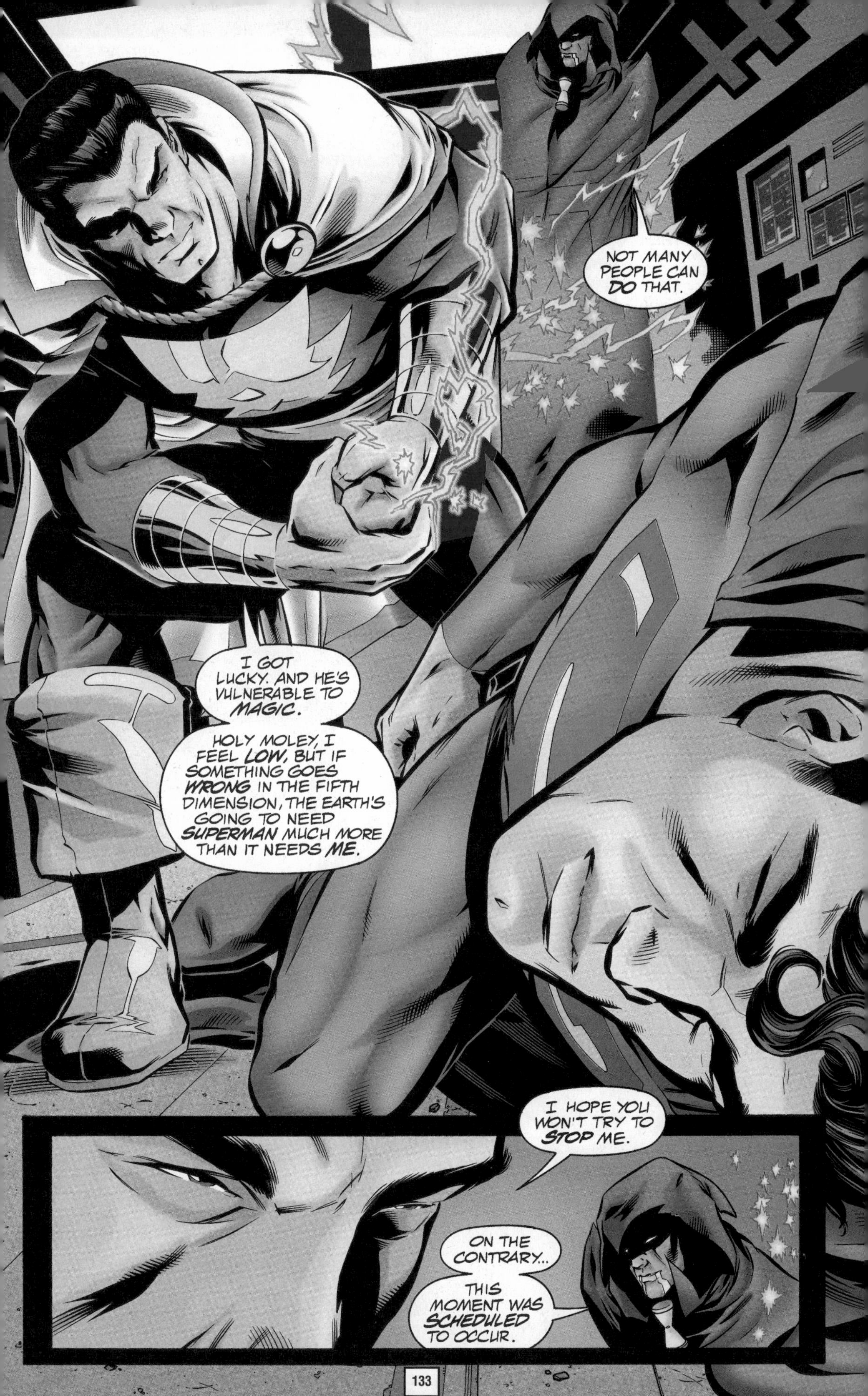
NOT MANY PEOPLE CAN DO THAT.
I GOT LUCKY. AND HE'S VULNERABLE TO MAGIC.
HOLY MOLEY, I FEEL LOW, BUT IF SOMETHING GOES WRONG IN THE FIFTH DIMENSION, THE EARTH'S GOING TO NEED SUPERMAN MUCH MORE THAN IT NEEDS ME.
I HOPE YOU WON'T TRY TO STOP ME.
ON THE CONTRARY...
THIS MOMENT WAS SCHEDULED TO OCCUR.

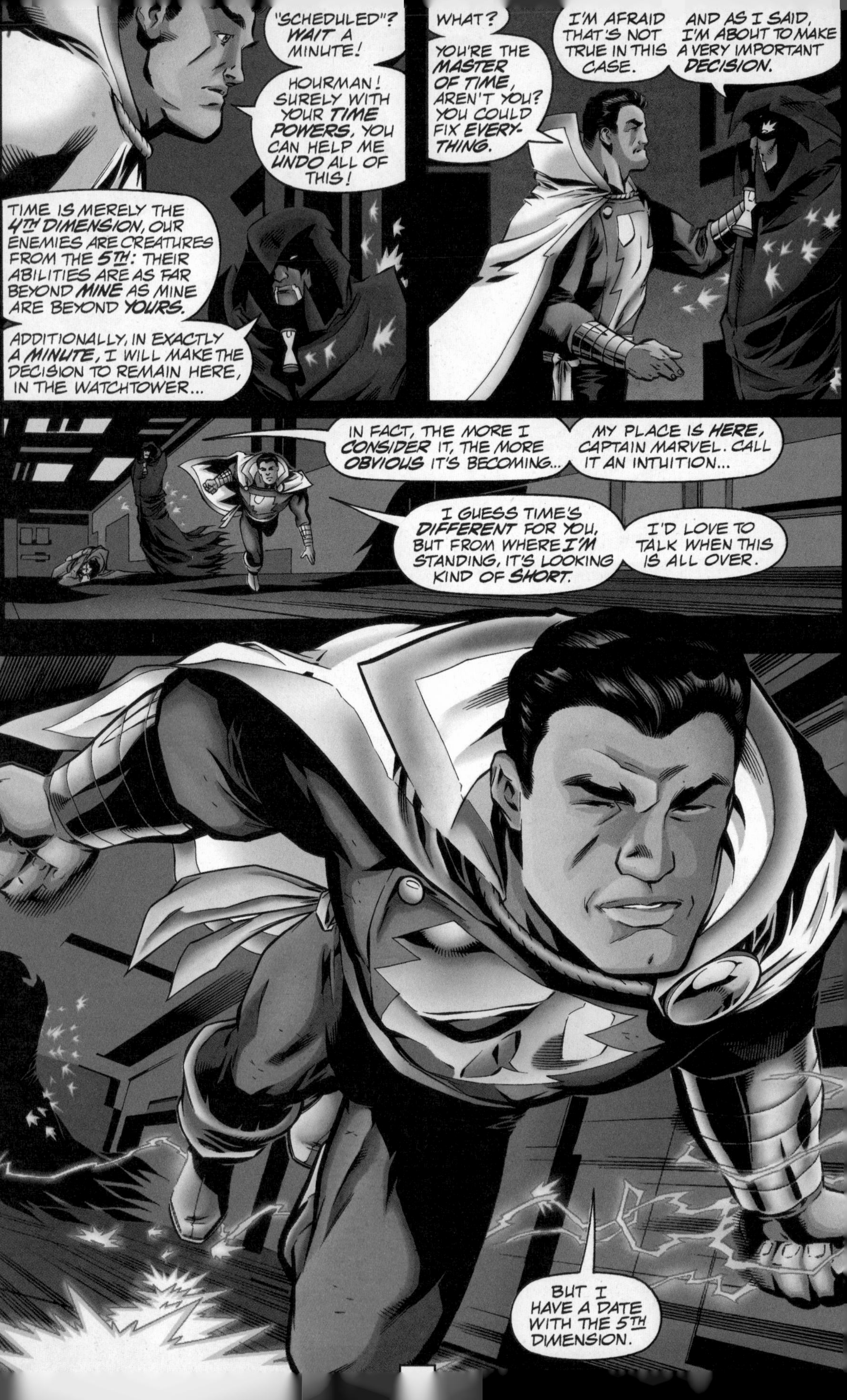
"SCHEDULED"? WAIT A MINUTE!
HOURMAN! SURELY WITH YOUR TIME POWERS, YOU CAN HELP ME UNDO ALL OF THIS!
TIME IS MERELY THE 4TH DIMENSION, OUR ENEMIES ARE CREATURES FROM THE 5TH: THEIR ABILITIES ARE AS FAR BEYOND MINE AS MINE ARE BEYOND YOURS.
ADDITIONALLY, IN EXACTLY A MINUTE, I WILL MAKE THE DECISION TO REMAIN HERE, IN THE WATCHTOWER...
WHAT?
YOU'RE THE MASTER OF TIME, AREN'T YOU? YOU COULD FIX EVERYTHING.
I'M AFRAID THAT'S NOT TRUE IN THIS CASE.
AND AS I SAID, I'M ABOUT TO MAKE A VERY IMPORTANT DECISION.
IN FACT, THE MORE I CONSIDER IT, THE MORE OBVIOUS IT'S BECOMING...
MY PLACE IS HERE, CAPTAIN MARVEL. CALL IT AN INTUITION...
I GUESS TIME'S DIFFERENT FOR YOU, BUT FROM WHERE I'M STANDING, IT'S LOOKING KIND OF SHORT.
I'D LOVE TO TALK WHEN THIS IS ALL OVER.
BUT I HAVE A DATE WITH THE 5TH DIMENSION.

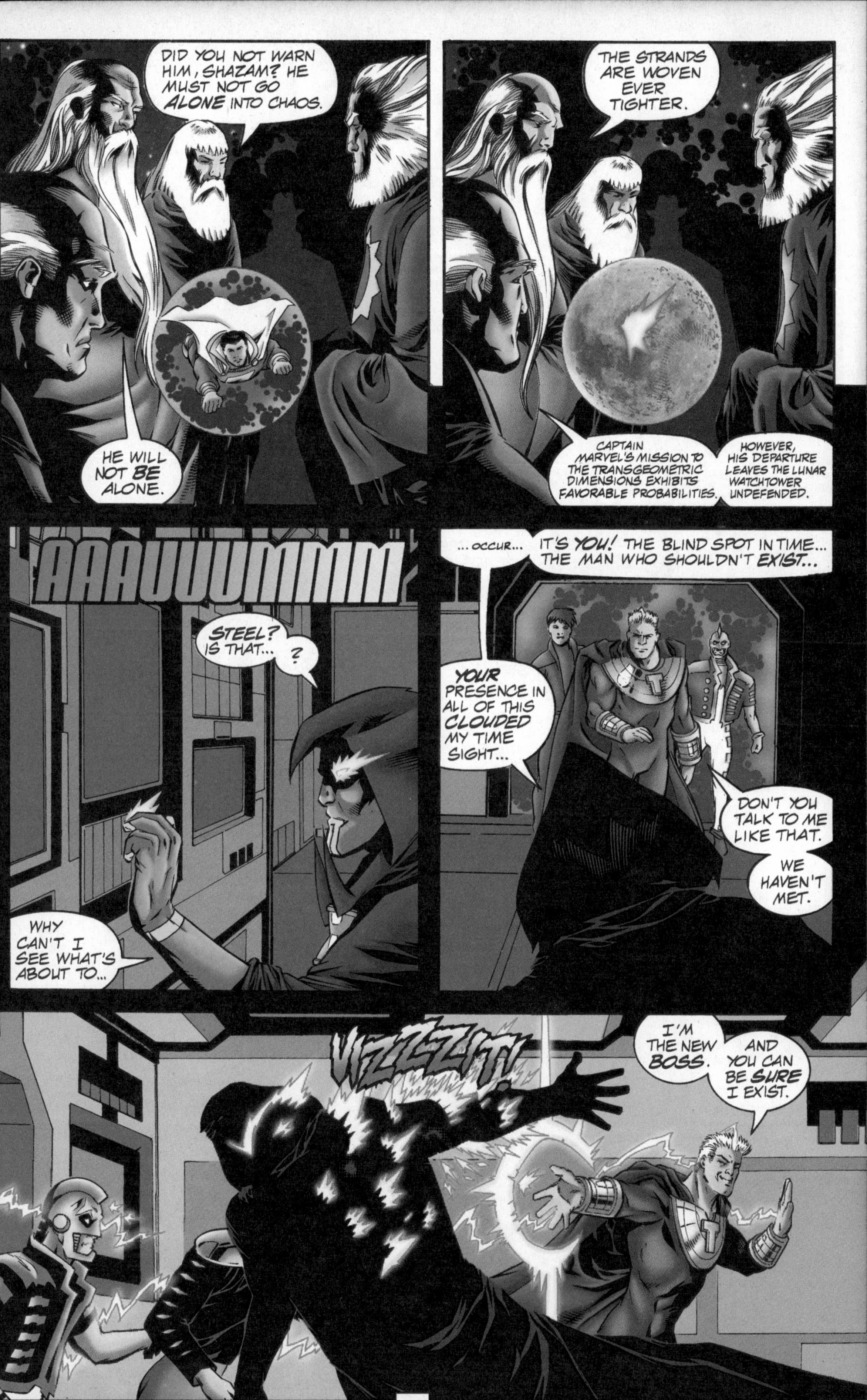

DID YOU NOT WARN HIM, SHAZAM? HE MUST NOT GO ALONE INTO CHAOS.
HE WILL NOT BE ALONE.
THE STRANDS ARE WOVEN EVER TIGHTER.
CAPTAIN MARVEL'S MISSION TO THE TRANSGEOMETRIC DIMENSIONS EXHIBITS FAVORABLE PROBABILITIES.
HOWEVER, HIS DEPARTURE LEAVES THE LUNAR WATCHTOWER UNDEFENDED.
AAAVVVUMMMM
STEEL? IS THAT... ?
WHY CAN'T I SEE WHAT'S ABOUT TO...
... OCCUR...
IT'S YOU! THE BLIND SPOT IN TIME... THE MAN WHO SHOULDN'T EXIST...
YOUR PRESENCE IN ALL OF THIS CLOUDED MY TIME SIGHT...
DON'T YOU TALK TO ME LIKE THAT.
WE HAVEN'T MET.
VIZZZZIT!
I'M THE NEW BOSS.
AND YOU CAN BE SURE I EXIST.

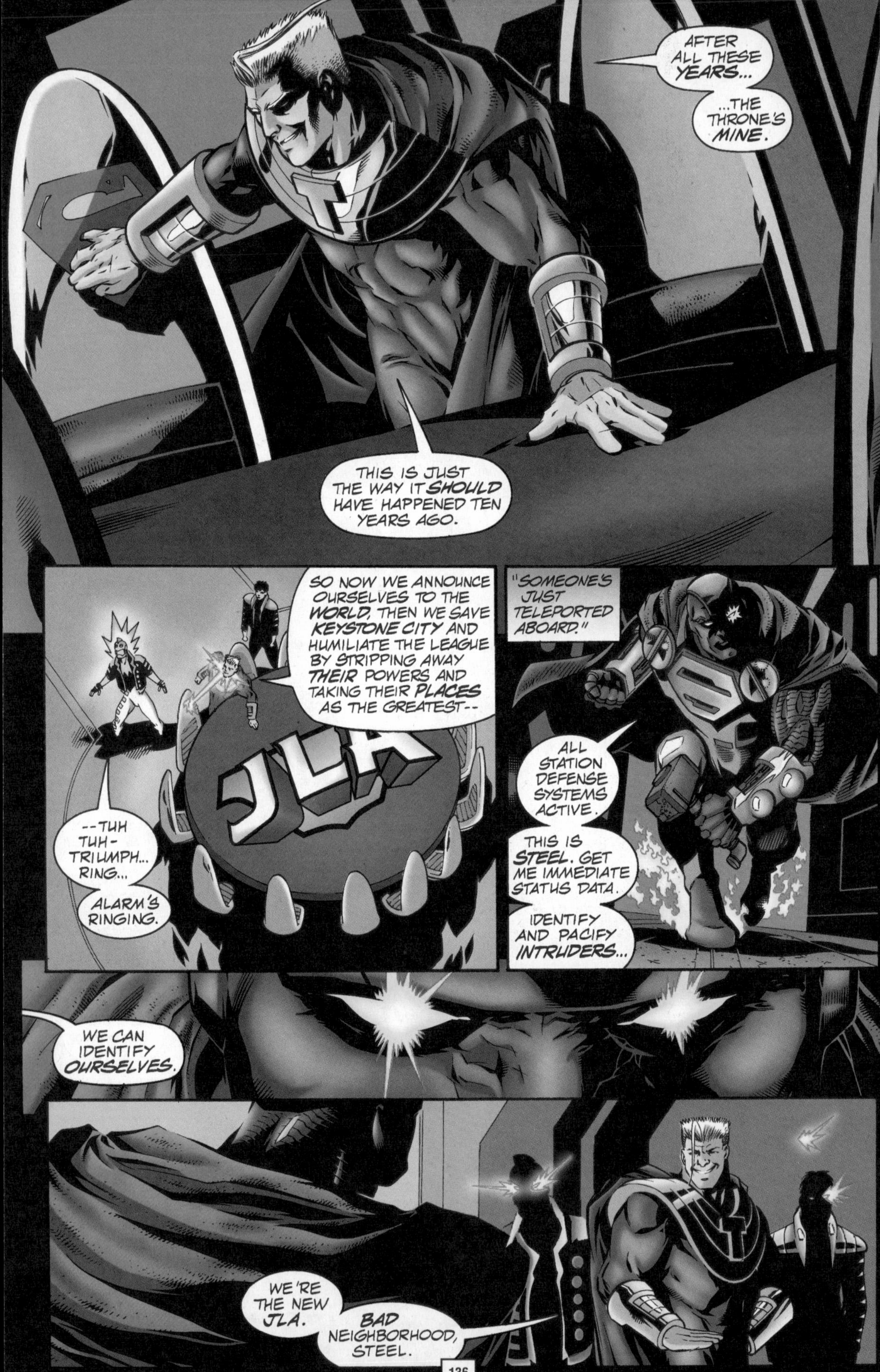
AFTER ALL THESE YEARS...
...THE THRONE'S MINE.
THIS IS JUST THE WAY IT SHOULD HAVE HAPPENED TEN YEARS AGO.
SO NOW WE ANNOUNCE OURSELVES TO THE WORLD, THEN WE SAVE KEYSTONE CITY AND HUMILIATE THE LEAGUE BY STRIPPING AWAY THEIR POWERS AND TAKING THEIR PLACES AS THE GREATEST--
JLA
--TUH TUH-TRIUMPH... RING...
ALARM'S RINGING.
"SOMEONE'S JUST TELEPORTED ABOARD."
ALL STATION DEFENSE SYSTEMS ACTIVE.
THIS IS STEEL. GET ME IMMEDIATE STATUS DATA.
IDENTIFY AND PACIFY INTRUDERS...
WE CAN IDENTIFY OURSELVES.
WE'RE THE NEW JLA.
BAD NEIGHBORHOOD, STEEL.

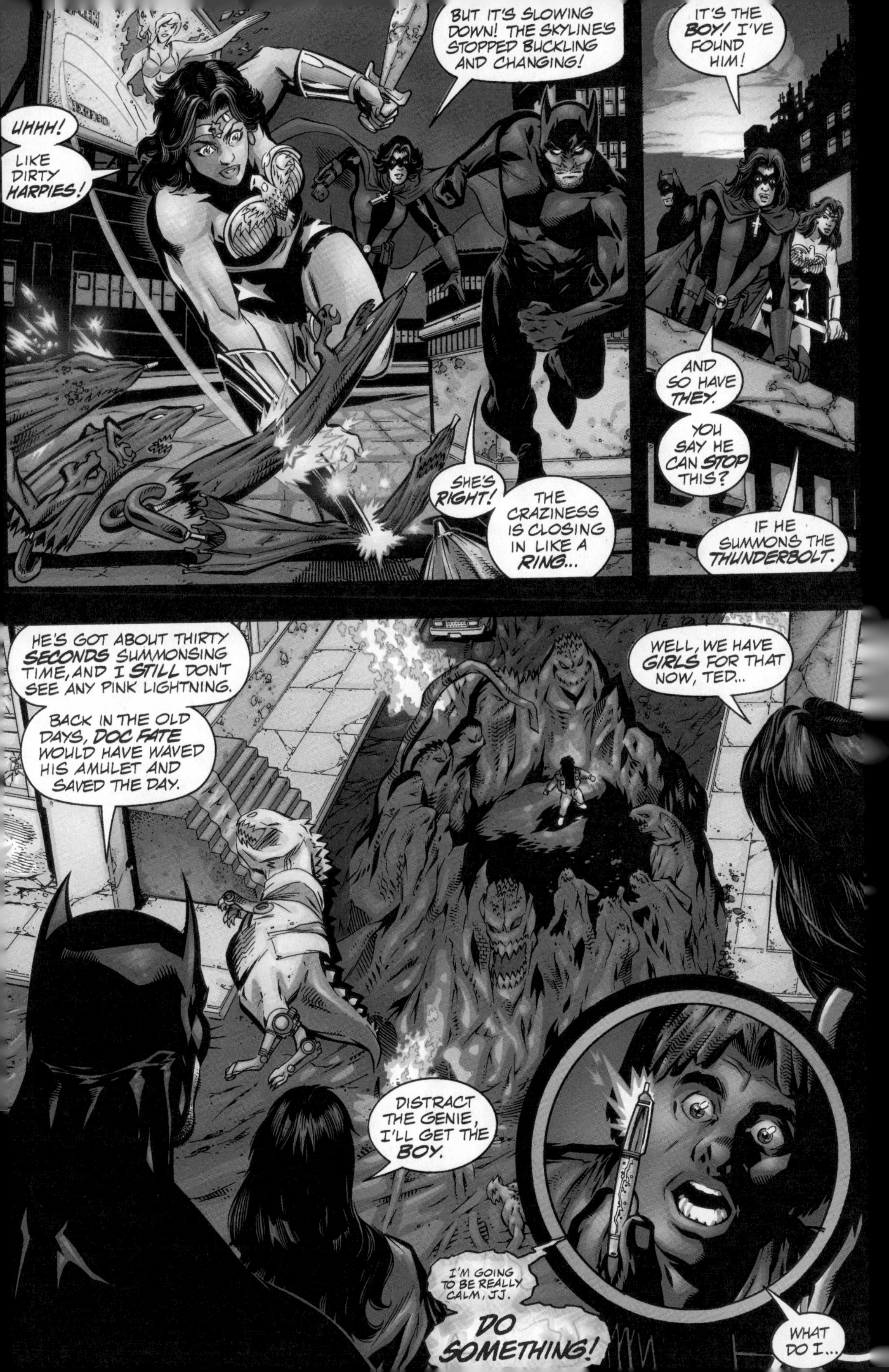
UHHH!
LIKE DIRTY HARPIES!
BUT IT'S SLOWING DOWN! THE SKYLINE'S STOPPED BUCKLING AND CHANGING!
SHE'S RIGHT!
THE CRAZINESS IS CLOSING IN LIKE A RING...
IT'S THE BOY! I'VE FOUND HIM!
AND SO HAVE THEY.
YOU SAY HE CAN STOP THIS?
IF HE SUMMONS THE THUNDERBOLT.
HE'S GOT ABOUT THIRTY SECONDS SUMMONSING TIME, AND I STILL DON'T SEE ANY PINK LIGHTNING.
BACK IN THE OLD DAYS, DOC FATE WOULD HAVE WAVED HIS AMULET AND SAVED THE DAY.
WELL, WE HAVE GIRLS FOR THAT NOW, TED...
DISTRACT THE GENIE, I'LL GET THE BOY.
I'M GOING TO BE REALLY CALM, JJ.
DO SOMETHING!
WHAT DO I...

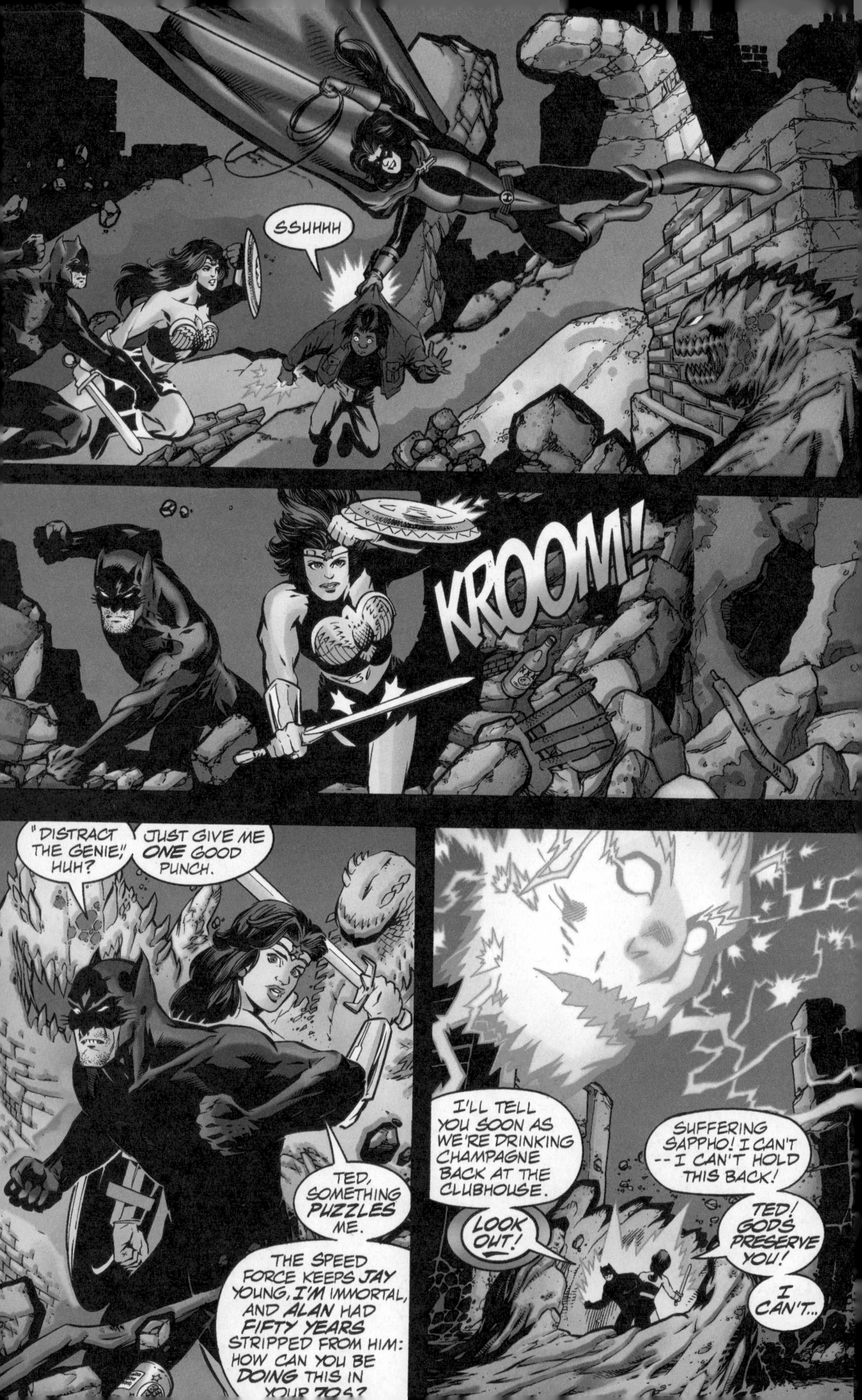
SSUHHH
KROOM!!
"DISTRACT THE GENIE," HUH?
JUST GIVE ME ONE GOOD PUNCH.
TED, SOMETHING PUZZLES ME.
THE SPEED FORCE KEEPS JAY YOUNG, I'M IMMORTAL, AND ALAN HAD FIFTY YEARS STRIPPED FROM HIM: HOW CAN YOU BE DOING THIS IN YOUR 70S?
I'LL TELL YOU SOON AS WE'RE DRINKING CHAMPAGNE BACK AT THE CLUBHOUSE.
LOOK OUT!
SUFFERING SAPPHO! I CAN'T -- I CAN'T HOLD THIS BACK!
TED! GODS PRESERVE YOU!
I CAN'T...

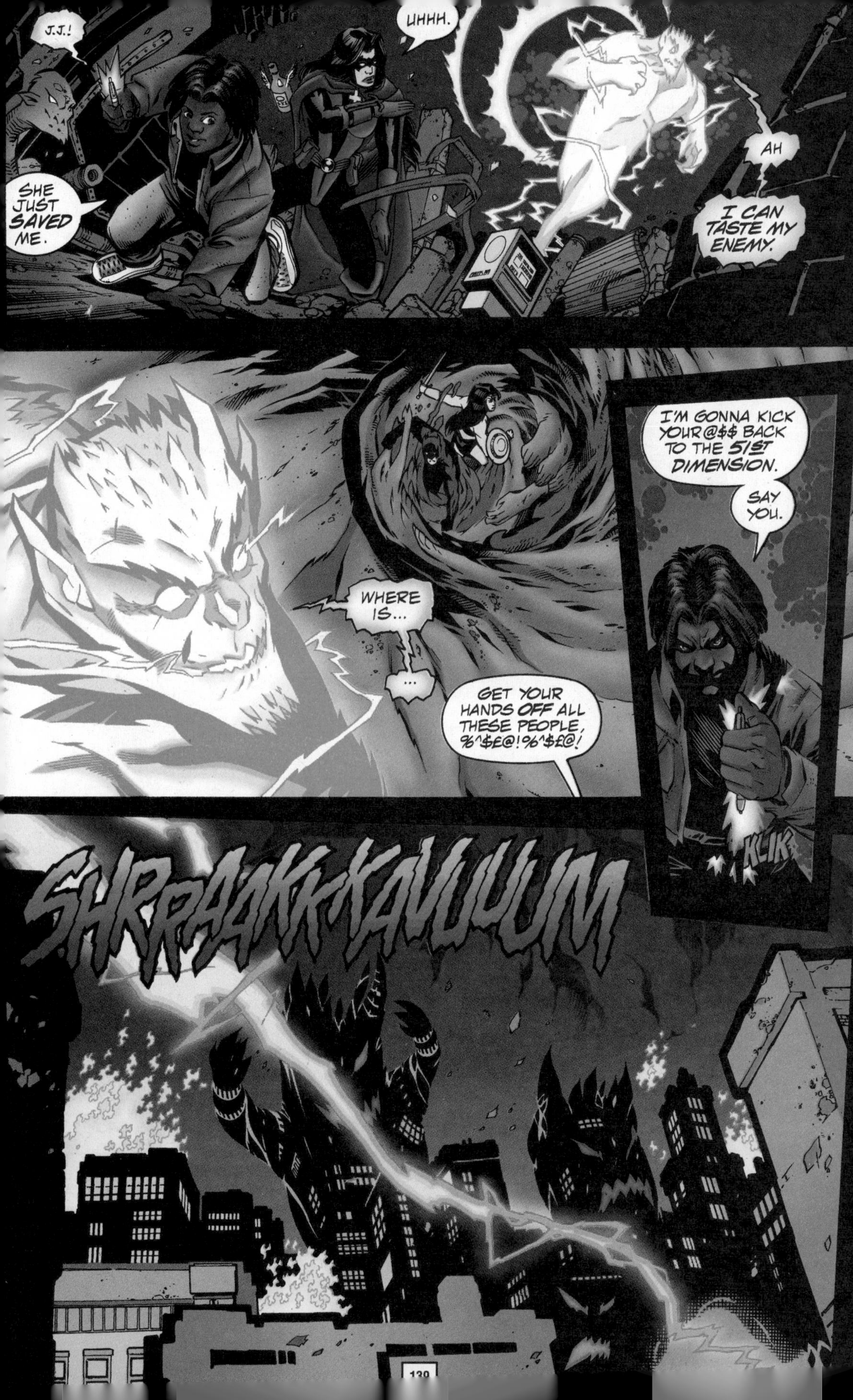
J.J.!
UHHH.
SHE JUST SAVED ME.
AH
I CAN TASTE MY ENEMY.
I'M GONNA KICK YOUR@$$ BACK TO THE 51ST DIMENSION.
SAY YOU.
WHERE IS...
...
GET YOUR HANDS OFF ALL THESE PEOPLE, %^$£@!%^$£@!
KLIK
SHRAAKK-KAVUUUM

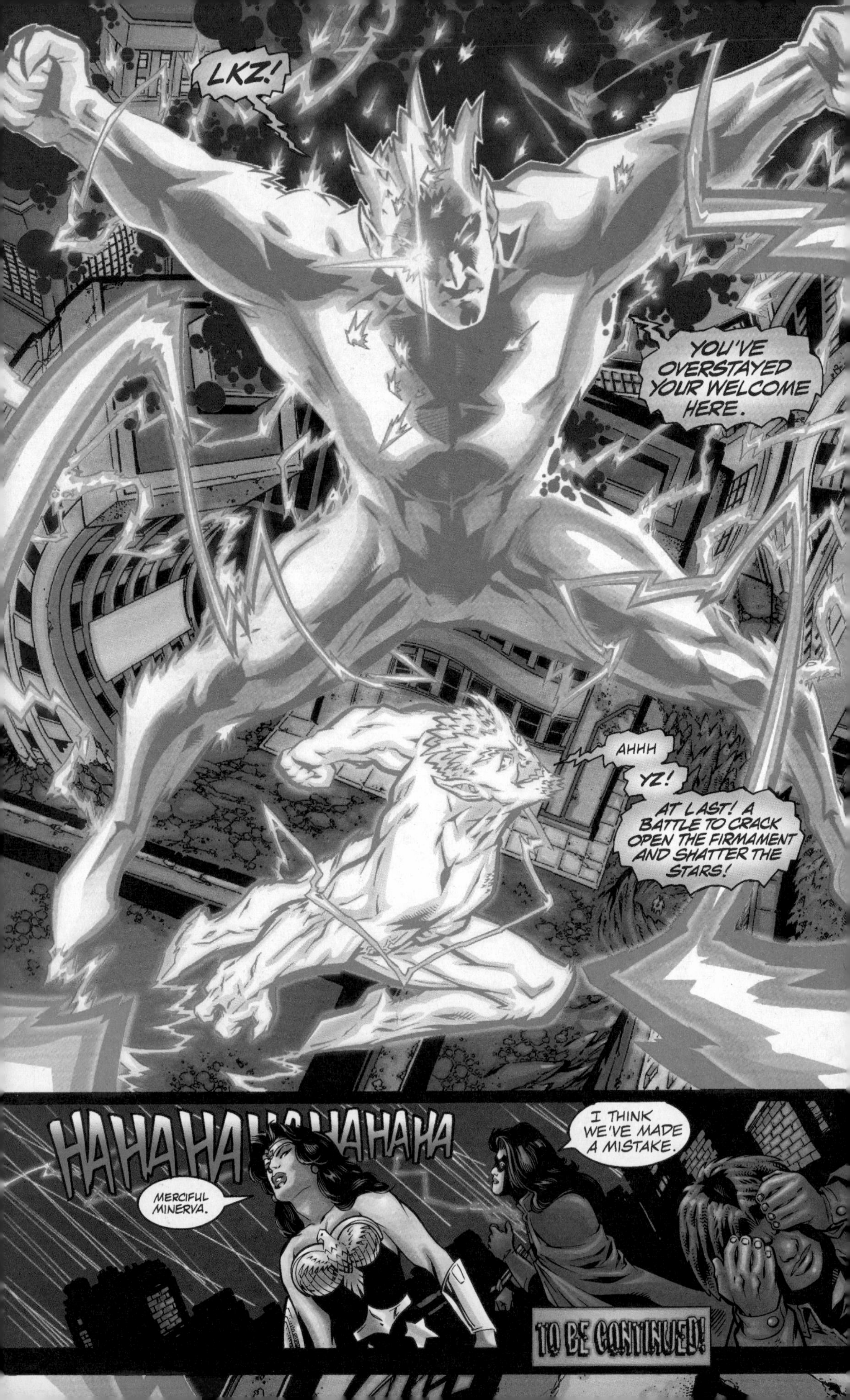
LKZ!
YOU'VE OVERSTAYED YOUR WELCOME HERE.
AHHH
YZ!
AT LAST! A BATTLE TO CRACK OPEN THE FIRMAMENT AND SHATTER THE STARS!
HAHAHAHAHAHAHAHA
MERCIFUL MINERVA.
I THINK WE'VE MADE A MISTAKE.
TO BE CONTINUED!

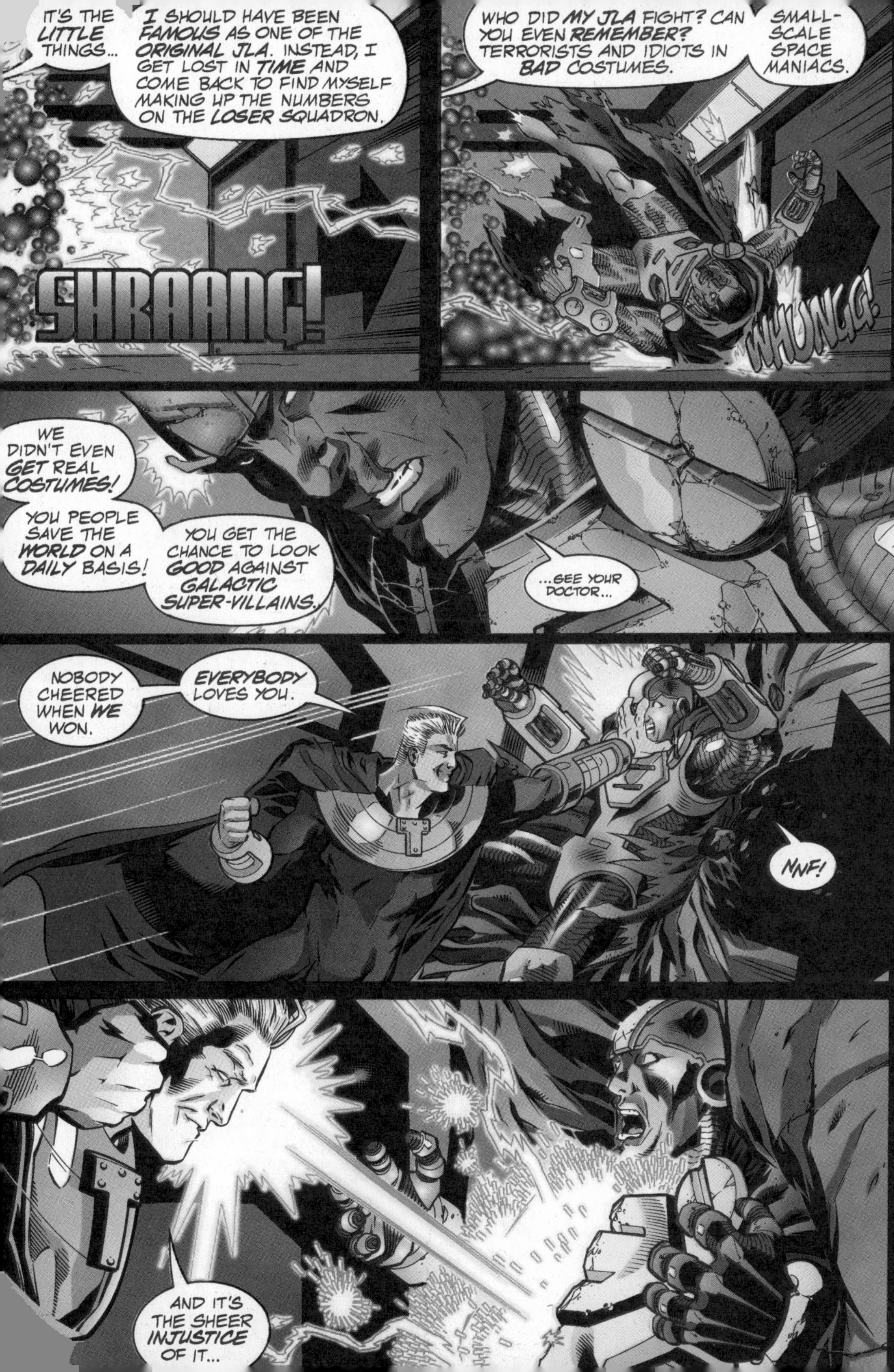
IT'S THE LITTLE THINGS...
I SHOULD HAVE BEEN FAMOUS AS ONE OF THE ORIGINAL JLA. INSTEAD, I GET LOST IN TIME AND COME BACK TO FIND MYSELF MAKING UP THE NUMBERS ON THE LOSER SQUADRON.
SHRAANG!
WHO DID MY JLA FIGHT? CAN YOU EVEN REMEMBER? TERRORISTS AND IDIOTS IN BAD COSTUMES.
SMALL-SCALE SPACE MANIACS.
WHUNGG!
WE DIDN'T EVEN GET REAL COSTUMES!
YOU PEOPLE SAVE THE WORLD ON A DAILY BASIS!
YOU GET THE CHANCE TO LOOK GOOD AGAINST GALACTIC SUPER-VILLAINS.
...SEE YOUR DOCTOR...
NOBODY CHEERED WHEN WE WON.
EVERYBODY LOVES YOU.
NNF!
AND IT'S THE SHEER INJUSTICE OF IT...

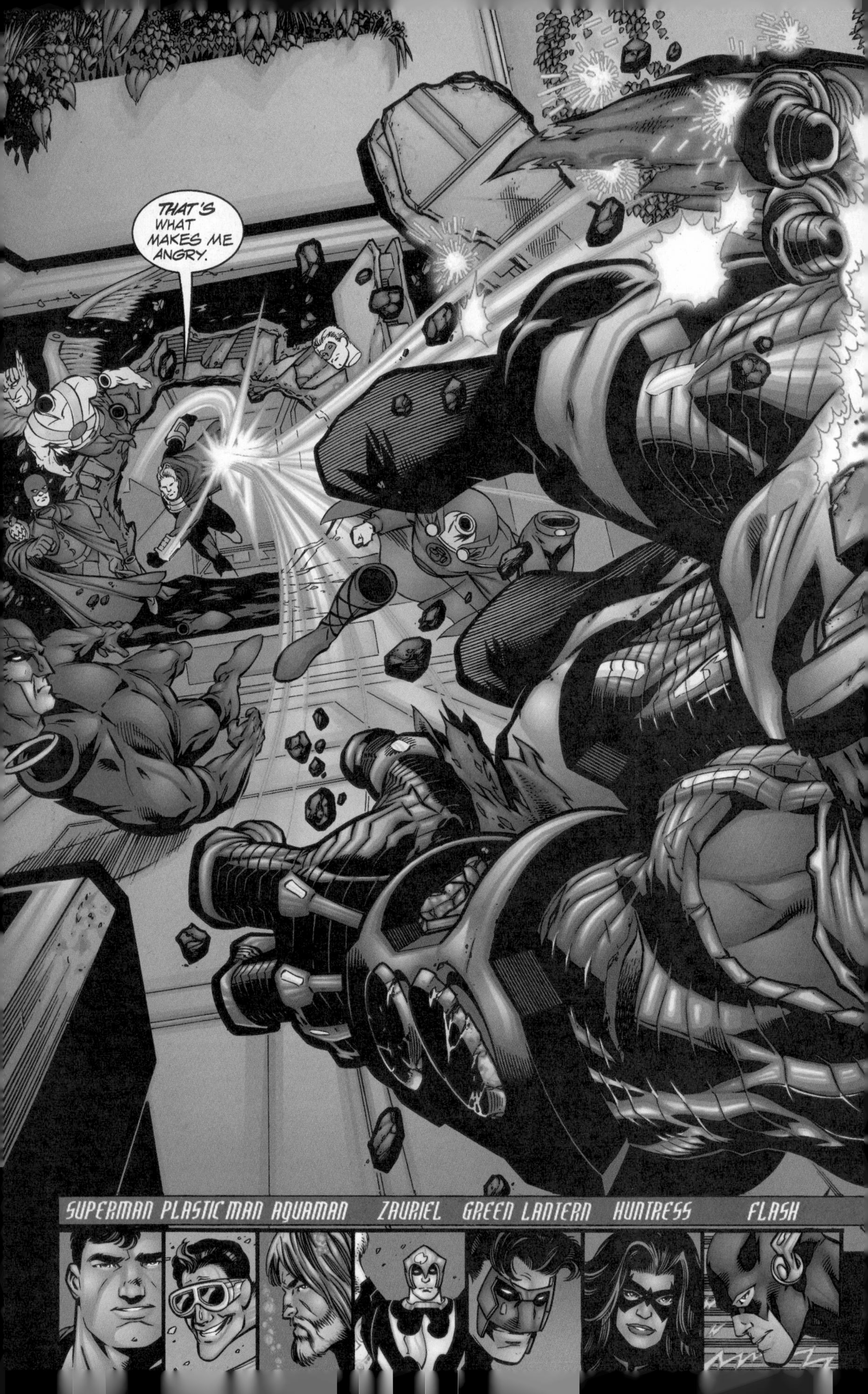
THAT'S WHAT MAKES ME ANGRY.
SUPERMAN
PLASTIC MAN
AQUAMAN
ZAURIEL
GREEN LANTERN
HUNTRESS
FLASH

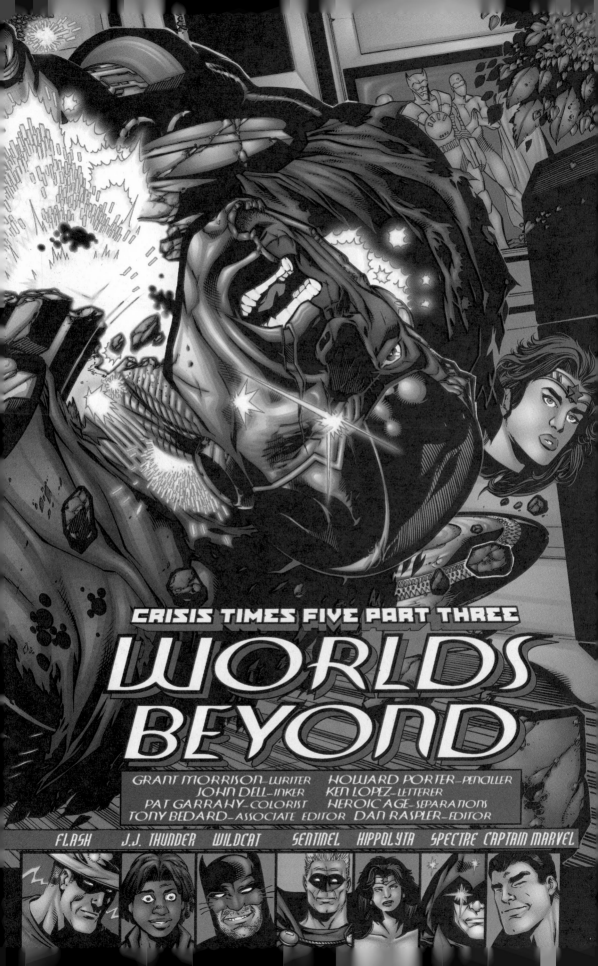

CRISIS TIMES FIVE PART THREE

WORLDS BEYOND

GRANT MORRISON—WRITER   HOWARD PORTER—PENCILLER
JOHN DELL—INKER   KEN LOPEZ—LETTERER
PAT GARRAHY—COLORIST   HEROIC AGE—SEPARATIONS
TONY BEDARD—ASSOCIATE EDITOR   DAN RASPLER—EDITOR

FLASH   J.J. THUNDER   WILDCAT   SENTINEL   HIPPOLYTA   SPECTRE   CAPTAIN MARVEL

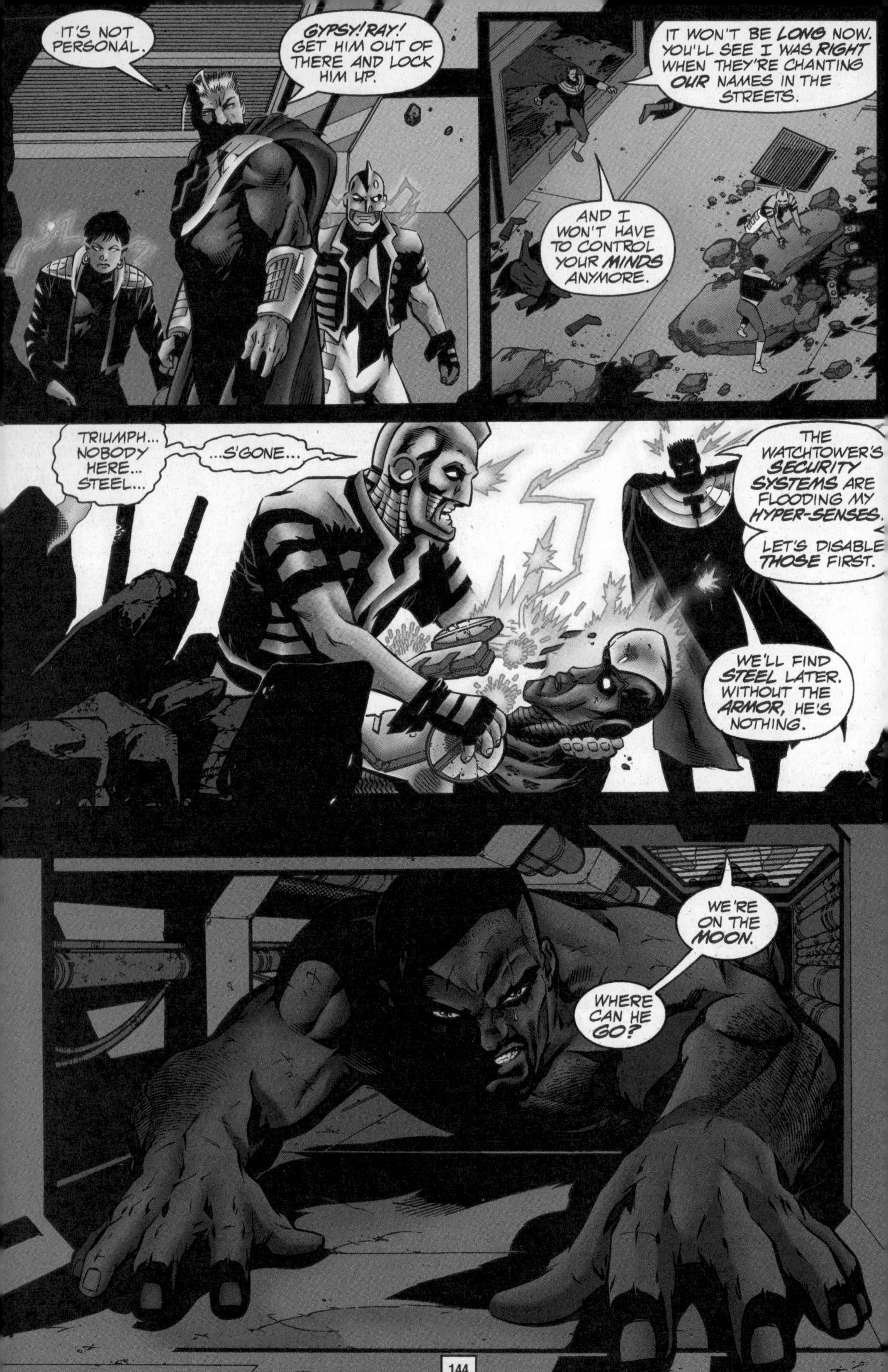
IT'S NOT PERSONAL.
GYPSY! RAY! GET HIM OUT OF THERE AND LOCK HIM UP.
IT WON'T BE LONG NOW. YOU'LL SEE I WAS RIGHT WHEN THEY'RE CHANTING OUR NAMES IN THE STREETS.
AND I WON'T HAVE TO CONTROL YOUR MINDS ANYMORE.
TRIUMPH... NOBODY HERE... STEEL...
...S'GONE...
THE WATCHTOWER'S SECURITY SYSTEMS ARE FLOODING MY HYPER-SENSES.
LET'S DISABLE THOSE FIRST.
WE'LL FIND STEEL LATER. WITHOUT THE ARMOR, HE'S NOTHING.
WE'RE ON THE MOON.
WHERE CAN HE GO?

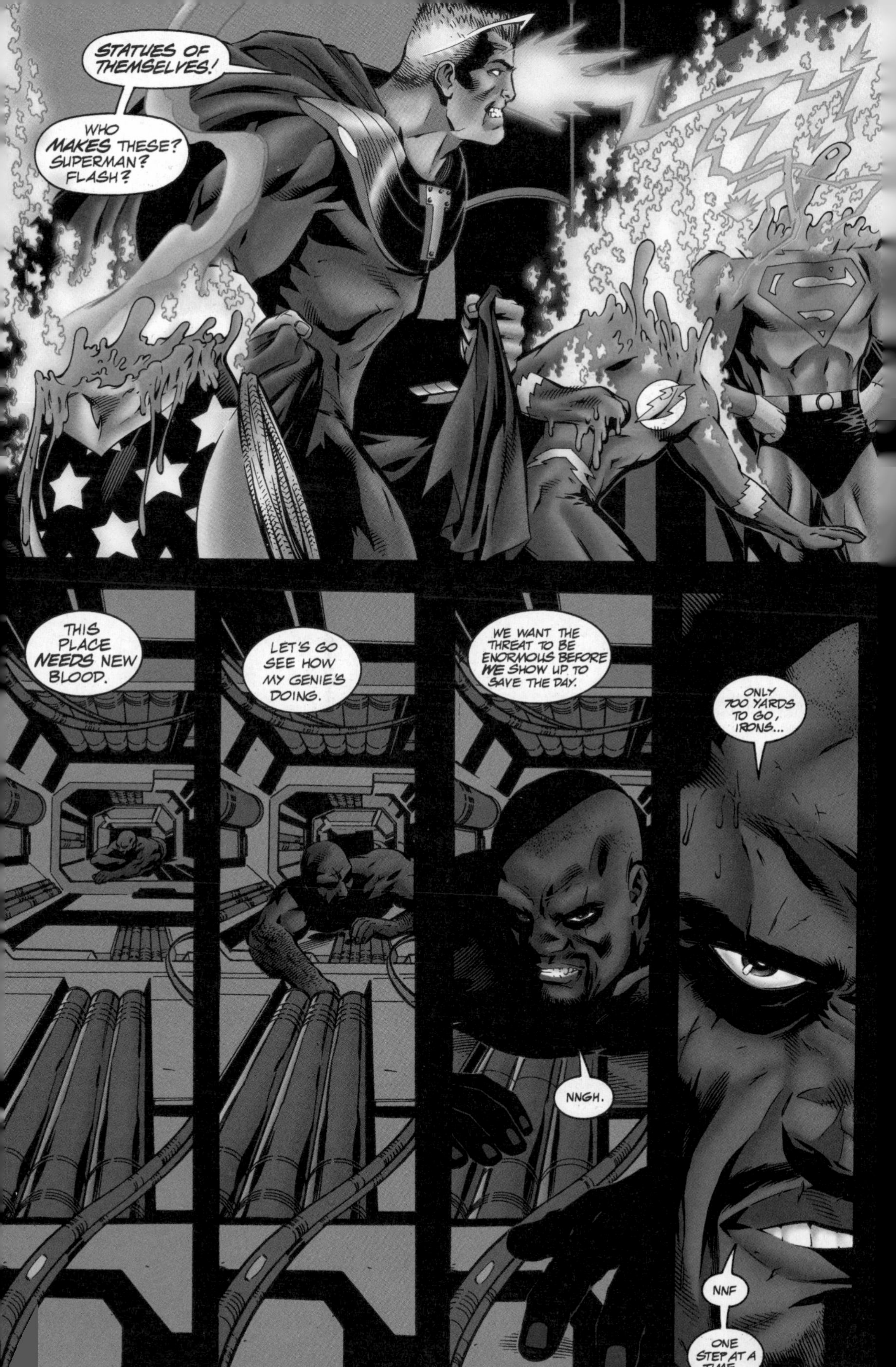
STATUES OF THEMSELVES!
WHO MAKES THESE? SUPERMAN? FLASH?
THIS PLACE NEEDS NEW BLOOD.
LET'S GO SEE HOW MY GENIE'S DOING.
WE WANT THE THREAT TO BE ENORMOUS BEFORE WE SHOW UP TO SAVE THE DAY.
NNGH.
ONLY 700 YARDS TO GO, IRONS...
NNF
ONE STEP AT A TIME.

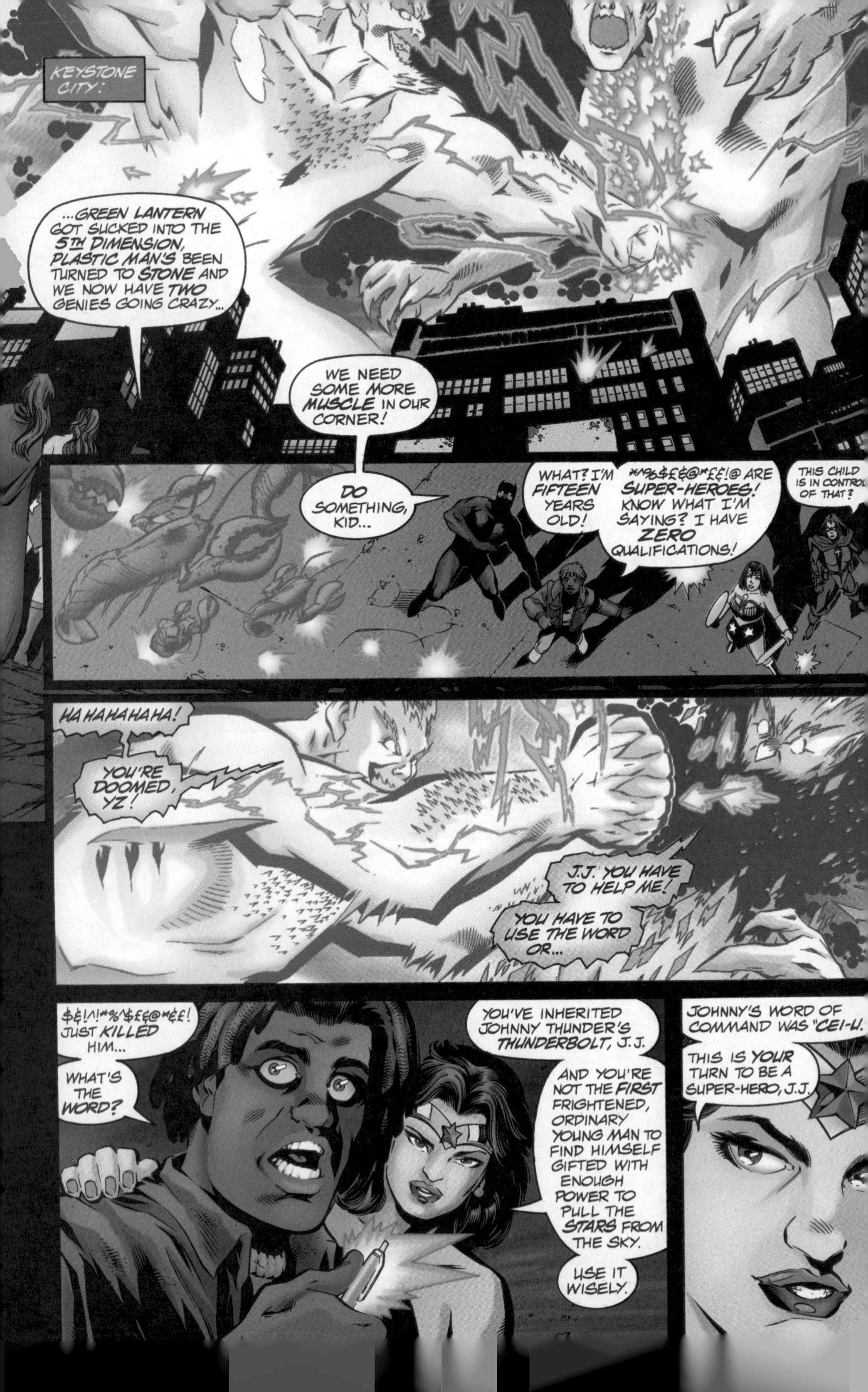
KEYSTONE CITY:
...GREEN LANTERN GOT SUCKED INTO THE 5TH DIMENSION, PLASTIC MAN'S BEEN TURNED TO STONE AND WE NOW HAVE TWO GENIES GOING CRAZY...
WE NEED SOME MORE MUSCLE IN OUR CORNER!
DO SOMETHING, KID...
WHAT? I'M FIFTEEN YEARS OLD!
^%$£€@£€!@ ARE SUPER-HEROES! KNOW WHAT I'M SAYING? I HAVE ZERO QUALIFICATIONS!
THIS CHILD IS IN CONTROL OF THAT?
HA HA HA HA HA HA!
YOU'RE DOOMED, YZ!
J.J. YOU HAVE TO HELP ME!
YOU HAVE TO USE THE WORD OR...
$€!^!*%^$£€@*€£! JUST KILLED HIM...
WHAT'S THE WORD?
YOU'VE INHERITED JOHNNY THUNDER'S THUNDERBOLT, J.J.
AND YOU'RE NOT THE FIRST FRIGHTENED, ORDINARY YOUNG MAN TO FIND HIMSELF GIFTED WITH ENOUGH POWER TO PULL THE STARS FROM THE SKY.
USE IT WISELY.
JOHNNY'S WORD OF COMMAND WAS "CEI-U."
THIS IS YOUR TURN TO BE A SUPER-HERO, J.J.

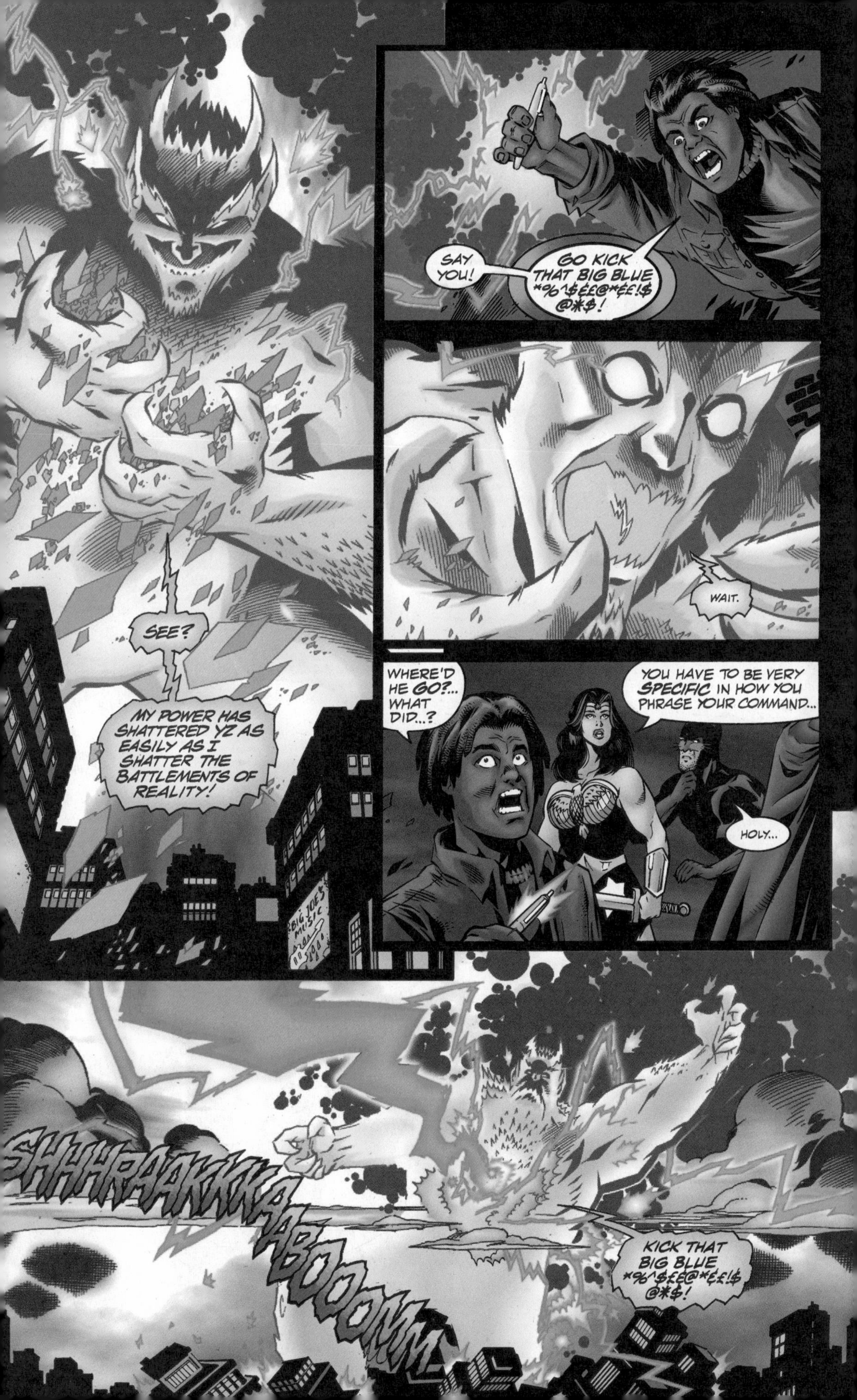
SEE?
MY POWER HAS SHATTERED YZ AS EASILY AS I SHATTER THE BATTLEMENTS OF REALITY!
SAY YOU!
GO KICK THAT BIG BLUE *%^$££@*££!$ @*$!
WAIT.
WHERE'D HE GO?... WHAT DID...?
YOU HAVE TO BE VERY SPECIFIC IN HOW YOU PHRASE YOUR COMMAND...
HOLY...
BIG JOE'S MUSIC
SHHRAAKKKABOOOMM
KICK THAT BIG BLUE *%^$££@*££!$ @*$!

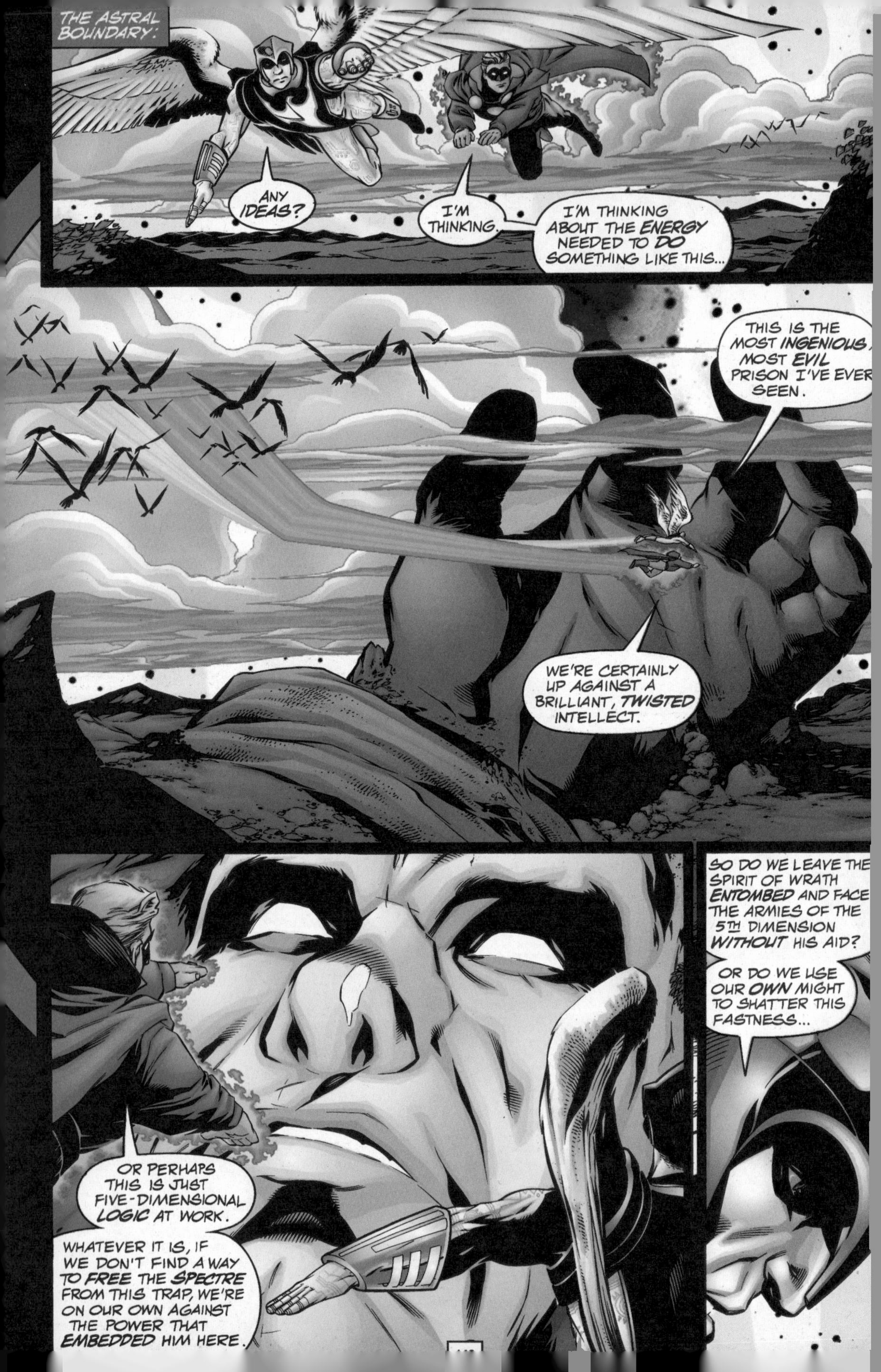
THE ASTRAL BOUNDARY:
ANY IDEAS?
I'M THINKING.
I'M THINKING ABOUT THE ENERGY NEEDED TO DO SOMETHING LIKE THIS...
THIS IS THE MOST INGENIOUS, MOST EVIL PRISON I'VE EVER SEEN.
WE'RE CERTAINLY UP AGAINST A BRILLIANT, TWISTED INTELLECT.
OR PERHAPS THIS IS JUST FIVE-DIMENSIONAL LOGIC AT WORK.
WHATEVER IT IS, IF WE DON'T FIND A WAY TO FREE THE SPECTRE FROM THIS TRAP, WE'RE ON OUR OWN AGAINST THE POWER THAT EMBEDDED HIM HERE.
SO DO WE LEAVE THE SPIRIT OF WRATH ENTOMBED AND FACE THE ARMIES OF THE 5TH DIMENSION WITHOUT HIS AID?
OR DO WE USE OUR OWN MIGHT TO SHATTER THIS FASTNESS...

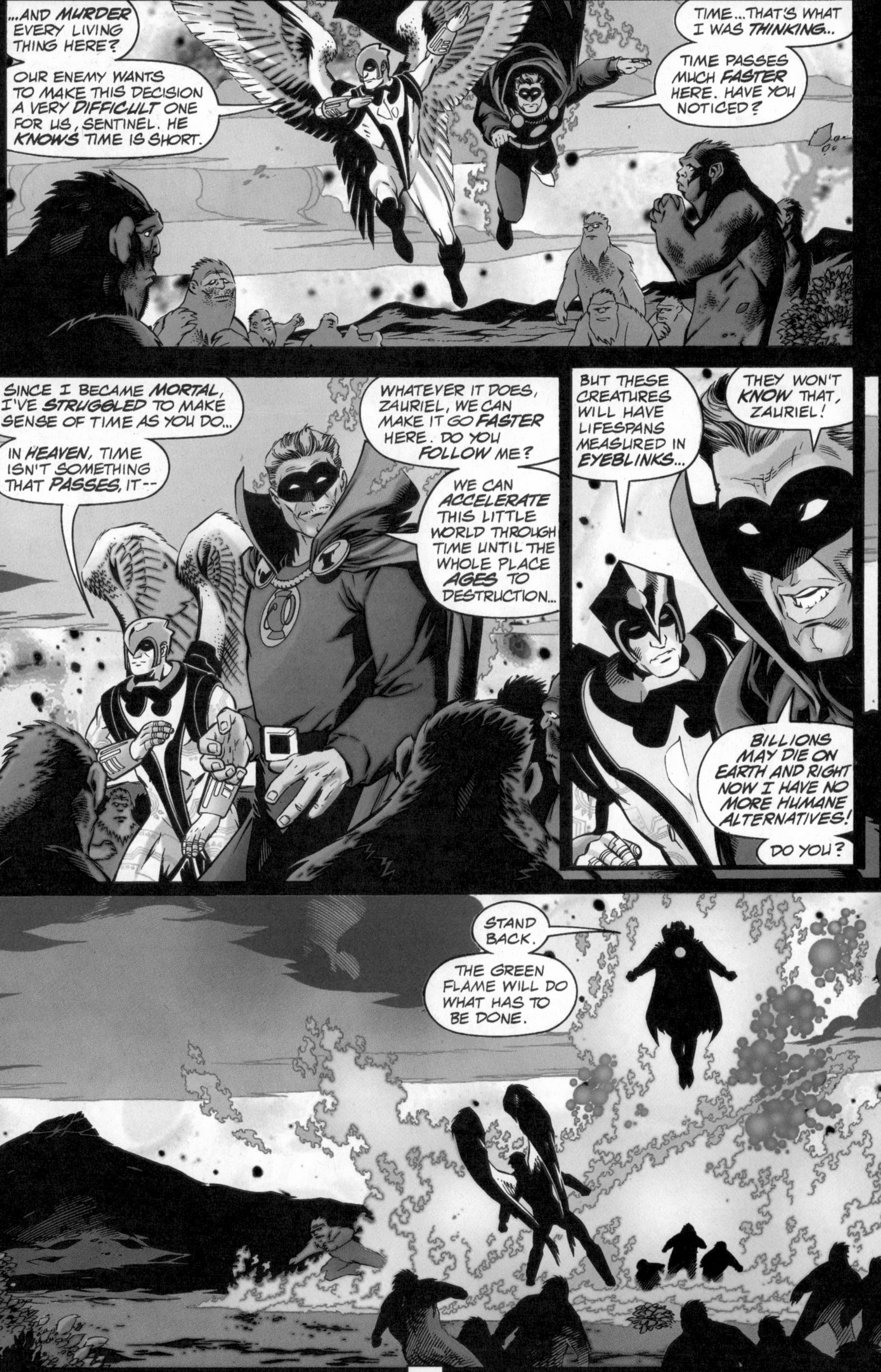
...AND MURDER EVERY LIVING THING HERE?
OUR ENEMY WANTS TO MAKE THIS DECISION A VERY DIFFICULT ONE FOR US, SENTINEL. HE KNOWS TIME IS SHORT.
TIME...THAT'S WHAT I WAS THINKING...
TIME PASSES MUCH FASTER HERE. HAVE YOU NOTICED?
SINCE I BECAME MORTAL, I'VE STRUGGLED TO MAKE SENSE OF TIME AS YOU DO...
IN HEAVEN, TIME ISN'T SOMETHING THAT PASSES, IT--
WHATEVER IT DOES, ZAURIEL, WE CAN MAKE IT GO FASTER HERE. DO YOU FOLLOW ME?
WE CAN ACCELERATE THIS LITTLE WORLD THROUGH TIME UNTIL THE WHOLE PLACE AGES TO DESTRUCTION...
BUT THESE CREATURES WILL HAVE LIFESPANS MEASURED IN EYEBLINKS...
THEY WON'T KNOW THAT, ZAURIEL!
BILLIONS MAY DIE ON EARTH AND RIGHT NOW I HAVE NO MORE HUMANE ALTERNATIVES!
DO YOU?
STAND BACK.
THE GREEN FLAME WILL DO WHAT HAS TO BE DONE.

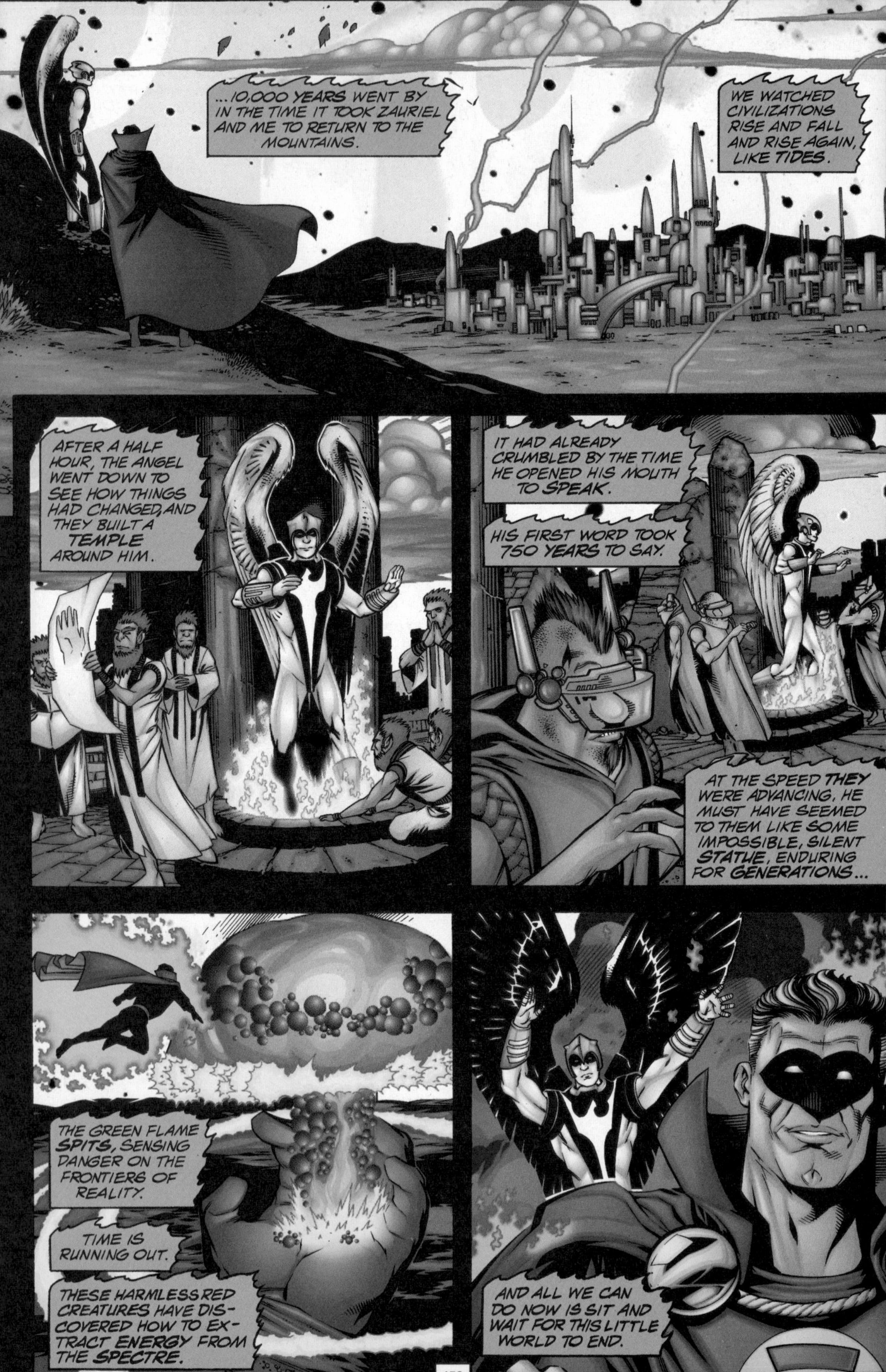
...10,000 YEARS WENT BY IN THE TIME IT TOOK ZAURIEL AND ME TO RETURN TO THE MOUNTAINS.
WE WATCHED CIVILIZATIONS RISE AND FALL AND RISE AGAIN, LIKE TIDES.
AFTER A HALF HOUR, THE ANGEL WENT DOWN TO SEE HOW THINGS HAD CHANGED, AND THEY BUILT A TEMPLE AROUND HIM.
IT HAD ALREADY CRUMBLED BY THE TIME HE OPENED HIS MOUTH TO SPEAK.
HIS FIRST WORD TOOK 750 YEARS TO SAY.
AT THE SPEED THEY WERE ADVANCING, HE MUST HAVE SEEMED TO THEM LIKE SOME IMPOSSIBLE, SILENT STATUE, ENDURING FOR GENERATIONS...
THE GREEN FLAME SPITS, SENSING DANGER ON THE FRONTIERS OF REALITY.
TIME IS RUNNING OUT.
THESE HARMLESS RED CREATURES HAVE DISCOVERED HOW TO EXTRACT ENERGY FROM THE SPECTRE.
AND ALL WE CAN DO NOW IS SIT AND WAIT FOR THIS LITTLE WORLD TO END.

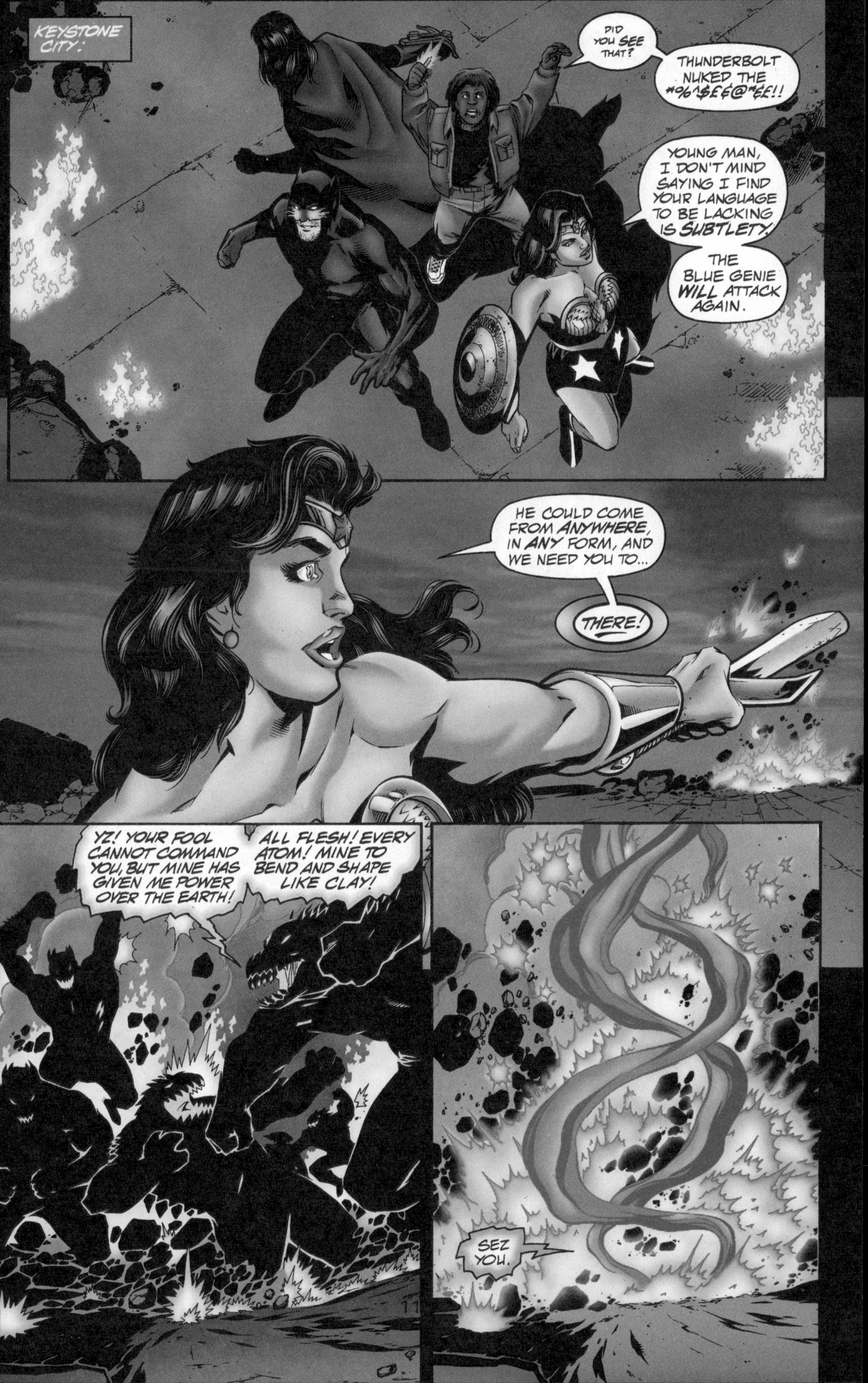
KEYSTONE CITY:
DID YOU SEE THAT?
THUNDERBOLT NUKED THE #%^$£€@*££!!
YOUNG MAN, I DON'T MIND SAYING I FIND YOUR LANGUAGE TO BE LACKING IS SUBTLETY.
THE BLUE GENIE WILL ATTACK AGAIN.
HE COULD COME FROM ANYWHERE, IN ANY FORM, AND WE NEED YOU TO...
THERE!
YZ! YOUR FOOL CANNOT COMMAND YOU, BUT MINE HAS GIVEN ME POWER OVER THE EARTH!
ALL FLESH! EVERY ATOM! MINE TO BEND AND SHAPE LIKE CLAY!
SEZ YOU.

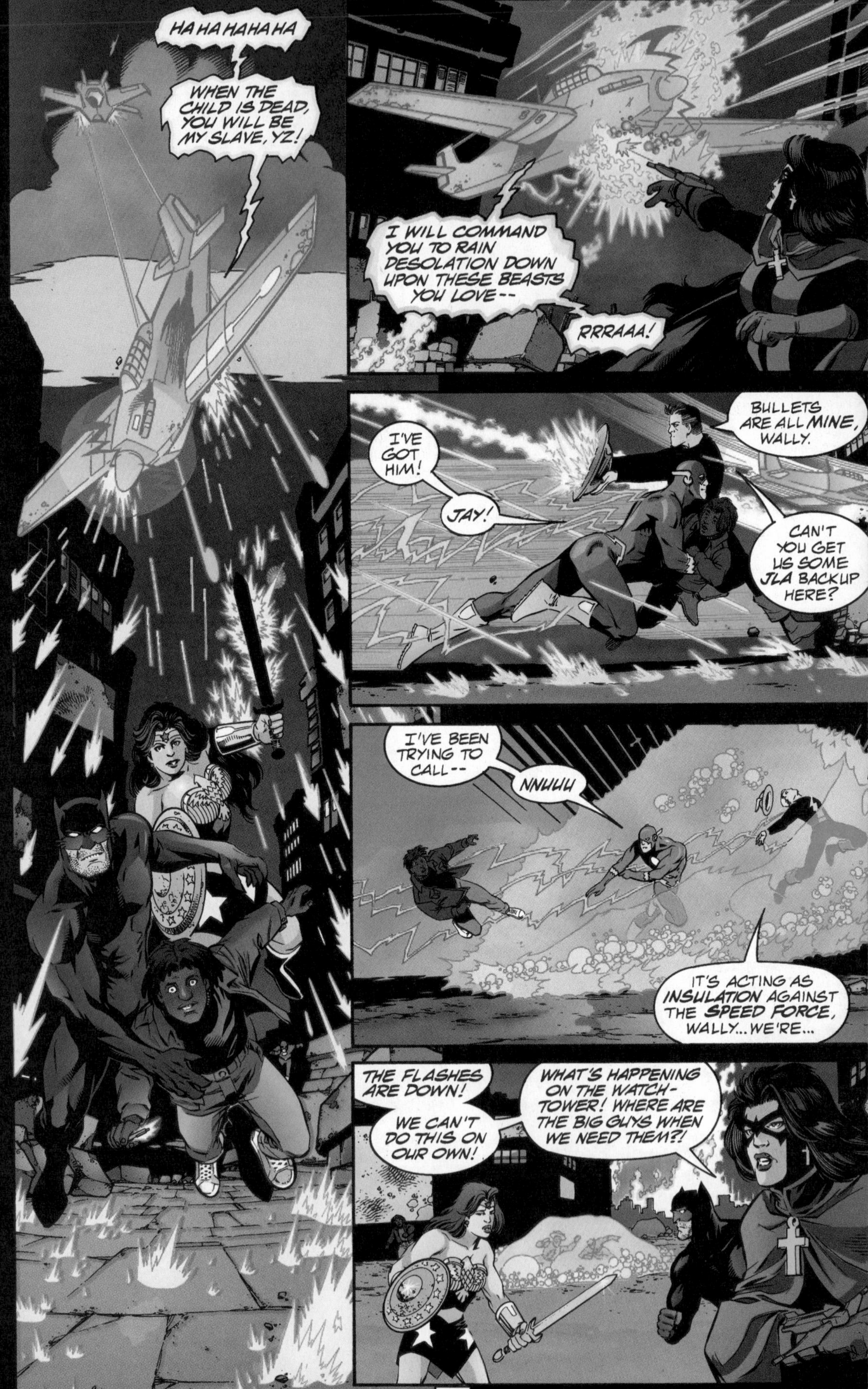
HA HA HA HA HA HA
WHEN THE CHILD IS DEAD, YOU WILL BE MY SLAVE, YZ!
I WILL COMMAND YOU TO RAIN DESOLATION DOWN UPON THESE BEASTS YOU LOVE--
RRRAAA!
I'VE GOT HIM!
JAY!
BULLETS ARE ALL MINE, WALLY.
CAN'T YOU GET US SOME JLA BACKUP HERE?
I'VE BEEN TRYING TO CALL--
NNUUU
IT'S ACTING AS INSULATION AGAINST THE SPEED FORCE, WALLY... WE'RE...
THE FLASHES ARE DOWN!
WE CAN'T DO THIS ON OUR OWN!
WHAT'S HAPPENING ON THE WATCH-TOWER! WHERE ARE THE BIG GUYS WHEN WE NEED THEM?!

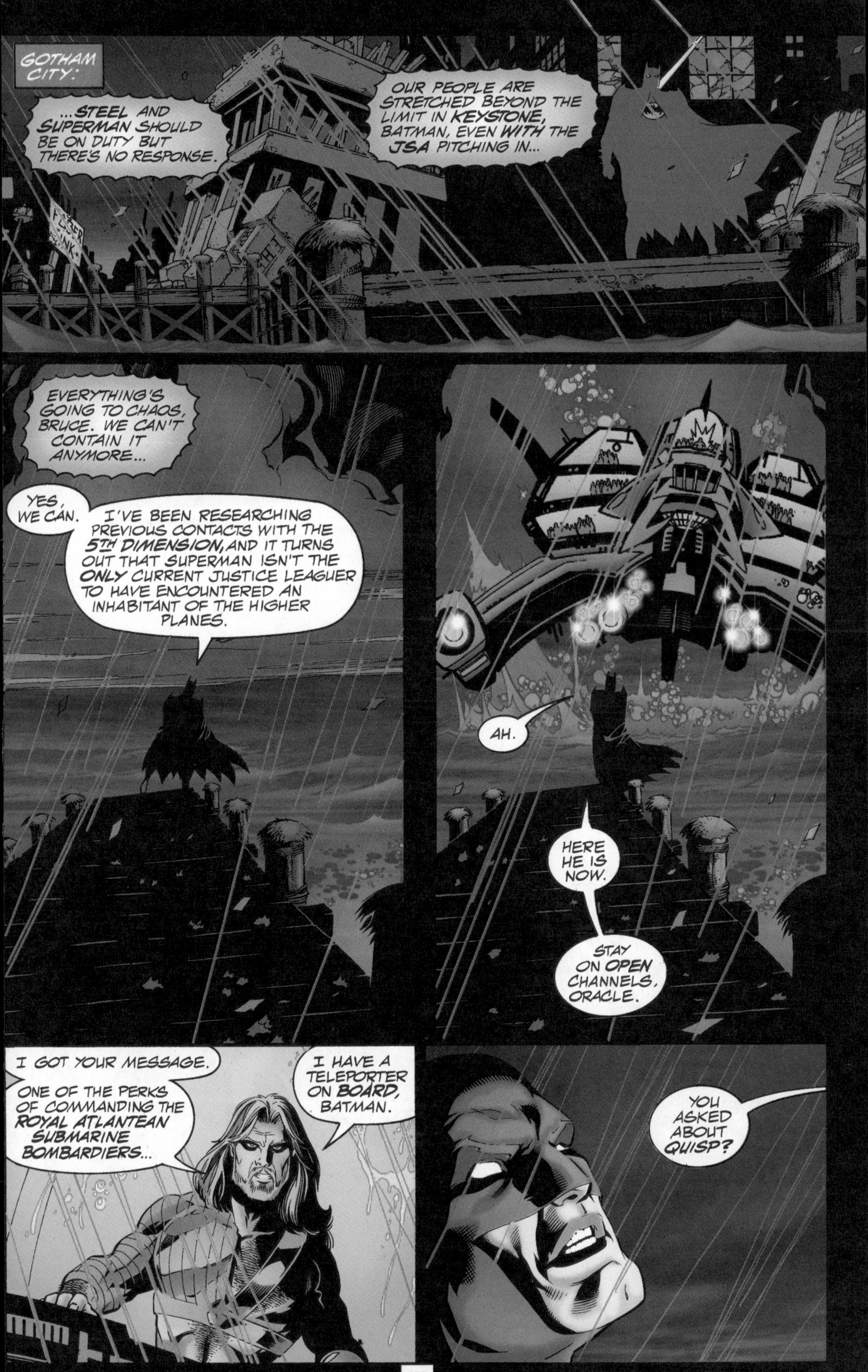
GOTHAM CITY:
...STEEL AND SUPERMAN SHOULD BE ON DUTY BUT THERE'S NO RESPONSE.
OUR PEOPLE ARE STRETCHED BEYOND THE LIMIT IN KEYSTONE, BATMAN, EVEN WITH THE JSA PITCHING IN...
EVERYTHING'S GOING TO CHAOS, BRUCE. WE CAN'T CONTAIN IT ANYMORE...
YES, WE CAN.
I'VE BEEN RESEARCHING PREVIOUS CONTACTS WITH THE 5TH DIMENSION, AND IT TURNS OUT THAT SUPERMAN ISN'T THE ONLY CURRENT JUSTICE LEAGUER TO HAVE ENCOUNTERED AN INHABITANT OF THE HIGHER PLANES.
AH.
HERE HE IS NOW.
STAY ON OPEN CHANNELS, ORACLE.
I GOT YOUR MESSAGE.
ONE OF THE PERKS OF COMMANDING THE ROYAL ATLANTEAN SUBMARINE BOMBARDIERS...
I HAVE A TELEPORTER ON BOARD, BATMAN.
YOU ASKED ABOUT QUISP?

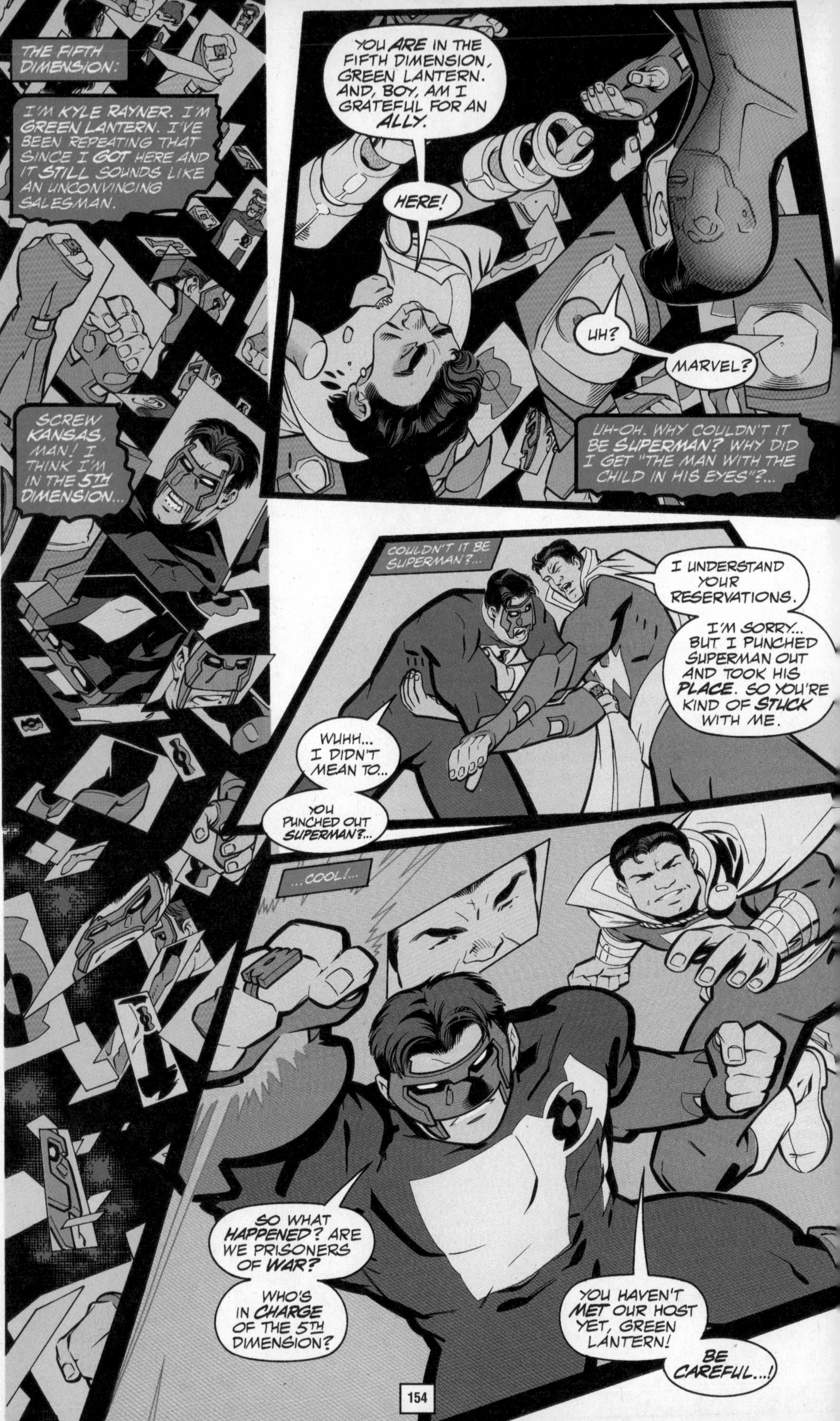

THE FIFTH DIMENSION:
I'M KYLE RAYNER. I'M GREEN LANTERN. I'VE BEEN REPEATING THAT SINCE I GOT HERE AND IT STILL SOUNDS LIKE AN UNCONVINCING SALESMAN.
YOU ARE IN THE FIFTH DIMENSION, GREEN LANTERN. AND, BOY, AM I GRATEFUL FOR AN ALLY.
HERE!
UH?
MARVEL?
SCREW KANSAS, MAN! I THINK I'M IN THE 5TH DIMENSION...
UH-OH. WHY COULDN'T IT BE SUPERMAN? WHY DID I GET "THE MAN WITH THE CHILD IN HIS EYES"?...
COULDN'T IT BE SUPERMAN?...
I UNDERSTAND YOUR RESERVATIONS.
I'M SORRY... BUT I PUNCHED SUPERMAN OUT AND TOOK HIS PLACE. SO YOU'RE KIND OF STUCK WITH ME.
WUHH... I DIDN'T MEAN TO...
YOU PUNCHED OUT SUPERMAN?...
...COOL!...
SO WHAT HAPPENED? ARE WE PRISONERS OF WAR?
WHO'S IN CHARGE OF THE 5TH DIMENSION?
YOU HAVEN'T MET OUR HOST YET, GREEN LANTERN!
BE CAREFUL...!

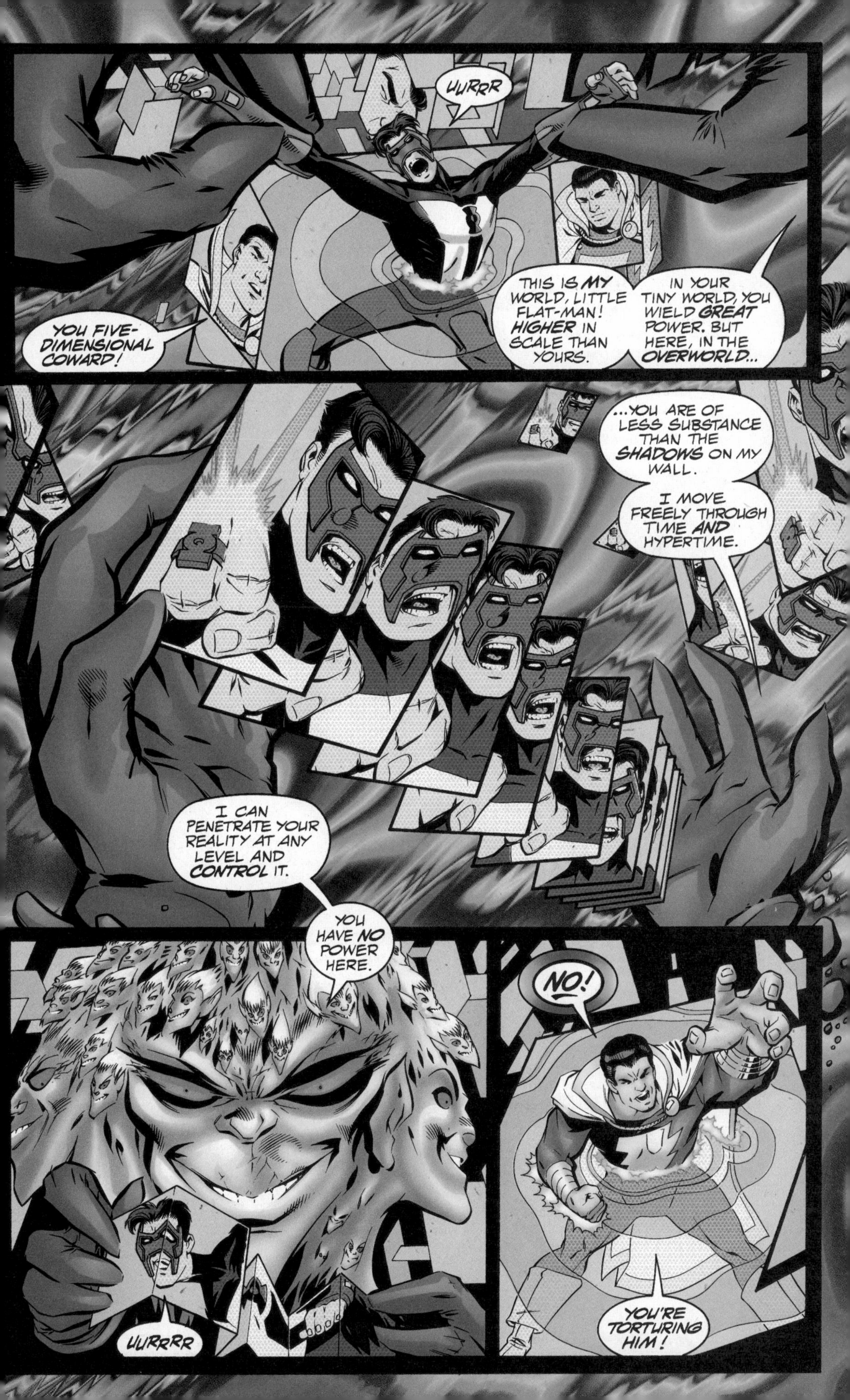
UURRR
YOU FIVE-DIMENSIONAL COWARD!
THIS IS MY WORLD, LITTLE FLAT-MAN! HIGHER IN SCALE THAN YOURS.
IN YOUR TINY WORLD, YOU WIELD GREAT POWER. BUT HERE, IN THE OVERWORLD...
...YOU ARE OF LESS SUBSTANCE THAN THE SHADOWS ON MY WALL.
I MOVE FREELY THROUGH TIME AND HYPERTIME.
I CAN PENETRATE YOUR REALITY AT ANY LEVEL AND CONTROL IT.
YOU HAVE NO POWER HERE.
UURRRR
NO!
YOU'RE TORTURING HIM!

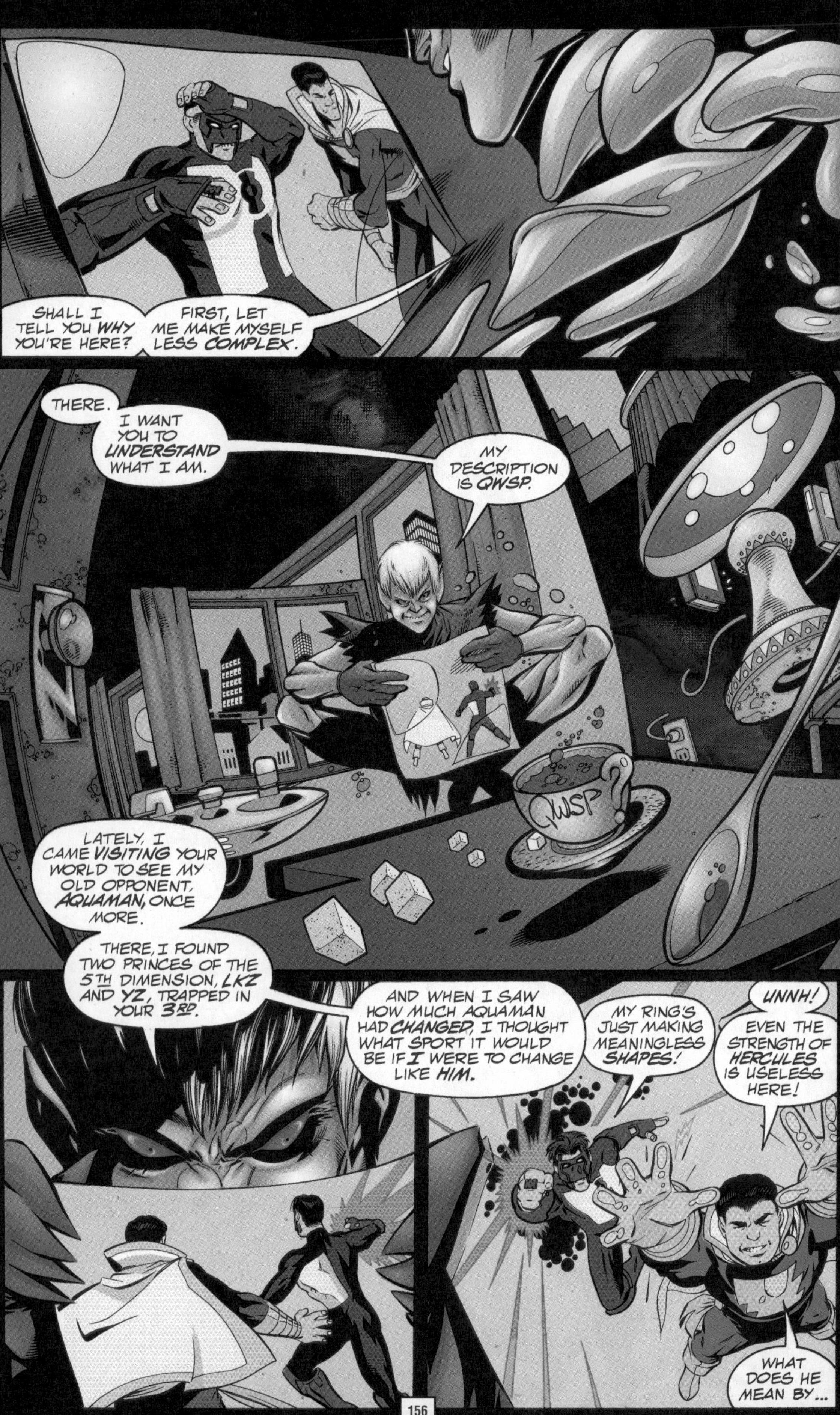
SHALL I TELL YOU WHY YOU'RE HERE?
FIRST, LET ME MAKE MYSELF LESS COMPLEX.
THERE.
I WANT YOU TO UNDERSTAND WHAT I AM.
MY DESCRIPTION IS QWSP.
QWSP
LATELY, I CAME VISITING YOUR WORLD TO SEE MY OLD OPPONENT, AQUAMAN, ONCE MORE.
THERE, I FOUND TWO PRINCES OF THE 5TH DIMENSION, LKZ AND YZ, TRAPPED IN YOUR 3RD.
AND WHEN I SAW HOW MUCH AQUAMAN HAD CHANGED, I THOUGHT WHAT SPORT IT WOULD BE IF I WERE TO CHANGE LIKE HIM.
MY RING'S JUST MAKING MEANINGLESS SHAPES!
UNNH!
EVEN THE STRENGTH OF HERCULES IS USELESS HERE!
WHAT DOES HE MEAN BY...

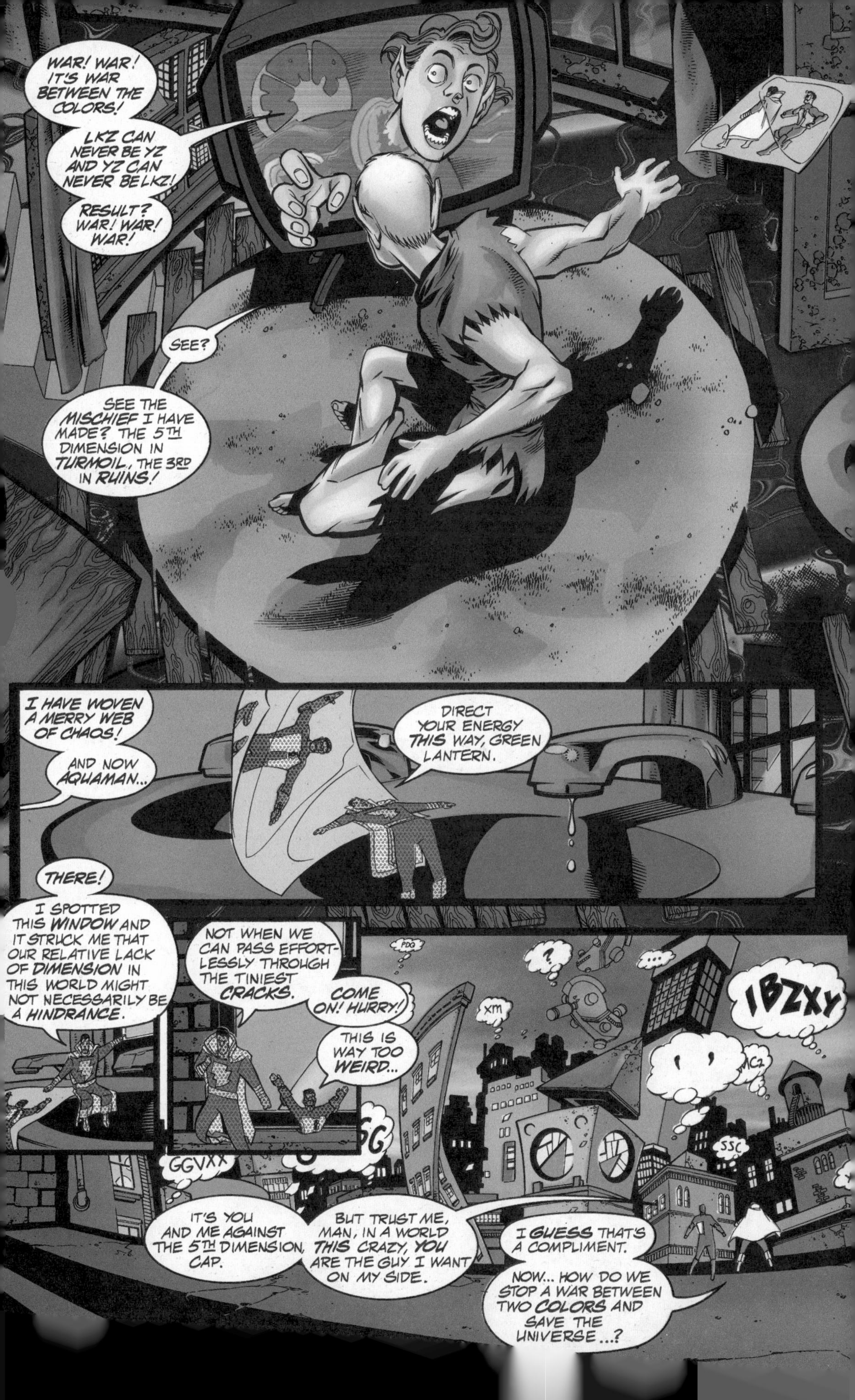
WAR! WAR! IT'S WAR BETWEEN THE COLORS!
LKZ CAN NEVER BE YZ AND YZ CAN NEVER BE LKZ!
RESULT? WAR! WAR! WAR!
SEE?
SEE THE MISCHIEF I HAVE MADE? THE 5TH DIMENSION IN TURMOIL, THE 3RD IN RUINS!
I HAVE WOVEN A MERRY WEB OF CHAOS!
AND NOW AQUAMAN...
DIRECT YOUR ENERGY THIS WAY, GREEN LANTERN.
THERE!
I SPOTTED THIS WINDOW AND IT STRUCK ME THAT OUR RELATIVE LACK OF DIMENSION IN THIS WORLD MIGHT NOT NECESSARILY BE A HINDRANCE.
NOT WHEN WE CAN PASS EFFORTLESSLY THROUGH THE TINIEST CRACKS.
COME ON! HURRY!
THIS IS WAY TOO WEIRD...
PDQ
?
xm
IBZXY
MC2
SSC
GGVXX
IT'S YOU AND ME AGAINST THE 5TH DIMENSION, CAP.
BUT TRUST ME, MAN, IN A WORLD THIS CRAZY, YOU ARE THE GUY I WANT ON MY SIDE.
I GUESS THAT'S A COMPLIMENT.
NOW... HOW DO WE STOP A WAR BETWEEN TWO COLORS AND SAVE THE UNIVERSE...?

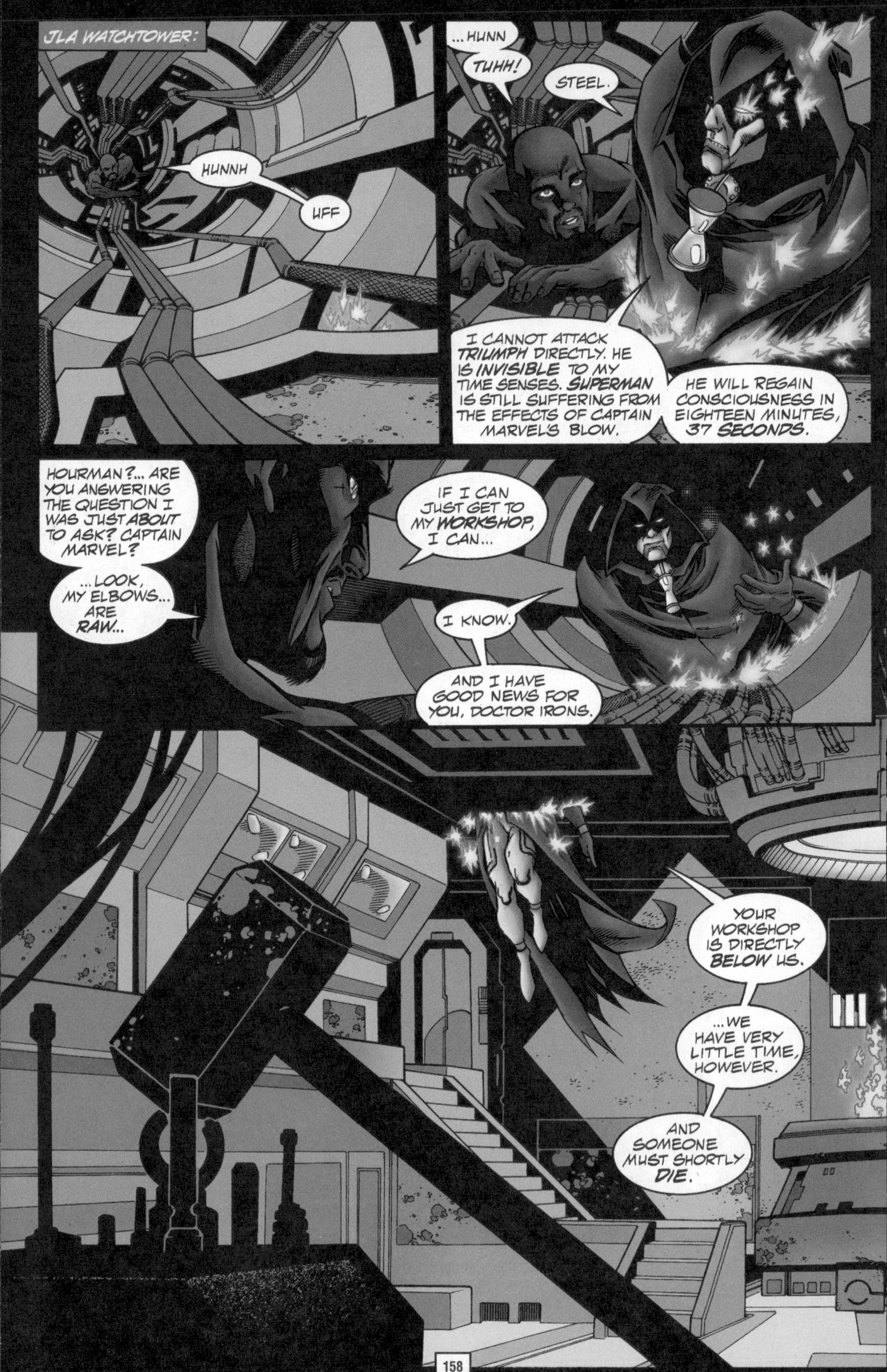

JLA WATCHTOWER:
HUNNH
UFF
...HUNN
TUHH!
STEEL.
I CANNOT ATTACK TRIUMPH DIRECTLY. HE IS INVISIBLE TO MY TIME SENSES. SUPERMAN IS STILL SUFFERING FROM THE EFFECTS OF CAPTAIN MARVEL'S BLOW.
HE WILL REGAIN CONSCIOUSNESS IN EIGHTEEN MINUTES, 37 SECONDS.
HOURMAN?... ARE YOU ANSWERING THE QUESTION I WAS JUST ABOUT TO ASK? CAPTAIN MARVEL?
...LOOK, MY ELBOWS... ARE RAW...
IF I CAN JUST GET TO MY WORKSHOP, I CAN...
I KNOW.
AND I HAVE GOOD NEWS FOR YOU, DOCTOR IRONS.
YOUR WORKSHOP IS DIRECTLY BELOW US.
...WE HAVE VERY LITTLE TIME, HOWEVER.
AND SOMEONE MUST SHORTLY DIE.

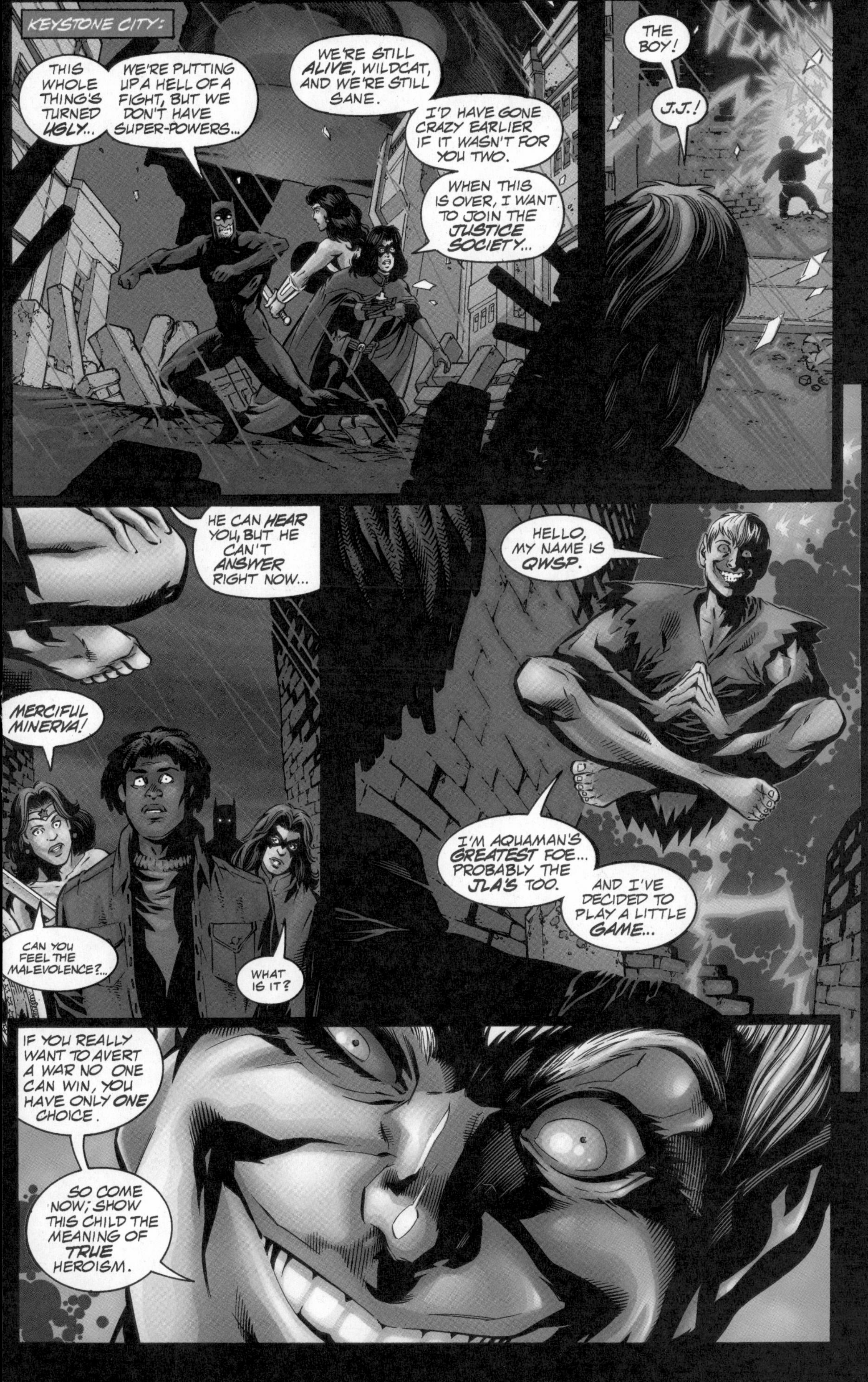
KEYSTONE CITY:
THIS WHOLE THING'S TURNED UGLY...
WE'RE PUTTING UP A HELL OF A FIGHT, BUT WE DON'T HAVE SUPER-POWERS...
WE'RE STILL ALIVE, WILDCAT, AND WE'RE STILL SANE.
I'D HAVE GONE CRAZY EARLIER IF IT WASN'T FOR YOU TWO.
WHEN THIS IS OVER, I WANT TO JOIN THE JUSTICE SOCIETY...
THE BOY!
J.J.!
HE CAN HEAR YOU, BUT HE CAN'T ANSWER RIGHT NOW...
HELLO, MY NAME IS QWSP.
I'M AQUAMAN'S GREATEST FOE... PROBABLY THE JLA'S TOO.
AND I'VE DECIDED TO PLAY A LITTLE GAME...
MERCIFUL MINERVA!
CAN YOU FEEL THE MALEVOLENCE?...
WHAT IS IT?
IF YOU REALLY WANT TO AVERT A WAR NO ONE CAN WIN, YOU HAVE ONLY ONE CHOICE.
SO COME NOW; SHOW THIS CHILD THE MEANING OF TRUE HEROISM.

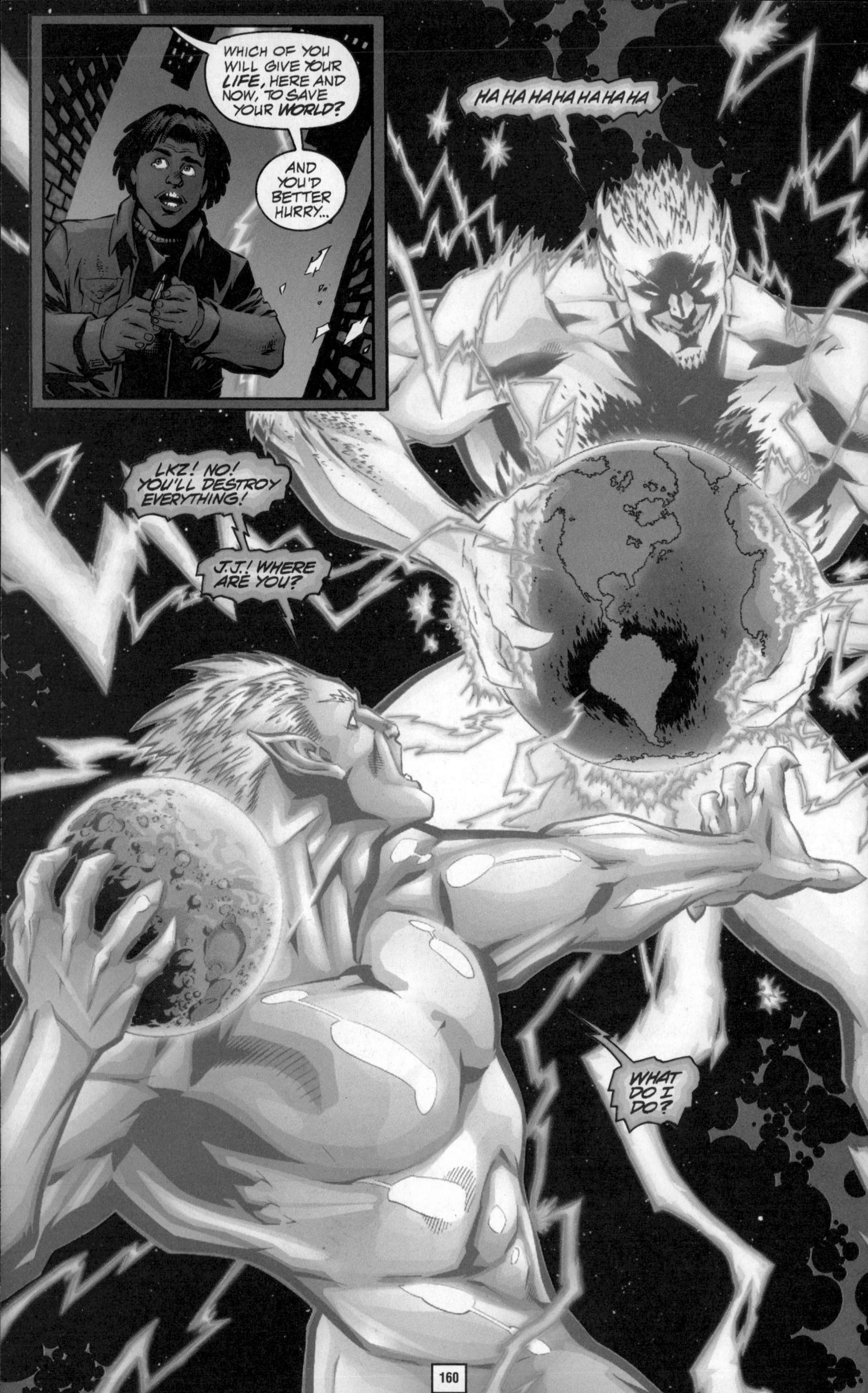
WHICH OF YOU WILL GIVE YOUR LIFE, HERE AND NOW, TO SAVE YOUR WORLD?
AND YOU'D BETTER HURRY...
HA HA HA HA HA HA HA HA HA
LKZ! NO! YOU'LL DESTROY EVERYTHING!
J.J.! WHERE ARE YOU?
WHAT DO I DO?

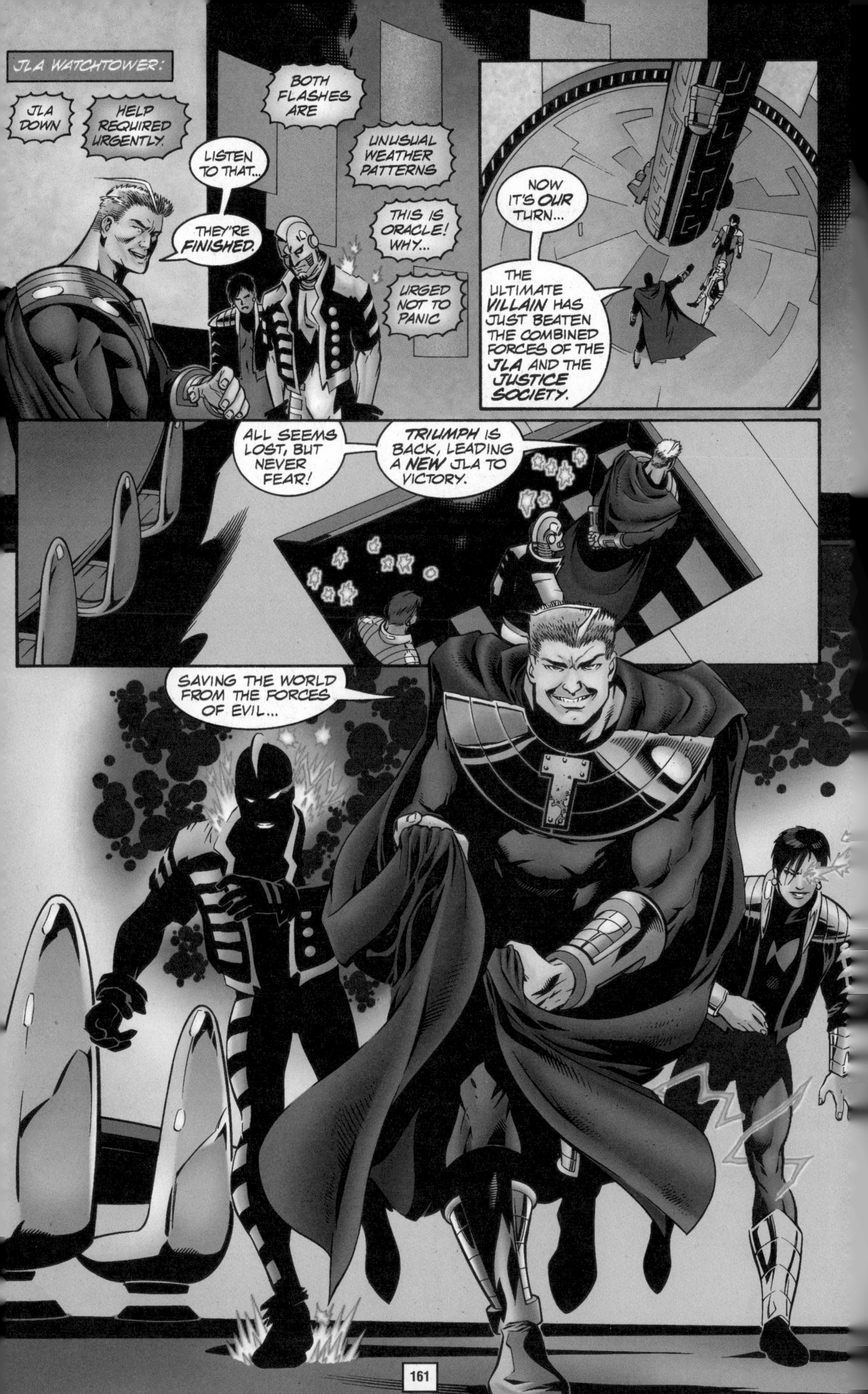
JLA WATCHTOWER:
JLA DOWN
HELP REQUIRED URGENTLY.
LISTEN TO THAT...
BOTH FLASHES ARE
UNUSUAL WEATHER PATTERNS
THIS IS ORACLE! WHY...
URGED NOT TO PANIC
THEY'RE FINISHED.
NOW IT'S OUR TURN...
THE ULTIMATE VILLAIN HAS JUST BEATEN THE COMBINED FORCES OF THE JLA AND THE JUSTICE SOCIETY.
ALL SEEMS LOST, BUT NEVER FEAR!
TRIUMPH IS BACK, LEADING A NEW JLA TO VICTORY.
SAVING THE WORLD FROM THE FORCES OF EVIL...

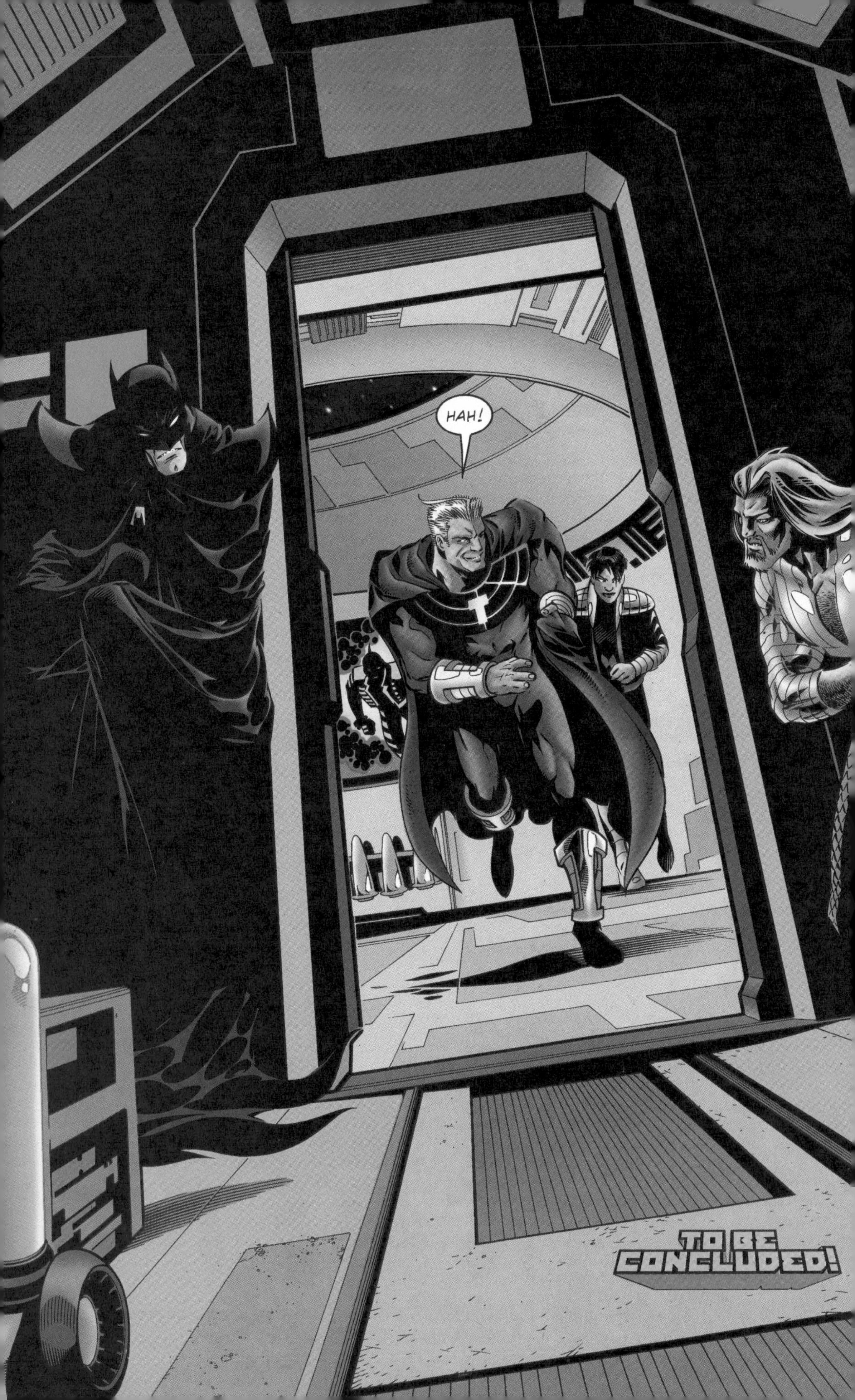
HAH!
TO BE CONCLUDED!

THE QUINTESSENCE:

THUS THE DRAMA *PAUSES*, THE PLAYERS CATCH THEIR BREATH THE *CHORUS* BEGINS...

AND WE LORDS AND GUARDIANS OF ETERNITY, THE QUINTESSENCE OF WISDOM, MUST ONLY BEAR *WITNESS*...

NOW THE FATAL HOUR ARRIVES.

"THE *WRATH OF GOD*, IMPRISONED BY MAGIC FROM BEYOND SPACE AND TIME, SHAKES OFF HIS MIGHTY *CHAINS*."

"BEHOLD THE ANGEL *ZAURIEL*, A WHOLE WORLD DEAD IN HIS HANDS: THE *PRICE* OF THE DREAD SPECTRE'S RELEASE..."

"*TWO COLORS* CONTINUE TO WAGE WAR IN THE 5TH DIMENSION, THREATENING THE 3RD."

"*HUMANITY'S FATE* HANGS UPON A WHIM OF THE IMPS."

"AND THE *JUSTICE LEAGUE*, AS EVER, STAND FOURSQUARE AGAINST THE CHAOS."

"BUT SEE! THE FINAL BATTLE DAWNS."

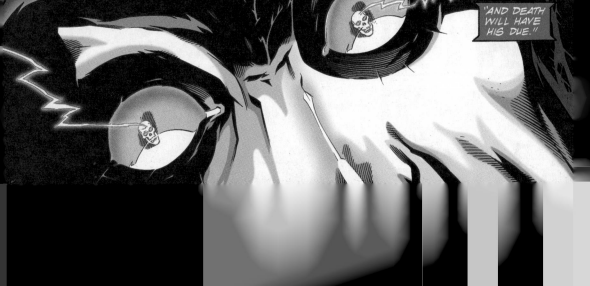

"AND DEATH WILL HAVE HIS DUE."

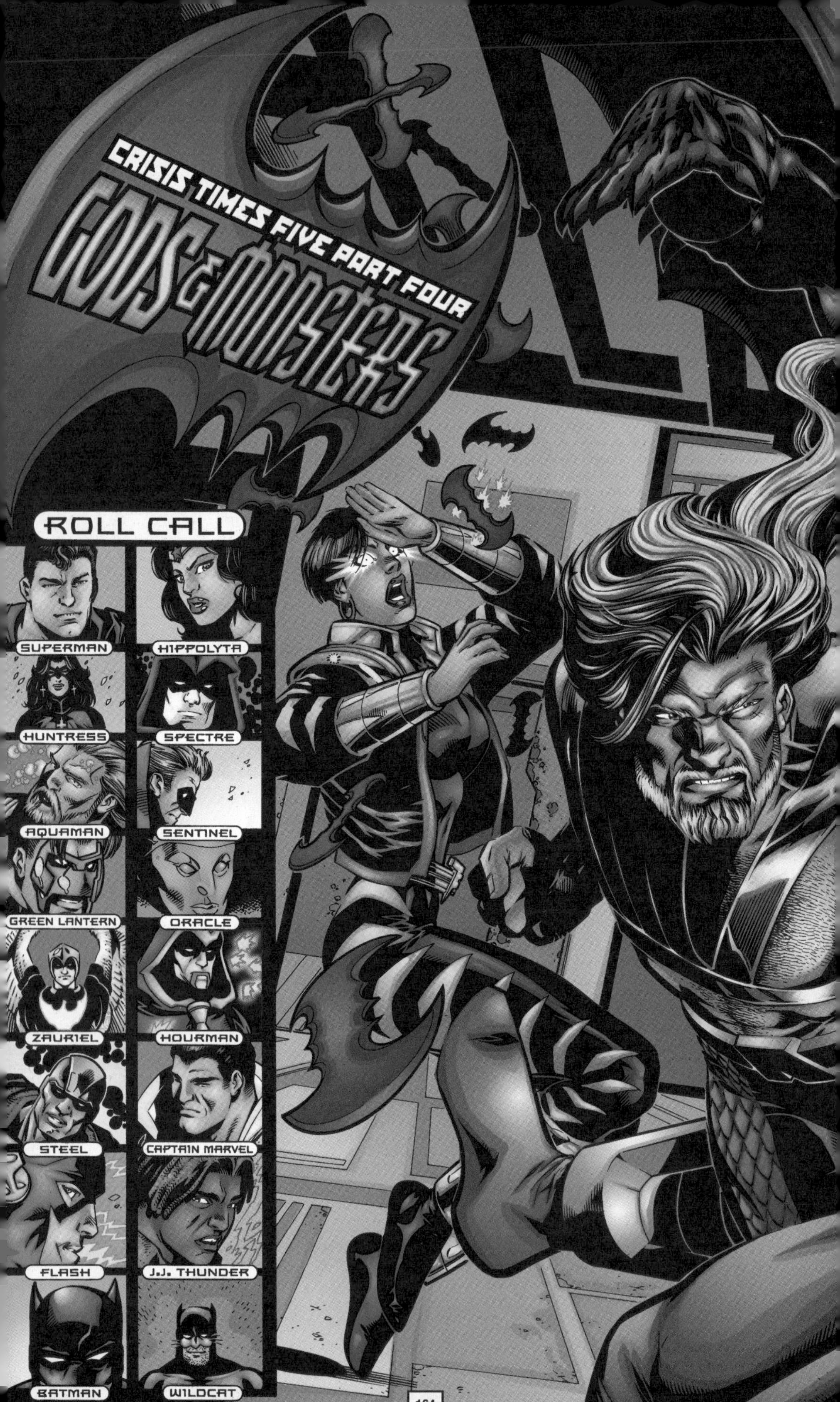

CRISIS TIMES FIVE PART FOUR
GODS & MONSTERS
ROLL CALL
SUPERMAN
HIPPOLYTA
HUNTRESS
SPECTRE
AQUAMAN
SENTINEL
GREEN LANTERN
ORACLE
ZAURIEL
HOURMAN
STEEL
CAPTAIN MARVEL
FLASH
J.J. THUNDER
BATMAN
WILDCAT

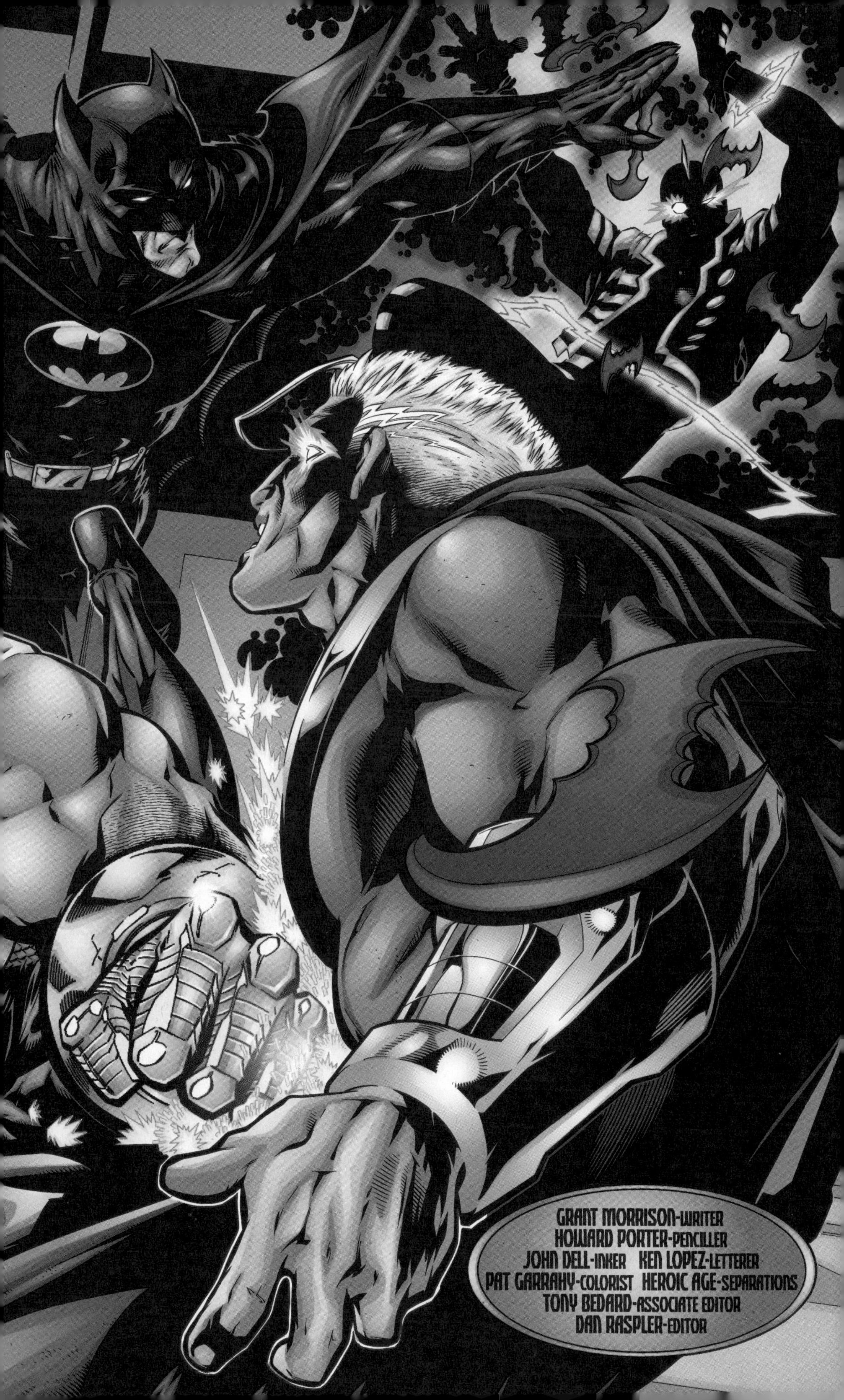
GRANT MORRISON-WRITER
HOWARD PORTER-PENCILLER
JOHN DELL-INKER KEN LOPEZ-LETTERER
PAT GARRAHY-COLORIST HEROIC AGE-SEPARATIONS
TONY BEDARD-ASSOCIATE EDITOR
DAN RASPLER-EDITOR

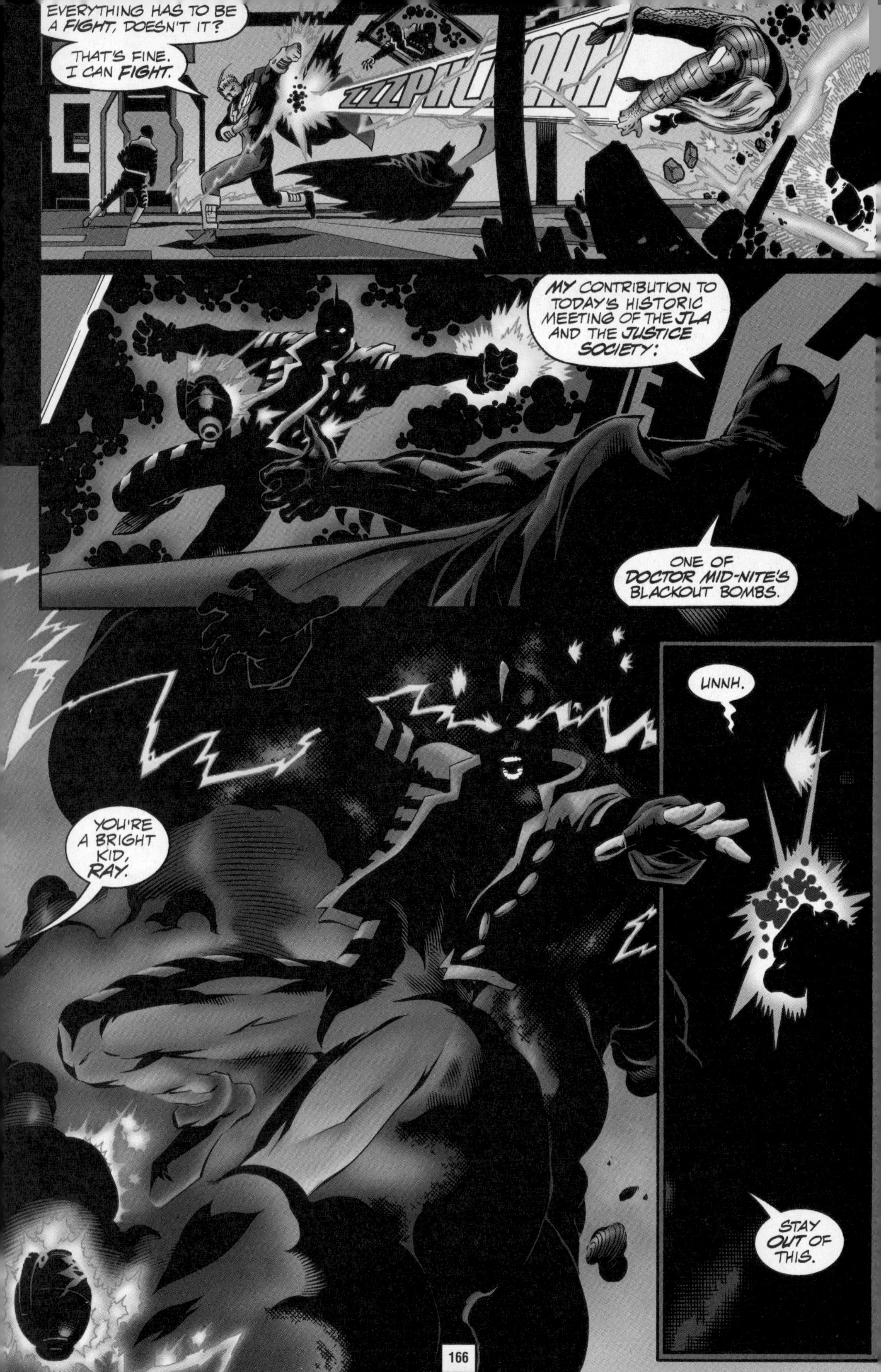

EVERYTHING HAS TO BE A FIGHT, DOESN'T IT?
THAT'S FINE. I CAN FIGHT.
ZZZPHOOOAAA
MY CONTRIBUTION TO TODAY'S HISTORIC MEETING OF THE JLA AND THE JUSTICE SOCIETY:
ONE OF DOCTOR MID-NITE'S BLACKOUT BOMBS.
UNNH.
YOU'RE A BRIGHT KID, RAY.
STAY OUT OF THIS.

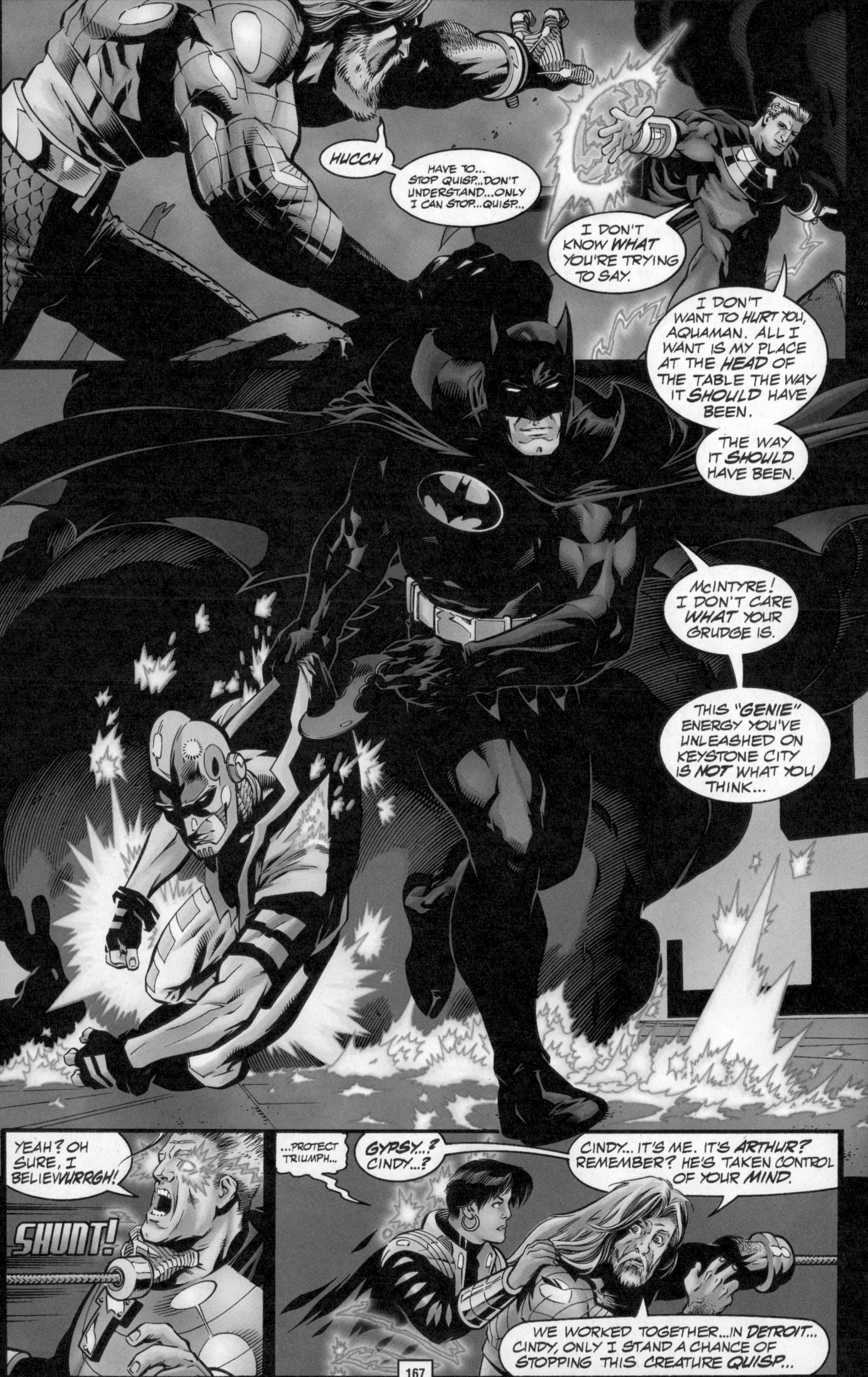
HUCCH
HAVE TO... STOP QUISP...DON'T UNDERSTAND...ONLY I CAN STOP...QUISP...
I DON'T KNOW WHAT YOU'RE TRYING TO SAY.
I DON'T WANT TO HURT YOU, AQUAMAN. ALL I WANT IS MY PLACE AT THE HEAD OF THE TABLE THE WAY IT SHOULD HAVE BEEN.
THE WAY IT SHOULD HAVE BEEN.
McINTYRE! I DON'T CARE WHAT YOUR GRUDGE IS.
THIS "GENIE" ENERGY YOU'VE UNLEASHED ON KEYSTONE CITY IS NOT WHAT YOU THINK...
YEAH? OH SURE, I BELIEVURRGH!
SHUNT!
...PROTECT TRIUMPH...
GYPSY...? CINDY...?
CINDY... IT'S ME. IT'S ARTHUR? REMEMBER? HE'S TAKEN CONTROL OF YOUR MIND.
WE WORKED TOGETHER...IN DETROIT... CINDY, ONLY I STAND A CHANCE OF STOPPING THIS CREATURE QUISP...

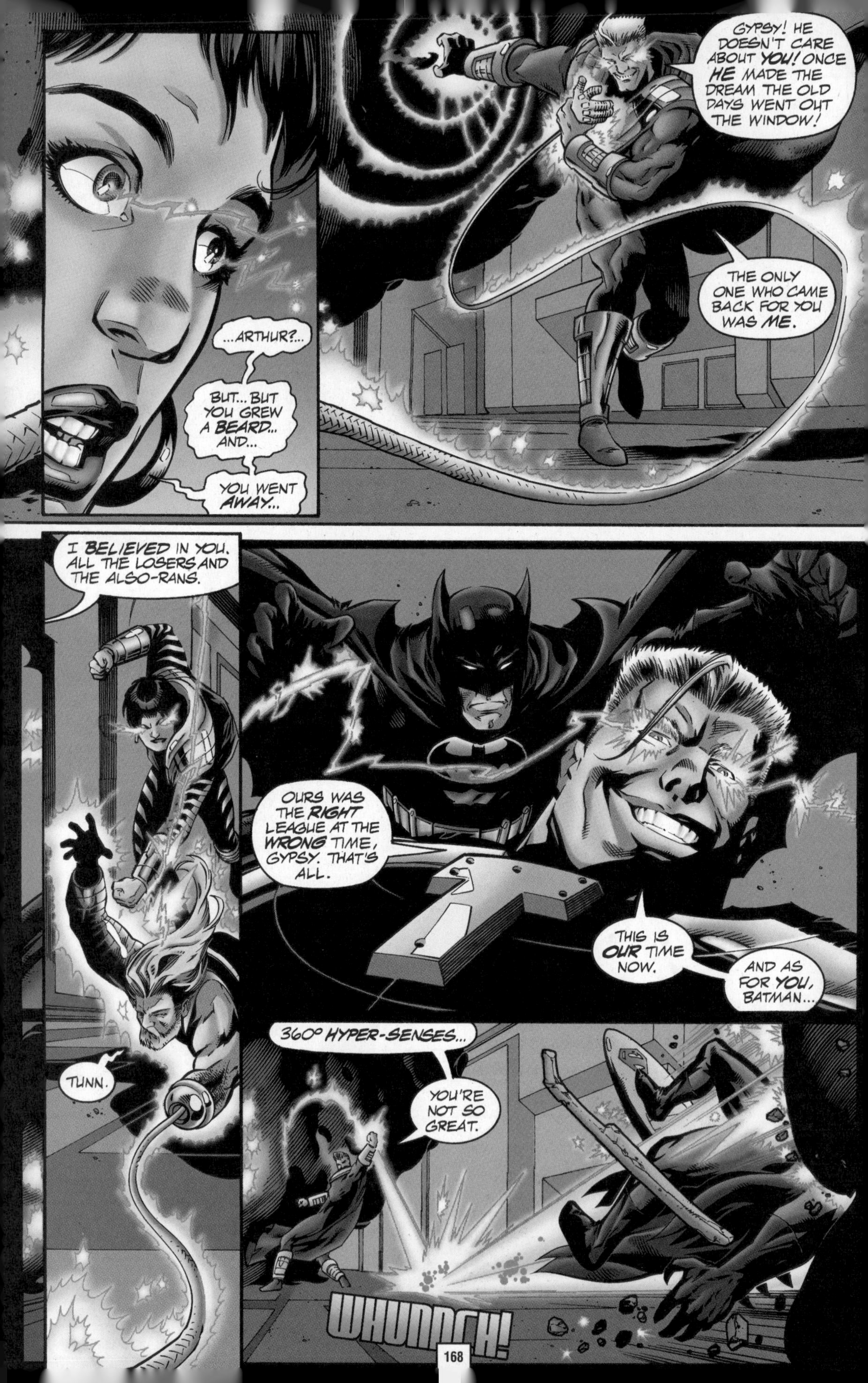
GYPSY! HE DOESN'T CARE ABOUT YOU! ONCE HE MADE THE DREAM THE OLD DAYS WENT OUT THE WINDOW!
THE ONLY ONE WHO CAME BACK FOR YOU WAS ME.
...ARTHUR?...
BUT... BUT YOU GREW A BEARD... AND...
YOU WENT AWAY...
I BELIEVED IN YOU. ALL THE LOSERS AND THE ALSO-RANS.
OURS WAS THE RIGHT LEAGUE AT THE WRONG TIME, GYPSY. THAT'S ALL.
THIS IS OUR TIME NOW.
AND AS FOR YOU, BATMAN...
TUNN.
360° HYPER-SENSES...
YOU'RE NOT SO GREAT.
WHUNNCH!

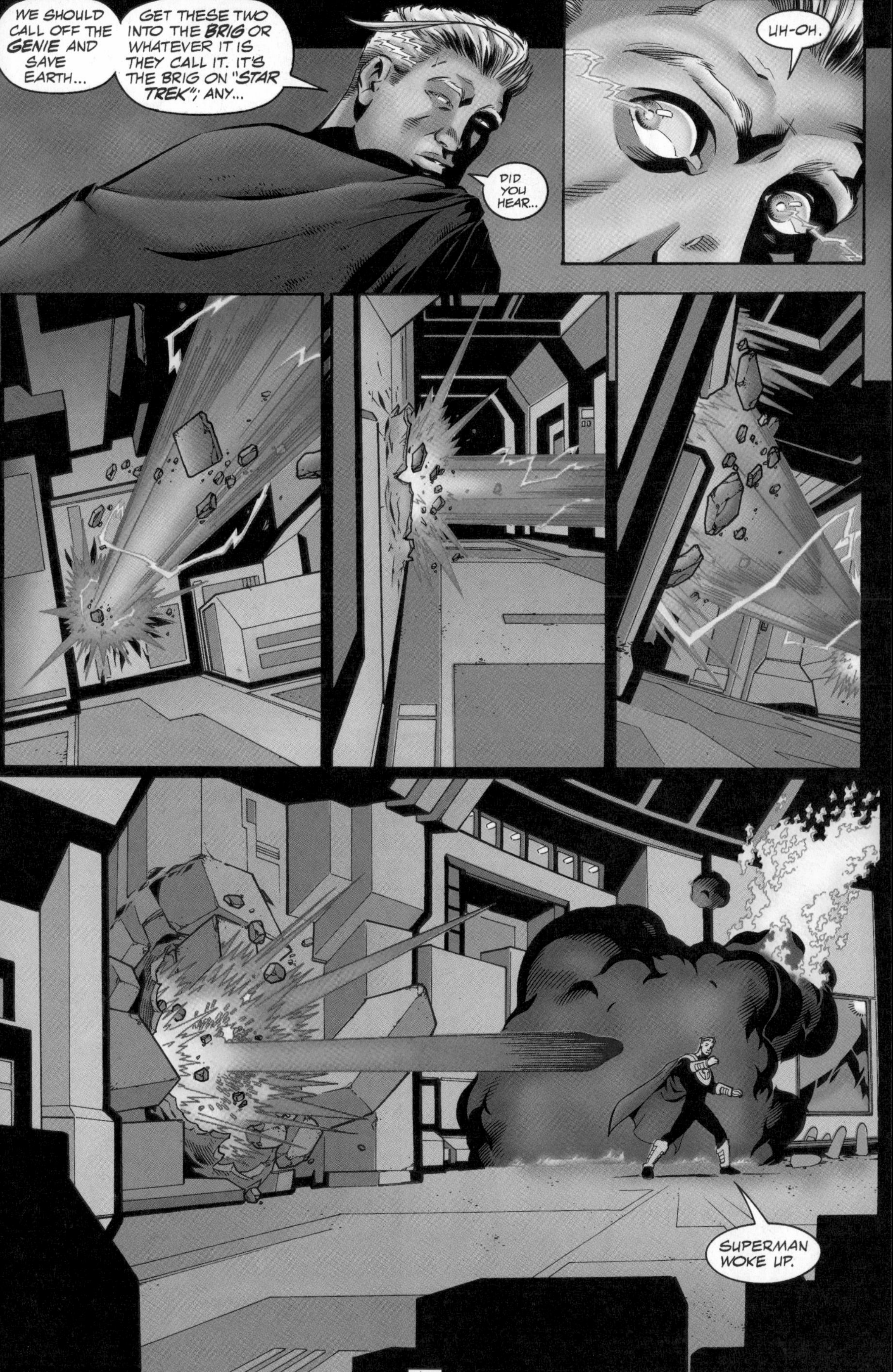
WE SHOULD CALL OFF THE GENIE AND SAVE EARTH...
GET THESE TWO INTO THE BRIG OR WHATEVER IT IS THEY CALL IT. IT'S THE BRIG ON "STAR TREK"; ANY...
DID YOU HEAR...
UH-OH.
SUPERMAN WOKE UP.

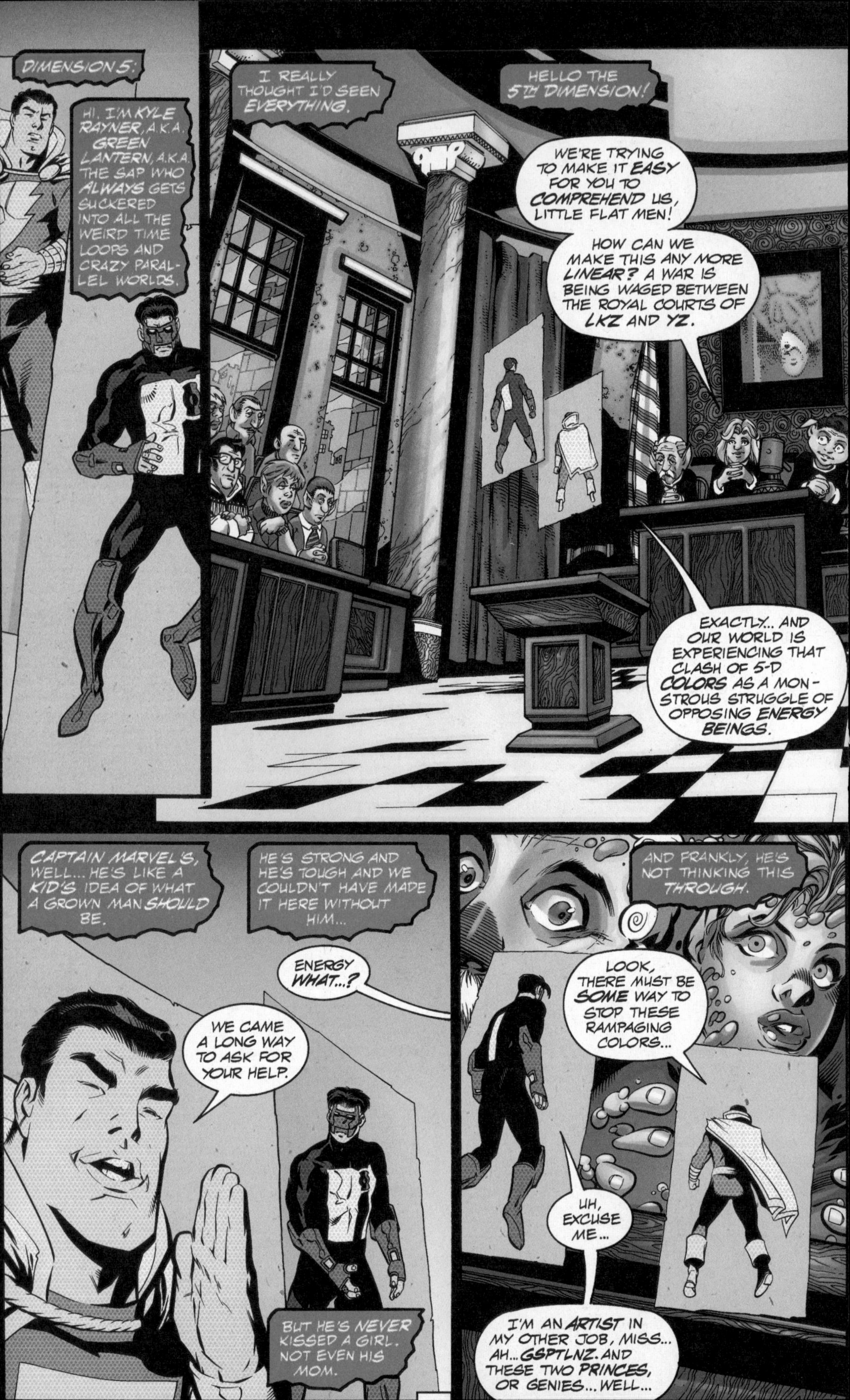
DIMENSION 5:
HI. I'M KYLE RAYNER, A.K.A. GREEN LANTERN, A.K.A. THE SAP WHO ALWAYS GETS SUCKERED INTO ALL THE WEIRD TIME LOOPS AND CRAZY PARALLEL WORLDS.
I REALLY THOUGHT I'D SEEN EVERYTHING.
HELLO THE 5TH DIMENSION!
WE'RE TRYING TO MAKE IT EASY FOR YOU TO COMPREHEND US, LITTLE FLAT MEN!
HOW CAN WE MAKE THIS ANY MORE LINEAR? A WAR IS BEING WAGED BETWEEN THE ROYAL COURTS OF LKZ AND YZ.
EXACTLY... AND OUR WORLD IS EXPERIENCING THAT CLASH OF 5-D COLORS AS A MONSTROUS STRUGGLE OF OPPOSING ENERGY BEINGS.
CAPTAIN MARVEL'S, WELL... HE'S LIKE A KID'S IDEA OF WHAT A GROWN MAN SHOULD BE.
HE'S STRONG AND HE'S TOUGH AND WE COULDN'T HAVE MADE IT HERE WITHOUT HIM...
ENERGY WHAT...?
WE CAME A LONG WAY TO ASK FOR YOUR HELP.
BUT HE'S NEVER KISSED A GIRL. NOT EVEN HIS MOM.
AND FRANKLY, HE'S NOT THINKING THIS THROUGH.
LOOK, THERE MUST BE SOME WAY TO STOP THESE RAMPAGING COLORS...
UH, EXCUSE ME...
I'M AN ARTIST IN MY OTHER JOB, MISS... AH... GSPTLNZ. AND THESE TWO PRINCES, OR GENIES... WELL...

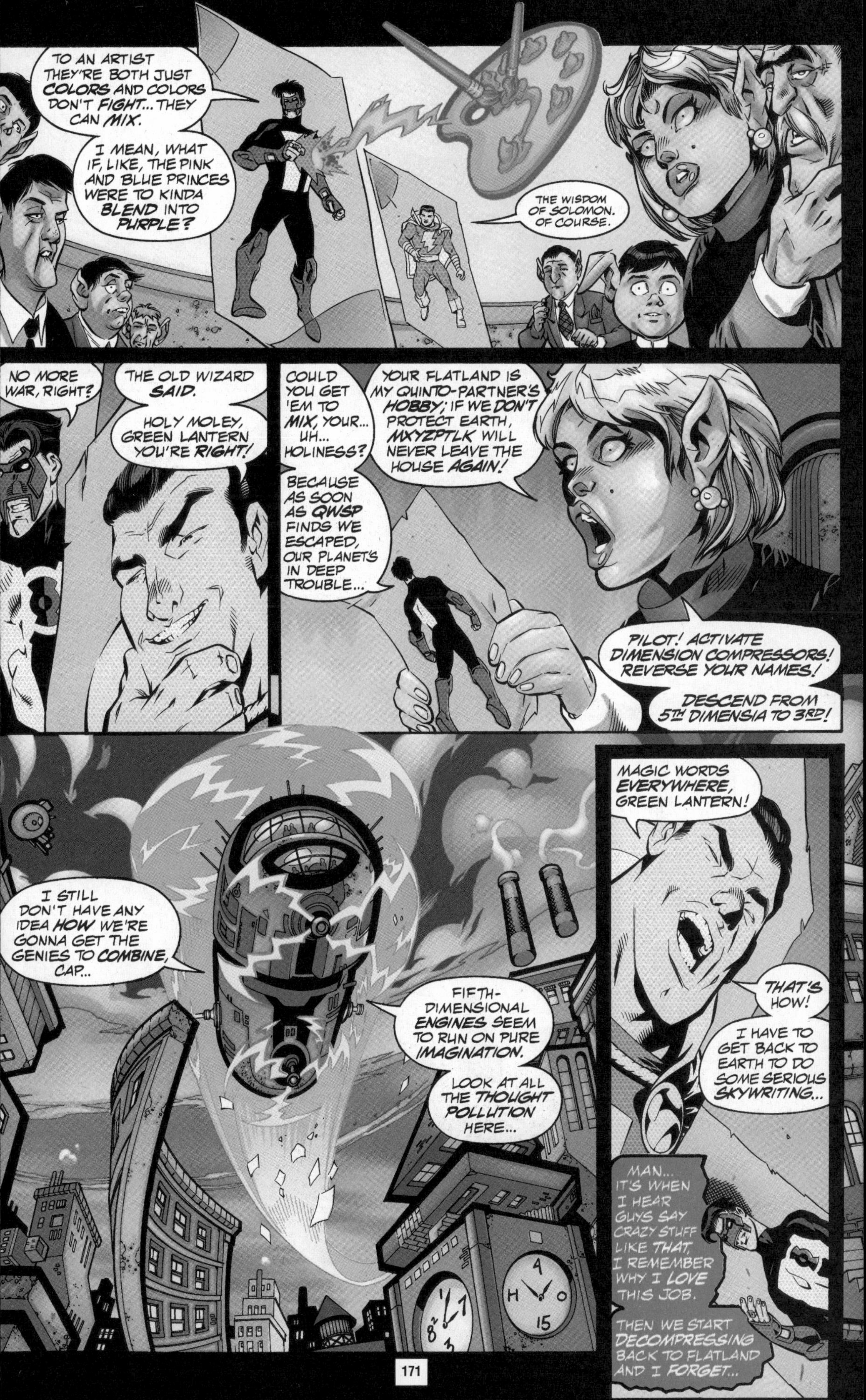
TO AN ARTIST THEY'RE BOTH JUST COLORS AND COLORS DON'T FIGHT... THEY CAN MIX.
I MEAN, WHAT IF, LIKE, THE PINK AND BLUE PRINCES WERE TO KINDA BLEND INTO PURPLE?
THE WISDOM OF SOLOMON. OF COURSE.
NO MORE WAR, RIGHT?
THE OLD WIZARD SAID.
HOLY MOLEY, GREEN LANTERN YOU'RE RIGHT!
COULD YOU GET 'EM TO MIX, YOUR... UH... HOLINESS?
BECAUSE AS SOON AS QWSP FINDS WE ESCAPED, OUR PLANET'S IN DEEP TROUBLE...
YOUR FLATLAND IS MY QUINTO-PARTNER'S HOBBY; IF WE DON'T PROTECT EARTH, MXYZPTLK WILL NEVER LEAVE THE HOUSE AGAIN!
PILOT! ACTIVATE DIMENSION COMPRESSORS! REVERSE YOUR NAMES!
DESCEND FROM 5TH DIMENSIA TO 3RD!
I STILL DON'T HAVE ANY IDEA HOW WE'RE GONNA GET THE GENIES TO COMBINE, CAP...
FIFTH-DIMENSIONAL ENGINES SEEM TO RUN ON PURE IMAGINATION.
LOOK AT ALL THE THOUGHT POLLUTION HERE...
MAGIC WORDS EVERYWHERE, GREEN LANTERN!
THAT'S HOW!
I HAVE TO GET BACK TO EARTH TO DO SOME SERIOUS SKYWRITING...
MAN... IT'S WHEN I HEAR GUYS SAY CRAZY STUFF LIKE THAT, I REMEMBER WHY I LOVE THIS JOB.
THEN WE START DECOMPRESSING BACK TO FLATLAND AND I FORGET...

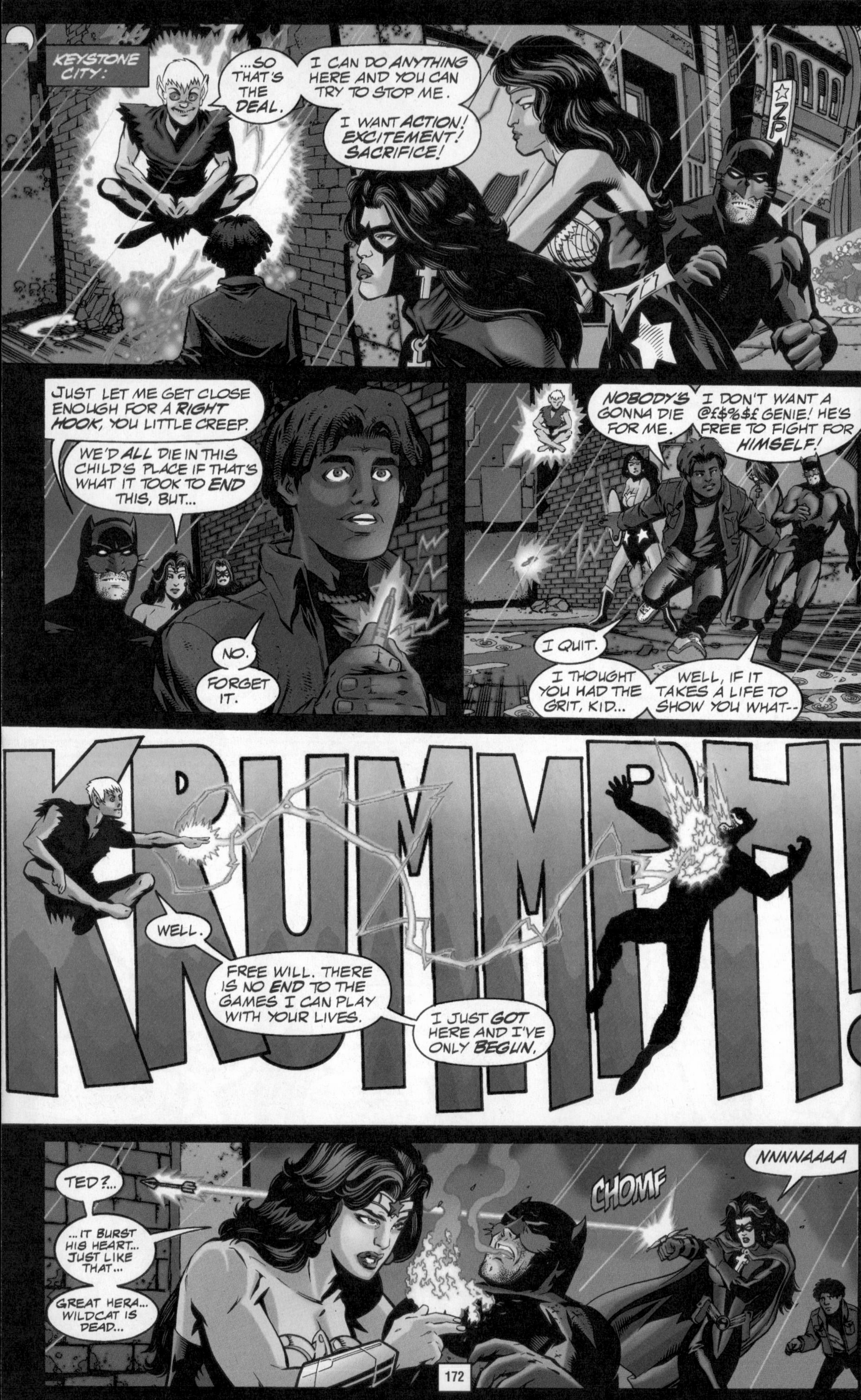
KEYSTONE CITY:
...SO THAT'S THE DEAL.
I CAN DO ANYTHING HERE AND YOU CAN TRY TO STOP ME.
I WANT ACTION! EXCITEMENT! SACRIFICE!
JUST LET ME GET CLOSE ENOUGH FOR A RIGHT HOOK, YOU LITTLE CREEP.
WE'D ALL DIE IN THIS CHILD'S PLACE IF THAT'S WHAT IT TOOK TO END THIS, BUT...
NO.
FORGET IT.
NOBODY'S GONNA DIE FOR ME.
I DON'T WANT A @£$%$£ GENIE! HE'S FREE TO FIGHT FOR HIMSELF!
I QUIT.
I THOUGHT YOU HAD THE GRIT, KID...
WELL, IF IT TAKES A LIFE TO SHOW YOU WHAT--
KRUMMPH!
WELL.
FREE WILL. THERE IS NO END TO THE GAMES I CAN PLAY WITH YOUR LIVES.
I JUST GOT HERE AND I'VE ONLY BEGUN.
TED?...
...IT BURST HIS HEART... JUST LIKE THAT...
GREAT HERA... WILDCAT IS DEAD...
CHOMF
NNNNAAAA

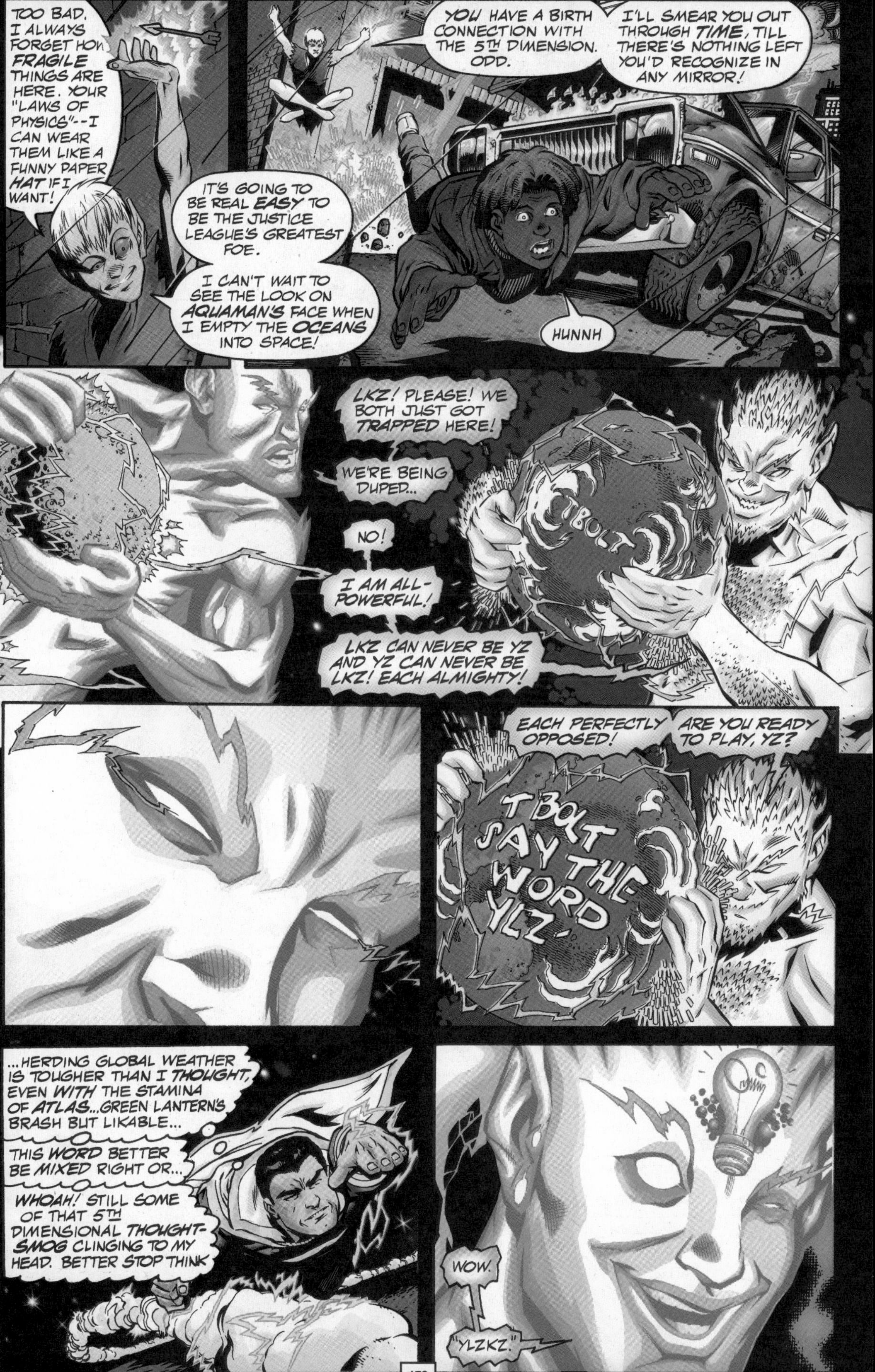
TOO BAD. I ALWAYS FORGET HOW FRAGILE THINGS ARE HERE. YOUR "LAWS OF PHYSICS"--I CAN WEAR THEM LIKE A FUNNY PAPER HAT IF I WANT!
IT'S GOING TO BE REAL EASY TO BE THE JUSTICE LEAGUE'S GREATEST FOE.
I CAN'T WAIT TO SEE THE LOOK ON AQUAMAN'S FACE WHEN I EMPTY THE OCEANS INTO SPACE!
YOU HAVE A BIRTH CONNECTION WITH THE 5TH DIMENSION. ODD.
I'LL SMEAR YOU OUT THROUGH TIME, TILL THERE'S NOTHING LEFT YOU'D RECOGNIZE IN ANY MIRROR!
HUNNH
LKZ! PLEASE! WE BOTH JUST GOT TRAPPED HERE!
WE'RE BEING DUPED..
NO!
I AM ALL-POWERFUL!
LKZ CAN NEVER BE YZ AND YZ CAN NEVER BE LKZ! EACH ALMIGHTY!
T BOLT
EACH PERFECTLY OPPOSED!
ARE YOU READY TO PLAY, YZ?
T BOLT SAY THE WORD YLZ-
...HERDING GLOBAL WEATHER IS TOUGHER THAN I THOUGHT, EVEN WITH THE STAMINA OF ATLAS...GREEN LANTERN'S BRASH BUT LIKABLE...
THIS WORD BETTER BE MIXED RIGHT OR...
WHOAH! STILL SOME OF THAT 5TH DIMENSIONAL THOUGHT-SMOG CLINGING TO MY HEAD. BETTER STOP THINK
WOW.
"YLZKZ."

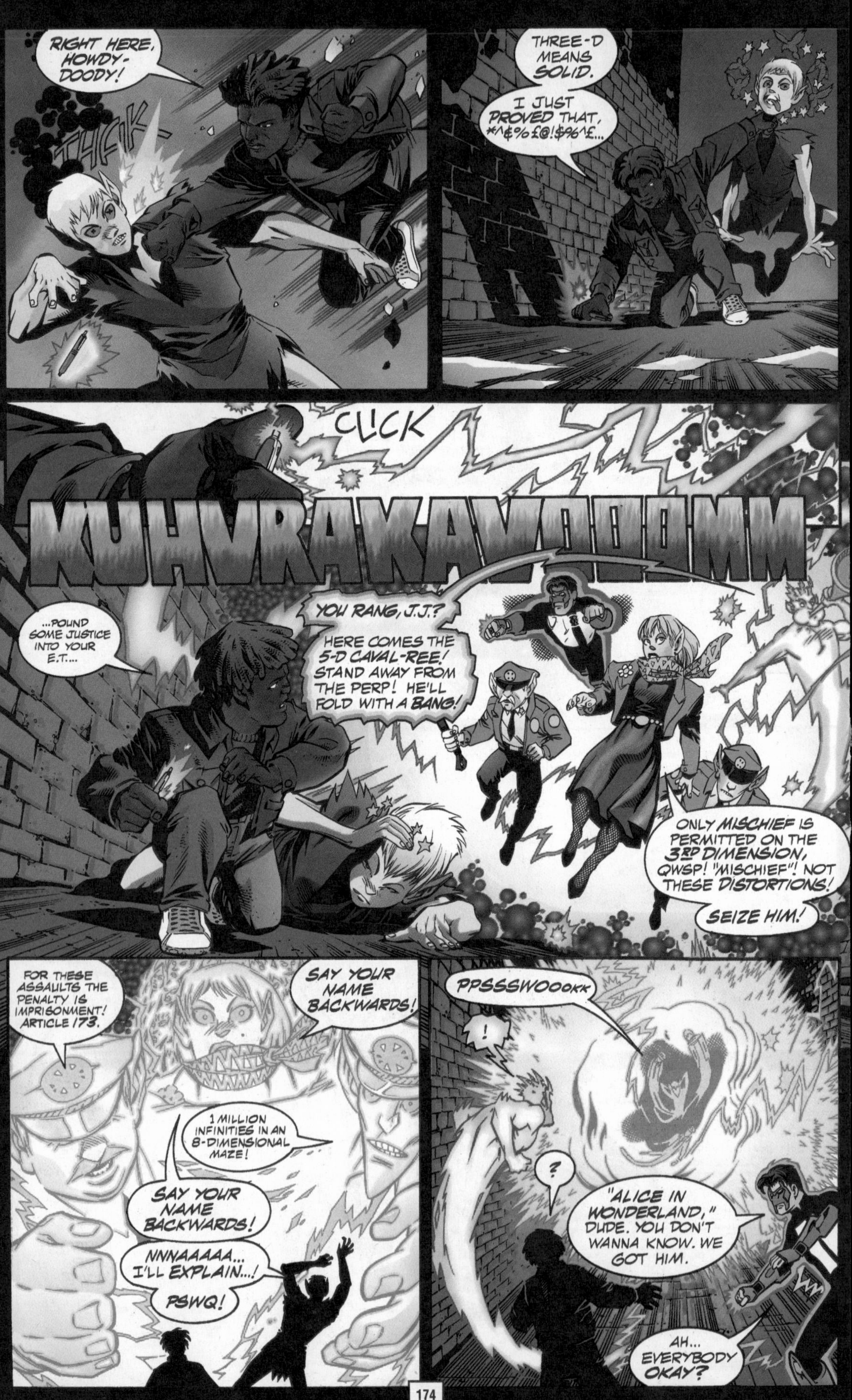
RIGHT HERE, HOWDY-DOODY!
THWAK
THREE-D MEANS SOLID.
I JUST PROVED THAT, *^¢%£@!$%^£...
CLICK
KUHVRAKAVOOMM
...POUND SOME JUSTICE INTO YOUR E.T....
YOU RANG, J.J.?
HERE COMES THE 5-D CAVAL-REE! STAND AWAY FROM THE PERP! HE'LL FOLD WITH A BANG!
ONLY MISCHIEF IS PERMITTED ON THE 3RD DIMENSION, QWSP! "MISCHIEF"! NOT THESE DISTORTIONS!
SEIZE HIM!
FOR THESE ASSAULTS THE PENALTY IS IMPRISONMENT! ARTICLE 173.
SAY YOUR NAME BACKWARDS!
1 MILLION INFINITIES IN AN 8-DIMENSIONAL MAZE!
SAY YOUR NAME BACKWARDS!
NNNAAAAA... I'LL EXPLAIN...!
PSWQ!
PPSSSWOOOokk
!
?
"ALICE IN WONDERLAND," DUDE. YOU DON'T WANNA KNOW. WE GOT HIM.
AH... EVERYBODY OKAY?

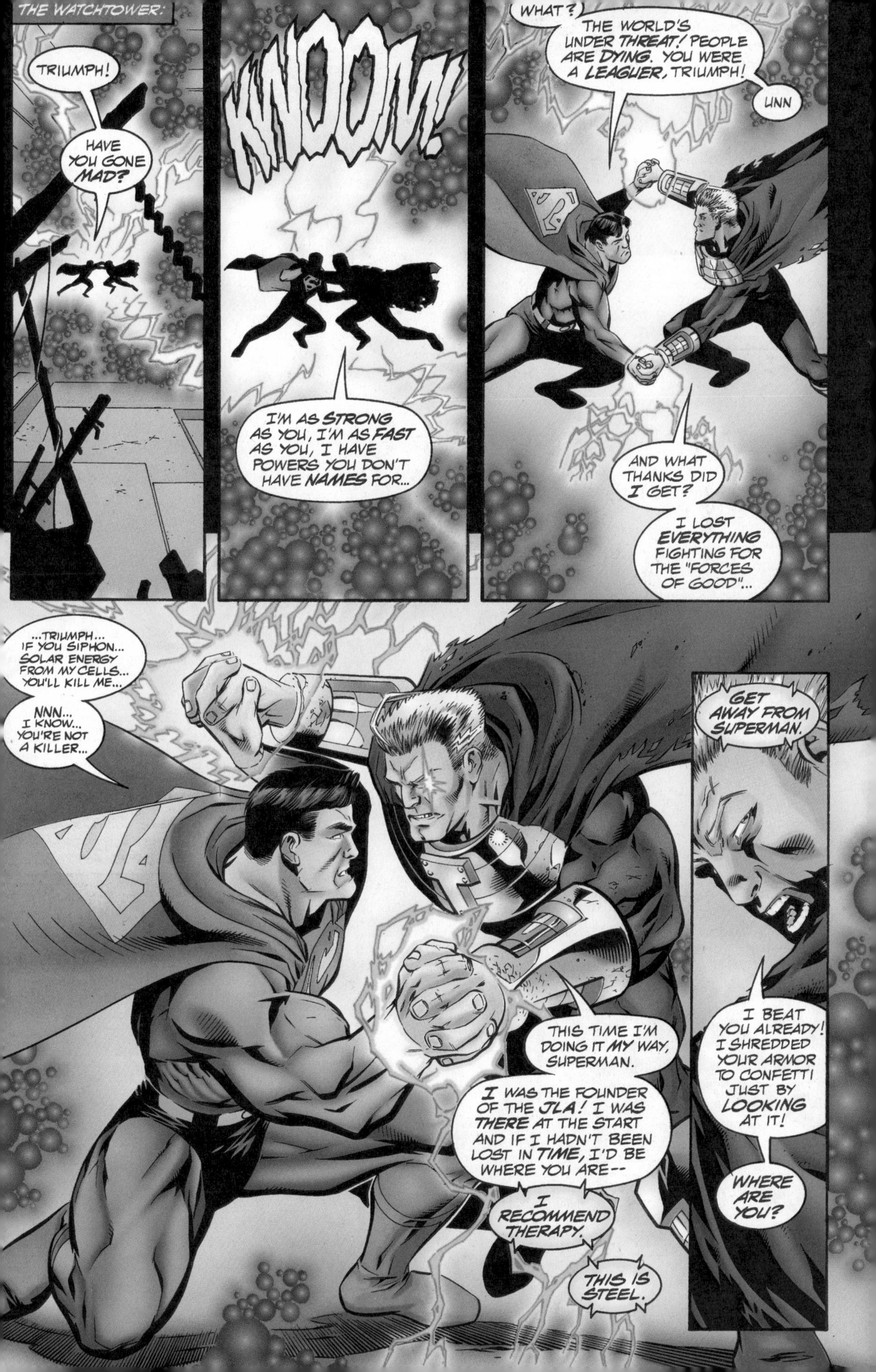
THE WATCHTOWER:
TRIUMPH!
HAVE YOU GONE MAD?
KNOOM!
I'M AS STRONG AS YOU, I'M AS FAST AS YOU, I HAVE POWERS YOU DON'T HAVE NAMES FOR...
WHAT?
THE WORLD'S UNDER THREAT! PEOPLE ARE DYING. YOU WERE A LEAGUER, TRIUMPH!
UNN
AND WHAT THANKS DID I GET?
I LOST EVERYTHING FIGHTING FOR THE "FORCES OF GOOD"...
...TRIUMPH... IF YOU SIPHON... SOLAR ENERGY FROM MY CELLS... YOU'LL KILL ME...
NNN... I KNOW... YOU'RE NOT A KILLER...
THIS TIME I'M DOING IT MY WAY, SUPERMAN.
I WAS THE FOUNDER OF THE JLA! I WAS THERE AT THE START AND IF I HADN'T BEEN LOST IN TIME, I'D BE WHERE YOU ARE--
I RECOMMEND THERAPY.
THIS IS STEEL.
GET AWAY FROM SUPERMAN.
I BEAT YOU ALREADY! I SHREDDED YOUR ARMOR TO CONFETTI JUST BY LOOKING AT IT!
WHERE ARE YOU?

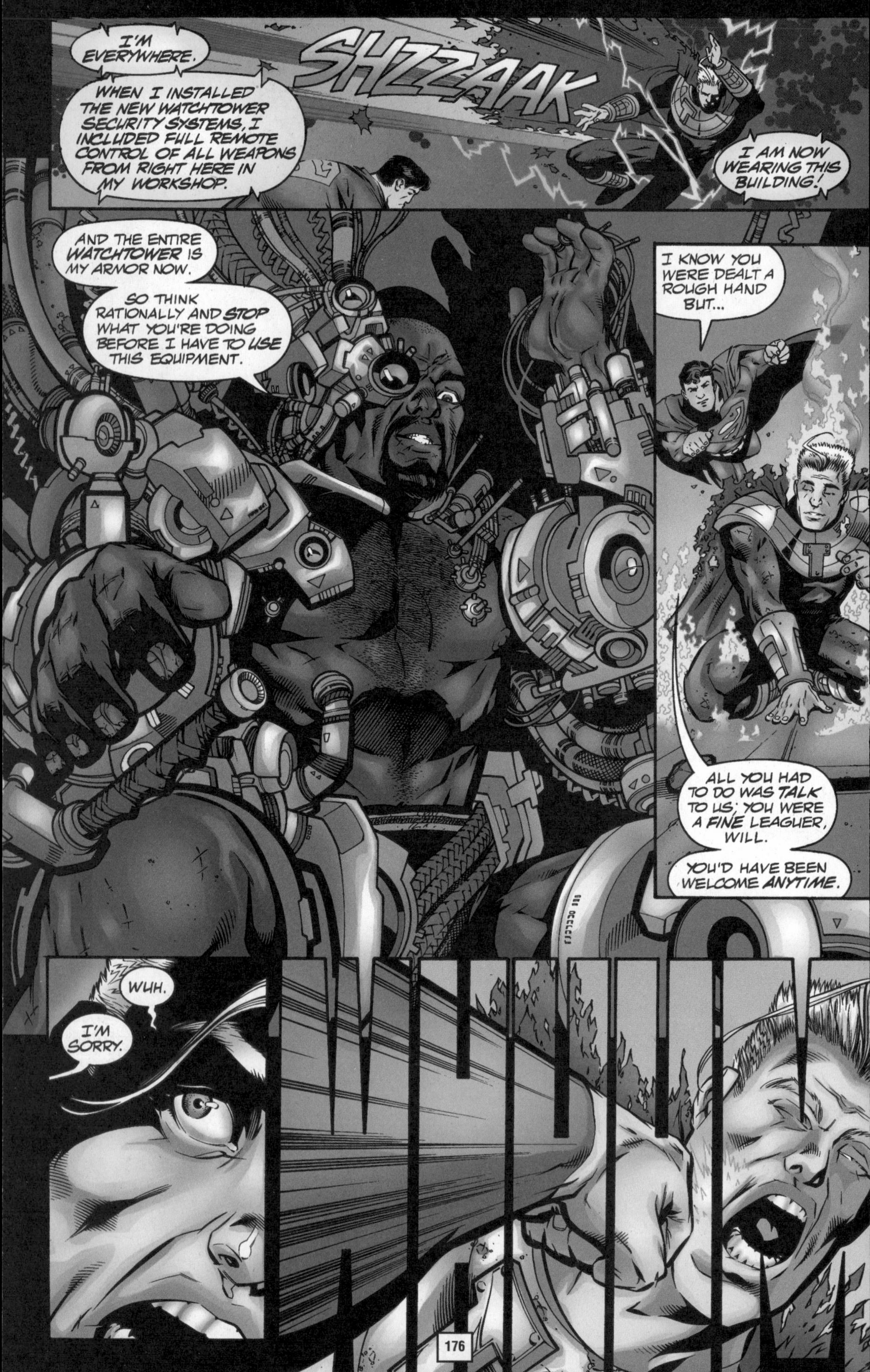
I'M EVERYWHERE.
SHZZAAK
WHEN I INSTALLED THE NEW WATCHTOWER SECURITY SYSTEMS, I INCLUDED FULL REMOTE CONTROL OF ALL WEAPONS FROM RIGHT HERE IN MY WORKSHOP.
I AM NOW WEARING THIS BUILDING!
AND THE ENTIRE WATCHTOWER IS MY ARMOR NOW.
SO THINK RATIONALLY AND STOP WHAT YOU'RE DOING BEFORE I HAVE TO USE THIS EQUIPMENT.
I KNOW YOU WERE DEALT A ROUGH HAND BUT...
ALL YOU HAD TO DO WAS TALK TO US; YOU WERE A FINE LEAGUER, WILL.
YOU'D HAVE BEEN WELCOME ANYTIME.
WUH.
I'M SORRY.

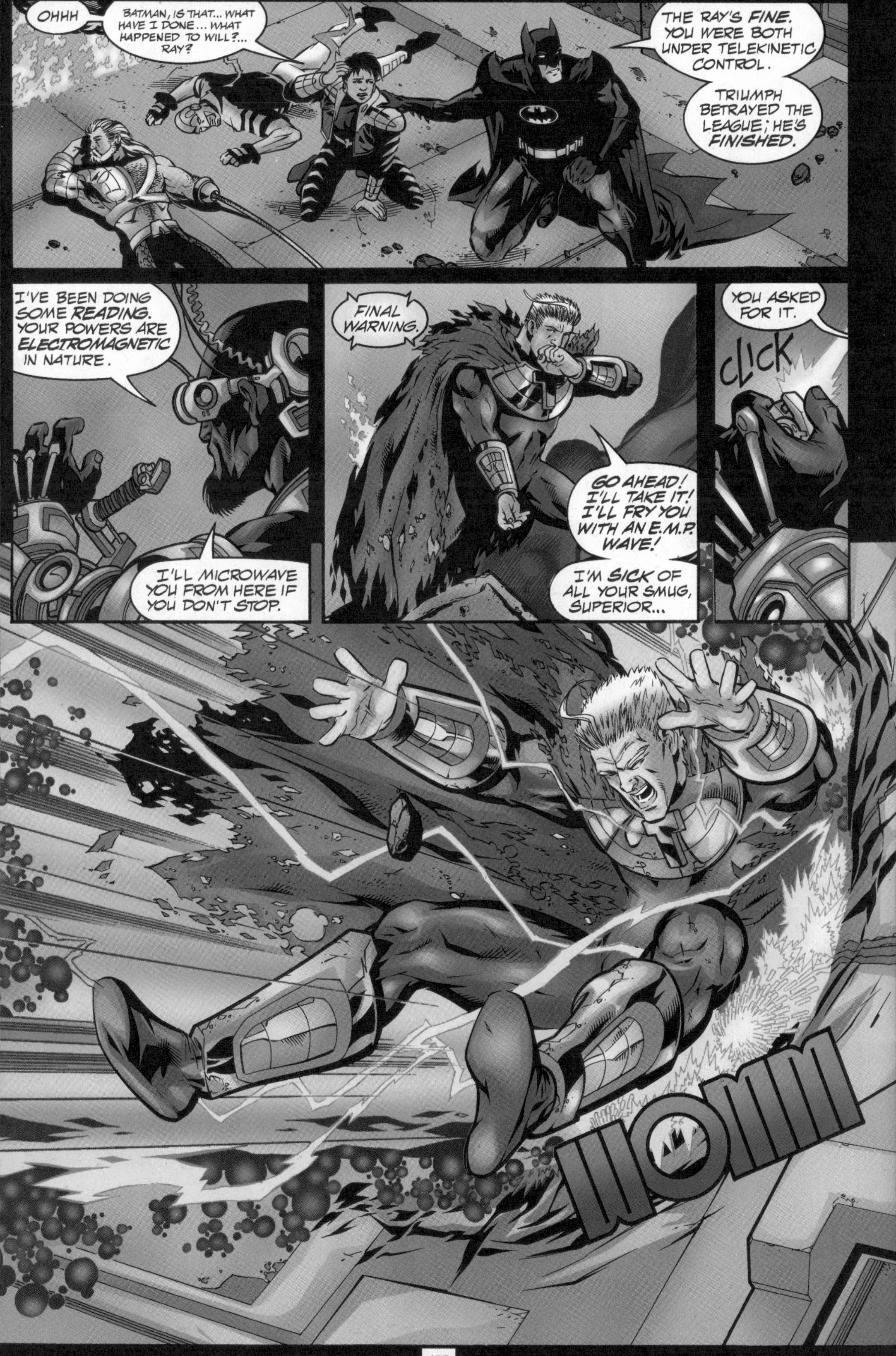

OHHH
BATMAN, IS THAT... WHAT HAVE I DONE... WHAT HAPPENED TO WILL?... RAY?
THE RAY'S FINE. YOU WERE BOTH UNDER TELEKINETIC CONTROL.
TRIUMPH BETRAYED THE LEAGUE; HE'S FINISHED.
I'VE BEEN DOING SOME READING. YOUR POWERS ARE ELECTROMAGNETIC IN NATURE.
I'LL MICROWAVE YOU FROM HERE IF YOU DON'T STOP.
FINAL WARNING.
GO AHEAD! I'LL TAKE IT! I'LL FRY YOU WITH AN E.M.P. WAVE!
I'M SICK OF ALL YOUR SMUG, SUPERIOR...
YOU ASKED FOR IT.
CLICK
WOMM

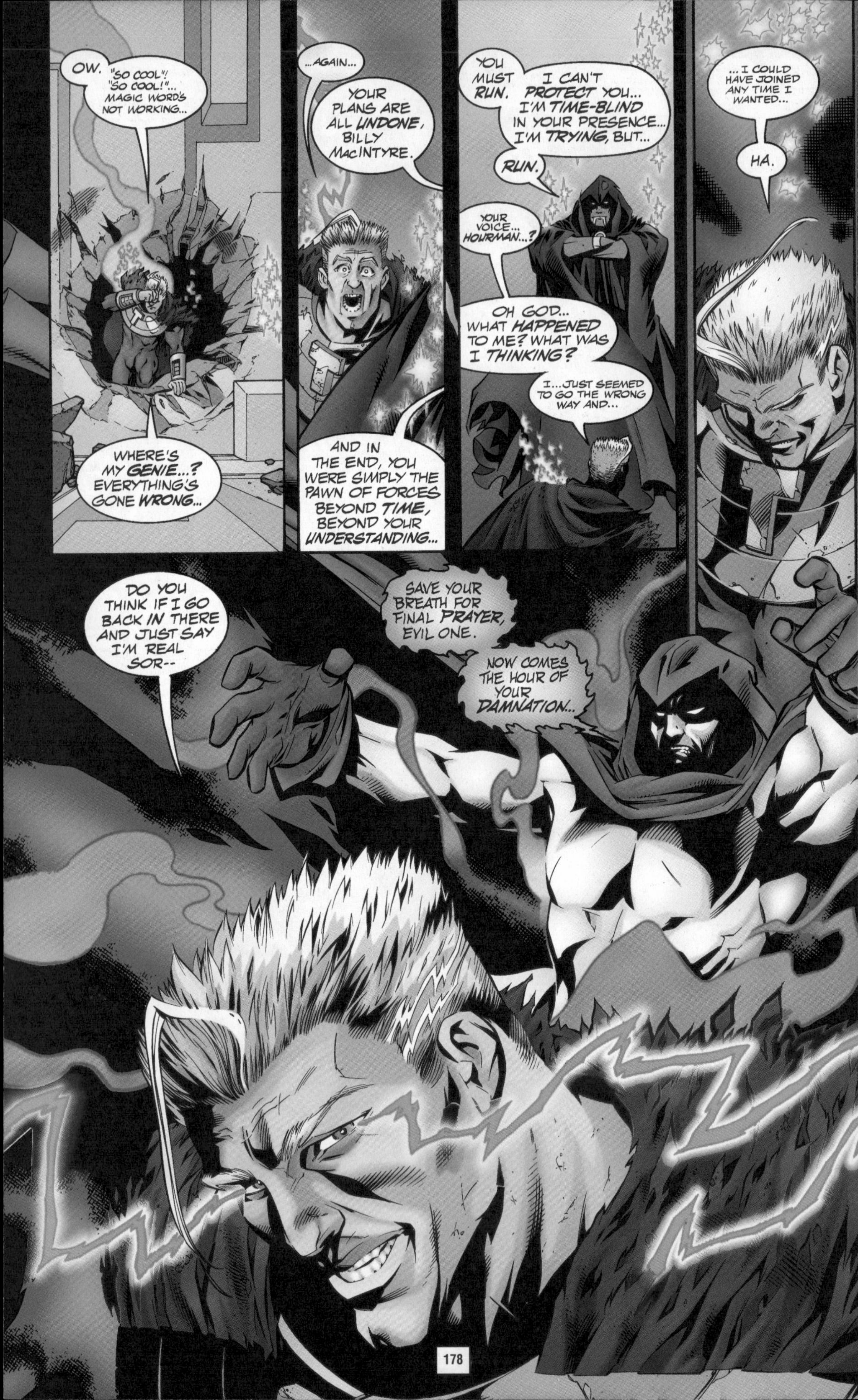
OW. "SO COOL"! "SO COOL!"... MAGIC WORD'S NOT WORKING...
WHERE'S MY GENIE...? EVERYTHING'S GONE WRONG...
...AGAIN...
YOUR PLANS ARE ALL UNDONE, BILLY MacINTYRE.
AND IN THE END, YOU WERE SIMPLY THE PAWN OF FORCES BEYOND TIME, BEYOND YOUR UNDERSTANDING...
YOU MUST RUN.
I CAN'T PROTECT YOU... I'M TIME-BLIND IN YOUR PRESENCE... I'M TRYING, BUT...
RUN.
YOUR VOICE... HOURMAN...?
OH GOD... WHAT HAPPENED TO ME? WHAT WAS I THINKING?
I...JUST SEEMED TO GO THE WRONG WAY AND...
...I COULD HAVE JOINED ANY TIME I WANTED...
HA.
DO YOU THINK IF I GO BACK IN THERE AND JUST SAY I'M REAL SOR--
SAVE YOUR BREATH FOR FINAL PRAYER, EVIL ONE.
NOW COMES THE HOUR OF YOUR DAMNATION...

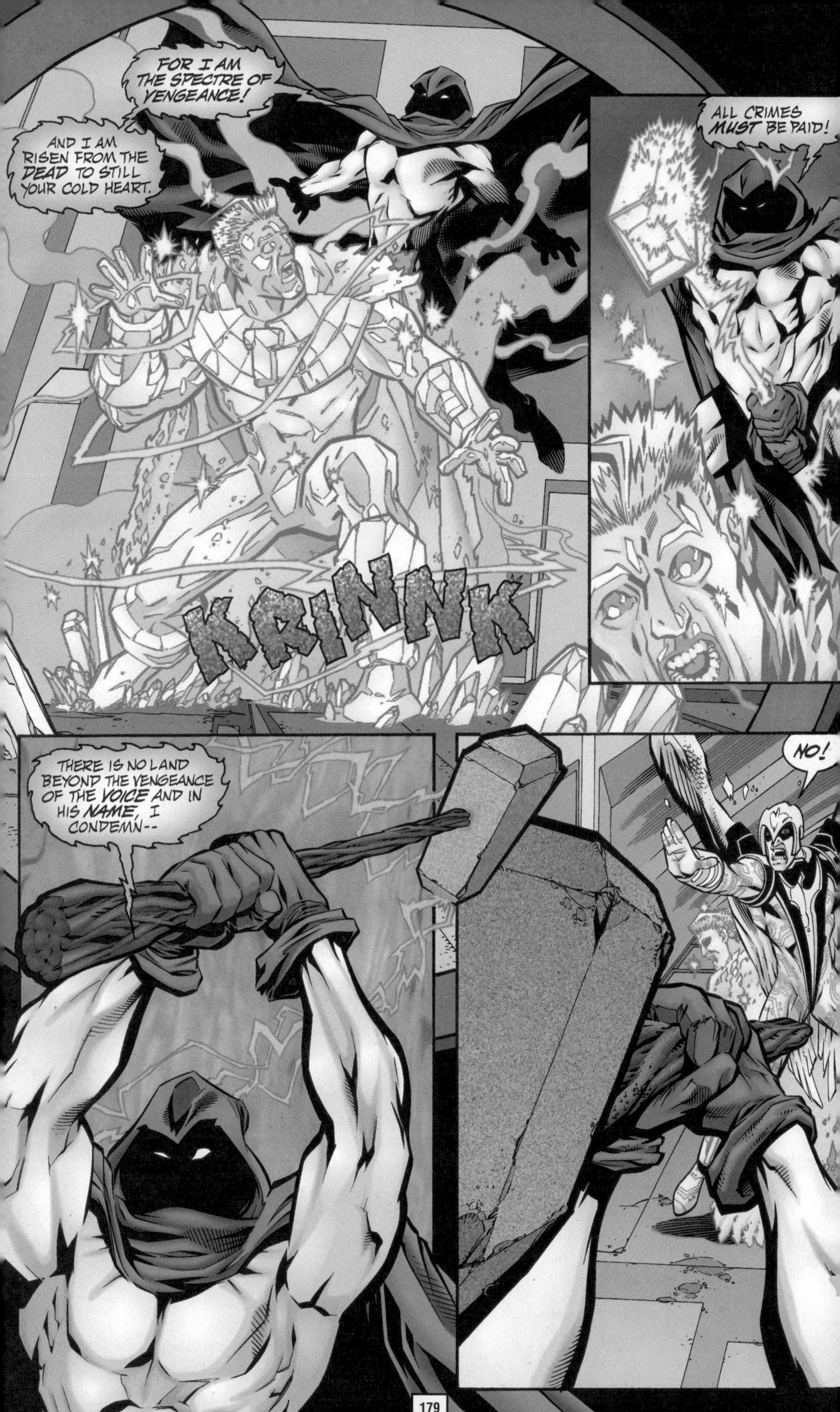
FOR I AM THE SPECTRE OF VENGEANCE!
AND I AM RISEN FROM THE DEAD TO STILL YOUR COLD HEART.
ALL CRIMES MUST BE PAID!
KRINNK
THERE IS NO LAND BEYOND THE VENGEANCE OF THE VOICE AND IN HIS NAME, I CONDEMN--
NO!

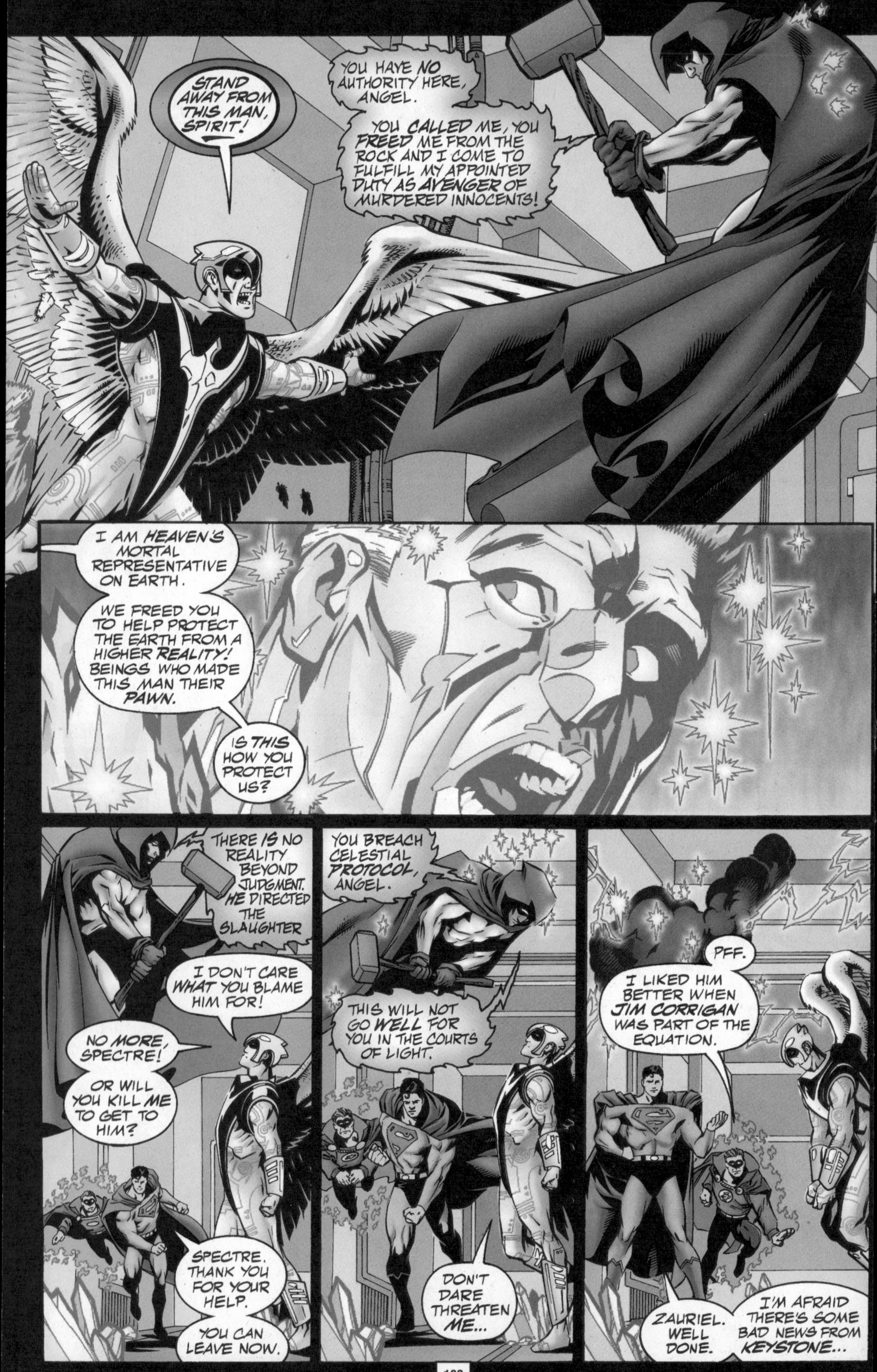
STAND AWAY FROM THIS MAN, SPIRIT!
YOU HAVE NO AUTHORITY HERE, ANGEL.
YOU CALLED ME, YOU FREED ME FROM THE ROCK AND I COME TO FULFILL MY APPOINTED DUTY AS AVENGER OF MURDERED INNOCENTS!
I AM HEAVEN'S MORTAL REPRESENTATIVE ON EARTH.
WE FREED YOU TO HELP PROTECT THE EARTH FROM A HIGHER REALITY! BEINGS WHO MADE THIS MAN THEIR PAWN.
IS THIS HOW YOU PROTECT US?
THERE IS NO REALITY BEYOND JUDGMENT. HE DIRECTED THE SLAUGHTER
I DON'T CARE WHAT YOU BLAME HIM FOR!
NO MORE, SPECTRE!
OR WILL YOU KILL ME TO GET TO HIM?
SPECTRE. THANK YOU FOR YOUR HELP.
YOU CAN LEAVE NOW.
YOU BREACH CELESTIAL PROTOCOL, ANGEL.
THIS WILL NOT GO WELL FOR YOU IN THE COURTS OF LIGHT.
DON'T DARE THREATEN ME...
PFF.
I LIKED HIM BETTER WHEN JIM CORRIGAN WAS PART OF THE EQUATION.
ZAURIEL. WELL DONE.
I'M AFRAID THERE'S SOME BAD NEWS FROM KEYSTONE...

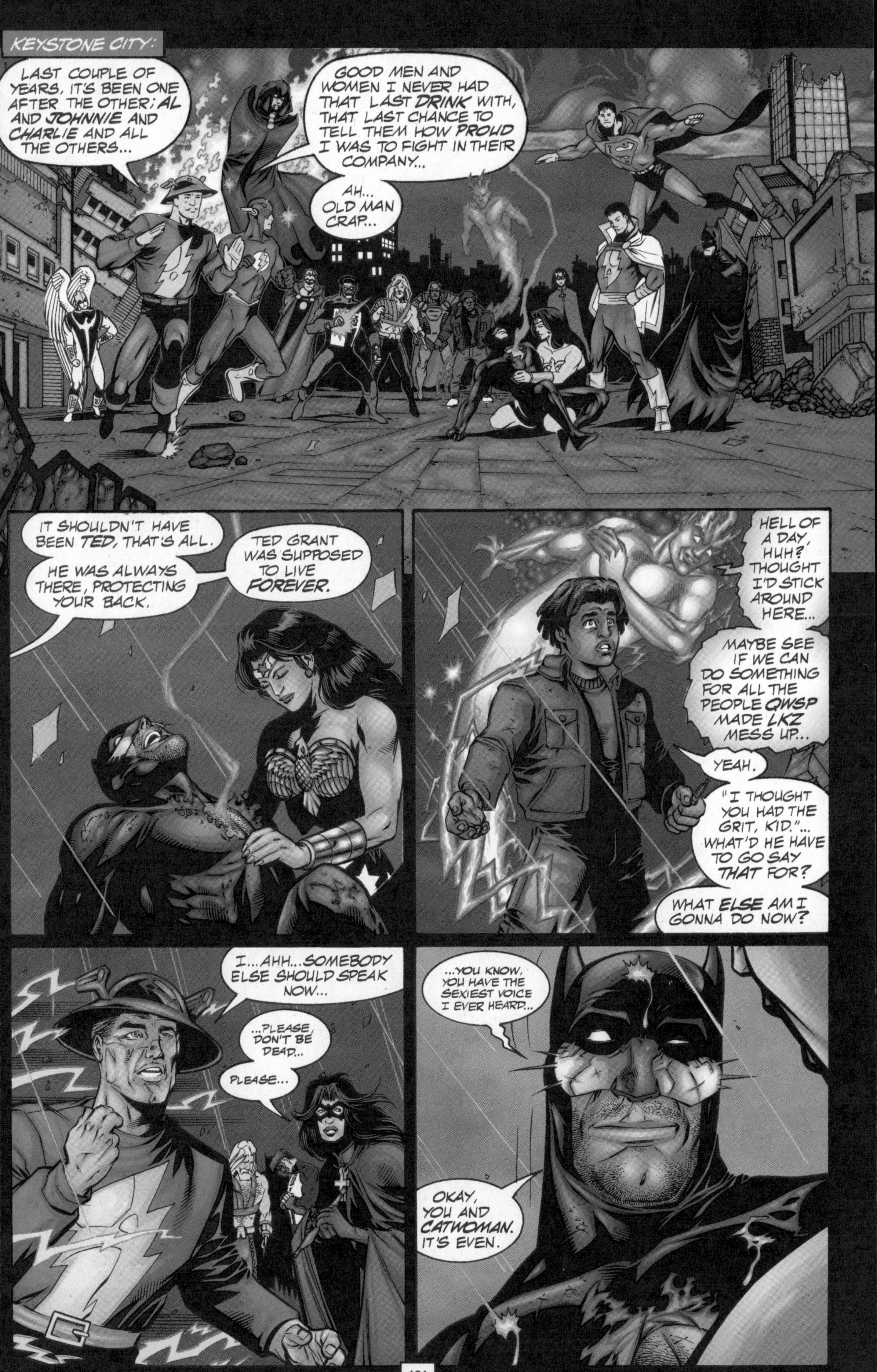

KEYSTONE CITY:
LAST COUPLE OF YEARS, IT'S BEEN ONE AFTER THE OTHER; AL AND JOHNNIE AND CHARLIE AND ALL THE OTHERS...
GOOD MEN AND WOMEN I NEVER HAD THAT LAST DRINK WITH, THAT LAST CHANCE TO TELL THEM HOW PROUD I WAS TO FIGHT IN THEIR COMPANY...
AH... OLD MAN CRAP...
IT SHOULDN'T HAVE BEEN TED, THAT'S ALL.
HE WAS ALWAYS THERE, PROTECTING YOUR BACK.
TED GRANT WAS SUPPOSED TO LIVE FOREVER.
HELL OF A DAY, HUH? THOUGHT I'D STICK AROUND HERE...
MAYBE SEE IF WE CAN DO SOMETHING FOR ALL THE PEOPLE QWSP MADE LKZ MESS UP...
YEAH.
"I THOUGHT YOU HAD THE GRIT, KID."... WHAT'D HE HAVE TO GO SAY THAT FOR?
WHAT ELSE AM I GONNA DO NOW?
I...AHH...SOMEBODY ELSE SHOULD SPEAK NOW...
...PLEASE, DON'T BE DEAD...
PLEASE...
...YOU KNOW, YOU HAVE THE SEXIEST VOICE I EVER HEARD...
OKAY, YOU AND CATWOMAN. IT'S EVEN.

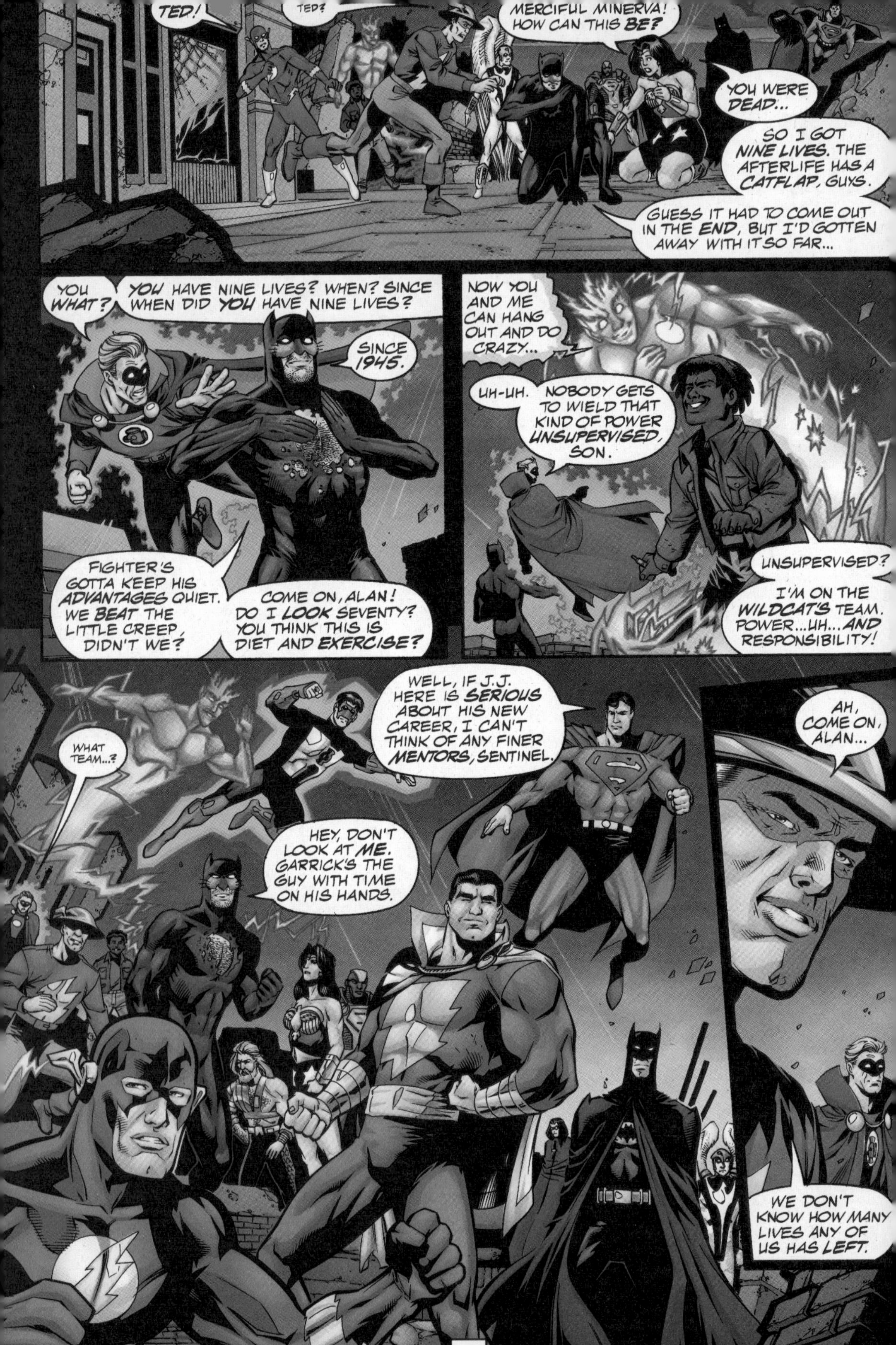
TED!
TED?
MERCIFUL MINERVA! HOW CAN THIS BE?
YOU WERE DEAD...
SO I GOT NINE LIVES. THE AFTERLIFE HAS A CATFLAP, GUYS.
GUESS IT HAD TO COME OUT IN THE END, BUT I'D GOTTEN AWAY WITH IT SO FAR...
YOU WHAT?
YOU HAVE NINE LIVES? WHEN? SINCE WHEN DID YOU HAVE NINE LIVES?
SINCE 1945.
FIGHTER'S GOTTA KEEP HIS ADVANTAGES QUIET. WE BEAT THE LITTLE CREEP, DIDN'T WE?
COME ON, ALAN! DO I LOOK SEVENTY? YOU THINK THIS IS DIET AND EXERCISE?
NOW YOU AND ME CAN HANG OUT AND DO CRAZY...
UH-UH.
NOBODY GETS TO WIELD THAT KIND OF POWER UNSUPERVISED, SON.
UNSUPERVISED?
I'M ON THE WILDCAT'S TEAM. POWER...UH...AND RESPONSIBILITY!
WHAT TEAM...?
WELL, IF J.J. HERE IS SERIOUS ABOUT HIS NEW CAREER, I CAN'T THINK OF ANY FINER MENTORS, SENTINEL.
HEY, DON'T LOOK AT ME. GARRICK'S THE GUY WITH TIME ON HIS HANDS.
AH, COME ON, ALAN...
WE DON'T KNOW HOW MANY LIVES ANY OF US HAS LEFT.

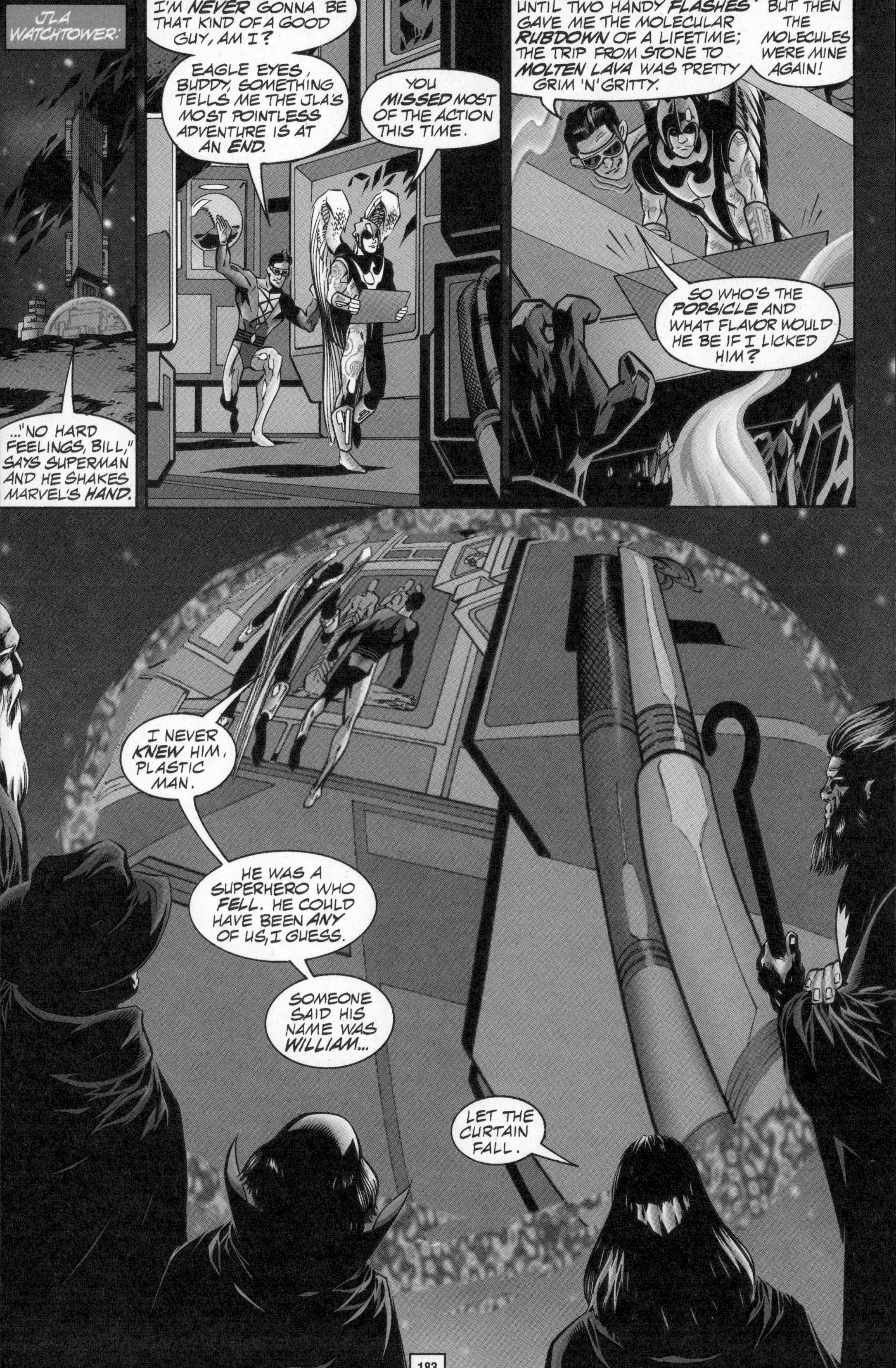

JLA WATCHTOWER:
..."NO HARD FEELINGS, BILL," SAYS SUPERMAN AND HE SHAKES MARVEL'S HAND.
I'M NEVER GONNA BE THAT KIND OF A GOOD GUY, AM I?
EAGLE EYES, BUDDY, SOMETHING TELLS ME THE JLA'S MOST POINTLESS ADVENTURE IS AT AN END.
YOU MISSED MOST OF THE ACTION THIS TIME.
UNTIL TWO HANDY FLASHES GAVE ME THE MOLECULAR RUBDOWN OF A LIFETIME; THE TRIP FROM STONE TO MOLTEN LAVA WAS PRETTY GRIM 'N' GRITTY.
BUT THEN THE MOLECULES WERE MINE AGAIN!
SO WHO'S THE POPSICLE AND WHAT FLAVOR WOULD HE BE IF I LICKED HIM?
I NEVER KNEW HIM, PLASTIC MAN.
HE WAS A SUPERHERO WHO FELL. HE COULD HAVE BEEN ANY OF US, I GUESS.
SOMEONE SAID HIS NAME WAS WILLIAM...
LET THE CURTAIN FALL.

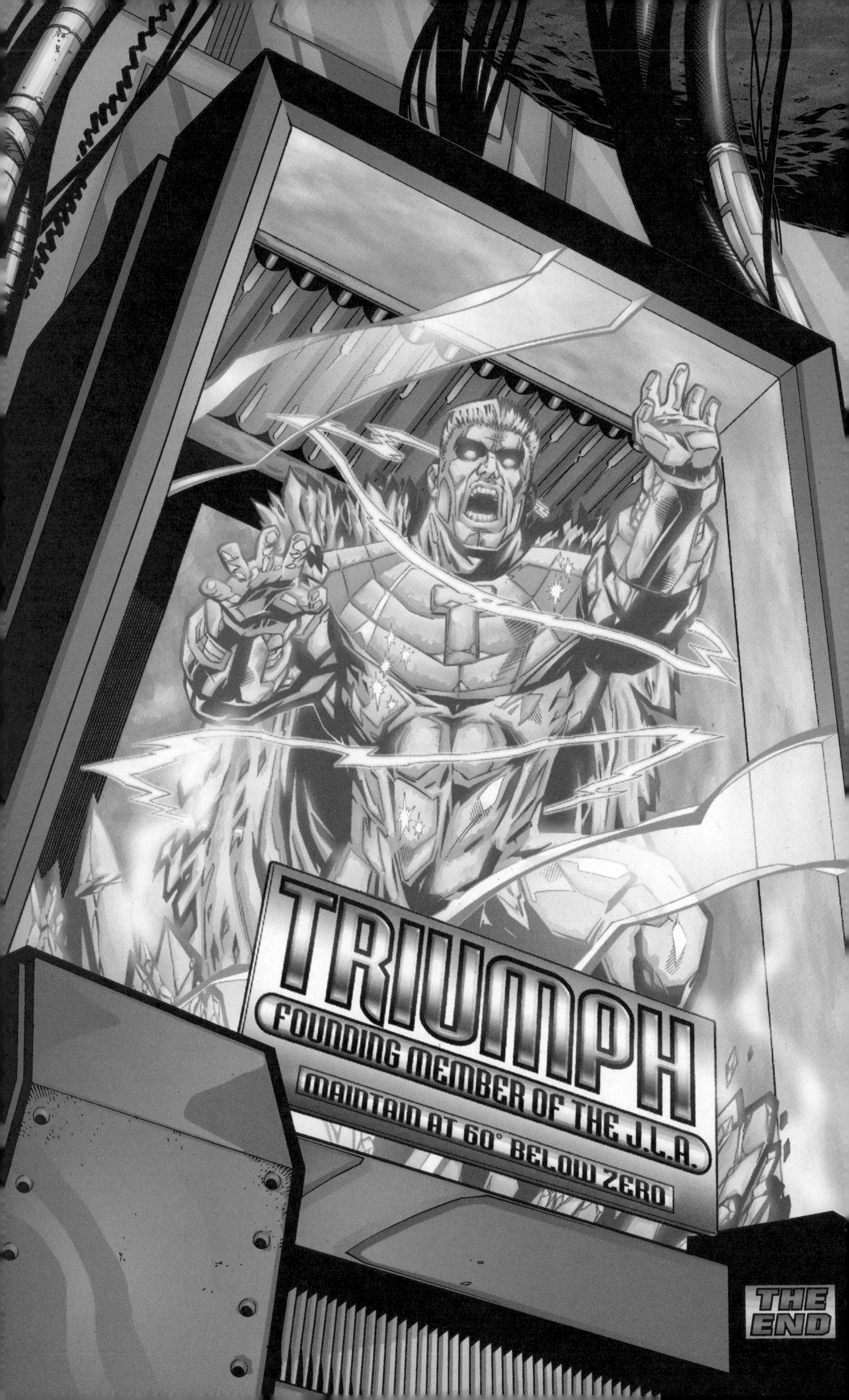
TRIUMPH
FOUNDING MEMBER OF THE J.L.A.
MAINTAIN AT 60° BELOW ZERO
THE END

INSIDE JOB

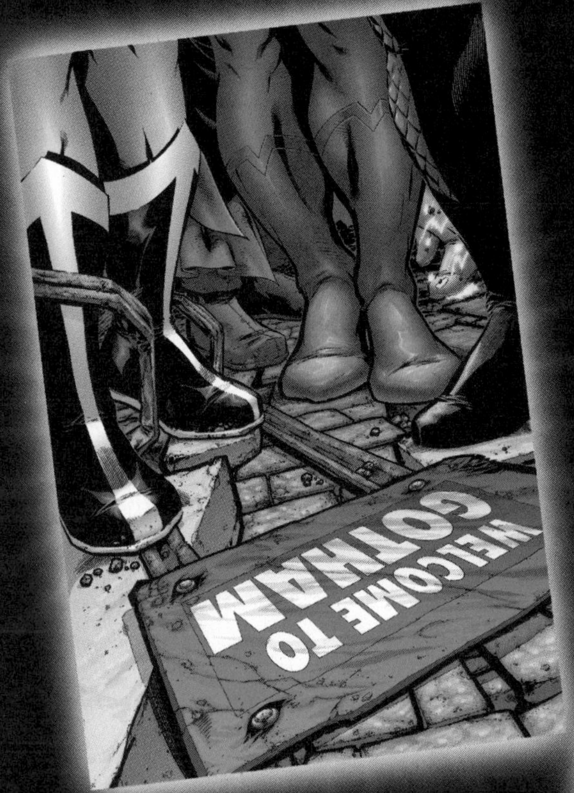
WELCOME TO GOTHAM

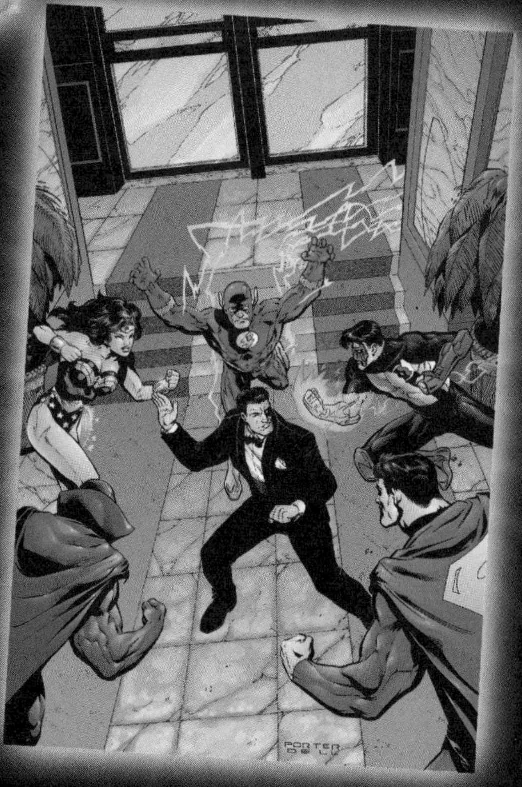

ALTERED EGO

...BELIEVE WHAT YOU READ IN THE NEWSPAPERS. POLLS INDICATED THAT, AFTER ITS PLAGUES AND ITS EARTHQUAKE, MOST AMERICANS WERE WILLING TO WRITE GOTHAM CITY OFF.
...BUT IT DOESN'T CHANGE THE CONSEQUENCES. FEDERAL AID DENIED, UTILITIES SHUT DOWN... THE CITY ACTUALLY SEALED OFF...
...AND SO, SO MANY PEOPLE REFUSING TO EVACUATE BEFORE THE NATIONAL GUARD CLOSED ALL EXITS.
I CHOOSE TO BELIEVE THAT THEY FELT SO WITH DEEP REGRET...
THOSE WHO LEFT AND THOSE WHO STAYED-- ALL DENIED SHELTER, ALL LEFT HOMELESS. I WISH THERE WERE MORE I COULD DO TO HELP.
WHICH IS WHY YOU'RE STANDING AT THE EDGE OF THE IONOSPHERE.

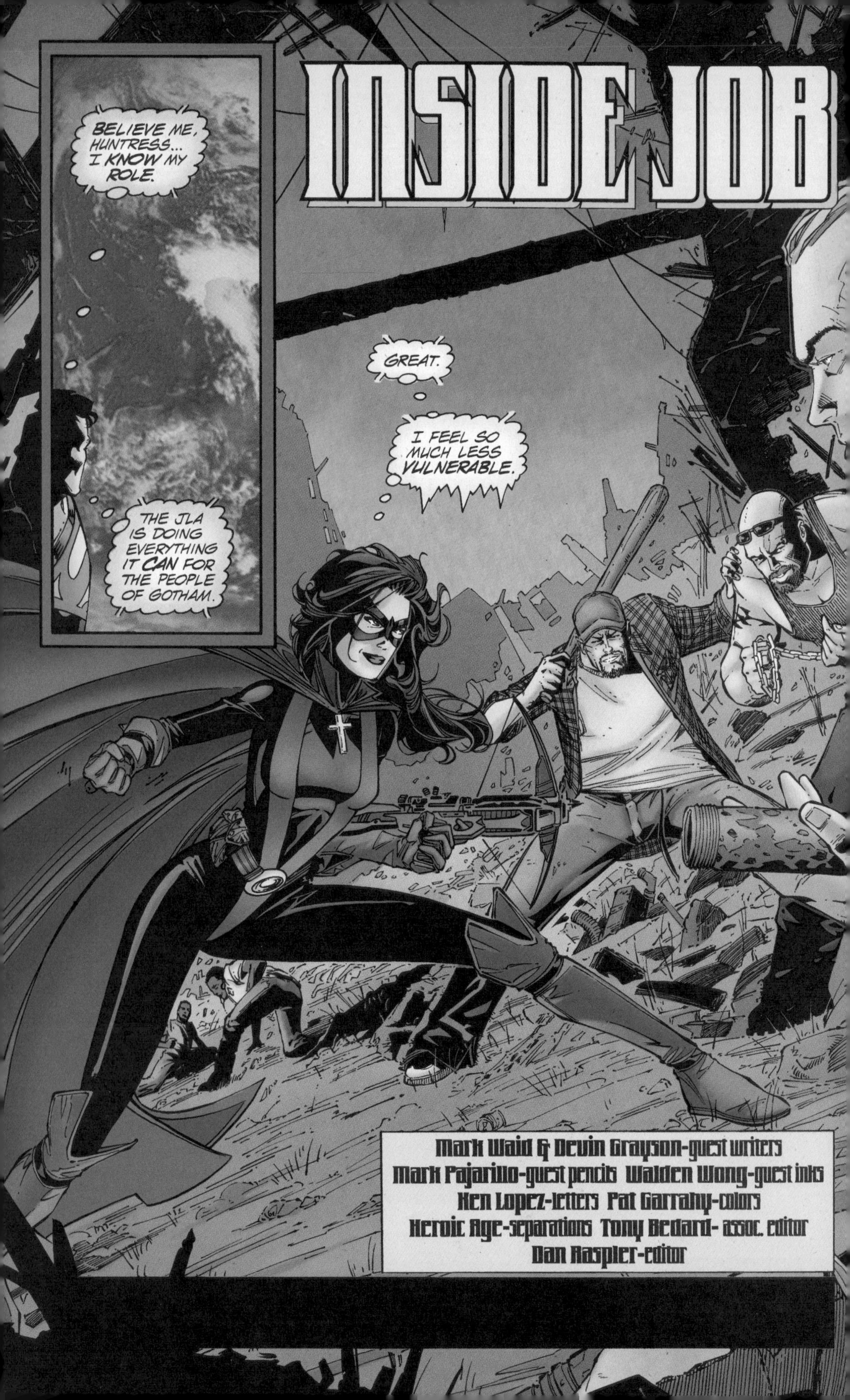
INSIDE JOB
BELIEVE ME, HUNTRESS... I KNOW MY ROLE.
THE JLA IS DOING EVERYTHING IT CAN FOR THE PEOPLE OF GOTHAM.
GREAT.
I FEEL SO MUCH LESS VULNERABLE.
Mark Waid & Devin Grayson-guest writers
Mark Pajarillo-guest pencils Walden Wong-guest inks
Ken Lopez-letters Pat Garrahy-colors
Heroic Age-separations Tony Bedard- assoc. editor
Dan Raspler-editor

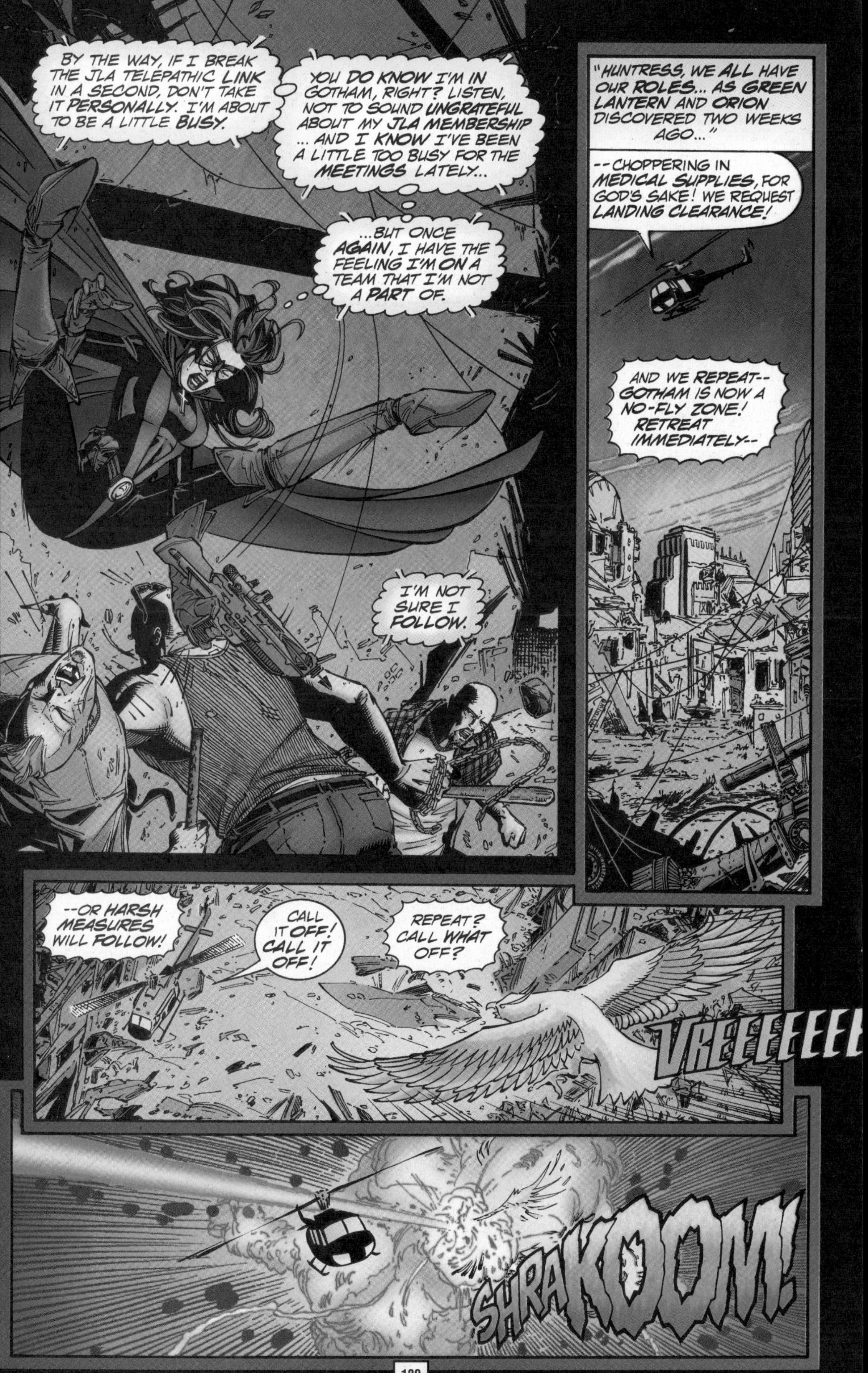

BY THE WAY, IF I BREAK THE JLA TELEPATHIC LINK IN A SECOND, DON'T TAKE IT PERSONALLY. I'M ABOUT TO BE A LITTLE BUSY.
YOU DO KNOW I'M IN GOTHAM, RIGHT? LISTEN, NOT TO SOUND UNGRATEFUL ABOUT MY JLA MEMBERSHIP ... AND I KNOW I'VE BEEN A LITTLE TOO BUSY FOR THE MEETINGS LATELY...
...BUT ONCE AGAIN, I HAVE THE FEELING I'M ON A TEAM THAT I'M NOT A PART OF.
I'M NOT SURE I FOLLOW.
"HUNTRESS, WE ALL HAVE OUR ROLES... AS GREEN LANTERN AND ORION DISCOVERED TWO WEEKS AGO..."
--CHOPPERING IN MEDICAL SUPPLIES, FOR GOD'S SAKE! WE REQUEST LANDING CLEARANCE!
AND WE REPEAT-- GOTHAM IS NOW A NO-FLY ZONE! RETREAT IMMEDIATELY--
--OR HARSH MEASURES WILL FOLLOW!
CALL IT OFF! CALL IT OFF!
REPEAT? CALL WHAT OFF?
VREEEEEEE
SHRAKOOM!

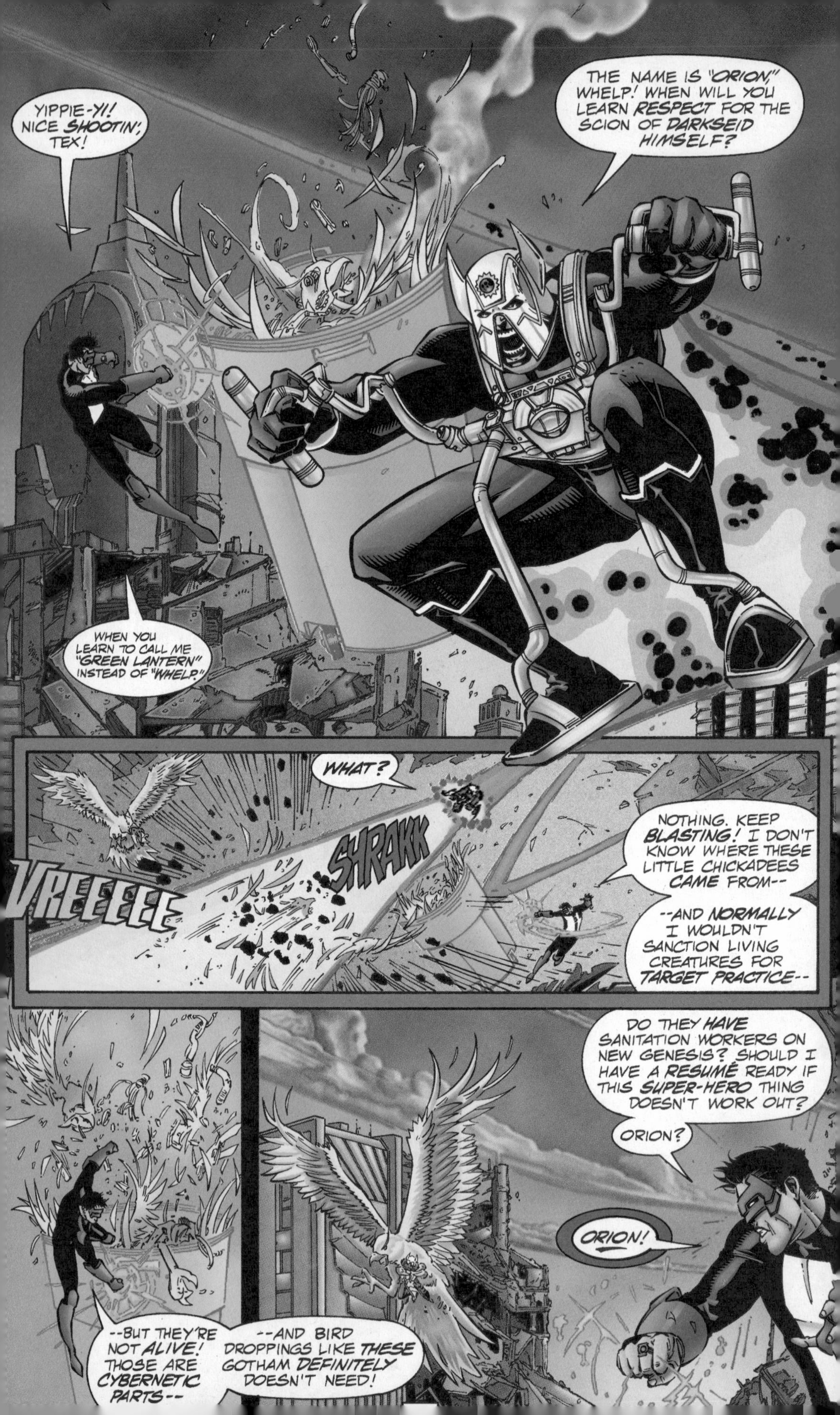
YIPPIE-YI! NICE SHOOTIN', TEX!
THE NAME IS "ORION," WHELP! WHEN WILL YOU LEARN RESPECT FOR THE SCION OF DARKSEID HIMSELF?
WHEN YOU LEARN TO CALL ME "GREEN LANTERN" INSTEAD OF "WHELP."
WHAT?
SHRAKK
VREEEEE
NOTHING. KEEP BLASTING! I DON'T KNOW WHERE THESE LITTLE CHICKADEES CAME FROM--
--AND NORMALLY I WOULDN'T SANCTION LIVING CREATURES FOR TARGET PRACTICE--
--BUT THEY'RE NOT ALIVE! THOSE ARE CYBERNETIC PARTS--
--AND BIRD DROPPINGS LIKE THESE GOTHAM DEFINITELY DOESN'T NEED!
DO THEY HAVE SANITATION WORKERS ON NEW GENESIS? SHOULD I HAVE A RESUMÉ READY IF THIS SUPER-HERO THING DOESN'T WORK OUT?
ORION?
ORION!

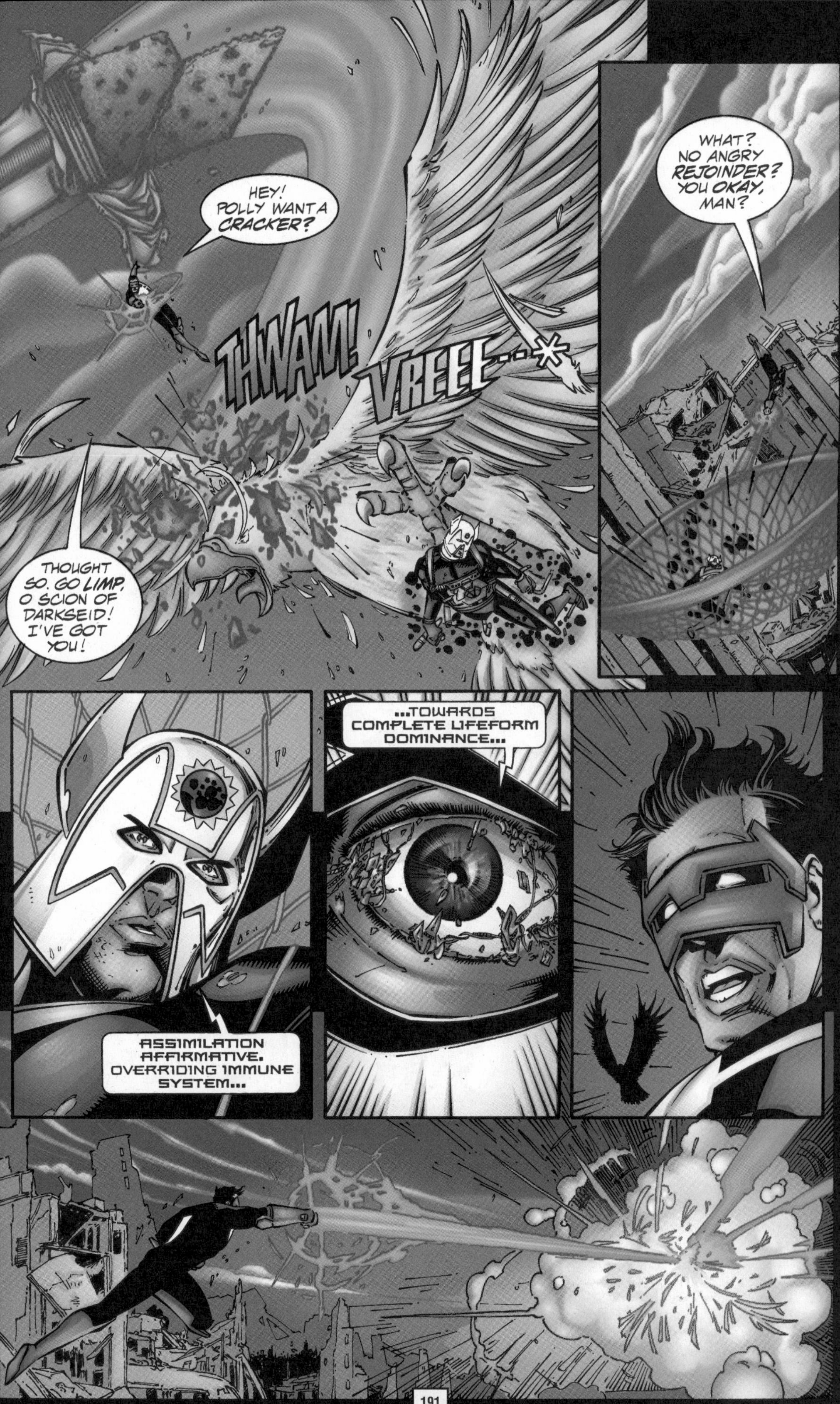
HEY! POLLY WANT A CRACKER?
THWAM!
VREEE...
THOUGHT SO. GO LIMP, O SCION OF DARKSEID! I'VE GOT YOU!
WHAT? NO ANGRY REJOINDER? YOU OKAY, MAN?
ASSIMILATION AFFIRMATIVE. OVERRIDING IMMUNE SYSTEM...
...TOWARDS COMPLETE LIFEFORM DOMINANCE...

ARTIFICIAL LIFE...

...IN THE FORM OF A MECHANICAL VIRUS.

GENANITE TECHNOLOGY.

EXCUSE ME?

MICROSCOPIC *NANITES* GENETI-CALLY ENGINEERED TO TRANSFORM *ORGANIC* CELLS INTO *MACHINE* CELLS ON *CONTACT*--PRESUMABLY TURNING THOSE *AFFECTED* INTO *DRONES*.

IN ORION'S CASE, WE CAUGHT IT *QUICKLY* ENOUGH TO *TREAT* IT--AND ONLY *THEN* BECAUSE OF HIS *EXTRATERRESTRIAL PHYSIOLOGY*. THE *GOTHAM-ITES* WOULD NOT HAVE BEEN SO *FORTUNATE*.

CLEARLY, THE BIRDS WERE DESIGNED AS *CARRIERS* FOR A GENGINEERED *DISEASE*... AND THE *IMPLICATION* IS *STAGGERING*.

LOCUS.

AGAIN... EXCUSE ME?

"*LOCUS*. A ROGUE GROUP OF *GENETICISTS* THE JLA FOUGHT LONG BEFORE YOUR *TIME*.* APPARENTLY, THEY'RE UP AND *RUNNING* AGAIN--

"--BECAUSE THE *YELLOW BIRDS* ARE *THEIRS*--AN AVIAN MAPPED FROM *ALIEN DNA*."

SO NOW THAT GOTHAM'S BEEN SEVERED FROM THE *MAINLAND*, THEY SEE IT AS ONE BIG *PETRI DISH*?

PERHAPS...OR PERHAPS THE *REVERSE*. DID THEY *SEE* IT AS A POTENTIAL LABORATORY-- AND HAVE IT QUARANTINED BY THE GOVERNMENT?

NO *WAY!* YOU'RE SAYING THIS "*NO MAN'S LAND*" LEG-ISLATION IS *THEIR...*

DOES LOCUS *OWN* THE SENATORS IT WOULD *TAKE* TO PULL SOMETHING LIKE THAT *OFF*?

*JLA: YEAR ONE --DAN.

192

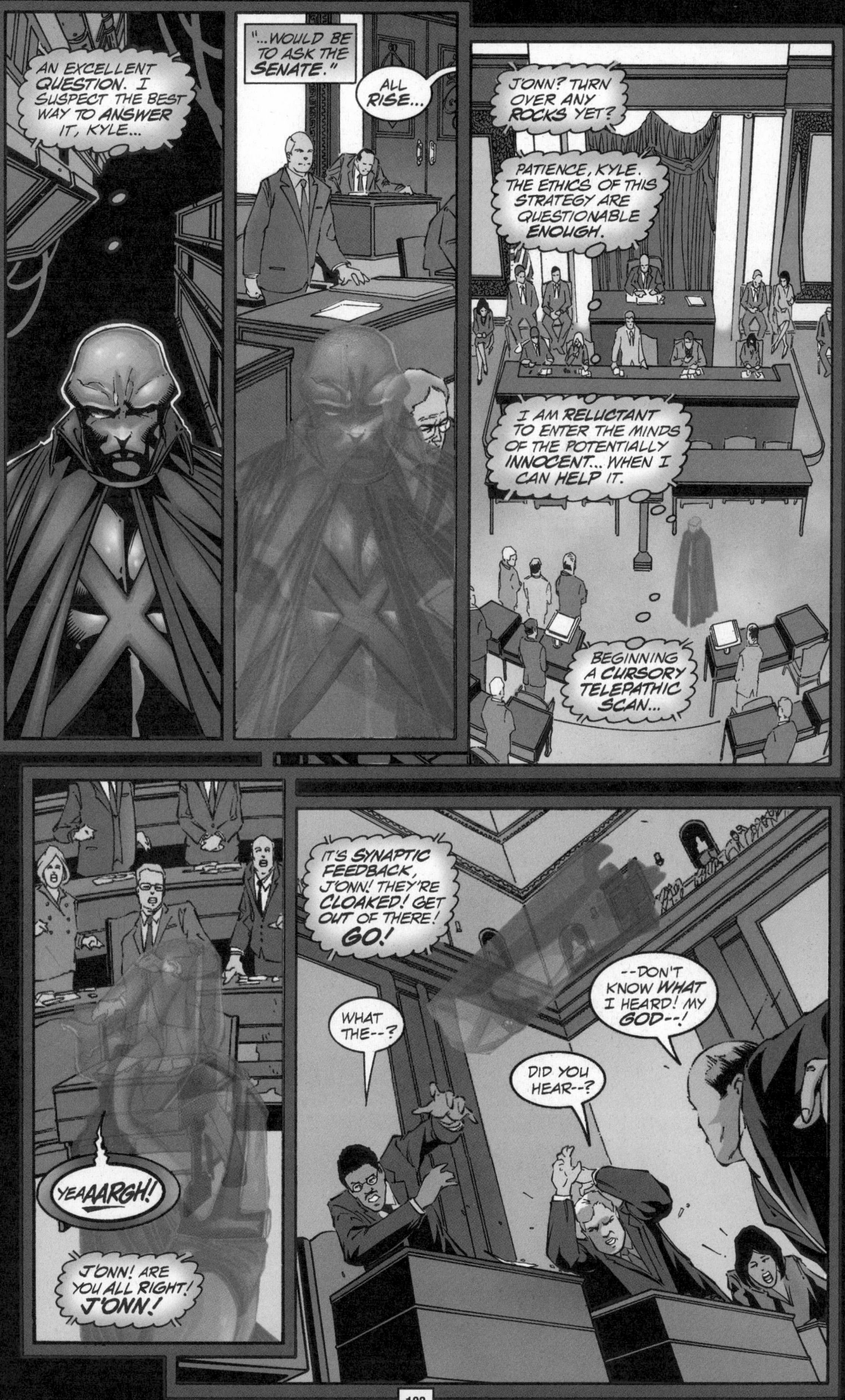
AN EXCELLENT QUESTION. I SUSPECT THE BEST WAY TO ANSWER IT, KYLE...
"...WOULD BE TO ASK THE SENATE."
ALL RISE...
J'ONN? TURN OVER ANY ROCKS YET?
PATIENCE, KYLE. THE ETHICS OF THIS STRATEGY ARE QUESTIONABLE ENOUGH.
I AM RELUCTANT TO ENTER THE MINDS OF THE POTENTIALLY INNOCENT... WHEN I CAN HELP IT.
BEGINNING A CURSORY TELEPATHIC SCAN...
YEAAARGH!
J'ONN! ARE YOU ALL RIGHT! J'ONN!
IT'S SYNAPTIC FEEDBACK, J'ONN! THEY'RE CLOAKED! GET OUT OF THERE! GO!
WHAT THE--?
--DON'T KNOW WHAT I HEARD! MY GOD--!
DID YOU HEAR--?

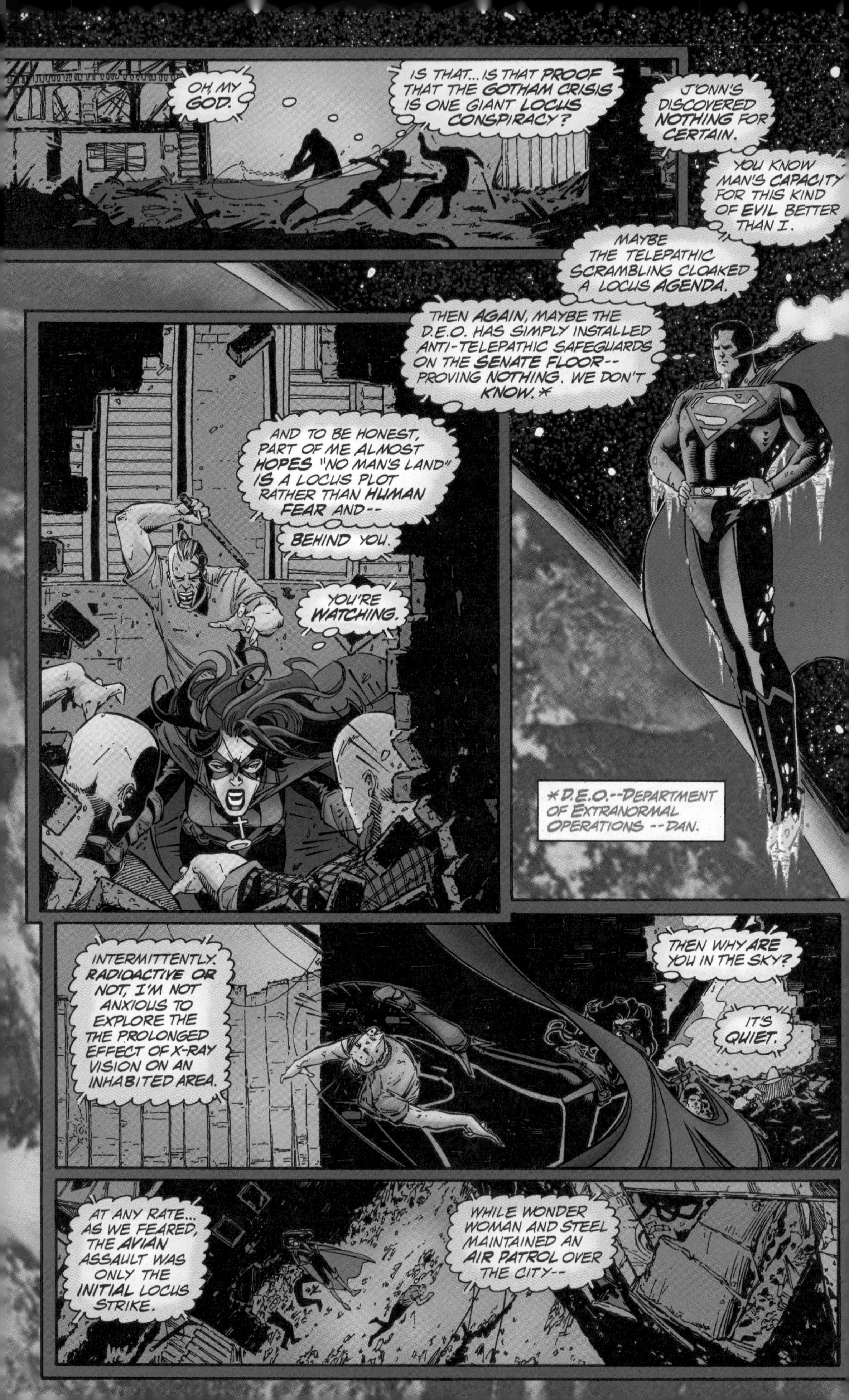
OH, MY GOD.
IS THAT... IS THAT PROOF THAT THE GOTHAM CRISIS IS ONE GIANT LOCUS CONSPIRACY?
J'ONN'S DISCOVERED NOTHING FOR CERTAIN.
YOU KNOW MAN'S CAPACITY FOR THIS KIND OF EVIL BETTER THAN I.
MAYBE THE TELEPATHIC SCRAMBLING CLOAKED A LOCUS AGENDA.
THEN AGAIN, MAYBE THE D.E.O. HAS SIMPLY INSTALLED ANTI-TELEPATHIC SAFEGUARDS ON THE SENATE FLOOR-- PROVING NOTHING. WE DON'T KNOW.*
AND TO BE HONEST, PART OF ME ALMOST HOPES "NO MAN'S LAND" IS A LOCUS PLOT RATHER THAN HUMAN FEAR AND--
BEHIND YOU.
YOU'RE WATCHING.
*D.E.O.--DEPARTMENT OF EXTRANORMAL OPERATIONS --DAN.
THEN WHY ARE YOU IN THE SKY?
IT'S QUIET.
INTERMITTENTLY. RADIOACTIVE OR NOT, I'M NOT ANXIOUS TO EXPLORE THE THE PROLONGED EFFECT OF X-RAY VISION ON AN INHABITED AREA.
AT ANY RATE... AS WE FEARED, THE AVIAN ASSAULT WAS ONLY THE INITIAL LOCUS STRIKE.
WHILE WONDER WOMAN AND STEEL MAINTAINED AN AIR PATROL OVER THE CITY--

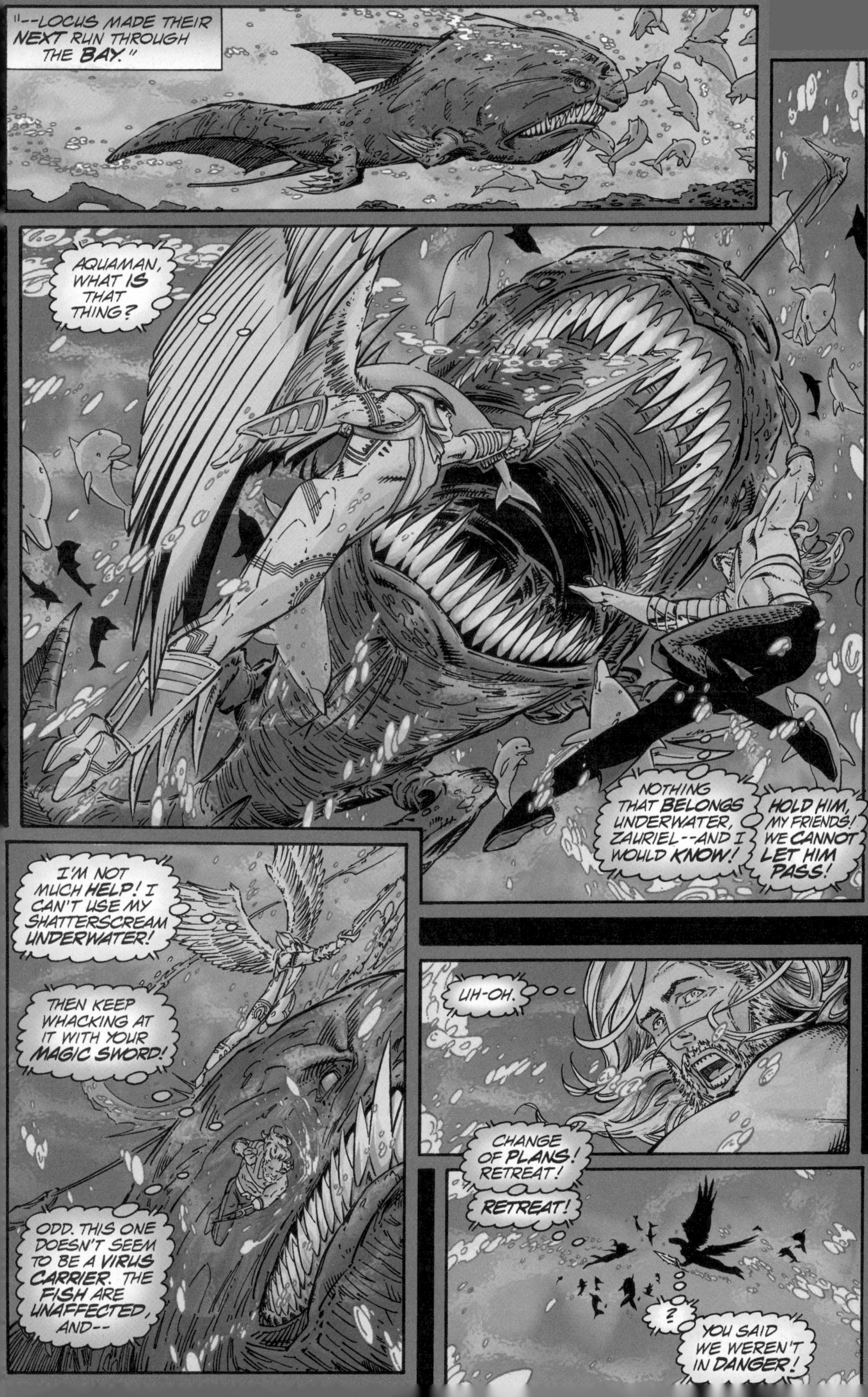
"--LOCUS MADE THEIR NEXT RUN THROUGH THE BAY."
AQUAMAN, WHAT IS THAT THING?
NOTHING THAT BELONGS UNDERWATER, ZAURIEL--AND I WOULD KNOW!
HOLD HIM, MY FRIENDS! WE CANNOT LET HIM PASS!
I'M NOT MUCH HELP! I CAN'T USE MY SHATTERSCREAM UNDERWATER!
THEN KEEP WHACKING AT IT WITH YOUR MAGIC SWORD!
ODD. THIS ONE DOESN'T SEEM TO BE A VIRUS CARRIER. THE FISH ARE UNAFFECTED, AND--
UH-OH.
CHANGE OF PLANS! RETREAT!
RETREAT!
?
YOU SAID WE WEREN'T IN DANGER!

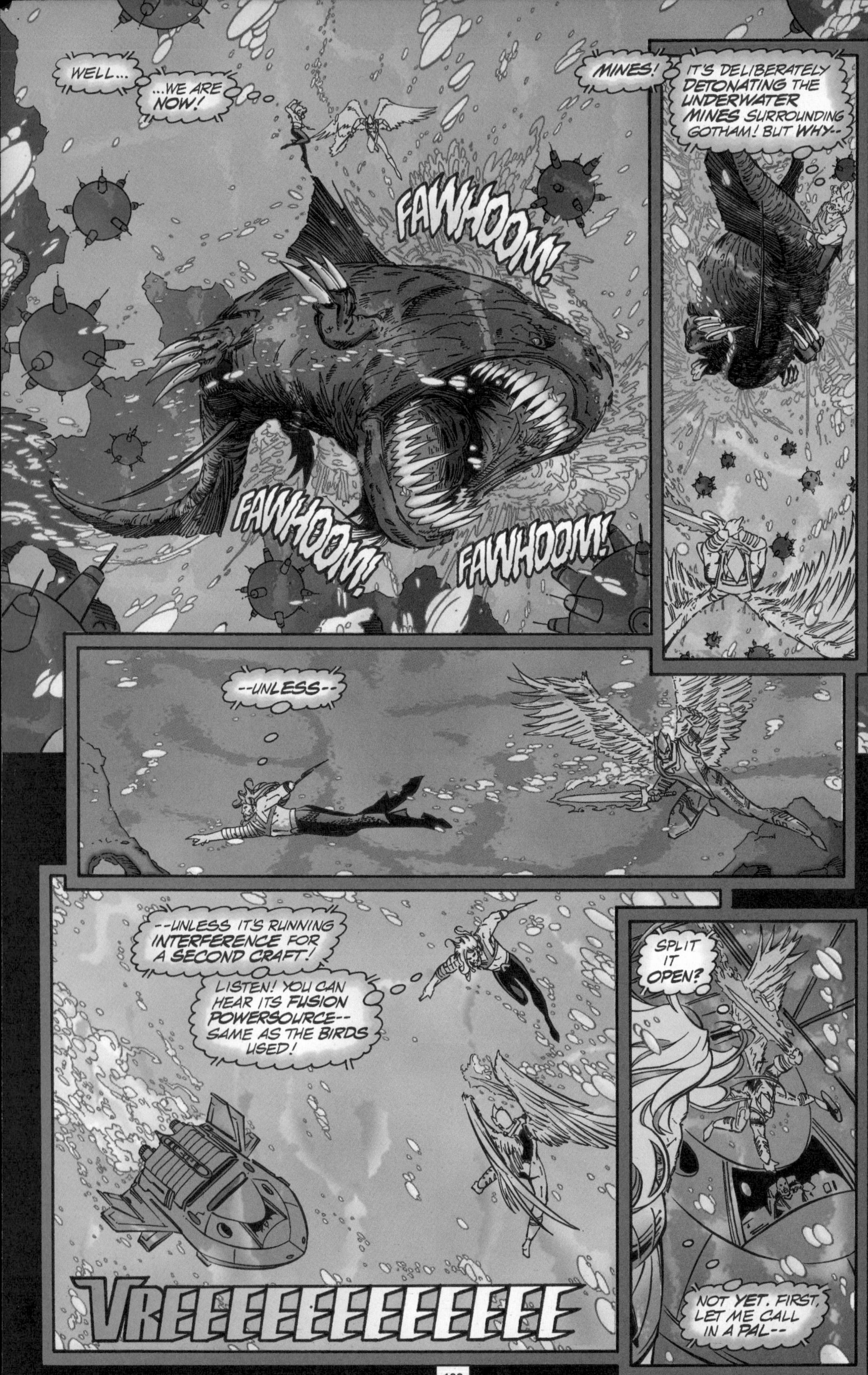
WELL...
...WE ARE NOW!
MINES!
IT'S DELIBERATELY DETONATING THE UNDERWATER MINES SURROUNDING GOTHAM! BUT WHY--
FAWHOOM!
FAWHOOM!
FAWHOOM!
--UNLESS--
--UNLESS IT'S RUNNING INTERFERENCE FOR A SECOND CRAFT!
LISTEN! YOU CAN HEAR ITS FUSION POWERSOURCE-- SAME AS THE BIRDS USED!
VREEEEEEEEEEEEE
SPLIT IT OPEN?
NOT YET. FIRST, LET ME CALL IN A PAL--

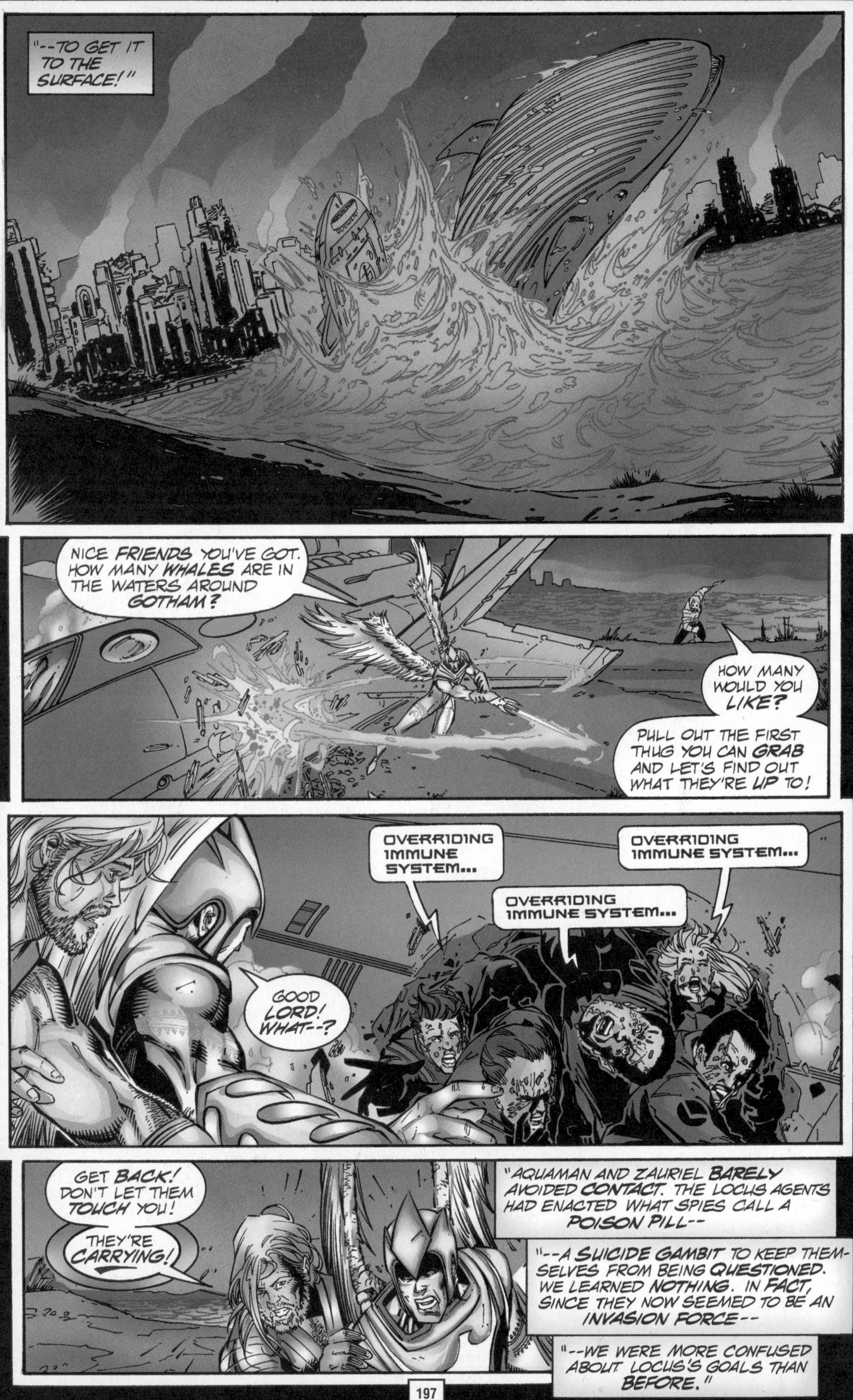
"--TO GET IT TO THE SURFACE!"
NICE FRIENDS YOU'VE GOT. HOW MANY WHALES ARE IN THE WATERS AROUND GOTHAM?
HOW MANY WOULD YOU LIKE?
PULL OUT THE FIRST THUG YOU CAN GRAB AND LET'S FIND OUT WHAT THEY'RE UP TO!
OVERRIDING IMMUNE SYSTEM...
OVERRIDING IMMUNE SYSTEM...
OVERRIDING IMMUNE SYSTEM...
GOOD LORD! WHAT--?
GET BACK! DON'T LET THEM TOUCH YOU!
THEY'RE CARRYING!
"AQUAMAN AND ZAURIEL BARELY AVOIDED CONTACT. THE LOCUS AGENTS HAD ENACTED WHAT SPIES CALL A POISON PILL--
"--A SUICIDE GAMBIT TO KEEP THEMSELVES FROM BEING QUESTIONED. WE LEARNED NOTHING. IN FACT, SINCE THEY NOW SEEMED TO BE AN INVASION FORCE--
"--WE WERE MORE CONFUSED ABOUT LOCUS'S GOALS THAN BEFORE."

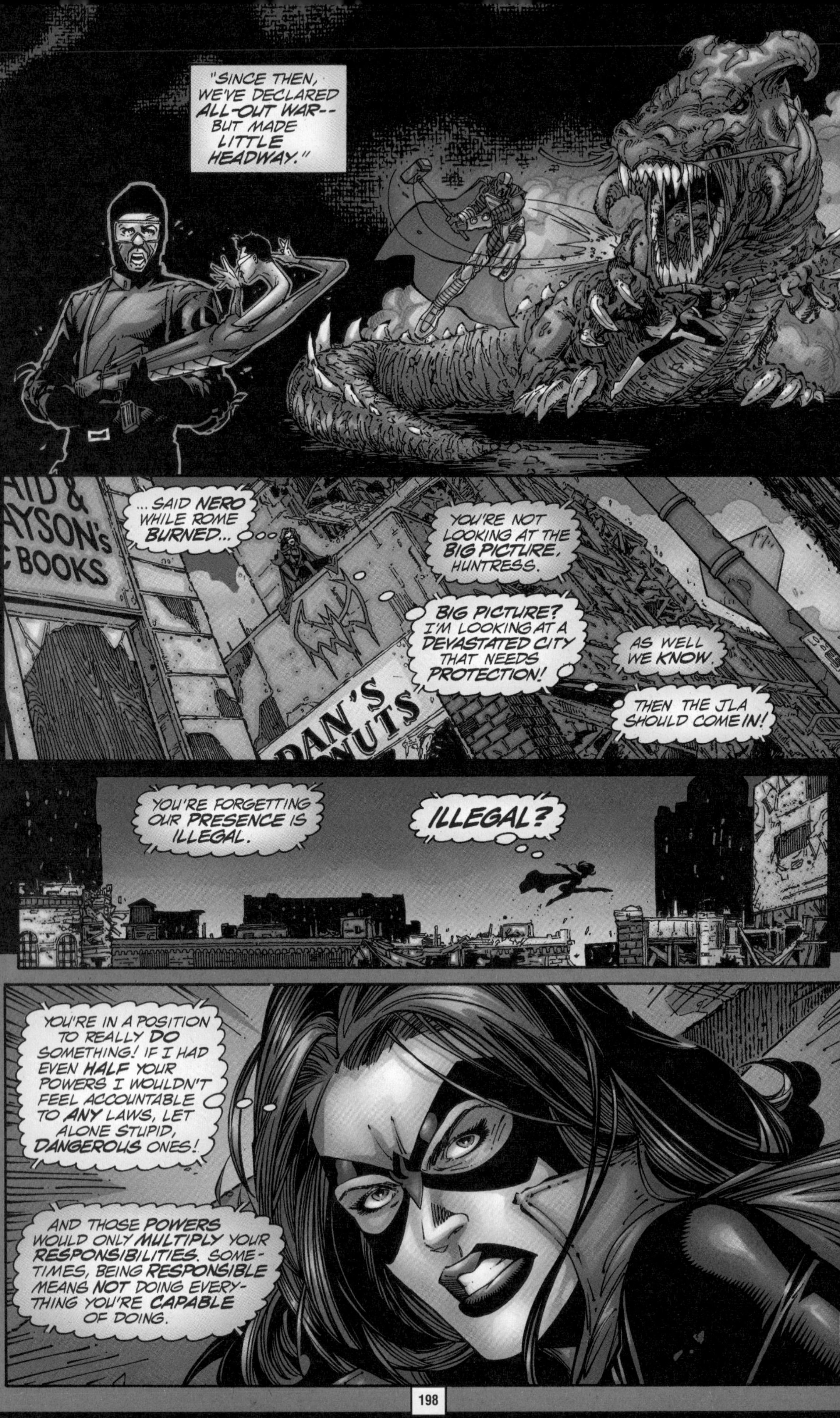
"SINCE THEN, WE'VE DECLARED ALL-OUT WAR-- BUT MADE LITTLE HEADWAY."
...SAID NERO WHILE ROME BURNED...
YOU'RE NOT LOOKING AT THE BIG PICTURE, HUNTRESS.
BIG PICTURE? I'M LOOKING AT A DEVASTATED CITY THAT NEEDS PROTECTION!
AS WELL WE KNOW.
THEN THE JLA SHOULD COME IN!
YOU'RE FORGETTING OUR PRESENCE IS ILLEGAL.
ILLEGAL?
YOU'RE IN A POSITION TO REALLY DO SOMETHING! IF I HAD EVEN HALF YOUR POWERS I WOULDN'T FEEL ACCOUNTABLE TO ANY LAWS, LET ALONE STUPID, DANGEROUS ONES!
AND THOSE POWERS WOULD ONLY MULTIPLY YOUR RESPONSIBILITIES. SOMETIMES, BEING RESPONSIBLE MEANS NOT DOING EVERYTHING YOU'RE CAPABLE OF DOING.

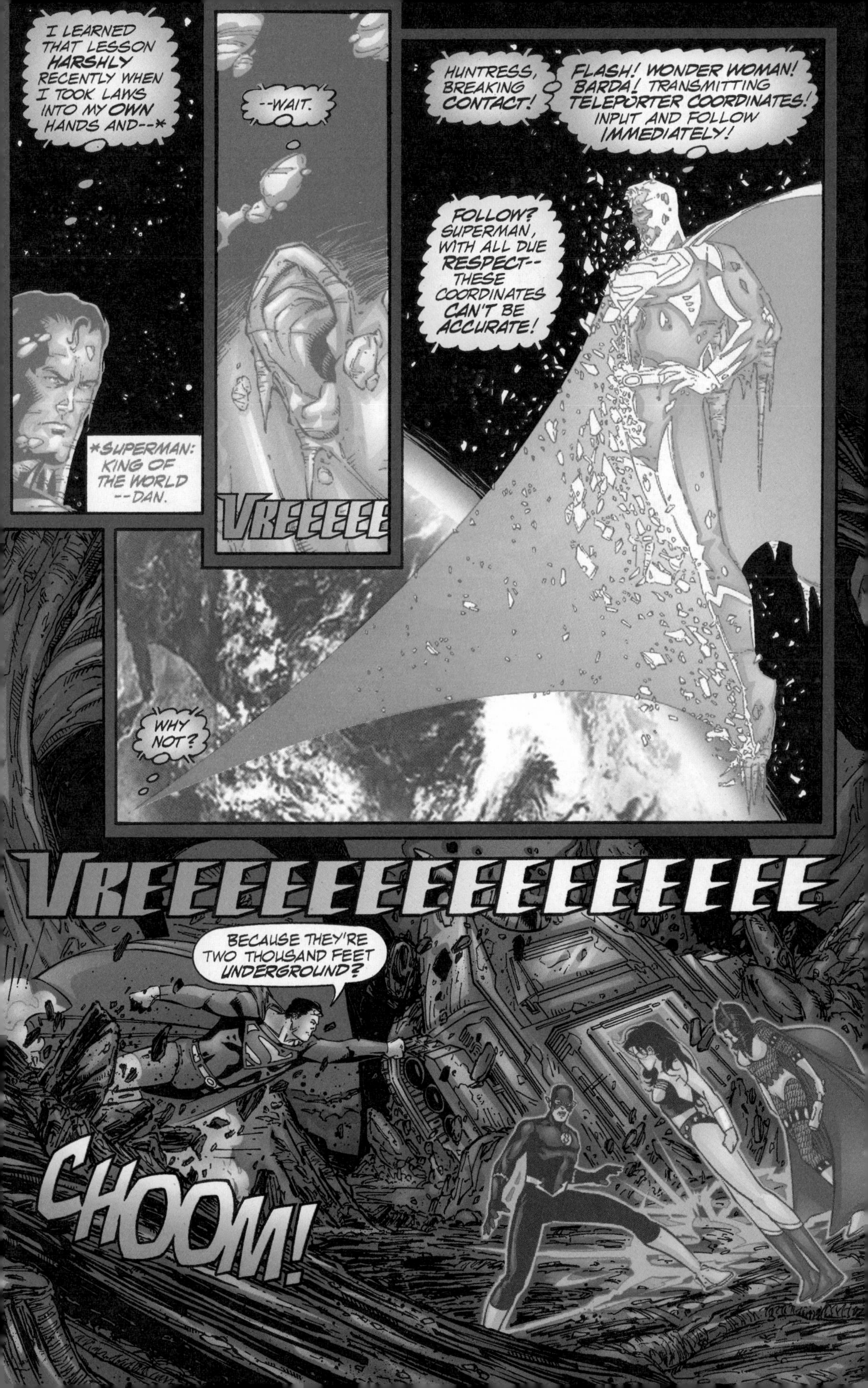
I LEARNED THAT LESSON HARSHLY RECENTLY WHEN I TOOK LAWS INTO MY OWN HANDS AND--*
*SUPERMAN: KING OF THE WORLD --DAN.
--WAIT.
VREEEEE
HUNTRESS, BREAKING CONTACT!
FLASH! WONDER WOMAN! BARDA! TRANSMITTING TELEPORTER COORDINATES! INPUT AND FOLLOW IMMEDIATELY!
FOLLOW? SUPERMAN, WITH ALL DUE RESPECT-- THESE COORDINATES CAN'T BE ACCURATE!
WHY NOT?
VREEEEEEEEEEEEEEE
BECAUSE THEY'RE TWO THOUSAND FEET UNDERGROUND?
CHOOM!

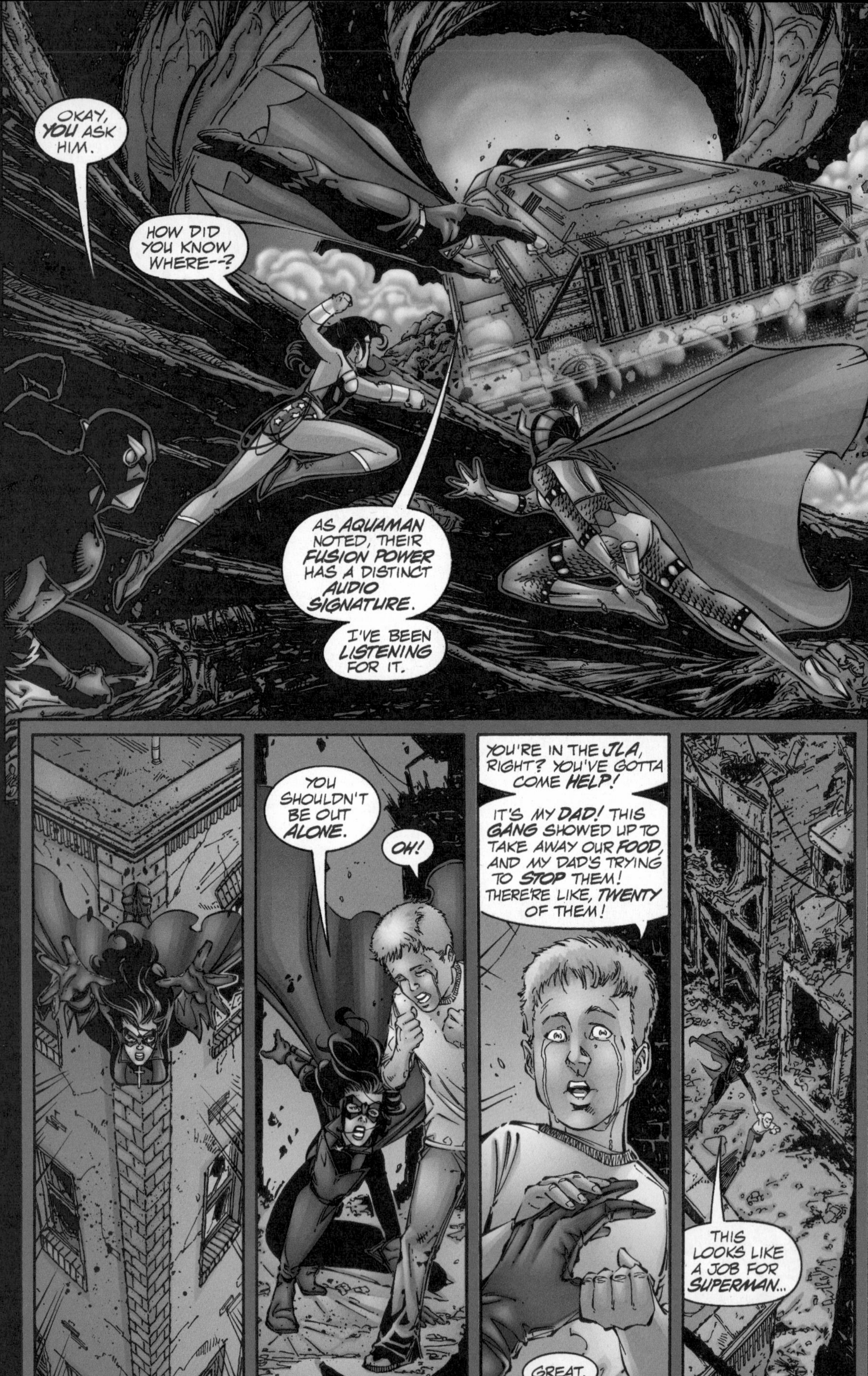
OKAY, YOU ASK HIM.
HOW DID YOU KNOW WHERE--?
AS AQUAMAN NOTED, THEIR FUSION POWER HAS A DISTINCT AUDIO SIGNATURE.
I'VE BEEN LISTENING FOR IT.
YOU SHOULDN'T BE OUT ALONE.
OH!
YOU'RE IN THE JLA, RIGHT? YOU'VE GOTTA COME HELP!
IT'S MY DAD! THIS GANG SHOWED UP TO TAKE AWAY OUR FOOD, AND MY DAD'S TRYING TO STOP THEM! THERE'RE LIKE, TWENTY OF THEM!
GREAT.
THIS LOOKS LIKE A JOB FOR SUPERMAN...

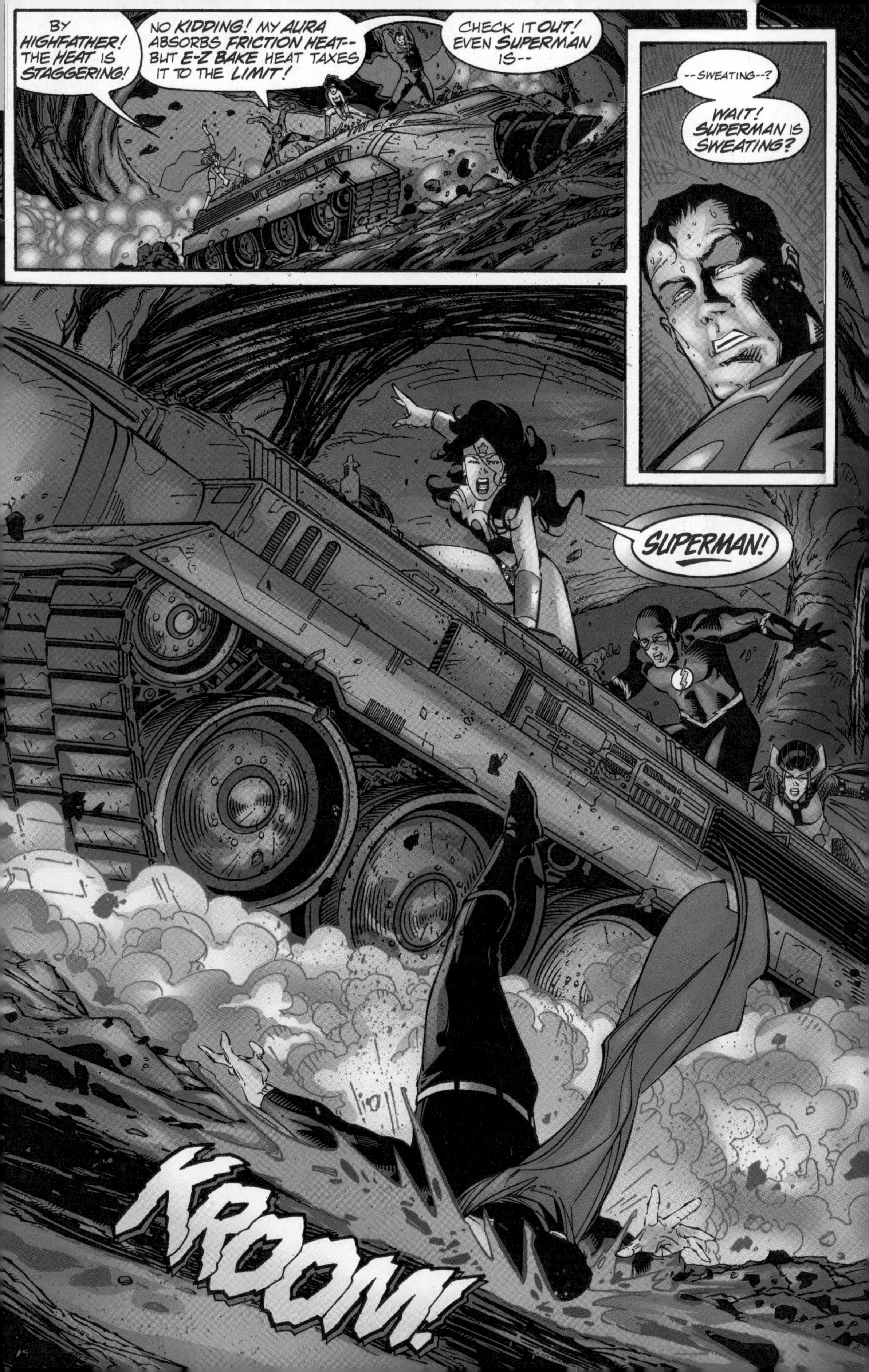
BY HIGHFATHER! THE HEAT IS STAGGERING!
NO KIDDING! MY AURA ABSORBS FRICTION HEAT-- BUT E-Z BAKE HEAT TAXES IT TO THE LIMIT!
CHECK IT OUT! EVEN SUPERMAN IS--
--SWEATING--?
WAIT! SUPERMAN IS SWEATING?
SUPERMAN!
KROOM!

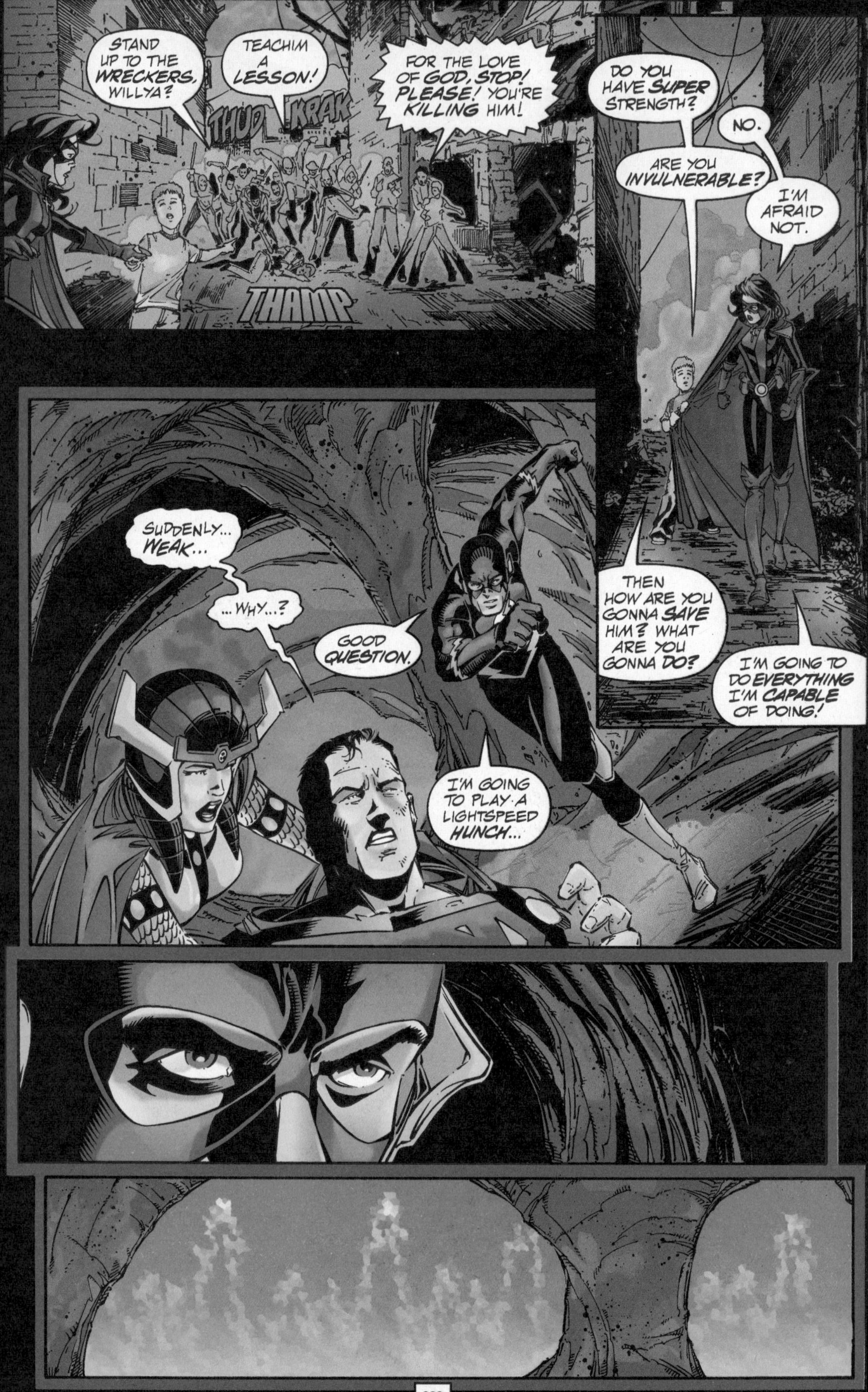
STAND UP TO THE WRECKERS, WILLYA?
TEACHIM A LESSON!
THUD
KRAK
FOR THE LOVE OF GOD, STOP! PLEASE! YOU'RE KILLING HIM!
THAMP
DO YOU HAVE SUPER STRENGTH?
NO.
ARE YOU INVULNERABLE?
I'M AFRAID NOT.
THEN HOW ARE YOU GONNA SAVE HIM? WHAT ARE YOU GONNA DO?
I'M GOING TO DO EVERYTHING I'M CAPABLE OF DOING!
SUDDENLY... WEAK...
...WHY...?
GOOD QUESTION.
I'M GOING TO PLAY A LIGHTSPEED HUNCH...

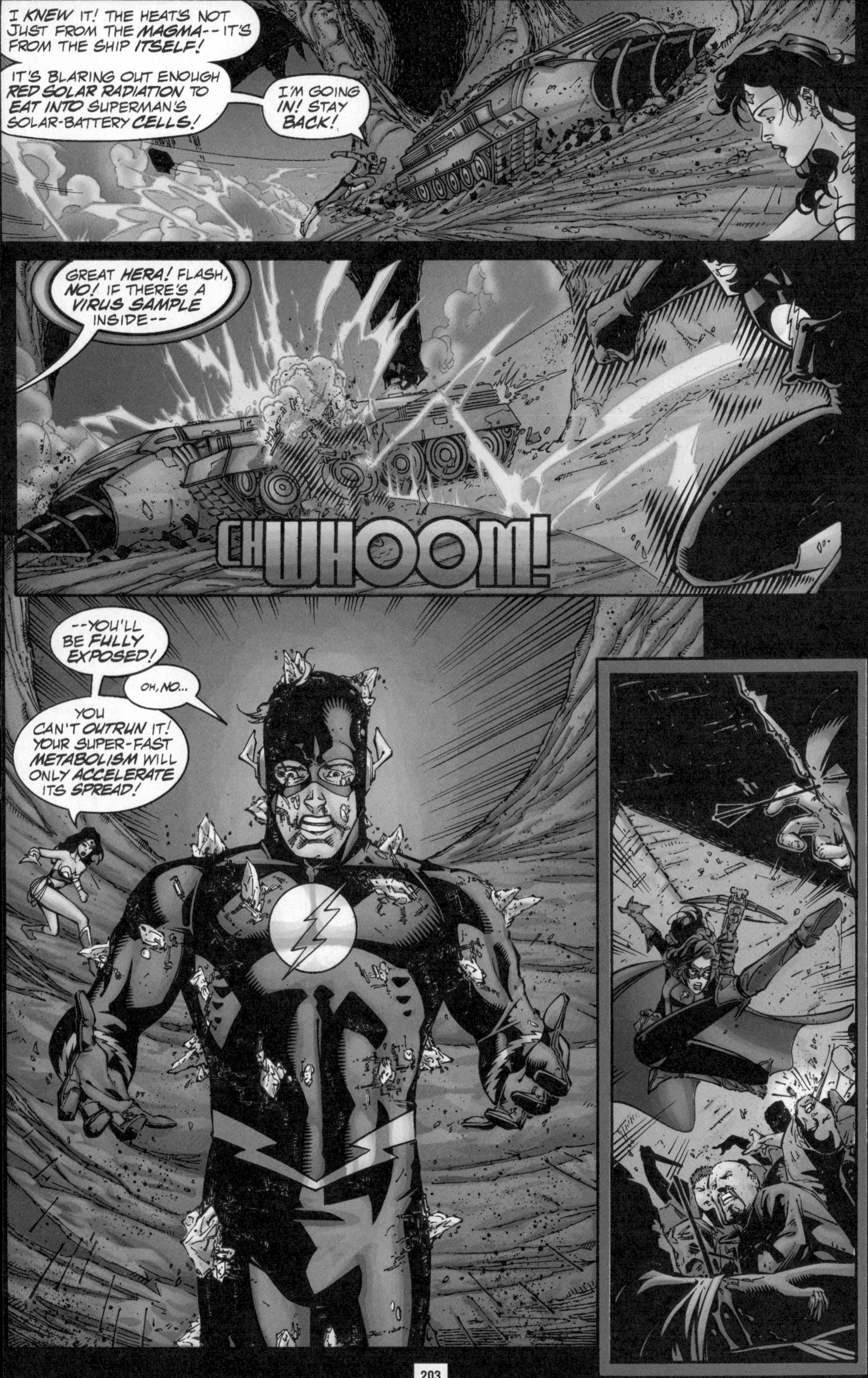
I KNEW IT! THE HEAT'S NOT JUST FROM THE MAGMA-- IT'S FROM THE SHIP ITSELF!
IT'S BLARING OUT ENOUGH RED SOLAR RADIATION TO EAT INTO SUPERMAN'S SOLAR-BATTERY CELLS!
I'M GOING IN! STAY BACK!
GREAT HERA! FLASH, NO! IF THERE'S A VIRUS SAMPLE INSIDE--
CHWHOOM!
--YOU'LL BE FULLY EXPOSED!
OH, NO...
YOU CAN'T OUTRUN IT! YOUR SUPER-FAST METABOLISM WILL ONLY ACCELERATE ITS SPREAD!

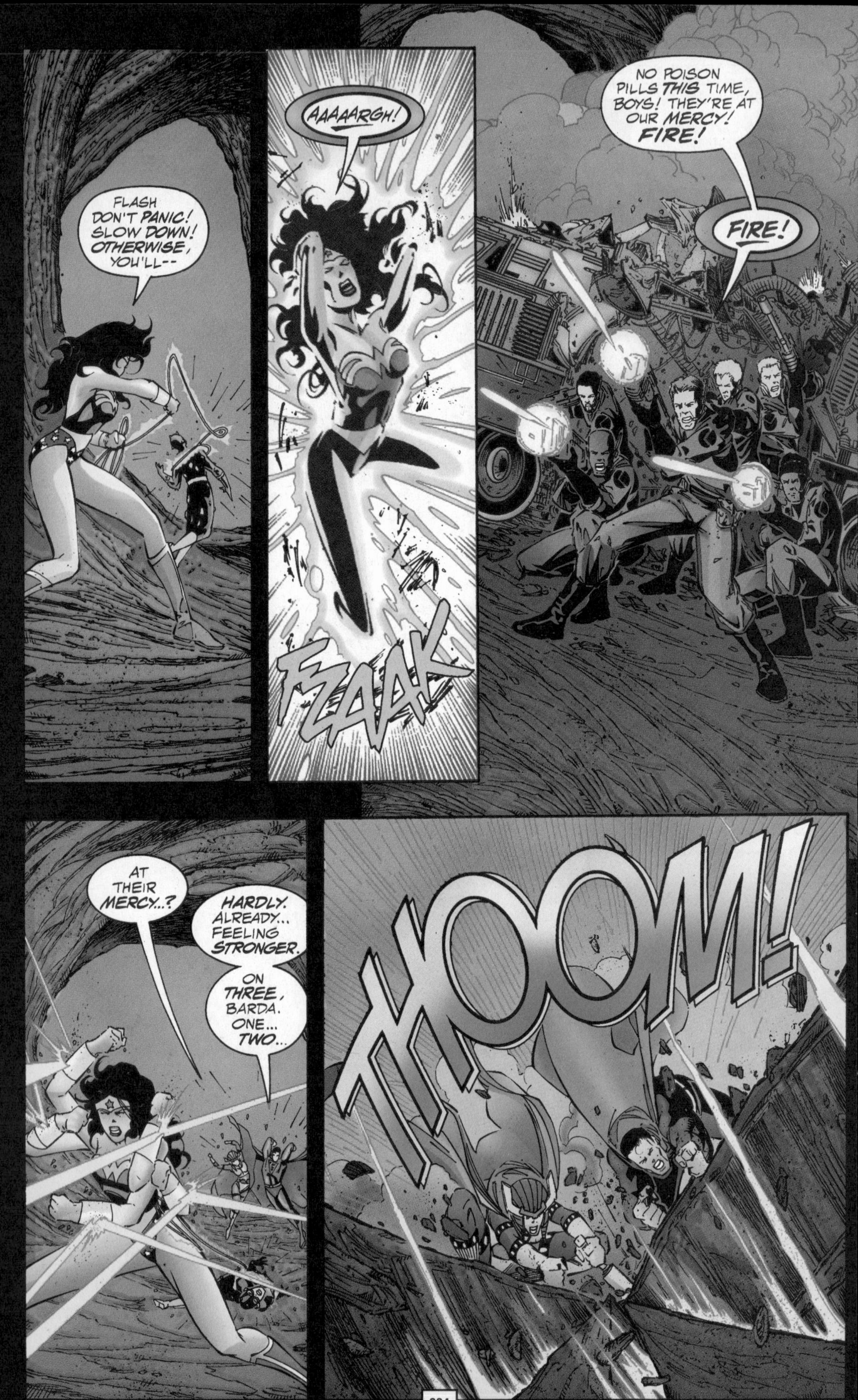

FLASH DON'T PANIC! SLOW DOWN! OTHERWISE, YOU'LL--
AAAAARGH!
FZAAK
NO POISON PILLS THIS TIME, BOYS! THEY'RE AT OUR MERCY! FIRE!
FIRE!
AT THEIR MERCY..?
HARDLY. ALREADY... FEELING STRONGER.
ON THREE, BARDA. ONE... TWO...
THOOM!

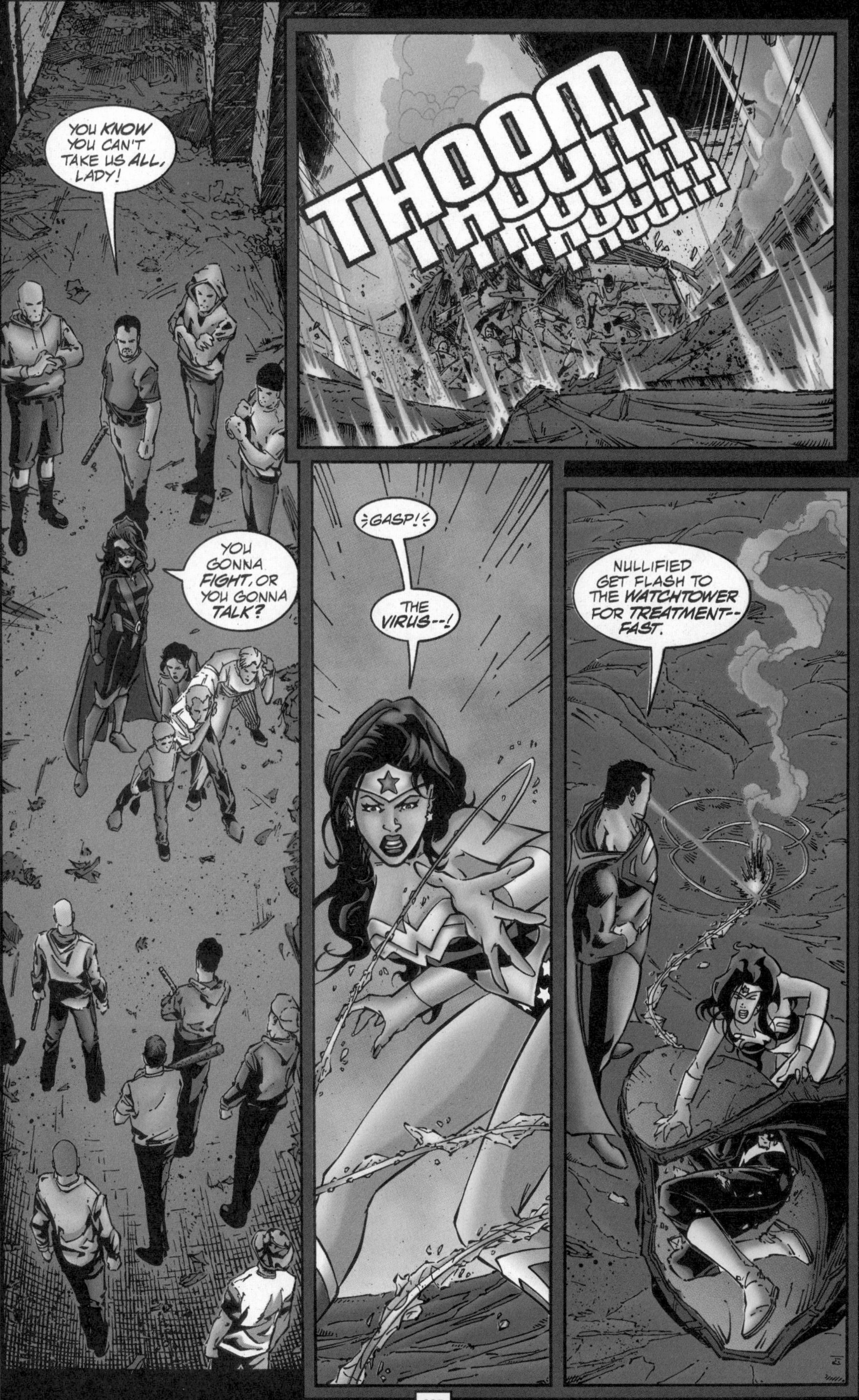

YOU KNOW YOU CAN'T TAKE US ALL, LADY!
YOU GONNA FIGHT, OR YOU GONNA TALK?
THOOM
THOOM
THOOM
GASP!
THE VIRUS--!
NULLIFIED GET FLASH TO THE WATCHTOWER FOR TREATMENT-- FAST.

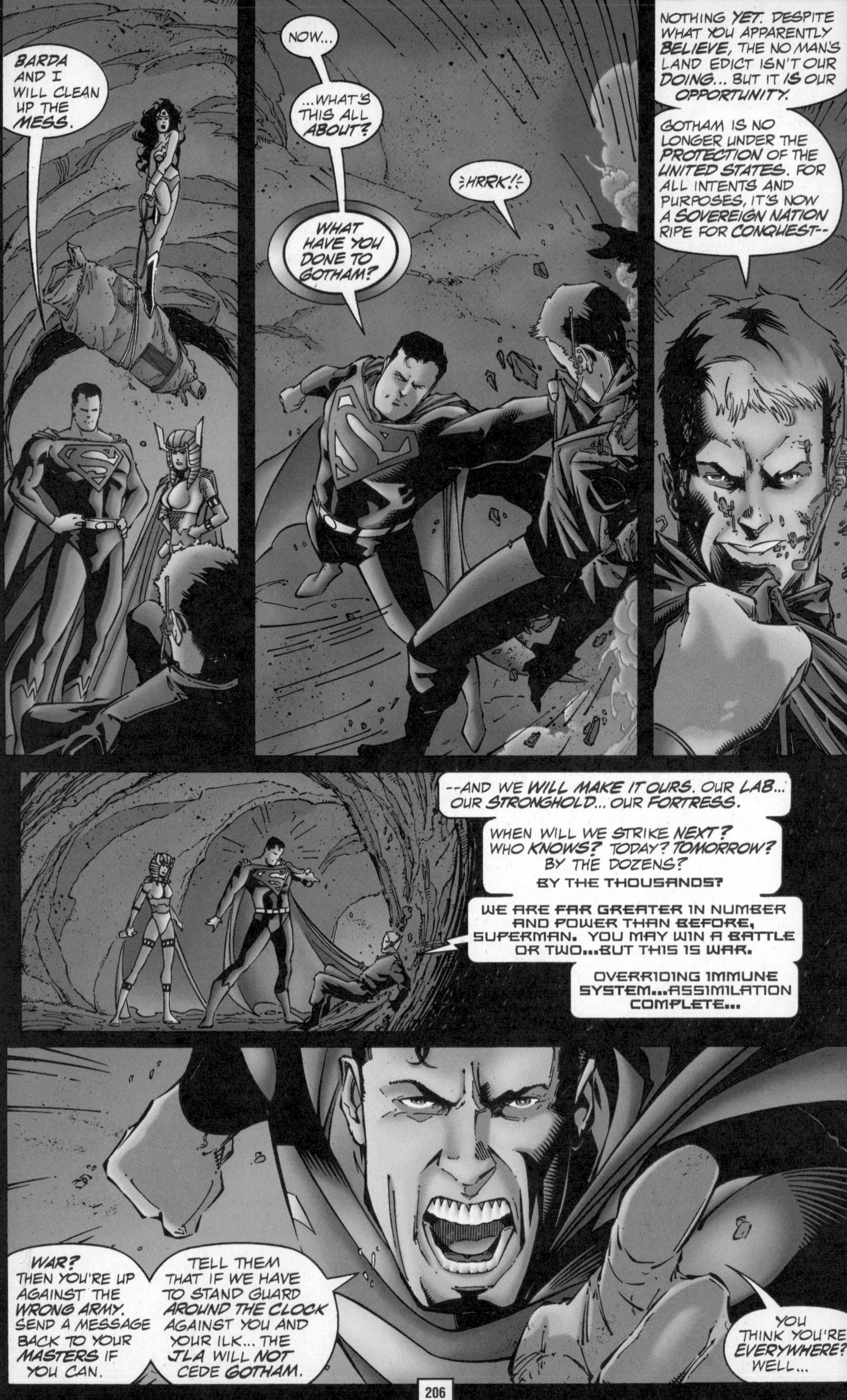
BARDA AND I WILL CLEAN UP THE MESS.
NOW...
...WHAT'S THIS ALL ABOUT?
WHAT HAVE YOU DONE TO GOTHAM?
HRRK!
NOTHING YET. DESPITE WHAT YOU APPARENTLY BELIEVE, THE NO MAN'S LAND EDICT ISN'T OUR DOING... BUT IT IS OUR OPPORTUNITY.
GOTHAM IS NO LONGER UNDER THE PROTECTION OF THE UNITED STATES. FOR ALL INTENTS AND PURPOSES, IT'S NOW A SOVEREIGN NATION RIPE FOR CONQUEST--
--AND WE WILL MAKE IT OURS. OUR LAB... OUR STRONGHOLD... OUR FORTRESS.
WHEN WILL WE STRIKE NEXT? WHO KNOWS? TODAY? TOMORROW? BY THE DOZENS?
BY THE THOUSANDS?
WE ARE FAR GREATER IN NUMBER AND POWER THAN BEFORE, SUPERMAN. YOU MAY WIN A BATTLE OR TWO...BUT THIS IS WAR.
OVERRIDING IMMUNE SYSTEM...ASSIMILATION COMPLETE...
YOU THINK YOU'RE EVERYWHERE? WELL...
WAR? THEN YOU'RE UP AGAINST THE WRONG ARMY. SEND A MESSAGE BACK TO YOUR MASTERS IF YOU CAN.
TELL THEM THAT IF WE HAVE TO STAND GUARD AROUND THE CLOCK AGAINST YOU AND YOUR ILK... THE JLA WILL NOT CEDE GOTHAM.

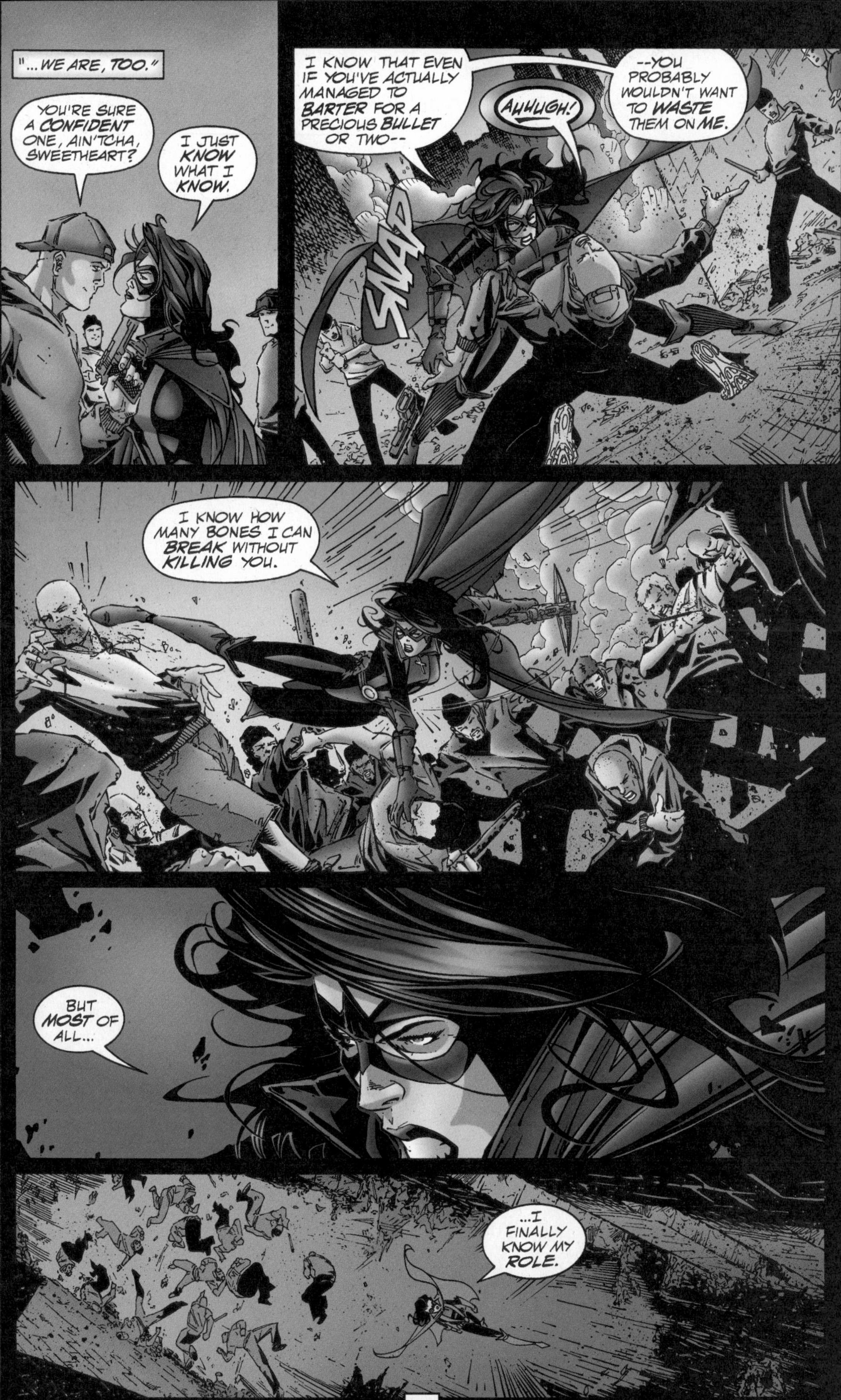
"...WE ARE, TOO."
YOU'RE SURE A CONFIDENT ONE, AIN'TCHA, SWEETHEART?
I JUST KNOW WHAT I KNOW.
I KNOW THAT EVEN IF YOU'VE ACTUALLY MANAGED TO BARTER FOR A PRECIOUS BULLET OR TWO--
AHHUGH!
--YOU PROBABLY WOULDN'T WANT TO WASTE THEM ON ME.
SNAP
I KNOW HOW MANY BONES I CAN BREAK WITHOUT KILLING YOU.
BUT MOST OF ALL...
...I FINALLY KNOW MY ROLE.

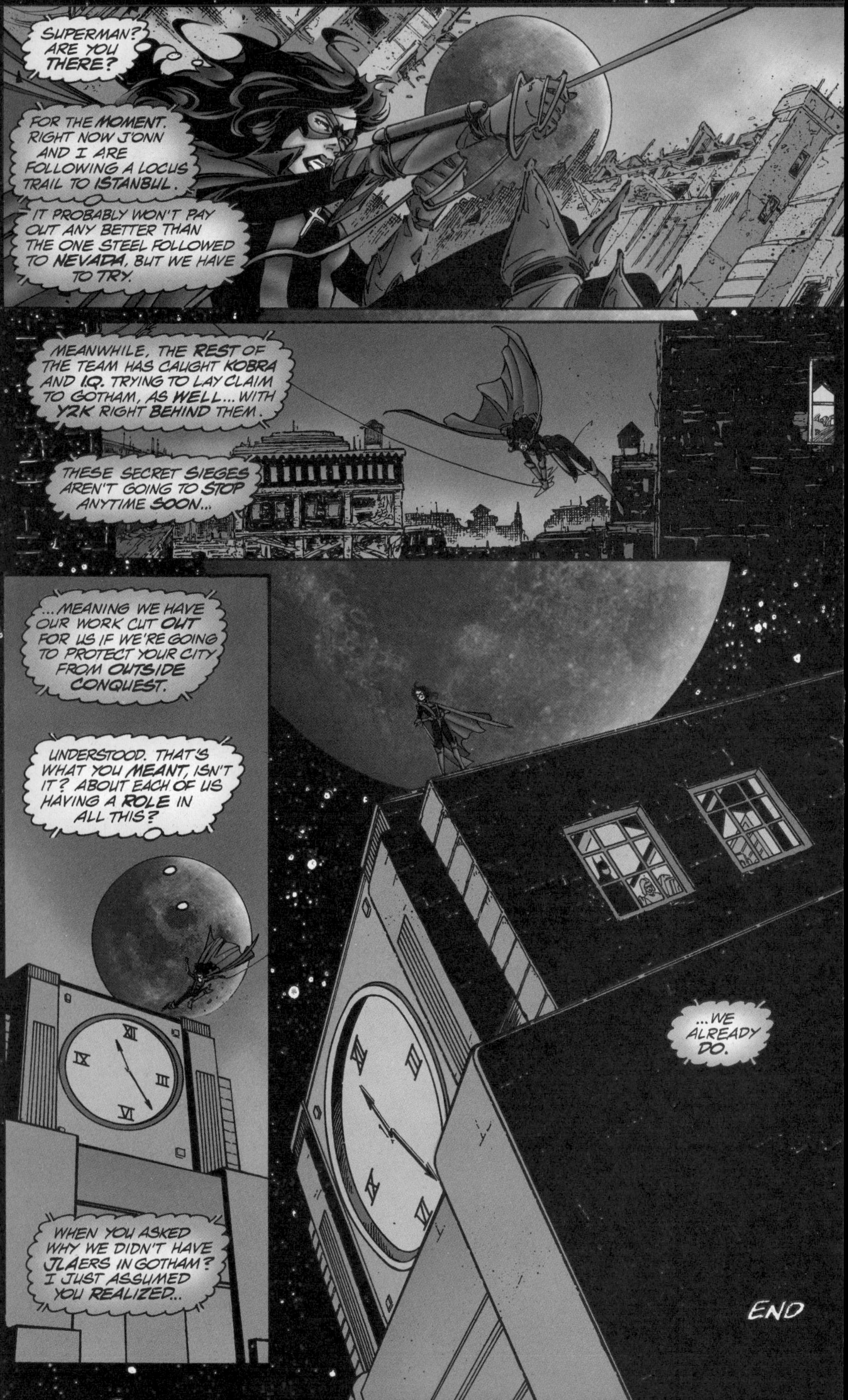
SUPERMAN? ARE YOU THERE?
FOR THE MOMENT. RIGHT NOW J'ONN AND I ARE FOLLOWING A LOCUS TRAIL TO ISTANBUL.
IT PROBABLY WON'T PAY OUT ANY BETTER THAN THE ONE STEEL FOLLOWED TO NEVADA, BUT WE HAVE TO TRY.
MEANWHILE, THE REST OF THE TEAM HAS CAUGHT KOBRA AND I.Q. TRYING TO LAY CLAIM TO GOTHAM, AS WELL... WITH Y2K RIGHT BEHIND THEM.
THESE SECRET SIEGES AREN'T GOING TO STOP ANYTIME SOON...
...MEANING WE HAVE OUR WORK CUT OUT FOR US IF WE'RE GOING TO PROTECT YOUR CITY FROM OUTSIDE CONQUEST.
UNDERSTOOD. THAT'S WHAT YOU MEANT, ISN'T IT? ABOUT EACH OF US HAVING A ROLE IN ALL THIS?
WHEN YOU ASKED WHY WE DIDN'T HAVE JLAERS IN GOTHAM? I JUST ASSUMED YOU REALIZED...
...WE ALREADY DO.
END

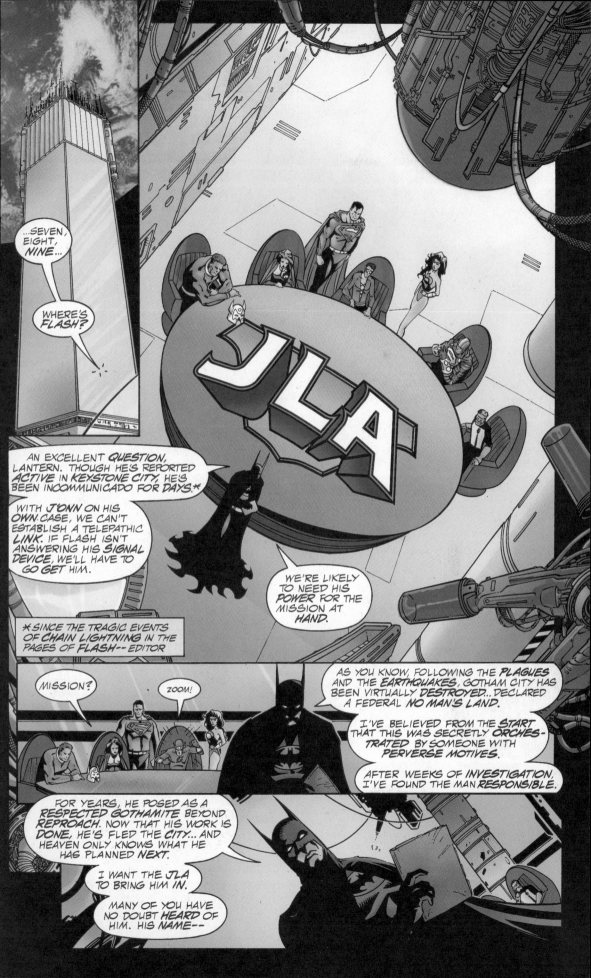

...SEVEN, EIGHT, *NINE*...

WHERE'S *FLASH*?

AN EXCELLENT *QUESTION*, *LANTERN*. THOUGH HE'S REPORTED *ACTIVE* IN *KEYSTONE CITY*, HE'S BEEN *INCOMMUNICADO* FOR *DAYS*.*

WITH *J'ONN* ON HIS *OWN* CASE, WE CAN'T ESTABLISH A TELEPATHIC *LINK*. IF FLASH ISN'T ANSWERING HIS *SIGNAL DEVICE*, WE'LL HAVE TO *GO GET* HIM.

WE'RE *LIKELY* TO NEED HIS *POWER* FOR THE MISSION AT *HAND*.

*SINCE THE TRAGIC EVENTS OF *CHAIN LIGHTNING* IN THE PAGES OF *FLASH*-- EDITOR

MISSION?

ZOOM!

AS YOU KNOW, FOLLOWING THE *PLAGUES* AND THE *EARTHQUAKES*, GOTHAM CITY HAS BEEN VIRTUALLY *DESTROYED*...DECLARED A FEDERAL *NO MAN'S LAND*.

I'VE BELIEVED FROM THE *START* THAT THIS WAS SECRETLY *ORCHES-TRATED* BY SOMEONE WITH *PERVERSE* MOTIVES.

AFTER WEEKS OF *INVESTIGATION*, I'VE FOUND THE MAN *RESPONSIBLE*.

FOR YEARS, HE POSED AS A *RESPECTED GOTHAMITE* BEYOND *REPROACH*. NOW THAT HIS WORK IS *DONE*, HE'S FLED THE *CITY*... AND HEAVEN ONLY KNOWS WHAT HE HAS PLANNED *NEXT*.

I WANT THE *JLA* TO BRING HIM *IN*.

MANY OF YOU HAVE NO DOUBT *HEARD* OF HIM. HIS *NAME*--

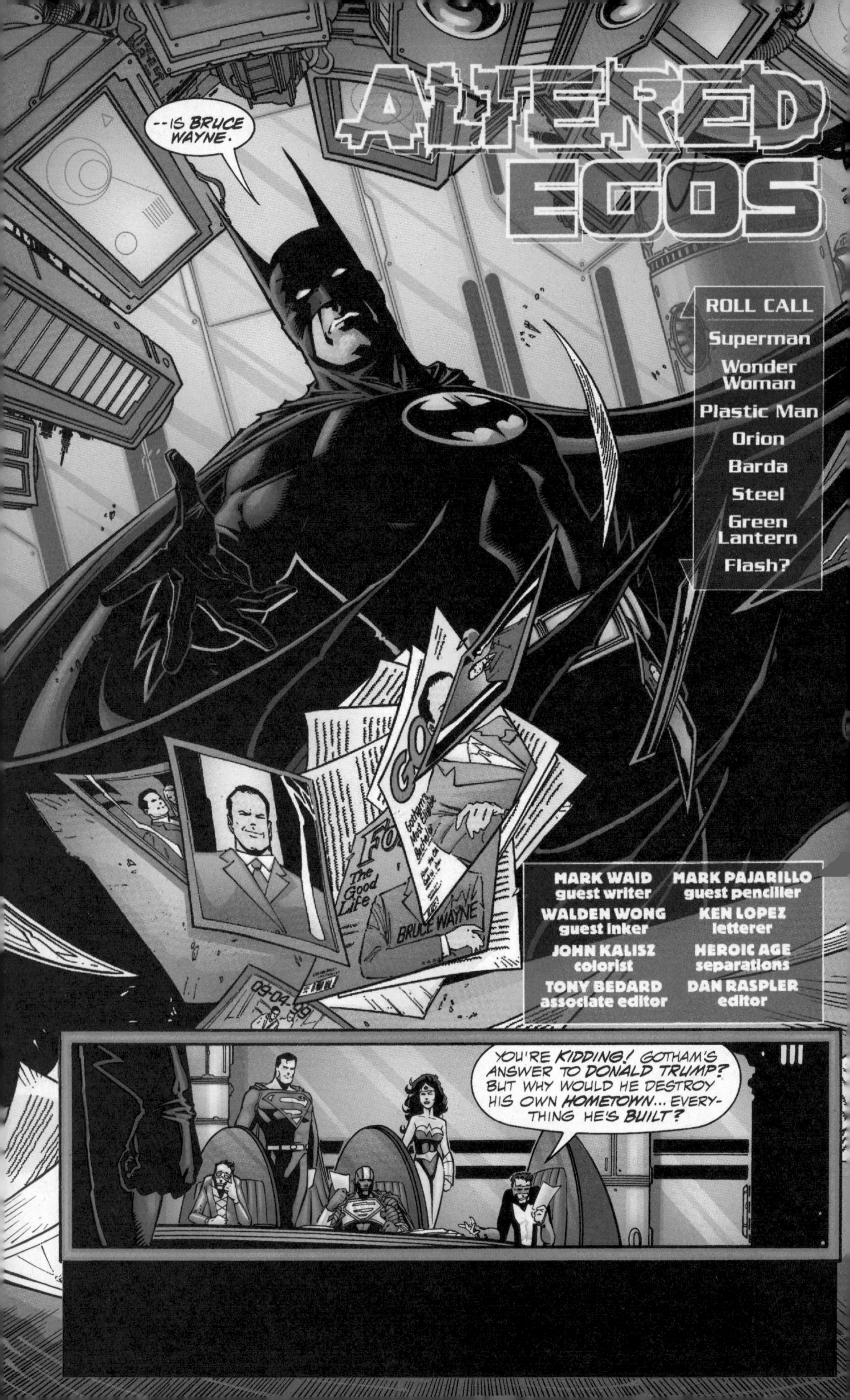
--IS BRUCE WAYNE.
ALTERED EGOS
ROLL CALL
Superman
Wonder Woman
Plastic Man
Orion
Barda
Steel
Green Lantern
Flash?
The Good Life
Gotham's Most Eligible Bachelor
BRUCE WAYNE
MARK WAID guest writer
MARK PAJARILLO guest penciller
WALDEN WONG guest inker
KEN LOPEZ letterer
JOHN KALISZ colorist
HEROIC AGE separations
TONY BEDARD associate editor
DAN RASPLER editor
YOU'RE KIDDING! GOTHAM'S ANSWER TO DONALD TRUMP? BUT WHY WOULD HE DESTROY HIS OWN HOMETOWN... EVERYTHING HE'S BUILT?

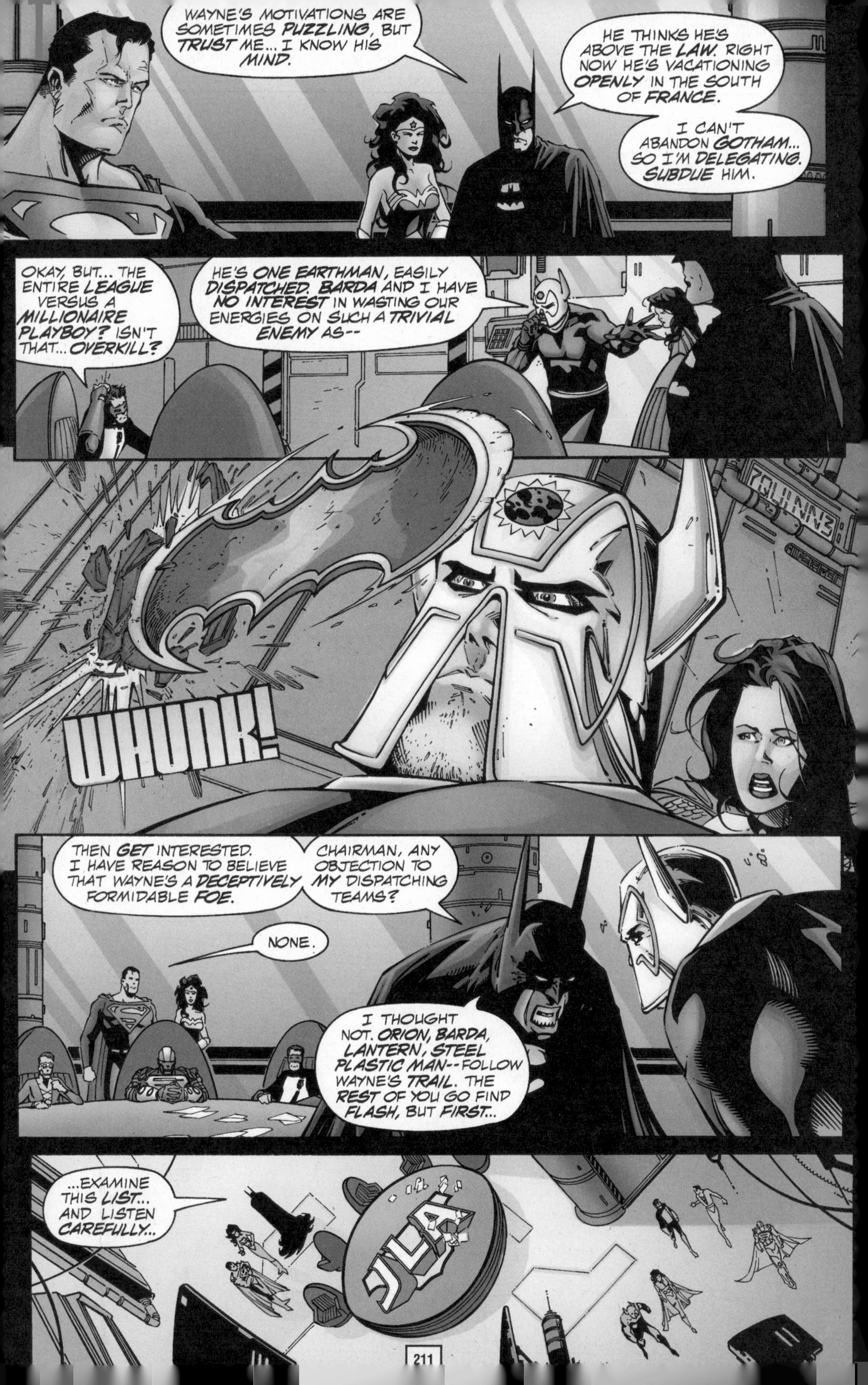
WAYNE'S MOTIVATIONS ARE SOMETIMES PUZZLING, BUT TRUST ME... I KNOW HIS MIND.
HE THINKS HE'S ABOVE THE LAW. RIGHT NOW HE'S VACATIONING OPENLY IN THE SOUTH OF FRANCE.
I CAN'T ABANDON GOTHAM... SO I'M DELEGATING. SUBDUE HIM.
OKAY, BUT... THE ENTIRE LEAGUE VERSUS A MILLIONAIRE PLAYBOY? ISN'T THAT... OVERKILL?
HE'S ONE EARTHMAN, EASILY DISPATCHED. BARDA AND I HAVE NO INTEREST IN WASTING OUR ENERGIES ON SUCH A TRIVIAL ENEMY AS--
WHUNK!
THEN GET INTERESTED. I HAVE REASON TO BELIEVE THAT WAYNE'S A DECEPTIVELY FORMIDABLE FOE.
CHAIRMAN, ANY OBJECTION TO MY DISPATCHING TEAMS?
NONE.
I THOUGHT NOT. ORION, BARDA, LANTERN, STEEL PLASTIC MAN--FOLLOW WAYNE'S TRAIL. THE REST OF YOU GO FIND FLASH, BUT FIRST...
...EXAMINE THIS LIST... AND LISTEN CAREFULLY...
JLA

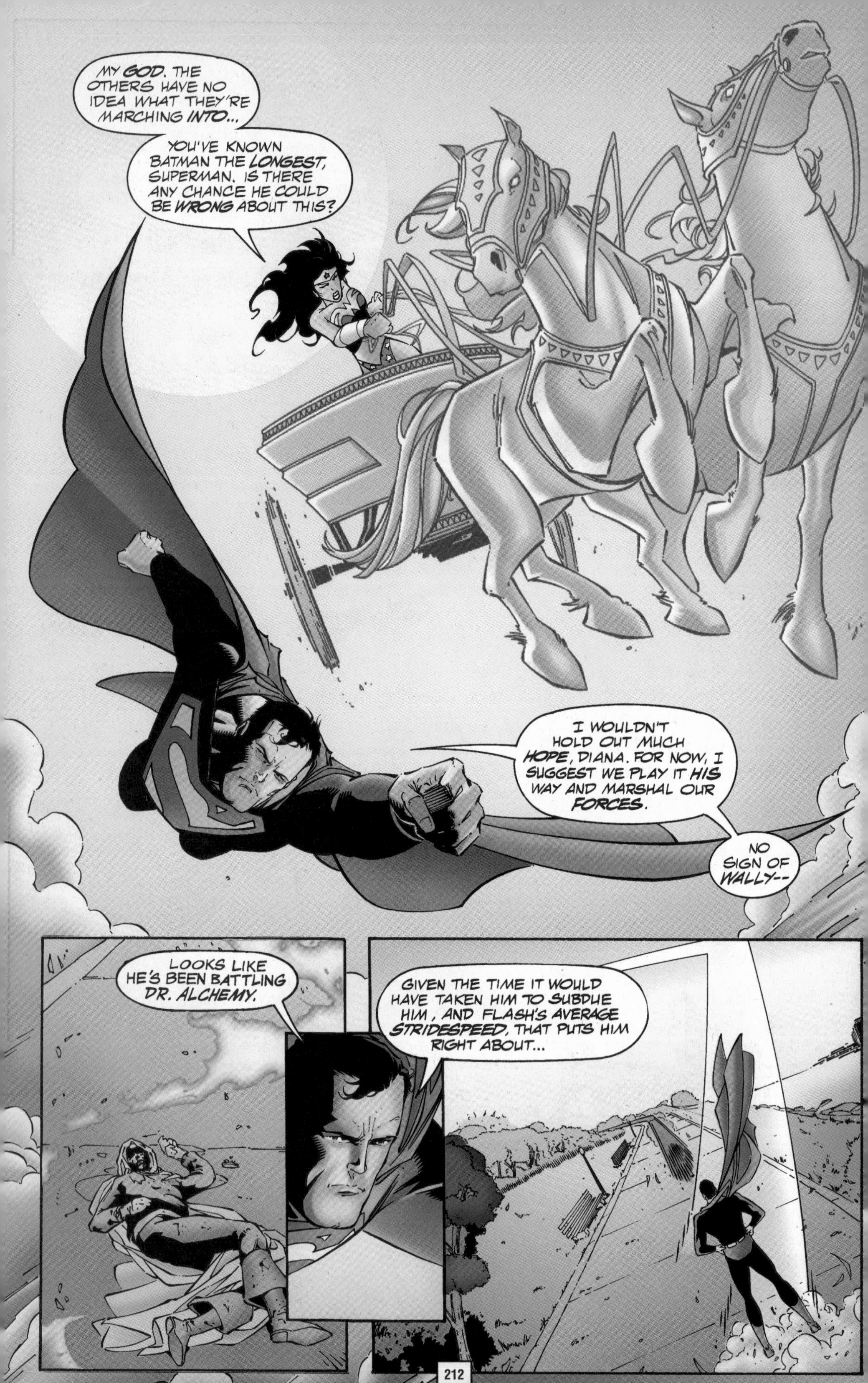
MY GOD. THE OTHERS HAVE NO IDEA WHAT THEY'RE MARCHING INTO...
YOU'VE KNOWN BATMAN THE LONGEST, SUPERMAN. IS THERE ANY CHANCE HE COULD BE WRONG ABOUT THIS?
I WOULDN'T HOLD OUT MUCH HOPE, DIANA. FOR NOW, I SUGGEST WE PLAY IT HIS WAY AND MARSHAL OUR FORCES.
NO SIGN OF WALLY--
LOOKS LIKE HE'S BEEN BATTLING DR. ALCHEMY.
GIVEN THE TIME IT WOULD HAVE TAKEN HIM TO SUBDUE HIM, AND FLASH'S AVERAGE STRIDESPEED, THAT PUTS HIM RIGHT ABOUT...

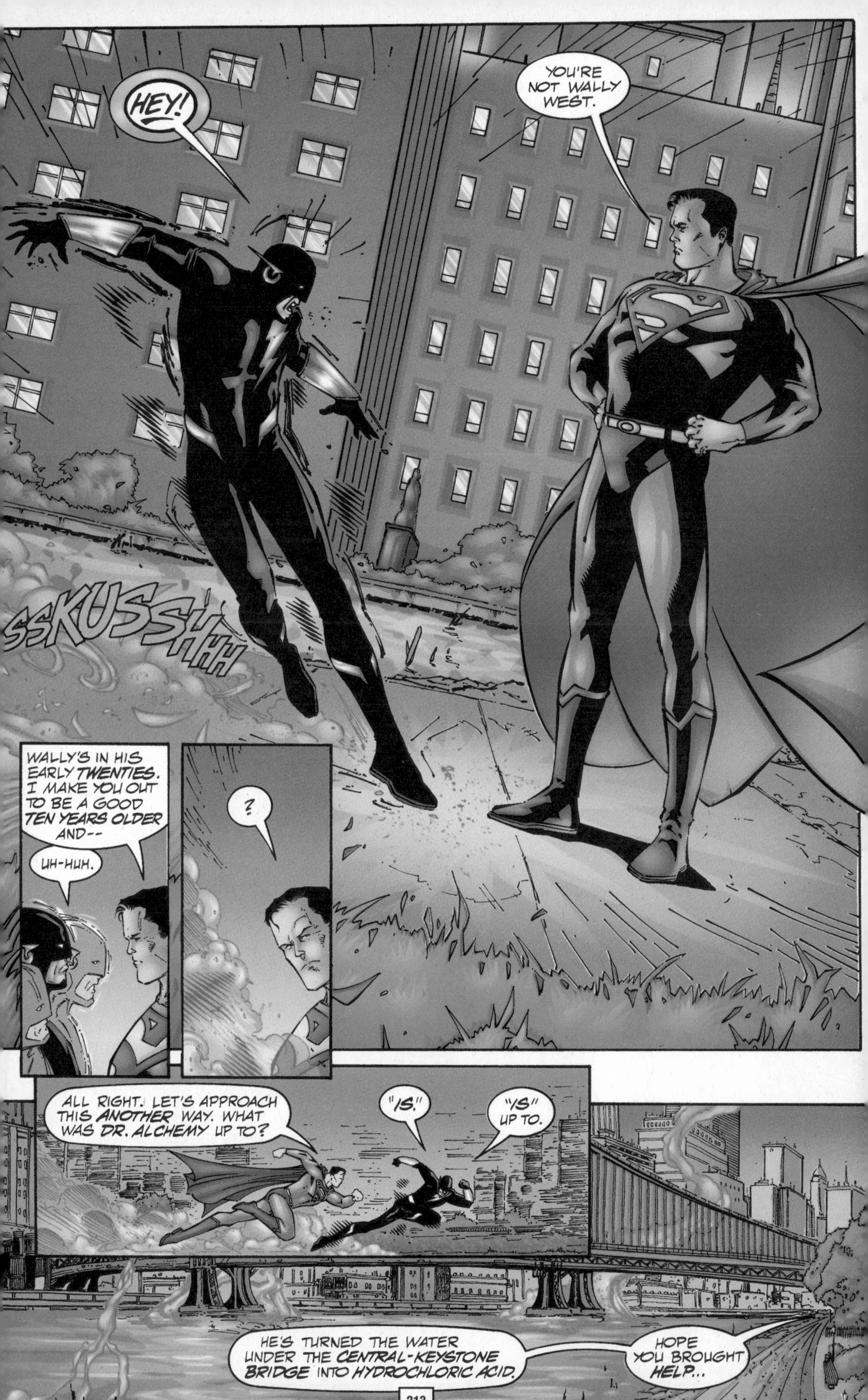
HEY!
YOU'RE NOT WALLY WEST.
SSKUSSHHH
WALLY'S IN HIS EARLY TWENTIES. I MAKE YOU OUT TO BE A GOOD TEN YEARS OLDER AND--
UH-HUH.
?
ALL RIGHT. LET'S APPROACH THIS ANOTHER WAY. WHAT WAS DR. ALCHEMY UP TO?
"IS."
"IS" UP TO.
HE'S TURNED THE WATER UNDER THE CENTRAL-KEYSTONE BRIDGE INTO HYDROCHLORIC ACID.
HOPE YOU BROUGHT HELP...

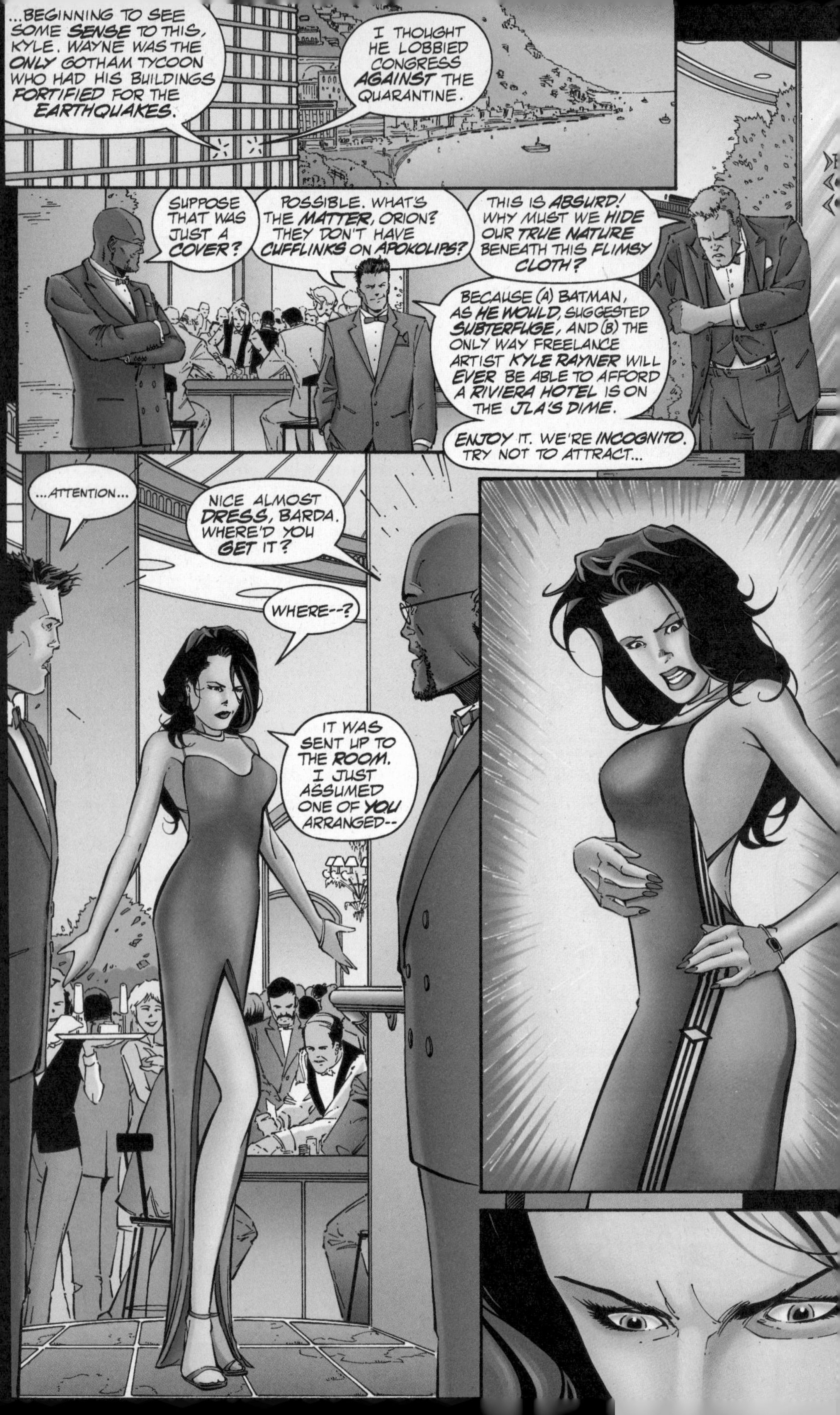
...BEGINNING TO SEE SOME SENSE TO THIS, KYLE. WAYNE WAS THE ONLY GOTHAM TYCOON WHO HAD HIS BUILDINGS FORTIFIED FOR THE EARTHQUAKES.
I THOUGHT HE LOBBIED CONGRESS AGAINST THE QUARANTINE.
SUPPOSE THAT WAS JUST A COVER?
POSSIBLE. WHAT'S THE MATTER, ORION? THEY DON'T HAVE CUFFLINKS ON APOKOLIPS?
THIS IS ABSURD! WHY MUST WE HIDE OUR TRUE NATURE BENEATH THIS FLIMSY CLOTH?
BECAUSE (A) BATMAN, AS HE WOULD, SUGGESTED SUBTERFUGE, AND (B) THE ONLY WAY FREELANCE ARTIST KYLE RAYNER WILL EVER BE ABLE TO AFFORD A RIVIERA HOTEL IS ON THE JLA'S DIME.
ENJOY IT. WE'RE INCOGNITO. TRY NOT TO ATTRACT...
...ATTENTION...
NICE ALMOST DRESS, BARDA. WHERE'D YOU GET IT?
WHERE--?
IT WAS SENT UP TO THE ROOM. I JUST ASSUMED ONE OF YOU ARRANGED--

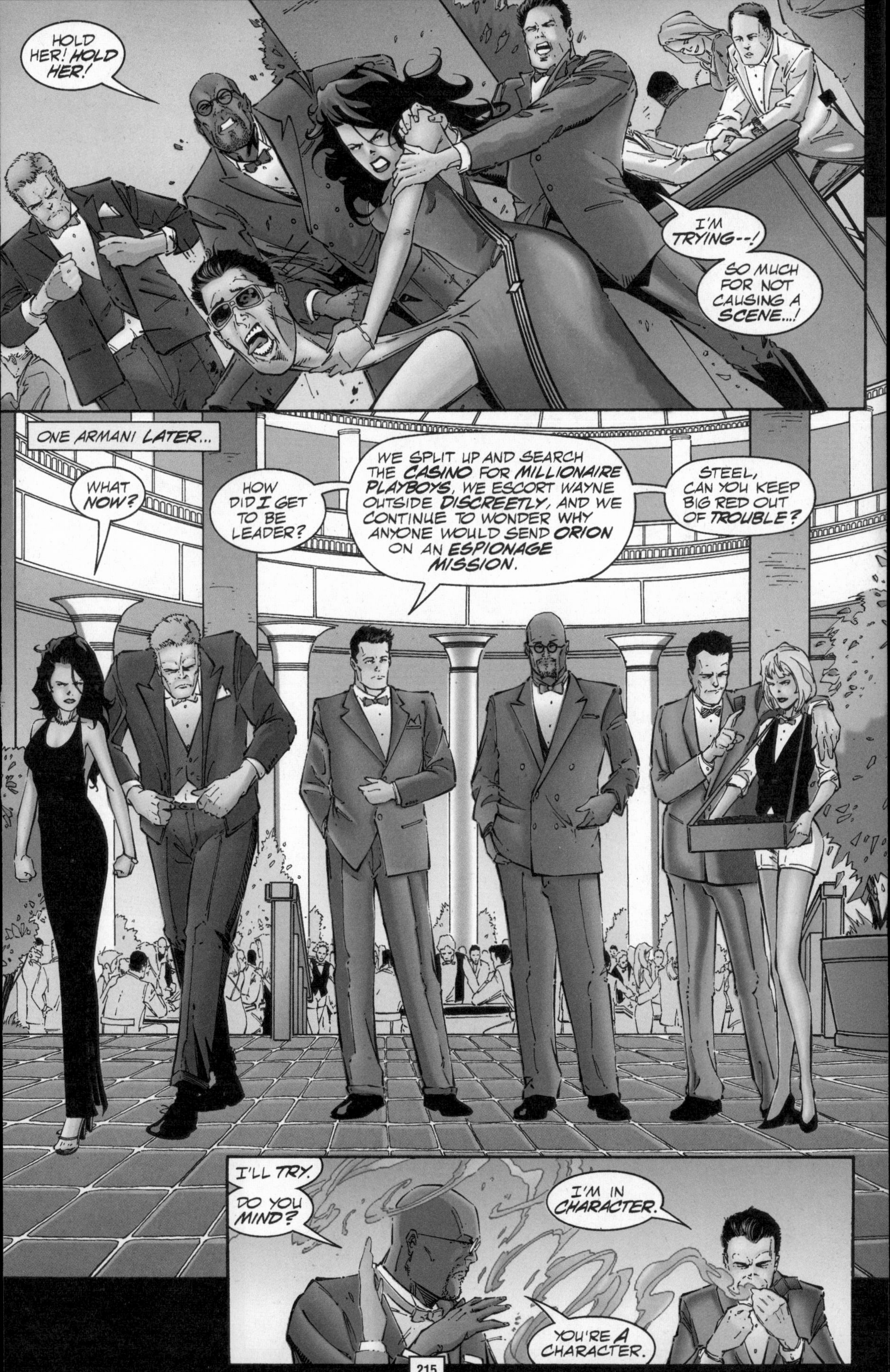
HOLD HER! HOLD HER!
I'M TRYING--!
SO MUCH FOR NOT CAUSING A SCENE...!
ONE ARMANI LATER...
WHAT NOW?
HOW DID I GET TO BE LEADER?
WE SPLIT UP AND SEARCH THE CASINO FOR MILLIONAIRE PLAYBOYS, WE ESCORT WAYNE OUTSIDE DISCREETLY, AND WE CONTINUE TO WONDER WHY ANYONE WOULD SEND ORION ON AN ESPIONAGE MISSION.
STEEL, CAN YOU KEEP BIG RED OUT OF TROUBLE?
I'LL TRY.
DO YOU MIND?
I'M IN CHARACTER.
YOU'RE A CHARACTER.

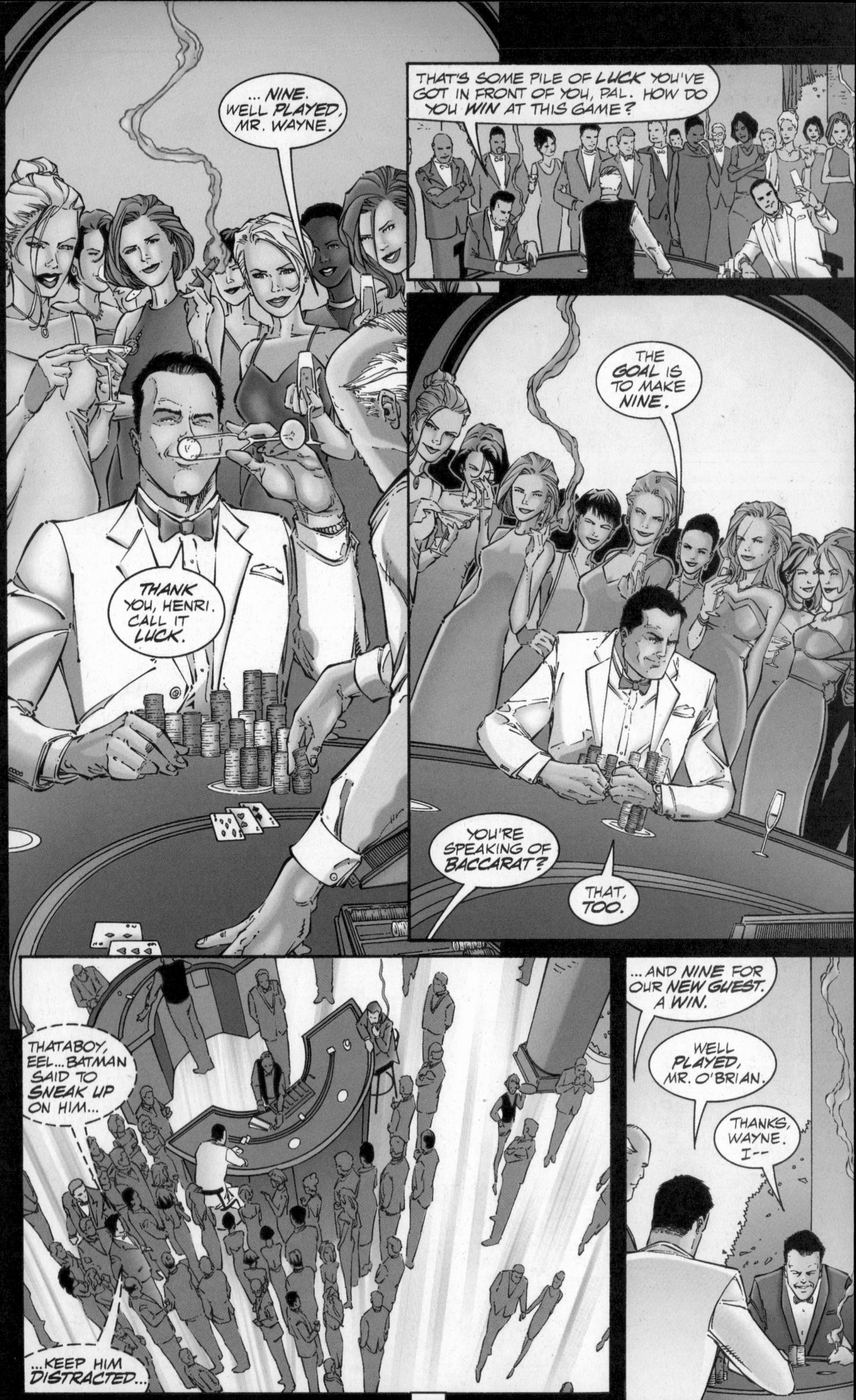

...NINE. WELL PLAYED, MR. WAYNE.
THANK YOU, HENRI. CALL IT LUCK.
THAT'S SOME PILE OF LUCK YOU'VE GOT IN FRONT OF YOU, PAL. HOW DO YOU WIN AT THIS GAME?
THE GOAL IS TO MAKE NINE.
YOU'RE SPEAKING OF BACCARAT?
THAT, TOO.
THATABOY, EEL...BATMAN SAID TO SNEAK UP ON HIM...
...KEEP HIM DISTRACTED...
...AND NINE FOR OUR NEW GUEST. A WIN.
WELL PLAYED, MR. O'BRIAN.
THANKS, WAYNE. I--

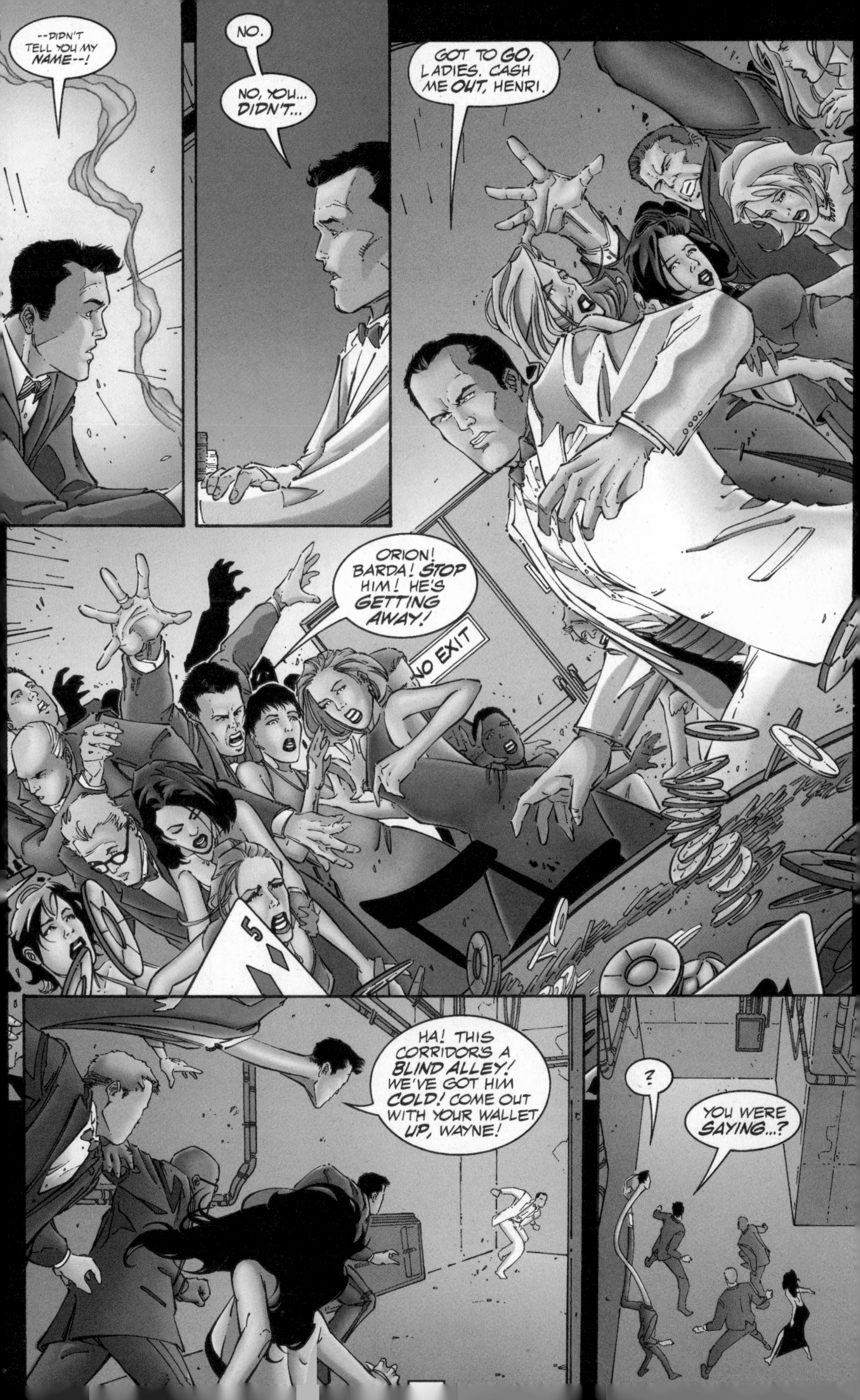
--DIDN'T TELL YOU MY NAME--!
NO.
NO, YOU... DIDN'T...
GOT TO GO, LADIES. CASH ME OUT, HENRI.
ORION! BARDA! STOP HIM! HE'S GETTING AWAY!
NO EXIT
HA! THIS CORRIDOR'S A BLIND ALLEY! WE'VE GOT HIM COLD! COME OUT WITH YOUR WALLET UP, WAYNE!
?
YOU WERE SAYING...?

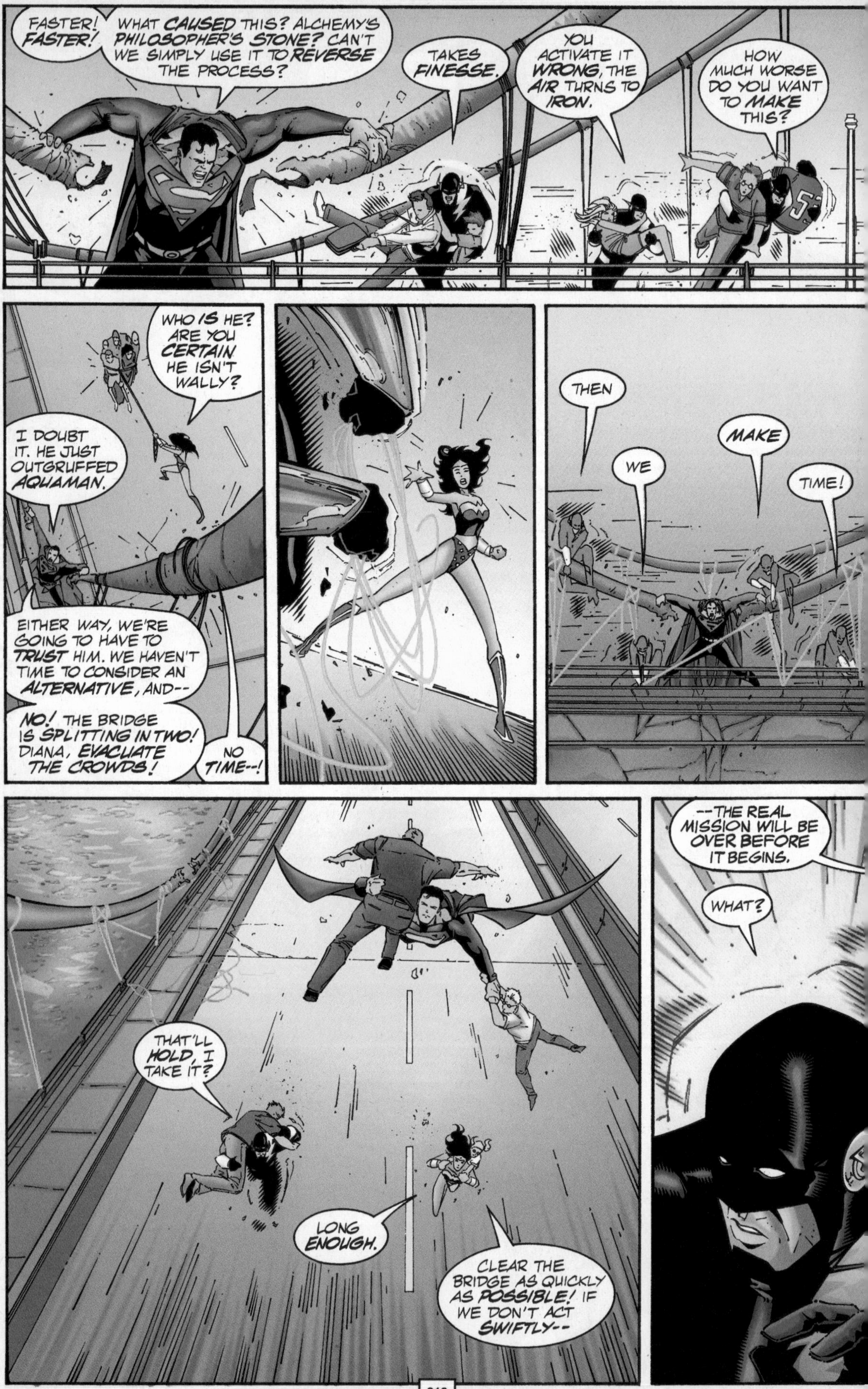
FASTER! FASTER!
WHAT CAUSED THIS? ALCHEMY'S PHILOSOPHER'S STONE? CAN'T WE SIMPLY USE IT TO REVERSE THE PROCESS?
TAKES FINESSE.
YOU ACTIVATE IT WRONG, THE AIR TURNS TO IRON.
HOW MUCH WORSE DO YOU WANT TO MAKE THIS?
WHO IS HE? ARE YOU CERTAIN HE ISN'T WALLY?
I DOUBT IT. HE JUST OUTGRUFFED AQUAMAN.
EITHER WAY, WE'RE GOING TO HAVE TO TRUST HIM. WE HAVEN'T TIME TO CONSIDER AN ALTERNATIVE, AND--
NO! THE BRIDGE IS SPLITTING IN TWO! DIANA, EVACUATE THE CROWDS!
NO TIME--!
THEN
WE
MAKE
TIME!
THAT'LL HOLD, I TAKE IT?
LONG ENOUGH.
CLEAR THE BRIDGE AS QUICKLY AS POSSIBLE! IF WE DON'T ACT SWIFTLY--
--THE REAL MISSION WILL BE OVER BEFORE IT BEGINS.
WHAT?

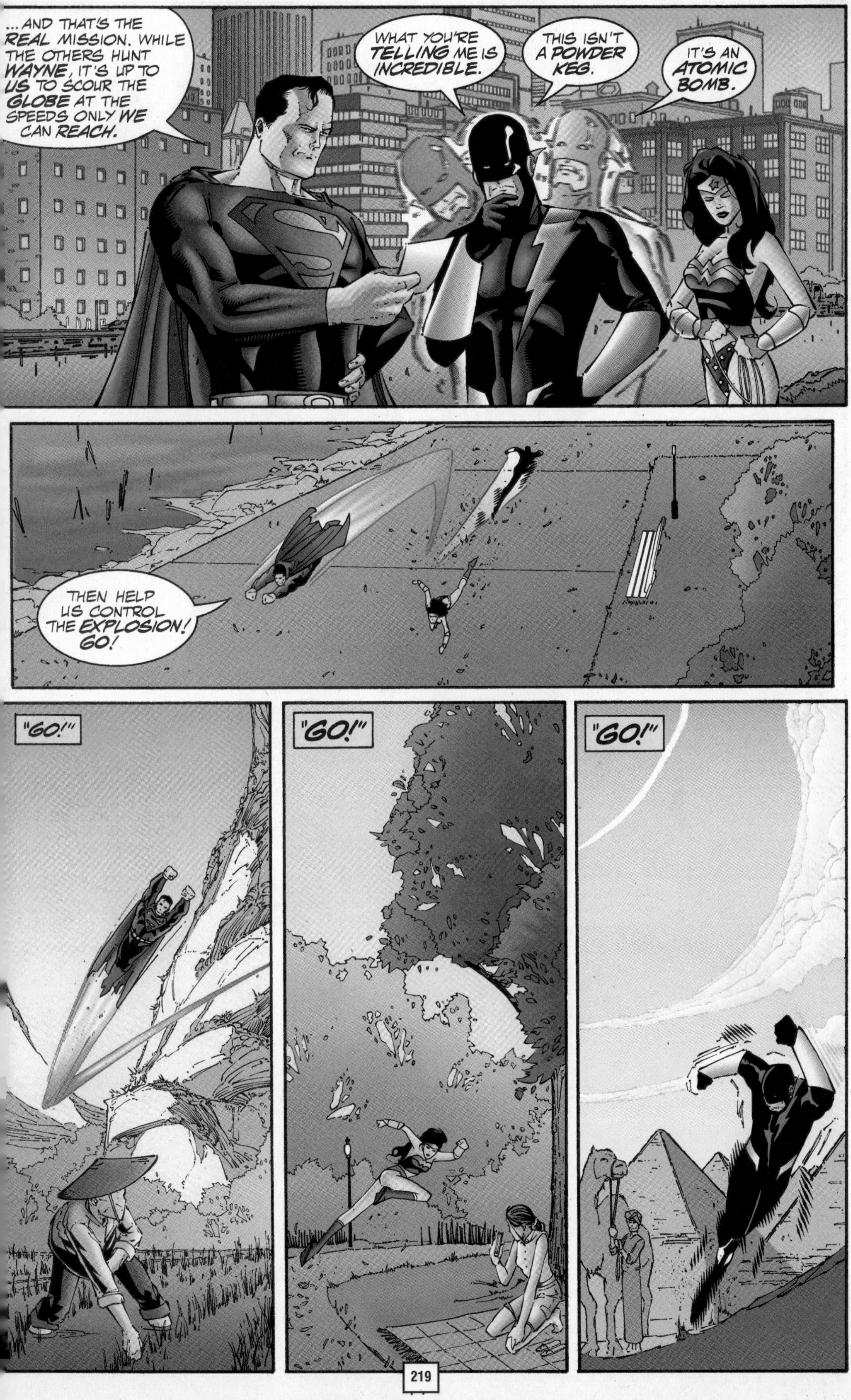
...AND THAT'S THE REAL MISSION. WHILE THE OTHERS HUNT WAYNE, IT'S UP TO US TO SCOUR THE GLOBE AT THE SPEEDS ONLY WE CAN REACH.
WHAT YOU'RE TELLING ME IS INCREDIBLE.
THIS ISN'T A POWDER KEG.
IT'S AN ATOMIC BOMB.
THEN HELP US CONTROL THE EXPLOSION! GO!
"GO!"
"GO!"
"GO!"

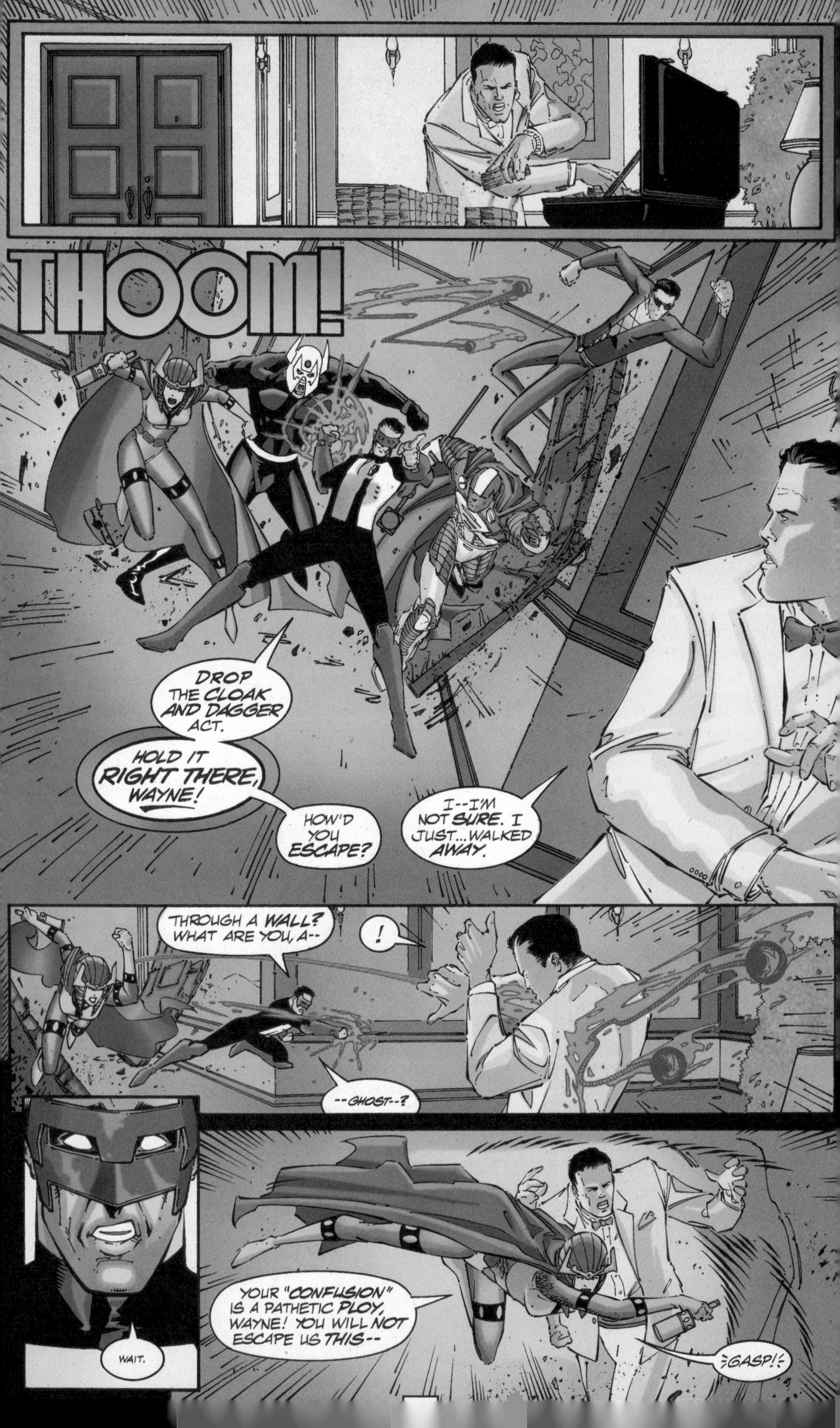
THOOM!
DROP THE CLOAK AND DAGGER ACT.
HOLD IT RIGHT THERE, WAYNE!
HOW'D YOU ESCAPE?
I--I'M NOT SURE. I JUST...WALKED AWAY.
THROUGH A WALL? WHAT ARE YOU, A--
!
--GHOST--?
WAIT.
YOUR "CONFUSION" IS A PATHETIC PLOY, WAYNE! YOU WILL NOT ESCAPE US THIS--
GASP!

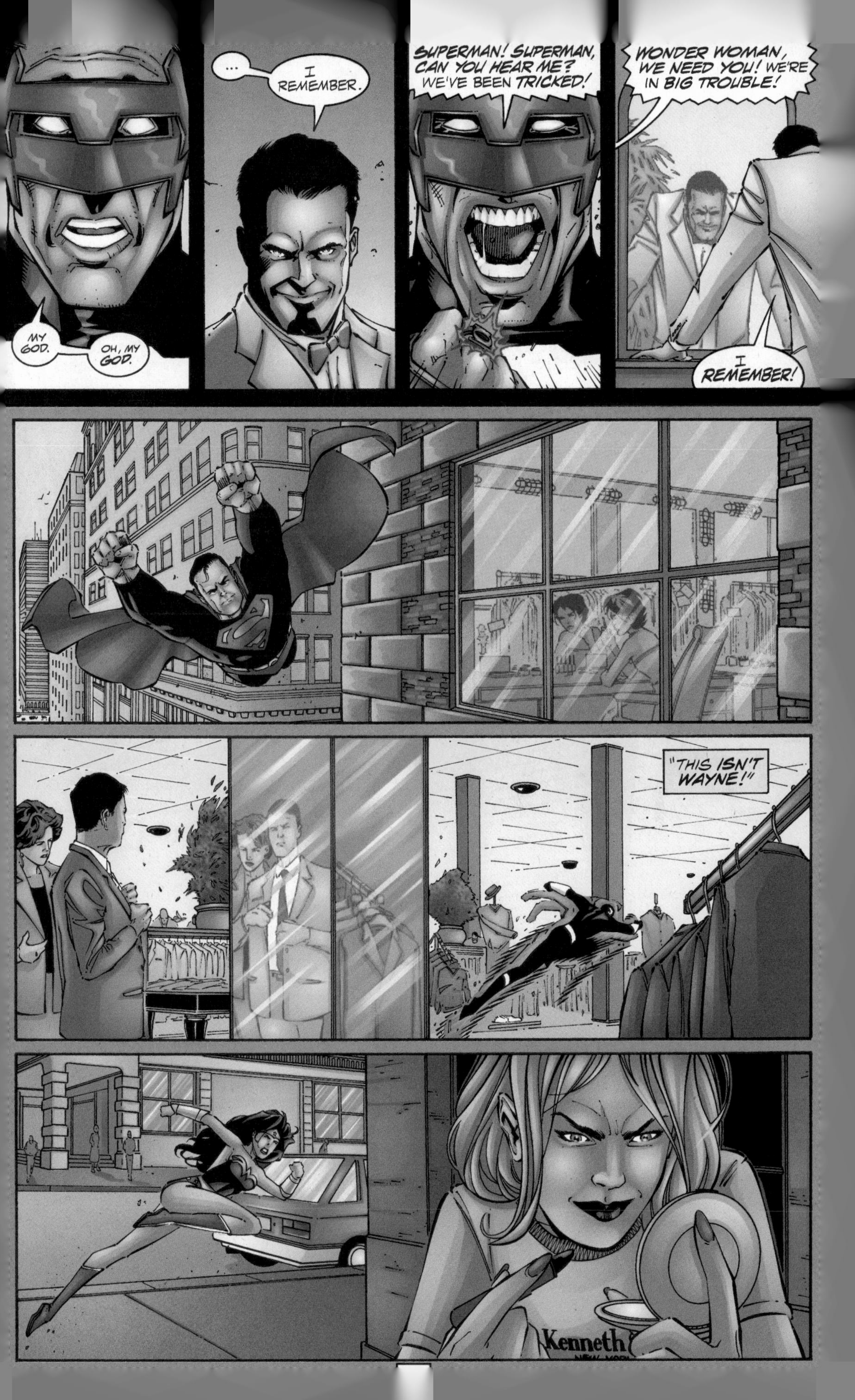
MY GOD.
OH, MY GOD.
...
I REMEMBER.
SUPERMAN! SUPERMAN, CAN YOU HEAR ME? WE'VE BEEN TRICKED!
WONDER WOMAN, WE NEED YOU! WE'RE IN BIG TROUBLE!
I REMEMBER!
"THIS ISN'T WAYNE!"
Kenneth

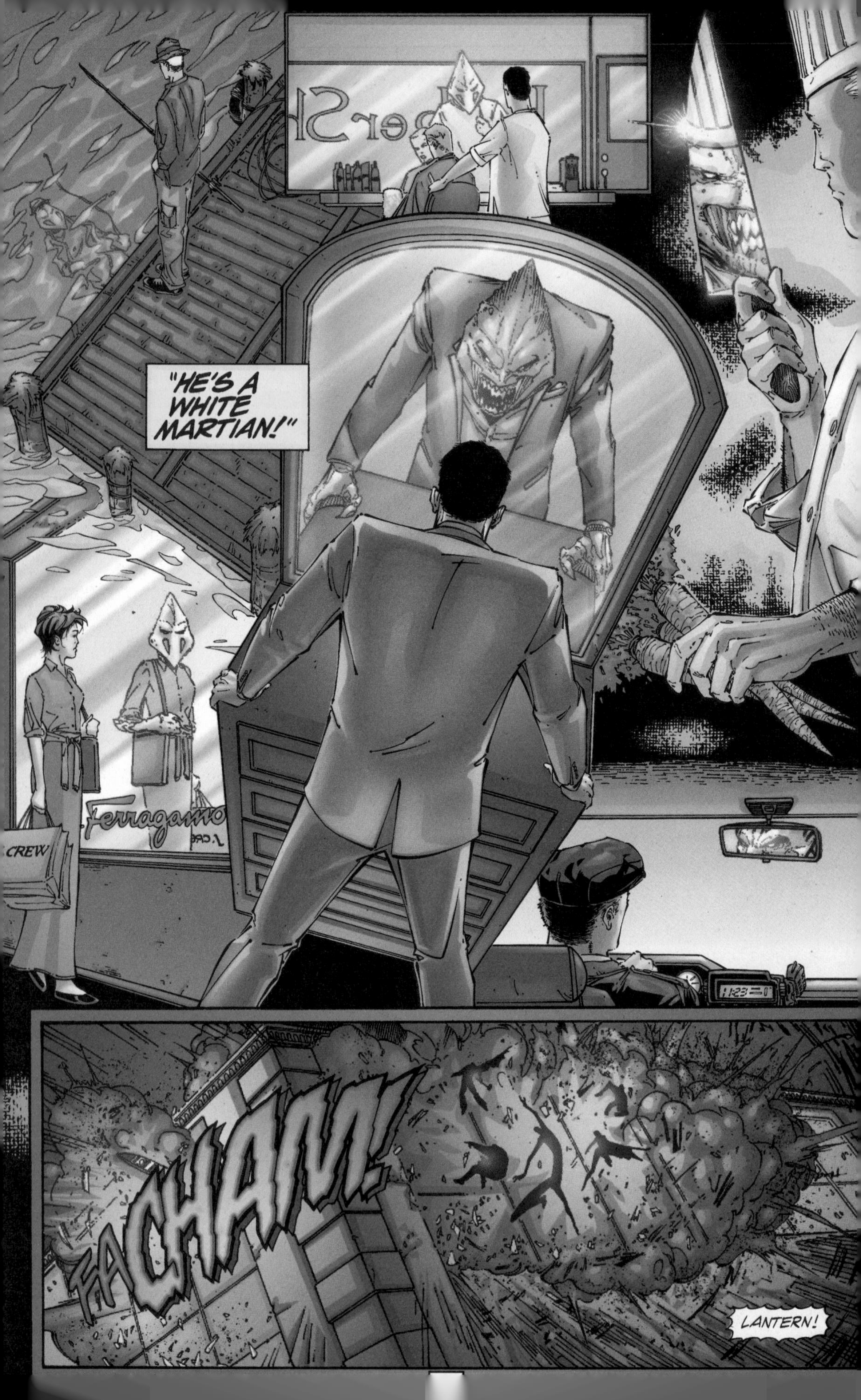
"HE'S A WHITE MARTIAN!"
Ferragamo
J.CREW
FACHAM!
LANTERN!

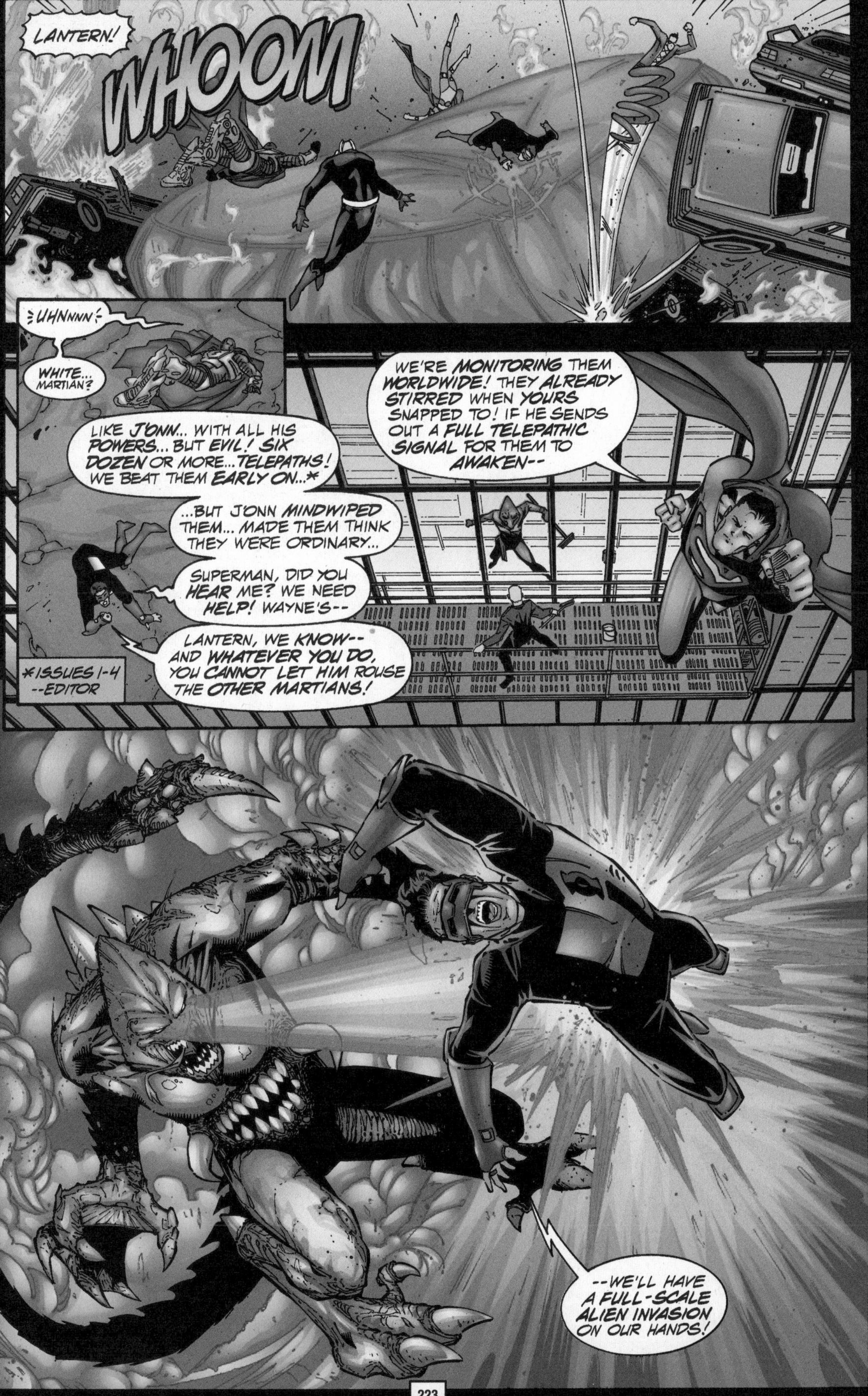
LANTERN!
WHOOM
UHNNNN
WHITE... MARTIAN?
LIKE J'ONN... WITH ALL HIS POWERS... BUT EVIL! SIX DOZEN OR MORE... TELEPATHS! WE BEAT THEM EARLY ON...*
...BUT J'ONN MINDWIPED THEM... MADE THEM THINK THEY WERE ORDINARY...
SUPERMAN, DID YOU HEAR ME? WE NEED HELP! WAYNE'S--
LANTERN, WE KNOW-- AND WHATEVER YOU DO, YOU CANNOT LET HIM ROUSE THE OTHER MARTIANS!
*ISSUES 1-4 --EDITOR
WE'RE MONITORING THEM WORLDWIDE! THEY ALREADY STIRRED WHEN YOURS SNAPPED TO! IF HE SENDS OUT A FULL TELEPATHIC SIGNAL FOR THEM TO AWAKEN--
--WE'LL HAVE A FULL-SCALE ALIEN INVASION ON OUR HANDS!

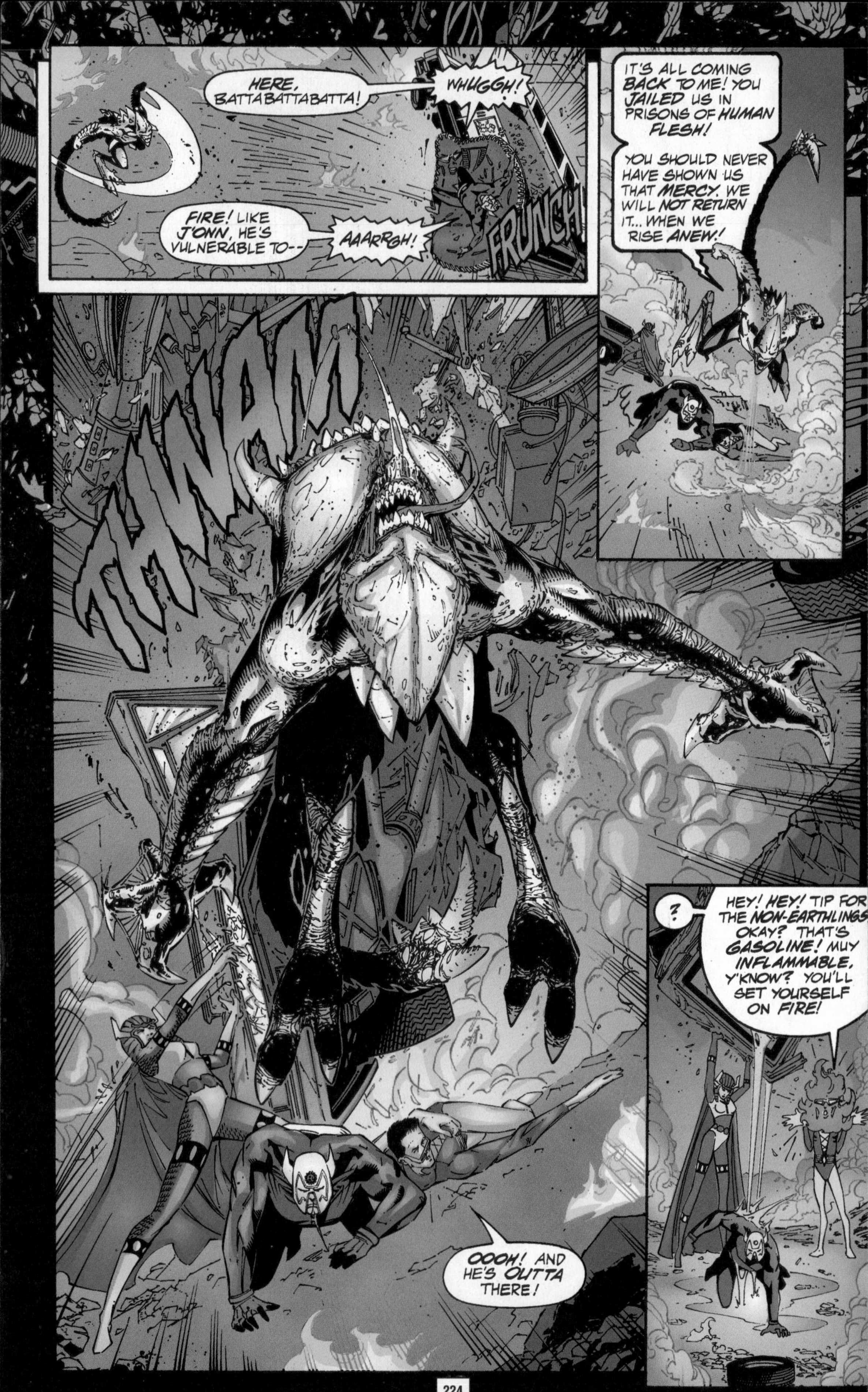
HERE, BATTABATTABATTA!
WHUGGH!
FIRE! LIKE J'ONN, HE'S VULNERABLE TO--
AAARRGH!
FRUNCH!
IT'S ALL COMING BACK TO ME! YOU JAILED US IN PRISONS OF HUMAN FLESH!
YOU SHOULD NEVER HAVE SHOWN US THAT MERCY. WE WILL NOT RETURN IT... WHEN WE RISE ANEW!
THWAM!
OOOH! AND HE'S OUTTA THERE!
?
HEY! HEY! TIP FOR THE NON-EARTHLINGS OKAY? THAT'S GASOLINE! MUY INFLAMMABLE, Y'KNOW? YOU'LL SET YOURSELF ON FIRE!

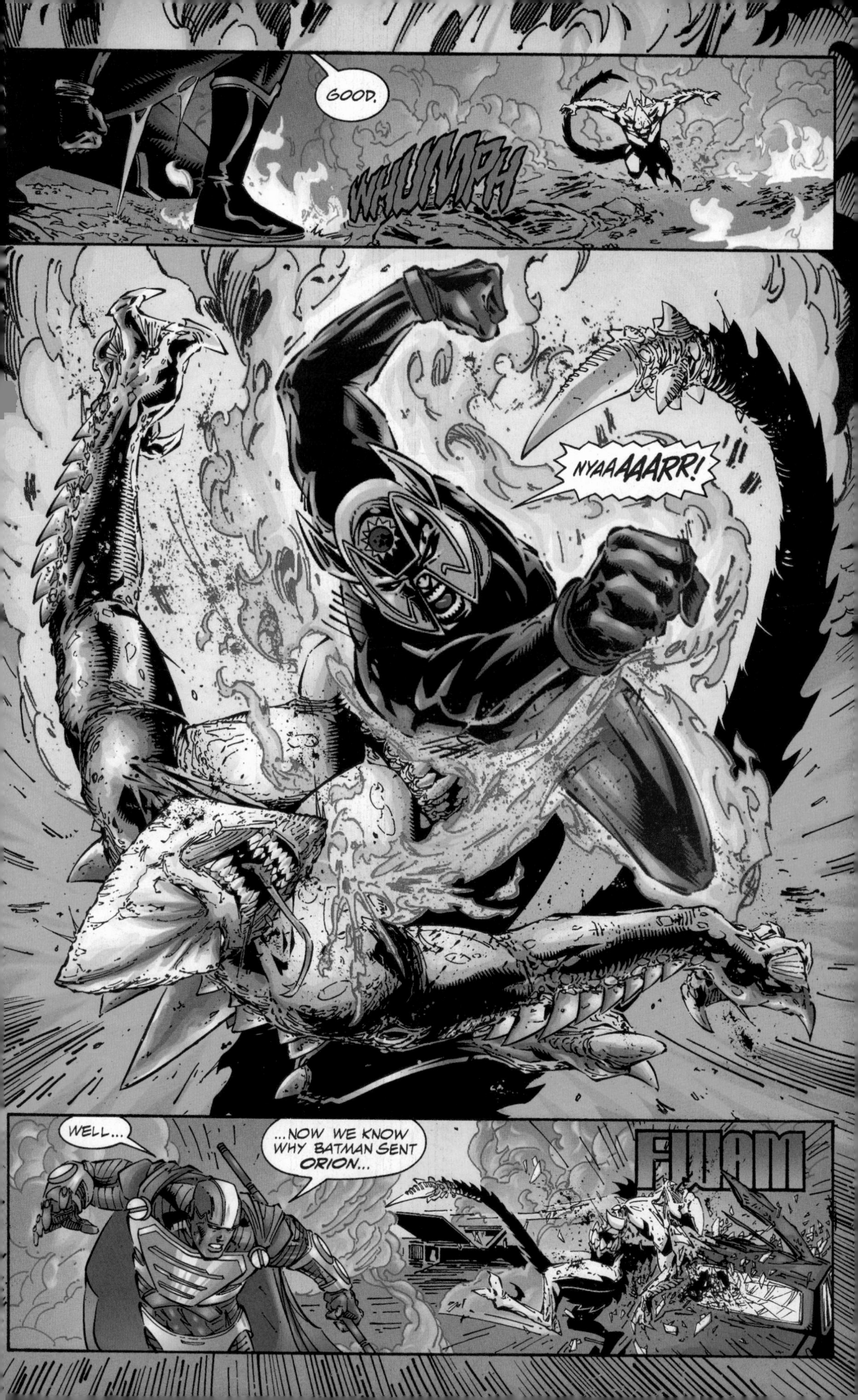

GOOD.
WHUMPH
NYAAAAARR!
WELL...
...NOW WE KNOW WHY BATMAN SENT ORION...
FWAM

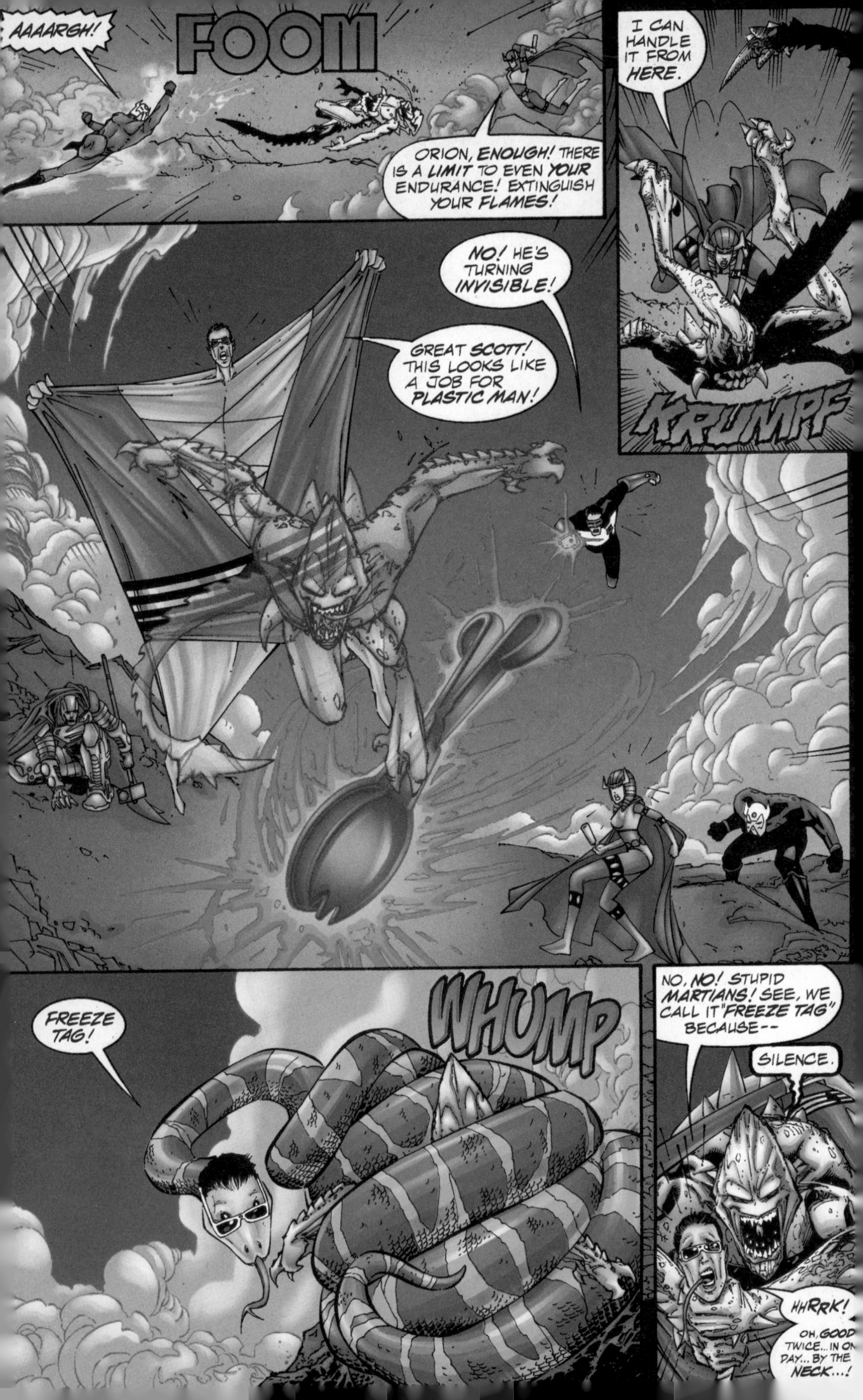
AAAARGH!
FOOM
ORION, ENOUGH! THERE IS A LIMIT TO EVEN YOUR ENDURANCE! EXTINGUISH YOUR FLAMES!
I CAN HANDLE IT FROM HERE.
KRUMPF
NO! HE'S TURNING INVISIBLE!
GREAT SCOTT! THIS LOOKS LIKE A JOB FOR PLASTIC MAN!
FREEZE TAG!
WHUMP
NO, NO! STUPID MARTIANS! SEE, WE CALL IT "FREEZE TAG" BECAUSE--
SILENCE.
HHRRK!
OH, GOOD TWICE... IN ON DAY... BY THE NECK...!

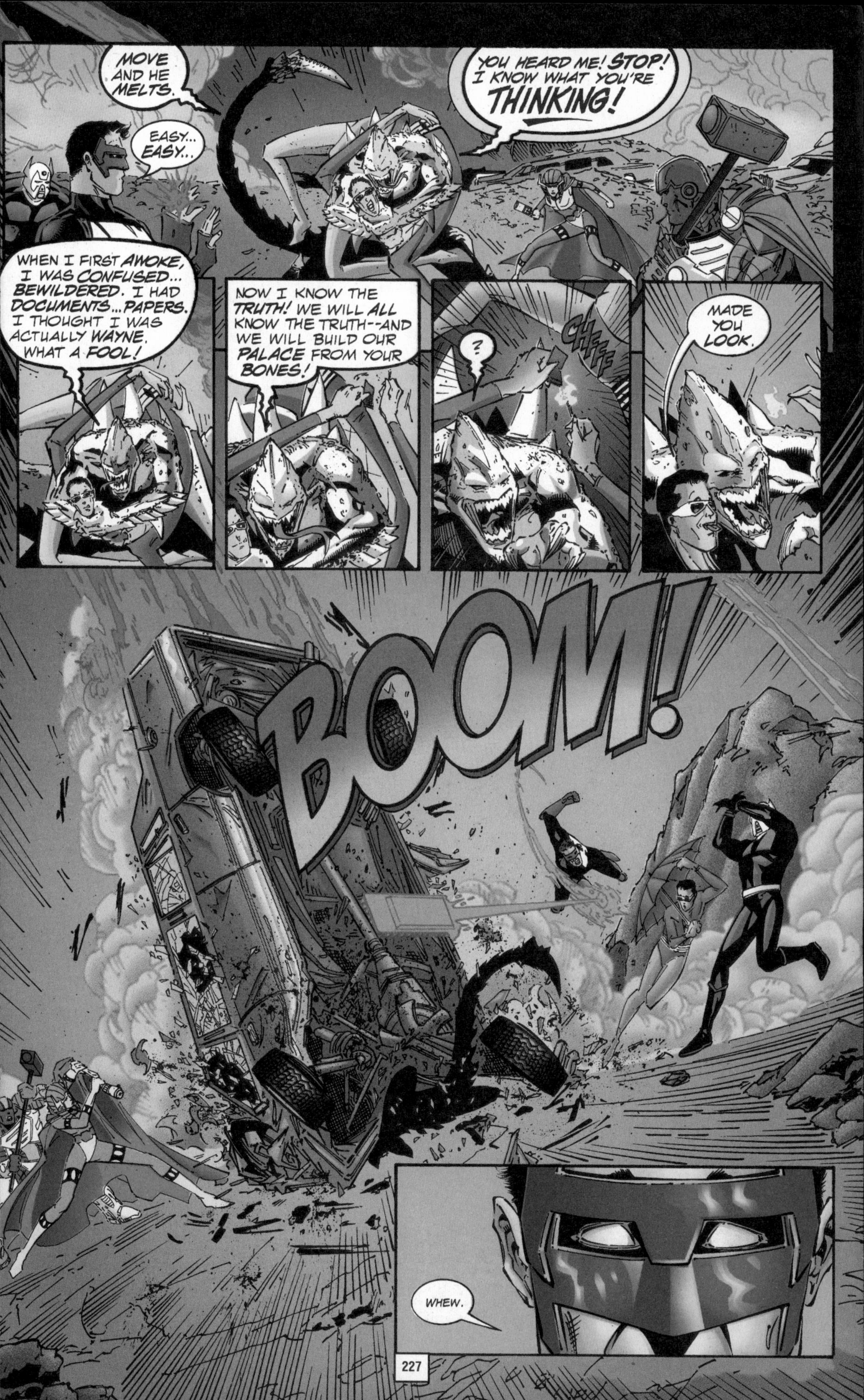

MOVE AND HE MELTS.
EASY... EASY...
YOU HEARD ME! STOP! I KNOW WHAT YOU'RE THINKING!
WHEN I FIRST AWOKE, I WAS CONFUSED... BEWILDERED. I HAD DOCUMENTS... PAPERS. I THOUGHT I WAS ACTUALLY WAYNE. WHAT A FOOL!
NOW I KNOW THE TRUTH! WE WILL ALL KNOW THE TRUTH--AND WE WILL BUILD OUR PALACE FROM YOUR BONES!
?
CHFFF
MADE YOU LOOK.
BOOM!
WHEW.

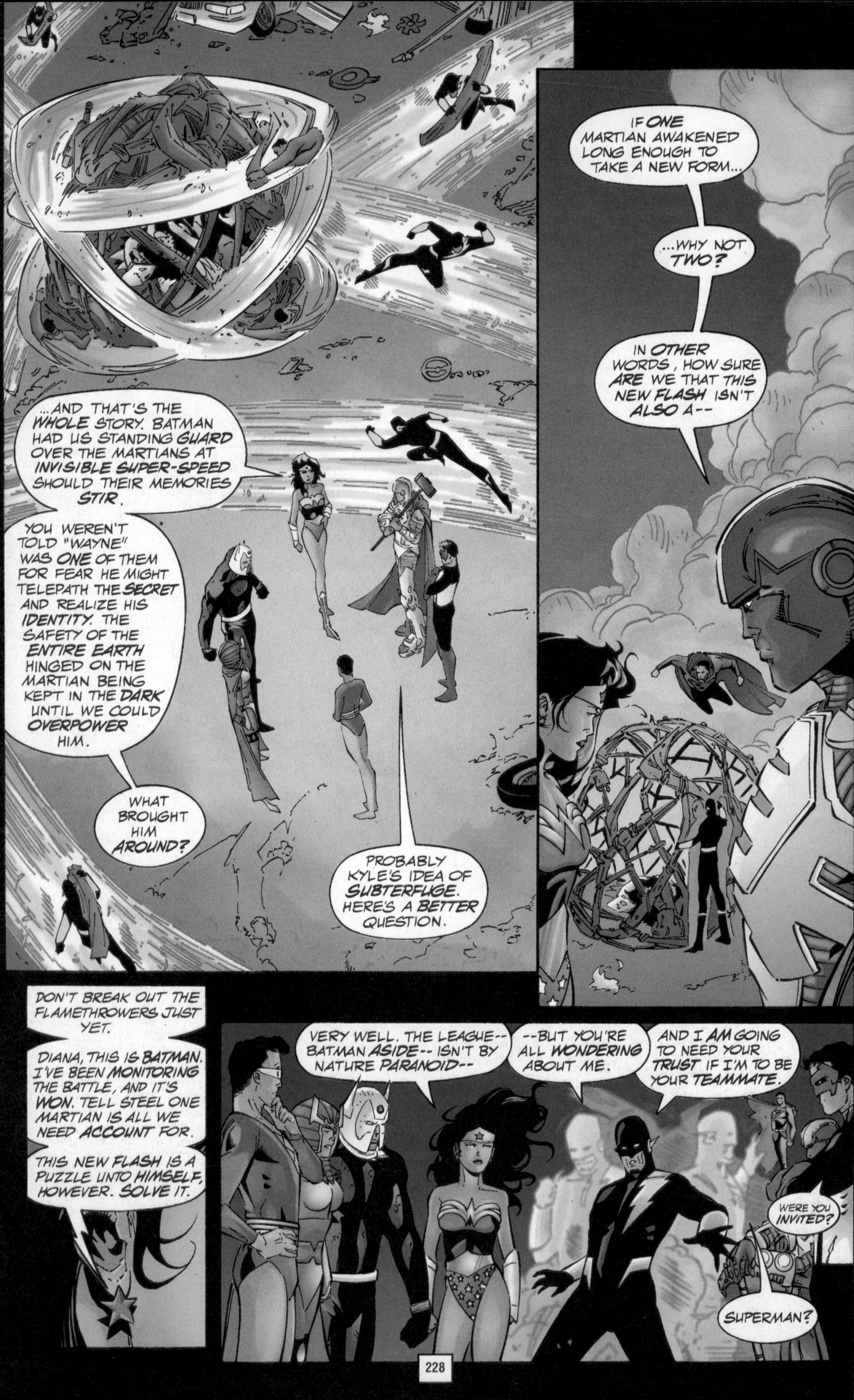
...AND THAT'S THE WHOLE STORY. BATMAN HAD US STANDING GUARD OVER THE MARTIANS AT INVISIBLE SUPER-SPEED SHOULD THEIR MEMORIES STIR.
YOU WEREN'T TOLD "WAYNE" WAS ONE OF THEM FOR FEAR HE MIGHT TELEPATH THE SECRET AND REALIZE HIS IDENTITY. THE SAFETY OF THE ENTIRE EARTH HINGED ON THE MARTIAN BEING KEPT IN THE DARK UNTIL WE COULD OVERPOWER HIM.
WHAT BROUGHT HIM AROUND?
PROBABLY KYLE'S IDEA OF SUBTERFUGE. HERE'S A BETTER QUESTION.
IF ONE MARTIAN AWAKENED LONG ENOUGH TO TAKE A NEW FORM...
...WHY NOT TWO?
IN OTHER WORDS, HOW SURE ARE WE THAT THIS NEW FLASH ISN'T ALSO A--
DON'T BREAK OUT THE FLAMETHROWERS JUST YET.
DIANA, THIS IS BATMAN. I'VE BEEN MONITORING THE BATTLE, AND IT'S WON. TELL STEEL ONE MARTIAN IS ALL WE NEED ACCOUNT FOR.
THIS NEW FLASH IS A PUZZLE UNTO HIMSELF, HOWEVER. SOLVE IT.
VERY WELL. THE LEAGUE-- BATMAN ASIDE-- ISN'T BY NATURE PARANOID--
--BUT YOU'RE ALL WONDERING ABOUT ME.
AND I AM GOING TO NEED YOUR TRUST IF I'M TO BE YOUR TEAMMATE.
WERE YOU INVITED?
SUPERMAN?

"I DON'T LIKE THIS."

"YOU DON'T LIKE ANYTHING."

"WHAT IN THE WORLD ARE THEY TALKING ABOUT?"

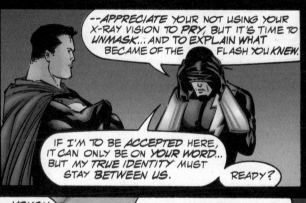

"--APPRECIATE YOUR NOT USING YOUR X-RAY VISION TO PRY, BUT IT'S TIME TO UNMASK... AND TO EXPLAIN WHAT BECAME OF THE FLASH YOU KNEW.

IF I'M TO BE ACCEPTED HERE, IT CAN ONLY BE ON YOUR WORD... BUT MY TRUE IDENTITY MUST STAY BETWEEN US.

READY?"

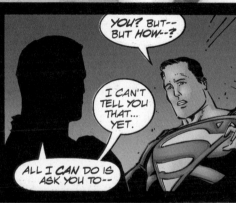

"YOU? BUT-- BUT HOW--?"

"I CAN'T TELL YOU THAT... YET.

ALL I CAN DO IS ASK YOU TO--"

"--VOUCH FOR THIS MAN WITHOUT RESERVATION.

I CAN'T GIVE DETAILS... BUT TRUST ME. HE IS AS MUCH JLA MATERIAL AS ANYONE I'VE EVER KNOWN."

"WHOA. WHOA! NOT THAT I MISS HIM OR ANYTHING, BUT... WHERE'S WALLY?"

"QUESTION'S TABLED--"

"--BUT THERE ARE PLENTY OF OTHERS THAT NEED ANSWERING. I'LL MEET YOU AT THE WATCHTOWER."

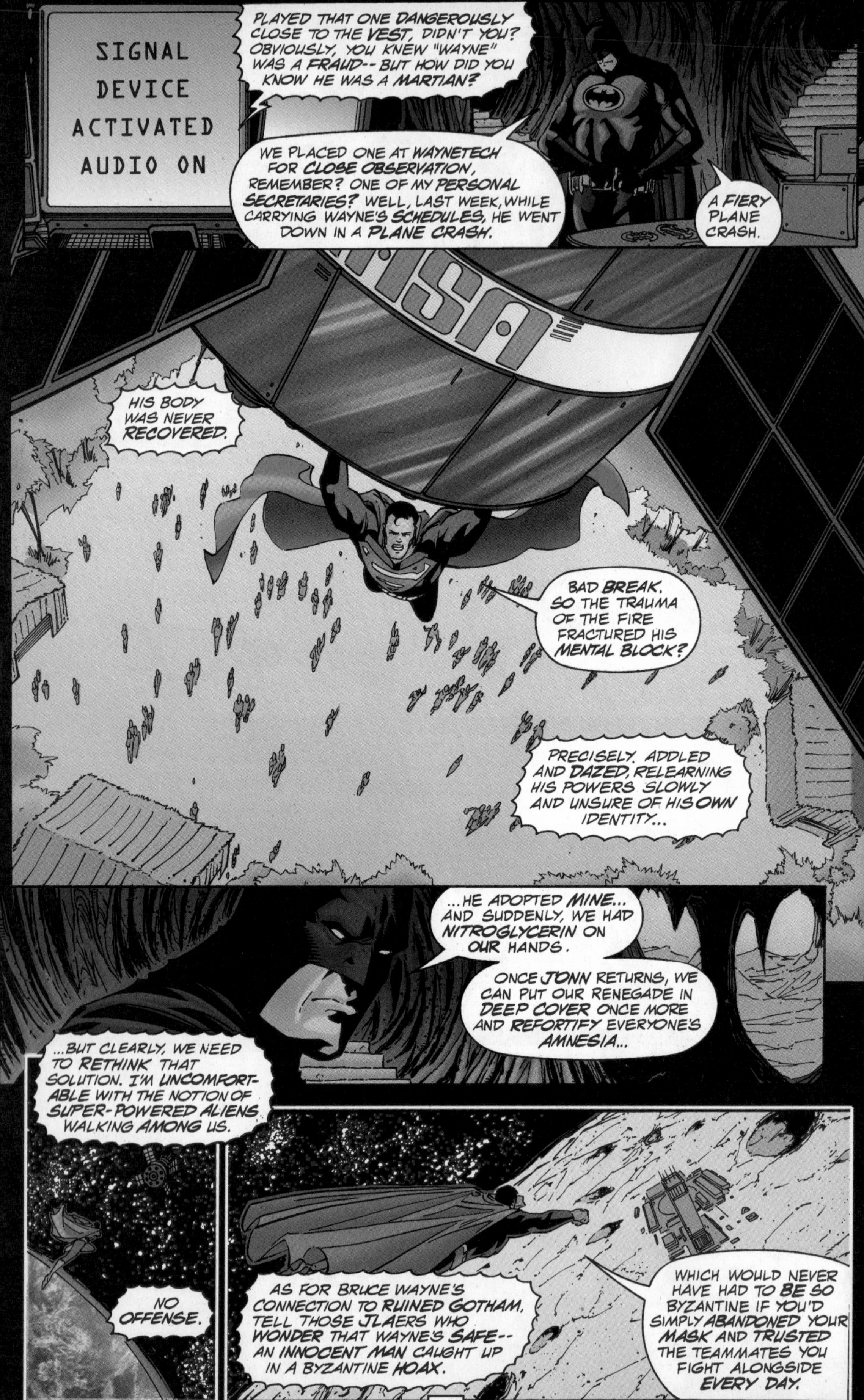
SIGNAL DEVICE ACTIVATED AUDIO ON
PLAYED THAT ONE DANGEROUSLY CLOSE TO THE VEST, DIDN'T YOU? OBVIOUSLY, YOU KNEW "WAYNE" WAS A FRAUD-- BUT HOW DID YOU KNOW HE WAS A MARTIAN?
WE PLACED ONE AT WAYNETECH FOR CLOSE OBSERVATION, REMEMBER? ONE OF MY PERSONAL SECRETARIES? WELL, LAST WEEK, WHILE CARRYING WAYNE'S SCHEDULES, HE WENT DOWN IN A PLANE CRASH.
A FIERY PLANE CRASH.
JLA
HIS BODY WAS NEVER RECOVERED.
BAD BREAK. SO THE TRAUMA OF THE FIRE FRACTURED HIS MENTAL BLOCK?
PRECISELY. ADDLED AND DAZED, RELEARNING HIS POWERS SLOWLY AND UNSURE OF HIS OWN IDENTITY...
...HE ADOPTED MINE... AND SUDDENLY, WE HAD NITROGLYCERIN ON OUR HANDS.
ONCE JONN RETURNS, WE CAN PUT OUR RENEGADE IN DEEP COVER ONCE MORE AND REFORTIFY EVERYONE'S AMNESIA...
...BUT CLEARLY, WE NEED TO RETHINK THAT SOLUTION. I'M UNCOMFORTABLE WITH THE NOTION OF SUPER-POWERED ALIENS WALKING AMONG US.
NO OFFENSE.
AS FOR BRUCE WAYNE'S CONNECTION TO RUINED GOTHAM, TELL THOSE JLAERS WHO WONDER THAT WAYNE'S SAFE-- AN INNOCENT MAN CAUGHT UP IN A BYZANTINE HOAX.
WHICH WOULD NEVER HAVE HAD TO BE SO BYZANTINE IF YOU'D SIMPLY ABANDONED YOUR MASK AND TRUSTED THE TEAMMATES YOU FIGHT ALONGSIDE EVERY DAY.

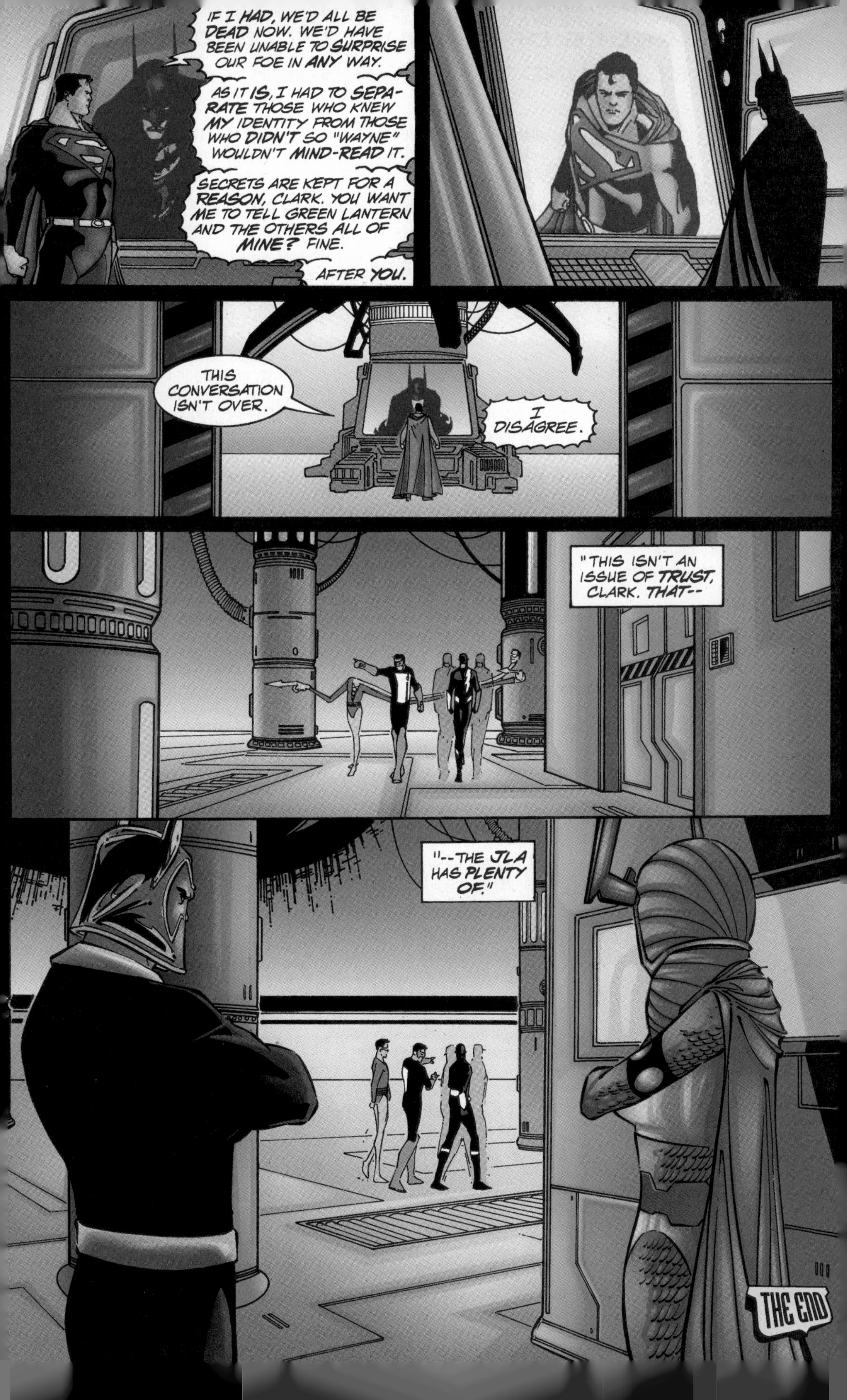
IF I HAD, WE'D ALL BE DEAD NOW. WE'D HAVE BEEN UNABLE TO SURPRISE OUR FOE IN ANY WAY.
AS IT IS, I HAD TO SEPARATE THOSE WHO KNEW MY IDENTITY FROM THOSE WHO DIDN'T SO "WAYNE" WOULDN'T MIND-READ IT.
SECRETS ARE KEPT FOR A REASON, CLARK. YOU WANT ME TO TELL GREEN LANTERN AND THE OTHERS ALL OF MINE? FINE.
AFTER YOU.
THIS CONVERSATION ISN'T OVER.
I DISAGREE.
"THIS ISN'T AN ISSUE OF TRUST, CLARK. THAT--
"--THE JLA HAS PLENTY OF."
THE END

THE HEROES OF THE JUSTICE LEAGUE CAN ALSO BE FOUND IN THESE BOOKS FROM DC:

GRAPHIC NOVELS

JLA/WILDC.A.T.S: CRIME MACHINE
Grant Morrison/Val Semeiks/
Kevin Conrad

JUSTICE RIDERS
Chuck Dixon/J.H. Williams/Mick Gray

COLLECTIONS

JUSTICE LEAGUE: A NEW BEGINNING
Keith Giffen/J. M. DeMatteis/
Kevin Maguire

**JUSTICE LEAGUE:
A MIDSUMMER'S NIGHTMARE**
Mark Waid/Fabian Niciezo/
Jeff Johnson/Darick Robertson/
John Holdredge/Anibal Rodriguez

JLA: NEW WORLD ORDER
Grant Morrison/Howard Porter/
John Dell

JLA: AMERICAN DREAMS
Grant Morrison/Howard Porter/
John Dell/various

JLA: ROCK OF AGES
Grant Morrison/Howard Porter/
John Dell/various

JLA: STRENGTH IN NUMBERS
Morrison/Waid/Porter/various writers
and artists

JLA: WORLD WITHOUT GROWN-UPS
Dezago/Nauck/Ramos/McKone/
various artists

THE KNIGHTFALL Trilogy
  BATMAN: KNIGHTFALL Part 1:
  Broken Bat
  Various writers and artists
  BATMAN: KNIGHTFALL Part 2:
  Who Rules the Night
  Various writers and artists
  BATMAN: KNIGHTSEND
  Various writers and artists

THE DEATH OF SUPERMAN Trilogy
  THE DEATH OF SUPERMAN
  Various writers and artists
  WORLD WITHOUT A SUPERMAN
  Various writers and artists
  THE RETURN OF SUPERMAN
  Various writers and artists

AQUAMAN: TIME & TIDE
Peter David/Kirk Jarvinen/
Brad Vancata

THE FLASH: TERMINAL VELOCITY
Mark Waid/various

GREEN LANTERN: A NEW DAWN
Ron Marz/Darryl Banks/
Romeo Tanghal/various

GREEN LANTERN: EMERALD KNIGHTS
Marz/Dixon/Banks/Pelletier/Johnson/
Braithwaite/various

JACK KIRBY'S NEW GODS
Jack Kirby/Vince Colletta/Mike Royer

JACK KIRBY'S MISTER MIRACLE
Jack Kirby/Vince Colletta/Mike Royer

STEEL: THE FORGING OF A HERO
Various writers and artists

WONDER WOMAN: THE CONTEST
William Messner-Loebs/
Mike Deodato, Jr.

**WONDER WOMAN: THE CHALLENGE
OF ARTEMIS**
William Messner-Loebs/
Mike Deodato, Jr.

WONDER WOMAN: SECOND GENESIS
John Byrne

WONDER WOMAN: LIFELINES
John Byrne

**DC VERSUS MARVEL/
MARVEL VERSUS DC**
Marz/David/Jurgens/Castellini/
Rubinstein/Neary

**THE AMALGAM AGE OF COMICS:
THE DC COMICS COLLECTION**
Various writers and artists

**RETURN TO THE AMALGAM AGE
OF COMICS: THE DC COMICS
COLLECTION**
Various writers and artists

THE FINAL NIGHT
K. Kesel/Marz/Immonen/McKone/
Marzan, Jr./McKenna

KINGDOM COME
Mark Waid/Alex Ross

LEGENDS: THE COLLECTED EDITION
John Ostrander/Len Wein/
John Byrne/Karl Kesel

UNDERWORLD UNLEASHED
Waid/Porter/Peterson/Jimenez/Williams/
various

ARCHIVE EDITIONS

**THE FLASH ARCHIVES Volume 1
(FLASH COMICS 104, SHOWCASE 4, 8,
13, 14, and THE FLASH 105-108)**
John Broome/Robert Kanigher/
Carmine Infantino/Frank Giacoia/
Joe Giella/Joe Kubert

**GREEN LANTERN ARCHIVES Volume 1
(SHOWCASE 22-23 and
GREEN LANTERN 1-5)**
John Broome/Gil Kane/Joe Giella/
various

**JUSTICE LEAGUE OF AMERICA
ARCHIVES Volume 1
(THE BRAVE AND THE BOLD 28-30 and
JUSTICE LEAGUE OF AMERICA 1-6)**
Gardner Fox/Mike Sekowsky/various

**JUSTICE LEAGUE OF AMERICA
ARCHIVES Volume 2
(JUSTICE LEAGUE OF AMERICA 7-14)**
Gardner Fox/Mike Sekowsky/various

**JUSTICE LEAGUE OF AMERICA
ARCHIVES Volume 3
(JUSTICE LEAGUE OF AMERICA 15-22)**
Gardner Fox/Mike Sekowsky/various

**JUSTICE LEAGUE OF AMERICA
ARCHIVES Volume 4
(JUSTICE LEAGUE OF AMERICA 23-30)**
Gardner Fox/Mike Sekowsky/various

**PLASTIC MAN ARCHIVES Volume 1
(POLICE COMICS 1-20)**
Jack Cole

**WONDER WOMAN ARCHIVES Volume 1
(ALL STAR COMICS 8, SENSATION
COMICS 1-12, and WONDER WOMAN 1)**
William Moulton Marston/Harry G. Peter

FOR THE NEAREST COMICS SHOP CARRYING COLLECTED EDITIONS
AND MONTHLY TITLES FROM DC COMICS, CALL 1-888-COMIC BOOK.

JLA9811